London

"All you've got to do is decide to go
and the hardest part is over.

So go!"

TONY WHEELER, COFOUNDER – LONELY PLANET

D0250735

THIS EDITION WRITTEN AND RESEARCHED BY
Damian Harper, Steve Fallon, Emilie Filou,
Vesna Maric, Sally Schafer

Contents

Left: London Eye (p169), designed by David Marks and Julia Barfield

Top: St Paul's Cathedral (p147)

Right: Victoria Park (p221)

Welcome to London

One of the world's most visited cities, London has something for everyone: from history to culture, art to architecture.

Time Travel

London is immersed in history. Not so much that it's precious, but there's sufficient antiquity and historic splendour (Tower of London, Westminster Abbey, Hampton Court) to blow you away. London's buildings are eye-catching milestones in the city's unique and compelling biography. There's more than enough funky innovation (the Shard, the Aquatics Centre, the Gherkin) to put a crackle in the air, but it never drowns out London's well-preserved, centuries-old narrative. Architectural grandeur rises up all around you in the West End, ancient remains dot the City and charming pubs punctuate the Thames riverside. Take your pick.

Art & Culture

A tireless innovator of art and culture, London's a city of ideas and the imagination. British people are fiercely independent thinkers (and critics) so London's creative milieu is naturally streaked with leftfield attitude, from theatrical innovation to contemporary art, pioneering music, writing and design. And that's even truer in these testing recessionary times. The artistic bar has been nudged higher, the audience is more demanding and the Olympic Games are limbering up, so London is moving heaven and earth to entertain. Revel in the choice.

Diversity

English may be the national tongue, but over 300 languages shape London's linguistic soundscape. These languages also represent cultures that season the culinary aromas on London's streets, the clothing you glimpse and the music you hear. It can seem like the whole world has come to town. Museums, such as the British Museum and the Victoria & Albert Museum, have collections as diverse as they are magnificent, while flavours at markets such as Borough and Exmouth range across the gourmet spectrum. London's diverse cultural dynamism makes it quite possibly the world's most international city, while being somehow intrinsically British.

A Tale of Two Cities

London is as much about high-density, sight-packed exploration (the West End, South Bank, the City) and urban dynamism as it is about wide-open spaces and leafy escapes. Central London is where you will find all the major museums, galleries and most iconic sights, but escape to Hampstead Heath or Greenwich Park to flee the crowds and put the city's greener hues into gorgeous perspective. Or venture even further out to Kew Gardens, Richmond or Hampton Court Palace for effortlessly good-looking panoramas of riverside London.

Why I love London

By Damian Harper

Growing up in Notting Hill was fantastic but what truly made me adore London was living all around it. Many Londoners are defiantly local, but to me it's not all about one area. It's the pumping vitality that animates one part of the city and the leafy tranquillity of others. Much of London's a whole mosaic of local histories and teasing them apart linguistically is magic. Take any name and see what you unearth: Aldwych (Auld-Wych – meaning the 'Old Settlement') is slap-bang in the centre of town and unsurprisingly the innocuous Holywell Lane in Shoreditch once bubbled over with sacred waters, while Chiswick was *the* place to go for cheese.

For more about our authors, see p464.

Tower Bridge (p150) on the River Thames

London's
Top 16

National Gallery (p93)

1 This superlative collection of (largely pre-modern) art at the heart of London is one of the world's largest and a roll-call of some of the world's most outstanding artistic compositions. With highlights including work from Leonardo Da Vinci, Michelangelo, Gainsborough, Constable, Turner, Monet, Renoir and Van Gogh, it's a bravura performance and one not to be missed. On-site restaurants and cafes are also exceptional, rounding out a terrific experience and putting the icing on an already eye-catching cake.

◉ *The West End*

British Museum (p83)

2 With five million visitors trooping through its doors annually, the British Museum in Bloomsbury is London's most popular tourist attraction. A vast and hallowed collection of artefacts, art and age-old antiquity, you could spend a lifetime here and still make daily discoveries (admission is free, so you could just do that, if so inclined). Otherwise join everyone else on the highlights tours (or eyeOpener tours) for a précis of the museum's treasures. GREAT COURT AT THE BRITISH MUSEUM

◉ *The West End*

ORIEN HARVEY / LONELY PLANET IMAGES ©

Tate Modern (p164)

3 The favourite of Londoners (and, quite possibly, the world), this contemporary art collection enjoys a triumphant position right on the River Thames. Housed in the former Bankside Power Station, the Tate Modern is a vigorous statement of modernity, architectural renewal and accessibility. The permanent collection is free, but make sure you enter down the ramp into the Turbine Hall, where the gallery's standout temporary exhibitions push the conceptual envelope and satisfy more cerebral art-hunters.

⊙ *The South Bank*

Tower of London (p141)

4 Few parts of the UK are as steeped in history or as impregnated with legend and superstition, as the titanic stonework of this fabulous fortress. A strong candidate for London's Top Sight, not only is the tower an architectural odyssey but there's also a diamond almost as big as the Ritz, free tours from its magnificently attired 'beefeaters', a dazzling array of armour and weaponry and a palpable sense of ancient history at every turn. Because there is simply so much to see, it's well worth getting here early as you will need at least half a day of exploration (probably more). It's definitely worth tagging along with one of the Yeoman Warders (beefeaters) on their fascinating and eye-opening tours.

⊙ *The City*

Sporting London (p72)

5 You may not land tickets to the FA Cup Final at Wembley Stadium or front-row seats for the men's 100m finals at the Olympic Stadium, but there are plenty of ways to enjoy sport in London. Whether you find yourself watching first-round matches at Wimbledon, cheering runners at the London Marathon, hopping on a Barclay's Bike to weave through the central London traffic or jogging around Battersea Park, there's lots on offer. And why not check out the impressive new facilities in Olympic Park, which hosts the Olympic Stadium, the stunning Aquatics Centre and the cutting-edge Velodrome. NOVAK DJOKOVIC, 2011 MEN'S SINGLES FINAL, WIMBLEDON

🏃 *Sports & Activities*

Natural History Museum *(p187)*

6 With its thunderous, animatronic Tyrannosaurus Rex, towering diplodocus skeleton, magical Wildlife Garden, outstanding Darwin Centre and architecture straight from a Gothic fairy tale, the Natural History Museum is quite simply a work of great curatorial imagination. Kids are the target audience but, when you look around, adults are equally mesmerised. Popular sleepovers in the museum have young ones snoozing alongside the diplodocus, while winter brings its own magic, as the glittering ice rink by the east lawn swarms with skaters.

⊙ *Kensington & Hyde Park*

National Maritime Museum *(p273)*

7 Exploring this shipshape museum is not just a first-rate lesson in England's rich maritime traditions but also an occasion to come to Greenwich and soak up its manifold riverine charms. Due to be boosted in size with a new wing in 2012, the museum is an inspiring flick through the brine-soaked pages of English history, fashioning an absorbing experience from a dramatic and often violent seafaring chronicle. Kids are well catered for, with ample hands-on stuff to keep young salty sea dogs occupied.

⊙ *Greenwich & South London*

London Eye (p169)

8 You may have eyed up London from altitude as you descended into Heathrow, but your pilot won't have lingered over the supreme views of town that extend in every direction from London's great riverside Ferris wheel. The queues move as slowly as the Eye rotates (there are ways to fast-track your way on), but that makes the occasion even more rewarding once you've lifted off and London unfurls beneath you. Avoiding grey days is the top tip – but with London's notoriously overcast skies that may be a tall order. If you've only a few days in the capital, make this your first stop and you can at least say you've seen the sights. LONDON EYE DESIGNED BY DAVID MARKS AND JULIA BARFIELD

⊙ *The South Bank*

Westminster Abbey (p80)

9 Adorers of medieval ecclesiastic architecture will be in seventh heaven at this sublime abbey and hallowed place of coronation for England's sovereigns. Within the Abbey, almost every nook and adorable cranny has a story attached to it but few sights in London are as beautiful, or as well preserved, as the Henry VII chapel. Elsewhere you will find the oldest door in the UK, Poet's Corner, the Coronation Chair, 14th-century cloisters, a 900-year-old garden, royal sarcophagi and much more. Be warned that the crowds are almost as solid as the Abbey's unshakeable stonework, so try to be as close to the front of the queue as you can first thing in the morning.

⊙ *The West End*

Hyde Park & Kensington Gardens (p192 & p191)

10 London's urban parkland is virtually second to none and is *the* place to see locals at ease and in their element. Hyde Park alone ranges across a mighty 142 hectares; throw in Kensington Gardens and you have even more space to roam and everything you could want: a central London setting, a royal palace, extravagant Victoriana, boating opportunities, open-air concerts, an art gallery, magnificent trees and a thoughtful and tasteful granite memorial to Princess Diana. HYDE PARK

⊙ *Kensington & Hyde Park*

Shakespeare's Globe (p168)

11 Few London experiences can beat a Bard's eye view of the stage at the recreated Globe and it's even more fun to get a ticket to stand (Elizabethan style) as one of the all-weather 'groundlings' (in the open-air yard before the stage, taking whatever the London skies deliver). But if you want a more comfortable perspective on Shakespeare, pay a bit more and grab one of the seats in the galleries. The theatre is a triumph of authenticity, right down to the nail-less construction, English oak beams, original joinery and thatching (sprinklers are a modern touch, as is the roar of overflying aircraft). If you've a soft spot for Shakespeare, architecture and the English climate, you'll have an absolute ball.

⊙ *The South Bank*

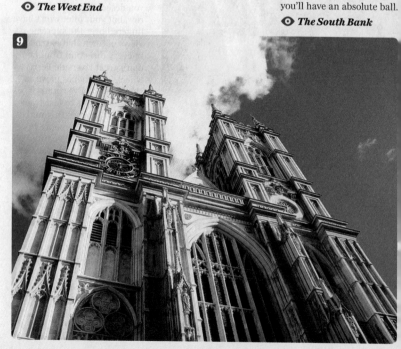

Notting Hill Carnival (p260)

12 Every August, trendy Notting Hill throws a big, long and loud party. Europe's leading street festival is a vibrantly colourful three-day celebration of Afro-Caribbean music, culture and food. Over a million people visit every year, taking part in the celebrations, thronging the streets and letting their hair down. The festival is a must if you want a spirited glimpse of multicultural London and its cross-pollination of music, food, clothing, language and culture.

⊙ *Notting Hill & West London*

Victoria & Albert Museum (p183)

13 You could spend your entire London trip in this huge museum and still be astounded at its variety and depth. Located in stylish South Kensington, the world's leading collection of decorative arts has something for everyone, from imposing 19th-century architecture to antique Chinese ceramics, Japanese armour, Islamic textiles, works by Raphael, a beautiful collection of jewellery and the revolutionary Sony Walkman (plus other modern design classics). And don't overlook the fabulous architecture of the museum, another major attraction in itself.

⊙ *Kensington & Hyde Park*

SIMON GREENWOOD / LONELY PLANET IMAGES ©

Camden Town (p240)

14 A foray into trendy North London is a crucial part of the London experience away from the central sights. Camden's market – actually four markets in one great melange – may be a hectic and tourist-oriented attraction, but snacking on the go from the international food stalls is a great way to enjoy browsing the merchandise, while Camden's terrific dining scene, throbbing nightlife and well-seasoned pub culture is well known to night owls citywide. DOC MARTENS FOR SALE, CAMDEN TOWN

⊙ *Hampstead & North London*

London Pubs (p54)

15 London minus its pubs would be like Paris sans cafes or Beijing shorn of its charming *hutong*. Pub culture is an indispensable element of London DNA and it's the place to be if you want to see local people in their hop-scented element. Longer hours for many pubs have only cemented them as the cornerstone for a good night out across the capital. Once no-go zones for discerning foodies, pubs long ago upped their game: standout gastropubs now dot London's culinary cosmos in highly tasty and appetising proportions, frequently putting top-tier restaurants to shame.

🍷 *Drinking & Nightlife*

CHRISTIAN HELMAGSSON / LONELY PLANET IMAGES ©

DOUG MCKINLAY / LONELY PLANET IMAGES ©

Kew Gardens (p296)

16 Where else in London can you size up an 18th-century 10-storey Chinese pagoda and a Japanese gateway while finding yourself among one of the world's most outstanding botanical collections? Kew Gardens is loved by Londoners for its 19th-century palm house, Victorian glasshouses, conservatories, tree canopy walkway, architectural follies and mind-boggling plant variety. You'll need a day to do it justice, but you could find yourself heading back for more.

◉ *Richmond, Kew & Hampton Court*

What's New

Olympic Park

Begun in 2008, the huge Olympic Park (p222) in Stratford has seen the conversion of a neglected and forgotten part of East London into a shimmering sporting development for the 2012 Games and beyond. Standout design highlights include the stunning Aquatics Centre, the Olympic Stadium and the state-of-the-art Velodrome. The entire park will be rebranded the Queen Elizabeth Olympic Park upon its reopening after the Games in 2013, in a bid to make the park a top destination for visitors and residents beyond the 2012 Games.

Barclay's Cycle Hire Scheme

London's enthusiastic, tousle-haired mayor Boris Johnson spearheaded this immensely popular bike-hire scheme, with the affectionately named 'Boris bikes' dotting the capital since 2010. All you need to hire a bike is your debit or credit card, a reasonably fit pair of legs and lungs, plus a basic sense of direction. There are over 400 well-marked docking stations (p393) around London and short trips are free!

Westfield Stratford City

Europe's largest urban shopping centre opened next to the Olympic Park in autumn 2011, with an astonishing 300 stores, 70 restaurants, a 17-screen cinema, three hotels, bowling alley and the UK's largest casino.

London Bridge Quarter Project

In a costly development, London Bridge station and the surrounding district is receiving a facelift, including erection of the already iconic (yet incomplete at the time of writing) Shard (p367), set to glitter high above South London in 2012.

East London Line Extension

Extensions to the East London Line now see stations in the southeast of London lashed onto the overground network and linked directly to Dalston Junction and Highbury & Islington. Visitors will enjoy a high-frequency service to sights in southeast London, such as the Horniman Museum and Crystal Palace Park plus the chance to rapidly shuttle between north and southeast London. A further extension from Surrey Quays to Clapham Junction will open in 2012.

British Museum Extension

The World Conservation and Exhibitions Centre is currently undergoing construction at the British Museum, with a late 2013 target completion date. The extension will house a new exhibition space plus conservation and science facilities.

New Routemaster Buses

Phased out (except for a few heritage routes) and sorely missed by both Londoners and visitors, London's classic Routemaster buses (hop-on, hop-off double-decker buses) are being resurrected in a modern and more environmentally friendly guise. A fleet of buses is expected to be routemastering the capital's streets from 2012.

Leicester Square

This famously underwhelming epicentral square has long punched way beneath its weight and is undergoing a revamp in preparation for a 2012 relaunch.

For more up-to-the-minute recommendations, see **lonelyplanet.com/london**

Need to Know

Currency
Pound sterling (£).
100 pence = £1.

Language
English (and over 300 others).

Visas
Not required for US, Canadian, Australian, New Zealand or South African visitors for stays up to six months. European Union nationals can stay indefinitely.

Money
ATMs widespread. Major credit cards accepted everywhere.

Mobile Phones
Buy local SIM cards for European and Australian phones, or a pay-as-you-go phone. Set other phones to international roaming.

Time
London is on GMT; during British Summer Time (BST; late March to late October), London clocks are one hour ahead of GMT.

Tourist information
Britain Visitor Centre (Map p422; www.visitbritain.com; 1 Regent St SW1; ⊘9.30am-6pm Mon, 9am-6pm Tue-Fri, 9am-4pm Sat, 10am-4pm Sun & bank holidays Sep-May, to 5pm Sat Jun-Sep; ⊖Piccadilly Circus) can book accommodation.

Your Daily Budget
The following are average costs per day.

Budget under £60
➜ Dorm beds £10-30

➜ Supermarkets, markets, lunchtime specials for food

➜ Loads of free or cheap museums and sights (p37)

➜ Reduced-price standby tickets or bargain cinema tickets

➜ Barclays Cycle Hire Scheme (p393)

Midrange £60-150
➜ Double room £100

➜ Two-course dinner with glass of wine £30

➜ Theatre ticket £10-50

Top End over £150
➜ Four-star/boutique hotel room £200

➜ Three-course dinner in top restaurant with wine £80-100

➜ Black cab trips £30

➜ Best-seats theatre tickets £65

Advance Planning

Three months Book weekend performance of top shows; dinner bookings at renowned restaurants; book tickets for must-see exhibitions; book a room at a popular hotel.

One month Check listings on entertainment sites such as www.timeout.com for fringe theatre, live music, festivals and book tickets.

A few days Check the weather on www.tfl.gov.uk/weather.

Websites

Lonely Planet (www.lonelyplanet.com/london

Visit London (www.visitlondon.com)

London Town (www.londontown.com)

Evening Standard (www.thisislondon.com)

Time Out (www.timeout.com/london)

Transport for London (www.tfl.gov.uk)

WHEN TO GO

Summer is peak season: days are long, festivals are afoot, but it's busy and crowded; spring and autumn are cooler, but delightful. Winter is cold but quiet.

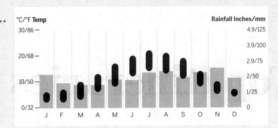

Arriving in London

Heathrow Airport Trains, London Underground (tube) and buses to central London 5.25am to midnight (night buses run later) £5-17; taxi £45-65.

Gatwick Airport Trains to central London 4.30am to 1.35am £7-18; buses run to central London hourly 6am to 9.45pm £7.50-10; taxi £90.

Stansted Airport Trains run to central London 5.30am to around midnight £21. Buses to central London run round the clock £9-10.50; taxi £90.

Luton Airport Trains run to central London 7am to 10pm £12.50. Buses run to central London round the clock £10-16; taxi £90.

London City Airport Trains run to central London 5.30am to 12.30am Mon to Sat, 7am to 11.30pm Sunday; taxi £30.

St Pancras International Train Station In Central London (for Eurostar train arrivals from Europe) and connected by many underground lines to other parts of the city.

For much more on Arrival, see p388.

Getting Around

Prepaid Oyster cards can be used across London's transport network, offering the cheapest fares. Buy one (and top up) at most tube stations, most train stations and many newsagents.

Underground (tube) The quickest way to get around; trains run 5.30am to 12.30am (7am to 11.30pm Sunday).

Bus Slow going but ace views from double-deckers. Large number of night buses.

Train Mostly useful for outlying areas such as Hampton Court and day trips (p307).

Bicycle The Barclays Cycle Hire Scheme (p393) is excellent value, and free for short hops.

Taxi Black cabs can be hailed on the street when the yellow light is lit.

Boat Good for such destinations as Hampton Court Palace and Kew Gardens, but slow.

Walking A lot of central sightseeing is best done on foot.

Car hire It's generally better to use a combination of the above; if you drive, beware the congestion charge (p394).

For much more on Getting Around, see p391.

Sleeping

Hanging your hat in London can be expensive and as the city is busy at the best of times, you'll need to book your room well in advance to secure your top choice.

Decent, centrally located hostels are easy enough to find and also offer reasonably priced double rooms. Bed and breakfasts are a dependable and inexpensive, if rather simple, option. Hotels range from cheap, no-frills chains through boutique choices to luxury five-star historic hotels fit to sleep royalty.

Websites

For general traveller information on London and hotel bookings, try:

➡ **Lonely Planet** (www.lonelyplanet.com/london) Destination information, hotel bookings, traveller forum and more.

➡ **Visit London** (www.visitlondon.com) Wide range of accommodation options by area within town.

➡ **London Town** (www.londontown.com) Great deals and special offers.

For much more on Sleeping, see p322.

Top Itineraries

Day One

The West End (p78)

 First stop, **Trafalgar Square** for its architectural grandeur and photo-op views down Whitehall to **Big Ben**. Art lovers will make an instant break for the **National Gallery** while the **Houses of Parliament**, **Westminster Abbey** and **Buckingham Palace** can all be reached on foot. If the sun's out, seize a sandwich and race to the grass of leafy **St James's Park**.

> **Lunch** National Dining Rooms (p121) in the National Gallery: fantastic choice.

South Bank (p162)

Walk across Westminster Bridge to Waterloo and, with your pre-booked ticket for the **London Eye**, enjoy a revolution in the city skies and astronomical views (if the weather's clear). Sashay along the South Bank and head down the ramp into the bowels of the **Tate Modern** for some grade-A art. Aim your camera at **St Paul's Cathedral** on the far side of the elegant **Millennium Bridge** and don't forget **Shakespeare's Globe**.

> **Dinner** Skylon (p173) for top views, but book well ahead.

Southwark & South Bank (p162)

 Southwark Cathedral is well worth a gander and if **Borough Market**'s open, follow your nostrils to some fine snacking on the move. Take to the terrace of the **Anchor Bankside** to sup on a post-dinner glass but have your camera primed again for the views. Alternatively, sink a drink in the historic **George Inn** on Borough High St or have theatre tickets booked for the **Globe**, the **National Theatre** or the **Old Vic**.

Day Two

The City (p139)

 London's finance-driven Square Mile is home to the must-see sights of **St Paul's Cathedral** and the **Tower of London**, both of which will require time. This is the oldest part of town, so there are plentiful churches and historic buildings, while innovative chunks of modern architecture also pierce the sky. Don't overlook the **Museum of London** if there's time and, of course, views of iconic **Tower Bridge** and the river.

> **Lunch** The Restaurant at St Paul's (p157) is a handy choice.

The West End (p78)

Stand amid the swirling traffic at **Piccadilly Circus** before exploring well-heeled Mayfair, bustling **Chinatown** and historic **Soho**, then head to **Covent Garden Piazza** to watch the street performers and shop. Alternatively, save some calories for tackling the immensity of the **British Museum** in Bloomsbury or window shop your way along Oxford Street to **Marble Arch** and on into **Hyde Park**.

> **Dinner** Yauatcha (p116) for excellent Chinese food.

The West End (p78)

 Relax on the grass of **Green Park** or **St James's Park** as lights prepare to sparkle across the West End. Squeeze into **French House** for a quick pint, aim for one of the neighbourhood's outstanding dining options and have theatre tickets booked way ahead for a hit musical in London's 'theatreland'.

Day Three

Kensington, Chelsea & Knightsbridge (p181)

 Make for South Kensington to explore the **Victoria & Albert Museum** or the **Natural History Museum**, before roaming around **Hyde Park** and **Kensington Palace**. Shop along Kensington High Street, the **King's Road** or head to Knightsbridge and get swept away by the crowds in **Harrods**. For peace and quiet, head to the **Chelsea Physic Garden**, a walled botanical haven near the **River Thames**, or explore tranquil **Carlyle's House**. For full-on historic grandeur, take in **Apsley House**.

> **Lunch** Zuma (p196) for top-notch Japanese cuisine.

Clerkenwell, Shoreditch & Spitalfields (p201)

 Wander around **Georgian Spitalfields** and explore the cultural diversity along **Brick Lane**, size up contemporary art at the **White Cube Gallery** and the intriguing interiors of the **Geffrye Museum** before digging out some history at **St John's Gate**. For a quiet escape, hunt down the tombs and graves of the famous in **Bunhill Fields**.

> **Dinner** Moro (p205) serves splendid North African–Spanish fusion food.

North London (p233)

For nightlife, head north – weekends, especially, are buzzing: head to Dalston for ultra-hip clubs, Camden for live music. You can find excellent gastropubs, pubs, bars and DJ bars right across the neighbourhood, but focal points are Hampstead, Islington, Camden and King's Cross.

Day Four

Greenwich (p268)

 Greenwich's architectural and maritime sights are world-renowned but there are also lovely village charms and some tremendous pubs, some of them right on the riverbank. Sights such as the **Royal Observatory**, **National Maritime Museum** and **Old Royal Naval College** are near each other, so sightseeing can easily be done on foot.

> **Lunch** The Old Brewery (p282) is great for Modern British cuisine.

Kew Gardens, Hampton Court Palace (p291)

Choose between one of these two spectacular sights to flee urban London and swallow up an afternoon of sightseeing: **Hampton Court Palace** for astonishing Tudor brickwork and interiors, **Kew Gardens** for a botanical wonderland, some magnificent Victorian glasshouse architecture and an 18th-century Chinese pagoda. Alternatively, head to Richmond for its leisurely riverside ambience and views.

> **Dinner** Tatra (p261) for classic Polish dishes.

Notting Hill and West London (p256)

Round off the day with a pint in the garden at the **Windsor Castle** pub or another of the drinking houses between Kensington High Street and Notting Hill Gate. For something different, dress up and ascend to the nightclub in the **Kensington Roof Gardens** – a club high above Kensington High St with half a hectare of gardens and four pink flamingos.

If You Like...

Art

Tate Modern A breathtaking collection of modern and contemporary art in a power station setting right on South Bank (p164).

National Gallery Overdose on culture at this stupendous collection of more than 2000 pre-20th-century paintings housed in fabulous premises right at the heart of London (p93).

Tate Britain Works by JMW Turner are the standout pieces here, but this excellent museum has a sublime collection of pre-Raphaelite art and hosts the annual Turner Prize (p98).

Wallace Collection An astonishing treasure trove of art, furniture, porcelain and armour housed in a sublime Italianate mansion (p113).

National Portrait Gallery Celebrated British people creatively captured by equally famous artists over five hundred years (p97).

Royalty

Tower of London Castle, tower, prison, medieval execution site and home of the dazzling Crown Jewels (p142).

Buckingham Palace The Queen Mother of all London's royal palaces, with lovely gardens and – the popular drawcard – Changing of the Guard (p88).

Hampton Court Palace Magnificent Tudor palace, located within beautiful grounds on the Thames (p293).

MICHAEL COYNE / LONELY PLANET IMAGES ©

Changing of the Guard (p89), Buckingham Palace

Kensington Palace Princess Diana's former home, this stately (and recently restored) and stunning royal palace is the highlight of Kensington Gardens (p194).

St James's Palace The official Tudor residence of English sovereigns for more than three hundred years (p104).

Views

St Paul's Cathedral Climb up into London's largest ecclesiastical dome for gobsmacking views of town (p147).

London Eye For gently rotating, tip-top views of London – but choose a fair-weather day (p169).

Parliament Hill Skyscraping views across London from Hampstead Heath (p241).

Anchor Bankside Hop up to the terrace of this riverside pub for picture-postcard panoramas across the Thames (p177).

Trafalgar Square Take a long, long look down Whitehall to Big Ben (p96).

5th View Mouthwatering views of Westminster top the menu (p118).

Greenwich Park Clamber up to the statue of General Wolfe for superlative views (p271).

Parks & Gardens

Hampstead Heath Woods, hills, meadows and top scenic views, all rolled into one sublime sprawl (p241).

Hyde Park Grand gardens, lovely lawns, a head-turning variety of trees and inviting expanses of greenery (p192).

Dulwich Park Hire one of the park's low-slung bikes and cycle round this terrific area of grass and trees (p281).

Richmond Park Europe's largest urban parkland has everything from herds of deer to tranquil pockets of woodland, seemingly infinite wild tracts and beautiful vistas (p298).

St James's Park Feast on some sublime views in one of London's most attractive royal parks (p103).

Kew Gardens A botanist's paradise, a huge expanse of greenery and a great day out with the kids (p296).

Chelsea Physic Garden Tranquil and particularly tidy botanical enclave just a stone's throw from the Thames (p193).

Animals & Wildlife

London Zoo With a new tiger enclosure planned, this is one of the world's oldest and most famous zoos (p237).

Natural History Museum An A–Z of the natural world displayed in an iconic chunk of South Kensington Victorian architecture (p187).

Sea Life London Aquarium Tremendous collection of creatures from the world's saltwater depths on display next to the Thames (p169).

Horniman Museum Huge stuffed walrus, moon jellyfish, a swarm of bees, sumptuous gardens...and loads of kids (p279).

Mudchute Park & Farm Lovely city farm on the Isle of Dogs: cows, sheep and llamas with a Canary Wharf backdrop (p224).

Kensington Roof Gardens Not many rooftop bars come equipped with their own pink flamingos (p263).

For more top London spots, see

➡ Museums & Galleries (p39)

➡ Eating (p44)

➡ Drinking & Nightlife (p53)

➡ Gay & Lesbian (p59)

➡ Entertainment (p61)

➡ Shopping (p67)

➡ Sports & Activities (p72)

PLAN YOUR TRIP IF YOU LIKE...

Cemeteries

Highgate Cemetery Gothic and sublimely overgrown 20-hectare Victorian place of the dead, including Karl Marx (p245).

Abney Park Cemetery Tangled with weeds, reclaimed by nature, with moments of magic (p242).

Brompton Cemetery Some of this cemetery's dead found immortality in the names of Beatrix Potter's animal characters (p258).

Tower Hamlets Cemetery Park Another specialist in the wild and sublime Victorian ruin look (p222).

Squares

Trafalgar Square London's iconic central square, lorded over by Lord Nelson – and four magnificent felines (p96).

Soho Square Serene spot for a sandwich in the sun at the heart of the West End (p92).

Trinity Square Gardens Picturesque and well-tended one-time location of the notorious Tower Hill scaffold (p150).

Squares of Bloomsbury Elegant, historic and tranquil squares dotted around literary Bloomsbury (p101).

Covent Garden Piazza
Fine-looking West End square originally laid out in the 17th century, and popular with street performers (p107).

Music

Proud Camden Leading North London bar with foot-stomping live music and a superb terrace (p248).

Royal Albert Hall Venue of the proms and the UK's most iconic concert venue (p192).

Fabric Three-floor first port of call for hip clubbers in town (p210).

Horniman Museum Eclectic Forest Hill museum with an astonishing exhibition of musical instruments and hands-on musical displays (p279).

606 Club Get into the subterranean swing of things at this atmospheric and world-famous jazz club (p198).

Royal Festival Hall Fantastic acoustics and an excellent program of music across the aural spectrum (p178).

Church Recitals Take a pew at one of the many free afternoon church recitals around town (p38).

Cultural Diversity

Chinatown At the heart of London and the place to be for dim sum dining or the Chinese New Year (p92).

Brick Lane Take a wander and a gander and go shopping around this vibrant London outpost of the Bangladeshi community (p204).

Brixton Village Great dining and shopping converge in South London's most famous multicultural neighbourhood (p289).

Kingsland Road If Vietnamese cuisine is on your list, you can't go wrong (p209).

Whitechapel Road Lively, vibrant and cacophonous tangle of cultures and languages (p219).

Rivers and Canals

Regent's Canal Amble along the historic trade route and take a shortcut across North London at the same time (p239).

Richmond Home to some spectacular views of the Thames with enchanting pastoral shade in Petersham Meadows (p300).

Greenwich Pop into a riverside pub and toast the fine views of the river with a pint (p268).

South Bank Hop on our South Bank Walk and walk from County Hall to City Hall past some outstanding waterside sights (p175).

Hampton Court Palace Take a riverboat up the Thames to Henry VIII's spectacular palace (p293).

Village Charms

Primrose Hill With lovely restaurants, boutiques and pubs, this North London village has genuine appeal (and celebrity-spotting ops) (p239).

Richmond Perhaps the archetypal London village, with village green, a river perspective, a fabulous bridge and gorgeous parkland. (p298).

Greenwich Beyond Greenwich's stately sights, its back streets exude a village tempo, with rows of charming terraced two-floor cottages (p273).

Dulwich Village After viewing the Dulwich Picture Gallery, wander around Dulwich Village

with its towering horse chestnut trees to experience some of London's easy-going and tranquil charms (p281).

Wimbledon Well-heeled Wimbledon's leafy atmosphere is the perfect antidote to central London's urban density (p302).

Putney & Barnes Barnes is more village-like but parts of Putney are a joy as well (p299).

Walking

Hampstead Heath Wild, hilly, carefree heathland and woodland with some excellent views from London's highest open space (p241).

Regent's Canal Take a canalside hike across North London (p239).

South Bank Take our riverside walk from the County Hall to Tower Bridge (p175).

Putney to Barnes Amble along the delightful riverside on this do-able segment of the Thames Path (p295).

The West End Jump on our highlights tour from Covent Garden to Trafalgar Square (p115).

Wimbledon Common Follow nature trails or just branch off in any direction for woodland, heath, grassland and bracing exploration (p302).

Churches

St Paul's Cathedral Sir Christopher Wren's 300-year old domed masterpiece and London's most iconic historic church (p147).

Westminster Abbey Ancient and sublime site of coronation for English monarchs since William the Conqueror (p80).

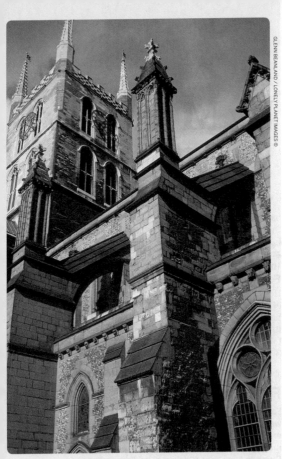

Above: Southwark Cathedral (p172)

Below: London Eye (p169), designed by David Marks and Julia Barfield

Westminster Cathedral The gaunt interior sparkles fitfully with dazzling Byzantine mosaics (p195).

Brompton Oratory Sublime, incense-wreathed Catholic church in dapper Knightsbridge (p193).

Southwark Cathedral Rich in intriguing detail, from 12th-century remains to a fine Elizabethan sideboard (p172).

St James's Piccadilly Another Wren church and home to an arts and crafts fair, music recitals and concerts (p104).

Modern Architecture

Aquatics Centre Striking and dramatic masterpiece of the Olympic Park (p222).

30 St Mary Axe Colloquially dubbed 'the Gherkin' and the city's most iconic modern edifice (p151).

Shard A crystalline spike slowly forming over South Bank (p366).

Lloyd's of London Richard Rogers' inside-out London masterpiece (p151).

London Eye Unsurprisingly visible from many remote parts of town (p169).

City Hall Does it look like a woodlouse or Darth Vader's helmet? Your call (p172).

Month by Month

January

January in London kicks off with a big bang at midnight at the end of the year. London has yet to shake off winter, but the London Art Fair brings splashes of colour.

New Year's Celebration

On 31 December, the famous countdown to midnight in Trafalgar Square is met with terrific fireworks and massive crowds.

London Art Fair

Over 100 major galleries participate in this contemporary art fair (www.londonartfair.co.uk; Business Design Centre, Islington), now one of the largest in Europe, with thematic exhibitions, special events and the best emerging artists.

London International Mime Festival

Held in the last two weeks of January, this festival is a must for lovers of originality, playfulness, physical talent and the unexpected (www.mimefest.co.uk).

February

February is usually chilly, wet and even snow-encrusted, but spring may peek through. The Chinese New Year (Spring Festival) is fun, and Londoners lark about with pancakes on Shrove Tuesday.

Chinese New Year

In late January but usually early February, Chinatown fizzes, crackles and pops in this colourful street festival, which includes a Golden Dragon parade, eating and partying.

Pancake Races

On Shrove Tuesday, in late February/early March, you can catch pancake races and associated silliness at various venues around town (Spitalfields Market, Covent Garden & Lincoln's Inn Fields).

March

March sees spring in the London air and trees beginning to flower, most colourfully in parks and gardens (p274). London is getting in the mood to head outdoors again.

Head of the River Race

Some 400 crews take part in this colourful annual boat race (www.horr.co.uk) held over a 7km course on the Thames, from Mortlake to Putney.

Kew Gardens Spring Festival

For flower aficionados, this is the best time (continuing through April) to see Kew Gardens (p296).

St Patrick's Day Parade & Festival

Top festival for the Irish in London, held on the Sunday closest to 17 March, with a colourful parade through central London and other festivities in and around Trafalgar Square.

April

April sees London in bloom with warmer days and a spring in everyone's step. Runners spill onto the streets for the London Marathon and some sights previously shut for winter reopen.

🏃 London Marathon

Some 35,000 runners – most running for charity – pound London in one of the world's biggest road races (www.virginlondonmarathon.com), heading from Greenwich Park to the Mall.

🏃 Oxford & Cambridge Boat Race

Crowds line the banks of the Thames for the country's two most famous universities going oar-to-oar from Putney to Mortlake. Dates vary, due to each university's Easter breaks, so check the website (www.theboatrace.org).

May

A delightful time to be in London: days are warming up and Londoners begin to start lounging around in parks, popping sunshades on and enjoying bank holiday weekends.

◉ Chelsea Flower Show

The world's most renowned horticultural event (www.rhs.org.uk) attracts the cream of London's green-fingered and flower-mad gardeners.

June

The peak season begins with long, warm days, the arrival of Wimbledon and other alfresco events.

◉ Royal Academy Summer Exhibition

Beginning in June and running through August, this exhibition (www.royalacademy.org.uk) showcases works submitted by artists from all over Britain, distilled to a thousand or so pieces.

◉ Trooping the Colour

The Queen's official birthday is celebrated with much flag-waving, parades, pageantry and noisy flyovers (www.trooping-the-colour.co.uk).

🏃 Wimbledon Lawn Tennis Championships

For two weeks a year the quiet South London village of Wimbledon falls under a sporting spotlight as the world's best tennis players gather to battle for the championship (www.wimbledon.com).

◉ Open Garden Squares Weekend

Over one weekend, more than 200 gardens (www.opensquares.org) in London that are usually inaccessible to the public fling open their gates for exploration.

July

July features the capital's major gay parade, a host of outdoor festivities and the music calendar hits a high note with the Proms.

🎭 Pride London

The gay community paints the town pink in this annual extravaganza (www.pridelondon.org), featuring a morning parade and a huge afternoon event on Trafalgar Square (locations frequently change).

☆ BBC Promenade Concert (the Proms)

Two months of outstanding classical concerts (www.bbc.co.uk/proms) at various prestigious venues, centred on the Royal Albert Hall (p198).

August

Schools have broken up for summer, families are holidaying and the hugely popular annual Caribbean carnival dances into Notting Hill.

🎭 Notting Hill Carnival

Europe's biggest – and London's most vibrant – outdoor carnival (www.thecarnival.tv) is a celebration of Caribbean London, featuring music, dancing and costumes over the summer bank holiday weekend.

✨ Great British Beer Festival

Organised by CAMRA (Campaign for Real Ale), this boozy festival (http://gbbf.camra.org.uk) cheerfully cracks open casks of ale from the UK and abroad at Earls Court Exhibition Centre.

September

The end of summer and start of autumn is a lovely time to be in town, with comedy festivals and a chance to look at London properties normally shut to the public.

✨ The Mayor's Thames Festival

Celebrating the River Thames, this cosmopolitan festival (www.thamesfestival.org) sees fairs, street theatre, music, food stalls, fireworks and river races culminating in the superb Night Procession.

✨ Greenwich Comedy Festival

Bringing giggles to Greenwich over a week in early September.

⊙ London Open House

For a weekend in late September, the public is invited in to see over 700 heritage buildings throughout the capital that are normally off-limits (www.londonopenhouse.org), p363.

🏃 Great Gorilla Run

It looks bananas, but this gorilla-costume charity run (www.greatgorillarun.org/london) along a 7km route from the City to Bankside

Above: Great Gorilla Run
Below: Lord Mayor's Show

and back again is all in aid of gorilla conservation.

October

The weather is getting colder, the clocks go back an hour and London's parkland is splashed with autumnal colours.

🌠 Dance Umbrella

London's annual festival of contemporary dance (www.danceumbrella. co.uk) features five weeks of performances by British and international dance companies at venues across London.

🌠 London Film Festival

The city's premier film event (www.lff.org.uk) attracts big overseas names and you can catch over 100 British and international films before their cinema release. Masterclasses are

given by world-famous directors.

November

London nights are getting longer but they crackle with fireworks in the first week of November.

☆ Guy Fawkes Night (Bonfire Night)

Bonfire Night commemorates Guy Fawkes' foiled attempt to blow up Parliament in 1605. Bonfires and fireworks light up the night on 5 November. Primrose Hill, Highbury Fields, Alexandra Palace, Clapham Common and Crystal Palace Park all have the best firework displays.

◉ Lord Mayor's Show

In accordance with the Magna Carta of 1215, the newly elected Lord Mayor

of the City of London travels in a state coach from Mansion House to the Royal Courts of Justice to take an oath of allegiance to the Crown. The floats, bands and fireworks that accompany the Mayor were added later (www.lordmay orsshow.org).

December

London may see snow and a festive mood reigns as Christmas approaches and shops are dressed up to the nines.

◉ Lighting of the Christmas Tree & Lights

A celebrity is normally carted in to switch on all the festive lights that line Oxford, Regent and Bond streets, and a towering Norwegian spruce is set up in Trafalgar Square.

With Kids

London is a fantastic place for children. The city's museums will fascinate all ages, and you'll find theatre, dance and music performances perfect for older kids. Playgrounds and parks, city farms and nature reserves are perfect for either toddler energy busting or relaxation.

Summer fountain, Royal Festival Hall, Southbank Centre (p170)

DOUG MCKINLAY / LONELY PLANET IMAGES ©

Central London Kid Picks

Hyde Park and St James's Park
Open spaces, playgrounds, water and wildlife. See p192 and p103.

West End
Museum and gallery activities. See p78.

Coram's Fields
Sand pits, swings, animals, and areas for all kinds of acrobatics. See www.corams fields.org.

Kensington Gardens
A ship-shaped playground and wonderful paddling fountain. See p191.

East London Kid Picks

V&A Museum of Childhood
Active and gregarious fun in the numerous play areas. See p220.

Hackney City Farm
Best combined with a nearby market (Columbia Rd or Broadway Market) for teens. See www.hackneycityfarm.co.uk.

Mudchute City Farm
The biggest city farm in town. See p224.

South London Kid Picks

Southbank Centre
Car free and full of fun, music events at the Royal Festival Hall (p170) for teens.

Battersea Park
Leafy and with its own zoo. See p278.

Horniman Museum
Has an array of free-to-touch objects, such as puppets and masks, and interactive exhibits in the Nature Base. The Music Gallery is a true highlight, with 1,600 instruments on display; not only can the little ones listen to the instruments' sounds, they can also bash on a selection in the Hands On room. See www.horni man.ac.uk.

Vauxhall City Farm

Animal petting and picnicking on the grass. See p283.

North London Kid Picks

London Zoo

Where the wild things are. See p237.

Hampstead Heath

The closest your child will get to a real forest within the city. See p241.

Kentish Town City Farm

A lovely place to get in touch with the gentle beasts. See www.ktcityfarm.org.uk.

Best Museums

London's museums are anything if not child friendly. You'll find storytelling at the National Gallery (three years and over; p93), arts and crafts workshops at the Victoria & Albert Museum (p183), train-making workshops at the Transport Museum (p107), tons of finger-painting opportunities at Tate Modern (p164) and Tate Britain (p98), or performance, art and crafts at Somerset House (p110). And what's better, they're all free (check websites for details). You'll also find that many arts and cultural festivals aimed at adults also cater to children – an example is the annual Opera Holland Park Opera (p265) with its opera performances aimed at children.

Get behind the wheel at the London Transport Museum

Twenty of London Transport buses and trains are on display and available for touching, climbing on and general child-handling, while also providing valuable learning opportunities on the history of the development of London and its transport. There is a modest picnic area too. Check the website for workshop information. See p107.

Meet the mummies at the British Museum

London's, and Britain's, best museum has hours of fun for all the family, but plan your visit in advance since the place is vast. The mummies are always a favourite with children over three. See p83.

Interact till you drop at the Science Museum

This is the definitive children's museum, with interactive displays, fascinating learning and educational displays, as well as a basement Garden play area. There are also great storytelling sessions and a fantastic cafe for families. See p190.

Gawp at the dinosaurs at the Natural History Museum

The weekend and half-term time queues attest to this museum's immense popularity with families, thanks to its fascinating permanent display of around 70 million plant, animal, fossil, rock and mineral specimens, a Wildlife Garden, and the excellent temporary exhibitions, such as the 2011 'Age of the Dinosaur', with life-size moving dinosaur animatronics. See p187.

Museum Sleepovers

What better fun than to spend the night curled up with the mummies (of the ancient kind) or next to a dinosaur's paw?

British Museum

Bed down in the Egyptian and Mesopotamian galleries, but not before storytelling and activities relating to the museum's

VERONICA GARBUTT / LONELY PLANET IMAGES ©

Palm House, Kew Gardens (p296)

current exhibitions. Excellent fun. Quarterly only. See p83.

Natural History Museum

Dino Snore in the grand Central Hall under the watchful eye of the 150-million-year-old Diplodocus, having first explored the museum's darkest nooks and crannies with only a torch to light your way. See p187.

Science Museum

Running for nearly 20 years, this is the young Londoners' favourite, with IMAX 3D film screenings and science workshops to lull you to sleep. See p190.

Museum Ice Skating

In winter months (November to January), a section by the East Lawn of the Natural History Museum is transformed into a glittering and highly popular ice rink. Book your slot well ahead (www.ticketmaster.co.uk). See p72 for more ice-skating rinks in London.

Eating with Kids

OK, it's not Italy, Spain or France in its uber-relaxed approach to small diners, but most of London's restaurants and cafes are child friendly and offer baby-changing facilities and high chairs. Pick your places with some awareness – avoid high-end and more quiet, small restaurants and cafes if you have toddlers or small babies (and those with the 'No Children' signs on the doors!), and go for noisier restaurants and more relaxed cafes, and you'll find that you'll be welcomed and probably even given that hardest of London's currencies to come by – a smile.

London is a great opportunity for your kids to taste all the world's cuisines in close proximity to each other, so pick from good- quality (and MSG-free) Chinese, to Italian, French, Mexican, Japanese and Indian restaurants. Many places have kids' menus, but ask for smaller portions of adult dishes if your children have a more adventurous palatte; you'll find that most places will be keen to oblige. Otherwise, kids' menus range from the usual burgers, pastas (tomato/bolognese sauce), sausage and mash, and so on, and cost anything from £2.50 to £5.

Best Kid-Friendly Eateries

Cibo at Mamas & Papas

Best for babies. See www.mamasandpapas.com.

That Place on the Corner

Great food and tons of workshops and classes and birthday party catering. See www.thatplaceonthecorner.co.uk.

Huggle

A chic cafe with workshops and a play area. See www.huggle.co.uk.

Frizzante @ City Farm

Great cafe (p227) for a big lunch before or after animal sightings.

NEED TO KNOW

→ Under-16s travel free on buses, under-11s travel free on the tube and under-5s go free on the trains.

→ Get a babysitter or nanny at Greatcare (www.greatcare.co.uk).

→ The best way to see London is to walk – public transport can be crowded and hot in the summer months.

→ If you are a new London resident, check your local council for information on child-friendly activities in your area.

Parks & Playgrounds

Great parks abound in London and, within them, an abundance of playgrounds and wildlife. Here are some favourites.

St James's Park

Admiring the ducks and squirrels and watching the pelicans' teatime is a must at St James's Park (p103), followed by running around the rocky playground and sandpit. Finish up with a break at Inn the Park.

Coram's Fields

Almost three hectares of lawns, sandpit, shallow pool, animal yard, swings and other contraptions are all yours at Coram's Fields, a local favourite.

Hyde Park

Row your boat on the Serpentine Lake or hire a pedalo and go out onto the water *en famille*. You can also cycle (hire a 'Boris bike' in the park) and hit the ship-shaped playground at the Princess Diana Memorial, in Kensington Gardens. See p192.

Battersea Park

A leafy haven that contains its own zoo and provides some great playing opportunities. See p278.

Regent's Park

A truly wonderful park (p238), with lots of peaceful green spaces that your child can enliven – and it is home to London Zoo (p237), which makes it cool without even trying.

Off-Beat Activities

If you're a London resident, or if you're just after a bit of off-beat fun for your children, take them to one of these courses:

Children's cookery classes

Try **La Cucina Caldesi** (www.caldesi.com) in Marylebone who aim their courses from six-year-olds to teens or **Kiddy Cook** (www. kiddycook.co.uk) in Twickenham, who will let a two-year-old get busy with the raw ingredients.

Circus skills

Get those unicycling skills up to scratch at **Albert & Friends Instant Circus** (www. albertandfriendsinstantcircus.co.uk; 3+).

Mushroom Hunting

Fungi to be With (www.fungitobewith.org) mushroom hunting in Hampstead Heath, Epping Forest and Wimbledon Common.

City Farms & Nature Reserves

City kids need a daily, or at least weekly, fix of their animal buddies, and London obliges with the UK's most diverse pick of the animal kingdom through its city farms, zoos and nature reserves.

Freightliners City Farm

A fantastic working **farm** (www.freightlinersfarm.org.uk) in the inner city that's home to cows, sheep, pigs and Giant Flemmish rabbits. It's also a community centre with an own-built cafe and opportunities to buy eggs and vegies grown on the farm.

Hackney City Farm

A retreat from the urbane East London surroundings, the **Hackney City Farm** (www.hackneycityfarm.co.uk) has goats, sheep, pigs and a donkey named Larry. It also has a vegetable and herb garden and sells eggs; the on-site Frizzante @City Farm (p227) has won awards for its excellent food.

Greenwich Peninsula Ecology Park

The perfect place to meander on the marshland paths and bird watch. Lose yourself in nature in the midst of industrial London. See www.urbanecology.org.uk.

Kentish Town City Farm

London's oldest city **farm** (www.ktcityfarm. org.uk) has been going since 1972 and was the example for the rest of the capital's farms. Apart from petting the animals, kids can get involved in feeding and cleaning; there are popular pony-riding and pottery-throwing workshops too.

Highgate Wood & Queen's Wood

Once part of the ancient Forest of Middlesex, **Highgate Wood** (www.cityoflondon. gov.uk/openspaces) is a huge woodland area that feels worlds away from the traffic-laden streets of London. The entire place is just heavenly for kids with its carefully thought-out playground and outdoor storytelling sessions and treasure hunts.

Mudchute City Farm

This is the largest city farm in town, though the view of the nearby Canary Wharf skyscrapers excludes the chance of the farm imagining itself to be a bucolic idyll. There's a 9am duck walk and other daily activities, as well as a great picnic area. See p224.

Epping Forest

Twelve miles in length and nearly as many across, Epping Forest is popular for horse riding, cycling and walking, and is also the place to spot a grazing cow. Best for older kids and their families, and those keen on getting plenty of exercise.

Like a Local

...ocal life envelops you in London, ...ut you might notice it only in ...natches. Londoners know how ...o avoid the tourist crowds, so go ...here they go and be surprised. ...ocals wait till late-opening ...ights before slipping into ...useums or galleries; the sun ...ops out and they swarm to parks.

GREG BALFOUR EVANS / ALAMY©

...n Park (p105)

Drinking Like a Local

The British and Londoners get bad press for binge drinking. But most drinking in London is actually warmly sociable, gregarious and harmless fun. Londoners drink at the 'local', shorthand for the 'pub round the corner'. It's a community mainstay and a local haven. Prices may be high but generosity is commonplace and drinkers always step up to buy the next round. Aim for pubs with a sense of quirky history and a great range of ales and you can't go wrong. For more information on the London pub scene, see p53.

Dining Like a Local

Londoners can be found queuing for seats or reserving tables at stylish restaurants across the city. As a rule of thumb, however, they'll dine at their local fish and chip shop rather than trek across town, but once a week they'll don their glad rags and blow their savings on a treat. You'll find them stocking up at Borough Market (p176) and other food markets, and picking up organic vegetables at farmers markets across town. But you'll also find them piling on the peri-peri sauce at Nando's, downing bowls of noodles at Wagamama or grabbing a sandwich from Marks & Spencer to sit out in Hyde Park. Sunday roast in a pub is a local weekend institution. For more information on eating out in London, see p44.

Shopping Like a Local

They are on home turf, so Londoners know precisely where to shop. They'll be in charity shops hunting for overlooked first editions and hard-to-find clothing, skimming market stalls for vintage togs off Brick Lane, browsing along Portobello Rd, rifling through Brixton Village or retreating to small, independent bookshops for peace, quiet and old-school service. But you'll also find them in well-heeled Mayfair, bargain hunting along Kensington High St and Oxford St. For more information on shopping in London, see p67.

Taking to the Park

Greenwich locals may have only a minute courtyard garden, but one of the largest parks in town is right on their doorstep. Some Richmond folk are in the same boat. Despite being urban creatures, Londoners have a very, very low tolerance for concrete compared to, say, the Chinese. They also have access to some of the world's most beautiful urban parks and consequently are, more often than not, reading a book, playing football or simply chatting with friends on the grass. After, or during, a day of sightseeing, it can be the perfect way to recharge. For more on parks, see p274.

Sightseeing Like a Local

Londoners are habitually off the beaten track, taking the back route into their local park, exploring London's wilder fringes or making short cuts like following Regent's Canal (p239) across North London. Go exploring in London and see what you find. Many Londoners bide their time till late-night openings at museums (p40), for less crowds and more space.

Local Obsessions

The Weather

Londoners are highly skilled at meteorological conversations (talking about the weather), so if you don't know what to chat about with a local, just chuck in the weather and watch the conversation blossom before your eyes. House prices, the chronic traffic and the National Health Service are other conversation-starters. Alternatively, there's...

Politics

Traditional rabble-rousers, the British always talk about politics. Once their teeth are truly stuck in, they won't let a political debate go; so if you like politics, you'll

NEED TO KNOW

Everyone's getting about town on two wheels these days, so why not hop on a Barclay's Bike (p393): it's fun, cheap, practical, definitively local and there are docking stations everywhere. All Londoners who travel by public transport invest in an Oyster card (p391), which nets excellent discounts and avoids queues for tickets. On the buses, Routemaster heritage lines 9 and 15 are excellent for sightseeing, so grab a seat upstairs.

find company. Head to Speakers' Corner (p192) to find out what bees are in whose bonnets.

Postcodes

The existential divide between North and South London remains as wide as ever. Londoners forget that exclusive areas such as Cheyne Row in Chelsea were once deeply uncool. Postcode vanity determines virtually everything in some Londoners' lives – especially for the moneyed classes – serving as a kind of potted CV, burnished medal or unmentionable stigma. Some postcodes up their game (SE22, East Dulwich) to nurture cachet within just a few years, others are seemingly beyond help (Thornton Heath). And Londoners all know exactly what the latest developments are.

Supper Clubs

Always drawn to the experimental and novel, Londoners have taken to supper clubs. With everything from secret restaurants, underground eateries, dinner dates with films, themes and compulsory fancy dress, or rarely seen dishes from across the world; see http://supperclubfangroup.ning.com for leads and suggestions on how to locate a supper club near you. For more information see p49.

For Free

London may be one of the world's most expensive cities, but it won't always cost the earth. Many sights and experiences are free, gratis, complimentary, thrown in or won't cost you a penny (or very little). Become a London freeloader for the day and cash in on some tip-top freebies.

Houses of Parliament (p90)

Free Sights

Houses of Parliament

When parliament is in session, it's free to attend and watch UK parliamentary democracy in action.

Changing of the Guard

London's most famous open-air freebie, the Changing of the Guard at Buckingham Palace takes place at 11.30am from May to July (alternate days, weather permitting, August to March). Grab your spot early. Alternatively, catch the changing of the mounted guard at Horse Guard's Parade at 11am (10am on Sundays).

Daily Unlocking of the Tower of London

Daily ritual performed at the Tower at 9am (10am on Sundays). The more elaborate evening Ceremony of the Keys (p141) is also free, but you'll have to apply in writing well in advance.

Free Museums & Galleries

All state-funded museums and galleries are free, as long as you avoid the temporary exhibitions. Many of them are in the West End (p79).

Victoria & Albert Museum

The spectacular V & A can easily consume a day of totally complimentary exploration.

National Gallery

The Trafalgar Square corner shops charge a king's ransom but this magnificent art collection is totally on the house.

Tate Modern

The art here may have a combined value larger than the GDP of a small nation, but it won't cost you a penny.

Free Guided Tours

Some museums, galleries and churches, such as the National Gallery, the Tate Britain, Brompton Cemetery (p258) and All Hallows-by-the-Tower (p150), offer free guided tours (on top of free admission).

Other attractions (such as the Churchill War Rooms) or St Paul's Cathedral offer free audioguides, but general admission might not be free. A number of attractions, such as the Courtauld Gallery (p110) and the Natural History Museum, host free talks and lectures.

Free Buildings

For one weekend in September, London Open House (p363) opens the front doors to over 700 private buildings for free.

Walking in London

Walking around town is possibly the best way to get a sense of the city and its history. Several of the neighbourhood chapters in this book include inspiring walks within that area of London. Check out London Footprints (www.london-footprints.co.uk) for further excellent London walks.

Shopping

At Borough Market (p176), you'll be offered loads of free samples to gnaw while you're browsing. Wedge Card (www.wedgecard.co.uk; per card £10) encourages people to shop locally by giving them a discount in shops that have signed up to the scheme.

Picnicking in Hyde Park

Few pastimes can beat lying around on the grass or hurling a Frisbee in one of London's parks. And the alfresco views are five-star.

Low-Cost Transport

Bikes from Barclay's Cycle Hire Scheme (p393) are free for the first 30 minutes. Use a one-day Travel Card or an Oyster Card to travel as much as you can on London Transport.

NEED TO KNOW

➡ **Websites** Click on London for Free (www.londonforfree.net).

➡ **Discount Cards** The London Pass (www.londonpass.com; from £16 per day; p397) can be a good investment.

➡ **Wi-fi Access** Many cafes offer free wi-fi to customers (p398).

➡ **Newspapers** The *Evening Standard* and *Metro* are both free.

➡ **Children** Under-16s travel free on buses, under-11s travel free on the tube, under-5s go free on the trains.

Free Music

Free gigs and music events take place all the time: in pubs, bars and churches.

Notting Hill Arts Club

Rough Trade's free showcase of live indie bands between 4pm and 8pm on Saturdays.

St Martin-in-the-Fields

This magnificent church hosts free lunchtime concerts at 1pm on Monday, Tuesday and Friday.

St James's Piccadilly

Free 50-minute lunchtime recitals (suggested donation) on Monday, Wednesday and Friday at 1.10pm.

St Giles-in-the-Fields

Free 40-minute recitals held every Friday at 1.10pm.

Free Films

Snoop around and you'll find pubs and cafes showing free films – although they'd expect you to buy a drink perhaps.

Garrison Public House

Free films every Sunday at 7pm in its basement cinema.

Scootercaffe

Free films every other Sunday.

British Museum (p83)

Museums & Galleries

London's museums and galleries top the list of the city's must-see attractions and not just for rainy days that frequently send locals scurrying for cover. Some of London's museums and galleries display incomparable collections that make them acknowledged leaders in their field. A big constellation of top-name museums awaits in South Kensington, and there is a similar concentration in the West End.

NEED TO KNOW

Tickets

➡ National museum collections (eg British Museum, National Gallery, Victoria & Albert Museum) are free, except for temporary exhibitions.

➡ Smaller museums will charge an entrance fee, typically around £5.

➡ Private galleries are usually free, or have a small admission fee.

➡ Book online at some museums (eg the British Music Experience) for discounted tickets.

Opening Hours

➡ National collections are generally open 10am to around 6pm, with one or two late nights a week (see p40); nights are an excellent time to visit museums as there are far fewer visitors.

Dining

➡ Many of the top museums also have fantastic restaurants, worthy of a visit in their own right (p121).

Useful Websites

Most London Museums – especially the most visited museums, such as the British Museum, the National Gallery etc – have sophisticated and highly resourceful websites, worth clicking on before your visit to explore the full range of activities available and the museum highlights. Many of the larger collections also have information zones where you can explore the collection electronically.

➡ **London Galleries** (www.london galleries.co.uk) A-Z list of all London's galleries, with links.

➡ **Culture 24** (www.culture24.org.uk) Reams of museum and gallery info.

The Big Hitters

London's most famous museums are all central, easy to get to and free to enter. Right at the heart of town, the National Gallery on Trafalgar Square displays masterpieces of Western European art from the 13th to the 19th centuries, ranging from Leonardo da Vinci to Turner and Monet. Right next door, the National Portrait Gallery celebrates famous British

Tyrannosaurus Rex, Natural History Museum (p187)

faces through a staggering collection of 160,000 paintings, sculptures and photographs from the 16th century to the present day. A short tube or bus trip north is the British Museum in Bloomsbury, housing an astonishing collection of antiquities. Affluent South Kensington is the home of three of London's leading museums, the Victoria & Albert Museum, with its vast range of historical exhibits from the decorative arts, and the kid-friendly Natural History Museum and Science Museum. Modern and contemporary art lovers will enjoy the Tate Modern on the South Bank, linked by boat to its sister museum across the Thames, the Tate Britain, venue of the annual Turner Prize and home to artworks across the centuries, including Constable, Turner, the Pre-Raphaelites and Francis Bacon.

Art Galleries

London's vibrant creative faculty and artistic scene finds expression in galleries across the city. Despite these challenging financial times, art remains a major cultural commodity and can be viewed and snapped up, as well as admired, in many London neighbourhoods. Mayfair has long been strong on private galleries in the more highbrow, traditional schools of painting, while more contemporary art finds its way into Spitalfields and Hoxton.

Museums at Night

Many museums open late once or twice a week, but several museums organise special nocturnal events to extend their range

Top: Tate Modern, South Bank (p164)
Bottom: Egyptian mummies, British Museum (p83)

ALEX SEGRE / ALAMY®

of activities and to present the collection in a different mood. It's often worth hopping onto a museum's website to see what activities it has. Some museums arrange night events only once a year, in May.

Museums with special nocturnal events or late-night opening hours include the following:

Sir John Soane's Museum (p100) Evenings of the first Tuesday of each month are illuminated by candlelight, so the atmosphere is even more magical (very popular, so there are always long queues).

National Portrait Gallery (p97) Open till 9pm Thursday and Friday.

Tate Modern (p164) Open till 10pm Friday and Saturday.

Tate Britain (p98) Open till 10pm on first Friday of the month.

British Museum (p83) Open till 8.30pm on Friday.

Science Museum (p190) Open till 7pm during school holidays.

Natural History Museum (p187) Organises night safaris and sleepovers (see p31).

Horniman Museum (p279) Sleepovers (with the walrus).

Courses, Talks & Lectures

Museums and galleries are excellent places to pick up specialist skills from qualified experts in their field. If you'd like to learn a new skill, brush up on an old one, or attend a fascinating lecture, there are many to choose from. Here are just a few:

Dulwich Picture Gallery (p281) Art classes for adults and children at all levels, holiday workshops, creative workshops, architecture education classes and three-day summer courses.

National Gallery (p93) Hosts a variety of art-themed talks, lectures and free drawing sessions, plus school holiday activities; some free.

National Portrait Gallery (p97) Range of art-centred activities, workshops, drop-in drawing sessions and talks; some free.

Tate Modern (p164) A whole range of fascinating workshops, classes and talks, plus online art courses; some free.

British Museum (p83) Range of activities, study days, workshops and short courses.

Tate Britain (p98) Art courses (including introduction to drawing), workshops, talks and discussions.

Victoria & Albert Museum (p183) Workshops, classes, lectures and more.

Specialist Museums

Whether you've a penchant for fans, toys, design, cartoons, London transport or ancient surgical techniques, you'll find museums throughout the city with their own niche collections. Even for nonspecialists these museums can be fascinating to browse and share the enthusiasm the curators instil in their collections. Most are centrally located and easy to reach, while others are worth a special trip to get to as they are frequently one of many sights in a particular part of London. See p43.

Museums & Galleries by Neighbourhood

➜ **The West End** (p78) The British Museum, National Gallery, National Portrait Gallery, Tate Britain and lots of smaller museums and galleries.

➜ **The City** (p139) Barbican, the Museum of London.

➜ **The South Bank** (p162) Tate Modern, Hayward Gallery, Design Museum, Fashion & Textile Museum and small art galleries.

➜ **Kensington & Hyde Park** (p181) Victoria & Albert Museum, Natural History Museum, Science Museum and others.

➜ **Clerkenwell, Shoreditch & Spitalfields** (p201) Geffrye Museum, 19 Princelet St, White Cube Gallery.

➜ **The East End & Docklands** (p217) Museum of London Docklands, Ragged School Museum, Whitechapel Gallery.

➜ **Hampstead & North London** (p233) Wellcome Collection, London Canal Museum, Burgh House, Estorick Collection of Modern Italian Art, Sir John Ritblat Gallery.

➜ **Notting Hill & West London** (p256) Museum of Brands, Packaging & Advertising.

➜ **Greenwich & South London** (p268) National Maritime Museum, Ranger's House, Astronomy Centre at the Royal Observatory, Imperial War Museum, Horniman Museum, Dulwich Picture Gallery.

Lonely Planet's Top Choices

British Museum (p83) Supreme collection of international artefacts and an inspiring testament to human creativity.

Victoria & Albert Museum (p183) Uniquely eclectic collection of decorative arts and design in a simply awe-inspiring setting.

National Portrait Gallery (p97) Admire the evolving style of British portraiture.

Tate Modern (p164) A feast of modern and contemporary art, housed within a transformed riverside power station.

Museum of London (p154) Get a firm handle on the history of the city at this fantastic museum.

Wellcome Collection (p238) Brings the sciences, medicine, art and life together with an astonishing collection.

Best Big Museums & Galleries

National Gallery (p93)

Tate Britain (p98)

Science Museum (p190)

Churchill War Rooms (p99)

Museum of London Docklands (p224)

Natural History Museum (p187)

Best Museum Architecture

National Gallery (p93)

Horniman Museum (p279)

National Maritime Museum (p273)

Tate Britain (p98)

Imperial War Museum (p276)

Natural History Museum (p187)

Best Small Museums

London Transport Museum (p107)

London Canal Museum (p238)

Geffrye Museum (p204)

Old Operating Theatre Museum & Herb Garret (p171)

Horniman Museum (p279)

Best Small Galleries

Photographers' Gallery (p106)

Courtauld Gallery (p110)

White Cube Gallery (p204)

Dulwich Picture Gallery (p281)

Barbican Gallery (p155)

Guildhall Art Gallery (p153)

Best House Museums

Apsley House (p191)

Dickens House Museum (p102)

Dennis Severs' House (p206)

Carlyle's House (p194)

Leighton House (p258)

Keats' House (p240)

Best Collections

National Gallery (p93)

Wallace Collection (p113)

Estorick Collection of Modern Italian Art (p241)

Imperial War Museum (p276)

Science Museum (p190)

Natural History Museum (p187)

Best Free Museums

National Gallery (p93)

Tate Britain (p98)

Geffrye Museum (p204)

Photographers' Gallery (p106)

Science Museum (p190)

Natural History Museum (p187)

Best Non-Free Museums & Galleries

Courtauld Gallery (p110)

Churchill War Rooms (p99)

London Transport Museum (p107)

Dulwich Picture Gallery (p281)

Best Specialist Museums

Fan Museum (p273)

Old Operating Theatre Museum & Herb Garret (p171)

Design Museum (p172)

Ragged School Museum (p221)

Best Quirky Museums

Sir John Soane's Museum (p100)

Hunterian Museum (p112)

Old Operating Theatre Museum & Herb Garret (p171)

Best-Located Museums

National Gallery (p93)

Photographers' Gallery (p106)

London Transport Museum (p107)

Science Museum (p190)

Natural History Museum (p187)

ORGANIC JUICE BAR

Spitalfields Market (p215)

Eating

Once the laughing stock of the cooking world, London has got its culinary act together in the last 20 years and is now an undisputed dining destination. There are plenty of fine, Michelin-starred restaurants, but it is the sheer diversity on offer that is extraordinary: from Afghan to Vietnamese, London is a virtual A to Z of world cuisine.

raditional British roast dinner

Specialities
ENGLISH FOOD

England may have given the world beans on toast, mushy peas and chip butties (French fries between two slices of buttered – and untoasted – white bread), but that's hardly the whole story. When well prepared – be it a Sunday lunch of roast beef and Yorkshire pudding (light batter baked until fluffy and eaten with gravy) or a cornet of lightly battered fish and chips sprinkled with salt and malt vinegar – English food can have its moments. And nothing beats a fry-up (or full English breakfast) with bacon, sausages, beans, eggs and mushrooms the morning after a big night out.

Modern British food has become a cuisine in its own right, by championing traditional (and sometimes underrated) ingredients such as root vegetables, smoked fish, shellfish, game and other meats such as sausages and black pudding (a kind of sausage stuffed with oatmeal, spices and blood). Dishes can be anything from game served with a traditional vegetable such as Jerusalem artichoke, seared scallops with orange-scented black pudding and roast pork with chorizo on rosemary mash.

SEAFOOD

Many who travel to England comment on the fact that for an island, Brits seem to make surprisingly little of their seafood, with the exception of the ubiquitous fish and chips. Modern British restaurants have started catching up, however, and many now offer local specialities such as Dover sole, Cornish oysters, Scottish

NEED TO KNOW

Opening Hours

In this book opening hours are listed in individual reviews only when they significantly differ from standard opening hours, as indicated below:

➡ Chain restaurants: noon-11pm

➡ Most restaurants: noon-2.30pm and 6-11pm

Price Ranges

The symbols below indicate the average cost per main course at the restaurant in question.

£	less than £10
££	£10-20
£££	more than £20

Reservations

➡ Make reservations at weekends, if you're keen on a particular place, or if you're in a group of more than four people.

➡ Top-end restaurants often run multiple sittings, with allocated time slots (generally two hours); pick a late slot if you don't want to be rushed.

Tipping

Most restaurants automatically tack a 'discretionary' service charge (usually 12.5%) onto the bill; this should be clearly advertised. If you feel the service wasn't adequate, you can tip separately (or not tip at all).

Haute Cuisine, Low Prices

➡ Top-end restaurants offer set lunch menus that are great value; à la carte prices are sometimes cheaper for lunch.

➡ Many West End restaurants offer good-value pre- or post-theatre menus.

➡ The reliable internet booking service **Top Table** (www.toptable.co.uk) offers substantial discounts (up to 50% off the food bill) at selected restaurants.

BYO

➡ BYO is common among budget establishments; some charge corkage (£1 to £1.50 per bottle of wine).

➡ **Wine Pages** (www.wine-pages.com) keeps a useful directory of BYO restaurants.

Top: Ottolenghi, Islington (p245)
Bottom: Full English breakfast

Eating by Neighbourhood

Hampstead & North London
Myriad options, with
hidden gems (p243)

Clerkenwell, Shoreditch & Spitalfields
Famous, creative restaurants
and great bargains (p205)

Notting Hill & West London
Eclectic, from vegetarian
to Eastern European
(p259)
(1mi)

The City
Geared towards
the business
lunch (p157)

East End & Docklands
Superb ethnic
food (p224)
(1mi)

The West End
Great for Asian,
European and
fusion (p113)

Kensington & Hyde Park
Chic, cosmopolitan
and often pricey
(p195)

London Eye

The South Bank
Excellent gastropubs
and fine river
dining (p173)

Richmond, Kew & Hampton Court
Sophisticated restaurants,
with style and substance
(p302)
(2mi)

Greenwich & South London
Exquisite cafes and
well-known restaurants
(p281)

scallops, smoked Norfolk eel, Atlantic herring and mackerel. There are some excellent restaurants specialising in seafood, as well as fish-and-chips counters trading in battered cod, haddock and plaice.

WORLD FOOD

One of the joys of eating out in London is the profusion of choice. For historical reasons Indian cuisine is widely available (curry has been labelled a national dish), but Asian cuisines in general are very popular: you'll find dozens of Chinese, Thai, Japanese and Korean restaurants, as well as elaborate fusion establishments blending flavours from different parts of Asia.

Food from continental Europe – French, Italian, Spanish, Greek, Scandinavian – is another favourite, with many classy Modern European establishments. Restaurants serving other cuisines tend to congregate where their home community is based:

Eastern European in Shepherd's Bush, Turkish in Dalston etc.

DESSERTS

England does a mean dessert and establishments serving British cuisine revel in these indulgent treats. Among our favourites are bread-and-butter pudding, sticky toffee pudding (a steamed pudding that contains dates and is topped with a divine caramel sauce), the alarmingly named spotted dick (a steamed suet pudding with currants and raisins), Eton mess (meringue, cream and strawberries mixed into a gooey, heavenly mess) and seasonal musts such as Christmas pudding (a steamed pudding with candied fruit and brandy) and fruity crumbles (rhubarb, apple etc).

Those with a sweet tooth should make sure they treat themselves to an afternoon tea, complete with cupcakes, scones and other pastries.

Gastropubs

While not so long ago the pub was where you went for a drink, with maybe a packet of potato crisps to soak up the alcohol, the birth of the gastropub in the 1990s means that today just about every pub has full meals. But the quality varies widely, from defrosted on the premises to Michelin-star worthy.

Breakfast & Brunch

The Brits were always big on breakfast – they even invented one, the full English breakfast. It's something of a protein overload but there's nothing quite like it to mop up the excesses of the night before. A typical plate will include bacon, sausages, baked beans in tomato sauce, eggs (fried or scrambled), mushrooms, tomatoes and toast (maybe with Marmite). You'll find countless grotty cafes – nicknamed 'greasy spoons' – serving these monster plates. They're also a must in gastropubs.

Making a comeback on the breakfast table is porridge, boiled oats in water or milk, served hot, sweet or savoury. Top-end restaurants serving breakfast, such as the Wolseley (p117), have played a big part in glamming up what was essentially a poor man's meal. We love it with banana and honey, fruit compote or even plain with just some chocolate powder.

Londoners have also gotten into brunch of late. It isn't quite New York yet, but the offerings are getting better all the time. A number of gastropubs, cafes and top-end restaurants now serve a range of treats,

Inn the Park restaurant, St James's Park (p116)

from pancakes to eggs Benedict to elaborate breakfast omelettes, waffles and more.

Vegetarians & Vegans

London has been one of the best places for vegetarians to dine out since the 1970s. It was initially due mostly to its many Indian restaurants, which, for religious reasons, always cater for people who don't eat meat. But a number of dedicated vegetarian restaurants have since cropped up, offering imaginative, filling and truly delicious meals. Most nonvegetarian places generally offer a couple of dishes for those who don't eat meat; vegans, however, will find it harder outside Indian or dedicated restaurants.

Celebrity Chefs

London's food renaissance was partly led by a group of telegenic chefs who built food empires around their names and their TV programs. Gordon Ramsay is the most (in) famous of the lot but his London venues are still standard-bearers for top-quality cuisine. Other big names include Jamie Oliver, whose restaurant trains disadvantaged young people, and Heston Blumenthal,

> ### MARMITE, LOVE IT!
>
> Marmite is a savoury spread made from yeast extract (a by-product of beer brewing). Its origin makes it a tough sale to foreigners, although take our word for it, lightly spread on buttered toast, it is totally delicious: salty, with a slight nutty flavour. It is undoubtedly an acquired taste, though, a fact that the manufacturers have embraced in their marketing: 'Love it or hate it', says the strapline.
>
> Australia and New Zealand champion their own versions of the savoury spread but many Brits deem them inferior to the original article!

whose mad-professor-like experiments with food (molecular gastronomy, as he describes it) have earned him rave reviews.

Cafes

While tea remains a quintessential English beverage, Londoners long ago adopted espresso and steamy latte as the hot drinks de rigueur. There are Starbucks and other coffee chains seemingly at every corner, but plenty of smaller cafes fly the independent flag too. Many sell pastries for breakfast and sandwiches for lunch and are great for a quick bite on the go or a break from pounding the pavement.

Food Markets

The boom in London's eating scene has extended to its markets, which come in three broad categories: food stalls that are part of a broader market and appeal to visitors keen to soak up the atmosphere (eg Spitalfields, Borough or Camden); farmers markets, which sell pricey local and/or organic products (check out www.lfm.org.uk for a selection of the best, such as Broadway and Marylebone); and the many colourful food markets, where the oranges

and lemons come from who knows where and the barrow boys and girls speak with cockney accents straight out of central casting (Brixton, Ridley Rd, Berwick St).

For something a little different you could also pay a visit to London's wholesale markets, where retailers and restaurants get their supplies.

Billingsgate Fish Market (Map p421; Trafalgar Way E14; ☺5-8.30am Tue-Sat; DLR West India Quay) This wholesale fish market is open to the public, but you'll have to be up at the crack of dawn. People will tell you that you have to buy in bulk, but most of the wise-crackin' vendors are prepared to do a deal.

Smithfield Market (p155) London's last surviving meat market and the most modern of its kind in Europe.

Supper Clubs

If you think restaurants are so last season, you'll love supper clubs: half restaurant, half dinner party, they combine the quality of the former with the informality of the latter. They're run by average Joes with a penchant for cooking and generally cater for 10 to 20 people; meals are set three- or

Spitalfields Market (p215)

four-course menus (£20 to £40), and the clientele couldn't be more eclectic. For visitors it is a chance to meet Londoners over dinner, get off the beaten track and check out what the locals' living rooms look like.

The difficulty is that these underground restaurants are rarely permanent (the cook might move or decide that his/her day job is quite enough) and so recommending a supper club can be tricky. The following will help:

Supper club hostess **Ms Marmite** has set up an excellent directory of London supper clubs at http://supperclubfangroup.ning.com.

Food blog the **London Foodie** (www.thelondon foodie.co.uk) features regular supper club reviews.

Facebook is the way forward; hosts post details of their forthcoming events on their pages.

Another place to look is **newspapers**: all the broadsheets regularly write about new ventures.

London Chain Gang

While the usual bleak offerings of US-based chain restaurants are to be found all over the capital, London also boasts some excellent chains of inventive and interesting restaurants, which locals patronise frequently. They're all good value and made even cheaper by regular voucher offers: check out www.vouchercodes.co.uk and www. myvouchercodes.co.uk for the latest offers.

The following are some of our favourites; check their websites for a full list of outlets.

Benugo (www.benugocafedeli.com) This mini-chain of cafe delis does great sandwiches: choose your bread (baguette, bagel, wrap etc), pick your filling (so many!) and off you go.

Busaba Eathai (www.busaba.com) A relatively small chain, with just six outfits, Busaba does divine Thai food, served without fuss among beautiful, modern Asian decor.

Byron (www.byronhamburgers.com) Simple but excellent burgers, cooked medium and accompanied by the bare essentials (lettuce, tomato, red onion).

Carluccio's (www.carluccios.com) The Italian restaurants at this ever-expanding chain have a somewhat upmarket ambience; there's also a deli selling takeaway goodies.

Canteen (www.canteen.co.uk) All-day, casual dining is how Canteen styles itself. Drop in any

Top: Afternoon tea at Bea's of Bloomsbury (p117)
Middle: Shanghai Blues (p122), High Holborn
Bottom: Skylon (p173), atop Royal Festival Hall

PIE & MASH

From the middle of the 19th century until just after WWII, the staple lunch for many Londoners was a spiced-eel pie (eels were once plentiful in the Thames) served with mashed potatoes and liquor (a parsley sauce). Pies have been replaced by sandwiches nowadays, although they remain popular in the East End. A popular modern-day filling is beef and mashed potato (curried meat is also good), with eel served smoked or jellied as a side dish. To try it, head to a pie & mash shop: F. Cooke (p227), Clark's (p207) and M Manze (p176) are great options.

time for great English staples such as porridge for breakfast, or pies and roast for lunch.

Giraffe (www.giraffe.net) There's a kind of sunny-Californian feel to Giraffe, where the likes of burritos, brunch and vegetarian salad wraps are served with a smile.

Gourmet Burger Kitchen (www.gbk.co.uk) The burgers at GBK are the real deal, made from prime Scottish beef and enlivened by specially created sauces and superb chips.

Le Pain Quotidien (www.lepainquotidien.com) A simple, stripped-down, French-style chain of cafes that serves salads, soups, filled baguettes and excellent cakes.

Masala Zone (www.masalazone.com) An excellent – and excellent-value – Indian chain that specialises in thalis (a meal made of several small dishes). The contemporary Indian decor is another hit.

Nando's (www.nandos.co.uk) Flame-grilled chicken with peri-peri sauce – who would have thought this Portuguese recipe could become so popular? There are dozens of outlets in London.

Ping Pong (www.pingpongdimsum.com) The dim-sum fever that has taken over London shows

no sign of abating and Ping Pong keeps growing; it is reliably good and has sleek decor.

Pizza Express (www.pizzaexpress.com) London's original pizza chain is still going strong, with regular new recipes and excellent locations throughout the capital.

Pret à Manger (www.pret.com) London's most popular sandwich chain, Pret has made its name on freshly made, tasty sandwiches. It also does delicious, chunky soups.

Real Greek (www.therealgreek.com) Serving beautifully presented meze and souvlaki, this chain is great for sharing lots of dishes between friends.

Strada (www.strada.co.uk) A cut (and a slice) above when it come to chain pizzerias, Strada does lovely pizzas from its wood-fired ovens. The pasta is also pretty good.

Tas (www.tasrestaurant.com) An established chain of good Turkish restaurants with a roll-call of stews, grills and mezes that rarely disappoints.

Wagamama (www.wagamama.com) The turnover is pretty quick at this fusion noodle place, which is great if you're in a hurry, but not so if you like a little service with your food.

Lonely Planet's Top Choices

Providores & Tapa Room (p122) Fusion food at its best.

Wapping Food (p229) A perfect East End recipe: industrial decor meets haute cuisine.

franco manca (p283) London's finest pizzas, locally prepared but with Italian flair.

Gordon Ramsay (p197) Three Michelin stars and a celeb chef.

Gaucho Grill (p244) Fabulous restaurant specialising in succulent Argentinian beef.

Best by Budget

£
Honest Burgers (p283)
E Pellici (p225)
Mangal Ocakbasi (p247)
Nevada Street Deli (p282)
Busaba Eathai (p114)
Taquería (p259)

££
Moro (p205)
Ottolenghi (p245)
Magdalen (p174)
Al Boccon di'Vino (p302)
Kazan (p196)

£££
Les Trois Garçons (p207)
Gordon Ramsay at Claridge's (p124)
Chez Bruce (p284)
Zuma (p196)
Le Boudin Blanc (p123)

Best by Cuisine

Modern European
Whitechapel Gallery Dining Room (p225)

Vincent Rooms (p113)
Launceston Place (p195)
Andrew Edmunds (p118)
Wild Honey (p124)

Indian
Tayyabs (p224)
Café Spice Namasté (p225)
Mooli's (p117)
Rasoi Vineet Bhatia (p197)
Cinnamon Club (p113)

Chinese
Yauatcha (p116)
Bar Shu (p118)
Hunan (p197)
Baozi Inn (p120)
Pearl Liang (p262)

Vegetarian
Gate (p261)
Mildreds (p118)
Manna (p246)
Gallery Cafe (p227)
Diwana Bhel Poori House (p246)

Italian
Bocca di Lupo (p117)
Fifteen (p208)
Locanda Locatelli (p123)
Polpetto (p118)

British
St John (p205)
Penny Black (p197)
Laughing Gravy (p174)
Inn the Park (p116)

Best Gastropubs

Gun (p229)
Anchor & Hope (p174)
Garrison Public House (p174)

Duke of Cambridge (p246)
Lots Road Pub & Dining Room (p304)

Best for Views

Skylon (p173)
Formans (p228)
Oxo Tower Restaurant & Brasserie (p173)
River Café (p262)
Min Jiang (p196)

Best Afternoon Teas

Dean Street Townhouse (p117)
Orangery (p196)
Volupté (p160)
Bea's of Bloomsbury (p117)
Wolseley (p117)

Best Food Markets

Borough Market (p176)
Broadway Market (p231)
Portobello Road Market (p259)
Marylebone Farmers Market (p124)

Best Gourmet Shops

Jones Dairy (p232)
Fortnum & Mason (p132)
Algerian Coffee Stores (p134)
Vintage House (p134)

Best Celebrity Chef Restaurants

Viajante (p225)
Dinner by Heston Blumenthal (p196)
Nobu (p124)
HIX (p118)

West London pub

🍷 Drinking & Nightlife

There's little Londoners like to do more than party. From Hogarth's 18th-century Gin Lane prints to Mayor Boris Johnson's decision to ban all alcohol on public transport in 2008, the capital's history has been shot through with the population's desire to imbibe as much alcohol as possible and revel like there is no tomorrow.

NEED TO KNOW

Opening Hours

Unless otherwise stated all pubs and bars reviewed in this book open at 11am and close at 11pm from Monday to Saturday and at 10.30pm on Sunday. Thanks to a change in the law in 2005, some pubs and bars now stay open longer, although most close around 2am or 3am at the latest.

Clubs generally open at 10pm and close between 4am and 7am.

Costs

Midweek prices are reasonable, and there are plenty of student nights or those oriented to a budget crowd. If you want to go to a big club on a Saturday night (*the* night for clubbing), expect to pay at least £20.

Tickets & Guest Lists

Queuing in the cold at 11pm can be frustrating; get there early and/or book tickets for bigger events if you can't bear being left in door-whore limbo.

Some clubs will require you to sign up on their guest list beforehand; check ahead.

Dress Code

London's clubs are generally relaxed. Posh clubs in areas such as Kensington will want a glam look, so dress to impress (no jeans or trainers); the further east, the more laid-back and edgy the fashion.

What's On?

Check the listings in *Time Out* or the *Evening Standard* – part of the charm of London's nightlife is that it's always changing, so keep your eyes peeled!

The Pub

The pub (public house) is at the heart of London's existence and is one of the capital's great social levellers. Virtually every Londoner has a 'local' and looking for your own is one of the highlights of any visit to the capital.

Pubs in central London are mostly drinking dens, busy from 5pm onwards with the postwork crowd during the week and revellers at weekends. But in more

Ale on tap

residential areas in East, South, West and North London, pubs come into their own at weekends, when long lunches turn into afternoons and groups of friends settle in for the night. Many also run popular quizzes on week nights.

You'll be able to order almost anything you like in a pub, from beer to wine, soft drinks, spirit and mixer (whisky and coke etc) and sometimes hot drinks too. Some specialise in beer and real ales, offering drinks from local microbreweries, fruit beers, organic ciders and other rarer beverages; others have invested in a good wine list (often the case in gastropubs serving good food).

In winter a number of pubs offer mulled wine; in summer the must-have drink is Pimms and lemonade (if it's properly done it should have fresh mint leaves, citrus fruit, strawberries and cucumber).

BEER

The raison d'être of a pub is first and foremost to serve beer – be it lager, ale or stout in a glass or a bottle. On draught (drawn from the cask) it is served by the pint (570mL) or half-pint (285mL) and, more occasionally, third-of-a-pint for real ale tasting.

Pubs generally serve a good selection of lager (what most people would refer to as 'beer': highly carbonated and drunk cool or cold) and a smaller selection of real ales or 'bitter' (slightly gassy or still, drunk at room temperature, with strong flavours). In London the best-known home brews are Tennent's and Carling,

Top: Roof terrace, Queen of Hoxton (p212)

Bottom: Loungelover (p212)

JAMES WINSPEAR/PHOTOLIBRARY©

Drinking by Neighbourhood

Hampstead & North London
Atmospheric pubs and live music (p248)

Clerkenwell, Shoreditch & Spitalfields
Edgy clubs and hip bars (p210)

Notting Hill & West London
Traditional pubs, river views, relaxed evenings (p263)
(1mi)

The City
Post-work punters, quiet after 10pm (p159)

East End & Docklands
Increasingly trendy, with excellent bars (p229)
(1mi)

The West End
Legendary establishments, up-for-it crowds (p125)

Kensington & Hyde Park
Favourite of Royals and A-listers (p198)

London Eye

The South Bank
Franchises and good ol' boozers (p177)

Richmond, Kew & Hampton Court
Pubs with a village feel (p305)
(2mi)

Greenwich & South London
Vibrant parties and old-school pubs (p285)

although you'll find everything from Fosters to San Miguel.

Among the multitude of ales on offer in London pubs, London Pride, Courage Best, Burton Ale, Adnam's, Theakston (in particular Old Peculiar) and Old Speckled Hen are among the best.

Stout, the best known of which is Irish Guinness, is a slightly sweet, dark beer with a distinct flavour that comes from malt that is roasted before fermentation.

Once considered something of an old man's drink, real ale is enjoying a renaissance among young Londoners keen to sample flavours from the country's brewing tradition. Staff at bars serving good selections of real ales are often hugely knowledgeable, just like a sommelier in a restaurant with a good cellar, so ask them for recommendations if you're not sure what to order.

Clubbing

When it comes to clubbing, London's where it's at. Most people who come here want a piece of the action. You'll probably know what you want to experience – it might be big clubs such as Fabric or the Ministry of Sound, or sweaty shoebox clubs with the latest DJ talent – but there's plenty to tempt you to branch out from your usual tastes and try something new: from thumping techno, rock, nu rave, Latin, ska, pop, country, grime, minimal electro, hip hop or 1950s lindy hopping, there's something going on every night.

Thursdays are loved by those who want to have their fun before the office workers mob the streets on Friday. Saturdays are the busiest and best if you're a serious clubber, and Sundays often see surprisingly good events throughout London.

There are clubs across town, though East London is the top area for cutting-edge clubs; King's Cross still retains a couple of good clubs but is a shadow of what it once was.

Bars

In the small party space left by pubs and clubs, bars have managed to grow into a popular alternative for a London night out. Generally opened later than pubs, but closing earlier than clubs, they tempt those keen to skip bedtime at 11pm but not keen enough to go clubbing. They generally have DJs (sometimes a small dance floor too), door charges after 11pm (sometimes), a more modern decor than pubs and fancier (and pricier) drinks, including cocktails. They also tend to be smaller than bona fide nightclubs.

Specialist cocktail bars are in a league of their own in London, with fantastic drinks, often the barmen's own creations, and some fancy moves that would make Tom Cruise proud.

Burlesque

After years of low-profile parties with high-glitter gowns, the burlesque scene burst onto the mainstream in the noughties, showering London with nipple tassels, top hats, sexy lingerie and some of the best parties in town. Subsequently, the 'alternative' burlesque scene became overwhelmingly mainstream, and club-night organisers, passionately dedicated to dressing up and taking fun seriously, raised prices in many of the venues to ward off those who

NIGHT MOVES

Most Londoners will start the night in a pub or a bar, and then move on to a late-opening bar or a club. Pub crawls are another favourite: one drink per pub, until you've exhausted your liver or your drinking options for the night.

wouldn't buck up and dress up. So prepare to pay an average of £25 for some (but not all) of the city's best burlesque nights, and make sure you look like a million dollars.

Expect anything from male burlesque contests to girls on roller skates hosting tea parties on a good burlesque night. Venues and events to look out for:

Volupté (p160) The queen of London burlesque, with shows, parties, dinners and much more.

Last Tuesday Society (www.thelasttues daysociety.org) Runs fantastic masked balls on various occasions (St Valentine's Day, summer party, Halloween etc).

Lady Luck Night (www.ladyluckclub.co.uk) The city's top night for rockabilly and old jazz.

If you're not quite confident about your tease routine yet, **Burlesque Baby** (www.burlesquebaby.com) runs a burlesque academy where you can perfect your moves and brush up your pin-up hair and make-up skills. It also runs its own burlesque shows, **Va Va Voom Club**, in various clubs.

PLAN YOUR TRIP DRINKING & NIGHTLIFE

Lonely Planet's Top Choices

Jerusalem Tavern (p210) Tiny but delightful, with original beers from a Norfolk brewery.

Book Club (p211) A modern temple to good times, with great offbeat events.

Draft House (p287) A standout watering hole, popular with high-flyers and families alike.

Proud Camden (p248) Great drinks, music and fun in Camden's old stables.

Greenwich Union (p285) Championing drinks from local microbreweries.

Troubadour (p264) A bohemian bar where wine and conversation keep flowing.

Best Pubs

White Cross (p305)

Grapes (p230)

Ye White Hart (p305)

Edinboro Castle (p248)

Golden Heart (p213)

Windsor Castle (p264)

Best Cocktail Bars

Worship St Whistling Shop (p212)

Experimental Cocktail Club (p126)

Purl (p129)

Happiness Forgets (p212)

Academy (p126)

Best Clubs

Fabric (p210)

Cargo (p211)

Passing Clouds (p251)

Kensington Roof Gardens (p263)

Plastic People (p212)

Best for Ale

Mason & Taylor (p211)

Old Brewery (p286)

Rake (p178)

Ye Olde Watling (p160)

Carpenter's Arms (p230)

White Horse (p305)

Best Bars

Bar 23 (p251)

Boogaloo (p249)

Queen of Hoxton (p212)

Barrio North (p250)

Green Room (p265)

Best Beer Gardens

Garden Gate (p249)

Britannia (p230)

Spaniard's Inn (p249)

Grand Union (p263)

Best for Views

Vertigo 42 (p159)

Galvin at Windows (p198)

Ye White Hart (p305)

White Swan (p306)

Best Riverside Pubs

Dove (p263)

Waterway (p263)

Anchor Bankside (p177)

Cutty Sark Tavern (p286)

Trafalgar Tavern (p286)

Best Wine Bars

Gordon's Wine Bar (p129)

El Vino (p160)

Vinoteca (p210)

French House (p126)

Best for Sport

Junction (p250)

Sports Cafe (p128)

Camino (p248)

Bar Kick (p211)

Best Historic Pubs

Ye Olde Cheshire Cheese (p160)

Prospect of Whitby (p231)

George Inn (p177)

Spaniard's Inn (p249)

London Apprentice (p306)

Prince Alfred (p265)

Gay & Lesbian

The city of Oscar Wilde, Quentin Crisp and Elton John does not disappoint its queer visitors, proffering a fantastic mix of brash, camp, loud and edgy parties, bars, clubs and events year-round. A world capital of gaydom on par with New York and San Francisco, London's gay and lesbian communities have turned good times into an art form.

Gay Rights

Protection from discrimination is now enshrined in law, and civil partnerships now allow gay couples the same rights as straight couples. That's not to say homophobia doesn't exist – outside the bubble of Soho, abuse on the street at public displays of affection is still not unusual.

Drinking

The queer drinking scene in London is wonderfully varied. Whether you fancy a quiet pint in a traditional boozer that just happens to be gay, or want a place to wet your whistle before going out dancing, you'll be spoiled for choice.

Clubbing

London has some of the most exciting and varied gay clubbing in the world, but it's a moveable feast, as the clubbing scene is about club nights rather than venues, meaning a club that was fantastic and full of drag queens one night might well be straight and full of Goths the next. Here's some of the best:

Popcorn (Heaven, p128) A fun and cheap night out, Popcorn is an Ibiza-style club night with a great selection of music on offer and refreshingly priced drinks offers. Mondays.

Industri (Barcode, p128) The hottest midweek party, Industri recently relocated from Vauxhall to Soho for a change of scene. Befriending the DJs, flirting with door whores and dancing with go-go boys are all on the menu.

Room Service (Diu, Map p422; www.diulondon. com; 12-13 Greek St W1; ⊖Tottenham Court Rd) Run by uberpromoter, socialite and trannie extraordinaire Jodie Harsh, Room Service has go-go dancers, famous DJs, celebs and a very up-for-it crowd. Thursdays.

A:M (Fire, p288) As the name suggests this is an after-party party, starting at 3am and clocking off at 11am on Saturdays. The music features some of the best techno and electro DJs on the London scene and the whole place is pure hedonism.

G-A-Y (Heaven, p128) Love it or hate it, G-A-Y is a centre of gravity for the gay scene and seemingly where half of Soho is headed on a Saturday night. Its new home at Heaven has helped the ageing club get a new lease on life. Bring your tight T-shirt!

Horsemeat (The Eagle, p127) One of the biggest Sunday nights in town, especially popular at bank holidays, when you can expect to queue for at least an hour.

Lesbian

The lesbian scene in London is far less visible than the flamboyant gay one, though there are a couple of excellent lesbian bars in Soho and plenty going on elsewhere around the city. Certain areas of the capital are well known to have thriving lesbian communities and are worth a visit in their own

NEED TO KNOW

Free Press

London has a lively gay press charting the ever-changing scene. Pick up these publications at any gay venue; their listings are the most up-to-date available.

➡ **Boyz** (www.boyz.co.uk)

➡ **QX** (www.qxmagazine.com)

➡ **Pink Paper** (www.pinkpaper.com)

Magazines

Available at most news-agents in Soho.

➡ **Gay Times** (www.gaytimes.co.uk)

➡ **Diva** (www.divamag.co.uk)

➡ **Attitude** (www.atitude.co.uk)

➡ **AXM** (www.axm-mag.com)

Blogs & Other Resources

➡ **Ginger Beer** (www.gingerbeer.co.uk)

➡ **Me Me Me** (www.me-me-me.tv)

➡ **Time Out** (www.timeout.com/london/gay)

➡ **Visit London** (www.visitlondon.com/people/gay)

Help

➡ Always report homophobic crimes to the **police** (☎999).

➡ **London Lesbian & Gay Switchboard** (☎0300 330 0630; www.llgs.org.uk) provides free advice, counselling and other help to anyone who needs a sympathetic ear.

right – particularly Stoke Newington and Hackney in northeast London. Check out www.gingerbeer.co.uk for the full low-down on events, club nights and bars.

Gay & Lesbian by Neighbourhood

➡ **Shoreditch** (p201) Fashionable Shoreditch is home to London's more alternative gay scene, often very well mixed in with local straight people. Here you'll find arty parties and the hipper bars and clubs, where the muscle boys fear to tread.

➡ **Soho** (p78) The long-established gay village of Soho, once so central to any gay experience of London, has somewhat lost its pre-eminence to the edgy East End.

➡ **Vauxhall** (p268) Vauxhall, once a bleak concrete jungle, is now home to London's mainstream muscle boys.

Best Gay & Lesbian Events

Lesbian & Gay Film Festival (www.bfi.org.uk/llgff) A

renowned film festival, now in its 25th year, hosted by the British Film Institute, with screenings, premieres, awards and talks. Early April.

Gay Pride (www.pridelondon.org) One of the world's largest gay prides, complete with speakers, stalls, performers and parties across town. Late June, early July.

Soho Pride (www.sohopride.net) Smaller, more intimate, less activism and more fun! It's also been promoted as GayDar Days. August.

Best Gay Bars

George & Dragon (p211)

Joiners Arms (p230)

Edge (p126)

Two Brewers (p287)

Village (p126)

Best Gay Clubs

AREA (p287)

RVT (p287)

Fire (p288)

Heaven (p128)

London's West End (p130)

 # Entertainment

London's cultural life is the richest and most varied in the English-speaking world. Whatever soothes your soul, flicks your switch or floats your boat, from inventive theatre to dazzling musicals, comedy venues, dance, opera or live music, London has an energetic and innovative answer. In fact, you could spend several lifetimes in London and still only sample a fraction of the astonishing range of entertainment the city has to offer.

NEED TO KNOW

Tickets

➡ Book well ahead for live performances.

➡ Cut-price standby tickets are sometimes available at several theatrical venues, including the National Theatre, the Barbican and the Southbank Centre.

➡ Student standby tickets are sometimes available one hour before performances start.

➡ Midweek matinees at such venues as the Royal Opera House are usually much cheaper than evening performances; restricted-view seats can be very cheap (from 10p).

➡ For gigs, be wary of touts outside the venue on the night. Be sure to check with the holder of a genuine ticket before buying, to avoid forgeries.

➡ Most mainstream and art-house cinemas offer discounts all day Monday and most weekday afternoon screenings.

➡ On the day of performance, you can buy discounted tickets, sometimes up to 50% off, for West End productions from **tkts Leicester Sq** (Map p432; ⊙10am-7pm Mon-Sat, noon-3pm Sun; ⊕Leicester Sq).

➡ If you can, buy direct from the venue. Events sell out rapidly and agencies tend to have tickets after the venue has sold out. **Ticketmaster** (☑0870 154 4040; www.ticketmaster.co.uk) and **Stargreen** (☑7734 8932; www.stargreen.com) have 24-hour telephone and online booking services.

Useful Magazines

➡ The weekly **Time Out** (www.timeout.com/london) has current theatre listings.

Useful Websites

➡ **Taste Theatre** (www.tastetheatre.com) Browse by genre or theatre.

➡ **London Theatre** (www.londontheatre.co.uk) Good general overview of London theatre.

➡ **London Dance** (www.londondance.com) Handy listing for dance events.

Music festival in Hyde Park (p192)

Theatre

A night out at the theatre in London is a must-do experience. London's Theatreland in the dazzling West End – from Aldwych in the east, past Shaftesbury Ave to Regent St in the west – has a concentration of English-speaking theatres rivalled only by New York's Broadway. With the longest history, London theatre is also the world's most diverse, from Shakespeare's classics performed with traditional authenticity, to innovative productions that push new boundaries, to raise-the-roof musicals that run and run.

With over 40 theatres in the West End alone, more theatre tickets sell here than anywhere else on Earth, many for musicals and shows that have performed for decades. But the West End is just the shiniest aspect of the multifaceted London theatre world, where actors walk the boards across town, from highbrow theatres to tiny fringe stages tucked away above pubs.

With its cosmopolitan DNA and multicultural roots, London is a hotbed of theatrical creativity: even Hollywood stars are abandoning their pampered lives for a season treading the boards in London. The celebrated National Theatre is the regular home of innovative new shows, creative directing and much-loved classics that often migrate to other theatres in the West End. The Barbican hosts foreign drama companies to massive acclaim. Traditional stagecraft is also on offer, particularly at the lovely old-school

Top: Shakespeare's Globe (p179)
Bottom: Royal Albert Hall (p192)

Shakespeare's Globe, where the emphasis is on Shakespearian authenticity.

At the edges are more peripheral, subsidised shows from experimental groups, where conceptual ideas find expression to a sometimes bewildered audience. In summer open-air theatres ride out both balmy days and sudden showers entertaining crowds in parks, most famously in Regent's Park. For more on theatre see p372.

Opera

With one of the world's leading opera companies at the Royal Opera House in Covent Garden, and impressive direction from Edward Gardner at the English National Opera (the Coliseum), as well as other operatic venues and events, London has more than enough for opera goers. It's not just the classics that are produced, as innovative productions bring operatic expression to a host of modern-day subjects. Holland Park (p265) is the summer venue for operatic productions. Opera is expensive to produce and, consequently, tickets are pricey.

Classical Music

Music lovers will be spoiled for choice in this leading city of classical sounds, with four world-class symphony orchestras, two opera companies, various smaller ensembles and fantastic venues (and reasonable ticket prices). The Southbank Centre, Barbican and Royal Albert Hall all maintain an alluring program of performances, further solidifying London's outstanding reputation as a venue for classical music with traditional crowd-pleasers as well as innovative compositions and sounds. The Proms (p198) is the largest event on the festival calendar.

Dance

London is home to five major dance companies and a host of small and experimental ones. The **Royal Ballet** (www.roh.org.uk), the best classical-ballet company in the land, is based at the Royal Opera House in Covent Garden. The **English National Ballet** (www.ballet.org.uk) often performs at the London Coliseum, especially at Christmas and in summer. Sadler's Wells (p214) is excellent for experimental dance.

The annual contemporary dance event in London is **Dance Umbrella** (www.dance umbrella.co.uk). For more information about dance in the capital, visit the website of **London Dance** (www.londondance.com); see also p374).

Live Rock, Pop, Jazz & Blues

Musically diverse and defiantly different, London has long ploughed its own musical furrow, generating edgy and creative sounds. Local bands and singers have again swung the spotlight on London Town's musical talent, with soulful Adele, Lily Allen and the late Amy Winehouse, folk rockers Mumford & Sons, South London rapper Tinie Tempah and Coldplay all waving the London flag. Mega-names from across the planet all see London as an essential stop on their transglobal stomps, so be prepared for massive international artists bringing their tunes to adoring crowds and tickets selling out faster than you can find your credit card. If it's jazz or blues you're after, London has a host of excellent clubs and pubs where you can catch classics and contemporary tunes. The city's major jazz event is the **London Jazz Festival** (www.londonjazzfestival.org.uk) in November. Also look out for summer jazz weekends at Fulham Palace and Hampton Court Palace.

For more on London music, see p379.

Comedy

They look a miserable bunch on the underground, and the winter gloom, drizzly rain and recession blues don't help, but Londoners have a solid sense of humour. And despite – or because of – the recession, comedy is still flourishing in the capital. You can roll up at any one of the 20-plus major comedy clubs or countless other venues (including pubs), and tickle your ribs or snort your drink down the wrong way.

Most comedy acts have both eyes on the critical Edinburgh Festival season: April to July, new acts are being tried out on audiences; August is the cruellest month for comedy in London, because everyone's shifted up north for the festival itself; and winter has comedians doing the stuff that went down well at the festival. Check Edinburgh Comedy Awards for the new bright stars.

Some of the world's most famous modern comedians hail from, or made their names in, London, including Ben Elton, Alexei Sayle, Victoria Wood, Julian Clary, Rowan Atkinson, Reeves & Mortimer, Eddie Izzard, Jo Brand, Sacha Baron Cohen (aka Ali G, Borat and Brüno), Ricky Gervais, Matt Lucas, David Walliams, Russell Brand, Josie Long, Paul Sinha, Tiernan Douieb, Russell Howard and Alan Carr.

London's leading comedy event is the **Greenwich Comedy Festival** (www.greenwichcomedyfestival.co.uk) and Union Chapel (p253) is a wonderful venue that hosts a monthly **Live at the Chapel** (http://liveatthechapel.co.uk), with big names and live music.

Film

Londoners have a passion for all things celluloid and digital, from the vast BFI IMAX in Waterloo, to the huge screen at the Empire Leicester Sq, to small 40-seater cinemas, to a host of art-house and independent cinemas and local pub film clubs that cram in beer-quaffing film buffs. For some ambient class with your popcorn, try the Edwardian interior of the **Coronet** (p264) in Notting Hill Gate, or the nearby **Electric Cinema** (p264), the UK's oldest cinema, on Portobello Rd. For back-catalogue classics, turn to the **BFI** (p179) at South Bank, but keep an eye out for film festivals at independent cinemas, which bring in reels of foreign movies. For further eclectic tastes, shorts, foreign cinema as well as mainstream movies, London's independent cinemas allow you to put your feet up, sip a glass of wine and feel right at home. You can catch monthly seasons and premieres, as well as actors and directors chatting about their work and answering questions. Cinemas such as the **Prince Charles** (p130) have cheap tickets, run minifestivals and screen popular singalong classics. Many major premieres are held in Leicester Sq, the priciest part of London for cinema tickets. Look out also for the **Summer Screen** at Somerset House (p110), **Movies on the Lawn** at Fulham Palace (p299) and other open-air cinema screenings. See p383 for more information about film and film festivals in London.

Entertainment by Neighbourhood

➡ **The West End** (p78) Entertainment central for theatres, musicals, opera, classical-music concert halls and small live-music venues.

➡ **The City** (p139) Barbican Arts Centre and church concerts.

➡ **The South Bank** (p162) Major theatre concentration: the National Theatre, Royal Festival Hall, Shakespeare's Globe and the Old Vic.

➡ **Kensington & Hyde Park** (p181) Royal Albert Hall and the Royal Court Theatre.

➡ **Clerkenwell, Shoreditch & Spitalfields** (p201) Sadler's Wells, live music bars and comedy.

➡ **The East End & Docklands** (p217) Cabaret and theatre.

➡ **Hampstead & North London** (p233) The works: indie rock, open-air live music, comedy, theatre, jazz and opera.

➡ **Notting Hill & West London** (p256) Tremendous independent cinemas, live music, summer opera.

➡ **Greenwich & South London** (p268) Live music, dance, theatre and cinema.

➡ **Richmond, Kew & Hampton Court** (p291) Live jazz, open-air concerts and live-music pubs.

Up the Creek comedy club (p289)

NEIL SETCHFIELD / LONELY PLANET IMAGES ©

Lonely Planet's Top Choices

12 Bar (p130)
Southbank Centre (p178)
Proud Camden (p251)
Royal Opera House (p130)
Barbican (p160)
Wilton's (p231)

Best Mainstream Theatre

Shakespeare's Globe (p179)
National Theatre (p178)
Soho Theatre (p131)
Royal Court Theatre (p198)
Old Vic (p180)
Hampstead Theatre (p253)

Best Fringe Theatre

Arcola Theatre (p253)
Bush Theatre (p265)
Battersea Arts Centre (p288)
Young Vic (p180)

Best for Classical Music

Wigmore Hall (p131)
Royal Albert Hall (p198)
Royal Festival Hall (p178)
Cadogan Hall (p198)

Best Church Venues for Music

St Martin-in-the-Fields (p108)
St John's, Smith Square (p101)
St James's Piccadilly (p104)
St Paul's Cathedral (p147)
Westminster Abbey (p80)

Best Dance Performance Venues

London Coliseum (p132)
Sadler's Wells (p214)
Laban (p288)
Royal Festival Hall (p178)
Place (p131)

Best Live Rock & Pop Venues

Barfly (p252)
O2 Shepherd's Bush Empire (p265)
O2 Academy Brixton (p289)
O2 (p289)
Royal Albert Hall (p198)
KOKO (p251)

Best for Live Jazz

606 Club (p198)
Pizza Express Jazz Club (p131)
Vortex Jazz Club (p253)
Ronnie Scott's (p131)

Best Pubs for Live Music

Boogaloo (p249)
Old Blue Last (p213)
Lock Tavern (p249)
Macbeth (p213)

Best Open-Air Venues for Live Performances

Shakespeare's Globe (p168)
Kenwood House (p251)
Opera Holland Park (p265)
Regent's Park's open-air theatre (p238)
Hyde Park (p192)
Fulham Palace (p299)

Best for Comedy

Comedy Store (p130)
Comedy Camp (p131)
Up the Creek (p289)
Amused Moose Soho (p132)

Best for Street Performance

Covent Garden (p107)
Trafalgar Sq (p96)

Best Cinemas

Rio Cinema (p252)
BFI Southbank (p179)
Everyman Hampstead (p252)
Curzon Soho (p131)
Ritzy Picturehouse (p289)
Electric Cinema (p264)

Liberty department store (p134)

Shopping

From charity-shop finds to designer 'it bags', there are thousands of ways to spend your hard-earned cash in London. Many of the big-name shopping attractions, such as Harrods, Hamleys, Camden and Spitalfields Market, have become must-sees in their own right, but chances are that with so many temptations, you'll give your wallet a full workout.

NEED TO KNOW

Opening Hours

➡ Shops generally open from 9am or 10am to 6pm or 7pm Monday to Saturday.

➡ The majority of shops in the West End (Oxford St, Soho and Covent Garden), Chelsea, Knightsbridge, Kensington, Greenwich, Hampstead and Islington also open on Sunday, typically from noon to 6pm but sometimes 10am to 4pm.

➡ Shops in the West End open late (to 9pm) on Thursday; those in Chelsea, Knightsbridge and Kensington open late on Wednesday.

➡ If there's a major market on a certain day – say, Columbia Road Flower Market on a Sunday morning – it's a good bet that neighbouring stores will also fling their doors open.

Taxes & Refunds

In certain circumstances visitors from non-EU countries are entitled to claim back the 20% value-added tax (VAT) they have paid on purchased goods. The rebate applies only to items purchased in stores displaying a 'tax free' sign (there are plenty of these along Bond St). For details on how to claim it, see p401.

Carnaby St, Soho

Markets

Perhaps the biggest draw for visitors is the capital's famed markets. A treasure trove of small designers, unique jewellery pieces, original framed photographs and posters, colourful vintage pieces and bric-a-brac, they are the antidote to impersonal, carbon-copy high-street shopping.

The most popular markets are Camden, Spitalfields and Portobello Road, which are in full swing at the weekend. Although they're all more or less outdoors (Spitalfields is now covered, as are the Stables in Camden), they are always busy, rain or shine.

Designers

British designers are well established in the fashion world and a visit to Stella McCartney, Matthew Williamson, Burberry or Mulberry is an experience in its own right.

Vintage Fashion

Gripped as it is by looking good, and with a permanent shopping fever, London's love affair with vintage apparel seems to be a lasting one. Vintage designer pieces from Chanel, Dior, Miu Miu, Vivienne Westwood, you name it – and odd bits and pieces from the 1920s to the 1980s – are all busting the rails in shops that are often as extravagant as the clothes they stock.

The rise of burlesque and cabaret club nights has meant that 1920s to 1950s costume dresses and jewellery have become much coveted, pushing prices up. It's not unusual for designer and rare pieces to cost up to £300, but you can find cheaper things (between £10 and £50) if you dig deep.

Charity shops in areas such as Chelsea, Notting Hill and Kensington usually have cheap designer wear (usually, the richer the area, the better the secondhand shops).

High Street Chains

Many bemoan the fact that chains have taken over the high street, leaving independent shops struggling to balance the books. But since they're cheap, fashionable and always conveniently located, Londoners (and others) keep going back for more. As well as familiar overseas retailers, such as Gap, H&M, Urban Outfitters and Zara, you'll find a number of home-grown chains (for a full list of outlets, check the websites):

French Connection UK (Map p428; www.frenchconnection.com; 396 Oxford St W1; ⊖Bond St) This chain's clothes are more sober than the

Top: Selfridges (p136)
Bottom: Tatty Devine (p215)

Shopping by Neighbourhood

Hampstead & North London
It's all about Camden Market (p254)

Clerkenwell, Shoreditch & Spitalfields
Vintage, vintage, vintage, fashion and jewellery (p214)

Notting Hill & West London
Famous market, vintage and lovely boutiques (p266)
(1mi)

The City
Good for suits but little else (p161)

East End & Docklands
Wonderful markets, discounted fashion (p231)
(1mi)

The West End
Shopping galore, from franchises to boutiques (p132)

Kensington & Hyde Park
High fashion and glamorous shopping (p199)

London Eye

The South Bank
Fabulous food and small designer shops (p180)

Richmond, Kew & Hampton Court
Antiques, delis and independent shops (p306)
(2mi)

Greenwich & South London
Eclectic markets, up-and-coming fashion (p289)

FCUK sobriquet suggests, though its advertising is always risqué.

Jigsaw (Map p432; www.jigsaw-online.com; 21 Long Acre WC2; ⊖Covent Garden) Classic women's clothes, with an emphasis on tweeds and knits, plus some chiffon and glitter.

Joseph (Map p440; 77 Fulham Rd SW3; ⊖South Kensington) Show them who wears the trousers, with classically smart pants and pants suits, plus a whole range of other fashion.

Karen Millen (Map p432; www.karenmillen. com; 32-33 James St WC2; ⊖Covent Garden) An upmarket womenswear store, with glam suit-trousers, voluptuous knits, shiny trench coats and evening frocks.

Marks & Spencer (Map p428; www.marks andspencer.co.uk; 458 Oxford St W1; ⊖Bond St) Rising from the years of being synonymous with 'quality knickers', M&S has pulled its socks up with some fabulous fashion lines.

Miss Selfridge (Map p422; www.missselfridge. com; 325 Oxford St W1; ⊖Oxford Circus or Bond St) Fun, throwaway fashion for female teens.

Oasis (Map p432;www.oasis-stores.com; 13 James St WC2; ⊖Covent Garden) Good catwalk copies that are sure to keep you in fashion.

Reiss (Map p422;www.reiss.co.uk; 14-17 Market Pl W1; ⊖Oxford Circus) Reiss suddenly came out of the shadows when the Duchess of Cambridge (aka Kate Middleton) was photographed wearing one of its numbers. Now a classic English label of understated fashion.

TopShop (p133) The mother of fast fashion seldom needs introducing; mass hysteria is guaranteed for the launch of special collections such as Kate Moss's.

Warehouse (Map p422;www.warehouse.co.uk; Argyll St W1; ⊖Oxford Circus) Somewhere be-tween TopShop and Oasis in the fashion stakes.

Lonely Planet's Top Choices

Silver Vaults (p161) The world's largest collection of silver, from cutlery to jewellery.

Harrods (p199) Garish, stylish, kitsch, yet perennially popular department store.

John Sandoe Books (p199) A treasure trove of literary gems, with excellent staff recommendations.

Sister Ray (p135) A top independent music shop, with an ever-changing collection of vinyls and CDs.

Best Fashion Shops

Tatty Devine (p215)

Joy (p133)

Sting (p136)

Laden Showroom (p215)

Start (p216)

Best Markets

Spitalfields (p215)

Camden Market (p240)

Columbia Road (p231)

Portobello Road Market (p259)

Greenwich Market (p282)

Brixton Market (p290)

Best Vintage

Beyond Retro (p232)

Absolute Vintage (p215)

Limelight Movie Art (p199)

Bang Bang Exchange (p133)

Beehive (p290)

Rellik (p266)

Best Bookshops

Village Books (p290)

Books for Cooks (p266)

Daunt Books (p137) Guides, maps and tales from every corner of the world.

Magma (p215)

Gosh! (p137)

Best Music Shops

Rough Trade East (p215)

Sister Ray (p135)

Ray's Jazz (p135)

Sounds of the Universe (p135)

Best Department Stores

Harvey Nichols (p199)

Selfridges (p136)

Liberty (p134)

Fortnum & Mason (p132)

Best Shopping Streets

Marylebone High St (p136)

Brick Lane (p214)

King's Road (p199)

Covent Garden (p106)

Knightsbridge (p199)

Best for Gifts

Labour & Wait (p215)

Compendia (p290)

Penhaligon's (p132)

Greenwich Market (p282)

Roullier White (p290)

Shepherds (p133)

Best for Antiques

Portobello Road Market (p259)

Camden Passage (p254)

Silver Vaults (p161)

Sports & Activities

London bristles with cutting-edge sports facilities and the choice of activities is enormous. And with the Olympic Games towel-flicking sedentary locals into action, every other Londoner, from the grocer to your local librarian, seems to be training for a half-marathon or triathlon, cycling to work, jogging on the spot at zebra crossings, dusting off their football boots or pumping iron.

Health & Fitness

London parks swarm with joggers but when the skies open overhead they hit the treadmill.

Fitness First (☎01202-845000; www.fitnessfirst.co.uk) Branches all over the city.

La Fitness (☎7366 8080; www.lafitness.co.uk) Over 20 gyms in town.

Virgin active (☎0845 130 4747; www.virginactive.co.uk) Biggest chain in the UK; top end.

Football

Stadiums where you can watch matches (or, more realistically, take tours) include:

Wembley Stadium (www.wembleystadium.com) The city's landmark national stadium where England traditionally plays its international matches and where the FA Cup final is contested. The 2013 Champions League final will be played here.

Arsenal Emirates Stadium (www.arsenal.com; Holloway, Islington; ⊖Arsenal)

Chelsea (www.chelseafc.com; Stamford Bridge Stadium, Fulham Rd SW6; ⊖Fulham Broadway)

Swimming

London has some lovely 1930s art deco lidos, while swimming pools and public baths can be found across town (see p323).

Cricket

The **English Cricket Board** (☎0870 533 8833; www.ecb.co.uk) has full details of match schedules and tickets. Test matches are regularly played at Lords (p255) and the Oval (p280).

Ice Skating

A combined ice rink and bowling venue, **Queens Ice & Bowl** (☎7229 0172; www.queensiceandbowl.co.uk; 17 Queensway W2; ⊖Queensway) has skating year-round. In winter, ice rinks appear at Somerset House (p110), Natural History Museum (p187), Kew Gardens (p296), Hampton Court Palace (p293) and Tower of London (p141).

Rugby Union

Between January and March, England competes against Scotland, Wales, Ireland, France and Italy in the Six Nations Championship. Three games take place at Twickenham Stadium. For details, click on www.rfu.com.

Tennis

Wimbledon (p302) becomes the centre of the sporting universe for a fortnight in June/July when the world-famous tennis tournament takes place. Numerous parks around London have tennis courts, many free.

Lonely Planet's Top Choices

Barclays Cycle Hire Scheme (p393) A handy and versatile way to get about town and excellent for short hops.

Wembley Stadium (p72) Take a tour at this colossus of a modern stadium.

Hampstead Heath Ponds (p254) Open all year and tested daily for water quality, luring bands of swimmers whatever the season.

Porchester Spa (p267) Warm your toes in the Finnish log sauna and Turkish hot rooms and submit to a restorative massage.

Top Sporting Events

2012 Olympic Games (p222)

London Marathon (p27)

Wimbledon Lawn Tennis Championships (p27)

FA Cup Final (p72)

Oxford & Cambridge Boat Race (p27)

Best for Swimming

Parliament Hill Lido (p255)

London Fields Lido (p220)

Brockwell Park Lido (p290)

Shoreditch Rooms (p333)

Haymarket (p325)

Best Parks for Sports & Activities

Regent's Park (p238)

Battersea Park (p278)

Hampstead Heath (p241)

Dulwich Park (p281)

Best Walking Tours

The West End Walk (p115)

The South Bank Walk (p175)

Putney to Barnes (p292)

A Taste of the City (p158)

PLAN YOUR TRIP SPORTS & ACTIVITIES

NEED TO KNOW

Opening Hours

As a rule, most gyms open very early, usually from 6.30am, to ensure early risers get their workout on time. Equally they are open until at least 9pm. However, it's best to call ahead. Parks are generally open dawn to dusk.

Tickets

Getting tickets for Premier League matches during the August–mid-May football season in London is tricky, as seats are snapped up by season-ticket holders. Stadium tours are, however, available for an inside look. Tickets for all other enclosed sporting events need to be booked well in advance. The entertainment weekly **Time Out** (www.timeout.com) has the best information on fixtures, times, venues and ticket prices.

Explore London

LONDON'S TOP SIGHTS

London Eye (p169), designed by David
Marks and Julia Barfield

Neighbourhoods at a Glance

① The West End (p78)

With many of London's premier sights, postcodes and superlative restaurants, hotels and shops, the West End should be your first port of call. Iconic sights (Trafalgar Square, Piccadilly Circus), buildings and museums (Buckingham Palace, Westminster Abbey, British Museum), history and nightlife (Soho), shopping, parks (St James's Park) and theatres, they are all here.

② The City (p139)

London's historic core is a tale of two cities: all go during the week and deserted at weekends. But there are ancient streets and spectacular architecture while history waits at every turn. St Paul's Cathedral and the Tower of London are hallmark sights.

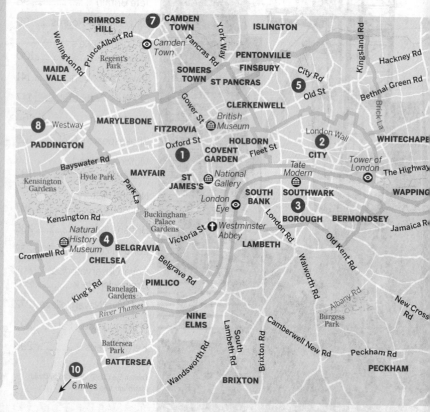

❸ The South Bank (p162)

The Tate Modern effect has done much to re-energise the South Bank, a must-visit area for art lovers, theatre-goers, culture hounds and iconic Thames views. There's also a super food market, first-rate pubs, dollops of history, dashing modern architecture and a sprinkling of fine gastropubs and restaurants.

❹ Kensington & Hyde Park (p181)

Splendidly well groomed, Kensington is one of London's most pleasant neighbourhoods. You'll find three fine museums here: the V&A, the Natural History Museum and the Science Museum as well as excellent dining, shopping and graceful parkland.

❺ Clerkenwell, Shoreditch & Spitalfields (p201)

This redeveloped area boasts top sights (Geffrye Museum, Georgian Spitalfields, White Cube Gallery), excellent markets (Exmouth, Spitalfields, Brick Lane) and a creative frisson, but truly comes alive at night.

❻ The East End & Docklands (p217)

Anyone with an interest in multicultural London needs to visit the East End. There's standout Asian cuisine, superlative museums, excellent pubs and markets but potentially it's the Olympic Park that will entice.

❼ Hampstead & North London (p233)

Leafy Hampstead, Primrose Hill, Islington and Highgate are splendidly upmarket, but there's also stunning wild parkland, grade-A gastropubs, markets, overgrown Victorian cemeteries and a great zoo. With top-notch nightlife, it's a round-the-clock experience.

❽ Notting Hill & West London (p256)

Portobello Market, fabulous cinemas, canal-side charms, superb pubs and clubs, swish parkland and mansions, varied shopping and ethnic eats makes Notting Hill and West London an eclectic must-see.

❾ Greenwich & South London (p268)

Regal riverside Greenwich complements its village feel with some grand architecture, grassy parkland and riverside pubs. Clapham has the restaurants, Brixton the clubs, while Dulwich Village is all leafy charm.

❿ Richmond, Kew & Hampton Court (p291)

Wander by the Thames, explore haunted Tudor palaces (Hampton Court), get lost in beautiful Kew Gardens, go deer-spotting in Richmond Park and down a pint by the riverside at sunset.

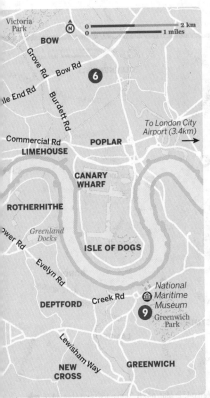

The West End

WESTMINSTER | BLOOMSBURY | FITZROVIA |ST JAMES'S | SOHO | CHINATOWN | COVENT GARDEN | LEICESTER SQUARE |
WHITEHALL | HOLBORN | THE STRAND | MARYLEBONE | MAYFAIR

Neighbourhood Top Five

1 Visiting the **Houses of Parliament** (p90): few countries allow such unrestricted access to their parliament and it is a unique experience to be able to watch Members of Parliament debate the latest laws. The building itself is stunning too.

2 Enjoying fabulous Chinese cuisine in **Soho and Chinatown** (p116).

3 Hiring a deckchair in **St James's Park** (p103) and enjoy regal views of London.

4 Exploring the history of ancient civilisations at the excellent – and free – **British Museum** (p83).

5 Hitting the shops and boutiques of **Covent Garden** (p134) and soak up the atmosphere.

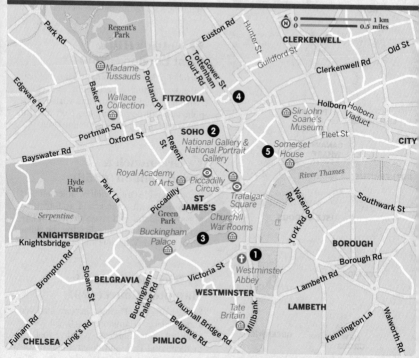

For more detail of this area, see Map p422, Map p432, Map p428, Map p430 and Map p426 ➡

Explore the West End

It may be a compact area, but the West End packs it in when it comes to sights. You'll need to allow half a day for the big museums (such as the British Museum or the National Gallery) and at least a couple of hours for places like Westminster Abbey and Buckingham Palace. All involve a fair amount of traipsing so plan a pub stop or a meal afterwards.

One of the delights of the West End is its energy and there is no better way to enjoy it than by walking around and taking it all in. Atmospheric places for a breather include Covent Garden, Trafalgar Square and St James's Park.

Westminster and Whitehall are deserted in the evenings, with little in the way of bars and restaurants. The same goes for St James's. Instead head to vibrant Soho for fantastic bars and restaurants, or the streets surrounding Covent Garden.

Local Life

➡ **Eating out** Soho is unrivalled when it comes to eating out. Andrew Edmunds (p118) and Mildreds (p118) never seem to go out of fashion, while new, hip places such as Spice Market (p120) and Spuntino (p117) open all the time.

➡ **Late-night openings** Be it for catching the latest exhibition or simply enjoying the permanent collections without the weekend crowds, many Londoners make the best of late-night openings at the National Gallery (p93), the National Portrait Gallery (p97) and the British Museum (p83). It's also popular for original first dates!

➡ **Shopping** Love it or loathe it, most Londoners will hit Oxford Street at some stage to do some shopping; it's smack bang in the centre of town and has every franchise under the sun as well as good department stores such as Selfridges (p136) and John Lewis (p138).

Getting There & Away

➡ **Underground** Every tube line goes through the West End so wherever you're staying in London, you'll have no difficulty getting there. The tube is also good for getting from one end of the West End to the other (Russell Square to Green Park, or Baker St to Embankment).

➡ **Walking** The West End is relatively compact so it'll be cheaper and generally more enjoyable to walk from one place to another rather than take public transport.

➡ **Barclays Bikes** There are docking stations everywhere within the West End and cycling is your best bet for short journeys.

Lonely Planet's Top Tip

London, the West End especially, can be expensive but there are plenty of tricks to make your pennies last. Many of the top museums are free so give them priority over the more commercial attractions. The West End is compact, so walk or take the bus (cheaper than the tube).

THE WEST END

✕ Best Places to Eat

➡ Providores & Tapa Room (p122)
➡ Yauatcha (p116)
➡ Le Boudin Blanc (p123)
➡ Mooli's (p117)
➡ Vincent Rooms (p113)

For reviews, see p113 ➡

🍷 Best Places to Drink

➡ Experimental Cocktail Club (p126)
➡ Purl (p129)
➡ Gordon's Wine Bar (p129)
➡ Newman Arms (p125)
➡ Queen's Larder (p125)

For reviews, see p125 ➡

◉ Best Free Sights

➡ British Museum (p83)
➡ Houses of Parliament (p90)
➡ National Gallery (p93)
➡ National Portrait Gallery (p97)
➡ Photographers' Gallery (p106)
➡ Wallace Collection (p113)

For reviews, see p101

WESTMINSTER ABBEY

Westminster Abbey is such an important commemoration site for both the British royalty and the nation's political and artistic idols that it's difficult to overstress its symbolic value or imagine its equivalent anywhere else in the world. With the exception of Edward V and Edward VIII, every English sovereign has been crowned here since William the Conqueror in 1066, and most of the monarchs from Henry III (died 1272) to George II (died 1760) were also buried here.

There is an extraordinary amount to see at the Abbey. The interior is chock-a-block with small chapels, elaborate tombs of monarchs, and monuments to various luminaries down through the ages. And, as you might expect for one of the most visited churches in Christendom, it can get intolerably busy.

A Regal History

The Abbey is a magnificent sight. Though a mixture of architectural styles, it is considered the finest example of Early English Gothic (1180–1280). The original church was built in the 11th century by King (later St) Edward the Confessor, who is buried in the chapel behind the main altar. Henry III (r 1216–72) began work on the new building but didn't complete it; the French Gothic nave was finished in 1388. Henry VII's huge and magnificent chapel was added in 1519.

The Abbey was initially a monastery for Benedictine monks. Many of the building's features attest to this collegial past (the octagonal chapter room, the quire and cloisters). In 1540, Henry VIII separated the Church of England from the Catholic Church and dissolved the monastery. The

DON'T MISS...

➡ Coronation Chair
➡ Henry VII's Lady Chapel
➡ Pyx Chamber
➡ College Garden
➡ Chapter House
➡ Poets' Corner

PRACTICALITIES

➡ Map p430
➡ www.westminster abbey.org
➡ Dean's Yard SW1
➡ adult/child £16/6
➡ ⊘9.30am-4.30pm Mon-Fri, to 6pm Wed, to 2.30pm Sat, last entry 1hr before closing
➡ ⊝Westminster or St James's Park

King became head of the Church of England and the Abbey acquired its 'royal peculiar' status (administered directly by the Crown and exempt from any ecclesiastical jurisdiction).

North Transept, Sanctuarium & Quire

Visitors enter the Abbey by the north door. The North Transept is often referred to as Statesmen's Aisle: politicians and eminent public figures are commemorated by staggeringly large marble statues and imposing marble plaques. The Whig and Tory prime ministers who dominated late Victorian politics, Gladstone (who is buried here) and Disraeli (who is not), have their monuments uncomfortably close to one another. Nearby is a monument to Robert Peel, who, as home secretary in 1829, created the Metropolitan Police. Robert's policemen became known as 'Bobby's boys' and later, simply, 'bobbies'.

At the heart of the Abbey is the **sanctuary** where coronations, royal weddings and funerals take place. George Gilbert Scott designed the ornate **high altar** in 1897. In front of the altar is a rare **marble pavement** dating back to 1268. It has intricate designs of small pieces of marble inlaid into plain marble.

The Quire, a sublime structure of gold, blue and red Victorian Gothic by Edward Blore, dates back to the mid-19th century. It sits where the original choir for the monks worship would have been but bears no resemblance to the original. Nowadays, the Quire is still used for singing but its regular occupants are now the Westminster Choir – 22 boys and 12 'lay vicars' (men) who sing the daily services.

Chapels

The Sanctuary is surrounded by several chapels. **Henry VII's Lady Chapel**, in the easternmost part of the Abbey, is the most spectacular with its circular vaulting on the ceiling, colourful banners and dramatic oak stalls. Behind the chapel's altar is the elaborate sarcophagus of Henry VII and his queen, Elizabeth of York.

Beyond the chapel's altar is the Royal Air Force (RAF) Chapel, with a stained-glass window commemorating the force's finest hour, the Battle of Britain. Next to it, a plaque marks the spot where Oliver Cromwell's body lay for two years until the Restoration, when it was disinterred, hanged and beheaded. The bodies believed to be those of the two child princes (allegedly) murdered in the Tower of London in 1483 are buried here.

There are two small chapels either side of Lady Chapel with the tombs of famous monarchs: on the left is where Elizabeth I and her half-sister 'Bloody

REFRESHMENTS

You can get drinks and snacks at the Coffee Club in the Cloister; you're allowed to take them to the College Garden for quiet enjoyment but not inside the buildings.

On 29 April 2011, Prince William married his girlfriend Catherine Middleton at Westminster Abbey. The couple had chosen the Abbey for the relatively intimate setting of the Sanctuary – because of the Quire, three-quarters of the 1900 or so guests couldn't see a thing! Unusually, the couple decided to decorate the Abbey with trees; less controversial was the bride's decision to opt for a gown by a British designer, Sarah Burton (of Alexander McQueen).

RESTAURANTS

There are two superb restaurants within 10 minutes' walk of the church: the Cinnamon Club (p113) serves fabulous (and expensive) Indian cuisine with a European twist, while the Vincent Rooms (p113) is the place to go for top-notch modern European cuisine at rock-bottom prices.

Mary' rest. On the right is the **tomb of Mary Queen of Scots**, beheaded on the orders of her cousin Elizabeth and with the acquiescence of her son, the future James I.

Opposite the entrance to the Lady Chapel is the rather ordinary-looking **Coronation Chair**, upon which almost every monarch since the late 13th century is said to have been crowned.

Shrine of St Edward the Confessor

The most sacred spot in the Abbey lies behind the high altar; access is generally restricted to protect the 13th-century floor. St Edward was the founder of the Abbey and the original building was consecrated a few weeks before his death. His tomb was slightly altered after the original was destroyed during the Reformation.

Outer Buildings & Gardens

The entrance to the Cloister is 13th century, while the cloister itself dates from the 14th. Eastwards down a passageway off the Cloister are three museums run by English Heritage. The octagonal **Chapter House** has one of Europe's best-preserved medieval tile floors and retains traces of religious murals. It was used as a meeting place by the House of Commons in the second half of the 14th century. To the right of the entrance to Chapel House is what is claimed to be the oldest door in the UK – it's been there 950 years.

The adjacent **Pyx Chamber** is one of the few remaining relics of the original Abbey and contains the Abbey's treasures and liturgical objects. Note the enormous trunks, which were made inside the room and used to store valuables from the Exchequer.

Next door, the **Abbey Museum** exhibits the death masks of generations of royalty, wax effigies representing Charles II and William III (who is on a stool to make him as tall as his wife Mary), as well as armour and stained glass.

To reach the 900-year-old **College Garden** (⊙10am-6pm Tue-Thu Apr-Sep, to 4pm Tue-Thu Oct-Mar), enter Dean's Yard and the Little Cloisters off Great College St.

Nave & South Transept

The south transept contains **Poets' Corner**, where many of England's finest writers are buried and/or commemorated; a memorial here is the highest honour the monarch can bestow.

On the western side of the cloister is **Scientists' Corner**, where you will find **Sir Isaac Newton's tomb**; a nearby section of the northern aisle of the nave is known as **Musicians' Aisle** where baroque composers Henry Purcell and John Blow are buried. (George Frederic Handel is also buried at the Abbey but in the south transept.)

The two towers above the west door are the ones through which you exit. These were designed by Nicholas Hawksmoor and completed in 1745. Just above the door, perched in 15th-century niches, are the latest sacred additions to the Abbey: 10 stone statues of international 20th-century martyrs. These were unveiled in 1998 and they include the likes of Martin Luther King and the Polish priest St Maximilian Kolbe, who was murdered by the Nazis at Auschwitz.

To the right as you exit is a memorial to innocent victims of oppression, violence and war around the world. 'All you who pass by, is it nothing to you?' it asks poignantly.

One of London's most visited attractions, the British Museum draws an average of five million punters each year. The museum was founded in 1753 following the bequest of royal physician Hans Sloane's 'cabinet of curiosities'. The collection opened to the public in 1759 and the museum has since kept expanding its collection through judicious acquisitions and the controversial plundering of imperialism. It's an exhaustive and exhilarating stampede through world cultures, with galleries devoted to ancient civilisations, from Egypt to Western Asia, the Middle East, the Romans and Greece, India, Africa, prehistoric and Roman Britain and medieval antiquities.

The museum is huge, so make a few focused visits if you have time, and consider the choice of tours. There are 15 free 30- to 40-minute **eyeOpener tours** of individual galleries throughout the day. The museum has also developed excellent **audioguides** (adult/child £5/3.50). They offer six themed tours lasting 30 to 90 minutes, as well as special children's trails. Finally, you can download one- or three-hour itineraries from the museum's website that take in various highlights.

Great Court
Covered with a spectacular glass-and-steel roof designed by Norman Foster in 2000, the Great Court is the largest covered public square in Europe. In its centre is the world-famous **Reading Room**, formerly the British Library, which has been frequented by all the big brains of history, from Mahatma Gandhi to Karl Marx.

DON'T MISS...

➡ Rosetta Stone
➡ Mummy of Katebet
➡ Parthenon Sculptures
➡ Oxus Treasure
➡ Mosaic Mask of Tezcatlipoca
➡ Lindow Man
➡ Sutton Hoo Ship-Burial artefacts

PRACTICALITIES

➡ Map p426
➡ www.british museum.org
➡ Great Russell St WC1
➡ admission free; £3 donation suggested
➡ ⊙10am-5.30pm Sat-Thu, to 8.30pm Fri
➡ ⊜Tottenham Court Rd or Russell Sq

A HISTORY OF THE WORLD IN 100 OBJECTS

In 2010, the British Museum launched an outstanding radio series on BBC Radio 4 called *A History of the World in 100 Objects*. The series, presented by British Museum director Neil MacGregor, retraces two million years of history through 100 objects from the museum's collections. Each object is described in a 15-minute program, its relevance and significance analysed. Anyone with access to an MP3 player would be encouraged to download the podcasts, available from www.bbc.co.uk/ahistoryoftheworld/programme. Neil MacGregor has also written a book on the topic, *A History of the World in 100 Objects*, published by Allen Lane (2010).

The British Museum is building a major new extension called the World Conservation and Exhibitions Centre in its northwestern corner, which will be completed in late 2013. The new building will host a new special exhibition space and state-of-the-art facilities for the preservation and research of the museum's collections.

Ancient Egypt

The star of the show at the British Museum is the Ancient Egypt collection. It comprises sculptures, fine jewellery, papyrus texts, coffins and mummies, including the beautiful and intriguing **Mummy of Katebet** (room 63). Perhaps the most prized item in the collection is the **Rosetta Stone** (room 4), the key to deciphering Egyptian hieroglyphics.

Ancient Greece

Another highlight of the museum is the **Parthenon Sculptures** (aka Parthenon Marbles; room 18). The marble works are thought to show the great procession to the temple that took place during the Panathenaic Festival, on the birthday of Athena, one of the grandest events in the Greek world.

Roman and Medieval Britain

Amid all the highlights from ancient Egypt, Greece and Rome, it almost comes as a surprise to see treasures from Britain and nearby Europe (rooms 40 to 51). Many go back to Roman times, when the empire spread across much of the continent, but not all.

The **Lindow Man** (room 50), for instance, is the remains of a 1st-century man discovered in a bog near Manchester in northern England in 1984. Thanks to the conditions in the bog, many of the internal organs, skin and hair were preserved and scientists from the British Museum were able to determine that the Lindow Man had met a horrific death: killed by an axe stroke on the head and garrotted.

Equally fascinating are artefacts from the **Sutton Hoo Ship-Burial** (room 41), an elaborate Anglo-Saxon burial site from Suffolk (Eastern England) dating back to the 7th century; items include coins and a stunning helmet complete with face mask.

Other Highlights

Kids will love the North American (room 26) and Mexican (room 27) galleries, with the 15th-century Aztec **Mosaic Mask of Tezcatlipoca** (or Skull of the Smoking Mirror), a human skull decorated with turquoise mosaic.

There are also superb collections on ancient Middle East civilisations, including rare artefacts from the **Royal Tombs of Ur** (room 56) in modern-day Iraq and the exquisite gold figurines from the **Oxus Treasure** (room 52), originating from the ancient Persian capital of Persepolis around 400 BC.

The 1820 **King's Library** is a stunning neoclassical space, and retraces how such disciplines as biology, archaeology, linguistics and geography emerged during the Enlightenment of the 18th century.

BRITISH MUSEUM

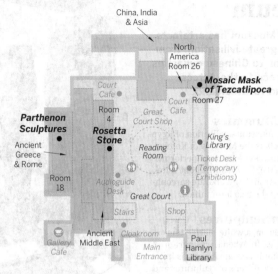

China, India
& Asia

North
America
Room 26

**Mosaic Mask
of Tezcatlipoca**
Room 27

Court
Cafe

Room
4

Court
Cafe

Great
Court Shop

King's
Library

**Parthenon
Sculptures**

**Rosetta
Stone**

Reading
Room

Ticket Desk
(Temporary
Exhibitions)

Ancient
Greece
& Rome

Room
18

Audioguide
Desk

Great Court

Stairs

Shop

Ancient
Middle East

Cloakroom

Paul
Hamlyn
Library

Gallery
Cafe

Main
Entrance

Great Russell Street

Ground Floor

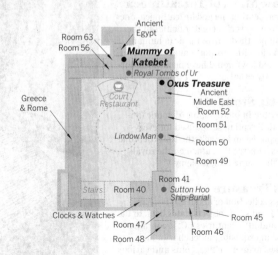

Ancient
Egypt

Room 63

Room 56

**Mummy of
Katebet**

Royal Tombs of Ur

Oxus Treasure
Ancient
Middle East
Room 52

Greece
& Rome

Court
Restaurant

Room 51

Room 50

Lindow Man

Room 49

Room 41

Stairs

Room 40

Sutton Hoo
Ship-Burial

Room 45

Clocks & Watches

Room 47

Room 46

Room 48

Upper Floor

Treasures of the British Museum

The British Museum has artefacts from every great civilisation, from the Pharaohs to Chinese dynasties, Ancient Greece to the Aztecs, Easter Island to Greenland.

Egyptian Mummies

1 Among the museum's collection of Egyptian artefacts is the Mummy of Katebet, an elderly Chantress of Amun (a performer for temple rituals). Everything about Katebet is unusual: from her elaborate sarcophagus to the way she was mummified.

Parthenon Sculptures

2 The Parthenon, a white marble temple dedicated to Athena, was part of a grandiose complex on the Acropolis in Athens. There are dozens of sculptures and friezes as well as interactive displays explaining how they all once fitted together.

Mosaic Mask of Tezcatlipoca

3 Representing the god Tezcatlipoca, one of four powerful creator deities in the Mexican pantheon, this 'mask' (a human skull inlaid with turquoise mosaic, with an articulated jaw) would have been worn during priestly rituals.

Rosetta Stone

4 Written in hieroglyphic, demotic (ancient Egyptian script used for everyday purposes) and Greek, the Rosetta Stone features a decree that affirmed the royal cult of the young king Ptolemy V.

Oxus Treasure

5 This collection of about 170 Persian gold and silver objects dates back to the fourth and fifth centuries BC. It contains vessels, an exquisite model chariot and figurines, armlets, rings, coins and various personal objects.

....

Clockwise from top left
1. Egyptian mummies **2.** Parthenon sculptures **3.** Mosaic Mask of Tezcatlipoca **4.** Rosetta Stone

Built in 1705 as Buckingham House for the duke of the same name, this palace has been the Royal Family's London lodgings since 1837, when Queen Victoria moved in. St James's Palace was judged too old-fashioned and insufficiently impressive, although Buckingham underwent a number of modifications until it was deemed fit for purpose.

The palace's first resident is commemorated in great pomp outside the palace, on the **Queen Victoria Memorial**, with its 25m-high column. The forecourt, gates and railings were all added at the same time as part of the memorial scheme. The memorial was dedicated by her grandson George V in 1911. The palace was open to the public in the 1990s in a bid to revive popular support for the monarchy after tumultuous times. Commoners now get a peek of the State Rooms, a mere 19 of the 775 rooms of the palace, and only during August and September, when Her Majesty is holidaying in Scotland. The Queen's Gallery is open year-round, however, and the Royal Mews from April to December.

State Rooms

The tour starts in the Guard Room (too small for the Ceremonial Guard, who use adjoining quarters). It takes in the State Dining Room (all red damask and Regency furnishings); then moves on to the Blue Drawing Room (which has a gorgeous fluted ceiling by John Nash) and the White Drawing Room, where foreign ambassadors are received.

The Ballroom, where official receptions and state banquets are held, was a late addition to the palace: Queen Victoria thought Buckingham lacked a proper room for entertaining;

DON'T MISS...

➡ Picture Gallery

➡ Royal Mews

➡ Gardens

➡ Changing of the Guard

➡ Throne Room

PRACTICALITIES

➡ Map p430

➡ www.royalcollection.org.uk

➡ Buckingham Palace Rd SW1

➡ adult/child £18/10

➡ ⊙9.30am-6.30pm late Jul–late Sep, timed ticket with admission every 15min

➡ ⊖St James's Park, Victoria or Green Park

the Ballroom was built between 1853 and 1855 and opened with a ball a year later to celebrate the end of the Crimean War. The **Throne Room** is rather kitsch with its his-and-hers pink chairs initialled 'ER' and 'P', sitting smugly under a theatre arch.

Picture Gallery & Gardens

The most interesting part of the tour (for all but royal sycophants) is the 76.5m-long Picture Gallery, featuring splendid works by such artists as Van Dyck, Rembrandt, Canaletto, Poussin, Canova and Vermeer.

Wandering the gardens is another highlight here – as well as admiring some of the 350 or so species of flowers and plants and listening to the many birds, you'll get beautiful views of the palace and a peek of the famous lake.

Queen's Gallery

Over the last 500 years, the Royal Family has amassed paintings, sculpture, ceramics, furniture and jewellery. The splendid **Queen's Gallery** (www.royalcollection.org.uk; southern wing, Buckingham Palace, Buckingham Palace Rd SW1; adult/child £9/4.50; ☺10am-5.30pm) showcases some of the palace's treasures on a rotating basis, through temporary exhibitions.

The gallery was originally designed as a conservatory by John Nash. It was converted into a chapel for Queen Victoria in 1843, destroyed in a 1940 air raid and reopened as a gallery in 1962. A £20-million renovation for Elizabeth II's Golden Jubilee in 2002 enlarged the entrance and added a Greek Doric portico, a multimedia centre and three times as much display space. Entrance to the gallery is through Buckingham Gate. Combined tickets with the Royal Mews cost £16/9 for adult/child.

Royal Mews

South of the palace, the **Royal Mews** (www.royalcollection.org.uk; Buckingham Palace Rd SW1; adult/child £8/5; ☺10am-5pm Apr-Oct, to 4pm Mon-Sat Nov-Dec) started life as a falconry but is now a working stable looking after the royals' immaculately groomed horses, along with the opulent vehicles the monarch uses for transport. The Queen is well known for her passion for horses and she names every horse that resides at the mews.

Highlights for visitors include the enormous and opulent gold coach of 1762, which has been used for every coronation since that of George III, the 1910 Glass Coach used for royal weddings (Prince William and Catherine Middleton actually used the 1902 State Landau to make the best of the good weather) and a Rolls-Royce Phantom IV from the royal fleet.

CHANGING OF THE GUARD

At 11.30am daily from May to July, and on alternate days, weather permitting, from August to March, the old guard (Foot Guards of the Household Regiment) comes off duty to be replaced by the new guard on the forecourt of Buckingham Palace. Crowds come to watch the carefully choreographed marching and shouting of the guards in their bright red uniforms and bearskin hats. It lasts about half an hour and is very popular so arrive early if you want to get a good spot.

One of the main uses of the Throne Room is for official wedding photographs, most recently for those of the Duke and Duchess of Cambridge (Prince William and Catherine Middleton).

ROYAL CHRISTENINGS

Another room at the centre of Royal Family life is the music room, where four royal babies were christened: the Prince of Wales (Prince Charles), the Princess Royal (Princess Anne), the Duke of York (Prince Andrew) and the Duke of Cambridge (Prince William).

The House of Commons and House of Lords are housed here in the sumptuous Palace of Westminster. The House of Commons is where Members of Parliament (MPs) meet to propose and discuss new legislation, and to grill the prime minister and other ministers.

When Parliament is in session, visitors are allowed to attend the debates in the House of Commons and the House of Lords. Enter via **St Stephen's Entrance**. It's not unusual to have to wait up to two hours to access the chambers. The best time to watch a debate is during Prime Minister's Question Time on Wednesday, but it's also the busiest.

Towers

The most famous feature of the Houses of Parliament is the Clock Tower, commonly known as **Big Ben**. Ben is the bell hanging inside and is named after Benjamin Hall, the commissioner of works when the tower was completed in 1858. Thirteen-tonne Ben has rung in the New Year since 1924.

Westminster Hall

One of the most stunning features of the Palace of Westminster, seat of the English monarchy from the 11th to the early 16th centuries, is Westminster Hall. The building was originally built in 1099 and is today the oldest surviving part of the complex. The awe-inspiring roof was added between 1394 and 1401; it is the earliest known example of a hammer-beam roof and has been described as 'the greatest surviving achievement of medieval English carpentry'.

Westminster Hall was used for coronation banquets in medieval times, and also served as a courthouse until the 19th century. The trials of William Wallace (1305), Thomas More

DON'T MISS...

➜ Westminster Hall
➜ House of Commons
➜ House of Lords
➜ Big Ben

PRACTICALITIES

➜ Map p430
➜ www.parliament.uk
➜ St Stephen's Entrance, St Margaret St SW1
➜ admission free
➜ ⏱during parliamentary sessions 2.30-10.30pm Mon & Tue, 11.30-7pm Wed, 11.30am-6.30pm Thu, 9.30am-3pm Fri
➜ ⊖Westminster

(1535), Guy Fawkes (1606) and Charles I (1649) all took place here. In the 20th century, monarchs and Winston Churchill lay in state here.

House of Commons

The layout of the Commons Chamber is based on that of St Stephen's Chapel in the original Palace of Westminster. The current chamber, designed by Giles Gilbert Scott, replaced the earlier one destroyed by a 1941 bomb.

Although the Commons is a national assembly of 646 MPs, the chamber has seating for only 437. Government members sit to the right of the Speaker and Opposition members to the left. During debates, MPs wanting to speak stand up to catch the Speaker's eye.

House of Lords

The **House of Lords** (⊘2.30-10pm Mon & Tue, 3-10pm Wed, 11am-7.30pm Thu, 10am to close of session Fri) is also open for visits, via the amusingly named 'Strangers' Gallery'. The intricate Gothic interior led its poor architect, Pugin (1812–52), to an early death from overwork and nervous strain.

Most of the members of the House of Lords are life peers (appointed for their lifetime by the monarch); there is also a small number of hereditary peers and a group of 'crossbench' members (not affiliated to the main political parties).

Tours

On Saturdays and when Parliament is in recess (July to September, and then holidays around Christmas, Easter and a couple of weeks in February and June), visitors can join a 75-minute **guided tour** (www.parliament.uk; ☑ booking 0844 847 1672; adult/child £15/6) of both chambers, Westminster Hall and other historic buildings. Tour schedules change with every recess, so check ahead. It's best to book.

DEBATES

To find out what's being debated on a particular day, check the notice board beside the entrance, or check online at www.parliament.uk. The debating style in the Commons is well known for being quite combative but not all debates are flamboyant arguing duels. In fact, many are rather boring and long-winded, although they are an essential feature of British democracy.

After campaign group 'Fathers 4 Justice' lobbed a condom full of purple powder at Tony Blair in May 2004 and prohunt campaigners broke into the Commons that September, security was further tightened, and a bulletproof screen now sits between members of the public and the debating chamber.

TOP SIGHTS
SOHO

Soho's reputation as the epicentre of nightlife and a proud gay neighbourhood is legendary and well deserved (see box p119). It definitely comes into its own in the evenings, but during the day you'll be charmed by the area's bohemian side and the sheer energy of the place.

DON'T MISS...

➡ Chinatown
➡ Soho Square
➡ Old Compton Street
➡ Dean Street

PRACTICALITIES

➡ Map p422
➡ ⊖Oxford Circus, Tottenham Court Rd, Leicester Sq, Piccadilly Circus

Chinatown

Immediately north of Leicester Square – but a world away in atmosphere – are Lisle and Gerrard Sts, the focal point for London's Chinese community. Although not as big as Chinatowns in many other cities – it's just two streets really – this is a lively quarter with fake oriental gates, Chinese street signs, red lanterns, many, many restaurants and great Asian supermarkets.

London's original Chinatown was further east, near Limehouse, but moved here after heavy bombardments in WWII. To see it at its effervescent best, time your visit for Chinese New Year in late January/early February (p26). Do be aware that the quality of food here varies enormously – many places are mediocre establishments aimed squarely at the tourist market. For the best of the lot, see our recommendations (p116).

Soho Square

At Soho's northern end, leafy **Soho Square** is the area's back garden. This is where people come to laze in the sun on spring and summer days, and where office workers have their lunch. It was laid out in 1681, and originally named King's Square, which is why the statue of Charles II stands in its northern half. In the centre is a tiny mock-Tudor house – the gardener's shed – whose lift was a passage to underground shelters during WWII.

Dean Street

Heading south of Soho Square, you'll find **Dean Street**. No 28 was the home of Karl Marx and his family from 1851 to 1856. Marx, his wife Jenny and their four children lived in extreme poverty, without a toilet or running water, and three of their children died of pneumonia in this flat. While the father of communism spent his days researching *Das Kapital* in the British Museum, his main sources of income were from writing articles for newspapers and financial help from his friend and colleague Friedrich Engels. The Marx family was eventually saved by a large inheritance from Mrs Marx's relatives, after which they upped sticks and moved to the more salubrious surroundings of Primrose Hill (p239).

Today Dean Street is a lively place lined with bars and restaurants that no doubt would have given Marx indigestion.

Other Streets

Old Compton Street is the epicentre of the gay village. As one gay aficionado put it, it's the perfect place to 'clock and cruise'. That said, it is a street loved by all, gay or other, for its great bars, risqué shops and general good vibes.

Seducer and heart-breaker Casanova and opium-addicted writer Thomas de Quincey lived on **Greek Street**, whereas the parallel **Frith Street** (No 20) housed Mozart for a year from 1764.

NATIONAL GALLERY

With more than 2000 Western European paintings on display, this is one of the largest galleries in the world. There are seminal paintings from every important epoch in the history of art, including works by Leonardo da Vinci, Michelangelo, Titian, Van Gogh and Renoir.

The Sainsbury Wing on the gallery's western side houses paintings from 1260 to 1510. In these 16 rooms you will find plenty of fine religious paintings commissioned for private devotion as well more unusual masterpieces such as Boticelli's *Venus & Mars*.

The High Renaissance (1510–1600) is covered in the West Wing where Michelangelo, Titian, Correggio, El Greco and Bronzino hold court, while Rubens, Rembrandt and Caravaggio can be found in the North Wing (1600–1700). There are notably two self-portraits of Rembrandt and the beautiful *Rockeby Venus* by Velázquez.

The most crowded part of the gallery is likely to be the East Wing (1700–1900), with a great collection of 18th-century British landscape artists such as Gainsborough, Constable and Turner, and highbrow impressionist and postimpressionist masterpieces. Visitors will no doubt recognise Van Gogh's *Sunflowers* and Degas' *Dancers*.

The comprehensive **audioguides** (£3.50) are highly recommended, as are the free one-hour introductory guided tours that leave from the information desk in the Sainsbury Wing daily at 11.30am and 2.30pm. There are also special trails and activity sheets for children.

For sustenance, look no further than the **National Dining Rooms** (p121) run by Irish chef Oliver Peyton, which has high-quality British food and an all-day bakery.

DON'T MISS...

➡ *Sunflowers*, by Van Gogh

➡ *Venus & Mars*, by Botticelli

➡ *The Arnolfini Portrait*, by van Eyck

➡ *Rockeby Venus*, by Velázquez

➡ *Rain, Steam & Speed: The Great Western Railway*, by Turner

PRACTICALITIES

➡ Map p432

➡ www.nationalgallery.org.uk

➡ Trafalgar Sq WC2

➡ admission free; prices vary for temporary exhibitions

➡ ⊘10am-6pm Sat-Thu, to 9pm Fri

➡ ⊕Charing Cross or Leicester Sq

National Gallery Masterpieces

The collection of the National Gallery spans seven centuries of European painting. It's a whirl of masterpieces, displayed in sumptuous, airy galleries.

Venus & Mars, Botticelli

1 The scene depicts Venus, goddess of love, intently looking at Mars, god of war, fast asleep and content. The message is that love conquers all.

Sunflowers, Van Gogh

2 This masterpiece seldom needs introduction; it is one of four that Van Gogh painted to decorate a room in the house he used to share with fellow impressionist Gauguin in Arles, southern France.

Rockeby Venus, Velázquez

3 This painting is significant because it is the only known surviving example of a nude by the Spanish master, a topic that was frowned upon in Catholic Spain. It shows Venus with her son Cupid.

Arnolfini Portrait, van Eyck

4 Often thought to represent a wedding, this is actually a portrait of a rich merchant, Giovanni di Nicolao Arnolfini, and his wife. The woman looks pregnant but she is in fact wearing a full-skirted dress, fashionable at the time.

Rain, Steam & Speed: The Great Western Railway, Turner

5 One of JMW Turner's great paintings, it shows Maidenhead railway bridge across the River Thames. It is characteristic of Turner's blurry strokes and pastel colours.

Clockwise from top left
1. Botticelli's *Venus & Mars* 2. Van Gogh's *Sunflowers*
3. *Rockeby Venus* by Velázquez 4. *The Arnolfini Portrait* by van Eyck

TOP SIGHTS
TRAFALGAR SQUARE

In many ways this is the centre of London, where rallies and marches take place, tens of thousands of revellers usher in the New Year and locals congregate for anything from communal open-air cinema to various political protests.

The great square was neglected over many years, ringed with gnarling traffic and given over to flocks of feral pigeons. But things changed in 2000 when Ken Livingstone became London Mayor and embarked on a bold and imaginative scheme to transform it into the kind of space John Nash had intended when he designed it in the early 19th century. Traffic was banished from the northern flank in front of the National Gallery and a new pedestrian plaza built.

DON'T MISS...

➡ Nelson's Column
➡ Bronze Lions
➡ Fourth Plinth
➡ Admiralty Arch

PRACTICALITIES

➡ Map p432
➡ ⊖Charing Cross or Leicester Sq

Square

The square commemorates the victory of the British navy at the Battle of Trafalgar against the French and Spanish navies in 1805 during the Napoleonic wars. The main square contains two beautiful fountains, which are dramatically lit at night. At each corner of the square is a plinth (a small column topped with a statue), three of them topped with statues of military leaders and the fourth, in the northeast corner, now a ubiquitous art installation called, imaginatively, the **Fourth Plinth** (see p107).

The plaza at the north, in front of the National Gallery, is a favourite of street performers.

Nelson's Column

Standing in the centre of the square since 1843, the 52m-high Nelson's Column (upon which the admiral surveys his fleet of ships to the southwest) honours Admiral Lord Nelson, who led the fleet's victory over Napoleon. The column is flanked by four enormous bronze statues of lions sculpted by Sir Edwin Landseer and cast with seized Spanish and French cannons.

Buildings around Trafalgar Square

The pedestrianisation of Trafalgar Square has made it easier to appreciate not only the square but also the splendid buildings around it: the National Gallery (p93), the National Portrait Gallery (p97) and the newly renovated church of St Martin-in-the-Fields (p108).

The ceremonial Pall Mall runs west from the top of the square. To the west is Canada House (1827), designed by Robert Smirke. If you look southwest down Whitehall, you'll also get a glimpse of Big Ben at the Houses of Parliament (p90).

Events

Countless cultural events are held here, showcasing the city's multiculturalism, with celebrations for Christmas, Chinese New Year, African music concerts, film screenings and so on. In recent years, Trafalgar Square has become a top protest venue too, with demonstrations against the war in Iraq, conflicts in Gaza and Sri Lanka and other international hot potatoes taking place here.

Admiralty Arch

To the southwest of Trafalgar Square stands Admiralty Arch, where the Mall begins and leads to Buckingham Palace. It is a grand Edwardian monument, a triple-arched stone entrance designed by Aston Webb in honour of Queen Victoria in 1910. The large central gate is opened only for royal processions and state visits.

The **National Portrait Gallery (NPG) is a wonderful combination of art and history. What makes the collection so compelling is its familiarity; in many cases, you'll have heard of the subject (royals, scientists, politicians, celebrities) and/or the artist (Andy Warhol, Annie Leibovitz, Sam Taylor-Wood). The gallery houses a primary collection of some 10,000 works, which are regularly rotated.**

The NPG is organised chronologically (starting on the 2nd floor), and then by themes. One of the museum's highlights is the famous 'Chandos portrait' of Shakespeare; it is believed to be the only one to have been painted during the author's lifetime. Other highlights include a fascinating painting of Queen Elizabeth I displaying her might by standing over a map of England, and a touching sketch of novelist Jane Austen by her sister Cassandra.

The 1st floor is a captivating journey through the Victorian era and the 20th century, with portraits illustrating the rise and fall of the British Empire.

The ground floor is dedicated to modern figures, using a variety of media (sculpture, photography, video etc). Among the most popular displays are the iconic Blur portraits by Julian Opie and Sam Taylor-Wood's *David*, a video-portrait of David Beckham asleep after football training.

The gallery hosts brilliant temporary exhibitions and the excellent **audioguides** (£3) highlight 200 portraits and allow you to hear the voices of some of the people portrayed.

The **Portrait** restaurant (p121) on the top floor has superb views towards Westminster and does wonderful food, including decadent afternoon teas.

DON'T MISS...

➡ Blur portraits, by Julian Opie

➡ William Shakespeare, 'Chandos Portrait' attributed to John Taylor

➡ *Queen Elizabeth II*, by Andy Warhol

➡ *Jane Austen*, by Cassandra Austen

➡ *Queen Elizabeth I*, by Marcus Gheeraerts the Younger

PRACTICALITIES

➡ Map p432

➡ www.npg.org.uk

➡ St Martin's Pl WC2

➡ admission free; prices vary for temporary exhibitions

➡ ⊘10am-6pm, to 9pm Thu & Fri

➡ ⊜Charing Cross or Leicester Sq

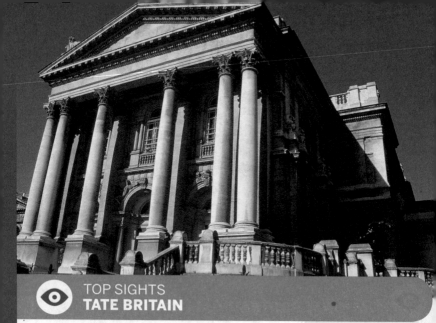

TATE BRITAIN

You'd think that Tate Britain might have suffered since its lavish, sexy sibling, Tate Modern (p164), took half its collection and all of the limelight upriver when it opened in 2000. But, on the contrary, the venerable Tate Britain, built in 1897, stretched out splendidly with its definitive collection of British art from the 16th to the late 20th centuries, while the Modern sister devoted its space to modern art.

The star of the show at Tate Britain is JMW Turner; after he died in 1851, his estate was settled by a decree declaring that whatever had been found in his studio – 300 oil paintings and about 30,000 sketches and drawings – would be bequeathed to the nation. The 'Turner Bequest', as it became known, forms the bulk of the Tate's Turner collection. You'll find such classics as *The Scarlet Sunset* and *Norham Castle, Sunrise*.

As well as Turner's art, there are seminal works by such artists as Constable, Gainsborough and Reynolds, but also more modern artists, such as Lucian Freud, Francis Bacon and Tracey Emin. Tate Britain also hosts the prestigious and often controversial Turner Prize for contemporary art from October to early December every year.

There are free one-hour **thematic tours** (⊙11am, noon, 2pm, 3pm Mon-Fri, noon & 3pm Sat & Sun), along with free 15-minute **Art in Focus talks** (⊙1.15pm Tue, 2.30pm Sat) on specific works. **Audioguides** (£3.50) are also available.

A good time to visit the gallery is **Late at Tate** night, on the first Friday of the month, when the gallery stays open until 10pm.

DON'T MISS...

➡ *The Scarlet Sunset*, JMW Turner

➡ *Three Studies for Figures at the Base of a Crucifixion*, by Francis Bacon

➡ *Norham Castle, Sunrise*, by JMW Turner

➡ *Flatford Mill*, by John Constable

➡ *Ophelia*, by Sir John Everett Millais

PRACTICALITIES

➡ Map p430

➡ www.tate.org.uk

➡ Millbank SW1

➡ admission free; prices vary for temporary exhibitions

➡ ⊙10am-6pm

➡ ⊖Pimlico

TOP SIGHTS
CHURCHILL WAR ROOMS

In 1938, with the prospect of war across Europe looming ever more seriously, the British government decided to look for a suitable site for a temporary emergency government shelter while plans for relocation to the suburbs were being finalised. The basement of what is now the treasury was selected and converted. But at the end of August 1939, with the relocation plans far from ready and the war imminent, the cabinet and chiefs of the armed forces decided to move underground for the foreseeable future. On 3 September Britain declared war on Germany.

The bunker served as nerve centre of the war cabinet until the end of WWII in August 1945: here chiefs of staff slept, ate and plotted Hitler's downfall, blissfully believing they were protected from Luftwaffe bombs (turns out it would have crumpled had the area taken a hit). The existence of the war rooms was revealed to the public in 1948, but it became a museum only in 1984.

Cabinet War Rooms

The Cabinet War Rooms have been left much as they were when the lights were turned off on 15 August 1945 when Japan surrendered and everyone headed off for a well-earned drink. Many rooms have been preserved, including the room where the cabinet held more than 100 meetings, the Telegraph Room with a hotline to Roosevelt, the cramped typing pool, the converted broom cupboard that was Churchill's office, and the all-important map room (which was the operational centre). There are also several bedrooms, where higher-ranking officers slept.

In the Chief of Staff's Conference Room, the walls are covered with huge, original maps that were discovered only in 2002. If you squint two-thirds of the way down the right wall, somebody (Churchill himself?) drew a little doodle depicting a cross-eyed and bandy-legged Hitler knocked to the ground.

The free audioguide is very informative and entertaining and features plenty of anecdotes, including some from people who worked here at the nerve centre of Britain's war effort – and weren't even allowed by their irritable boss to relieve the tension by whistling.

Churchill Museum

This whizz-bang multimedia museum was added during the 2003 refurbishment of the war rooms. There are more interactive displays than you'll know where to look, as well as some of Churchill's personal effects, from cigars to his formal Privy Council uniform, to his shockingly tasteless red velvet 'romper' outfit.

Even though the museum doesn't shy away from its hero's fallibilities – it portrays Churchill as having a legendary temper, being a bit of a maverick and, on the whole, a pretty lousy peace-time politician – it does focus on his strongest suit: his stirring speeches. Churchill's oratorions are replayed for each goose-bumped visitor who steps in front of the interactive displays: 'I have nothing to offer but blood, toil, tears and sweat', 'We will fight them on the beaches', 'Never in the course of human history has so much been owed by so many to so few'.

DON'T MISS...

➡ Map Room

➡ Cabinet Room

➡ Anecdotes from former War Rooms staff

➡ Extracts from Churchill's famous speeches

➡ The 'Hitler doodle' in the Conference Room

PRACTICALITIES

➡ Map p430

➡ http://cwr.iwm.org.uk

➡ Clive Steps, King Charles St SW1

➡ adult/child £16/free

➡ ⊘9.30am-6pm, last admission 5pm

➡ ⊖Westminster

TOP SIGHTS
SIR JOHN SOANE'S MUSEUM

This little museum is one of the most atmospheric and fascinating sights in London. The building is the beautiful, bewitching home of architect Sir John Soane (1753–1837), which he left brimming with surprising personal effects and curiosities, and the museum represents his exquisite and eccentric taste.

Soane was a country bricklayer's son, most famous for designing the Bank of England. In his work and life, he drew on ideas picked up while on an 18th-century grand tour of Italy. He married a rich woman and used the wealth to build this house and the one next door, which was opened as an exhibition and education space in late 2007.

The heritage-listed house is largely as it was when Sir John was carted out in a box, and is itself a main part of the attraction. It has a glass dome that brings light right down to the basement, a lantern room filled with statuary, rooms within rooms, and a picture gallery where paintings are stowed behind each other on folding wooden panes. This is where Soane's choice paintings are displayed, including *Riva degli Schiavoni, looking West* by Canaletto, drawings by Christopher Wren and Robert Adam, and the original *Rake's Progress*, William Hogarth's set of cartoon caricatures of late-18th-century London lowlife. You'll have to ask a guard to open the panes so that you can view all the paintings. Among Soane's more unusual acquisitions are an Egyptian hieroglyphic sarcophagus, an imitation monk's parlour, and slaves' chains.

The first Tuesday evening of each month is the choice time to visit as the house is lit by candles and the atmosphere is even more magical (it is very popular and there are always long queues).

DON'T MISS...

➡ *Riva degli Schiavoni, looking West* by Canaletto
➡ *Rake's Progress* by William Hogarth
➡ Sarcophagus of King Seti I
➡ Candlelit tours

PRACTICALITIES

➡ Map p432
➡ www.soane.org
➡ 13 Lincoln's Inn Fields WC2
➡ admission free
➡ ⏲10am-5pm Tue-Sat & 6-9pm 1st Tue of month
➡ ⊖Holborn

⊙ SIGHTS

The West End is a vague term – any Londoner you meet will give you their own take on which neighbourhoods it does and doesn't include – but what is striking is its variety: from reverentially quiet in Bloomsbury and Holborn to bustling with revellers and shoppers 24/7 in Soho, Piccadilly Circus and Oxford Street. The best way to get to know the West End is on foot. Most sights are within walking distance of one another and you'll get a much better sense of the area's atmosphere that way.

⊙ Westminster

WESTMINSTER ABBEY CHURCH
See p80.

HOUSES OF PARLIAMENT HISTORIC BUILDING
See p90.

TATE BRITAIN MUSEUM
See p98.

**ST JOHN'S,
SMITH SQUARE** HISTORIC BUILDING
Map p430 (www.sjss.org.uk; Smith Sq, Westminster SW1; ⊖Westminster or St James's Park) In the heart of Westminster, this eye-catching church was built by Thomas Archer in 1728 under the Fifty New Churches Act (1711), which aimed to build 50 new churches for London's rapidly growing metropolitan area. Though they never did build all 50 churches, St John's, along with a dozen others, saw the light of day. Unfortunately,

with its four corner towers and monumental facades, the structure was much maligned for the first century of its existence thanks to rumours that Queen Anne likened it to a footstool, though it's also said that she actually requested a church built in the shape of a footstool. Whatever the case, it's generally agreed now that the church is a masterpiece of English baroque, although it no longer serves as a church. After receiving a direct hit during WWII, it was rebuilt in the 1960s as a classical music venue, and is renowned for its crisp acoustics.

The brick-vaulted restaurant in the crypt is called, predictably, the **Footstool**, and is open for lunch Monday to Friday, as well as for pre- and postconcert dinner.

⊙ Bloomsbury & Fitzrovia

BRITISH MUSEUM MUSEUM
See p83.

SQUARES OF BLOOMSBURY SQUARE
Map p426 At the very heart of Bloomsbury is **Russell Square**. Originally laid out in 1800 by Humphrey Repton, it was dark and bushy until the striking facelift that pruned the trees, tidied up the plants and gave it a 10m-high fountain.

The centre of literary Bloomsbury was **Gordon Square** where, at various times, Bertrand Russell lived at No 57, Lytton Strachey at No 51 and Vanessa and Clive Bell, Maynard Keynes and the Woolf family at No 46. Strachey, Dora Carrington and Lydia Lopokova (the future wife of Maynard Keynes) all took turns living at No 41. Not all the buildings, many of which now

---

LITERARY BLOOMSBURY

Bloomsbury's beautiful squares were once colonised by the 'Bloomsbury Group', a group of artists and writers who included Virginia Woolf and EM Forster, and the stories of their many intricate love affairs are as fascinating as their books. Charles Dickens, Charles Darwin, William Butler Yeats and George Bernard Shaw also lived here or hereabouts, as attested by the many blue plaques dotted around.

Bedford Square was home to many London publishing houses until the 1990s, when they were swallowed up by multinational conglomerates and relocated. They included Jonathan Cape, Chatto and the Bodley Head (set up by Woolf and her husband Leonard), and were largely responsible for perpetuating the legend of the Bloomsbury Group by churning out seemingly endless collections of associated letters, memoirs and biographies.

Today Bloomsbury continues to teem with excellent bookshops and cafes, while remaining relatively uncommercial.

LOCAL KNOWLEDGE

BT TOWER

Map p426 (60 Cleveland St W1; ⊜Goodge St) Visible from virtually everywhere in central London, the 1960s BT Tower (which was once the highest structure in the city)was closed to the public many years ago as a result of terrorist threats. Incongruously for such a conspicuous structure, the building was officially a 'secret' and didn't appear on official maps until 1993, when Member of Parliament Kate Hoey used her parliamentary privilege to 'confirm' its existence.

The tower is still used as a communications hub and for air pollution monitoring. It is also a listed building, which means that those lovely satellite dishes are there to stay! The BT Tower reopened to the public for one day in 2010 as part of the Open House London (p363), when 480 lucky ballot winners got tickets for a guided tour. Following the success of the initiative, there are plans to open the tower annually as part of Open House.

belong to the university, are marked with blue plaques.

Lovely **Bedford Square** is the only completely Georgian square still surviving in Bloomsbury.

FREE NEW LONDON
ARCHITECTURE   ARCHITECTURE

Map p426 (www.newlondonarchitecture.org; Bldg Centre, 26 Store St WC1; ⊙9.30am-6pm Mon-Fri, 10am-5pm Sat; ⊜Goodge St) An excellent excursion to see which way London's architectural development is going, this is a frequently changing exhibition that will capture the imagination and interest of anyone who loves London. A large model of the capital highlights the new building areas, showing the extent of the 2012 Olympics plans and various neighbourhood regeneration programs. Photographs and details of individual buildings make it easy to locate each new structure, so that you can go and see it in real life.

DICKENS HOUSE MUSEUM   HISTORIC BUILDING

(www.dickensmuseum.com; 48 Doughty St WC1; adult/child £7/3; ⊙10am-5pm; ⊜Russell Sq) Charles Dickens, the great Victorian novelist, lived a nomadic life in the big city, moving around London so often that he left behind an unrivalled trail of blue plaques. This handsome four-storey house is his sole surviving residence before he upped and moved to Kent. Not that he stayed here for very long – he lasted a mere 2½ years (1837–39) – but this is where his work really flourished: he dashed off *The Pickwick Papers, Nicholas Nickleby* and *Oliver Twist* despite worry over debts, deaths and his ever-growing family. The house was saved from demolition and the museum opened in 1925, showcasing the family drawing room (restored to its original condition) and 10 rooms containing various memorabilia. At the time of writing, the museum was planning a substantial (and much-needed) refurbishment in time to commemorate the bicentenary of Dickens's birth in 2012. The museum is five minutes' walk from Russell Square tube station.

POLLOCK'S TOY MUSEUM   MUSEUM

Map p426 (www.pollockstoymuseum.com; 1 Scala St W1; adult/child £5/3; ⊙10am-5pm Mon-Sat; ⊜Goodge St) Aimed at both kids and adults, this museum is simultaneously creepy and mesmerising. You walk in through its shop, laden with excellent wooden toys and various games, and start your exploration by climbing up a rickety narrow staircase, where displays begin with framed dolls from Latin America, Africa, India and Europe. Upstairs is the museum's collection of toy theatres, many made by Benjamin Pollock himself, the leading Victorian manufacturer of the popular sets. Head up another set of stairs and you see tin toys and weird-looking dolls in cotton nighties. As you continue on the higgledy-piggledy trail of creaking stairs and floorboards, the dolls follow you with their glazed eyes. After you've climbed three flights of stairs, you'll descend four and, as if by magic, be led back to the shop.

BRUNSWICK CENTRE   MALL

Map p426 (www.brunswick.co.uk; The Brunswick WC1; ⊜Russell Sq) This now-wonderful 1960s complex consists of apartments, restaurants, shops and a cinema. A £24-million project transformed it from a dreary, stern space to a lovely, cream-coloured airy square in 2006, and the centre is now packed with people seven days a week. The original architect, Patrick Hodgkinson, worked on the renovations and claimed that the centre now looks like what he'd orginally planned in the '60s (but at the time the design was stunted by the local council). For more information and a complete listing of shops and restaurants, check the website.

FREE PETRIE MUSEUM OF EGYPTIAN ARCHAEOLOGY   MUSEUM

Map p426 (UCL; www.petrie.ucl.ac.uk; University College London, Malet Pl WC1; ◷1-5pm Tue-Sat; ◉Goodge St) You'll need to have a special interest in Egyptian archaeology to enjoy this fairly academic museum. There are some 80,000 objects in the collection, one of the most impressive of Egyptian and Sudanese archaeology in the world, but the displays – glass boxes with row upon row of artefacts – don't really do much to highlight them. The museum is named after Professor William Flinders Petrie (1853–1942), who uncovered many of the items during his excavations and donated the collection to the university in 1933.

ST GEORGE'S, BLOOMSBURY   CHURCH

Map p426 (Bloomsbury Way WC1; ◷9.30am-5.30pm Mon-Fri, 10.30am-12.30pm Sun; ◉Holborn or Tottenham Court Rd) Superbly restored in 2005, this Nicholas Hawksmoor church (1731) is distinguished by its classical portico of Corinthian capitals and a steeple that was inspired by the Mausoleum of Halicarnassus. It is topped with a statue of George I in Roman dress.

◉ St James's

BUCKINGHAM PALACE   PALACE

See p88.

ST JAMES'S PARK   PARK

Map p430 (www.royalparks.gov.uk; The Mall SW1; ◷5am-dusk; ◉St James's Park or Green Park) This is one of the smallest but most gorgeous of London's parks. It has brilliant views of the London Eye, Westminster, St James's Palace, Carlton Terrace and

TOP SIGHTS
ROYAL ACADEMY OF ARTS

Britain's first art school was founded in 1768 but the organisation moved here onlyin the following century. The collection contains drawings, paintings, architectural designs, photographs and sculptures by past and present Academicians such as John Constable, Sir Joshua Reynolds, Thomas Gainsborough, JMW Turner, David Hockney and Norman Foster. Highlights are displayed in the **John Madejski Fine Rooms**, which are accessible by **free guided tours** (1 hr; ◷1pm & 3pm Wed-Fri, 1pm Tue, 11.30am Sat). The displays change regularly.

The rooms themselves are a treat; it was in the Reynolds Room for instance that Charles Darwin first presented his groundbreaking ideas on evolutionary biology to the Linnean Society.

The famous **Summer Exhibition** (Jun to mid- Aug), which has showcased contemporary art for sale by (established as well as unknown) artists for nearly 250 years, is the Academy's biggest event.

Burlington House's courtyard features a stone-paved piazza with choreographed lights and fountains arranged to display the astrological star chart of founder Joshua Reynolds on the day he was born. (Reynolds' statue sits in the middle.)

DON'T MISS...

➡ Summer Exhibition
➡ John Madejski Fine Rooms

PRACTICALITIES

➡ Map p430
➡ www.royalacademy.org.uk
➡ Burlington House, Piccadilly W1
➡ ◷10am-6pm, to 10pm Fri
➡ ◉Green Park

Horse Guards Parade, and the view of Buckingham Palace from the footbridge spanning St James's Park Lake is the best you'll find. The central lake is full of different types of ducks, geese, swans and general fowl, and its southern side's rocks serve as a rest stop for pelicans (fed at 2.30pm daily). Some of the technicolour flowerbeds were modelled on John Nash's original 'floriferous' beds of mixed shrubs, flowers and trees. Spring and summer days see Londoners and tourists alike sunbathing, picnicking, admiring the squirrels and generally enjoying the sunshine. You can rent **deckchairs** (1hr £1.50; ☉Mar-Oct daylight hours) to make your lounging around more comfortable.

On the Mall's park edge stands the **National Police Memorial**, one column of marble and another of glass. Conceived by film director Michael Winner *(Death Wish)* and designed by architect Norman Foster and artist Per Arnoldi, it pays tribute to 1600 'bobbies' who have lost their lives in the line of duty.

BURLINGTON ARCADE   HISTORIC SITE

Map p430 (51 Piccadilly W1; ⊖Green Park) Flanking Burlington House (home of the Royal Academy of Arts) on its western side is the curious Burlington Arcade, built in 1819 and evocative of a bygone era. Today it is a shopping precinct for the very wealthy and is most famous for the Burlington Berties, uniformed guards who patrol the area keeping an eye out for punishable offences such as running, chewing gum or whatever else might lower the arcade's tone. The fact that the arcade once served as a brothel isn't mentioned.

ST JAMES'S PICCADILLY   CHURCH

Map p422 (197 Piccadilly W1; ☉8am-7pm; ⊖Piccadilly Circus) The only church Christopher Wren built from scratch and on a new site (most of the other London churches are replacements for ones razed in the Great Fire), this simple building is exceedingly easy on the eye and substitutes what some might call the pompous flourishes of Wren's most famous churches with a warm and elegant user-friendliness. The spire, although designed by Wren, was added only in 1968. This is a particularly sociable church; it houses a counselling service, stages lunchtime and evening concerts, provides shelter for an antiques market (10am to 5pm Tuesday) and an arts and crafts fair (10am to 6pm Wednesday to Saturday), has Caffé Nero attached on the side, and last but not least, teaches the word of God.

FREE WHITE CUBE GALLERY   GALLERY

Map p430 (www.whitecube.com; 25-26 Mason's Yard SW1; ☉10am-6pm Tue-Sat; ⊖Green Park or Piccadilly Circus) This central sister to the Hoxton original (p204) hosted Tracey Emin's first exhibition in five years, 'Those who suffer Love', in 2009. Together with the massively publicised Damien Hirst 'For the Love of God' exhibition two years before, it brought back some of the publicity for the (now not-so-young) Young British Artists (YBAs). Housed in Mason's Yard, a traditional courtyard with brick houses and an old pub, the White Cube looks like an ice block – white, straight-lined and angular. The two contrasting styles work well together and the courtyard often serves as a garden for the gallery on popular opening nights.

ST JAMES'S PALACE   PALACE

Map p430 (Cleveland Row SW1; closed to the public; ⊖Green Park) The striking Tudor gatehouse of St James's Palace, the only surviving part of a building initiated by the palace-mad Henry VIII in 1530, is best approached from St James's St to the north of St James's park. This was the official residence of kings and queens for more than three centuries.

Foreign ambassadors are still formally accredited to the Court of St James, although the tea and biscuits are actually served at Buckingham Palace. Princess Diana, who hated this place, lived here until her divorce from Charles in 1996, when she moved to Kensington Palace. Prince Charles and his sons stayed on at St James's until 2004, before decamping next door to Clarence House, leaving St James's Palace to a brace of minor royals including Charles's sister, Princess Anne.

CLARENCE HOUSE   PALACE

Map p430 (www.royalcollection.org.uk; Cleveland Row SW1; adult/child £9/5; ☉10am-4pm Mon-Fri, to 5.30pm Sat & Sun; Aug-Oct; ⊖Green Park) After his beloved granny the Queen Mum died in 2002, Prince Charles got the tradespeople into her former home and spent £4.6 million of taxpayers' money reshaping Clarence House to his own design yet the public have to pay to have a look at five official rooms when royal residents are on holidays.

The highlight is the late Queen Mother's small art collection, including one painting by playwright Noël Coward and others by WS Sickert and Sir James Gunn. The house was originally designed by John Nash in the early 19th century, but – as Prince Charles wasn't the first royal to call in the decorators – has been modified much since. Admission is by timed tickets, which must be booked in advance; book also for disabled access.

SPENCER HOUSE   PALACE

Map p430 (www.spencerhouse.co.uk; 27 St James's Pl SW1; admission & tour adult/concession £9/7; ⊘10.30am-5.45pm Sun, last entry 4.45pm, closed Jan & Aug; ⊜Green Park) Just outside Green Park, Spencer House was built in the Palladian style between 1756 and 1766 for the first Earl Spencer, an ancestor of Princess Diana. The Spencers moved out in 1927 and their grand family home was used as an office, until Lord Rothschild stepped in and returned it to its former glory in 1987 with an £18-million restoration.

Visits to the eight lavishly furnished rooms of the house are by guided tour only. The gardens, returned to their 18th-century design, are open only between 2pm and 5pm on a couple of Sundays in summer. Children under 10 are not admitted.

QUEEN'S CHAPEL   CHURCH

Map p430 (Marlborough Rd SW1; ⊘services only, 8.30am & 11.15am Sun Oct-Jul; ⊜Green Park) This small chapel is where contemporary royals from Princess Diana to the Queen Mother have lain in their coffins in the run-up to their funerals. The church was originally built by Inigo Jones in the Palladian style and was the first post-Reformation church in England built for Roman Catholic worship.

It was once part of St James's Palace but was separated after a fire. The simple interior has exquisite 17th-century fittings and is atmospherically illuminated by light streaming in through the large windows above the altar.

GREEN PARK   PARK

Map p430 (www.royalparks.gov.uk; Piccadilly W1; ⊘5am-dusk; ⊜Green Park) Less manicured than the adjoining St James's, beautiful Green Park has wonderful huge oaks and hilly meadows, and it's never as crowded as St James's. It was once a duelling ground and served as a vegetable garden during WWII.

GUARDS MUSEUM   MUSEUM

Map p430 (www.theguardsmuseum.com; Wellington Barracks, Birdcage Walk SW1; adult/child £4/free; ⊘10am-4pm; ⊜St James's Park) If you found the crowds at the Changing of the Guards tiresome and didn't see a thing, get here for 10.50am on any day from April to August to see the guards getting into formation outside the museum, for their march up to Buckingham Palace.

In addition, you can check out the history of the five regiments of foot guards and their role in military campaigns from Waterloo onwards at this little museum. There are uniforms, oil paintings, medals, curios and memorabilia that belonged to the soldiers. Perhaps the biggest draw here is the huge collection of toy soldiers for sale in the shop.

FREE **INSTITUTE OF CONTEMPORARY ARTS**   ARTS CENTRE

Map p430 (ICA; www.ica.org.uk; Nash House, The Mall SW1; ⊘noon-11pm Wed, to 1am Thu-Sat, to 9pm Sun; ⊜Charing Cross or Piccadilly Circus; 🛱) Housed in a traditional building along the Mall, the ICA is as untraditional as you can possibly get. This was where Picasso and Henry Moore had their first UK shows, and ever since then the institute has sat comfortably on the cutting and controversial edge of the British arts world, with an excellent range of experimental/progressive/radical/obscure films, music and club nights, photography, art, theatre, lectures, multimedia works and book readings. There's also the licensed **ICA Bar & Restaurant**. The complex includes an excellent bookshop.

ARCADE FUN

Just east of Piccadilly Circus is **London Trocadero** (Map p422; www.londontrocadero.com; 1 Piccadilly Circus W1; ⊘10am-1am), a huge indoor amusement arcade that has six levels of hi-tech, high-cost fun for youngsters, along with cinemas, US-themed restaurants and bowling alleys. Good to know in case the kids need a break from sightseeing.

◉ Soho & Chinatown

SOHO NEIGHBOURHOOD
See p92.

 PHOTOGRAPHERS' GALLERY GALLERY
Map p422 (www.photonet.org.uk; 16-18 Ramillies
St W1; admission free; ⊖Oxford Circus) This fantastic place was in the midst of a substantial refurbishment program at the time of writing and planned to reopen with a bang in early 2012, with three floors of exhibition space, a brand new cafe and a shop brimming with prints and photography books. The gallery awards the prestigious annual Deutsche Börse Photography Prize, which is of major importance for contemporary photographers; past winners include Richard Billingham, Luc Delahaye, Andreas Gursky, Boris Mikhailov and Juergen Teller.

REGENT STREET STREET
Map p422 Regent St is the border separating the hoi polloi of Soho and the high-society residents of Mayfair. Designed by John Nash as a ceremonial route, it was meant to link the Prince Regent's long-demolished city dwelling with the 'wilds' of Regent's Park, and was conceived by the architect as a grand thoroughfare that would be the centrepiece of a new grid for this part of town. Alas, it was never to be – too many toes were being stepped on and Nash had to downscale his plan.

There are some elegant shop fronts that look older than their 1920s origins (when the street was remodelled) but, as in the rest of London, the chain stores have almost completely taken over. The street's most famous retail outlet is undoubtedly Hamleys (p134), London's premier toy and game store. Regent Street is also famous for its Christmas lights displays, which are turned on with great pomp in late November every year.

◉ Covent Garden & Leicester Square

NATIONAL GALLERY MUSEUM
See p93.

TRAFALGAR SQUARE SQUARE
See p96.

TOP SIGHTS
PICCADILLY CIRCUS

John Nash had originally designed Regent St and Piccadilly to be the two most elegant streets in town but, curbed by city planners, Nash couldn't realise his dream to the full. He would certainly be disappointed with what Piccadilly Circus has become: swamped with visitors, flanked by **flashing advertisement panels** and surrounded by shops flogging tourist tat.

But despite the crowds and traffic, Piccadilly Circus has become a postcard for the city, buzzing with the liveliness that makes it exciting to be in London.

Designed in the 1820s, the hub was named after the street Piccadilly (going west from the square), which earned its name in the 17th century from the stiff collars (picadils) that were the sartorial staple of the time (and were the making of a nearby tailor's fortune).

At the centre of the circus is the famous aluminium statue, Anteros, twin brother of Eros, dedicated to the philanthropist and child-labour abolitionist Lord Shaftesbury. The sculpture was at first cast in gold, but it was later replaced by the present-day one. Down the years the angel has been mistaken for **Eros**, the God of Love, and the misnomer has stuck (you'll even see signs for 'Eros' from the Underground).

DON'T MISS...

➡ Piccadilly Circus's buzzing atmosphere
➡ 'Eros'
➡ Flashing ad panels

PRACTICALITIES

➡ Map p422
➡ ⊖Piccadilly Circus

FOURTH PLINTH

Three of the four plinths located at Trafalgar Square's corners are occupied by notables, King George IV on horseback, and military men General Sir Charles Napier and Major General Sir Henry Havelock. One, originally intended for a statue of William IV, has largely remained vacant for the past 150 years. The Royal Society of Arts conceived the unimaginatively titled **Fourth Plinth Project** (www.london.gov.uk/fourthplinth) in 1999, deciding to use the empty space for works by contemporary artists. They commissioned three works: *Ecce Homo* by Mark Wallinger (1999), a life-size statue of Jesus, which appeared tiny in contrast to the enormous plinth; Bill Woodrow's *Regardless of History* (2000) and Rachel Whiteread's *Monument* (2001), a resin copy of the plinth, turned upside down.

The Mayor's office has since taken over the Fourth Plinth Project, continuing with the contemporary-art theme. One of the most memorable commissions so far was Anthony Gormley's *One & Other* (2009), which featured no inanimate object but simply a space for individuals to occupy – each person spent an hour on the plinth, addressing the crowds on any chosen subject, performing or simply sitting quietly. The project ran 24 hours a day, every day for 100 days, and the rules specified that the participants spent their hour on the plinth alone, could do what they wanted as long as it wasn't illegal and were allowed to take with them anything they could carry.

Following Yinka Shonibare's *MBE Nelson's Ship in a Bottle* (2011), a wink to the square's dominant figure, Mayor Boris Johnson announced in early 2011 that artist duo Elmgreen & Dragset would present *Powerless Structures, Fig. 101*, a boy astride a rocking horse, in 2012 and that Katharina Fritsch would exhibit *Hahn/Cock*, a huge, bright blue sculpture of a cockerel, in 2013. Each artwork will be exhibited for 18 months.

NATIONAL PORTRAIT GALLERY   MUSEUM

See p97.

COVENT GARDEN PIAZZA   SQUARE

Map p432 (⊖Covent Garden) London's first planned square is now the exclusive preserve of tourists who flock here to shop in the quaint old arcades, be entertained by buskers, pay through the nose for refreshments at outdoor cafes and bars, and watch street performers pretend to be statues.

On its western flank is **St Paul's Church** (www.actorschurch.org; Bedford St WC2; ⊙8.30am-5.30pm Mon-Fri, 9am-1pm Sun). The Earl of Bedford, the man who had commissioned Inigo Jones to design the piazza, asked for the simplest possible church, basically no more than a barn. The architect responded by producing 'the handsomest barn in England'. It has long been regarded as the actors' church for its associations with the theatre, and contains memorials to the likes of Charlie Chaplin and Vivien Leigh. The first Punch and Judy show took place in front of it in 1662, and the church continues to host concerts, recitals and dance events. Check out the lovely courtyard at the back, perfect for a picnic.

LONDON TRANSPORT MUSEUM   MUSEUM

Map p432 (www.ltmuseum.co.uk; Covent Garden Piazza WC2; adult/child £14/free; ⊙10am-6pm Sat-Thu, 11am-6pm Fri; ⊖Covent Garden) This museum reopened in late 2007, after a £22-million refurbishment and redesign. You can now see the revitalised existing collection (consisting of buses from the horse age to today, plus taxis, trains and all other modes of transport) and new collections that feature other major cities' transport systems, fascinating insights into how the city developed as a result of better transport and tons of original advertising posters. Check out the museum shop for original and interesting souvenirs, including a great selection of posters.

ROYAL OPERA HOUSE   HISTORIC BUILDING

Map p432 (www.roh.org.uk; Bow St WC2; tours £8-10.50; ⊙general tour 4pm daily, backstage tour 10.30am, 12.30pm, 2.30pm Mon-Fri, 10.30am, 11.30am, 12.30pm & 1.30pm Sat; ⊖Covent Garden) On the northeastern flank of Covent Garden piazza is the gleaming, redeveloped – and practically new – Royal Opera House. You can take a tour of the opera: the pompously named 'Velvet, Gilt & Glamour Tour' is a general 45-minute tour of the auditorium;

COVENT GARDEN HISTORY

Covent Garden was originally the site of a convent (hence, 'covent') and its garden owned by Westminster Abbey in the 13th century. The site became the property of John Russell, the first Earl of Bedford, in 1552. The area developed thanks to his descendants, who employed Inigo Jones to convert a vegetable field into a piazza in the 17th century. He built the elegant Italian-style piazza, and its tall terraced houses soon started to draw rich socialites who coveted the central living quarters. The bustling fruit and veg market – immortalised in *My Fair Lady* where it was a flower market – dominated the piazza. London society, including such writers as Pepys, Fielding and Boswell, gathered here in the evenings looking for some action among the coffee houses, theatres, gambling dens and brothels.

Lawlessness became commonplace, leading to the formation of a volunteer police force known as the Bow Street Runners (see Georgian London, p352). In 1897 Oscar Wilde was charged with gross indecency in the now-closed Bow St magistrate's court. A flower market designed by Charles Fowler was added at the spot where London's Transport Museum now stands.

During the 1970s the city traffic made it increasingly difficult to maintain the fruit and veg market so it was moved in 1974. Property developers loomed over the space and there was even talk of the market being demolished for a road but, thanks to the area's dedicated residential community who demonstrated and picketed for weeks, the piazza was saved and transformed into what you see today.

more distinctive are the 1½-hr backstage tours that take you through the venue (although not always the auditorium), and let you experience the planning, excitement and hissy fits happening before a performance at one of the world's busiest opera houses. As it's a working theatre, backstage tours vary greatly from one day to the next.

Of course, the best way to enjoy the ROH is by seeing a performance (see p130).

LEICESTER SQUARE
SQUARE

Map p432 (⊖Leicester Sq) At the time of research, Leicester Square was undergoing an extensive – and much-needed – makeover to turn it into a lively plaza and glamorous premiere venue. The revamp is much overdue; although the square was very fashionable in the 19th century, in the last few decades it had become synonymous with antisocial behaviour, rampant pickpocketing and outrageous cinema ticket prices (a whopping £18!).

The square will retain its many cinemas and nightclubs, and city planners hope it will attract high-profile film premieres, with all the associated celeb-spotting and publicity.

Works on the square started in December 2010 and were scheduled to be complete in April 2012, in time for the Olympics. Expect sleek, open-plan design to replace the once- dingy little park. The Charlie Chaplin statue and the ticket booth will both be retained and, in the case of the latter, modernised.

ST MARTIN-IN-THE-FIELDS
CHURCH

Map p432 (www.stmartin-in-the-fields.org; Trafalgar Sq WC2; ⊙8am-6.30pm, evening concerts 7.30pm; ⊖Charing Cross) The 'royal parish church' is a delightful fusion of classical and baroque styles that was completed by James Gibbs (1682–1754) in 1726. The church is well known for its excellent classical music concerts, many by candlelight, and its links to the Chinese community (mass is held in English, Mandarin and Cantonese).

A £36-million refurbishment, completed at the end of 2007, provided a new entrance pavilion, a wonderful new cafe that hosts jazz evenings once a week, a foyer, and several new areas at the rear of the church, including spaces offering social care to the Chinese community and homeless people.

Refurbishment excavations unearthed a 1.5-tonne limestone Roman sarcophagus containing a human skeleton in the churchyard; the yard also holds the graves of 18th-century artists Reynolds and Hogarth.

⊙ Whitehall

CHURCHILL WAR ROOMS
MUSEUM

See p99.

NO 10 DOWNING STREET
HISTORICAL BUILDING

Map p430 (www.number10.gov.uk; 10 Downing St SW1; ⊖Westminster or Charing Cross) This has been the official office of British leaders since 1732, when George II presented No 10 to Robert Walpole and, since refurbishment in 1902, it's also been the Prime Minister's official London residence. As Margaret Thatcher, a grocer's daughter, famously put it, the PM 'lives above the shop' here.

But, for such a famous address, No 10 is a small-looking building on a plain-looking street, hardly warranting comparison with the White House, for example. The street was cordoned off with a rather large iron gate during Margaret Thatcher's time so you won't see much.

Breaking with tradition when he came to power, Tony Blair and his family (he has four children) swapped houses with the then-unmarried Chancellor Gordon Brown, who traditionally occupied the rather larger flat at No 11. When Gordon Brown became Prime Minister in 2007, he stayed at Number 11, having since married and had two children. New Prime Minister David Cameron did the same with his three children in the summer of 2011, following extensive refurbishment of the flat. The scale of the renovations caused a bit of a furore when photos were published of Mr Cameron's wife Samantha and US President Barack Obama's wife Michelle chatting in the fancy new kitchen: total renovations bill, £28,000.

HORSE GUARDS PARADE   HISTORIC SITE
Map p430 (⊙Changing of the Guard 11am Mon-Sat, 10am Sun; ⊖Westminster or St James's Park) In a more accessible version of Buckingham Palace's Changing of the Guard, the mounted troopers of the Household Cavalry change guard here daily, at the official entrance to the royal palaces (opposite the Banqueting House). A lite-pomp version takes place at 4pm when the dismounted guards are changed. On the Queen's official birthday in June, the Trooping of the Colour is also staged here.

Fittingly, as the parade ground and its buildings were built in 1745 to house the Queen's so-called Life Guards, this will be the pitch for the beach volleyball during the London 2012 Olympics (see www.london2012.org).

BANQUETING HOUSE   HISTORIC BUILDING
Map p430 (www.hrp.org.uk; Whitehall SW1; adult/child £5/free; ⊙10am-5pm Mon-Sat; ⊖Westminster or Charing Cross) This is the only surviving part of the Tudor Whitehall Palace, which once stretched most of the way down Whitehall and burned down in 1698. It was designed as England's first purely Renaissance building by Inigo Jones after he returned from Italy, and it looked like no other structure in the country at the time. Apparently, the English hated it for more than a century.

A bust outside commemorates 30 January 1649 when Charles I, accused of treason by Cromwell after the Civil War, was executed on a scaffold built against a 1st-floor window here. When the monarchy was reinstated with Charles II, it inevitably became something of a royalist shrine. In a huge, virtually unfurnished hall on the 1st floor there are nine ceiling panels painted by Rubens in 1635. They were commissioned by Charles I and depict the 'divine right' of kings.

ST GILES-IN-THE-FIELDS, A LITANY OF MISERIES

Built in what used to be countryside between the City and Westminster, **St Giles church** (Map p432; 60 St Giles High St; ⊙9am-4pm Mon-Fri; ⊖Tottenham Court Rd) isn't much to look at but its history is a chronicle of London's most miserable inhabitants.

The current structure is the third to stand on the site of an original chapel built in the 12th century to serve the leprosy hospital. Until 1547, when the hospital closed, prisoners on their way to be executed at Tyburn (p193) stopped at the church gate and sipped a large cup of soporific ale – their last refreshment – from St Giles's Bowl. From 1650 the prisoners were buried in the church grounds. It was also within the boundaries of St Giles that the Great Plague of 1665 took hold.

In Victorian times it was London's worst slum, oft name-checked by Dickens. Today the drug-users who hang out around the area make you feel like things haven't changed much.

An interesting relic in the church is the pulpit that was used for 40 years by John Wesley, the founder of Methodism.

Banqueting House is still occasionally used for state banquets and concerts, and if the house is rented for an event it will be closed to the public.

CENOTAPH
MEMORIAL

Map p430 (Whitehall SW1; ◉Westminster or Charing Cross) The Cenotaph (Greek for 'empty tomb'), built in 1920 by Edwin Lutyens, is Britain's main memorial to the British and Commonwealth victims who were killed during the two world wars. The Queen and other public figures lay poppies at its base on the second Sunday in November (Remembrance Sunday).

◉ Holborn & The Strand

FREE ROYAL COURTS OF JUSTICE
HISTORIC BUILDING

Map p432 (460 The Strand; ◎9am-4.30pm Mon-Fri; ◉Temple) Where The Strand joins Fleet St, you'll see the entrance to this gargantuan melange of Gothic spires, pinnacles and burnished Portland stone, designed by aspiring cathedral builder GE Street in 1874. (It took so much out of the architect that he died of a stroke shortly before its completion.) The Royal Courts of Justice is a public building and is therefore open to visitors. You're allowed to sit in on any of the court proceedings; the list of cases to be heard is displayed daily in the Great Hall. But cameras must be left at the entrance. There are displays of legal costumes scattered about the building.

ST CLEMENT DANES
CHURCH

Map p432 (www.raf.mod.uk/stclementdanes; The Strand WC2; ◎9am-4pm, except bank holidays; ◉Temple) An 18th-century English nursery rhyme that incorporates the names of London churches goes: 'Oranges and lemons, say the bells of St Clements', with the soothing final lines: 'Here comes a chopper to chop off your head/Chop, chop, chop, chop, the last man's dead!' Isn't that nice? Well, even though the bells of this church chime that nursery tune every day at 9am, noon and 3pm, this *isn't* the St Clements referred to in the first line of the verse – that's St Clements Eastcheap, in the City. But we all know that historical fact needn't get in the way of a good story.

◉ TOP SIGHTS
SOMERSET HOUSE

Passing beneath the arched entrance towards this splendid Palladian masterpiece, it's hard to believe that the magnificent courtyard in front of you, with its 55 dancing fountains, was a car park for tax collectors until a spectacular refurbishment in 2000. William Chambers designed the house in 1775 for royal societies and it now contains two fabulous galleries.

The **Courtauld Gallery** (www.courtauld.ac.uk; adult/child £6/free, 10am-2pm Mon free; ◎10am-6pm)is located immediately to your right as you enter Somerset House from The Strand. Here, you can have an uncrowded stroll among masterpieces by Rubens, Botticelli, Cézanne, Degas, Renoir, Manet and Monet, to mention but a few. There are free, 15-minute **lunchtime talks** on specific works or themes from the collection at 1.15pm every Monday and Friday. The **Embankment Galleries** host regular photographic exhibitions.

The courtyard is transformed into a popular **ice rink** in winter and used for concerts and events in summer; the **Summer Screen** (when the Great Court turns into an outdoor cinema for 10 evenings in early August) is particularly popular. Behind the house, there's a sunny terrace and cafe overlooking the embankment.

DON'T MISS...

➜ Courtauld Gallery masterpieces

➜ Skating in the winter

➜ Movies in the summer

PRACTICALITIES

➜ Map p432

➜ www.somerset-house.org.uk

➜ The Strand WC2

➜ admission free to courtyard & terrace

➜ ◎house 10am-6pm, Great Court 7.30am-11pm

➜ ◉Temple or Covent Garden

INNS OF COURT

For all of the West End's urban mania, the area hides some unexpected pockets of Zenlike calm. Clustered around Holborn and Fleet St are the Inns of Court, with quiet alleys, open spaces and a serene atmosphere. All London barristers work from within one of the four inns, and a roll-call of former members ranges from Oliver Cromwell and Charles Dickens to Mahatma Gandhi and Margaret Thatcher. It would take a lifetime working here to grasp the intricacies of the protocols of the inns – they're similar to the Freemasons, and both are 13th-century creations with centuries of tradition. It's best to just soak in the dreamy atmosphere and relax.

Lincoln's Inn (Map p432; Lincoln's Inn Fields WC2; ⊘grounds 9am-6pm Mon-Fri, chapel 12.30-2.30pm Mon-Fri; ⊖Holborn) Lincoln's Inn is the most attractive of the four inns and has a chapel, pleasant square and picturesque gardens that invite a stroll, especially early or late in the day when the legal eagles aren't flapping about. The court itself, although closed to the public, is visible through the gates and is relatively intact, with original 15th-century buildings, including the Tudor Lincoln's Inn Gatehouse on Chancery Lane. Inigo Jones helped plan the well-preserved chapel, which was built in 1623.

Inner Temple and Middle Temple (Map p432; King's Bench Walk EC4; ⊖Temple or Blackfriars) From The Strand, look for a studded black door labelled 'Middle Temple Lane', opposite the Royal Courts building, and you'll find yourself in the sprawling complex surrounding Temple Church (see p157). The church was originally planned and built by the secretive Knights Templar between 1161 and 1185. There are wonderful gardens and courtyards at every turn. At the weekend you'll usually have to enter from the Victoria Embankment side.

Staple Inn (Holborn; ⊖Chancery Lane) The 16th-century shop-front facade is the main interest at Staple Inn (1589), the last of eight Inns of Chancery whose functions were superseded by the Inns of Court in the 18th century. The buildings, mostly postwar reconstructions, are now occupied by the Institute of Actuaries and aren't actually open to the public, although nobody seems to mind a discreet and considerate look around. On the same side of Holborn but closer to Fetter Lane stood Barnard's Inn, redeveloped in 1991. Pip lived here with Herbert Pocket in Dickens' *Great Expectations*.

Gray's Inn (Gray's Inn Rd WC1; ⊘grounds 10am-4pm Mon-Fri, chapel 10am-6pm Mon-Fri; ⊖Chancery Lane) This inn – destroyed during WWII, rebuilt and expanded – is less interesting than Lincoln's Inn, although the peaceful gardens are still something of a treat. The walls of the original hall absorbed the first ever performance of Shakespeare's *Comedy of Errors*.

Sir Christopher Wren designed the original building in 1682 but only the walls and a steeple added by James Gibbs in 1719 survived the Luftwaffe bombing in 1941, and the church was rebuilt after the war as a memorial to Allied airmen. Today it is the chapel of the Royal Air Force (RAF), and there are some 800 slate badges of different squadrons set into the pavement of the nave. The statue in front of the church quietly and contentiously commemorates the RAF's Sir Arthur 'Bomber' Harris, who led the bombing raids that obliterated Dresden and killed up to 25,000 civilians during WWII.

STRAND STREET

Map p432 (⊖Charing Cross or Temple) From the time it was built, at the end of the 12th century, The Strand (from the Old English and German word for beach) ran by the Thames. Its grandiose stone houses, built by the nobility, counted as some of the most prestigious places to live, sitting as they did on a street that connected the City and Westminster, the two centres of power; indeed, its appeal lasted for seven centuries, with the 19th-century prime minister Benjamin Disraeli pronouncing it 'the finest street in Europe'. Buildings included the Cecil Hotel (now no more), the Savoy

Hotel, Simpson's, King's College and Somerset House.

But modern times haven't treated The Strand with the same sort of respect and awe; the street is now overrun by offices, cheap restaurants and odd souvenir shops, and despite the fact that the Savoy and the wonderful Somerset House still grace the street, it is hardly seen as the fine drag it once was. Still, there are some lovely things to see here, such as **Twinings** at No 216, a teashop opened by Thomas Twining in 1706. It's believed to be the oldest company in the capital still trading on the same site and owned by the same family. The Strand is also the centre of London philatelic life, with stamp- and coin-collectors' mecca **Stanley Gibbons** at No 339.

FREE HUNTERIAN MUSEUM   MUSEUM
Map p432 (www.rcseng.ac.uk/museums; Royal College of Surgeons, 35-43 Lincoln's Inn Fields WC2; ⊙10am-5pm Tue-Sat; ⊜Holborn) The collection of anatomical specimens of pioneering surgeon John Hunter (1728–93) inspired this fascinating, slightly morbid, little-known, yet fantastic London museum. Among the more bizarre items on display are the skeleton of a 2.3m giant, half of mathematician Charles Babbage's brain and, hilariously, Winston Churchill's dentures.

Thanks to a massive refurbishment some years back, the atmosphere is less gory and allows decent viewing of such things as animal digestive systems (forensically documented in formaldehyde) and the 'hearing organ' of a blue whale. Upstairs there's a display on surgery techniques, which will impress and disgust in equal measure. There's a free guided tour every Wednesday at 1pm.

⊙ Marylebone

SHERLOCK HOLMES MUSEUM   MUSEUM
Map p428 (www.sherlock-holmes.co.uk; 221b Baker St; adult/child £6/4; ⊙9.30am-6pm; ⊜Baker St) Though the museum gives its address as 221b Baker St, the actual fictional abode of Sherlock Holmes is the Abbey National building a bit further south. Fans of the books will enjoy examining the three floors of reconstructed Victoriana, deerstalkers, burning candles and flickering grates, but may baulk at the dodgy waxworks of Professor Moriarty and 'the Man

with the Twisted Lip'. It is disappointing too that there is so little information on Arthur Conan Doyle.

BROADCASTING HOUSE   BUILDING
Map p428 (www.bbc.co.uk/showsandtours; Portland Pl; tours adult/child £10/8; ⊙Sun; ⊜Oxford Circus) This is the iconic building from which the BBC began radio broadcasting in 1932 and from where much of its radio output still comes. You can visit Broadcasting House with a 1½-hour tour, generally held on Sunday. The tour takes you to the radio theatre as well as behind the scenes for a peek at the studios (and live recordings) of the various BBC channels.

ALL SOULS CHURCH   CHURCH
Map p428 (www.allsouls.org; Langham Pl W1; ⊙9am-6pm, closed Sat; ⊜Oxford Circus) This delightful church, designed by John Nash (the man behind Trafalgar Square, Regent's Street and Piccadilly Circus) features a circular columned porch and distinctive needle-like spire, reminiscent of an ancient Greek temple. Built from Bath stone, the church was very unpopular when completed in 1824 – a contemporary cartoon by George Cruikshank shows Nash rather painfully impaled on the spire through the bottom with the words 'Nashional Taste!!!' below it. It was bombed during the Blitz and renovated in 1951, and is now one of the most distinctive churches in central London.

⊙ Mayfair

HANDEL HOUSE MUSEUM   MUSEUM
Map p428 (www.handelhouse.org; 25 Brook St W1; adult/child £6/2; ⊙10am-6pm Tue-Sat, to 8pm Thu, noon-6pm Sun; ⊜Bond St) George Frederick Handel lived in this 18th-century Mayfair building for 36 years until his death in 1759; this is where he composed some of his finest works, including *Water Music, Messiah, Zadok the Priest* and *Fireworks Music*. The house opened as a museum in late 2001 after extensive restorations and looks as it would have when the great German-born composer was in residence.

Exhibits include early editions of Handel's operas and oratorios, portraits of musicians and singers who worked with Handel and musical instruments in the Rehearsal & Performance room on the first

TOP SIGHTS
WALLACE COLLECTION

Arguably London's finest small gallery, the Wallace Collection is an enthralling glimpse into 18th-century aristocratic life. The sumptuously restored Italianate mansion houses a treasure-trove of 17th- and 18th-century paintings, porcelain, artefacts and furniture collected by the same family and bequeathed to the nation by the widow of Sir Richard Wallace (1818–90) on condition it should always be on display in the centre of London.

Among the many highlights are paintings by Rembrandt, Delacroix, Titian, Rubens, Poussin, Velázquez and Gainsborough in the stunning **Great Gallery**. There's a spectacular array of medieval and Renaissance armour (including some to try on), stunning chandeliers and a sweeping staircase – deemed one of the best examples of French interior architecture in existence. The excellent audioguides (£4) can give you some insight into the plethora of objects and paintings.

There are also temporary exhibitions, popular themed events and ballroom dancing (check the website for schedules).

Have lunch at the excellent glass-roofed restaurant (**Wallace**, p121) and you'll have spent an outstanding day in London.

DON'T MISS...
➡ Great Gallery
➡ Furniture by famous cabinet-maker André-Charles Boulle
➡ François Boucher's *Madame de Pompadour*

PRACTICALITIES
➡ Map p428
➡ www.wallacecollection.org
➡ Hertford House, Manchester Sq W1
➡ admission free
➡ ⊙10am-5pm
➡ ⊜Bond St

floor; musicians regularly come to practice so you may be treated to a free concert. The staff attending the rooms are all Handel enthusiasts and wonderfully knowledgeable about the composer's life and his work.

Funnily enough, the house at No 23 (now part of the museum) was home to a musician as different from Handel as could be imagined: American guitarist **Jimi Hendrix** (1942–70) lived there from 1968 until his death.

Entrance to the museum is on Lancashire Court.

EATING

Many of the city's most eclectic, fashionable and, quite simply, best restaurants are dotted around the West End. As with most things in London, it pays to be in the know: while there's a huge concentration of mediocre places to eat along the main tourist drags, the best eating experiences are frequently tucked away on backstreets and not at all obvious.

✗ Westminster

VINCENT ROOMS TOP CHOICE   MODERN EUROPEAN £
Map p430 (✆7802 8391; www.thevincentrooms.com; Westminster Kingsway College, Vincent Sq SW1; mains £6-10.50; ⊙lunch noon-2pm Mon-Fri, dinner selected evenings only; ⊜Victoria) Here you're essentially offering yourself up as a guinea pig for the student chefs at Westminster Kingsway College, where celebrity chef Jamie Oliver was trained. Service is nervously eager to please, the atmosphere in both the Brasserie and the Escoffier Room is smarter than expected, and the food (including excellent vegie options) ranges from wonderful to exquisite – at prices that puts other culinary stars to shame.

CINNAMON CLUB INDIAN £££
Map p430 (✆7222 2555; www.cinnamonclub.com; Old Westminster Library, 30 Great Smith St SW1; mains £14-32; ⊙closed Sun; ⊜St James's Park) Domed skylights, high ceilings, parquet flooring and a book-lined mezzanine all convey an atmosphere reminiscent of a colonial club. The food is sumptuous: a mix of traditional Indian with a modern European twist. If money is no object, treat

yourself to a culinary adventure with one of the tasting menus (lunch/dinner £45/75). The club also does breakfast, with options ranging from European-style eggs to Indian *uttapam* (stuffed, crispy rice pancakes).

✗ Bloomsbury

ABENO   JAPANESE ££
Map p426 (www.abeno.co.uk; 47 Museum St WC1; mains £7.50-18; ⊙lunch & dinner; ⊖Tottenham Court Rd) This understated Japanese restaurant specialises in *okonomiyaki*, a savoury pancake from Osaka. The pancakes consist of cabbage, egg and flour combined with the ingredients of your choice (there are more than two dozen varieties, including anything from sliced meats and vegetables to egg, noodles and cheese) and they're cooked on the hotplate at your table. You'll also find the more traditional teppan-yaki and *yakisoba* dishes. All come beautifully presented.

HUMMUS BROS   MIDDLE EASTERN £
Map p426 (www.hbros.co.uk; Victoria House, 37-63 Southampton Row WC1; mains £2.50-6; ⊙11am-9pm Mon-Fri; 🕿 🍴 ⊖Holborn) The deal at this very popular outlet is a bowl of filling hummus with your choice of topping (beef, chicken, tabouleh etc) eaten with warm pita bread. It's very filling and you can eat in or take away.

CHILLI COOL   CHINESE £
Map p426 (www.chillicool.com; 15 Leigh St WC1; mains £7-19; ⊙lunch & dinner; ⊖Russell Sq) For genuine Szechuan cuisine, look no further than Chilli Cool. The restaurant itself is nothing to write home about but it's the food people come for: hot pots, dan dan noodles, Gong Bao Chicken and all the Szechuan favourites, which the clientele (almost exclusively Chinese) merrily tucks into.

NORTH SEA FISH RESTAURANT
FISH & CHIPS ££
Map p426 (7-8 Leigh St WC1; mains £9-20; ⊙closed Sun; ⊖Russell Sq) The North Sea sets out to cook fresh fish and potatoes – a simple ambition in which it succeeds admirably. Look forward to jumbo-sized plaice or halibut steaks, deep-fried or grilled, and a huge serving of chips. There's takeaway next door if you can't face the soulless dining room.

✗ Fitzrovia

BUSABA EATHAI   THAI £
Map p426 (www.busaba.com; 22 Store St WC1; mains £7-9; ⊙lunch & dinner; ⊖Goodge St) The Store St premises of this hugely popular mini-chain is slightly less hectic than some of the other West End outlets, but it retains all the signature features that have made it a roaring success: uberstyled Asian interior, large communal wooden tables, and heavenly cheap and tasty Thai food. You'll find perfectly executed big hitters such as Pad Thai, green and red curry as well as fragrant noodle soups, exquisite calamari and other delights such as jungle curry. This isn't the place to come for a long and intimate dinner, but it's a superb option for an excellent and speedy meal.

HAKKASAN   CHINESE £££
Map p426 (☎7927 7000; www.hakkasan.com; 8 Hanway Pl W1; mains £9.50-42; ⊖Tottenham Court Rd) This basement restaurant – hidden down a most unlikely back alleyway – successfully combines celebrity status, stunning design, persuasive cocktails and sophisticated Chinese food. The low, nightclub-style lighting (lots of red) makes it a good spot for dating or a night out with friends (the bar serves seriously creative cocktails). For dinner in the main dining room you'll have to book far in advance. Do what savvy Londoners do and have lunch in the more informal Ling Ling lounge.

FINO   SPANISH ££
Map p426 (www.finorestaurant.com; 33 Charlotte St (enter from Rathbone St) W1; tapas £4-17; ⊙lunch Mon-Fri, dinner Mon-Sat; ⊖Goodge St or Tottenham Court Rd) Critically acclaimed (and it's easy to see why), Fino represents an example of good Spanish cuisine in a London that's all too dominated by dreary and uninventive tapas bars. Set in a glamorous basement, Fino is a tapas restaurant with a difference. Try the Jerusalem artichoke cooked with mint, the prawn tortilla with wild garlic or the foie gras with chilli jam for a feast of innovative and delightful Spanish cooking.

ROKA   JAPANESE ££
Map p426 (☎7580 6464; www.rokarestaurant. com; 37 Charlotte St W1; mains £15-24; ⊙lunch & dinner; ⊖Goodge St or Tottenham Court Rd) This stunner of a Japanese restaurant

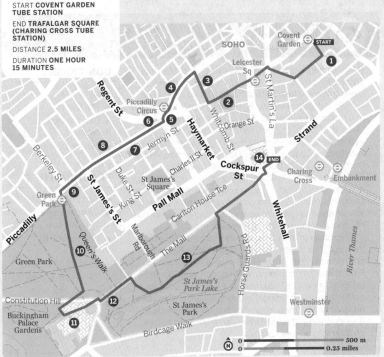

START **COVENT GARDEN TUBE STATION**

END **TRAFALGAR SQUARE (CHARING CROSS TUBE STATION)**

DISTANCE **2.5 MILES**

DURATION **ONE HOUR 15 MINUTES**

Neighbourhood Walk
The West End Walk

This walk takes you through the heart of the West End, from Covent Garden's chic shopping streets to Trafalgar Square via Chinatown and leafy St James's. From Covent Garden tube station, head to busy ❶ **Covent Garden Piazza** and enjoy the street performers outside St Paul's Church.

Continue on along King St and Garrick St; turn left on Long Acre and you'll arrive at ❷ **Leicester Square**, where many international blockbuster films premiere. Turn right on Wardour St; you'll soon come to the ersatz Oriental gates of ❸ **Chinatown** on your right hand side. The area is particularly beautiful around Chinese New Year, when hundreds of lanterns adorn the streets.

Turn left on ❹ **Shaftesbury Ave**; this is where you'll find some of the West End's most prestigious theatres. Hollywood stars such as Juliette Lewis and Christian Slater have performed here, as well as London's own Daniel Radcliffe (of Harry Potter fame). At the end of the avenue is the hectic ❺ **Piccadilly Circus**, 'London's Times Square', full of flashing ads, shops and tourists.

Make your way towards elegant ❻ **Piccadilly** from Piccadilly Circus; this avenue gives just a whiff of the nearby aristocratic St James's and Mayfair neighbourhoods. You can pop into ❼ **St James's Piccadilly**, the only church Wren built from scratch. Further along, you'll see the ❽ **Royal Academy of Arts**, home of Burlington House, and the famous ❾ **Ritz Hotel**.

Turn left into ❿ **Green Park**, a quiet space with some stunning oak trees and olde-worlde street lamps. ⓫ **Buckingham Palace** is at the bottom of the park, past the beautiful Canada Gates.

Walk down the grandiose ⓬ **Mall** and on the right is the lovely ⓭ **St James's Park**. Views of Buckingham palace and the nearby Whitehall are stunning. At the end of the Mall is ⓮ **Trafalgar Square**, dominated by Nelson's column and the National Gallery at the back. There are also great views of Big Ben from its southern side.

TOP SIGHTS
MADAME TUSSAUDS

Despite being kitsch and terribly overpriced, Madame Tussauds' (pronounced 'two-so') popularity doesn't seem to wane. The big attraction is getting a photo op with your dream celebrity: Kate Moss, Lady Gaga, David and Victoria Beckham, Hrithik Roshan of Bollywood fame, the Queen, Prince Charles and many more. If you're more into politics, then you could shake hands with Barack Obama or Tony Blair, or even London Mayor Boris Johnson with his signature mop haircut.

The whole place is shamefully commercial, with shops and spending opportunities in every room (ranging from snacks to a Formula 1 simulator, a get-your-hand-in-wax workshop or a print shop where you can get your 'celebrity shots' printed on a mug or mouse mat).

The museum has a long and interesting history since the eponymous Swiss model-maker (Marie Tussaud) started making death masks of people killed during the French Revolution. She came to London in 1803 and exhibited around 30 wax models in Baker St, on a site not far from this building. The models were an enormous hit in Victorian times, when they provided visitors with their only glimpse of the famous and infamous before photography was widespread.

DON'T MISS...

➡ Lady Gaga
➡ The Queen
➡ David & Victoria Beckham
➡ Barack Obama

PRACTICALITIES

➡ Map p428
➡ www.madame-tussauds.com
➡ Marylebone Rd NW1
➡ adult/child £29/25
➡ ◷9.30am-5.30pm Sep–mid-July, 9am-7pm mid-July–Aug
➡ ◉Baker St

---

mixes casual dining (wooden benches) with savoury titbits from the *robatayaki* (grill) kitchen in the centre. It has modern decor, the dominating materials being grey steel and glass.

RASA SAMUDRA　　　　　　　　INDIAN **££**
Map p426 (www.rasarestaurants.com; 5 Charlotte St W1; mains £8-14; ◷closed Sun; ◉Goodge St or Tottenham Court Rd) This bubblegum-pink eatery just up from Oxford Street showcases the seafood cuisine of Kerala state on India's southwest coast, supported by a host – eight out of 14 main courses – of more familiar vegetarian dishes. The fish soups are outstanding, the breads superb and the various curries divinely spiced. It is one of six Rasa restaurants in London.

✖ St James's

INN THE PARK　　　　　　　　BRITISH **££**
Map p430 (☎7451 9999; www.innthepark.com; St James's Park SW1; mains £13.50-18.50; ◷8am-11pm; ◉Trafalgar Sq) This stunning wooden cafe and restaurant in St James's Park (p103) is run by Irish wonderchef Oliver Peyton and offers cakes and tea as well

as excellent British food with a monthly-changing menu. The terrace, which overlooks one of the park's fountains with views of Whitehall's grand buildings, is wonderful on spring and summer days. If you're up for a special dining experience, come here for dinner when the park is quiet and slightly illuminated.

✖ Soho & Chinatown

TOP CHOICE **YAUATCHA**　　　　　　CHINESE **££**
Map p422 (www.yauatcha.com; 15 Broadwick St W1; dim sum £4-16; ◷lunch & dinner; ◉Oxford Circus) This most glamorous of dim sum restaurants (housed in the award-winning Ingeni building) is divided into two parts: the upstairs dining room offers a delightful blue-bathed oasis of calm from the chaos of Berwick Street Market, while downstairs has a smarter, more atmospheric feel with constellations of 'star' lights. Regardless of which option you take, you'll enjoy exquisite dim sum (steamed, fried and *cheung fun* – long, flat rice-flour rolls stuffed with meat, seafood or vegetables) as well as a fabulous range of teas.

TOP CHOICE MOOLI'S
INDIAN £

Map p422 (www.moolis.com; 50 Frith St W1; roti wrap £5; ⊘noon-10pm Mon-Wed, to 11.30pm Thu-Sat, closed Sun; ⊜Tottenham Court Rd or Leicester Sq) Started by a duo of Indian friends who'd had enough of the city life, Mooli's is a breath of fresh air in the quick-bite world (not least because it was partly funded through late-night poker sessions). A cheerful little eatery, it serves fresh, homemade rotis (Indian soft bread) with delicious filling (meat as well as paneer and chickpeas, all prepared with their own sauce and seasoning). There are also homemade chutneys, real lemonade, homemade mango lassis and a nice selection of bottled beers.

BOCCA DI LUPO
ITALIAN ££

Map p422 (⊘7734 2223; www.boccadilupo.com; 12 Archer St W1; mains £8.50-17.50; ⊘lunch & dinner Mon-Sat, lunch Sun; ⊜Piccadilly Circus) Hidden on a dark Soho backstreet, Bocca radiates elegant sophistication. The menu has dishes from across Italy (the menu tells you which region they're from) and every main can be served as small or large portions. Enjoy with an array of Italian wines and fantastic desserts. It's often full so make sure you book.

KOYA
NOODLES £

Map p422 (www.koya.co.uk; 49 Frith St W1; mains £7-14; ⊘lunch & dinner Mon-Sat; ⊜Tottenham Court Rd or Leicester Sq) Arrive early or late if you don't want to queue at this excellent Japanese eatery. Londoners come here for their fill of authentic udon noodles (hot or cold, served in broth or with a cold sauce), the efficient service and very reasonable prices.

SPUNTINO
AMERICAN ££

Map p422 (www.spuntino.co.uk; 61 Rupert St W1; mains £8-12; ⊘Mon-Sat 11am-midnight, to 11pm Sun; ⊜Piccadilly Circus) This eatery-cum-bar is Soho's latest craze. An unusual mix of speakeasy decor, staff who wouldn't look out of place in a truck stop and surprisingly

---

LONDON'S BEST AFTERNOON TEAS

The concept of afternoon tea (generally served between 3pm and 5pm) can be misleading to the non-initiated: of course, there will be a cup of tea (or coffee), but it's really all about the cakes! Cream tea includes scones with thick clotted cream and jam; afternoon tea is basically a meal, with finger sandwiches, pastries and scones, artfully presented on a tiered tray. The following are some of the best in town. Top-end hotels such as the Ritz and Claridges also offer afternoon tea but you will have to book six weeks in advance to guarantee a reservation.

Dean Street Townhouse (Map p422; www.deanstreettownhouse.com; 69-71 Dean St W1; tea £16; ⊘daily; 🖥 ⊜Tottenham Court Rd) Afternoon tea in the parlour of the Dean Street Townhouse hardly gets better; it's old-world cosy, with its upholstered furniture and roaring fireplace, and the pastries are divine. In summer, you can enjoy eating at one of the few tables on the street terrace.

Bea's of Bloomsbury (off Map p426; www.beasofbloomsbury.com; 44 Theobalds Rd WC1; tea £15; ⊘daily; ⊜Holborn or Chancery Lane) Bea's made its name with signature cupcakes so it was only natural for them to offer a full afternoon tea, too. The cafe is tiny but original with its mix of open kitchen and boutique decor. It's located 10 minutes' walk from the British Museum.

Wolseley (Map p430; ⊘7499 6996; www.thewolseley.com; 160 Piccadilly W1; cream/afternoon tea £9/21; ⊘daily; ⊜Green Park) This erstwhile Bentley car showroom has been transformed into an opulent Viennese-style brasserie, with golden chandeliers and stunning black-and-white tiled floors. It's a great place for spotting celebrities. Afternoon tea is a lavish affair, with the Wolseley's very own afternoon blend of English breakfast tea.

Portrait (see p121) The fabulous National Portrait Gallery restaurant does a wonderful Champagne cream tea (£30) with a glass of champagne and skyline views of London on a plate.

5th View (see p118) Homemade scones and jam with views of Westminster for a sophisticated afternoon tea (£15).

creative fusion American–Italian food, it's a delight at every turn. Try old favourites such as macaroni cheese, burgers and peanut-butter sandwiches, which have all been given a 21st-century facelift (we'll say no more!).

NORDIC BAKERY   SCANDINAVIAN £
Map p422 (www.nordicbakery.com; 14a Golden Sq W1; mains £4-5; ⊖Piccadilly Circus) The perfect place to escape the chaos that is Soho and relax in the dark-wood panelled space. Lunch on some Scandinavian smoked-fish sandwiches or have an afternoon break with tea/coffee and cake. The thick, sticky cinnamon buns are a naughty breakfast favourite.

5TH VIEW   INTERNATIONAL ££
Map p422 (www.5thview.co.uk; 5th fl, Waterstone's Piccadilly, 203-206 Piccadilly W1; mains £9-15; ⊙9am-9pm Mon-Sat, to 5pm Sun; ⊖Piccadilly Circus) The views of Westminster from the top of Waterstone's on Piccadilly are really quite dreamy. Add a relaxed, sophisticated dining room and some lovely food, and you have a gem of a place. We love the Lebanese meze or antipasti boards to share, and the selection of dishes from the chef's favourite cookbooks; if you enjoyed it, you'll know where to find the recipe!

BAR SHU   CHINESE ££
Map p422 (www.bar-shu.co.uk; 28 Frith St W1; mains £8-20; ⊙lunch & dinner; ⊖Leicester Sq) The story goes that a visiting businessman from Chengdu, capital of Szechuan Province in China, found London's Chinese food offerings so inauthentic that he decided to open up his own restaurant with five chefs from home. The result is authentic Szechuan cuisine, with dishes redolent of smoked chillies and the all-important ubiquitous peppercorn. Service is a little brusque but the food is delicious and the portions huge.

MILDREDS   VEGETARIAN £
Map p422 (www.mildreds.co.uk; 45 Lexington St W1; mains £9-10; ⊙closed Sun ⚲ ⊖Oxford Circus) Central London's most inventive vegie restaurant, Mildred's heaves at lunchtime so don't be shy about sharing a table in the skylit dining room. Expect the likes of roasted fennel and chickpea terrine and puy lentil casserole, Ethiopian stews, wonderfully exotic (and filling) salads as well as delicious stirfries. There are also vegan and gluten-free options, and a large range of organic wines.

VEERASWAMY   INDIAN £££
Map p422 (☎7734 1401; www.veeraswamy.com; 1st fl, 99 Regent St (enter from Swallow St) W1; mains £16-25; ⊙lunch & dinner; ⊖Piccadilly Circus) Having opened in 1926, this upmarket curry house can lay claim to being the oldest Indian restaurant in Britain. It's now owned by the same people who run Masala Zone (p247) and the standards are as high as ever, with the kitchen producing such crowd-pleasers as slow-cooked Hyderabad lamb biryani and Keralan-style sea bass. Booking is advisable.

ANDREW EDMUNDS   MODERN EUROPEAN ££
Map p422 (☎7437 5708; 46 Lexington St W1; mains £10-18; ⊙lunch & dinner; ⊖Piccadilly Circus) This cosy little place is exactly the sort of restaurant you wish you could find everywhere in Soho. Two floors of wood-panelled bohemia with a mouth-watering menu of French (confit of duck) and European (penne with goat's cheese) country cooking – it's a real find and reservations are essential.

STAR CAFÉ   CAFE £
Map p422 (www.thestarcafe.co.uk; 22 Great Chapel St W1; mains £6-9; ⊙7am-4pm Mon-Fri; ⊖Tottenham Court Rd) So very Soho, this wonderfully atmospheric cafe has vintage advertising and Continental decor that makes it feel like not much has changed since it opened in 1933. It's best known for its breakfasts, particularly the curiously named Tim Mellor Special of smoked salmon and scrambled eggs.

HIX   MODERN BRITISH ££
Map p422 (www.hixsoho.co.uk; ☎7292 3518; 66-70 Brewer St W1; mains £16-37; ⊙lunch & dinner; ⊖Piccadilly Circus) Celebrity chef Mark Hix's eponymous restaurant is all about seasonal British food. You'll find such classics as fish and chips and sticky toffee pudding given an elaborate makeover, as well as more unusual fare: lamb's tongue or silver mullet with whipped cauliflower. The decor is an eclectic collection of artworks from such renowned British artists as Tracy Emin and Damian Hirst.

POLPETTO   ITALIAN ££
Map p422 (www.polpetto.co.uk; upstairs at the French House, 49 Dean St W1; small plates £5-13; ⊙lunch & dinner Mon-Sat; ⊖Piccadilly Circus or Leicester Sq) This beautiful, tiny Italian bistro serves small plates of meat, fish and

SEX, DRUGS & ROCK'N'ROLL – THE HISTORY OF SOHO

Soho's character was formed by the many waves of immigration, and residential development started in the 17th century, after the Great Fire had levelled much of the city. An influx of Greek and Huguenot refugees and, later, the 18th-century influx of Italian, Chinese and other artisans and radicals into Soho replaced the bourgeois residents, who moved out of the area and into Mayfair. During the following century Soho was no more than a slum, with cholera frequently attacking the impoverished residents. But despite its difficulties, the cosmopolitan vibe attracted writers and artists, and the overcrowded area became a centre for entertainment, with restaurants, taverns and coffee houses springing up.

The 20th century was even more raucous, when a fresh wave of European immigrants settled in, making Soho a bona fide bohemian enclave for two decades after WWII. Ronnie Scott's famous club (p131), originally on Gerrard St, provided Soho's jazz soundtrack from the 1950s, while the likes of Jimi Hendrix, the Rolling Stones and Pink Floyd did their early gigs at the legendary Marquee club, which used to be on Wardour St. Soho had long been known for its seediness but when the hundreds of prostitutes who served the Square Mile were forced off the streets and into shop windows, it became the city's red-light district and a centre for porn, strip joints and bawdy drinking clubs. Gay liberation soon followed, and by the 1980s Soho was the hub of London's gay scene, as it remains today. The neighbourhood has a real sense of community, best absorbed on a weekend morning when Soho is at its most villagelike.

vegetables in the tradition of Venetian wine bars. Depending on your appetite you'll need to order three or four dishes between two. It's a tad expensive for what it is but the media types of Soho cannot get enough of the place; arrive early for dinner since you can't book.

ARBUTUS
MODERN EUROPEAN ££

Map p422 (☑7734 4545; www.arbutusrestaurant.co.uk; 63-64 Frith St W1; mains £16-20; ⊙lunch & dinner; ⊖Tottenham Court Rd) This Michelin-starred brainchild of Anthony Demetre does great British food, focuses on seasonal produce and just keeps on getting better. Try inventive dishes such as squid and mackerel 'burger', sweetbreads and artichokes or *pieds et paquets* (lamb tripe parcels with pig trotters) and don't miss the bargain £16.95 for a three-course lunch or £17.95 for a three-course pre- and post-theatre dinner. Booking is essential.

GAY HUSSAR
HUNGARIAN ££

Map p422 (☑7437 0973; www.gayhussar.co.uk; 2 Greek St W1; mains £13-18; ⊙closed Sun; ⊖Tottenham Court Rd) This is the Soho of the 1950s, when dining was still done grand style in wood-panelled rooms with brocade and sepia prints on the walls. Portions are huge; try the roast duck leg with all the trimmings or the 'Gypsy quick dish' of pork

medallions, onions and green peppers. A two-/three-course lunch is £19/22.

FERNANDEZ & WELLS
SPANISH £

Map p422 (www.fernandezandwells.com; 43 Lexington St W1; mains £4-14; ⊙11am-10pm Mon-Fri, noon-10pm Sat, 2-10pm Sun; ⊖Oxford Circus) A wonderful taste of Spain in Soho, Fernandez serves simple lunches and dinners of *jamón* (ham) and cured meats and cheese platters accompanied by quality wine. Grilled chorizo sandwiches are perfect for quick lunchtime bites. The place is usually busy, with a relaxed atmosphere and outside seating.

PRINCI
ITALIAN £

Map p422 (www.princi.co.uk; 135 Wardour St W1; mains £6-9; ⊙7am-midnight Mon-Sat, to 10pm Sun; 🛜; ⊖Oxford Circus or Tottenham Court Rd) Most people come to Princi by accident rather than design; they were just walking by and suddenly noticed a mouth-watering array of cakes and breads through the restaurant's huge bay windows. They come in 'just to have a look' and, before they know it, they're tucking in pesto gnocchi and a slice of tiramisu. That's the thing with Princi, it all looks so tempting! Prices are very reasonable too and the long opening hours mean you're guaranteed to have a decent meal almost round the clock.

BARRAFINA SPANISH ££

Map p422 (☎7813 8016; www.barrafina.co.uk; 54 Frith St W1; tapas £5-10; ☺lunch & dinner; ⊖Tottenham Court Rd) Tapas are always better value in Spain but the quality of the food here and the fact that its popularity just seems to rise may justify the price of what are essentially appetisers to go with your drink. Along with *gambas al ajillo* (prawns in garlic; £7.50), there are more unusual things such as tuna tartare and grilled quails with aioli. Because customers sit along the bar, it's not a good place for groups.

SPICE MARKET ASIAN ££

Map p422 (www.spicemarketlondon.co.uk; 10 Wardour St W1; mains £10.50-24, set lunch/dinner £18/48; ☺lunch & dinner; ⊖Leicester Sq or Piccadilly Circus) A very modern Asian establishment that blends flavours from across Southeast Asia. It's a tad try-hard and the men's uniforms look like pyjamas but the food is good and reasonably priced considering the location.

MILK BAR CAFE £

Map p422 (3 Bateman St W1; mains £4-6; ☺8am-7pm Mon-Fri, 9am-6pm Sat & Sun; ⊖Tottenham Court Rd) The diminutive Milk Bar has some of the best breakfasts in central London, with great big omelettes, homemade beans on toast, porridge, pancakes with fruit and honey – most for less than £5. The coffee is superb, too, and tea is served in mismatching flea-market bone-china cups.

KULU KULU JAPANESE £

Map p422 (www.kulukulu.co.uk; 76 Brewer St W1; sushi £2-4; ☺lunch & dinner Mon-Sat; ⊖Piccadilly Circus) This simple, bustling place just off Piccadilly Circus is one of the best and most affordable conveyor-belt Japanese places in London. The offering is pretty standard (tuna and salmon *maki* rolls, prawn tempura, teriyaki chicken etc) but it's all really tasty and fresh. At busy times, you're only allowed to sit in for 45 minutes.

NEW WORLD CHINESE £

Map p422 (1 Gerrard Pl W1; mains £7-10; ☺lunch & dinner; ⊖Leicester Sq) If you hanker after dim sum, the three-storey New World can oblige. All the old favourites – from *ha gau* (prawn dumpling) to *pai gwat* (steamed pork spare rib) – are available from steaming carts wheeled around the dining room daily 11am to 6pm.

✖ Covent Garden & Leicester Square

⬛TOP CHOICE BEN'S COOKIES BAKERY £

Map p432 (www.benscookies.com; 13Aa The Piazza, Covent Garden WC2; cookie £1.50; ☺10am-8pm Mon-Sat, 11am-7pm Sun; ⊖Covent Garden) The cookies at Ben's are, quite possibly, the best in the history of cookie-making. There are 18 different kinds to choose from, from triple chocolate to peanut butter, oatmeal and raisin to chocolate and orange, all wonderfully gooey and often warm (they're baked fresh on the premises throughout the day).

GREAT QUEEN STREET BRITISH ££

Map p432 (☎7242 0622; 32 Great Queen St WC2; mains £9-18; ☺lunch & dinner Mon-Sat, lunch Sun; ⊖Covent Garden or Holborn) One of Covent Garden's best places to eat, Great Queen Street is sister to the **Anchor & Hope** (p174) in Waterloo. The menu is seasonal (and changes daily), with an emphasis on quality, hearty dishes and good ingredients – there are always delicious stews, roasts and simple fish dishes. The atmosphere is lively, with a small bar downstairs. The staff are knowledgeable about what they serve, the wine list is good and booking is, as you may have guessed, essential.

BAOZI INN CHINESE £

Map p432 (25 Newport Ct WC2; mains £6-7; ☺closed Sun; ⊖Leicester Sq) The smaller sister of Bar Shu (p118) has its own personality and a unique (and cheap) menu. Decorated in a vintage style that plays at kitsch communist pop (complete with old Chinese communist songs tinkling out of the speakers), Baozi Inn serves quality Beijing and Chengdu-style street food, such as dan dan noodles with spicy pork and baozi buns (steamed buns with stuffing) handmade daily. It's authentic, delicious and cheap food-gold in often-unreliable Chinatown.

SCOOP ICE-CREAM £

Map p432 (www.scoopgelato.com; 40 Shorts Gardens WC2; ice creams £3-5; ☺noon-11pm; ⊖Covent Garden) The queue outside Scoop can stretch down the street on summer weekends, and it's no wonder: this is central London's only true *gelateria* and, boy, does it set a precedent. All the ingredients are natural and the servings are huge. Go for traditional flavours such as pistachio or

MUSEUM RESTAURANTS

National Dining Rooms (Map p432; www.peytonandbyrne.co.uk; Sainsbury Wing, National Gallery, Trafalgar Sq WC2; mains £15; ⊙10am-5.30pm Sat-Thu, to 8.30pm Fri; ⊜Charing Cross) Chef Oliver Peyton's restaurant at the National Gallery styles itself as 'proudly and resolutely British', and what a great idea. The menu features an extensive and wonderful selection of British cheeses for a light lunch. For something more filling, go for the county menu, a monthly changing menu honouring regional specialities from across the British Isles. The all-day bakery also churns out fresh cakes and pastries for mid-morning and afternoon treats.

Portrait (Map p432; ☑7312 2490; www.npg.org.uk/live/portrest.asp; 3rd fl, National Portrait Gallery, St Martin's Pl WC2; mains £14-29; ⊙lunch 11.45am-3pm daily, dinner Thu-Sat 5.30pm-8.15pm; ⊜Charing Cross) This stunningly located restaurant above the excellent National Portrait Gallery (p97) – with views over Trafalgar Square and Westminster – is a great place to relax after a morning or afternoon at the gallery; the brunch (weekends only) and afternoon tea (daily) come highly recommended. Unfortunately, Portrait is restricted in its opening times by the gallery, so dinner is rather early by London standards. Booking is advisable.

Wallace (Map p428; www.peytonandbyrne.co.uk/the-wallace-restaurant; Hertford House, Manchester Sq W1; mains £15-22; ⊙breakfast, lunch & dinner; ⊜Bond St) There are few more idyllically placed restaurants than this French brasserie in the courtyard of the Wallace Collection (p113). The emphasis is on seasonal Modern European dishes, with the menu du jour offering two- or three-course meals for £22/26.

chocolate or try original creations such as biscotto or green tea.

MONMOUTH COFFEE COMPANY   CAFE £
Map p432 (www.monmouthcoffee.co.uk; 27 Monmouth St WC2; cakes from £2.50; ⊙8am-6.30pm Mon-Sat; ⊜Tottenham Court Rd or Leicester Sq) Essentially a shop selling beans from just about every coffee-growing country in the world, Monmouth has a few wooden alcoves at the back where you can squeeze in and savour blends from around the world as well as cakes from local patisseries.

ROCK & SOLE PLAICE   FISH & CHIPS £
Map p432 (47 Endell St WC2; mains £10; ⊙lunch & dinner; ⊜Covent Garden) The approach at this no-nonsense fish-and-chip shop dating back to Victorian times is simplicity: basic wooden tables under the trees (in summer), simple decor inside and delicious cod, haddock or skate in batter served with a generous portion of chips. You can choose to eat in or take away.

WAHACA   MEXICAN £
Map p432 (www.wahaca.com; 66 Chandos Pl WC2; mains £7-10; ⊙noon-11pm Mon-Sat, to 10.30pm Sun; ⊜Covent Garden) This delightful cantina styles itself as a 'Mexican market eating' experience and the food is as authentic as you'll find in central London. You can

choose to share a selection of street snacks (tacos, tostadas, *quesadillas*) or go for more traditional mains such as grilled fish with chilli or a seafood salad. Wash it down with one of 12 tequilas – as the menu suggests, try sipping rather than shooting!

GIACONDA DINING ROOM   MODERN EUROPEAN ££
Map p432 (☑7240 3334; www.giacondadining. com; 9 Denmark St; mains £6.50-19.50; ⊙Tue-Fri lunch & dinner, dinner Sat; ⊜Tottenham Court Rd) A tiny room off Charing Cross Rd hides some of the best food around, with European staples such as duck confit, baked gnocchi, great steak tartare and good fresh fish of the day. The wine list is decent and you're greeted by friendly staff with a carafe of sparkling water.

J SHEEKEY   SEAFOOD £££
Map p432 (☑7240 2565; www.j-sheekey.co.uk; 28-32 St Martin's Ct WC2; mains £15-42; ⊙lunch & dinner; ⊜Leicester Sq) A jewel of the local scene, this incredibly smart restaurant, whose pedigree stretches back to 1896, has four elegant, discreet and spacious wood-panelled rooms in which to savour the riches of the sea, cooked simply and exquisitely. The oyster bar, popular with pre- and post-dinner punters, is another highlight. There is a three-course weekend lunch for £26.50.

CANELA
PORTUGUESE £

Map p432 (www.canelacafe.com; 33 Earlham St WC2; mains £8-9; ⊙lunch & dinner; ⊖Covent Garden) A small cafe serving tasty Portuguese and Brazilian dishes. The coffee is authentic, taken neat, very strong and with a cinnamon stick. Try the delicious *Pão de queijo*, a bread and cheese roll with one of the filling salads, or opt for the Portuguese national dish *feijoada*, a bean stew with smoked meat.

PRIMROSE BAKERY
CAFE £

Map p432 (www.primrosebakery.org.uk; 42 Tavistock St WC2; cakes £3; ⊙10.30am-7pm Mon-Sat, noon-5pm Sun; ⊖Covent Garden) Set in decor reminiscent of 1950s America, this little bakery specialises in the UK's latest food craze: the cupcake. There are more than 30 flavours to choose from, which can be savoured with a pot of tea in the tiny cafe.

RULES
BRITISH ££

Map p432 (www.rules.co.uk; 35 Maiden Lane WC2; mains £18-28; ⊙lunch & dinner Mon-Sat; ⊖Covent Garden) Established in 1798, this very posh and very British establishment is London's oldest restaurant. The menu is inevitably meat-oriented – Rules specialises in classic game cookery, serving up tens of thousands of birds between mid-August and January from its own estate – but fish dishes are also available. Puddings are traditional: trifles, treacles and lashings of custard.

ASSA
KOREAN £

Map p432 (53 St Giles High St WC2; mains £6-11; ⊙closed Sun; ⊖Tottenham Court Rd) The best of a trio of Korean restaurants behind the unsightly (and Heritage-listed) Centre Point building, Assa attracts a crowd of friendly young Asians who come for the cut-price soup noodles, *bibimbab* (rice served in a sizzling pot topped with thinly sliced beef, preserved vegetables and chilli-laced soybean paste) and potent *soju* (Korean saki).

✖ Holborn & The Strand

ASADAL
KOREAN ££

Map p432 (www.asadal.co.uk; 227 High Holborn WC1; mains £7-18; ⊙closed lunch Sun; ⊖Holborn) If you fancy Korean but want a bit more style thrown into the act, head for this spacious basement restaurant next to the Holborn tube station. The *kimchi* (pickled Chinese cabbage with chillies) is searing, the barbecues (£7 to £11.50) are done on your table and the *bibimbab* – rice served in a sizzling pot topped with thinly sliced beef, preserved vegetables and chilli-laced soybean paste – are the best in town.

SHANGHAI BLUES
CHINESE £££

Map p432 (☏7404 1668; www.shanghaiblues.co.uk; 193-197 High Holborn WC1; mains £15-52; ⊖Holborn) What was once the St Giles Library now houses one of London's most stylish Chinese restaurants. The dark and atmospheric interior – think black and blue tables and chairs punctuated by bright red screens – recalls imperial China with a modern twist. The menu is just as arresting, particularly the 'new style' dim sum served as appetisers, the *pipa* duck (roast duck) and the twice-cooked pork belly. There's a vast selection of teas, some of them quite rare. On Friday and Saturday nights, you can also enjoy live jazz.

KIMCHEE
KOREAN £

(www.kimchee.uk.com; 71 High Holborn WC1; mains £7-8; ⊙11.30am-11pm; ⊖Holborn) Named after Korea's signature dish, this latest addition to London's buzzing Asian food scene, Kimchee has combined a zen-like interior with neutral colours and the soft glow of dozens of enormous lampshades with the buzz of an open kitchen and vast dining room. The food is good and excellent value: try sharing a few dishes from the charcoal barbecue and the many sides, Korean style.

✖ Marylebone

TOP CHOICE PROVIDORES & TAPA ROOM
FUSION £££

Map p428 (☏7935 6175; www.theprovidores.co.uk; 109 Marylebone High St W1; mains £18-26; ⊙lunch & dinner; ⊖Baker St or Bond St) This place is split over two levels: tempting tapas (£2.80 to £15) on the ground floor (no bookings); and outstanding fusion cuisine in the elegant and understated dining room above. The food at Providores is truly original and tastes divine: the beef fillet with Szechuan-pickled shiitake mushrooms, chilli-glazed carrots, onion purée, walnut brioche crouton and béarnaise butter was exceptional, as was the grilled Scottish scallops on a tempura brown shrimp nori roll with *hijiki* (a seaweed), coconut sambal and dashi tapioca. There is also a fantastic brunch on Saturdays and Sundays.

LOCANDA LOCATELLI ITALIAN £££

Map p428 (☎7935 9088; www.locandalocatelli.com; 8 Seymour St W1; mains £14-33; ⊘lunch & dinner; ⊖Marble Arch) This dark but quietly glamorous restaurant in an otherwise unremarkable Marble Arch hotel is one of London's hottest tables, and you're likely to see some famous faces being greeted by celebrity chef Giorgio Locatelli at some point during your meal. The restaurant is renowned for its pasta dishes, which are sublime, but rather overpriced. Booking is essential.

PING PONG CHINESE £

Map p428 (www.pingpongdimsum.com; 10 Paddington St W1; dim sum from £3, set menus £10-15; ⊘lunch & dinner; ☑; ⊖Baker St) This popular chain serves dim sum all day. Customers tick their choices of steamed, griddled, baked or fried dim sum on a little paper menu and dishes arrive as and when they're ready. The flowering teas, with their exquisitely crafted flowers that open as the tea infuses, are a show-stopper.

FISHWORKS SEAFOOD ££

Map p428 (www.fishworks.co.uk; 89 Marylebone High St; mains £12.50-25; ⊘lunch & dinner; ⊖Baker St) As the name suggests, it's all about seafood here. The emphasis is on fresh products and, just to get the point home, you enter the restaurant via the fishmongers! There are some nice English specialities to try such as Dover sole, Devon ray and Cornish oysters, but you'll also find seafood delights from across the pond, including lobster or Mediterranean specialities such as tuna steak and fish soup.

IL BARETTO ITALIAN ££

Map p428 (www.ilbaretto.co.uk; 43 Blandford St W1; mains £10-32; ⊘lunch & dinner; ⊖Baker St or Bond St) An unpretentious trattoria that seems to be winning over the locals, Il Baretto specialises in good, wood-fired oven pizza and such simple Italian dishes as penne with tomato sauce and sausage, while sometimes venturing into exciting territory with its delicious langoustine grill.

LE PAIN QUOTIDIEN DELI £

Map p428; www.lepainquotidien.com; 72-75 Marylebone High St W1; mains £5-11; ⊘7am-9pm Mon-Fri, 8am-9pm Sat, 8am-7pm Sun; ☎

⊖Baker St) A simple, stripped-down French-style cafe that serves superfresh salads, soups and *tartines* (open-face sandwiches) throughout the day. There are some lovely breakfast options, with organic granolas, breads and preserves, and sinful cakes and pastries for afternoon tea (the fruit tartlets are to die for).

GOLDEN HIND FISH & CHIPS £

Map p428 (73 Marylebone Lane W1; mains £6.90-10.90; ⊘closed lunch Sat & all day Sun; ⊖Bond St) This 90-year-old chippie has a classic interior, chunky wooden tables and builders sitting alongside suits. And from the vintage fryer come ace fish and chips.

🌿 NATURAL KITCHEN CAFE £

Map p428 (www.thenaturalkitchen.com; 77-78 Marylebone High St W1; mains £8-13; ⊘8am-8pm Mon-Fri, 9am-7pm Sat, 9am-6pm Sun; ⊖Bond St) This is a decent, practical place to drop in for a relaxing pit-stop in between raiding the shops on Marylebone High Street. The organic shop – with fresh produce, butcher's, deli and wine – has a cafe on the 1st floor. It offers good-value breakfasts (£3 to £5) and quick lunch fixes such as warm sandwiches, salads and freshly baked quiches

REUBENS JEWISH ££

Map p428 (www.reubensrestaurant.co.uk; 79 Baker St W1; mains £10-24; ⊘11.30am-4pm & 5.30-10pm Sun-Thu, to 8pm Fri; ⊖Baker St) This kosher central cafe–restaurant has all the Ashkenazi favourites: gefilte fish, latkes and the famous salt beef as well as more complicated (and filling) main courses. It's pricey for what you get, but if you answer to a higher authority, it's money well spent.

✖ Mayfair

🔺 LE BOUDIN BLANC FRENCH £££
TOP CHOICE

Map p428 (☎7499 3292; www.boudinblanc.co.uk; 5 Trebeck St W1; mains £18-27; ⊘lunch & dinner; ⊖Green Park) This has to be (one of?) the best French restaurants in the capital: the meat is cooked to perfection, the sauces mouth-wateringly good and the portions huge. The *frites* (French fries) are the best you'll find this side of the pond. And there is, of course, a whopping 500 wines to choose from. No wonder it's always full.

WEST END FRUIT & VEG MARKETS

Berwick Street Market (Map p422; Berwick St W1; ⊙9am-5pm Mon-Sat; ⊖Piccadilly Circus or Oxford Circus) South of Oxford St and running parallel to Wardour St, this fruit-and-vegetable market has managed to hang onto its prime location since the 1840s. It's a great place to put together a picnic or shop for a prepared meal.

Marylebone Farmers Market (Map p428; Cramer St car park; ⊙10am-2pm Sun; ⊖Baker St) This weekly farmers market is the largest in town with three dozen producers coming from within a 100-mile radius of the M25. It's expensive but charming, reflecting the local demographic.

GORDON RAMSAY AT CLARIDGE'S
BRITISH £££

Map p428 (🖉7499 0099; www.gordonramsay.com; 55 Brook St W1; 3-course set lunch/dinner £30/80; ⊙lunch & dinner; ⊖Bond St) This match made in heaven – London's most celebrated chef in arguably its grandest hotel – will make you weak at the knees. A meal in the gorgeous art deco dining room is a special occasion indeed; the Ramsay flavours will have you reeling, from the Thai-spiced lobster ravioli with lemongrass and coconut to the chorizo-studded John Dory with Jersey Royals and asparagus and morel velouté, all the way to the cheese trolley, whether you choose from the French or British selections. Consider the six-course tasting menu (£80).

WILD HONEY
MODERN EUROPEAN £££

Map p428 (🖉7758 9160; www.wildhoneyrestaurant.co.uk; 12 St George St W1; mains £20-25; ⊙lunch & dinner; ⊖Oxford Circus or Bond St) Wild Honey receives consistently good reviews for its food and wine, stunning wood-panelled dining room and professional service. The menu is seasonal, so surprises await; you'll generally find a combination of inventive dishes, such as salad of crab with white peach and almonds and classic mains like grilled rib-eye of beef with bone marrow and young spring vegetables, all cooked to perfection.

NOBU
JAPANESE £££

(🖉7447 4747; www.noburestaurants.com; 1st fl, Metropolitan Hotel, 19 Old Park Lane W1; mains £12-33; ⊖Hyde Park Corner) You'll have to book a month in advance to eat here (or resign yourself to eating at 6pm or 10pm if you book just a few days before), but you'll get to chew and view the greatest celebrity restaurant magnet in town. Nobu has been lobbied for years to stop serving bluefin tuna, an endangered species, but it's been to no avail. Instead, you'll find a one-liner

asking you to 'ask your server for an alternative'. Whatever your stance, the Japanese food at Nobu is divine (the scallops are the biggest you'll ever see), if pricey. The decor is rather understated and the service discreet and efficient.

VILLANDRY
MODERN EUROPEAN ££

Map p428 (www.villandry.com; 170 Great Portland St W1; mains £12-24; ⊙closed dinner Sun; 🖝 ⊖Great Portland St) This excellent Modern European restaurant with a strong Gallic slant has an attractive market–delicatessen attached (not to mention a bar) so freshness and quality of ingredients is guaranteed. Try the cassoulet or one of the several daily fish dishes.

GREENHOUSE
MODERN EUROPEAN £££

Map p428 (🖉7499 3331; www.greenhouserestaurant.co.uk; 27a Hay's Mews W1; 2-/3-course set lunch £25/29, 3-course set dinner £65; ⊙lunch Mon-Fri, dinner Mon-Sat; ⊖Green Park) Located at the end of a wonderful sculpted 'garden', Greenhouse offers some of the best food in Mayfair served with none of the attitude commonly found in restaurants of this class. The tasting menu (£90) is only for the intrepid and truly hungry. Greenhouse doles out so many freebies – from *amuses-gueule* (appetisers) and inter-course sorbets to petits fours at the finale – you'll never get up.

MOMO
MOROCCAN £££

Map p422 (🖉7434 4040; www.momoresto.com; 25 Heddon St W1; mains £18-25, 2-/3-course set lunches £15/19; ⊙closed Sun lunch; ⊖Piccadilly Circus) This wonderfully atmospheric Moroccan restaurant is stuffed with cushions and lamps, and staffed by all-dancing, tambourine-playing waiters. It's a funny old place that manages to be all things to all diners, who range from romantic couples to raucous office-party ravers. Service is very friendly and the dishes are as exciting as you dare to be, so after the meze eschew the traditional and ordinary *tajine* (stew cooked in a traditional clay pot) and tuck into the splendid Moroccan speciality *pastilla,* a scrumptious nutmeg and pigeon pie. There's outside seating in this quiet backstreet in the warmer months.

EL PIRATA
SPANISH **££**

Map p440 (☏7491 3810; www.elpirata.co.uk; 5-6 Down St W1; tapas £5-8 ⊘closed Sun; ⊜Green Park) Silly name notwithstanding, this is a good Spanish restaurant, with a great list of tapas and traditional mains such as paella. There are two set menus if you can't decide which tapas to have. The selection of Spanish wines is one of the best in London.

SAKURA
JAPANESE **£**

Map p422 (23 Conduit St W1; mains £7-12; ⊜Oxford Circus) This very authentic Japanese restaurant has something for everyone throughout the day – from sushi and sashimi (£2 to £5) to tempura, sukiyaki and a host of sets (£9 to £24).

DRINKING & NIGHTLIFE

Over the last decade or so, the East End has trumped Soho and the West End as the coolest place in town. It is still a wonderful place for a night out – Friday and Saturday nights are buzzing with excitement and decadence, particularly the areas around Soho, Leicester Square and Covent Garden where you'll find people, booze and rickshaws in the streets till the early hours.

Bloomsbury & Fitzrovia

NEWMAN ARMS
PUB

Map p426 (www.newmanarms.co.uk; 23 Rathbone St W1; ⊜Goodge St or Tottenham Court Rd) A lovely local that is also one of the few family-run pubs in central London, Newman Arms is a one-tiny-room affair with a 150-year history of providing great beer to thirsty locals. George Orwell and Dylan Thomas were regulars in their day, and Michael Powell's *Peeping Tom* was filmed here in 1960. There's also an excellent pie room upstairs.

QUEEN'S LARDER
PUB

Map p426 (www.queenslarder.co.uk; 1 Queen Sq WC1; ⊜Russell Sq) In a lovely square southeast of Russell Square, this pub is so called because Queen Charlotte, wife of 'Mad' King George III, rented part of the pub's cellar to store special foods for him while he was being treated nearby. It's a tiny but wonderfully cosy pub; there are benches outside for fair-weather fans and a good dining room upstairs.

MUSEUM TAVERN
PUB

Map p426 (49 Great Russell St WC1; ⊜Tottenham Court Rd or Holborn) This is where Karl Marx used to retire for a well-earned pint after a hard day inventing communism in the British Museum Reading Room, and where George Orwell boozed after his literary musings. A lovely traditional pub set around a long bar, it has friendly staff and is popular with academics and students alike. While tourists check in for the atmosphere, the place retains its loyal regulars.

LAMB
PUB

(94 Lamb's Conduit St WC1; ⊜Russell Sq) The Lamb's central mahogany bar with beautiful Victorian dividers (also called 'snob screens' – they allowed famous and well-to-do punters to drink without having to suffer the curious gaze of lesser citizens!) has been a favourite with locals since the day it opened in 1729. Nearly 300 years later, its popularity hasn't waned, so come early to bag a booth. It has a decent selection of Young's bitters and a genial atmosphere perfect for unwinding. The Lamb is a five-minute walk from Russell Square tube station; walk down Guilford St then turn right at Guilford Pl.

LORD JOHN RUSSELL
PUB

Map p426 (91 Marchmont St WC1; ⊜Russell Sq) If you're pining for your student days or just want a cheap pint, head down to the Lord John Russell. Here you can blend in with the under- and post-grads who are escaping the local halls of residence. It's a traditional one-room bar and there is a lovely outdoor space in the adjoining mews.

BRADLEY'S SPANISH BAR
BAR

Map p426 (42-44 Hanway St W1; ⊜Tottenham Court Rd) Bradley's is only vaguely Spanish in decor, but much more authentic in its choice of booze: San Miguel, Cruzcampo, Tinto de Verano (red wine with rum and

THE WEST END DRINKING & NIGHTLIFE

lemonade) and – teenager favourite – Sangria. Punters are squeezed under low ceilings in the nooks of the basement, while a vintage vinyl jukebox plays out rock tunes of your choice.

TEMPUS BAR
BAR

Map p426 (Hotel Russell, Russell Sq WC1; ⊖Russell Sq) Nestled behind the awesome Victorian Gothic facade of the Hotel Russell, Tempus is a nice change from traditional pubs. With grand Edwardian decor, huge leather armchairs and table service, prices are a little inflated but there is a good selection of cocktails and wines, and you're generally guaranteed a seat.

🍸 Soho & Chinatown

TOP CHOICE EXPERIMENTAL COCKTAIL CLUB
COCKTAIL BAR

Map p422 (www.experimentalcocktailclub london.com; 13A Gerrard St W1; ⊖6pm-3am Mon-Sat, 5pm-midnight Sun; ⊖Leicester Sq or Piccadilly Circus) Once a late-night premises of a less reputable kind, the Experimental is now a sensational cocktail bar. The interior, with its soft lighting, mirrors, bare brick wall and elegant furnishings matches the sophistication of the cocktails: rare and original spirits (purple *shiso*-infused Ketel One Vodka, bird's-eye-chilli-infused Ocho Blanco Tequila etc), vintage martinis, Billecart and Krug Champagne and homemade fruit syrups. There is a £5 cover charge after 11pm.

ACADEMY
COCKTAIL BAR

Map p422 (www.labbaruk.com; 12 Old Compton St W1; ⊖4pm-midnight Mon-Sat, to 10.30pm Sun; ⊖Leicester Sq or Tottenham Court Rd) A longstanding favourite in Soho, the Academy has some of the best cocktails in town. The menu is the size of a small book but, fear not, if you can't be bothered to read through it, just tell the bartender what you feel like (gin and exotic fruit? Why, no problem, Madam!) and he'll mix you something divine.

WHITE HORSE
PUB

Map p422 (45 Rupert St W1; ⊖Piccadilly Circus or Leicester Sq) A lovely pub in a very busy part of Soho, the White Horse ticks all our boxes: friendly staff, cheap drinks (it's part of the Sam Smith brewery) and a great traditional

interior with etched glass and wood panels. The upstairs area is particularly cosy and generally quieter than downstairs.

FRENCH HOUSE
BAR

Map p422 (www.frenchhousesoho.com; 49 Dean St W1; ⊖Leicester Sq or Piccadilly Circus) French House is Soho's legendary boho boozer with a history to match: this was the meeting place of the Free French Forces during WWII, and de Gaulle is said to have drunk here often, while Dylan Thomas, Peter O'Toole and Francis Bacon all frequently ended up on the wooden floors. Come here to sip on Ricard, French wine or Kronenbourg and check out the quirky locals.

EDGE
GAY

Map p422 (www.edgesoho.co.uk; 11 Soho Sq W1; ⊖to 1am Mon-Sat; ⊖Tottenham Court Rd) Overlooking Soho Square in all its four-storey glory, the Edge is London's largest gay bar and heaves every night of the week: there are dancers, waiters in bunny (or other) outfits, good music and a generally super friendly vibe. There's a heavy straight presence, as it's so close to Oxford Street.

CANDY BAR
LESBIAN

Map p422 (www.candybarsoho.com; 4 Carlise St W1; ⊖to midnight Sun-Thu, to 2am Fri & Sat; ⊖Tottenham Court Rd) This brilliant bar has been the centre of London's small but fun lesbian scene for years and is showing no signs of waning. Busy most nights of the week, this is very much a girls' space (one male guest per two women are allowed, though) and this should definitely be your first port of call on the London lesbian scene.

MADAME JO JO'S
CLUB

Map p422 (www.madamejojos.com; 8 Brewer St W1; ⊖Leicester Sq or Piccadilly Circus) The renowned subterranean, crimson cabaret bar and all its sleazy fun comes into its own with Kitsch Cabaret on Saturday and Burlesque Idol on Fridays. Keb Darge's Lost & Found night on Saturday is legendary, attracting a cool crew of breakdancers, jazz dancers and people just out to have a good time. It's Tranny Schak Up (drag queen night) on Wednesdays.

VILLAGE
GAY

Map p422 (www.village-soho.co.uk; 81 Wardour St W1; ⊖4pm-1am Mon-Sat, to 11.30pm Sun; ⊖Piccadilly Circus or Leicester Sq) The Village is always up for a party, whatever the night

LOCAL KNOWLEDGE

GAY TIMES IN LONDON

Freelance journalist Stephen Unwin gives us the lowdown on his favourite places for good times in London. Stephen is a patron of Jake, a networking community for high-flying gay men and women, and associate editor of The Briefing, Jake's weekly e-zine.

For Weeknights and Weekend Afternoons

I like hanging out at **Boheme Bar & Kitchen** (Map p422; www.bohemekitchen.co.uk; 19-21 Old Compton St W1; ⊙11am-1am Mon-Wed, to 3am Thu-Sat, to midnight Sun; ⊖Leicester Sq). I just get a table outside, have some food and do some people watching.

For restaurants, **Polpetto** (p118) is good, and I love the sexy-rough atmosphere at **Spuntino** (p117).

For After-Work Drinks

The **Duke of Wellington** (Map p422; 77 Wardour St W1; ⊖Leicester Sq) is a relaxed pub with an older feel. It's a nice place for a drink and the crowd meshes with the after-work punters from the bars next door. I also love the balcony at the **Yard** (p127).

Partying until the Wee Hours

Room Service (p59), the Thursday club night at Diu, is doing very well. It's one of the few places to have go-go dancers and is unabashedly sexy. They have world-famous DJs playing.

Horsemeat at the **Eagle** (p288) in Vauxhall is great on Sunday, particularly during Bank Holidays. You'll have to queue for at least an hour but that's half the fun as everyone drinks and makes friends in the queue.

My favourite place to go is Shoreditch, however. For a great night out, we'll start at the **George & Dragon** (p211) or **Nelsons Head** (p230); we'll stay there until midnight and then head to the **Joiners Arms** (p230): it's really grotty but has great music and is always rammed!

of the week. There are karaoke nights, disco nights, go-go dancer nights, take your pick. And if you can't wait to strut your stuff until the clubs open, there is a dancefloor downstairs, complete with dancing pole, of course.

FRIENDLY SOCIETY   GAY
Map p422 (79 Wardour St W1; ⊙6-11pm Mon-Thu, to midnight Fri & Sat, to 10.30pm Sun; ⊖Piccadilly Circus) Definitely one of Soho's friendliest and more relaxed gay bars. A fun and up-for-it crowd assembles in the early evening: drink beer under S&M Barbie and Ken, and chill out to live DJs.

COACH & HORSES   PUB
Map p422 (29 Greek St W1; ⊖Leicester Sq) Famous as the place where *Spectator* columnist Jeffrey Bernard drank himself to death, this small, busy and thankfully unreconstructed boozer retains an old Soho bohemian atmosphere with a regular clientele of soaks, writers, hacks, tourists and those too drunk to lift their heads off the counter. Pretension will be prosecuted.

YARD   GAY
Map p422 (www.yardbar.co.uk; 57 Rupert St W1; ⊖Piccadilly Circus) This old Soho favourite attracts a great cross-section of the great and the good. It's a pretty attitude-free place, perfect for preclub drinks or just an evening out. There are DJs upstairs in the Loft most nights as well as a friendly crowd in the eponymous, atmospheric courtyard downstairs.

PROFILE   GAY
Map p422 (www.profilesoho.com; 84-86 Wardour St W1; ⊖Piccadilly Circus or Leicester Sq) This American-diner-meets-Soho bar serves an eclectic mix of Absolut vodka cocktails, unremarkable wine, draught beer and dangerously tasty alcoholic milkshakes. The food menu sports such American classics as burgers and Caesar salad. Happy hour is from 4pm to 7pm daily.

LOOP BAR   BAR
Map p428 (www.theloopbar.co.uk; 19 Dering St W1; admission £10 after 10pm; ⊙to 3am Thu-Sat, closed Sun; ⊖Oxford Circus) Right off Oxford Circus, Loop has three floors of fun: a street-level bar, a sleek basement bar with

leather booths and chandeliers and, on the level below, Groovy Wonderland, a disco-styled club with flashing dancefloors, platform shoes on the walls and disco balls everywhere.

LO PROFILE   GAY

Map p422 (www.gaydarprofile.com; 84-86 Wardour St W1; ☺10pm-4am Fri & Sat; ⊖Piccadilly Circus or Leicester Sq) This addition to the gay club scene, with its go-go dancers, smoke machine and colourful star-shaped lights, is hugely popular. It gets a surge at 11pm when punters from the Profile Bar above move en masse for a boogie downstairs.

BARCODE   GAY

Map p422 (www.bar-code.co.uk; 3-4 Archer St W1; ☺4pm-1am Mon-Sat, to 11pm Sun; ⊖Piccadilly Circus) Tucked away down a Soho side street, this fun gay bar is full of a diverse range of people enjoying a pint or two and some evening cruising. There are frequent club nights in the downstairs area, including the popular **Industri** on Wednesday (p59) and **Comedy Camp** (p131) on Tuesdays.

JOHN SNOW   PUB

Map p422 (39 Broadwick St W1; ⊖Oxford Circus or Piccadilly Circus) This used to be one of Soho's most popular pubs, but after throwing out a gay couple for kissing in April 2011, its popularity nose-dived. It's a shame because it is otherwise a classic pub, with no music, just plenty of chat and cheap ale, lager, bitter and stout from British brewery Sam Smith's.

ENDURANCE   PUB

Map p422 (90 Berwick St W1; ⊖Oxford Circus or Piccadilly Circus) A Soho favourite, the Endurance has a retro jukebox that's full of indie hits, there's good wine and draught ales to be savoured, and there's decent food too; Sundays tend to be very quiet. Often the crowd spills outside in the evening, and daytime drinks afford good views of Berwick Street Market (p124) buzz.

KU BAR FRITH ST   GAY

Map p422 (25 Frith St; ☺until midnight Fri & Sat; ⊖Leicester Sq) This venue is not quite the party place that the Lisle Street Bar is and it therefore tends to be popular with a slightly older, smarter gay crowd.

MILK & HONEY   COCKTAIL BAR

Map p422 (☎7065 6840; www.mlkhny.com; 61 Poland St W1; ⊖Leicester Sq or Piccadilly Circus)

Milk & Honey's number one 'House Rule' reads: 'No name-dropping, no star fucking'. This select, dark-lit den is a members' club that lets non-members in on weeknights (before 11pm), and you have to phone in advance to reserve your two-hour slot. This practice is heavenly if you like privacy and great drinks, and hellish if you prefer a more down-to-earth atmosphere.

🍷 Covent Garden & Leicester Square

HEAVEN   GAY

Map p432 (www.heavennightclub-london.com; Villiers St WC2; ☺11pm-6am Mon, 11pm-4am Thu & Fri, 10pm-5am Sat; ⊖Embankment or Charing Cross) This long-standing and perennially popular gay club, under the arches beneath Charing Cross station, has always been host to good club nights. Monday's Popcorn night (mixed dance party, all-welcome door policy) has to be one of the best for weeknight's clubbing in the capital. The celebrated G-A-Y now also takes place here on Thursday (G-A-Y Porn Idol), Friday (G-A-Y Camp Attack) and Saturday (plain ol' G-A-Y).

LAMB & FLAG   PUB

Map p432 (33 Rose St WC2; ⊖Covent Garden or Leicester Sq) Pocket-sized but packed with charm and history, the Lamb & Flag is still going strong after more than 350 years. Rain or shine, you'll have to elbow your way to the bar through the merry crowd drinking outside. Inside, it's all brass fittings and creaky wooden floors. The main entrance is on top of a tiny cobbled street, but you can also reach it from the backstreet donkey path that'll make you think of Victorian England.

SALISBURY   PUB

Map p432 (90 St Martin's Lane WC2; ⊖Leicester Sq) Facing off the superchic St Martin's Lane Hotel, the Salisbury offers everything its opposite number doesn't: warmth, centuries of history and a glorious, traditionally British pub interior. It has a vast range of beers, including lots of ales and rarer continental lagers such as Stella Black and Estrella Damn.

SPORTS CAFE   BAR

(www.thesportscafe.com; 80 Haymarket SW1; ☺Mon-Sat noon-3am, to 10.30pm Sun ☎; ⊖Piccadilly Circus) For those keen to watch the latest ice hockey, American football, baseball or even soccer fixtures, the Sports Cafe is the place to be. It's a huge place, with four bars over two floors, giant screens everywhere and sports posters and memorabilia on the walls. The late licence means it's often raucous in the evenings, although it tends to be pretty quiet during the day.

KU BAR LISLE ST   GAY
Map p432 (www.ku-bar.co.uk; 30 Lisle St WC2; ☺noon-3am Mon-Sat, to 10.30pm Sun; ⊖Leicester Sq) With its smart interior, geometric black-and-white patterns on the walls and busy events schedule (disco, cabaret, DJ sets etc) in the basement, the Lisle street branch of this mini-chain attracts a young, fun-loving crowd. It's student night on Mondays.

CROSS KEYS   PUB
Map p432 (31 Endell St WC2; ⊖Covent Garden) Covered in ivy and frequented by loyal locals who come here for pints of Young's and spicy fry-ups, the Cross Keys is Covent Garden's tourist-free local pub. Eccentric landlord Brian has displayed his pop purchases as bar decorations (such as his £500 Elvis Presley napkin); brass pots, kettles and diving gear hang off the ceiling, and the punters range from bar props to Covent Garden professionals, all of whom spill onto the pavement and outside tables on summer days.

FREUD   BAR
Map p432 (198 Shaftesbury Ave WC2; ☺to 1am Thu & Sat, to 2am Fri; ⊖Covent Garden) Make this the first stop on your crawl because there's no way you'll make it down the stairs (not much more than a ladder) after a few drinks. It's a small basement bar–cafe–gallery with regular artworks from up and coming artists featured on the walls. The decor and punters are suitably scruffy, the cocktails are fancy, but beer is – sadly – only by the bottle.

🍷 Holborn & The Strand

TOP CHOICE GORDON'S WINE BAR   WINE BAR
Map p432 (www.gordonswinebar.com; 47 Villiers St WC2; ⊖Embankment or Charing Cross) Gordon's is somewhat a victim of its popularity; it is relentlessly busy and unless you arrive before the office crowd does (generally around 6pm), you can forget getting a table. It's cavernous and dark, and the French and New World wines are heady and reasonably priced. You can nibble on bread, cheese and olives.

PRINCESS LOUISE   PUB
Map p432 (208 High Holborn WC1; ⊖Holborn) This late-19th-century Victorian pub is spectacularly decorated with a riot of fine tiles, etched mirrors, plasterwork and a stunning central horseshoe bar. The old Victorian wood partitions give punters plenty of nooks and alcoves to hide in. Beers are Sam Smith's only but cost just over £2 a pint, so it's no wonder many elect to spend the whole evening here.

SEVEN STARS   PUB
Map p432 (53-54 Carey St WC2; ⊖Holborn or Temple) Even though it's packed with lawyers in the after-office booze rush hour, the tiny Seven Stars is still a relative secret to many Londoners. Sitting behind the Royal Courts of Justice (p110) and originally a sailors' hang-out, this is the place to come for real ale and ravishing game dishes (the eccentric landlady and chef, Roxy Beaujolais, is a former TV chef and raconteur).

POLSKI BAR   BAR
Map p432 (11 Little Turnstile WC1; ☺closed Sun; ⊖Holborn) With around 60 different types of vodka, from coffee to fruity to wheat-flavoured, simple old Polish *slivowica* (plum brandy) to kosher, everyone should find something that tickles their taste buds. There's great Polish food here, too, but the bare and cold interior leaves something to be desired.

🍷 Marylebone

TOP CHOICE PURL   COCKTAIL BAR
Map p428 (☎7935 0835; www.purl-london.com; 50-54 Blandford St W1; ⊖Baker St) A 'purveyor of fine matches and alcoholic libations', Purl is a fabulous underground drinking den. Decked out in vintage furniture, it serves original and intriguingly named cocktails ('What's Your Poison?' or 'Mr Hyde's No 2' spring to mind) and a punch of the day. The atmosphere is all subdued lighting and hushed-tone conversations, which only adds to the mysterious air of the place. Booking is recommended.

PRINCE REGENT

PUB

Map p428 (www.theprinceregentw1.co.uk; 71 Marylebone High St W1; ⊖Baker St) With a flamboyant decor of upholstered furniture, regal colours on the walls and gold-framed mirrors, the Prince Regent has gone all out on atmosphere. Drinks are pretty good too, with changing ales, a good selection of draught beers and wines and some decent food. There's also a small street terrace.

MARYLEBONE

PUB

Map p428 (www.themarylebonelondon.com; 93 Marylebone High St W1; ⊖Baker St) An upmarket pub with overpriced drinks, the Marylebone's redeeming feature is its regular live music sessions (Tuesdays and Thursdays) and DJ sets (Saturday). The sophisticated interior of light greys and soft furnishings is easy on the eye, too.

🍸 Mayfair

PUNCH BOWL

PUB

Map p428 (www.punchbowllondon.com; 41 Farm St W1; ⊖Bond St) Partly owned by film director Guy Ritchie (*Lock, Stock & Two Smoking Barrels; Snatch*), the Punch Bowl attracts a young and happening crowd sipping cask ales, fine wines and whisky rather than run-of-the-mill pints. The pub retains many of its original 18th-century features (wood panels, cornicing etc), although the dining room at the back definitely has a more modern feel to it.

GUINEA

PUB

Map p428 (www.theguinea.co.uk; 30 Bruton Pl W1; ⊖Green Park or Bond St) This quiet and friendly pub in London's most exclusive neighbourhood has something of a gentlemen's club about it, what with the shining brass fittings, heavy upholstery and good selection of ales. There are very few places to sit but if you do manage to bag a seat, you could order one of the famous pies from the rear restaurant.

☆ ENTERTAINMENT

TOP CHOICE 12 BAR

LIVE MUSIC

Map p432 (www.12barclub.com; Denmark St WC2; ⏰7pm-3am Mon-Sat, to 12.30am Sun; ⊖Leicester Sq) Small, intimate, with a rough-and-ready feel, the 12 Bar is one of our favourite live music venues in town, with anything from solo acts to bands performing every night of the week. The emphasis is on songwriting and the music is very much indie rock, with anything from folk and jazzy influences to full-on punk and metal sounds. Admission is £7.

TOP CHOICE ROYAL OPERA HOUSE

OPERA

Map p432 (www.roh.org.uk; Bow St WC2; ⊖Covent Garden) The £210 million redevelopment for the millennium gave classic opera a fantastic setting, and coming here for a night is a sumptuous prospect. Although the program has been fluffed up by modern influences, the main attractions here are still the classical ballet and opera – all are wonderful productions and feature world-class performers.

Midweek matinees are usually much cheaper than evening performances and restricted-view seats cost as little as £7. There are same-day tickets (one per customer available to the first 67 people in the queue) from 10am for £8 to £40. Half-price stand-by tickets are only occasionally available. Otherwise, full-price tickets go for anything up to £120.

TOP CHOICE COMEDY STORE

COMEDY

Map p422 (www.thecomedystore.co.uk; Haymarket House, 1a Oxendon St SW1; ⊖Piccadilly Circus) This was one of the first (and is still one of the best) comedy clubs in London. Although it's a bit like conveyor-belt comedy, it gets some of the biggest names. Wednesday and Sunday night's Comedy Store Players is the most famous improvisation outfit in town, with the wonderful Josie Lawrence; on Thursdays, Fridays and Saturdays it's Best in Stand Up, which features (you guessed it) the best on London's comedy circuit. Tickets are generally around £20.

PRINCE CHARLES

CINEMA

Map p422 (www.princecharlescinema.com; Leicester Pl WC2; ⊖Leicester Sq) You'd be right to think that ticket prices at Leicester Square cinemas are daylight robbery, so wait until the first-runs have finished and moved to the Prince Charles, central London's cheapest cinema; this is where non-members have to pay only £5.50–6.50 (or £8–10 for new releases). There are also mini-festivals, Q&As with film directors, old classics and, most famously, sing-along screenings of *Grease, The Sound of Music* and *Rocky Horror Picture Show.*

PIZZA EXPRESS JAZZ CLUB   JAZZ

Map p422 (www.pizzaexpresslive.com; 10 Dean St W1; ⊖Tottenham Court Rd) Believe it or not, this is one of the best and most consistently popular jazz venues in London. It's a bit of a strange arrangement, having a small basement venue beneath the main chain restaurant, but it seems to work well. Lots of big names perform here, as well as promising artists – Norah Jones, Jamie Cullum and Amy Winehouse (RIP) all played here in their early days. Admission is £15–20.

RONNIE SCOTT'S   JAZZ

Map p422 (www.ronniescotts.co.uk; 47 Frith St W1; ⊖Leicester Sq) Ronnie Scott originally opened his jazz club on Gerrard St in 1959 under a Chinese gambling den. The club moved to its current location six years later and became widely known as Britain's best jazz club. Such luminaries as Miles Davis, Charlie Parker, Thelonious Monk, plus Ella Fitzgerald, Count Basie and Sarah Vaughan have all played here.

The club continues to build upon its formidable reputation by hosting a range of big names and new talent. The atmosphere is great, but talking during music is a big no-no. Door staff can be terribly rude and the service slow, but that's how it's always been. Gigs are nightly and usually last until 2am. Expect to pay between £18 and £40.

COMEDY CAMP   COMEDY

Map p422 (www.comedycamp.co.uk; 3-4 Archer St W1; ☺8.30pm Tue & 1st Sat of every month; ⊖Piccadilly Circus) This gay (but very straight-friendly) comedy club, hosted by Simon Happily, has become one of Soho's favourites. It's held in the basement area of one of Soho's more enjoyable gay bars, **Barcode** (p128). Comedy Camp (£10) features both up-and-coming queer comedy acts as well as more established gay and lesbian comics.

SOHO THEATRE   THEATRE

Map p422 (www.sohotheatre.com; 21 Dean St W1; ⊖Tottenham Court Rd) Soho Theatre has developed a superb reputation for showcasing new writing talent and quality comedy. It's also hosted some top-notch stand-up or sketch-based comedians; US acts (such as Louis CK and Kirsten Schaal) frequently come here to perform. Tickets cost around £10–20.

BORDERLINE   CONCERT VENUE

Map p422 (http://venues.meanfiddler.com/borderline/home; Orange Yard W1; ⊖Tottenham Court Rd) Through the Tex-Mex entrance off Orange Yard and down into the basement you'll find a packed, 275-capacity venue that really punches above its weight. Read the writing on the walls (literally, there's a gig list): Crowded House, REM, Blur, Counting Crows, PJ Harvey, Lenny Kravitz, Debbie Harry, plus many anonymous indie outfits, have all played here. The crowd's equally diverse but full of music journos and talent-spotting record-company A&Rs.

PLACE   DANCE

Map p426 (www.theplace.org.uk; 17 Duke's Rd WC1; ⊖Euston Square) One of the most exciting modern-dance venues, the Place was the birthplace of modern British dance. It concentrates on challenging, contemporary and experimental choreography. Behind the late-Victorian facade you'll find a 300-seat theatre, an arty, creative cafe atmosphere and six training studios. The Place sponsors an annual dance award, 'Place Prize', which strives to seek out and award new and outstanding dance talent. Tickets cost £5-15.

CURZON SOHO   CINEMA

Map p422 (www.curzoncinemas.com; 99 Shaftesbury Ave W1; ⊖Leicester Sq or Piccadilly Circus) Curzon Soho is one of London's best cinemas. It has fantastic programming with the best of British, European, world and American indie films; regular Q&As with directors; shorts and mini-festivals; a Konditor & Cook cafe upstairs with tea and cakes to die for, and an ultracomfortable bar.

WIGMORE HALL   CLASSICAL MUSIC

Map p428 (www.wigmore-hall.org.uk; 36 Wigmore St W1; ⊖Bond St) This is one of the best concert venues in town, not only because of its fantastic acoustics, beautiful art nouveau hall and great variety of concerts and recitals, but also because of the sheer standard of the performances. Built in 1901 as the recital hall for Bechstein Pianos, it has remained one of the top places in the world for chamber music. The Sunday-morning coffee concerts (adult/concession £12/10) and the lunchtime concerts at 1pm on Monday (adult/senior £12/10) are both excellent value. Flagship evening concerts can cost up to £50.

AMUSED MOOSE SOHO
COMEDY

Map p422 (www.amusedmoose.com; Moonlighting, 17 Greek St W1; ⊜Tottenham Court Rd) One of the city's best clubs, Soho's Amused Moose is popular with audiences and comedians alike, perhaps helped along by the fact that heckling is 'unacceptable' and all of the acts are 'first-date friendly' in that they're unlikely to humiliate the front row.

LONDON COLISEUM
OPERA

Map p432 (www.eno.org; Coliseum, St Martin's Lane WC2; ⊜Leicester Sq or Charing Cross) The Coliseum is home to the English National Opera (ENO), celebrated for making opera modern and relevant; all operas here are sung in English. After several years in the wasteland, the ENO has been receiving better reviews and welcoming much bigger audiences since the arrival of music director Edward Gardner.

The building, built in 1904 and lovingly restored 100 years later, is very impressive. The English National Ballet also does regular performances at the Coliseum.

100 CLUB
LIVE MUSIC

Map p426 (www.the100club.co.uk; 100 Oxford St W1; ⊜Tottenham Court Rd) This legendary London venue has always concentrated on jazz, but it's also spreading its wings to swing and rock nowadays. It once showcased Chris Barber, BB King and the Stones, and was at the centre of the punk revolution as well as the '90s indie scene. It hosts dancing swing gigs and local jazz musicians, as well as the occasional big name.

DONMAR WAREHOUSE
THEATRE

Map p432 (www.donmarwarehouse.com; 41 Earlham St WC2; ⊜Covent Garden) The small Donmar Warehouse is the 'thinking man's theatre' in London. But it has taken a step back from the days when Nicole Kidman administered 'theatrical Viagra' nightly by peeling off her clothes in Sam Mendes' production of *The Blue Room* and Zoë Wanamaker really did Gothic Southern as Amanda Wakefield in Tennessee Williams' *Glass Menagerie*. Still, artistic director Michael Grandage stages interesting and somewhat inventive productions such as Ibsen's *Doll's House* with Gillian Anderson and *Hamlet* with the blue-eyed Jude Law.

ICA CINEMA
CINEMA

Map p430 (www.ica.org.uk; Nash House, The Mall SW1; ⊜Charing Cross or Piccadilly Circus) The Institute of Contemporary Arts (ICA) is a treasure for all lovers of indie cinema – its program always has material no one else is showing, such as the latest American independents, films showing out of season, all-night screenings and rare documentaries. The two cinemas are quite small, but comfortable enough.

SHOPPING

The West End's shopping seldom needs introducing. Oxford St is heaven or hell, depending on what you're after; it's all about chains, from Marks & Spencer to H&M, TopShop to Gap. Covent Garden is also beset with high-street outlets but they tend to be smaller and counterbalanced by independent boutiques, vintage in particular. As well as fashion, the West End is big on music. There are some great independent record shops, especially in Soho.

Westminster & St James's

PENHALIGON'S
ACCESSORIES

Map p430 (www.penhaligons.com; 16-17 Burlington Arcade W1; ⊜Piccadilly or Green Park) Most people's perfume-buying experience nowadays is limited to picking up their favourite scent at the airport duty-free. Penhaligon's is the antidote to such an anonymous and soulless process: here, attendants will ask you about your favourite smells, take you on a little exploratory tour of their signature range and help you discover new scents. There is a range of products, from traditional perfumes to home fragrances and bath and body products. All products are made in Devon, England.

FORTNUM & MASON
FOOD

Map p430 (www.fortnumandmason.co.uk; 181 Piccadilly W1; ⊜Piccadilly Circus) London's oldest grocery store celebrated its 300th birthday in 2007 by not yielding to modern times (its staff are still dressed in old-fashioned tailcoats) and keeping its glam food hall supplied with its famed food hampers, cut marmalade, speciality teas and so on. Downstairs is an elegant wine bar designed by the man behind the Wolseley (boxed text, p117). You'll also find elegant kitchenware, luxury gifts and perfumes.

D R HARRIS
BEAUTY

Map p430 (www.drharris.co.uk; 29 St James's St SW1; ⊗closed Sun; ⊖Green Park) Operating as chemist and perfumer since 1790 and the Prince of Wales's royal pharmacist, D R Harris can supply your moustache wax or perhaps some crystal eye drops to combat the red eyes after a late night. You can also combine it with D R Harris's own hangover cure: a bitter herbal concoction called D R Harris Pick-Me-Up.

TAYLOR OF OLD BOND STREET
BEAUTY

Map p430 (www.tayloroldbondst.co.uk; 74 Jermyn St SW1; ⊗closed Sun; ⊖Green Park) This shop has been plying its trade since the mid-19th century and has much contributed to the expression 'well-groomed gentleman'. It stocks every sort of razor, shaving brush and flavour of shaving soap imaginable.

SHEPHERDS
GIFTS

Map p430 (www.bookbinding.co.uk; 76 Rochester Row SW1; ⊗closed Sun; ⊖Victoria) Suckers for fine stationery, leather boxes, elegant albums and exquisite paper will get their fix at this wonderful bookbindery.

MINAMOTO KITCHOAN
FOOD

Map p422 (www.kitchoan.com; 44 Piccadilly W1; ⊗closed Sun; ⊖Piccadilly Circus) Walking into this Japanese sweet shop is a mind-blowing experience. *Wagashi* – Japanese sweets – are made out of all sorts of beans and rice and shaped into glazed red cherries, green-bean bunches or spiky kidney bean rolls. Order a couple, sit down and enjoy with a complimentary green tea, or buy a box for a sure-hit souvenir.

🏠 Bloomsbury & Fitzrovia

BANG BANG EXCHANGE
VINTAGE

Map p426 (www.myspace.com/bangbangexchange; 21 Goodge St W1; ⊖Goodge St) Got some designer pieces you're tired of? Bang Bang exchanges, buys and sells vintage pieces, proving the saying 'One girl's faded Prada dress is another girl's top new wardrobe piece'.

GAY'S THE WORD
BOOKS

Map p426 (http://freespace.virgin.net/gays.theword/; 66 Marchmont St WC1; ⊗10am-6.30pm Mon-Sat, 2-6pm Sun; ⊖Russell Sq or King's Cross) This London gay institution has been selling books nobody else stocks for three decades now, and still has a great range of gay- and lesbian-interest books and magazines as well as a real community spirit.

JAMES SMITH & SONS
ACCESSORIES

Map p432 (www.james-smith.co.uk; 53 New Oxford St WC1; ⊗closed Sun; ⊖Tottenham Court Rd) 'Outside every silver lining is a big black cloud', claim the cheerful owners of this quintessential English shop. Nobody makes and stocks such elegant umbrellas, walking sticks and canes as this traditional place and, thanks to bad English weather, they'll hopefully do great business for years to come.

🏠 Soho & Chinatown

JOY
FASHION

Map p422 (www.joythestore.com; 162-170 Wardour St W1; ⊖Oxford Circus or Tottenham Court Rd) Joy is an artistic blend of high street and vintage: there are excellent clothes, from silk dresses for women, fabulous shirts for men and timeless T-shirts for both, as well as funky gadgets such as a floating radio duck and dollar- and euro-shaped ice cube trays. Conventional shoppers abstain!

TOPSHOP & TOPMAN
FASHION

Map p422 (www.topshop.co.uk; 36-38 Great Castle St W1; ⊖Oxford Circus) Topshop is the 'It'-store when it comes to high-street shopping. Encapsulating London's supreme skill at bringing catwalk fashion to the youth market affordably and quickly, it constantly innovates by working with young designers and celebrities. It's the store that famously runs the popular Kate Moss collection. It has an entire floor dedicated to accessories (hair clips, tights, sunglasses, you name it). And if the store's five floors intimidate you, you can book an appointment with a personal shopper.

URBAN OUTFITTERS
FASHION

Map p422 (www.urbanoutfitters.co.uk; 200 Oxford St W1; ⊖Oxford Circus) Probably the trendiest of all chains, this cool American store serves both men and women and has the best young designer T-shirts, an excellent designer area (stocking Paul & Joe Sister, Vivienne Westwood's Red Label, Hussain Chalayan and See by Chloé, among others), 'renewed' secondhand pieces, saucy underwear, silly homewares and quirky gadgets.

PROWLER GAY ACCESSORIES

Map p422 (www.prowler-stores.co.uk; 5-7 Brewer St W1; ⊗11am-10pm Mon-Fri, 10am-10pm Sat, noon-8pm Sun; ⊖Piccadilly Circus) Prowler's flagship Soho store is a gay shopping mecca selling books, magazines, clothes and 'lifestyle accessories'. There's also a discreet 'adult' section with the usual array of DVDs and magazines, but the overall feel is of a respectable gay department store.

ALGERIAN COFFEE STORES COFFEE

Map p422 (www.algcoffee.co.uk; 52 Old Compton St W1; ⊗closed Sun; ⊖Leicester Sq) Stop and have a shot of espresso made in-store while you select your freshly ground coffee beans. Choose among dozens of varieties of coffees and teas.

VINTAGE HOUSE DRINK

Map p422 (42 Old Compton St W1; ⊗9am-11pm Mon-Fri, 9.30am-11pm Sat, noon-10pm Sun; ⊖Leicester Sq) A whisky connoisseur's paradise, this shop stocks more than 1000 single-malt Scotches, from smooth Macallan to peaty Lagavulin. It also stocks a huge array of spirits and liqueurs that you wouldn't find in your average wine shop.

MARSHMALLOW MOUNTAIN VINTAGE

Map p422 (www.marshmellowmountain.com; Kingly Ct, 49 Carnaby St W1; ⊖Oxford Circus) One of our favourites, with eccentric, well-chosen dresses and wonderful shoes and plenty of great accessories including hats and jewellery.

BEYOND THE VALLEY FASHION

Map p422 (www.beyondthevalley.com; 2 Newburgh St W1; ⊖Oxford Circus) An original boutique, ideal to discover new fashion talent, with clothes, jewellery, accessories and artwork on display inside the lovely shop. The Side Room, at the back of the shop, is a conservatory-style gallery space where small exhibitions regularly take place.

AGENT PROVOCATEUR LINGERIE

Map p422 (www.agentprovocateur.com; 6 Broadwick St W1; ⊖Oxford Circus) For women's lingerie that is to be worn and seen, and certainly *not* hidden, pull up to Joseph (son of Vivienne Westwood) Corre's wonderful Agent Provocateur. Its sexy and saucy corsets, bras and nighties for all shapes and sizes exude confident and positive sexuality.

HAMLEYS TOYS

Map p422 (www.hamleys.com; 188-196 Regent St W1; ⊖Oxford Circus) Reportedly the largest toy store in the world and certainly the most famous, Hamleys is a layer cake of playthings. Computer games are in the basement and the latest playground trends are at ground level. But that's just the start. Science kits are on the 1st floor, preschool toys on the 2nd, girls' playthings on the 3rd and model cars on the 4th, while the whole confection is topped off with Lego world and its cafe on the 5th.

LIBERTY DEPARTMENT STORE

Map p422 (www.liberty.co.uk; Great Marlborough St W1; ⊖Oxford Circus) An irresistible blend of contemporary styles in an old-fashioned mock-Tudor atmosphere, Liberty has a huge cosmetics department and an accessories floor, along with a breathtaking lingerie section, all at very inflated prices. A classic London souvenir is a Liberty fabric print.

AQUASCUTUM FASHION

Map p422 (www.aquascutum.co.uk; 100 Regent St W1; ⊖Piccadilly Circus) Despite the store's modern look, Aquascutum's mackintoshes, scarves, bags and hats remain traditional. For men, this means classic gabardine; for women, the look is straight lines, classic fashion and natural beauty, as worn by the super-rich.

🔒 Covent Garden & Leicester Square

URBAN OUTFITTERS FASHION

Map p432 (www.urbanoutfitters.co.uk; 42-56 Earlham St WC2; ⊖Covent Garden) Another great outlet of this ubertrendy chain (see review p133).

NEAL'S YARD DAIRY FOOD

Map p432 (www.nealsyarddairy.co.uk; 17 Shorts Gardens WC2; ⊗closed Sun; ⊖Covent Garden) A fabulous, smelly cheese house that would fit in rural England, this place is proof that the British can do just as well as the French when it comes to big rolls of ripe cheese. There are more than 70 varieties that the shopkeepers will let you taste, including independent farmhouse brands. Condiments, pickles, jams and chutneys are also available.

INDEPENDENT MUSIC STORES

It's sad that independent music stores find it difficult to keep going, especially in central London. That said, Britons buy more music per head than any other nation on earth (much of it in London), so here's hoping that little fish don't get munched by the big chains. This is a selection of the West End's best.

Sister Ray (Map p422; www.sisterray.co.uk; 34-35 Berwick St W1; ⊖Oxford Circus or Tottenham Court Rd) If you were a fan of the late, great John Peel on the BBC/BBC World Service, this specialist in innovative, experimental and indie music is just right for you.

Ray's Jazz (Map p422; 3rd fl, Foyle's, 113-119 Charing Cross Rd WC2; ⊖Tottenham Court Rd) Quiet and serene with friendly and helpful staff, this is one of the best jazz shops in London.

Sounds of the Universe (Map p422; www.soundsoftheuniverse.com; 7 Broadwick St W1; ⊖Oxford Circus or Tottenham Court Rd) Outlet of Soul Jazz Records label (responsible for so many great soul, reggae, funk and dub albums), this place stocks CDs and vinyl plus some original 45s.

Harold Moore's Records (Map p422; www.hmrecords.co.uk; 2 Great Marlborough St W1; ⊖Oxford Circus or Tottenham Court Rd) London's finest classical-music store stocks an extensive range of vinyl, CDs and DVDs, plus jazz in the basement.

Reckless Records (Map p422; www.reckless.co.uk; 30 Berwick St W1; ⊖Oxford Circus or Tottenham Court Rd) Despite its numerous name changes, this outfit hasn't really changed in spirit. It still stocks new and secondhand records and CDs, from punk, soul, dance and independent to mainstream.

Phonica (Map p422; www.phonicarecords.co.uk; 51 Poland St W1; ⊖Tottenham Court Rd or Oxford Circus) A cool and relaxed Poland St store that stocks a lot of house, electro and hip hop, but you can find just about anything from reggae to dub, jazz and rock.

On the Beat (Map p426; 22 Hanway St W1; ⊖Tottenham Court Rd) Mostly '60s and '70s retro – along with helpful staff – in a tiny room plastered with posters.

MOLTON BROWN　　　　　BEAUTY

Map p432 (www.moltonbrown.co.uk; 18 Russell St WC2; ⊖Covent Garden) A fabulously fragrant British natural beauty range, Molton Brown is *the* choice for boutique hotel and posh restaurant bathrooms. Its skin-care products offer plenty of pampering for men and women. In this store you can also have a facial, and buy make-up and home accessories.

APPLE STORE　　　　　ELECTRONICS

Map p432 (www.apple.com/uk/retail/coventgarden; 1-7 The Piazza WC2; ⊖9am-9pm Mon-Sat, noon-6pm Sun; ⊖Covent Garden) Mac geeks of the world unite! Here's your temple, so come and warm your faces on the soft glow emanating from iPads to iPods, laptops to desktops, inside this white and airy emporium. There are daily workshops and talks to help make the best of your Apple ware, and the banks of iMacs are a free-for-all internet surfing base. Come and worship.

TED BAKER　　　　　FASHION

Map p432 (www.tedbaker.com; 9-10 Floral St WC2; ⊖Covent Garden) The one-time Glaswegian tailoring shop from Glasgow has grown into a superb brand of clothing with elegant men's and womenswear. Ted's forte is its formalwear, with beautiful dresses for women (lots of daring prints and exquisite material) and sharp tailoring for men; the casual collections (denim, beachwear etc) are excellent too.

FORBIDDEN PLANET MEGASTORE　　BOOKS

Map p432 (www.forbiddenplanet.com; 179 Shaftesbury Ave WC1; ⊖Covent Garden or Tottenham Court Rd) A trove of comics, sci-fi, horror and fantasy literature, this is an absolute dream for anyone into manga comics or off-beat genre titles.

PAUL SMITH　　　　　FASHION

Map p432 (www.paulsmith.co.uk; 40-44 Floral St WC2; ⊖Covent Garden) Paul Smith represents the best of British classics with innovative twists. Super-stylish menswear, suits and tailored shirts are all laid out on open shelves in this walk-in closet of a shop. Smith also does womenswear with its sharp tailoring for an androgynous, almost masculine, look.

LUCY IN DISGUISE — VINTAGE
Map p432 (www.lucyindisguiselondon.com; 10-13 Kings Street WC2; ⊖Covent Garden) Opened in 2010 and owned by singer Lily Allen, Lucy in Disguise is a high-end vintage boutique. The collection is a mix of haute couture (Yves St Laurent and Chanel numbers are not unusual) and unbranded garments. The large number of 1980s outfits can sometimes make you feel like you've walked into the dressing room of a *Dallas* or *Santa Barbara* filmset.

SPACE NK — BEAUTY
Map p432 (www.spacenk.co.uk; 32 Shelton St WC2; ⊖Covent Garden) Space NK specialises in skincare products and stocks such brands as Dr Hauschka, Eve Lom, Chantecaille, Kiehl's and Phyto, as well as anti-ageing products from the likes of 24/7 and Dr Sebagh. Men's products range from Anthony to Kiehl's.

BENJAMIN POLLOCK'S TOYSHOP — TOYS
Map p432 (www.pollocks-coventgarden.co.uk; 1st fl, 44 Covent Garden Market WC2; ⊖Covent Garden) Here's a traditional toyshop that's loved by kids of all ages. There are Victorian paper theatres, wooden marionettes and finger puppets, and antique teddy bears that might be too fragile to play with.

POSTE MISTRESS — SHOES
Map p432 (61-63 Monmouth St WC2; ⊖Leicester Sq or Covent Garden) This is where all shoe fetishists should head for the wonderful collection of women's shoes from Emma Hope, Vivienne Westwood, Miu Miu and Dries Van Noten. They're discounted from their original price, but still, this is for shoppers for whom money is no object.

🔒 Marylebone

CATH KIDSTON — HOMEWARES
Map p428 (www.cathkidston.co.uk; 51 Marylebone High St W1; ⊖Baker St) If you can rock the preppy look, you'll love Cath Kidston with her signature floral prints and 1950s fashion (dresses above the knee and cinched at the waist, cardigans, shawls and old-fashioned pyjamas). There is also a range of homeware.

MONOCLE SHOP — ACCESSORIES
Map p428 (www.monocle.com; 2a George St W1; ⊖Bond St) Run by the people behind the design and international current affairs magazine *Monocle,* this shop is pure understated heaven. True, most things cost more than many spend in a year, but if you're a fan of minimalist, quality design across the board (there are bicycles, clothes, bags and so on), you won't regret dropping in. Beautifully bound first editions are on sale here, as well as stunning photography.

🔒 Mayfair

STING — FASHION
Map p422 (www.thesting.nl; 1 Piccadilly Circus W1; ⊙10am-10pm Mon-Sat, noon-6pm Sun; ⊖Piccadilly Circus) The new kid on the fashion block, the Sting is a 'network of brands': most of the clothes it stocks are European labels that are little known in the UK. Spread over three floors, you'll find anything from casual sweatpants and fluoro T-shirts to elegant dresses, frilly tops and handsome shirts.

ABERCROMBIE & FITCH — FASHION
Map p422 (www.abercrombie.com; 7 Burlington Gardens W1; ⊖Piccadilly Circus) Abercrombie's signature wholesome look (denims, jersey tops, cosy knitwear, perfectly tailored cotton shirts) doesn't seem to wane in popularity, despite the relatively high price tag. This shop is busy from the minute it opens its doors, and at weekends queues for the till snake through the ground floor. The store itself is more nightclub than classic retail: loud dance music, dark, moody lighting, overpowering perfume and topless hunks greet you at the entrance.

APPLE STORE — COMPUTERS
Map p422 (www.apple.com/uk/retail/regent street; 235 Regent St W1; ⊙9am-9pm Mon-Sat, noon-6pm Sun; ⊖Oxford Circus) Another flagship Apple store, with daily workshops, hands-on advice and gleaming Apple products.

SELFRIDGES — DEPARTMENT STORE
Map p428 (www.selfridges.com; 400 Oxford St W1; ⊖Bond St) Selfridges loves innovation –

BOOKWORM PARADISE: THE WEST END'S BEST BOOKSHOPS

Daunt Books (Map p428; www.dauntbooks.co.uk; 83-84 Marylebone High St W1; ⊖Baker St) An original Edwardian bookshop, with oak panels and gorgeous skylights, Daunt is one of London's loveliest travel bookshops. It has two floors and the ground level is stacked with fiction and nonfiction titles; the lower ground is where to head if you're travel focused.

London Review Bookshop (Map p426; www.lrb.co.uk; 14 Bury Pl WC1; ⊖Russell Sq or Holborn) The bookshop of *London Review of Books* literary magazine doesn't believe in piles of books, taking the clever approach of stocking wide-ranging titles in one or two copies only. It often hosts high-profile author talks; there is also a charming **cafe** where you can peruse your new purchases.

Foyle's (Map p422; www.foyles.co.uk; 113-119 Charing Cross Rd WC2; ⊖Tottenham Court Rd) This is London's most legendary bookshop, where you can bet on finding even the most obscure of titles. The lovely **cafe** is on the 1st floor, and **Ray's Jazz** (see box, p135) is up on the 5th floor. In 2011, Foyle's also acquired **Grant & Cutler**, the UK's largest foreign-language bookseller, whose vast catalogue is now available on the 1st floor.

Stanford's (Map p432; www.stanfords.co.uk; 12-14 Long Acre WC2; ⊖Leicester Sq or Covent Garden) As a 150-year-old seller of maps, guides and literature, the grand-daddy of travel bookshops is a destination in its own right. Ernest Shackleton, David Livingstone, Michael Palin and even Brad Pitt have all popped in here.

Waterstone's (Map p422; www.waterstones.com; 203-206 Piccadilly W1; ⊖Piccadilly Circus) The chain's megastore is the largest bookshop in Europe, boasting knowledgeable staff and regular author readings and signings. The store spreads across four floors, and there is a cafe in the basement and a fabulous rooftop bar–restaurant, **5th View** (p118).

Gosh! (Map p426; www.goshlondon.com; 39 Great Russell St WC1; ⊖Tottenham Court Rd) Draw up here for graphic novels, manga, newspaper-strip collections and children's books, such as the Tintin and Asterix series. It's also perfect for finding presents for kids and teenagers.

it's famed for its inventive window displays by international artists, gala shows and, above all, its amazing range of products. It's the trendiest of London's one-stop shops, with labels such as Boudicca, Luella Bartley, Emma Cook, Chloé and Missoni; an unparalleled food hall; and Europe's largest cosmetics department.

MULBERRY ACCESSORIES

Map p428 (41-42 New Bond St W1; ⊘closed Sun; ⊖Bond St) Is there a woman in the world who doesn't covet a Mulberry bag? They are voluptuous, soft and a massive style statement. The brand followed in the footsteps of its other British design brethren, Burberry and Pringle, and modernised itself in recent years.

POSTE SHOES

Map p428 (10 South Molton St; ⊖Bond St) Sitting on one of London's most fashionable streets, this very cool shop is aimed at boys who like good shoes, and stocks everything from vintage street labels to razor-sharp Italian imports.

VIVIENNE WESTWOOD FASHION

Map p422 (www.viviennewestwood.com; 44 Conduit St W1; ⊘closed Sun; ⊖Bond St or Oxford Circus) The ex-punk who dressed the punks and created the punk look now says that 'fashion is boring' and that she disagrees with everything she used to say. Always a controversial character with a reputation for being a bit barmy (she flashed her privates to the paparazzi after receiving her OBE), Ms Westwood is, thankfully, still designing clothes as bold, innovative and provocative as ever, featuring 19th-century-inspired bustiers, wedge shoes, tartan and sharp tailoring.

BURBERRY FASHION

Map p428 (www.burberry.com; 21-23 New Bond St SW1; ⊖Bond St) The first traditional

British brand to reach the heights of fashion, Burberry is known for its innovative take on classic pieces (bright-coloured trench coats, khaki pants with large and unusual pockets), its brand check pattern and a tailored, groomed look. You'll see a lot of its catwalk pieces ripped off by high-street shops.

JOHN LEWIS
DEPARTMENT STORE

Map p428 (www.johnlewis.co.uk; 278-306 Oxford St W1; ⊖Oxford Circus) 'Never knowingly undersold' is the motto of this store, whose range of household goods, fashion and luggage is better described as reliable rather than cutting edge.

STELLA MCCARTNEY
FASHION

Map p428 (www.stellamccartney.co.uk; 30 Bruton St W1; ⊘closed Sun; ⊖Bond St) Her sharp tailoring, floaty designs and accessible style and 'ethical' approach to fashion (no leather or fur) is very of-the-moment. This three-storey terraced Victorian home is a minimalist showcase for the designer's current collections. Depending on your devotion and wallet, you'll feel right at ease or like an intruder.

WRIGHT & TEAGUE
JEWELLERY

Map p430 (www.wrightandteague.com; 35 Dover St W1; ⊘closed Sun; ⊖Green Park) The Wright & Teague gold charm bracelets are absolutely ravishing, as are its elegant silver and gold bangles, long necklaces and rings for men and women. What's more, many are very affordable.

KURT GEIGER
SHOES

Map p428 (www.kurtgeiger.com; 65 South Molton St W1; ⊖Bond St) Fashion, quality and affordability all come together at this superlative men's and women's shoe store, where footwear from the likes of Birkenstock, Chloé, Hugo Boss, Marc Jacobs, Paul Smith and United Nude adorns the shelves.

BUTLER & WILSON
ACCESSORIES

Map p428 (www.butlerandwilson.co.uk; 20 South Molton St SW1; ⊖Bond St) There's a sybaritic 1920s Shanghai vibe to Butler & Wilson's central branch, where costume jewellery, handbags, T-shirts and knick-knacks are sold beneath red Chinese lanterns.

RIGBY & PELLER
LINGERIE

Map p422 (www.rigbyandpeller.com; 22a Conduit St W1; ⊘closed Sun; ⊖Oxford Circus) This old-fashioned place makes the Queen's bras, but Rigby & Peller's fitting and alteration service – open to us plebs – is equally legendary. Get yourself measured – many a customer has been surprised to discover they've been wearing the wrong size for years. Off-the-peg underwear and swimwear is also available.

The City

Neighbourhood Top Five

1 Being bowled over by the spectacular Crown Jewels, the Yeoman Warders' (beefeaters') gruesome tales and the head-spinning wealth of history at the unmatchable **Tower of London** (p141).

2 Listening for whispers in the dome of **St Paul's Cathedral** (p147), before enjoying its awe-inspiring views.

3 Getting under the skin of the city at the excellent **Museum of London** (p154).

4 Imagining the spectacle of London ablaze as you climb the **Monument** (p152).

5 Marvelling at the ultramodern **30 St Mary Axe** (p151) and **Lloyd's of London** (p151).

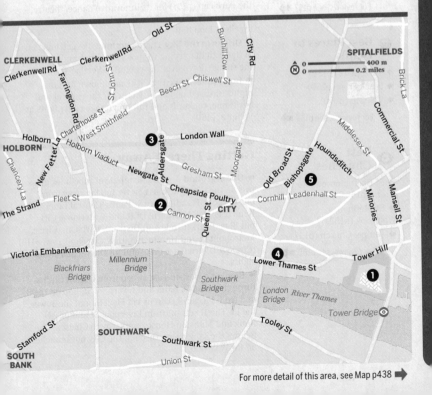

For more detail of this area, see Map p438 ➡

Lonely Planet's Top Tip

Designed by Jean Nouvel, **One New Change** (www.onenewchange.com; Cheapside EC2; ⊖St Paul's), a recently opened shopping centre, houses mainly run-of-the-mill, high-street brands, but take the lift to its 6th floor and a great open viewing platform will reward you with up-close views of the dome of St Paul's Cathedral and out over London.

✕ Best Places to Eat

➜ Sweeting's (p157)

➜ Café Below (p157)

➜ Restaurant at St Paul's (p157)

➜ City Càphê (p159)

For reviews, see p157 ➜

🍷 Best Places to Drink

➜ Vertigo 42 (p159)

➜ Black Friar (p159)

➜ Volupté (p160)

For reviews, see p159 ➜

👁 Best Churches

➜ St Bartholomew-the-Great (p155)

➜ St Stephen Walbrook (p152)

➜ Temple Church (p157)

For reviews, see p150 ➜

Explore: The City

For its size, the City punches well above its weight for attractions – there's literally an embarrassment of riches here when it comes to sightseeing. Start with the heavyweights – the Tower of London and St Paul's – and try to allow at least a half day for each. It's worth arriving early too, unless you like to queue. You can combine the other top sights with explorations of the City's lesser-known delights and quieter corners; the scores of churches make peaceful stops along the way.

While about 300,000 people work in the City of London, only 8000 actually live here. To really appreciate its frantic industry and hum, you're best to come during the week, which is when you'll find everything open. It empties quickly in the evening, though, as its workers retreat to the suburbs. Weekends have a very different appeal, giving you a lot more space for quiet contemplation, although you'll find most places shut tight until Monday. All of the big-hitting sights, however, open on at least one weekend day.

Local Life

➜ **Barbican** A powerhouse of culture, people flock to the Barbican (p154) for its innovative dance, theatre, music and art, stopping to enjoy lunch or a coffee in its excellent food hall.

➜ **Drinks in the Sky** There's nothing like getting a taste of the high life, trying to spot your house and watching the sun go down over the capital at Vertigo 42 (p159).

➜ **Burlesque** While the City's not known for late nights, dressed-up locals detour for the cabaret and burlesque, cocktails and full-on vintage club nights at Volupté (p160).

Getting There & Away

➜ **Underground** A veritable tangle of tube lines cross over in the City and you're never too far away from one of them. Handiest are St Paul's (Central Line) and Bank (Central, Northern, DLR and Waterloo & City), but Blackfriars (Circle and District), Barbican (Circle, Metropolitan and Hammersmith & City) and Tower Hill (Circle & District) are all useful for the further-flung sights.

➜ **Bus** For a west-to-east sweep from Oxford Circus through St Paul's, Bank and Liverpool St, hop on the 8; and from Piccadilly Circus via Fleet St and the Tower, the 15. The 11 sets off from Liverpool St and passes Bank and Mansion House on its way to Chelsea. The 26 follows the same route through the City but branches off for Waterloo.

The absolute kernel of London, with a history as bleak and bloody as it is fascinating, the Tower of London should be very near the top of anyone's list of London's sights. Begun during the reign of William the Conqueror (1066–87), the Tower is in fact a castle, and has served over the years as a palace, observatory, storehouse and mint. But it is, of course, most famous for its grizzly past as a prison and site of execution. Despite ever-growing ticket prices and the hordes of tourists, this is one of those rare pleasures: somewhere worth the hype.

You could spend days exploring the Tower and still have much left to see, but it's worth dedicating at least half a day to this incredible complex. Having a plan of attack is highly appropriate here and ours starts with one of the excellent Yeoman Warder's tours (p142).

Chapel Royal of St Peter ad Vincula

The culmination of your tour will leave you at the Chapel Royal of St Peter ad Vincula (St Peter in Chains), a rare example of ecclesiastical Tudor architecture and the burial place of those beheaded on the scaffold outside, most notably Anne Boleyn, Catherine Howard and Lady Jane Grey. Inside are monuments to luminaries from the Tower's history (although the chapel can only be accessed on a tour).

Tower Green Scaffold Site

Those 'lucky' enough to meet their fate here (rather than suffering the embarrassment of execution on Tower Hill) include the alleged adulterers Anne Boleyn and Catherine

DON'T MISS...

→ A Yeoman Warder's tour

→ Crown Jewels

→ White Tower and St John's Chapel

→ Tower Green scaffold site

→ Ravens

→ Medieval Palace

PRACTICALITIES

→ Map p438

→ www.hrp.org.uk

→ Tower Hill EC3

→ adult/child £19.80/10.45; audio guides £4

→ ⊙9am-5.30pm Tue-Sat, 10am-5.30pm Sun & Mon, closes 4.30pm daily Nov-Feb, last admission 30min before closing time

→ ⊖Tower Hill

Howard; the latter's lady-in-waiting, Jane Rochford; Margaret Pole, countess of Salisbury, descended from the House of York; 16-year-old Lady Jane Grey, who fell foul of Henry's daughter Mary I by being her rival for the throne; William, Lord Hastings; and Robert Devereux, Earl of Essex, once a favourite of Elizabeth I. In the case of Devereux, the authorities perhaps also feared a popular uprising in his support. The site is now commemorated by a commissioned sculpture by the artist Brian Catling, made up of two discs with a glass pillow resting on top, and a remembrance poem. To the left of the scaffold site is the Beauchamp Tower, where high-ranking prisoners have left behind unhappy inscriptions.

Crown Jewels

To the east of the chapel and north of the White Tower is the building that visitors most want to see: **Waterloo Barracks**, the home of the Crown Jewels. Here, you file past footage of Queen Elizabeth II's coronation, backed by stirring patriotic music, before you reach the vault itself (check out the doors as you go in – they look like they'd survive a nuclear attack). Once inside you'll be confronted with ornate sceptres, plates, orbs and, naturally, crowns. A travelator takes you past the dozen or so crowns that are the centrepiece, including the £27.5-million Imperial State Crown, set with diamonds (2868 of them, to be exact), sapphires, emeralds, rubies and pearls, and the platinum crown of the late Queen Mother, Elizabeth, which is famously set with the 105-carat Koh-i-Noor (Mountain of Light) diamond. Surrounded by myth and legend, the 14th-century diamond has been claimed by both India and Afghanistan. It reputedly confers enormous power on its owner, but male owners are destined to die a tormented death. At the time of writing, the Crown Jewels display was due to be redesigned in time for the Queen's Diamond Jubilee in June 2012, which should help reduce the sometimes very long queues.

Behind the Waterloo Barracks is the Bowyer Tower, where George, Duke of Clarence, brother and rival of Edward IV, was imprisoned and, according to a long-standing legend that has never been proved, was drowned in a barrel of malmsey (sweet Madeira wine).

White Tower

Begun in 1078 this was the original 'Tower' of London, built as a palace and fortress. While by modern standards it's not exactly tall, in the Middle Ages it would have dwarfed the huts of the peasantry surrounding the castle walls. Inside, along with St John's Chapel, the tower has retained a couple of remnants of Norman architecture, including a fireplace and garderobe (lavatory). Most of its interior, however, is given over to a Royal Armouries collection of cannons, guns and suits of armour for men and horses. Among the most remarkable exhibits on the 1st floor is Henry VIII's suit of armour, made for the monarch's bloated body in his forties. On the 2nd floor, check out the 2m suit of armour made for John of Gaunt (to see that coming towards you on a battlefield must have been terrifying) and, alongside it, a tiny child's suit of armour designed for James I's young son, Henry. Up on the 3rd floor you'll find the block and axe used at the last execution on Tower Hill in 1747, along with some amusing interactive displays.

St John's Chapel

This chapel, dating from 1080, with its vaulted ceiling, rounded archways and 12 stone pillars, is actually one of the finest examples of Romanesque architecture in the country. Elizabeth of York, wife of grief-stricken Henry VII, lay in state here for 12 days, surrounded by candles, having died after complications in childbirth in 1503. It has also served as a records office, but today is again a working chapel and holds services throughout the year.

The Ravens

Legend has it that Charles II requested that ravens always be kept at the Tower on the basis that if they were to leave, the kingdom would fall apart. Having lived through the plague and the Great Fire, disaster was probably fresh in his mind and he clearly wasn't willing to take any chances. Other camps, however, maintain that this may well be a Victorian fairy story. The stretch of green between the Wakefield and White Towers is where the famous ravens are found. There are usually eight ravens permanently at the Tower and their wings are clipped to placate the superstitious. The birds are all named and live much longer here than they would in the wild; watching them being fed chunks of meat is a fascinating sight.

Medieval Palace

Inside St Thomas' Tower, you can look at what the hall and bedchamber of Edward I might once have looked like. Here archaeologists have peeled back the layers of newer buildings to find what went before. Opposite St Thomas' Tower is Wakefield Tower, built by Henry III between 1220 and 1240. Its upper floor is

OTHER HIGHLIGHTS

On entering the Tower you'll cross the **moat**, which was finally drained of centuries of festering sewage in the 19th century, necessitated by persistent cholera outbreaks. A superbly manicured lawn now takes its place. Before you stands the **Bell Tower**, housing the curfew bells and one-time lock-up to Thomas More. The politician and author of *Utopia* was imprisoned here in 1534 before his execution for refusing to recognise King Henry VIII as head of the Church of England in place of the Pope.

Continuing along Water Lane you come to the famous **Traitors' Gate**, the gateway through which prisoners being brought by river entered the tower. Opposite Traitors' Gate is the huge portcullis of the **Bloody Tower**, taking its nickname from the 'princes in the tower', Edward V and his younger brother, who were held 'for their own safety' here and later murdered to annul their claims to the throne. The blame is usually laid at the door of their uncle, Richard III. An exhibition inside allows you to vote for your prime suspect. There are also exhibits on Elizabethan adventurer Sir Walter Raleigh, who was imprisoned here three times by the capricious Elizabeth I, most significantly from 1605 to 1616.

TACKLING THE TOWER

Although it's usually less busy in the late afternoon, don't leave your assault on the Tower until too late in the day. You could easily spend hours here and not see it all. Start by getting your bearings with the hour-long Yeoman Warder (Beefeater) tours; they're included in the cost of admission, entertaining and the only way to access the **Chapel Royal of St Peter ad Vincula 1** which is where they finish up.

When you leave the chapel, the **Tower Green scaffold site 2** is directly in front. The building immediately to your left is Waterloo Barracks , where the **Crown Jewels 3** are housed. These are the absolute highlight of a Tower visit, so keep an eye on the entrance and pick a time to visit when it looks relatively quiet. Once inside, take things at your own pace. Slow-moving travelators shunt you past the dozen or so crowns that are the treasury's centrepiece, but feel free to double-back for a second or even third pass – particularly if you ended up on the rear travelator the first time around. Allow plenty of time for the **White Tower 4** , the core of the whole complex, starting with the exhibition of royal armour. As you continue onto the 2nd floor, keep an eye out for **St John's Chapel 5** . The famous **ravens 6** can be seen in the courtyard around the White Tower. Head next through the towers that formed the **Medieval Palace 7** , then take the **East Wall Walk 8** to get a feel for the castle's mighty battlements. Spend the rest of your time poking around the many, many other fascinating nooks and crannies of the Tower complex.

BEAT THE QUEUES

➡ **Buy** your fast-track ticket in advance online or at the City of London Information Centre in St Paul's Churchyard.

➡ **Palacepalooza** An annual Historic Royal Palaces membership allows you to jump the queues and visit the Tower (and four other London palaces) as often as you like.

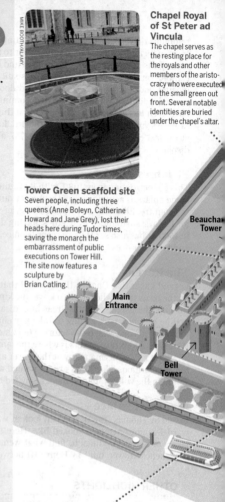

MIKE BOOTH/ALAMY.

Chapel Royal of St Peter ad Vincula
The chapel serves as the resting place for the royals and other members of the aristocracy who were executed on the small green out front. Several notable identities are buried under the chapel's altar.

Tower Green scaffold site
Seven people, including three queens (Anne Boleyn, Catherine Howard and Jane Grey), lost their heads here during Tudor times, saving the monarch the embarrassment of public executions on Tower Hill. The site now features a sculpture by Brian Catling.

Beaucha
Tower

Main
Entrance

Bell
Tower

White Tower
Much of the White Tower is taken up with this exhibition of 500 years of royal armour. Look for the virtually cuboid suit made to match Henry VIII's bloated body, complete with an oversized armoured pouch to protect his, ahem, crown jewels.

PAWEL LIBERA IMAGES/ALAMY.

St John's Chapel

Kept as plain and unadorned as it would have been in Norman times, the White Tower's 2nd-floor chapel is the oldest surviving church in London, dating from 1080.

Crown Jewels

When they're not being worn for affairs of state, Her Majesty's bling is kept here. Among the 23,578 gems, look out for the 530-carat Cullinan diamond at the top of the Royal Sceptre, the largest part of what was (until 1985) the largest diamond ever found.

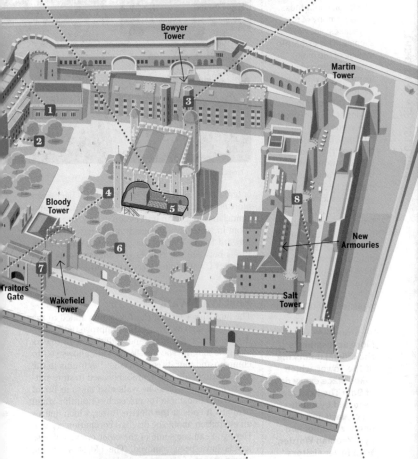

Bowyer Tower

Martin Tower

1

2

3

Bloody Tower

4

5

8

New Armouries

6

7

Traitors' Gate

Wakefield Tower

Salt Tower

Medieval Palace

This part of the Tower complex was commenced around 1220 and was home to England's medieval monarchs. Look for the recreations of the bedchamber of Edward I (1272–1307) in St Thomas's Tower and the throne room on the upper floor of the Wakefield Tower.

Ravens

This stretch of green is where the Tower's famous ravens are kept, fed on raw meat and blood-soaked bird biscuits. According to legend, if the birds were to leave the Tower, the kingdom would fall.

East Wall Walk

Follow the inner ramparts, starting from the 13th-century Salt Tower, passing through the Broad Arrow and Constable Towers, and ending at the Martin Tower, where the Crown Jewels were once stored.

CEREMONIES AT THE TOWER

As befits a building so steeped in history, the Tower still conducts a number of age-old ceremonies, some of which you can witness. The Ceremony of the Keys takes place every evening. This elaborate locking of the main gates has been performed daily without fail for more than 700 years. The ceremony begins at 9.53pm precisely, and it's all over by 10pm. Even when a bomb hit the Tower of London during the Blitz, the ceremony was only delayed by 30 minutes – the essence of the famed stiff upper lip. Entry to the ceremony begins at 9.30pm and is free but, in a suitably antiquated style, you have to apply for tickets by post as demand is so high. See the Tower website for details.

More accessible is the official unlocking of the Tower, which takes place every day at 9am The keys are escorted by a military guard and the doors are unlocked by a Yeoman Warder. With fewer visitors around, this is a great time to arrive, although you'll have to wait until 10am on a Sunday or Monday to begin your visit.

Yeoman Warders (beefeaters)

entered from St Thomas' Tower and has been even more enticingly furnished with a replica throne and candelabra to give an impression of how, as an anteroom in a medieval palace, it might have looked in Edward I's day. During the 15th-century War of the Roses between the Houses of Lancaster and York, Henry VI was almost certainly murdered in this tower.

East Wall Walk

The huge inner wall of the Tower was added to the fortress in 1220 by Henry III to improve the castle's defences. It is 36m wide and is dotted with towers along its length. The East Wall Walk allows you to climb up and tour its eastern edge, beginning in the 13th-century Salt Tower, probably used to store saltpetre for gunpowder. The walk also takes in Broad Arrow and Constable Towers, each containing small exhibits. It ends at the Martin Tower, which houses an exhibition about the original coronation regalia. Here you can see some of the older crowns, whose jewels have been removed. The oldest surviving crown is that of George I, which is topped with the ball and cross from James II's crown. It was from the Martin Tower that Colonel Thomas Blood attempted to steal the Crown Jewels in 1671, disguised as a clergyman.

TOP SIGHTS
TOWER OF LONDON

TOP SIGHTS
ST PAUL'S CATHEDRAL

Towering over Ludgate Hill, in a superb position that has been a place of worship for over 1400 years, St Paul's Cathedral is one of London's most majestic and recognisable buildings. For Londoners the vast dome, which still manages to dominate the skyline despite the far higher skyscrapers of the Square Mile, is a symbol of resilience and pride, standing tall for over 300 years. Viewing Sir Christopher Wren's masterwork from the inside, and climbing to its height for sweeping views of the capital, is an exhilarating experience.

Completed in 1710 (although this date is debated), and sporting the capital's largest church dome, this is the fifth church to stand on this site. Having undergone a huge restoration project to coincide with its 300th anniversary in 2010, the cathedral is today looking better than it has done for decades.

One of the best ways to explore the cathedral is by joining a free 1½-hour guided tour, which grants you access to the Geometric Staircase and Chapel of St Michael and St George. These usually take place four times a day (10.45am, 11.15am, 1.30pm and 2pm); head to the desk just past the entrance to book in. You can also enquire here about the shorter introductory talks available. If you'd rather go at your own pace, pick up one of the free 45-minute iPod tours (in multiple languages) at the entrance.

DON'T MISS...

➡ Climbing the dome

➡ Quire

➡ Tombs of Admiral Nelson and Duke of Wellington

PRACTICALITIES

➡ Map p149

➡ www.stpauls.co.uk

➡ St Paul's Church-yard EC4

➡ adult/child £14.50/5.50

➡ ⊘8.30am-4.30pm Mon-Sat, last admission 4pm

Dome

Despite all the fascinating history and its impressive interior, people are usually most interested in climbing the dome for one of the best views of London imaginable. It actually consists of three domes, one inside the other, and it made the cathedral Wren's tour de force. Exactly 528 stairs take you to the top, but it's a three-stage journey. Through a door on the

REFRESHMENTS & FACILITIES

In the crypt you'll find the **Crypt Café** (dishes £5.65-7.40; ⊘9am-5pm Mon-Sat, noon-4pm Sun) for light meals, and the excellent Restaurant at St Paul's (p157), in addition to a **shop** (⊘8.30am-5pm Mon-Sat, 10am-4.30pm Sun). Anyone is welcome to use the facilities in the cathedral crypt (for free), entering via the side door under the north transept; you can enter the cafe, restaurant and shop, use the toilet, shelter from bad weather, or even just enjoy a packed lunch here.

As part of the 300th anniversary celebrations, St Paul's has undergone a £40-million renovation project that has cleaned the cathedral inside and out – a painstakingly slow process that has been likened to carefully applying and removing a face pack. By the enormous Great West Door (opened only on special occasions), seek out a glass panel, known as the 'dirty panel', which has preserved a section of the wall to demonstrate just how black and gloomy St Paul's had become.

western side of the southern transept and some 30m and precisely 257 steps above, you reach the interior walkway around the dome's base. This is the **Whispering Gallery**, so called because if you talk close to the wall it really does carry your words around to the opposite side, 32m away. Climbing even more steps (another 119) you reach the **Stone Gallery**, an exterior viewing platform rather obscured by pillars and other suicide-preventing measures. The remaining 152 iron steps to the **Golden Gallery** are steeper and narrower than below but are really worth the effort. From here, 85m above London, you can enjoy superb 360-degree views of the city.

Interior

Back on the ground St Paul's offers plenty of riches for those who like to keep their feet firmly on its black-and-white tiled floor. Just beneath the dome is a compass and **epitaph** written for Wren by his son: *Lector, si monumentum requiris, circumspice* (Reader, if you seek his monument, look around you). In the northern aisle you'll find the grandiose **Duke of Wellington Memorial** (1875). In the north transept chapel is Holman Hunt's celebrated painting, **The Light of the World**, which depicts Christ knocking at an overgrown door that, symbolically, can only be opened from the inside. Beyond, in the cathedral's heart, are the particularly spectacular **quire** (or chancel) – its ceilings and arches dazzling with green, blue, red and gold mosaics – and the **high altar**. The ornately carved choir stalls by Grinling Gibbons on either side of the quire are exquisite, as are the ornamental wrought-iron gates, separating the aisles from the altar, by Jean Tijou (both men also worked on Hampton Court Palace). Walk around the altar, with its massive gilded oak canopy, to the **American Memorial Chapel**, a memorial to the 28,000 Americans based in Britain who lost their lives during WWII.

Around the southern side of the ambulatory is the **effigy of John Donne** (1573–1631), metaphysical poet and one-time dean of St Paul's.

Crypt

On the eastern side of both the north and south transepts are stairs leading down to the crypt and **OBE Chapel**, where services are held for members of the Order of the British Empire. The crypt has memorials to some 300 military demigods, including Florence Nightingale and Lord Kitchener, while both the Duke of Wellington and Admiral Nelson are actually buried here, Nelson having been placed in a black sarcophagus that is directly under the centre of the dome. On the surrounding walls are plaques in memory of those from the Commonwealth who died in various conflicts during the 20th century.

Wren's tomb is also in the crypt, and architect Edwin Lutyens, painter Joshua Reynolds and poet William Blake are remembered here too. The **Oculus**, opened in 2010 in the former treasury, projects four short films onto its walls (you'll need to have picked up the iPod audiotour to hear the sound). If you're not keen on scaling the dome, you can experience it here, audiovisually, from the ground.

Exterior

Just outside the north transept, there's a simple **monument** to the people of London, honouring the 32,000 civilians killed (and another 50,000 seriously injured) in the city during WWII. Also to the left as you face the entrance stairway is **Temple Bar**, one of the original gateways to the City of London. This medieval stone archway once straddled Fleet St at a site marked by a griffin but was removed to Middlesex in 1878. Temple Bar was restored and made a triumphal return to London (albeit in a totally new place) alongside the redevelopment of Paternoster Square in 2003.

ST PAUL'S CATHEDRAL

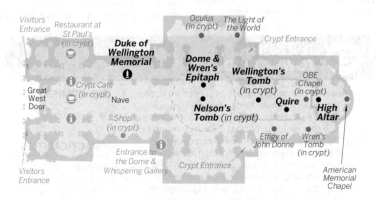

Ground Floor & Crypt

THE CITY ST PAUL'S CATHEDRAL

⊙ SIGHTS

TOWER OF LONDON HISTORICAL BUILDING
See p141.

ST PAUL'S CATHEDRAL CHURCH
See p147.

FREE **ALL HALLOWS-BY-THE-TOWER** CHURCH
Map p438 (www.ahbtt.org.uk; Byward St EC3;
⊘8am-6pm Mon-Fri, 10am-5pm Sat & Sun; ⊖Tower Hill) A church by the name All Hallows
(meaning 'All Saints') has stood on this site
since AD 675, and the best bit of the building today is undoubtedly its atmospheric
Saxon undercroft (crypt). There you'll find a
pavement of reused Roman tiles and walls
of the 7th-century Saxon church, as well
as coins and bits of local history. Above
ground it's a pleasant enough church, rebuilt after WWII. There's a copper spire
(added in 1957 to make the church stand
out more), a pulpit from a Wren church in
Cannon St that was destroyed in WWII
and a beautiful 17th-century font cover by
the master woodcarver Grinling Gibbons.
From April to September, free 20-minute
church tours leave at 2pm each day.

TRINITY SQUARE GARDENS GARDENS
Map p438 (⊖Tower Hill) Trinity Square Gardens, just to the west of Tower Hill tube
station, was once the site of the Tower Hill
scaffold where many met their fate, the last
in 1747. Now it's a much more peaceful little
place and home to Edwin Lutyens' memorial to the marines and merchant sailors
who lost their lives during WWI. Just outside Tower Hill tube station, a giant bronze
sundial depicts the history of London from
AD 43 to 1982, and on a grassy area next
to the tube's main exit there's a stretch of
the **medieval wall** built on Roman foundations, with a modern statue of Emperor Trajan (r AD 98–117) standing in front of it. At
the other end of the tunnel, to the right, is
a postern (gate) dating from the 13th century. You can see more of the **roman wall**
around the corner from the tube station,
in the forecourt of the **Grange Hotel** (8-14
Cooper's Row), where there's also a little information board.

FREE **ST OLAVE** CHURCH
Map p438 (www.sanctuaryinthecity.net; 8 Hart
St EC3; ⊘9am-5pm Mon-Fri, closed Aug; ⊖Tower
Hill) Tucked at the end of quiet Seething

⊙ TOP SIGHTS
TOWER BRIDGE

Perhaps second only to Big Ben as London's most recognisable symbol, Tower Bridge doesn't disappoint up
close. There's something about its neo-Gothic towers
and blue suspension struts that make it quite enthralling. Built in 1894 as a much-needed crossing point
in the east, it was equipped with a then revolutionary
bascule (see-saw) mechanism that could clear the way
for oncoming ships in three minutes. Although London's
days as a thriving port are long over, the bridge still does
its stuff, lifting around 1000 times a year and as often as
10 times a day in summer.

Housed within is the **Tower Bridge Exhibition**,
which explains the nuts and bolts of it all. If you're not
technically minded, it's still fascinating to get inside
the bridge and look along the Thames from its two
walkways. A lift takes you to the top of the structure,
42m above the river, from where you can walk along the
east- and west-facing walkways, lined with information
boards. There are a couple of stops on the way down
before you exit and continue on to the Engine Rooms,
which provide the real mechanical detail, and also house
a few interactive exhibits and a couple of short films.

DON'T MISS...
➡ Bridge lifting

PRACTICALITIES
➡ Map p438
➡ Bridge lift times
☑7940 3984 or
check web
➡ www.towerbridge.org.uk
➡ Tower Bridge Rd
SE1
➡ adult/child
£8/3.40
➡ ⊘10am-6.30pm
Apr-Oct, 9.30am-
6pm Nov-Mar, last
admission 1hr before
closing
➡ ⊖Tower Hill

Lane, St Olave's was built in the mid-15th century, and restored in the 1950s. Most famous of those who worshipped at the church is Samuel Pepys, who is buried here with his wife Elizabeth. Dickens called the place 'St Ghastly Grim' because of the skulls above its entrance, but today it's a lovely little spot.

30 ST MARY AXE (GHERKIN)   BUILDING

Map p438 (www.30stmaryaxe.co.uk; 30 St Mary Axe EC3; ⊖Aldgate or Bank) Known to one and all as 'the Gherkin' (for obvious reasons when you see its incredible shape), 30 St Mary Axe – as it is officially and far more prosaically named – remains London's most distinctive skyscraper, dominating the city despite actually being slightly smaller than the neighbouring NatWest Tower. The phallic Gherkin's futuristic, sci-fi exterior has become an emblem of modern London as recognisable as Big Ben or the London Eye.

Built in 2002–03 to a multi-award-winning design by Norman Foster, this is London's first ecofriendly skyscraper: Foster laid out the offices so they spiral around internal 'sky gardens'. The windows can be opened and the gardens are used to reprocess stale air, so air-conditioning is kept to a minimum. Its primary fuel source is gas, low-energy lighting is used throughout the building and the design maximises the amount of natural light let into the building, meaning that less electricity is used. You'll have to take our word for it though, as there's unfortunately no access to the public.

LLOYD'S OF LONDON   BUILDING

Map p438 (www.lloyds.com; 1 Lime St EC3; ⊖Aldgate or Bank) While the world's leading insurance brokers are inside underwriting everything from cosmonauts' lives to film stars' legs, people outside still stop to gawp at the stainless-steel external ducting and staircases of the Lloyd's of London building. The work of Richard Rogers, one of the architects of the Pompidou Centre in Paris, its brave-new-world postmodernism strikes a particular contrast with the olde-worlde Leadenhall Market next door. While you can watch people whizzing up and down the outside of the building in its all-glass lifts, sadly you can't experience it yourself.

LEADENHALL MARKET   MARKET

Map p438 (www.leadenhallmarket.co.uk; Whittington Ave EC3; ⊗public areas 24hr, shop opening times vary; ⊖Bank) Like stepping into a small slice of Victorian London, a visit to this covered mall off Gracechurch St is a minor time-travelling experience. There's been a market on this site since the Roman era, but the architecture that survives is all cobblestones and late-19th-century ironwork; even modern restaurants and chain stores decorate their facades in period style here. The market appears as Diagon Alley in *Harry Potter and the Philosopher's Stone*.

FREE BANK OF ENGLAND MUSEUM   MUSEUM

Map p438 (www.bankofengland.co.uk; Bartholomew Lane EC2; ⊗10am-5pm Mon-Fri; ⊖Bank) When William III declared war against France in the 17th century, he looked over his shoulder and soon realised he didn't have the funds to finance his armed forces. A Scottish merchant by the name of William Paterson came up with the idea of forming a joint-stock bank that could lend the government money and, in 1694, so began the Bank of England and the notion of national debt. The bank rapidly expanded in size and stature and moved to this site in 1734. During a financial crisis at the end of the 18th century, a cartoon appeared depicting the bank as a haggard old woman, and this is probably the origin of its nickname 'the Old Lady of Threadneedle St'. The institution is now in charge of maintaining the integrity of the British currency and financial system and, since 1997, also sets interest rates. Sir John Soane built the original structure, although unfortunately most of his splendid bank was demolished in the early 20th century and replaced with a more utilitarian model.

The centrepiece of the museum – which explores the evolution of money and the history of this venerable institution, and is not *nearly* as dull as it sounds – is a reconstruction of Soane's original stock office, complete with original mahogany counters. A series of rooms leading off the office are packed with exhibits ranging from silverware and coins to a gold bar you can lift up (it's amazingly heavy) and the muskets once used to defend the bank.

ROYAL EXCHANGE   HISTORIC BUILDING

Map p438 (www.theroyalexchange.com; Royal Exchange EC3; ⊗10am-11pm Mon-Fri; ⊖Bank) Founded by Thomas Gresham, this is the imposing, colonnaded building at the juncture of Threadneedle St and Cornhill to the east. It's the third building on a site originally chosen in 1564 by Gresham. It has not had a role as a financial institution since the 1980s and now houses a posh shopping centre and a cafe (Royal Exchange Grand Café & Bar; p159) and restaurant (Sauterelle; p159).

MANSION HOUSE   HISTORIC BUILDING
Map p438 (www.cityoflondon.gov.uk; guided tour adult/concession £6/4; ⊘tour 2pm Tue; ⊖Bank) Between King William St and Walbrook stands the grand, porticoed Mansion House, the official residence of the Lord Mayor of London, which was built in the mid-18th century by George Dance the Elder. It's not open to the public except on the weekly tour, which leaves from the porch entrance on Walbrook, with a maximum of 40 participants; tickets are sold on a first-come-first-served basis. Inside there are magnificent interiors, an impressive art collection and a stunning banqueting hall.

FREE ST STEPHEN WALBROOK   CHURCH
Map p438 (www.ststephenwalbrook.net; 39 Walbrook EC4; ⊘10am-4pm Mon-Fri; ⊖Bank) Along Walbrook, past the City of London Magistrates Court, is St Stephen Walbrook, built in 1672. Widely considered to be the finest of Wren's City churches and a forerunner to St Paul's Cathedral, this light and airy building is indisputably impressive. Some 16 pillars with Corinthian capitals rise up to support its dome and ceiling, while a large cream-coloured boulder lies at the heart of its roomy central space. There is a modern altar by sculptor Henry Moore, cheekily dubbed 'the Camembert' by critics.

FREE ST MARY WOOLNOTH   CHURCH
Map p438 (⊘9.30am-4.30pm Mon-Fri; ⊖Bank) In the angle between Lombard and King William Sts, Nicholas Hawksmoor's St Mary Woolnoth is recognisable by its distinctive twin towers. Completed in 1727, it is the architect's only City church and its interior Corinthian columns are a foretaste of his Christ Church in Spitalfields.

FREE ST MARY-LE-BOW   CHURCH
Map p438 (www.stmarylebow.co.uk; Cheapside EC2; ⊘7.30am-6pm Mon-Wed, to 6.30pm Thu, to 4pm Fri; ⊖Bank or St Paul's) Another of Wren's great churches, St Mary-le-Bow was built

TOP SIGHTS
MONUMENT

Sir Christopher Wren and Dr Robert Hooke's huge 1677 column, known simply as the Monument, is a memorial to the Great Fire of London of 1666, whose impact on London's history cannot be overstated. Tens of thousands of Londoners were left homeless and much of the city was destroyed.

An immense Doric column made of Portland stone, it is 4.5m wide, and 60.6m tall – the exact distance it stands from the bakery in Pudding Lane where the fire reputedly started – and is topped with a gilded bronze urn of flames that some call a big gold pincushion. Although a midget by today's standards, the Monument would have been gigantic, and towered over London, when first built.

Climbing up the column's 311 steps, which wind round an impressive circular staircase, rewards you with some of the best 360-degree views over London (due to its centrality as much as to its height). And after your descent, you'll also be the proud owner of a certificate that commemorates your achievement.

DON'T MISS...
➡ Fantastic views
➡ Claiming your certificate

PRACTICALITIES
➡ Map p438
➡ www.themonument.info
➡ Monument St EC3
➡ adult/child £3/1.50
➡ ⊘9.30am-5.30pm, last admission 5pm
➡ ⊖Monument

in 1673. It's famous as the church with the bells that dictate who is – and who isn't – a cockney; it's said that a true cockney has to have been born within earshot of Bow Bells, although before the advent of motor traffic this would have been a far greater area than it is today (see also p222). The church's delicate steeple is one of Wren's finest works and the modern stained glass is striking.

TEMPLE OF MITHRAS   RUIN

Map p438 (Queen Victoria St; ⊖Bank) A short way along Queen Victoria St, on the left, you'll find the remains of the 3rd-century AD Temple of Mithras. This potentially fascinating site was uncovered in the 1950s during the construction of Bucklersbury House, an office block on Walbrook St. The entire site was moved to its current location shortly afterwards for display. There's not a lot to see but if you're interested in this Persian god, artefacts found in the temple are on display at the Museum of London (p154). At the time of writing, the creation of Walbrook Square, an office and retail development, was underway, within which the remains are set to be displayed on their original site.

FREE GUILDHALL   HISTORIC BUILDING

Map p438 (www.cityoflondon.gov.uk; Gresham St EC2; ⊙9am-5pm unless closed for events, closed Sun Oct-Apr; ⊖Bank or St Paul's) Bang in the centre of the Square Mile, the Guildhall has been the City's seat of government for nearly 800 years. The present building dates from the early 15th century, making it the only secular stone structure to have survived the Great Fire of 1666, although it was severely damaged both then and during the Blitz of 1940.

Check in at reception to visit the impressive **Great Hall** (ring ahead as it often closes for formal functions), where you can see the banners and shields of London's 12 guilds (principal livery companies), which used to wield absolute power throughout the city. The lord mayor and sheriffs are still elected annually in the vast open hall, with its chunky chandeliers and church-style monuments. Among the monuments to look out for are statues of Winston Churchill, Admiral Nelson, the Duke of Wellington and the two prime ministers Pitt the Elder and Younger. In the minstrels' gallery at the western end are statues of the biblical giants Gog and Magog, traditionally

considered to be guardians of the city; today's figures replaced similar 18th-century statues destroyed in the Blitz. The Guildhall's stained glass was also blown out during the Blitz but a modern window in the southwestern corner depicts the city's history; look out for a picture of London's first lord mayor, Richard 'Dick' Whittington, and his famous cat.

The buildings to the west house Corporation of London offices and the **Guildhall Library** (Aldermanbury EC2; ⊙9.30am-5pm Mon-Sat), founded in 1425 under the terms of Dick Whittington's will. It specialises in the history of London and English local studies. Also here is the **Clockmakers' Museum** (www.clockmakers.org; admission free; ⊙9.30am-4.45pm Mon-Sat), which has a collection of more than 700 clocks and watches dating back some 500 years. It closes for an (unspecified) hour or two each week to wind the clocks.

FREE GUILDHALL ART GALLERY & ROMAN LONDON AMPHITHEATRE   GALLERY

Map p438 (www.guildhall-art-gallery.org.uk; Guildhall Yard EC2; charge for temporary exhibits; ⊙10am-5pm Mon-Sat, noon-4pm Sun; ⊖Bank) The gallery of the City of London provides a fascinating look at the politics of the Square Mile over the past few centuries, with a great collection of paintings of London in the 18th and 19th centuries, as well as the vast frieze entitled *The Defeat of the Floating Batteries* (1791), depicting the British victory at the Siege of Gibraltar in 1782. This huge painting was removed to safety just a month before the gallery was hit by a German bomb in 1941 – it spent 50 years rolled up before a spectacular restoration in 1999.

An even more recent arrival is a sculpture of former prime minister Margaret Thatcher, which has to be housed in a protective glass case as the Iron Lady was decapitated here by an angry punter with a cricket bat soon after its installation in 2002. Today, following some tricky neck surgery, Maggie has rejoined the gallery's collection, but her contentious legacy lives on.

The real highlight of the museum is deep in the darkened basement, where the archaeological remains of Roman London's amphitheatre (coliseum) lie. Discovered only in 1988 when work finally began on a new gallery following the original's destruction in the Blitz, they were immediately declared an ancient monument, and the new gallery was built around them. While only a few remnants of the stone walls lining the eastern entrance still stand, they're imaginatively fleshed out with a black-and-fluorescent-green *trompe l'oeil* of the missing seating, and computer-meshed outlines of spectators and gladiators. The roar of the crowd goes up as you reach the end of the entrance tunnel and hit the central stage, giving a real sense of how Roman London might have felt. Markings on the square outside the Guildhall indicate the original extent of the amphitheatre, allowing people to visualise its scale.

 ST LAWRENCE JEWRY CHURCH
Map p438 (www.stlawrencejewry.org.uk; Gresham St EC2; ⊙8am-4pm; ⊖Bank) To look at the Corporation of London's extremely well preserved official church, you'd barely realise that it was almost completely destroyed during WWII. Instead it does Sir Christopher Wren, who built it in 1677, and its subsequent restorers proud, with its immaculate alabaster walls and gilt trimmings. The arms of the City of London can be seen on the north wall and the Commonwealth Chapel is bedecked with the flags of member nations. Free piano recitals are held each Monday at 1pm; organ recitals at the same time on Tuesday.

As the church name suggests, this was once part of the Jewish quarter – the centre being Old Jewry, the street to the southeast. The district was sadly not without its pogroms. After some 500 Jews were killed in 1262 in mob 'retaliation' against a Jewish moneylender, Edward I expelled the entire community from London to Flanders in 1290. It did not return until the late 17th century.

BARBICAN HISTORIC BUILDING
Map p438 (www.barbican.org.uk; Silk St EC2; ⊙arts centre 9am-11pm Mon-Sat, noon-11pm Sun; ⊛; ⊖Barbican or Moorgate) Londoners remain fairly divided about the architectural legacy of this vast housing and cultural complex in the heart of the City. While the Barbican is named after a Roman fortification that may once have stood here protecting ancient Londinium, what you see today is very much a product of the 1960s and '70s. Built on a huge bomb site abandoned since WWII and opened progressively be-

---

TOP SIGHTS
MUSEUM OF LONDON

One of the capital's best museums, this is a fascinating walk through the various incarnations of the city from Anglo-Saxon village to 21st-century metropolis. The first gallery, London Before London, brings to life the ancient settlements that predated the capital and is followed by the Roman era, full of interesting displays and models. The rest of the floor takes you through the Saxon, medieval, Tudor and Stuart periods, culminating in the Great Fire of 1666. From here head down to the modern galleries, opened in 2010, where, in Expanding City, you'll find exquisite fashion and jewellery, the graffitied walls of a prison cell (1750) and the *Rhinebeck Panorama*, a detailed watercolour of London in the early 1800s. After a quick spin through the Pleasure Gardens, you emerge onto a glorious re-creation of a Victorian street. Highlights of the galleries leading up to the present day include a 1908 taxi cab, an art deco lift from Selfridges and an interactive water pump that makes clear the perils of the once insanitary water system. The testimonies from WWII are particularly moving, and in the last gallery you'll find the rather impressive Lord Mayor's Coach. There's also a great shop and two cafes.

DON'T MISS...
- ➡ Victorian Walk
- ➡ *Rhinebeck Panorama*
- ➡ Wellclose Square Prison Cell
- ➡ Roman London
- ➡ London Before London

PRACTICALITIES
- ➡ Map p438
- ➡ www.museum oflondon.org.uk
- ➡ London Wall EC2
- ➡ admission free
- ➡ ⊙10am-6pm
- ➡ ⊖Barbican or St Paul's

tween 1969 and 1982, it's fair to say that its austere concrete isn't everyone's cup of tea. Yet, although it has topped several polls as London's ugliest building, many Londoners see something very beautiful about its cohesion and ambition – incorporating Shakespeare's local church, **St Giles Cripplegate**, into its brave-new-world design and embellishing its public areas with lakes and ponds. With a £7-million refit bringing the complex a much-needed facelift in 2005, the Barbican is much better loved than London's other modernist colossus, the Southbank Centre (p170). Trendy urban architects have long prized apartments here, and the residences in the three high-rise towers that ring the cultural centre are some of the city's most sought-after living spaces. Guided **architectural tours** (£8; ⓦWed, Thu, Sat & Sun, check web for times) are fascinating and the best way to make sense of the purpose and beauty of the estate.

The Barbican is still London's preeminent cultural centre (see p160), boasting the Barbican Hall, two theatres, a cinema, and two well-regarded art galleries, the **Barbican Gallery** (ⓦ11am-8pm Fri-Tue, to 6pm Wed, to 10pm Thu), and the **Curve** (ⓦ11am-8pm Fri-Wed, to 10pm Thu). It also has three restaurants, including the highly recommended canteen-style **Barbican Foodhall** (ⓦ9am-8.30pm Mon-Sat, 11am-8pm Sun), offering a tempting array of freshly made sandwiches, cakes and pastries, daily changing hot meals and plenty of seating inside and on its lakeside terrace.

ST BARTHOLOMEW-THE-GREAT   CHURCH

Map p438 (www.greatstbarts.com; West Smithfield EC1; adult/concession £4/3.50; ⓦ8.30am-5pm Mon-Fri, 10.30am-4pm Sat & 8.30am-8pm Sun; ⓔFarringdon or Barbican) This spectacular Norman church dates from 1123. It was originally a part of the monastery of Augustinian Canons, but became the parish church of Smithfield in 1539 when King Henry VIII dissolved the monasteries. It sits on the corner of the grounds of St Bart's Hospital, on the side closest to Smithfield Market. Its authentic Norman arches, the weathered and blackened stone, the dark wood carvings and the low lighting lend the space an ancient calm. There are historical associations with William Hogarth, who was baptised here, and with politician Benjamin Franklin, who worked on site as an apprentice printer. Another selling point for modern audiences is that scenes

from *Shakespeare in Love, Four Weddings and a Funeral* and *Sherlock Holmes* were filmed here. The location managers for those movies knew what they were doing: St Bartholomew-the-Great is indeed one of the capital's most atmospheric places of worship. The cloisters house a lovely little **cafe** (ⓦ10am-4pm Mon-Fri, 9.30am-1.30pm & 5.15-6.30pm Sun, closed Saturday).

SMITHFIELD MARKET   MARKET

Map p438 (www.smithfieldmarket.com; West Smithfield EC1; ⓦ3am-noon Mon-Fri; ⓔFarringdon) Smithfield is central London's last surviving meat market. Its name derives from it being a smooth field where animals could be grazed, although its history is far from pastoral. Built on the site of the notorious St Bartholomew's fair, where witches were traditionally burned at the stake, this is where Scottish independence leader William Wallace was executed in 1305 (there's a large plaque on the wall of St Bart's Hospital south of the market), as well as the place where the leader of the Peasants' Revolt, Wat Tyler, met his end in 1381. Described in terms of pure horror by Dickens in *Oliver Twist*, this was once the armpit of London, where animal excrement and entrails created a sea of filth. Today it's a very smart annexe of Clerkenwell and full of bars and restaurants, while the market itself is a wonderful building. Visit before 7am to see it in full swing.

GOLDEN BOY OF PYE CORNER   MONUMENT

Map p438 (cnr Cock Lane & Giltspur St; ⓔSt Paul's or Farringdon) This small statue of a corpulent boy opposite St Bartholomew's Hospital has a somewhat odd dedication: 'In memory put up for the fire of London occasioned by the sin of gluttony 1666'. All becomes clear, however, when you realise the Great Fire started in a busy bakery on Pudding Lane and finally burned itself out in what was once called Pye (Pie) Corner, where the statue now stands. This was interpreted by many as a sign that the fire was an act of God as punishment for the gluttony of Londoners.

FREE CENTRAL CRIMINAL COURT
(OLD BAILEY)   HISTORIC BUILDING

Map p438 (www.cityoflondon.gov.uk; cnr Newgate & Old Bailey Sts; ⓦapprox 10am-1pm & 2-4pm Mon-Fri; ⓔSt Paul's) Just as fact is often better than fiction, taking in a trial in the 'Old Bailey' leaves watching a TV court-

THE CITY SIGHTS

room drama for dust. Of course, it's too late to see author Jeffrey Archer being found guilty of perjury here, watch the Guildford Four's convictions being quashed after their wrongful imprisonment for IRA terrorist attacks, or view the Yorkshire Ripper Peter Sutcliffe being sent down. However, the Old Bailey is a byword for crime and notoriety. So even if you sit in on a fairly run-of-the-mill trial, simply being in the court where such people as the Kray twins and Oscar Wilde (in an earlier building on this site) once appeared is memorable in itself.

Choose from 18 courts, of which the oldest – courts one to four – usually have the most interesting cases. As cameras, video equipment, mobile phones, large bags and food and drink are all forbidden inside, and there are no cloakrooms or lockers, it's important not to take these with you. Take a cardigan or something to cushion the hard seats though, and if you're interested in a high-profile trial, get there early.

The Central Criminal Court gets its nickname from the street on which it stands: *baillie* was Norman French for 'enclosed courtyard'. The current building opened in 1907 on the combined site of a previous Old Bailey and Newgate Prison. Intriguingly the figure of justice holding a sword and scales in her hands above the building's copper dome is *not* blindfolded (against undue influence, as is traditionally the case). That's a situation that has sparked many a sarcastic comment from those being charged here.

HOLBORN VIADUCT   BRIDGE

Map p438 (⊖St Paul's or Farringdon) This fine iron bridge was built in 1869 in an effort to smarten up the area, as well as to link Holborn and Newgate St above what had been a valley created by the River Fleet. The four bronze statues represent commerce and agriculture (on the southern side) and science and fine arts (on the north).

FREE ST ANDREW HOLBORN   CHURCH

Map p438 (www.standrewholborn.org.uk; Holborn Viaduct EC4; ⊗9am-5pm Mon-Fri; ⊖Chancery Lane) This church on the southeastern corner of Holborn Circus, first mentioned in the 10th century, was rebuilt by Wren in 1686 and was the largest of his parish churches. Even though the interior was bombed to smithereens during WWII, much of what you see inside today is origi-

nal 17th century, as it was brought from other churches.

DR JOHNSON'S HOUSE   MUSEUM

Map p438 (www.drjohnsonshouse.org; 17 Gough Sq EC4; adult/child £4.50/1.50; ⊗11am-5.30pm Mon-Sat May-Sep, to 5pm Mon-Sat Oct-Apr; ⊖Chancery Lane or Blackfriars) This wonderful house, built in 1700, is a rare surviving example of a Georgian city mansion. All around it today huge office blocks loom and tiny Gough Square can be quite hard to find. The house has been preserved, as it was the home of the great Georgian wit Samuel Johnson, the author of the first serious dictionary of the English language and the man who proclaimed 'When a man is tired of London, he is tired of life'.

The museum doesn't exactly crackle with Dr Johnson's immortal wit, yet it's still an atmospheric and worthy place to visit, with its antique furniture and artefacts from Johnson's life. The numerous paintings of Dr Johnson and his associates, including his black manservant Francis Barber and his clerk and biographer James Boswell, are, sadly, not particularly revealing of the great minds who would have considered the building a home from home. A more revealing object is a chair from Johnson's local pub, the Old Cock Tavern on Fleet St. Also on display is a copy of the first edition of the dictionary from 1755.

There's a rather ponderous video, plus leaflets telling how the lexicographer and six clerks (Boswell wasn't among them, yet) developed the first English dictionary in the house's attic during the period he lived here from 1748 to 1759. Children will love the Georgian dress-up clothes on the top floor, and there are also temporary exhibits in the attic.

Across Gough Square is a statue of Johnson's cat, Hodge, sitting above the full quote explaining why a man who is tired of London is also tired of life: 'For there is in London all that life can afford'.

FREE ST BRIDE'S, FLEET STREET   CHURCH

Map p438 (www.stbrides.com; St Bride's Lane EC4; ⊗8am-6pm Mon-Fri, hours vary Sat, 10am-6.30pm Sun; ⊖St Paul's or Blackfriars) Rupert Murdoch might have frogmarched the newspaper industry out to Wapping in the 1980s, but this small church off Fleet St remains 'the journalists' church' – William Caxton's first printing press was relocated to the churchyard after his death in 1500. Candles were kept burning here for reporters John McCarthy and Terry Anderson during their years as hostages in Lebanon in the 1990s, and a plaque commemorates journalists killed in the Iraq war alongside even more recent memorials. St Bride's is also of architectural interest. Designed by Sir Christopher Wren in 1671, its add-on spire (1703) reputedly inspired the first tiered wedding cake. In the crypt there's a well-presented history of the church, its surrounding areas and the printing industry. Guided tours (£5), which allow access to the charnel house, are conducted on Tuesdays at 3pm on selected dates (check the website for details).

TEMPLE CHURCH
CHURCH

Map p438 (www.templechurch.com; Temple EC4; £3; ⊙approx 2-4pm Wed-Sun, call or check website; ⊜Temple or Chancery Lane) This magnificent church lies within the walls of the Temple, built by the legendary Knights Templar, an order of crusading monks founded in the 12th century to protect pilgrims travelling to and from Jerusalem. The order moved here around 1160, abandoning its older headquarters in Holborn. Today the sprawling oasis of fine buildings and pleasant traffic-free green space is home to two Inns of Court (housing the chambers of lawyers practising in the City) and the Middle and the Lesser Temple.

The Temple Church has a distinctive design: the Round (consecrated in 1185 and designed to recall the Church of the Holy Sepulchre in Jerusalem) adjoins the Chancel (built in 1240), which is the heart of the modern church. Both parts were severely damaged by a bomb in 1941 and have been lovingly reconstructed. Its most obvious points of interest are the life-size stone effigies of nine knights that lie on the floor of the Round. These include the Earl of Pembroke, who acted as the go-between for King John and the rebel barons, eventually leading to the signing of the Magna Carta in 1215. In recent years the church has become a must-see for readers of *The Da Vinci Code* because a key scene was set here.

Check opening times in advance as they change frequently. During the week the easiest access to the church is via Inner Temple Lane, off Fleet St. At weekends you'll need to enter from Victoria Embankment.

EATING

The financial heart of London unsurprisingly caters for a well-heeled crowd and it can be a tough place to find a meal at the weekend, if not on a weekday evening. But neighbouring districts such as Shoreditch, Spitalfields and Clerkenwell offer a good selection of eating options if you get really stuck. During the week, Leadenhall Market stalls (p151) offer a delicious array of food, from steaming noodles to mountains of sweet treats (11am to 4pm).

SWEETING'S
SEAFOOD ££

Map p438 (www.sweetingsrestaurant.com; 39 Queen Victoria St EC4; mains £13.50-32; ⊙lunch Mon-Fri; ⊜Mansion House) Sweeting's is a City institution, having been around since 1830. It hasn't changed much, with its small sit-down dining area, mosaic floor and narrow counters, behind which stand waiters in white aprons. Dishes include sustainably sourced fish of all kinds (grilled, fried or poached), potted shrimps, eels and Sweeting's famous fish pie (£13.50).

CAFÉ BELOW
CAFE £

Map p438 (www.cafebelow.co.uk; St Mary-le-Bow church, Cheapside EC2; mains £8-12; ⊙7.30am-9pm Mon-Fri; ✎; ⊜Mansion House) This atmospheric cafe and restaurant is in the crypt of one of London's most famous old churches. From breakfast to dinner, the menus here are good value and offer tasty dishes such as fish cakes and steak sandwiches at lunch and fillet of sea bream or courgette filo pie in the evening. The menu includes a better-than-average choice for vegetarians too. In summer there are tables outside on the tree-lined courtyard next to the church.

RESTAURANT AT ST PAUL'S
MODERN BRITISH ££

Map p438 (www.restaurantatstpauls.co.uk; St Paul's Cathedral, St Paul's Churchyard EC4; 2/3 courses £21.50/25.95; ⊙noon-3pm; ✎; ⊜St Paul's) The quality of the dishes at this restaurant, set in the crypt of St Paul's, does a fair job of living up to the grandeur above. The short and simple menu offers two- or three-course lunches, including such dishes as potted lemon and thyme chicken and pork loin chop with a rarebit glaze. It also does a good-value daily express lunch (£15, including a glass of wine) and afternoon tea (served until 4.30pm Monday to Saturday).

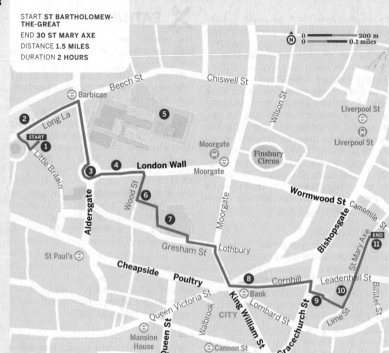

START **ST BARTHOLOMEW-THE-GREAT**
END **30 ST MARY AXE**
DISTANCE **1.5 MILES**
DURATION **2 HOURS**

Neighbourhood Walk
A Taste of the City

The City of London has as much history in its Square Mile as the rest of London put together, and this walk picks out just a few of its highlights. Start by exploring 12th-century ❶ **St Bartholomew-the-Great**, where the atmospheric interior has been frequently used as a film set. Head out through the Tudor gatehouse and turn right towards the Victorian arches of ❷ **Smithfield Market**. Take a right down Long Lane and again at Aldersgate St. Follow the roundabout to the right and nip up the stairs where you see the ❸ **Museum of London** sign. Once on the highwalk explore the museum's excellent galleries or head to the right to admire the ruins of the ❹ **Roman city walls** and behind them the ❺ **Barbican's** distinctive towers and balconies. Follow the painted lines on the highwalk for a closer look at the Barbican complex, or turn right at Pizza Express and ride the escalators to ground level. Turn right at Wood St to find the remaining tower of ❻ **St Alban's**, a Wren-designed church

destroyed in WWII. Turn left into Love Lane and right into Aldermanbury – the impressive 15th-century ❼ **Guildhall** is on your left. Crossing its courtyard continue east onto Gresham St, taking a right into Princes St and emerging onto the busy Bank intersection, lined with neoclassical temples to commerce. Behind the equestrian statue of the Iron Duke is a metal pyramid detailing the many significant buildings here. From the ❽ **Royal Exchange**, follow Cornhill and take a right down Gracechurch St. Turn left and into wonderful ❾ **Leadenhall Market**, roughly where the ancient forum once stood. As you wander out the far end, ❿ **Lloyd's of London** displays its innards for all to see. Once you turn left onto Lime St, ⓫ **30 St Mary Axe**, or 'the Gherkin', looms proudly before you. Built nearly 900 years after St Bartholomew-the-Great, it's testimony to the city's ability to constantly reinvent itself for the times.

CITY CÀPHÊ
VIETNAMESE £

Map p438 (www.citycaphe.com; 17 Ironmonger Lane EC2; dishes £3.85-6.40; ⊗11.30am-3pm Mon-Fri; ⊖Bank) Down a quiet little lane off Cheapside, this small cafe attracts queues of City workers for its excellent and good-value Vietnamese street food to eat in or takeaway. Choose from *pho* (noodle soup), salads or summer rolls, or go for the classic (and very reasonable) *banh mi* (baguettes), which are simply delicious.

SAUTERELLE
MODERN FRENCH £££

Map p438 (☎7618 2483; www.sauterelle -restaurant.co.uk; Royal Exchange EC3; mains £18-31; ⊗Mon-Fri; ⊖Bank) Up on the mezzanine level of the ornate Royal Exchange, Sauterelle ('grasshopper' in French) offers distinct yet subtlely flavoured fine dining, where beautifully cooked and presented dishes are accompanied by a comprehensive and well-chosen wine list. The setting is particularly romantic, with views to the covered courtyard below. Set menus (two/three courses £20/23.50) are good value.

BAR BATTU
FRENCH ££

Map p438 (☎7036 6100; www.barbattu.com; 48 Gresham St EC2; mains £11.50-24.50; ⊗11.30am-11pm Mon-Fri; ⊛; ⊖Bank) As well as the fantastic range of 'natural' wines (meaning they're made with as little outside intervention as possible) and helpful staff to advise on the list, this intimate place offers an enticing selection of dishes to accompany your tipple. From a sumptuous *boudin noir* (blood sausage) to grilled lemon sole, the food is well-executed, and smaller plates and charcuterie are also available if you just want to soak up the wine.

WINE LIBRARY
MODERN EUROPEAN ££

Map p438 (☎7481 0415; www.winelibrary.co.uk; 43 Trinity Sq EC3; set meals £17.25; ⊗11.30am-3pm Mon, 11.30am-8pm Tue-Fri; ⊖Tower Hill) This is a great place for a light but boozy lunch in the City. Buy a bottle of wine at retail price (no markup, £7.25 corkage fee) from the large selection on offer at the vaulted-cellar restaurant and then snack on a set plate of delicious pâtés, cheeses and salads. Reservations recommended for lunch.

WHITE SWAN PUB & DINING ROOM
GASTROPUB ££

Map p438 (www.thewhiteswanlondon.com; 108 New Fetter Lane EC4; pub mains £9.95-14.95; ⊗Mon-Fri; ⊛; ⊖Chancery Lane) Despite looking like any other anonymous City pub from the street, inside the White Swan is anything but typical – a smart downstairs bar that serves excellent pub food under the watchful eyes of animal trophies, and an upstairs dining room with a classic, meaty British menu (two-/three-course meal £26/29.75).

ROYAL EXCHANGE GRAND CAFÉ & BAR
MODERN EUROPEAN ££

Map p438 (www.danddlondon.com; Royal Exchange EC3; mains £12-16.50; ⊗8am-11pm Mon-Fri; ⊖Bank) This cafe sits in the middle of the covered courtyard of the beautiful Royal Exchange building. The food runs the gamut from breakfast, salads and sandwiches to oysters (from £11 a half-dozen) and duck confit (£13).

DRINKING & NIGHTLIFE

TOP CHOICE VERTIGO 42
BAR

Map p438 (☎7877 7842; www.vertigo42.co.uk; Tower 42, 25 Old Broad St EC2; ⊗noon-4.30pm & 5-11pm Mon-Fri, from 5pm Sat; ⊖Liverpool St or Bank) On the 42nd floor of a 183m-high tower, this circular bar has expansive views over the city that stretch for miles on a clear day, and are particularly stunning at sunset. The classic drinks list is, as you might expect, pricier than average – wine by the glass starts from £9.20 and champagne and cocktails from £14, and there's also a limited food menu. Reservations are essential and security is thorough.

BLACK FRIAR
PUB

Map p438 (174 Queen Victoria St EC4; ⊖Blackfriars) It may look like Friar Tuck just stepped out of this 'olde pubbe' just north of Blackfriars station, but the interior is actually an Arts and Crafts makeover dating back to 1905. Built on the site of a Dominican monastery, the theme is appealingly celebrated throughout the pub. There's a good selection of ales and bitters. Unusually for this part of town, it opens at the weekend.

COUNTING HOUSE
PUB

Map p438 (50 Cornhill EC3; ⊗Mon-Fri; ⊛; ⊖Bank or Monument) They say that old banks – with their counters and basement vaults – make

THE CITY ENTERTAINMENT

BAFFLED BY THE BARBICAN

Navigating your way around the Barbican can be a source of utter frustration. Built on a bomb site, the architects Chamberlin, Powell and Bon created an estate where the main focus was to look inward, rather than to what was a desolate city beyond its parameters. A structure (sometimes likened to a fortress) built for 4000 inhabitants, the complex was also designed to raise citizens above road level and allow them to move around with ease. Despite this, once inside, the Barbican is notoriously confusing. There are stairs from Barbican tube station that take you up onto the highwalks, from where a yellow line guides you to the arts complex, but if you're just heading straight there, most people opt to walk through the Beech St road tunnel to the recently added Silk St entrance, making the experience a little more straightforward.

perfect homes for pubs, and this award winner certainly looks and feels comfortable in the former headquarters of NatWest with its domed skylight and beautifully appointed main bar. This is a favourite of City boys – they come for the good range of real ales and the speciality pies (£9.75).

EL VINO
WINE BAR

Map p438 (www.elvino.co.uk; 47 Fleet St EC4; ⊙8.30am-10pm Mon-Fri; ⊖Blackfriars or Temple) A venerable institution that plays host to barristers, solicitors and other legal types from the Royal Courts of Justice across the way, this wine bar (one of five in a small chain) has one of the better wine lists in the City and prices at the attached shops are reasonable. El Vino featured as the wine bar Pomeroys in the TV series *Rumpole of the Bailey*.

YE OLDE CHESHIRE CHEESE
PUB

Map p438 (Wine Office Ct, 145 Fleet St EC4; ⊙Mon-Sat; ⊖Blackfriars) The entrance to this historic pub is via a narrow alley off Fleet St. Over its long history locals have included Dr Johnson, Thackeray and Dickens. Despite (or possibly because of) this, the Cheshire feels today like a bit of a museum piece, and a fairly shabby one at that. Nevertheless it's one of London's most famous pubs and it's well worth popping in for a pint.

YE OLDE WATLING
PUB

Map p438 (29 Watling St EC4; ⊙Mon-Fri; ⊖Mansion House) This small strip behind St Paul's has an almost village-like feel to it, and the centre of the village is definitely Ye Olde Watling, an old timer with a gorgeous wooden bar that is always busy from 5pm. Food is served and a there's a taste-before-you-try policy for the great selection of real ales.

ENTERTAINMENT

TOP CHOICE BARBICAN
CONCERT VENUE

Map p438 (✆7638 8891; www.barbican.org. uk; Silk St EC2; ⊖Moorgate or Barbican) Urging Londoners to 'do something different', the extensive program of events on offer at the Barbican always provides something new and adventurous. It's home to the wonderful London Symphony Orchestra, and the centre's associate orchestra, the lesser-known BBC Symphony Orchestra, also plays regularly, as do scores of leading international musicians. On the contemporary scene, it hosts all manner of high-quality musicians, focusing in particular on jazz, folk, world and soul artists. Dance is another strong point and its multidisciplinary festival, **Barbican International Theatre Events** (bite; www.barbican.org.uk/ theatre/about-bite), showcases some great performances, as well as the work of exciting overseas drama companies alongside local fringe-theatre troupes. It's also a dream to watch a film here, with an interesting line-up and brilliant sloping seating that ensures a full-screen view wherever you sit.

VOLUPTÉ
CABARET

Map p438 (www.volupte-lounge.com; 7-9 Norwich St EC4; ⊙from 11.30am Tue-Fri, from 7.30pm Sat; ☎; ⊖Chancery Lane) A gorgeous little cabaret venue just behind Fleet St, Volupté offers a real variety of burlesque, vaudeville, comedy and live music. The monthly Black Cotton Club is a hark-back to the 1920s in terms of dress code and music choice. At the weekend sit down to Tea & Tassels or an Afternoon Tease, a rather more alternative take on the classic afternoon tea, with live music, cabaret or burlesque performances.

SHOPPING

SILVER VAULTS   SILVERWARE

Map p438 (www.thesilvervaults.com; 53-64 Chancery Lane WC2; ⊙9am-5.30pm Mon-Fri, to 1pm Sat; ◉Chancery Lane) The shops that work out of these incredibly secure subterranean vaults make up the largest collection of silver under one roof in the world. The different businesses tend to specialise in particular types of silverware – from cutlery sets to picture frames and lots of jewellery. The quality of the goods is guaranteed, and even if you're not buying it's well worth visiting just to have a look around this extraordinary place.

THE CITY SHOPPING

The South Bank

WATERLOO | BANKSIDE | SOUTHWARK | BOROUGH | BERMONDSEY

Neighbourhood Top Five

1 Finding out what all the fuss is about, exploring the magnificent modern-art collection at the peerless **Tate Modern** (p164).

2 Revolving in leisurely fashion above London's panoramic cityscape in the iconic **London Eye** (p169).

3 Stimulating your taste buds on a gastronomic tour of discovery at **Borough Market** (p176).

4 Stopping by **Skylon** (p173) or the **Oxo Tower Restaurant & Brasserie** (p173) for riveting views of the Thames and the city, or dropping anchor at the **Anchor Bankside** (p177).

5 Getting a Bard's-eye view of Elizabethan theatrics as a groundling at the magnificent **Shakespeare's Globe** (p168).

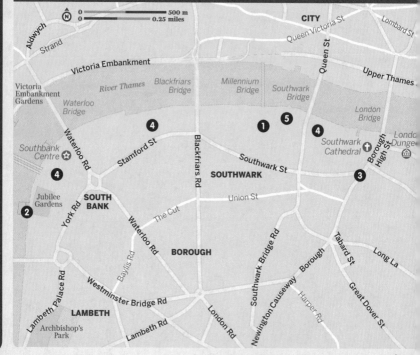

For more detail of this area, see Map p436

Explore: The South Bank

Once neglected beyond its arts venues, the South Bank today has transformed into one of London's must-see neighbourhoods. A roll call of riverside sights stretches along the Thames, commencing with the London Eye, running past the cultural enclave of the Southbank Centre and on to the Tate Modern, the Millennium Bridge and Shakespeare's Globe. It continues: waterside pubs, busy boutique shopping quarters, a cathedral, one of London's most-visited food markets and a handful of fun diversions for kids and irrepressible kidults. A stunning panorama unfolds on the far side of the Thames, as head-swivelling architecture rises up on either bank.

The drawcard sights stretch west-east in a manageable riverside melange, so doing it on foot is the best way. Located roughly halfway between the London Eye and Tower Bridge, the Tate Modern is by far the most time-intensive sight, and can easily hollow out a day's sightseeing; two to three days for the South Bank is optimum but if you're in a rush, one day may do for a (frazzling) whistle-stop look at the main sights.

Local Life

➡ **Hang-outs** Join locals picking through the gastronomic selection at Borough Market (p176) then take a courtyard seat outside Southwark Cathedral (p172) before a fish-and-chip lunch at Masters Super Fish (p174) or a pint at the galleried George Inn (p177).

➡ **Museums** Locals earmark Friday and Saturday late-night opening (till 10pm) at the Tate Modern (p164), when the art crowds have thinned.

➡ **Theatre** Londoners applaud Shakespeare's Globe (p168) and seats are stuffed with locals at impressive theatre venues such as the National Theatre (p169), the Old Vic (p180) and the Young Vic (p180).

Getting There & Away

➡ **Underground** The South Bank is lashed into the tube system by stations at Waterloo, Southwark, London Bridge and Bermondsey, all on the Jubilee Line; the Northern Line runs through London Bridge and Waterloo (the Bakerloo line runs through the latter).

➡ **On Foot** Cross to South Bank from the City over Tower Bridge, or from the West End across Westminster Bridge or any other vehicle and pedestrian bridges.

➡ **Bicycle** Jump on a Barclays Bike (p393) and wheel it!

➡ **Bus** The Riverside RV1 runs around the South Bank and Bankside, linking all the main sights (running between Covent Garden and Tower Gateway).

Lonely Planet's Top Tip

To collect the main sights, trace the Silver Jubilee Walk and the South Bank section of the Thames Path along the southern riverbank, with occasional inroads south for shopping, dining and drinking recommendations.

✕ Best Places to Eat

➡ Anchor & Hope (p174)
➡ Laughing Gravy (p174)
➡ Skylon (p173)
➡ Magdalen (p174)

For reviews, see p173 ➡

🍷 Best Places to Drink

➡ Rake (p178)
➡ George Inn (p177)
➡ Anchor Bankside (p177)
➡ Scootercaffe (p177)
➡ Baltic (p177)

For reviews, see p177 ➡

👁 Best Attractions

➡ Tate Modern (p164)
➡ London Eye (p169)
➡ Borough Market (p176)
➡ Shakespeare's Globe (p168)
➡ London Bridge Experience & London Tombs (p171)
➡ Sea Life London Aquarium (p169)

For reviews, see p169 ➡

THE SOUTH BANK

The public's love affair with this phenomenally successful modern art gallery shows no sign of cooling a decade after it opened. In fact, so enraptured are art goers with the Tate Modern that over 50 million visitors flocked to the former power station in its first 10 years. The world's most popular art gallery is naturally one of the most-visited sights in London and is set to expand its huge exhibition space even further in 2012 by adapting two of the power station's huge subterranean oil tanks, but visitors will have to wait until 2016 for the opening of the gallery's funky 11-storey geometric extension.

Power Station

The 200m-long Tate Modern is an imposing sight. The conversion of the empty Bankside Power Station – all 4.2 million bricks of it – to art gallery in 2000 was a masterstroke of design. The 'Tate Modern effect' is clearly as much about the building and its location as the mostly 20th-century art inside. The new Tate Modern Project extension will similarly be constructed of brick, but artistically devised as a lattice through which interior lights will be visible at eventide.

Turbine Hall

The first thing to greet you as you pour down the ramp off Holland St (the main entrance) is the cavernous 3300-sq-metre Turbine Hall. Originally housing the power station's humungous turbines, this vast space is the commanding venue for large-scale, temporary exhibitions; the sense of scale is astounding (enter from the river entrance and you'll end up on more-muted level 2). Some art critics

DON'T MISS...

➡ Turbine Hall
➡ *Sleeping Venus* (Paul Delvaux)
➡ Mark Rothko canvases
➡ *'Whaam!'* (Roy Lichtenstein)

PRACTICALITIES

➡ Map p436
➡ ♫Information & bookings 7887 8000
➡ www.tate.org.uk/modern
➡ Bankside SE1
➡ admission free, suggested donation £3, special exhibitions £8-10
➡ ⊙10am-6pm Sun-Thu, to 10pm Fri & Sat
➡ ☎
➡ ⊖St Paul's, Southwark or London Bridge

swipe at its populism, particularly the 'participatory art' (Carsten Höller's funfair-like slides *Test Site;* Doris Salcedo's enormous *Shibboleth* fissure in the floor; and Robert Morris' climbable geometric sculpture), but others insist this makes art more accessible. Originally visitors were invited to trample over Ai Weiwei's thoughtful and compelling *Sunflower Seeds* – a huge carpet of hand-painted ceramic seeds – until it was discovered people were making off with them in their shoes and turn-ups (to later appear on eBay) and the dust emitted by the 'seeds' was diagnosed a health risk.

Permanent Collection

Tate Modern's permanent collection on levels 3 and 5 is now arranged by both theme and chronology. More than 60,000 works are on constant rotation, and the curators have at their disposal paintings by Georges Braque, Henri Matisse, Piet Mondrian, Andy Warhol, Mark Rothko and Jackson Pollock, as well as pieces by Joseph Beuys, Damien Hirst, Rebecca Horn, Claes Oldenburg and Auguste Rodin.

Level 3: Surrealism to Painting & Sculpture of the 1940s and 1950s

Poetry and Dream submerges the viewer in the world of surrealism and the dreamlike mindscapes of Yves Tanguy, Max Ernst and other artists. Search out *Sleeping Venus* by Paul Delvaux, a haunting, erotic work. **Material Gestures** features European and American painting and sculpture of the 1940s and '50s, from Alberto Giacometti to Francis Bacon and Victor Pasmore. The contemplative series of canvases by Mark Rothko in room 3 is entrancing and beguiling.

Level 5: Dynamism & Revolutionary Art

Focussing on early-20th-century avant-garde movements, including cubism, futurism and vorticism, **States of Flux** opens with a dramatic pairing of Umberto Boccioni's *Unique Forms of Continuity in Space* and Roy Lichtenstein's pop icon *'Whaam!'*, pieces separated by half a century. In room 12 Richard Hamilton's replica of Marcel Duchamp's enigmatic *The Large Glass* (*The Bride Stripped Bare by Her Bachelors, Even*) is an intricate and thought-provoking highlight. **Energy and Process** highlights Arte Povera, revolutionary art of the 1960s, as its main focus.

Special Exhibitions

Special exhibitions (level 4) have included retrospectives on Edward Hopper, Frida Kahlo, August Strindberg, Nazism and 'Degenerate' Art, local 'bad boys' Gilbert & George, and Joan Miró. Other exhibitions are also held on level 2.

FURTHER INFORMATION

Audioguides, with four different tours, are available for £2. Free guided highlights tours depart at 11am, noon, 2pm and 3pm daily. You can grab a map from the information desk (£1) near the main entrance and river entrance.

Swiss architects Herzog & de Meuron scooped the prestigious Pritzker Prize for their transformation of empty Bankside Power Station, designed by Sir Giles Gilbert Scott, built between 1947 and 1963 and shut by high oil prices in 1981. Leaving the building's single central 99m-high chimney, adding a two-storey glass box onto the roof and employing the cavernous Turbine Hall as a dramatic entrance space were three strokes of genius.

TATE TO TATE BOAT

The **Tate Boat** (www.tate.org.uk/tatetotate; one way adult/child £5/2.50; ⊙every 40min 9.57am-4.44pm) operates between the Bankside Pier at Tate Modern and the Millbank Pier at its sister-museum, Tate Britain. Services from the latter depart from 10.17am to 5.04pm daily, also at 40-minute intervals.

THE SOUTH BANK TATE MODERN

◎ TOP SIGHTS
TATE MODERN

A FLOATING TOUR

London's history has always been determined by the Thames. The city was founded as a Roman port nearly 2000 years ago and over the centuries since then many of the capital's landmarks have lined the river's banks. A boat trip is a great way to experience the attractions.

There are piers dotted along both banks at regular intervals where you can hop-on/hop-off the regular services to visit places of interest. The best place to board is Westminster Pier, from where boats head downstream, taking you from the City of Westminster, the seat of government, to the original City of London, now the financial district and dominated by a growing band of skyscrapers. Across the river, the once shabby and neglected South Bank now bristles with as many top attractions as its northern counterpart.

In our illustration we've concentrated on the top highlights you'll enjoy at a fish's-eye view as you sail along. These are, from west

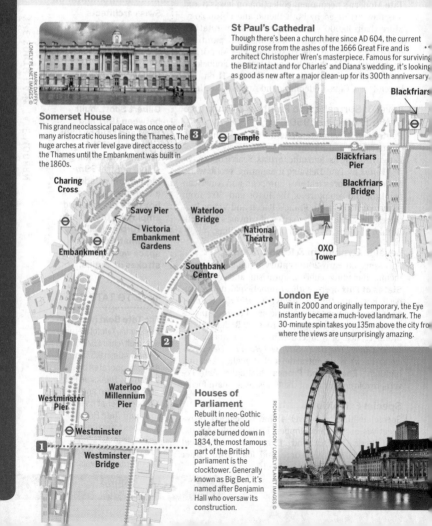

St Paul's Cathedral
Though there's been a church here since AD 604, the current building rose from the ashes of the 1666 Great Fire and is architect Christopher Wren's masterpiece. Famous for surviving the Blitz intact and for Charles' and Diana's wedding, it's looking as good as new after a major clean-up for its 300th anniversary.

Blackfriars

Somerset House
This grand neoclassical palace was once one of many aristocratic houses lining the Thames. The **3** huge arches at river level gave direct access to the Thames until the Embankment was built in the 1860s.

MARK DAFFEY / LONELY PLANET IMAGES ©

Temple

Blackfriars Pier

Blackfriars Bridge

Charing Cross

Savoy Pier

Waterloo Bridge

Victoria Embankment Gardens

National Theatre

Embankment

OXO Tower

Southbank Centre

London Eye
Built in 2000 and originally temporary, the Eye instantly became a much-loved landmark. The 30-minute spin takes you 135m above the city from where the views are unsurprisingly amazing.

2

Waterloo Millennium Pier

Westminster Pier

Houses of Parliament
Rebuilt in neo-Gothic style after the old palace burned down in 1834, the most famous part of the British parliament is the clocktower. Generally known as Big Ben, it's named after Benjamin Hall who oversaw its construction.

Westminster

1

Westminster Bridge

RICHARD I'ANSON / LONELY PLANET IMAGES ©

to east, the **Houses of Parliament** [1],
the **London Eye** [2], **Somerset House** [3],
St Paul's Cathedral [4], **Tate Modern** [5],
Shakespeare's Globe [6], the **Tower of
London** [7] and **Tower Bridge** [8].

Apart from covering this central
section of the river, boats can also be
taken upstream as far as Kew Gardens and
Hampton Court Palace, and downstream
to Greenwich and the Thames Barrier.

BOAT HOPPING

Thames Clippers hop-on/hop-off services
are aimed at commuters but are equally
useful for visitors, operating every 15 minutes on a loop from piers at Embankment,
Waterloo, Blackfriars, Bankside, London
Bridge and the Tower. Other services also
go from Westminster. Oyster cardholders
get a discount off the boat ticket price.

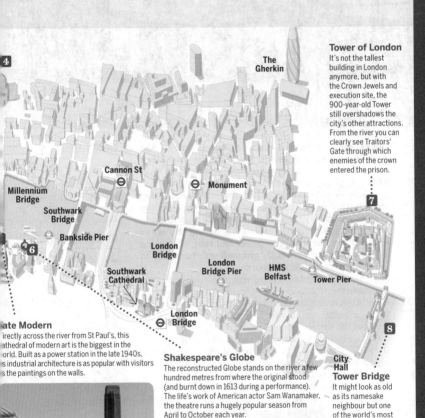

Tower of London
It's not the tallest
building in London
anymore, but with
the Crown Jewels and
execution site, the
900-year-old Tower
still overshadows the
city's other attractions.
From the river you can
clearly see Traitors'
Gate through which
enemies of the crown
entered the prison.

The Gherkin

Cannon St

Monument

Millennium Bridge

Southwark Bridge

Bankside Pier

[6]

London Bridge

London Bridge Pier

HMS Belfast

Tower Pier

[7]

Southwark Cathedral

London Bridge

[8]

ate Modern
irectly across the river from St Paul's, this
athedral of modern art is the biggest in the
orld. Built as a power station in the late 1940s,
s industrial architecture is as popular with visitors
s the paintings on the walls.

Shakespeare's Globe
The reconstructed Globe stands on the river a few
hundred metres from where the original stood
(and burnt down in 1613 during a performance).
The life's work of American actor Sam Wanamaker,
the theatre runs a hugely popular season from
April to October each year.

DOUG MCKINLAY / LONELY PLANET IMAGES ©

**City
Hall
Tower Bridge**
It might look as old
as its namesake
neighbour but one
of the world's most
iconic bridges was
only completed
in 1894. Not to be
confused with London
Bridge upstream, this
one's famous raising
bascules allowed
tall ships to dock
at the old wharves
to the west and are
still lifted up to 1000
times a year.

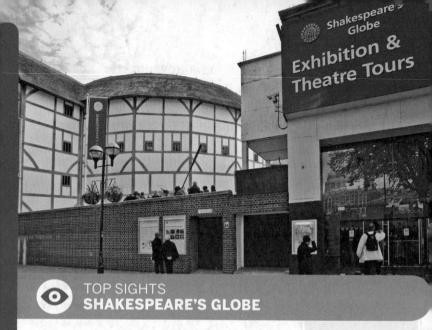

TOP SIGHTS
SHAKESPEARE'S GLOBE

Unlike other venues for Shakespearean plays, the new Globe was designed to resemble the original as closely as possible, painstakingly constructed with 600 oak pegs (nary a nail or a screw in the house), specially fired Tudor bricks and thatching reeds from Norfolk that pigeons supposedly don't like. Even the plaster contains goat hair, lime and sand, as it did in Shakespeare's time. It even means having the arena open to the fickle London skies and roar of passing aircraft, leaving the 700 'groundlings' to stand in London's notorious downpours.

Despite the worldwide popularity of Shakespeare over the centuries, the Globe was almost a distant memory when American actor (and, later, film director) Sam Wanamaker came searching for it in 1949. Undeterred by the fact that the theatre's foundations had vanished beneath a row of hertiage-listed Georgian houses, Wanamaker set up the Globe Playhouse Trust in 1970 and began fundraising for a memorial theatre. Work started only 200m from the original Globe site in 1987, but Wanamaker died four years before it opened in 1997.

Shakespeare's Globe consists of the reconstructed Globe Theatre and, beneath it, an exhibition hall, entry to which includes a tour (departing every 15 to 30 minutes) of the theatre, except when matinees are being staged in season. Then the tour shifts to the nearby Rose Theatre (p170) and costs less.

DON'T MISS...

➡ Exhibition Hall & Tour

➡ Interior of the Globe Theatre

PRACTICALITIES

➡ Map p436

➡ ☑ 7902 1400, bookings 7401 9919

➡ www.shakespeares globe.com

➡ 21 New Globe Walk SE1

➡ exhibition incl guided tour of theatre adult/child £11.50/7

➡ ⊘exhibition 9am-12.30pm & 1-5pm Mon-Sat, 9-11.30am & noon-5pm Sun late Apr–mid-Oct, 9am-5pm mid-Oct–late Apr

➡ ⊖St Paul's or London Bridge

⊙ SIGHTS

⊙ Waterloo

COUNTY HALL   HISTORIC BUILDING
Map p436 (Riverside Bldg, Westminster Bridge Rd SE1; 🚇; ⊖Westminster or Waterloo) Begun in 1909 but not completed until 1922, this grand building with its curved, colonnaded facade contains a vast aquarium and a museum devoted to the local film industry.

The excellent **Sea Life London Aquarium** (📞0871 663 1678; www.sealife.co.uk; adult/child £17/12.50; ⊙10am-6pm Mon-Thu, to 7pm Fri-Sun; 🚇) is one of the largest in Europe. Fish and other creatures from the briny deep are grouped in 15 zones according to their geographic origin, from the Pacific to the Atlantic Ocean and from temperate waters to tropical seas. There are over 40 sharks, a colony of gentoo penguins and other Antarctic creatures, ever-popular clownfish and a rewarding rainforests section.

The **London Film Museum** (📞7202 7040; www.londonfilmmuseum.com; adult/child £13.50/9.50; ⊙10am-5pm Mon-Wed & Fri, 11am-5pm Thu, 10am-6pm Sat, 11am-6pm Sun; 🚇) is surprisingly well done and because it looks at films made in the UK, not just British films, it includes exhibits such as the sets for *Star Wars* and the Indiana Jones films. There's a lot of participatory stuff and plenty of icons and props from the cinematic world (including the Rank Organisation gong and Christian Bale's Batman suit).

NATIONAL THEATRE   THEATRE
Map p436 (📞7452 3000; www.nationaltheatre.org.uk; South Bank SE1; 🚇; ⊖Waterloo) The nation's flagship theatre complex (p178) comprises three auditoriums: the Olivier, the Lyttelton and the Cottesloe. **Backstage tours** (adult/concession £7.50/6.50), lasting 1¼ hours, are available. There are six daily Monday to Friday, two on Saturday and one on Sunday. Consult the website for exact times.

⊙ Bankside & Southwark

TATE MODERN   GALLERY
See p164.

SHAKESPEARE'S GLOBE   THEATRE
See p168.

⊙ TOP SIGHTS
LONDON EYE

It's hard to remember what London looked like before the landmark London Eye (officially the EDF Energy London Eye) began twirling at the southwestern end of Jubilee Gardens in 2000. Not only has it fundamentally altered the South Bank skyline but, standing 135m tall in a fairly flat city, it is visible from many surprising parts of the city (eg Kennington, Mayfair or Honor Oak Park). A ride – or 'flight', as it is called here – in one of the wheel's 32 glass-enclosed eye pods holding up to 28 people draws 3.5 million visitors annually. At peak times (July, August and school holidays) it may seem like they are all in the queue with you; save money and shorten queues by buying tickets online, or cough up an extra £10 to showcase your fast-track swagger. Alternatively, visit before 11am or after 3pm to avoid peak density. It takes a gracefully slow 30 minutes and, weather permitting, you can see 25 miles in every direction from the top of the western hemisphere's tallest Ferris wheel. Together with its 23m-tall spindle, the hub of the London Eye weighs 330 tonnes, more than 20 times the weight of Big Ben.

DON'T MISS...

➤ Views of Hampton Court
➤ Views of the Tower of London

PRACTICALITIES

➤ Map p436
➤ 📞0870 500 0600
➤ www.londoneye.com
➤ Jubilee Gardens SE1
➤ adult/child £19/10
➤ ⊙10am-8.30pm Sep-Mar, to 9pm Apr-Jun, to 9.30pm Jul & Aug
➤ ⊖Waterloo

◉ TOP SIGHTS
SOUTHBANK CENTRE

The flagship venue of the Southbank Centre and its oldest standing building, the **Royal Festival Hall** with its gently curved facade of glass and Portland stone is more humane than its 1970s brutalist neighbours. A £90-million refit in 2007 added new pedestrian walkways, bookshops, music stores and food outlets, including the restaurant Skylon (p173), below it.

Just north, the austere **Queen Elizabeth Hall** is a brutalist icon, the second-largest concert venue in the centre, hosting chamber orchestras, quartets, choirs, dance performances and sometimes opera. It also contains the smaller **Purcell Room**, while underneath its elevated floor is a long-term, graffiti-decorated skateboarders' hang-out.

The opinion-dividing 1968 **Hayward Gallery** (✆0871 663 2509; www.southbankcentre.co.uk; admission £7-9; ◷10am-6pm Sat-Wed, to 8pm Thu & Fri) is one of London's premier exhibition spaces for major international art shows. Facilities include the upstairs Waterloo Sunset Pavilion, a Dan Graham–designed 'drop-in centre for children and old people and a space for viewing cartoons', offering wraparound views of London's brutalist horizons.

DON'T MISS...

➡ Royal Festival Hall
➡ Queen Elizabeth Hall
➡ Hayward Gallery

PRACTICALITIES

➡ Map p436
➡ ✆0871 663 2500
➡ www.southbank centre.co.uk
➡ Belvedere Rd SE1
➡ admission free; tickets for performances and exhibitions
➡ ⊖Waterloo

MILLENNIUM BRIDGE
BRIDGE

Map p436 The elegant Millennium Bridge staples the south bank of the Thames, in front of Tate Modern, with the north bank, at the steps of Peter's Hill below St Paul's Cathedral. The low-slung frame designed by Sir Norman Foster and Antony Caro looks spectacular, particularly lit up at night with fibre optics, and the view of St Paul's from the South Bank is one of London's iconic images.

ROSE THEATRE
THEATRE

Map p436 (✆7902 1400; www.rosetheatre.org.uk; 56 Park St SE1; adult/child £7.50/4.50; ◷1-5pm Mon-Sat, noon-5pm Sun late Apr–mid-Oct; ☏; ⊖London Bridge) The Rose, for which Christopher Marlowe and Ben Jonson wrote their greatest plays and in which Shakespeare learned his craft, is unique: its original 16th-century foundations were discovered in 1989 beneath an office building and given a protective concrete cover. Administered by the nearby Globe Theatre, the Rose is open to the public only when matinees are being performed at the Globe and can only be visited as part of a group.

GOLDEN HINDE
SHIP

Map p436 (✆7403 0123; www.goldenhinde.com; St Mary Overie Dock, Cathedral St SE1; adult/child £6/4.50; ◷10am-5.30pm; ⊖London Bridge) Okay, it looks like a dinky theme-park ride and kids love it, but stepping aboard this replica of Sir Francis Drake's famous Tudor ship will inspire genuine admiration for the admiral and his rather short (average height: 1.6m) crew, which counted between 40 and 60. A tiny five-deck galleon just like this was home to Drake and his crew from 1577 to 1580 as they became the first sailors to circumnavigate the globe.

Tickets are available from the **Golden Hinde Shop** (Pickfords Wharf, 1 Clink St SE1). On Sundays kids can party as pirates on deck; sleepovers on the gun deck (£39.95 per person) include grog, ship's biscuits, a Tudor dinner and a breakfast of bread and cheese.

VINOPOLIS
WINE TOURS

Map p436 (✆0870 241 4040, bookings 7940 8300; www.vinopolis.co.uk; 1 Bank End SE1; tours £21-38.50; ◷2-10pm Thu & Fri, noon-10pm Sat, noon-6pm Sun; ☏; ⊖London Bridge) Vinopolis, spread over a hectare of Victorian railway vaults in Bankside, provides a fairly sketchy tour of the world of wine, but it's interesting enough. You need to follow the audioguide to make sense of the exhibits, which introduce visitors to the history of wine-making, vineyards and grape varietals, regional characteristics and which wine goes with which food. All tours involve sampling at least five wines at various tasting stops along the way.

CLINK PRISON MUSEUM   MUSEUM
Map p436 (☑7403 0900; www.clink.co.uk; 1 Clink St SE1; adult/child £5/3.50; ☺10am-6pm Mon-Fri, to 9pm Sat & Sun; ☻London Bridge) This one-time private jail in the park of Winchester Palace, a 32-hectare area known as the Liberty of the Clink and under the jurisdiction of the bishops of Winchester and not the City, was used to detain debtors, prostitutes, thieves and even actors.

FREE BANKSIDE GALLERY   GALLERY
Map p436 (☑7928 7521; www.banksidegallery. com; 48 Hopton St SE1; ☺11am-6pm; ☎; ☻St Paul's, Southwark or London Bridge) Home of the Royal Watercolour Society and the Royal Society of Painter-Printmakers, this friendly, upbeat place has no permanent collection, but there are frequently changing exhibitions of watercolours, prints and engravings (many for sale). Call ahead or visit the website for details of events, such as evenings on which artists talk about their work.

◉ Borough & Bermondsey

LONDON BRIDGE EXPERIENCE
& LONDON TOMBS   MUSEUM
Map p436 (☑0800 043 4666; www.londonbridge experience.com; 2-4 Tooley St SE1; adult/child £23/17; ☺10am-5pm Mon-Fri, 10am-6pm Sat & Sun; ☻London Bridge) Winner of the 'Screamie' award (a prize for scary and haunted attractions in the UK) three years on the trot, this attraction marries history with hysteria. Stuffed away in the vaults beneath so-called New London Bridge (dating back to 1831), the history part takes you on a whistle-stop tour of London's most famous span – from the Romans to the Vikings, from Peter de Colechurch's 'Old London Bridge' (1209) with all the shops, to the American Robert McCulloch, who paid US$2.50 in 1967 for the privilege of transporting the dismantled bridge to Arizona. It's essentially for kids, so the roll call includes 'the Keeper of the Heads', who preserved (mummified) the severed heads of the executed for display on the bridge. Things

ratchet up as you descend into a series of tombs and plague pits dating as far back as the 14th century, where darkness, rodents (animatronics) and claustrophobia meet zombies-from-nowhere (actors). It's all great, occasionally heart-in-the-mouth entertainment and you save up to 50% by buying online.

HMS BELFAST   SHIP
Map p436 (☑7940 6300; www.iwm.org.uk; Morgan's Lane, Tooley St SE1; adult/child £13.50/ free; ☺10am-6pm Mar-Oct, to 5pm Nov-Feb; ☎; ☻London Bridge) White ensign flapping on the Thames breeze, HMS *Belfast* is a magnet for naval-gazing kids of all ages. A short walk west of testicular City Hall, this large, light cruiser – launched in 1938 – served in WWII, helping to sink the German battleship *Scharnhorst,* shelling the Normandy coast on D-Day and later participating in the Korean War. Her six-inch guns could bombard a target 14 land miles distant.

Ranging over five decks and four platforms, HMS *Belfast* is surprisingly interesting – even for landlubbers – as an insight into the way of life on board a cruiser, from boiler room to living quarters. The operations room has been reconstructed to show its role in the 1943 Battle of North Cape off Norway, which ended in the sinking of the *Scharnhorst*. On the bridge you can visit the admiral's cabin and sit in his chair, peer through the sights of the 4-inch HA/LA guns on the open deck, or sink a coffee in the aptly named Walrus cafe.

OLD OPERATING THEATRE MUSEUM &
HERB GARRET   MUSEUM
Map p436 (☑7188 2679; www.thegarret.org.uk; 9a St Thomas St SE1; adult/child £5.90/3.40; ☺10.30am-4.45pm; ☻London Bridge) This unique museum, 32 steps up the spiral stairway through the poorly marked door on the left leading into the tower of St Thomas Church (1703), focuses on the nastiness of 19th-century hospital treatment. Rediscovered in 1956 the garret was used by the apothecary of St Thomas's Hospital to store medicinal herbs and now houses a

MILLENNIUM BRIDGE
The Millennium Bridge got off on the wrong footing when it was closed just three days after opening in June 2000 due to an alarming swing; a costly 18-month refit put things right.

THE SOUTH BANK SIGHTS

TOP SIGHTS
SOUTHWARK CATHEDRAL

The earliest surviving parts of this relatively small cathedral are the **retrochoir** at the eastern end, which contains four chapels and was part of the 13th-century Priory of St Mary Overie, some ancient arcading by the southwest door, 12th-century wall cores in the north transept and an arch that dates to the original Norman church. But most of the cathedral is Victorian.

Enter via the southwest door and immediately to the left is a length of arcading dating to the 13th century; nearby is a selection of intriguing **medieval roof bosses** from the 15th century.

Walk up the north aisle of the nave and on the left you'll see the **tomb of John Gower**, the 14th-century poet who was the first to write in English.

Cross into the choir to admire the 16th-century **Great Screen** separating the choir from the retrochoir.

In the south aisle of the nave have a look at the green alabaster **monument to William Shakespeare**.

Beside the monument is a **plaque to Sam Wanamaker** (1919–93); nearby hangs a splendid **icon** of Jesus Christ illuminated by devotional candles. Do hunt down the exceedingly fine **Elizabethan sideboard** in the north transept.

DON'T MISS...

➡ Retrochoir
➡ Ancient arcading
➡ Great Screen

PRACTICALITIES

➡ Map p436
➡ ☑7367 6700
➡ www.southwark.anglican.org/cathedral
➡ Montague Close SE1
➡ admission free, requested donation £4
➡ ⊙8am-6pm Mon-Fri, from 9am Sat & Sun
➡ ⊖London Bridge

medical museum. Browse the natural remedies, including snail water for venereal disease and bladderwrack for goitre and tuberculosis. A fiendish array of amputation knives and blades is a presage to the 19th-century operating theatres and their rough-and-ready (pre-ether, pre-chloroform, pre-antiseptic) conditions. Surgeons had to be snappy; one minute for an amputation was judged about right. A box of sawdust beneath the table caught the blood, and contemporary accounts record the surgeons wearing frock coats 'stiff and stinking with pus and blood'. There's a demonstration on Victorian speed surgery at 2pm Saturday and one on how drugs were made at 2pm Sunday. Contact the museum for details of its spooky Surgery by Gaslight evenings. If you're wondering how they forced patients up the constricted spiral staircase, the original entrance was upstairs.

DESIGN MUSEUM
MUSEUM

Map p436 (☑7403 6933, recorded information 0870 833 9955; www.designmuseum.org; 28 Shad Thames SE1; adult/child £10/free; ⊙10am-5.45pm; ☎; ⊖Tower Hill or London Bridge) Housed in a 1930s-era warehouse, the rectangular galleries of the Design Museum stage a revolving program of special exhibitions devoted to contemporary design. Both populist and popular, past shows have ranged from Manolo Blahnik shoes to Formula One racing cars, the output of Dutch graphic designer Wim Crouwel and that miracle material, Velcro. The museum also hosts the annual Brit Insurance Design Awards for innovations in the field of design. The **Blueprint Café** (www.blueprintcafe.co.uk; ⊙noon-3pm Mon-Sat (till 4pm Sun) & 6-11pm Mon-Sat) has delicious views over Tower Bridge. The museum plans to move to a new site in the **former Commonwealth Institute** (Kensington High St W8; ⊖High St Kensington) in 2014.

FASHION & TEXTILE MUSEUM
MUSEUM

Map p436 (☑7407 8664; www.ftmlondon.org; 83 Bermondsey St SE1; adult/child £5/free; ⊙11am-6pm Wed-Sun; ☎; ⊖London Bridge) This brainchild of designer Zandra Rhodes has no permanent collection, just quarterly temporary exhibitions, which have included retrospectives on Swedish fashion and the evolution of underwear.

CITY HALL
BUILDING

Home to the Mayor of London, bulbous City Hall (☑7983 4100; www.london.gov.uk; The

Queen's Walk SE1; admission free; ⊕ 8.30am-6pm Mon-Thu, to 5.30pm Fri; ☎; ⊖Tower Hill or London Bridge) was designed by Foster and Partners and opened in 2002. The 45m, glass-clad building has been compared to a host of objects – from an onion, to Darth Vader's helmet, a woodlouse and a 'glass gonad'. Excellent green credentials include the use of cold ground water for its air conditioning system. The scoop amphitheatre outside the building is the venue for a variety of free entertainment in warmer weather, from music to theatre. Free exhibitions relating to London are also periodically held at City Hall.

EATING

Waterloo

SKYLON
MODERN EUROPEAN ££
Map p436 (☎7654 7800; www.skylonrestaurant. co.uk; 3rd fl, Royal Festival Hall, Southbank Centre, Belvedere Rd SE1; grillroom mains £12.50-19.50, restaurant 2-/3-course meal £40/45; ⊕grillroom noon-11pm, restaurant lunch daily, dinner to 10.30pm Mon-Sat; ⊖Waterloo) Named after the defunct 1950s tower, this excellent restaurant on top of the refurbished Royal Festival Hall is divided into grillroom and fine-dining sections by a large bar (open 11am to 1am). The decor is cutting-edge 1950s: muted colours and period chairs (trendy then, trendier now) while floor-to-ceiling windows bathe you in magnificent views of the Thames and the City. Weekday lunch is £24.50/28.50 for two/three courses. Dress smart casual (no sportswear).

OXO TOWER RESTAURANT & BRASSERIE
MODERN EUROPEAN £££
Map p436 (☎7803 3888; www.harveynichols. com; 8th fl, Barge House St SE1; restaurant dinner mains £19.50-32.50, 3-course set lunch £35, brasserie 2-/3-course set lunch £22.50/26.50; ⊕lunch & dinner ⊖Waterloo) The iconic Oxo Tower's conversion, with this restaurant on the 8th floor, helped spur much of the local dining renaissance. In the stunning glassed-in terrace you have a front-row seat for the best view in London, and you pay for this handsomely in the brasserie and stratospherically in the restaurant. Fish

THE SOUTH BANK EATING

TOP SIGHTS
LONDON DUNGEON

Under the arches of the Tooley St railway bridge, the London Dungeon has been milking it since 1974, spawning five other 'dungeons' in the UK and Europe. Starting with a stagger through a mirror maze (the Labyrinth of Lost Souls) and followed by a peep at the Great Plague, trip through torture and waltz through bedlam to head for a close shave with Sweeney Todd, the demon barber of Fleet St, and an encounter with Jack the Ripper.

The best bits are the vaudevillian delights of being sentenced by a mad, bewigged judge on trumped-up charges, the fairground-ride boat to Traitor's Gate and the Extremis Drop Ride to Doom that has you 'plummeting' to your death by hanging from the gallows. A new attraction is Vengeance - a spookily entertaining '5D laser ride' - where you are menaced by reawakened spirits which you fight off with lasers.

It's a good idea to buy tickets more cheaply online for this camped-up 90-minute gore-fest to avoid the mammoth queues. Hours vary according to season, so check the website.

DON'T MISS...
➡ The Great Plague
➡ Jack the Ripper
➡ Traitor's Gate
➡ Extremis Drop Ride to Doom

PRACTICALITIES
➡ Map p436
➡ ☎7403 7221, bookings 0871 423 2240
➡ www.thedungeons. com
➡ 28-34 Tooley St SE1
➡ adult/child £23/17
➡ ⊕usually 10am-5pm
➡ ⊖London Bridge

dishes – grilled sardines, squid with chorizo, sea bass with smoked aubergine purée – usually comprise half the fusion menu, but vegetarians and vegans will feel at home. Strong wine list.

ANCHOR & HOPE
GASTROPUB ££

Map p436 (36 The Cut SE1; mains £11.50-22; ☺lunch Tue-Sun, dinner Mon-Sat; ⊖Southwark or Waterloo) The hope is that you'll get a table without waiting hours because you can't book at this quintessential gastropub, except for Sunday lunch at 2pm. The anchor is gutsy, British food. Critics love this place inside out and despite the menu's heavy hitters (pork shoulder, salt marsh lamb shoulder cooked for seven hours and soy-braised shin of beef), vegetarians aren't completely stranded.

MASTERS SUPER FISH
FISH & CHIPS £

Map p436 (191 Waterloo Rd SE1; mains £7.25-16; ☺Mon-Sat; ⊖Waterloo) This popular place serves excellent fish (brought in fresh daily from Billingsgate Market and grilled rather than fried if desired); low on charm but full marks for flavour.

✗ Borough & Bermondsey

TOP CHOICE LAUGHING GRAVY
BRITISH ££

Map p436 (✆7998 1707; www.thelaughinggravy.co.uk; 154 Blackfriars Rd SE1; mains £8.50-17.50; ☺11am-late Mon-Fri, 5.30pm-late Sat, noon-6pm Sun; ⊖Southwark) It's hard not to warm to this cosy and very relaxed restaurant and

---

TOPOLSKI CENTURY

Within the arches below Hungerford Bridge is **Topolski Century** (Map p436 (✆7620 1275; www.topolskicentury.org.uk; 150-152 Hungerford Arches, Concert Hall Approach SE1; ☎; ⊖Waterloo), the lifework of Feliks Topolski (1907–89), a Polish-born British artist who painted mural after mural on board and canvas more than 180m long, tracing the history of the 20th century from the artist's early life in bohemian Warsaw to his death in 1989. At the time of writing, Topolski Century was shut, but there was a possibility it would reopen as a cafe, with some of the artwork intact.

---

bar in a former foundry building, christened after Laurel and Hardy's dog (also a colloquialism for whisky). Recently steered in a lucratively fresh direction by new owners, this is a true gem, with a sure-fire menu that's a combination of locally sourced food (cider-marinated lamb rump, pan-fried red mullet) and culinary talent from chef Michael Facey, with splendid roasts on Sunday. Few complain, many return for a second sitting.

TOP CHOICE MAGDALEN
MODERN BRITISH ££

Map p436 (www.magdalenrestaurant.co.uk; 152 Tooley St SE1; mains £13.50-21, 2-/3-course set lunch £15.50/18.50; ☺closed lunch Sat & all day Sun; ⊖London Bridge) You can't go wrong with this stylish dining room (with a couple of tables optimistically positioned outside). The Modern British fare adds its own appetising spin to familiar dishes (grilled calves' kidneys, creamed onion and sage, smoked haddock choucroute). The welcome is warm and the service excellent; a true diamond in the rough.

ROAST
MODERN BRITISH ££

Map p436 (www.roast-restaurant.com; 1st fl, Floral Hall, Borough Market, Stoney St SE1; mains £14-25; ☺closed dinner Sun; ⊖London Bridge) The focal point at this unique restaurant and bar perched directly above Borough Market is the glassed-in kitchen with an open spit, where ribs of beef, suckling pigs, birds and game are roasted. The emphasis is on roasted meats (featherblade of beef, lamb's kidneys) and seasonal vegetables, though there are lighter dishes such as salads and grilled fish. Also open for good breakfasts (Monday to Saturday), trading days at Borough Market (Thursday to Saturday) are the restaurant's busiest. If you're on the move, join the queue at the handy **takeaway** (☺7am-3pm Mon-Wed, 7am-6pm Thu-Sat) outside the main entrance at ground level for pork belly with Bramley apple sauce (£6), bacon butties (£3.20) or devil on horseback (£1.80).

GARRISON PUBLIC HOUSE
GASTROPUB ££

Map p436 (www.thegarrison.co.uk; 99-101 Bermondsey St SE1; mains £11.50-16; ☺breakfast, lunch & dinner daily, brunch Sat & Sun; ⊖London Bridge) The Garrison's traditional green-tiled exterior and rather distressed, beach-shack interior are both appealing. It boasts an actual cinema (free films every Sunday 7pm, intermissions for drinks provided) in

START **WATERLOO TUBE STATION**
END **LONDON BRIDGE TUBE STATION**
DISTANCE **1.5 MILES**
DURATION **2 HOURS**

Neighbourhood Walk
South Bank Walk

Across Westminster Bridge from the Houses of Parliament, grand **①** **County Hall** was the seat of London's local government from 1922 until Prime Minister Margaret Thatcher dissolved the Greater London Council in 1986. It now houses museums and hotels. The flashy headquarters of the **②** **British Film Institute Southbank** in South Bank is a mecca for film buffs and historians alike, screening thousands of films in four theatres each year, with archived films available for viewing in the Mediatheque. Carrying up to 10,000 pedestrians each day, a slender 'blade of light' designed by Sir Norman Foster lashing the north and south banks of the Thames, the **③** **Millennium Bridge** is everything contemporary architecture should be: modern, elegant and useful. The magnificently rebuilt **④** **Shakespeare's Globe** is a meticulous re-creation of the original open-air playhouse that stood here, only 200m from the current site, before being demolished in 1644. With ancient

pockets reaching back to the 12th century, the largely Victorian **⑤** **Southwark Cathedral** is often overlooked but well worth a visit, especially for its historical associations and peacefulness. A monument to Shakespeare, whose great works were originally written for the Bankside playhouses nearby, takes pride of place here. Nicknamed 'the egg' (or, more cheekily, 'the testicle'), **⑥** **City Hall** has an interior spiral ramp ascending above the assembly chamber to the building's roof, which has been fitted with energy-saving solar panels. Beyond rises splendid Tower Bridge (p150).

TOP SIGHTS
BOROUGH MARKET

Located here in some form or another since the 13th century, 'London's Larder' has enjoyed an astonishing renaissance in the past decade. Always overflowing with food lovers, inveterate gastronomes, wide-eyed newcomers, guidebook-toting visitors and all types in between, this fantastic market has become firmly established as a sight in its own right.

Along with a section devoted to quality fresh fruit, exotic vegetables and organic meat, there's a fine-foods retail market, with the likes of home-grown honey and homemade bread plus loads of free samples. Throughout, takeaway stalls supply sizzling gourmet sausages, chorizo sandwiches and quality burgers in spades, filling the air with meaty aromas. Shoppers get queuing for cheeses at Neal's Yard Dairy, wait in line at the Monmouth Coffee Company and the Spanish deli **Brindisa** (www.brindisa.com), line up for takeaways at Roast (p174), shop at butcher Ginger Pig and down pints of ale at Rake (p178). The market simply heaves on Saturdays (get here early for the best pickings).

DON'T MISS...

➡ Neal's Yard Dairy
➡ Brindisa
➡ Takeaways from Roast
➡ Rake

PRACTICALITIES

➡ Map p436
➡ ☑ 7407 1002
➡ www.borough market.org.uk
➡ cnr Southwark & Stoney Sts SE1
➡ ⏱11am-5pm Thu, noon-6pm Fri, 8am-5pm Sat
➡ ⊖London Bridge

---

its basement, but it's the food – razor clams, black face lamb gigot with roast squash, and pumpkin, chickpea and courgette cake – that lures punters to this evergreen Bermondsey gastropub. If you don't fancy nearly bashing your neighbour's elbow every time you lift your fork, though, come for breakfast (8am to 11.30am weekdays, 9am to 11.30am weekends).

CHAMPOR-CHAMPOR   ASIAN ££
Map p436 (www.champor-champor.com; 62-64 Weston St SE1; 2-/3-course set dinner £29.50/33.50; ⏱lunch Thu & Fri, dinner Mon-Sat; ⊖London Bridge) A restaurant whose name means 'mix and match' in Malay is going to ladle in a bit of imagination in the kitchen. The menu is ever-changing, but expect creations such as barbecued eel and spinach noodles, pigeon-and-plum hotpot, papaya and lime salad for dessert, plus all-important vegetarian options. Some dishes work better than others, but the eclectic Asian decor is a delight.

CANTEEN   BRITISH ££
Map p436 (Royal Festival Hall, Belvedere Rd, London SE1; mains £8.50-18.50; ⏱8am-11pm Mon-Fri, 9am-11pm Sat, 9am-10pm Sun; ⊖Waterloo)

Part of the design ethos, the institutional canteen-style furniture – plain wood tables, simple chairs – won't be a hit with everyone, but the outside seating in the shade of big umbrellas is immensely inviting on sunny days. The British food is homely and no-nonsense: all day breakfasts, shepherd's pie, steak and chips and daily roast.

M MANZE   BRITISH £
Map p436 (87 Tower Bridge Rd SE1; ⏱11am-2pm Mon, 10.30am-2pm Tue-Thu, 10am-2.15pm Fri, 10am-2.45pm Sat; ⊖London Bridge) Dating to 1902, M Manze (Italian roots) started off as an ice-cream seller before moving on to selling its legendary staples, today dished out by a band of chirpy staff. It's a classic operation, from the lovely tile work to the traditional working-man's menu: pie and mash (£3.20), pie and liquor (£2.25) and you can take your eels jellied or stewed (£3.20). David Beckham is rumoured to be a fan.

APPLEBEE'S FISH CAFÉ   SEAFOOD ££
Map p436 (www.applebeesfish.com; 5 Stoney St SE1; mains £13.50-39.50, 2-course seasonal set lunch £18.50; ⏱lunch & dinner Tue-Sat; ⊖London Bridge) Tempted by the seafood bounty of

Borough Market? Then head for this excellent fishmonger with a cafe-restaurant attached: all manner of fresher-than-fresh fish and shellfish dishes are on the ever-changing chalkboard, but the fish soup as a main (£9.50) is a meal in itself.

 DRINKING & NIGHTLIFE

The South Bank is a strange combination of good, down-to-earth boozers, which just happen to have been here for hundreds of years, and modern bars – all neon and alcopops – patronised by a younger, trendier crowd.

Waterloo

BALTIC
BAR

Map p436 (www.balticrestaurant.co.uk; 74 Blackfriars Rd SE1; ⊙noon-midnight Mon-Sat, to 10.30pm Sun; ⊖Southwark) This very stylish bar at the front of an Eastern European restaurant specialises – not surprisingly – in vodkas; some 50-plus, including bar-infused concoctions, along with cocktails. The bright and airy, high-ceilinged dining room, with a glass roof and lovely amber wall, is just behind, should you need some blotter.

CONCRETE
CAFE-BAR

Map p436 (www.southbankcentre.co.uk; Hayward Gallery, Southbank Centre, Belvedere Rd SE1; ⊙10am-6pm Sun & Mon, to 11pm Tue-Thu, to 1am Fri & Sat; ⊖Waterloo) By day this outlet in the Hayward Gallery (p170) is a discreet cafe serving tea and cake to an earnest, art-loving crowd. By night this Cinderella transforms into a wicked stepsister, with late-night bar, DJs, live music (Thursday to Saturday) and neon-pink cement mixers as props.

KING'S ARMS
PUB

Map p436 (25 Roupell St SE1; ⊖Waterloo or Southwark) Relaxed and charming when not crowded, this award-winning neighbourhood boozer at the corner of a terraced Waterloo backstreet was a funeral parlour in a previous life, so show some respect. The large traditional bar area, serving up a good selection of ales and bitters, gives way to a fantastically odd conservatory bedecked with junk-store eclectica of local interest and serving decent Thai food.

SCOOTERCAFFE
CAFE-BAR

Map p436 (132 Lower Marsh SE1; ⊙10am-11pm Mon-Thu, to midnight Fri & Sat; ⊖Waterloo) A real find in the elephants' graveyard we like to call Waterloo, this funky cafe-bar and former scooter repair shop with a Piatti scooter in the window serves killer hot chocolates and has free films every other Sunday (alternates with live music).

Bankside & Southwark

ANCHOR BANKSIDE
PUB

Map p436 (34 Park St SE1; ⊖London Bridge) Firmly anchored in many guidebooks (including this one) – but with good reason – this riverside boozer dates to the early 17th century (subsequently rebuilt after the Great Fire and again in the 19th century). Trips to the terrace are rewarded with superb views across the Thames but brace for a constant deluge of drinkers. Dictionary writer Samuel Johnson, whose brewer friend owned the joint, drank here, as did diarist Samuel Pepys.

SWAN AT THE GLOBE
BAR

(www.swanattheglobe.co.uk; 21 New Globe Walk SE1; ⊖London Bridge) At Shakespeare's Globe this fine pub-bar at the piazza level, with brasserie, is open for lunch and dinner (lunch only on Sunday) and has simply glorious views of the Thames and St Paul's from the 1st floor.

Borough & Bermondsey

GEORGE INN
PUB

Map p436 (Talbot Yard, 77 Borough High St SE1; ⊖Borough) This magnificent old boozer is London's last surviving galleried coaching inn, dating from 1676 and mentioned in

> ### LOCAL KNOWLEDGE
> #### DICKENSIAN HISTORY
> One of the old brick walls of Marshalsea Prison, where Charles Dickens' father and family were interred for debts, still stands along Angel Pl, an alley off Borough High St.

GLOBE HISTORY

The original Globe – known as the 'Wooden O' after its circular shape and roofless centre – was erected in 1599. Rival to the Rose Theatre, all was well but did not end well when the Globe burned to the ground within two hours during a performance of a play about Henry VIII in 1613 (a stage cannon ignited the thatched roof). A tiled replacement was speedily rebuilt only to be closed in 1642 by Puritans, who saw the theatre as the devil's workshop, and it was dismantled two years later.

Dickens' *Little Dorrit*. No wonder it falls under the protection of the National Trust. It is on the site of the Tabard Inn (thus the Talbot Yard address), where the pilgrims in Chaucer's *Canterbury Tales* gathered before setting out (well lubricated, we suspect) on the road to Canterbury, Kent.

RAKE PUB

Map p436 (14 Winchester Walk SE1; ⊘noon-11pm Mon-Fri, from 10am Sat; ⊖London Bridge) A place of superlatives – it's the only pub actually in Borough Market and the smallest boozer in London – the Rake tucks a strong line up of bitters and real ales (with one-third pint measures) into its pea-sized premises. Claustrophobics can find valuable elbow space on the bamboo-decorated decking outside.

ROYAL OAK PUB

Map p436 (44 Tabard St SE1; ⊘noon-11pm Mon-Sat, to 6pm Sun; ⊖Borough) Tucked away down a side street, this authentic Victorian place, owned by a small independent brewery in Sussex, is a mecca for serious beer drinkers. The literati might find their way here too since it's just a hop, skip and a handful of rice south of the Church of St George the Martyr, where Little Dorrit (aka Amy) was married in Dickens' eponymous novel.

ENTERTAINMENT

For theatre the National Theatre is a must for thoughtful and innovative drama. Into the South Bank's creative milieu will pirouette the Rambert Dance Company, leaping to new premises here in 2013.

TOP CHOICE NATIONAL THEATRE THEATRE

Map p436 (⊘7452 3000; www.nationalthea tre.org.uk; South Bank SE1; admission £10-41; ⊖Waterloo) England's flagship theatre showcases a mix of classic and contemporary plays performed by excellent casts in three

theatres (Olivier, Lyttelton and Cottesloe). Outstanding artistic director Nicholas Hytner has overseen some recent landmark productions and slashed ticket prices. There are constant surprises and recent triumphs have included the powerful *War Horse* with its life-sized equine puppets, *Phèdre* with the incomparable Helen Mirren, and the extraordinary musical *London Road* – focussing on the murder of five prostitutes in Ipswich.

Travelex tickets costing just £12 are available to certain performances during the peak period; otherwise, standby tickets (usually £20) are sometimes available 90 minutes before the performance. Students must wait until just 45 minutes before the curtain goes up to purchase £10 standby tickets. Entry Pass tickets for people aged 16 to 25 are £5. Sell-out performances allow for some standing room (£5).

SOUTHBANK CENTRE CONCERT VENUE

Map p436 (⊘0871 663 2500; www.southbank centre.co.uk; Belvedere Rd SE1; admission £8-45; ⊖Waterloo) The overhauled **Royal Festival Hall** (⊘7960 4242; admission £6-60) is London's premier concert venue and seats 3000 in a now-acoustic amphitheatre. It's one of the best places for catching world-music artists and hosts the fantastic Meltdown festival. Allies and Morrison architects worked on the £91-million renovations by using the existing 1950s materials – concrete, leather and wood – to superb effect. The sound is fantastic, the programming impeccable and there are frequent free gigs in the wonderfully expansive foyer.

There are more eclectic gigs at the smaller **Queen Elizabeth Hall** and **Purcell Room**. The three are also regular venues for the **Dance Umbrella** (www.danceumbrella. co.uk) citywide festival, as well as hosting independent dance productions year-round.

SHAKESPEARE'S GLOBE   THEATRE

Map p436 (⌖information 7902 1400, bookings 7401 9919; www.shakespeares-globe.org; 21 New Globe Walk SE1; adult £15-37.50, concession £12-34.50, standing £5; ⊖St Paul's or London Bridge) If you love Shakespeare and the theatre, the Globe will knock you off your feet. This authentic Shakespearean theatre (p168) is a wooden O without a roof over the central stage area, and although there are covered wooden bench seats in tiers around the stage, many people (there's room for 700) do as 17th-century 'groundlings' did, standing in front of the stage, shouting and heckling. Because the building is quite open to the elements, you may have to wrap up. No umbrellas are allowed, but cheap raincoats are on sale.

The theatre season runs from late April to mid-October and includes works by Shakespeare and his contemporaries such as Christopher Marlowe. The theatre's artistic director, Dominic Dromgoole, has decided to introduce a couple of new plays each season. A warning: two pillars holding up the stage canopy (the so-called Heavens) obscure much of the view in section D; you'd almost do better to stand. Cheapest tickets at Shakespeare's Globe are all-weather standing tickets.

MENIER CHOCOLATE FACTORY   THEATRE

Map p436 (⌖7378 1713; www.menierchocolate factory.com; 53 Southwark St SE1; ⊖London Bridge) Theatre and chocolate, two of many Londoners' major passions, have never been as gloriously paired as they are here – a theatre inside a gorgeous conversion of a 19th-century chocolate factory. To make matters better, the theatre's superb restaurant offers attractive combination deals: a two-course dinner and ticket.

BFI SOUTHBANK   CINEMA

Map p436 (⌖information 7928 3535, bookings 7928 3232; www.bfi.org.uk; Belvedere Rd SE1; ⊖Waterloo) Tucked almost out of sight under the arches of Waterloo Bridge is the British Film Institute, containing four cinemas that screen thousands of films each year, a gallery devoted to the moving image and the **Mediatheque** (⌖7928 3535; admission free; ⊖noon-8pm Tue-Sun), where you watch film and TV highlights from the BFI National Archive. There's also a gallery space with shows relating to film, a **film store** (⌖7815 1350) for books and DVDs, a restaurant and a gorgeous cafe. Largely a repertory or art-house theatre, the BFI runs regular retrospectives and is the major venue for the Times BFI London Film Festival,

THE SOUTH BANK ENTERTAINMENT

LOCAL KNOWLEDGE

DESIGNS ON LONDON

Winner of several Olivier awards for Best Set Designer, Rob Howell tells us where he likes to spend his time in London, when not creating his next production.

Rob's Picks

The middle of Waterloo Bridge (it has to be the middle) is a very special place to stop and soak in the beauty of London's skyline. The Thames flowing beneath, St Paul's (p147) to one side, and the Houses of Parliament (p90) with Big Ben to the other. There's something for everyone here: politics, history and nature.

Before a show, I'm with friends and colleagues in a restaurant close to the theatre we're working in. For me the best room in London to eat or drink in at any time of the day is the National Dining Rooms (p121). Breakfast is excellent and lunch, charcuterie or cheese will fit any moment up until cocktails are allowed. All of this in a magnificent room with generous space and fine art adjacent.

For theatre visits it's hard at present to top the National Theatre (p178). With three different theatres in one building, on any night you can witness some of the best performances and most vivid creative thinking in the city. The Royal Court Theatre (p198) on Sloane Square is the epicentre of new writing in London. New plays have high production values, and many jewels of British theatre history have been discovered here.

When lost for ideas with my work, I may find myself in Foyle's (p137). While it isn't the fabulously shabby (and frustrating) shop it was, it's a great place to lose a couple of hours (and a few quid) solving the puzzles my job throws up!

SOUTH BANK BOOK MARKET

The **South Bank Book Market** (⏰11am-7pm; Riverside Walk SE1) is great for secondhand books long out of print, and is held in all weather in front of the BFI Southbank, under the arches of Waterloo Bridge.

which screens 300 films from 60 countries in the second half of October.

OLD VIC
THEATRE

Map p436 (☎0844 871 7628; www.oldvictheatre. com; Waterloo Rd SE1; ⊖Waterloo) Never has there been a London theatre with a more famous artistic director. American actor Kevin Spacey took the theatrical helm in 2003, looking after this glorious theatre's program. Spacey keeps going from strength to strength, with such recent pickings as Brian Friel's *Dancing at Lughnasa* with singer Andrea Corr (who knew?) and *Richard III,* directed by ex-Donmar Warehouse honcho Sam Mendes and starring the Oscar-winning Spacey in the lead role. Breathtaking.

YOUNG VIC
THEATRE

Map p436 (☎7922 2922; www.youngvic.org; 66 The Cut SE1; ⊖Waterloo) One of the capital's most respected theatre troupes – bold, brave and talented – the Young Vic grabs audiences with winning performances such as the astonishing *Kafka's Monkey,* starring Kathryn Hunter, which returned to the Young Vic in 2011 after a triumphant world tour. There's a lovely two-level bar-restaurant with an open-air terrace upstairs.

BFI IMAX CINEMA
CINEMA

Map p436 (☎0870 787 2525; www.bfi.org.uk/ imax; 1 Charlie Chaplin Walk SE1; adult/child from £9/5.75; ⏰6 screenings 11am-9pm, ad-

ditional screening 11.30pm Sat; ☎; ⊖Waterloo) The British Film Institute IMAX Cinema screens 2-D and IMAX 3-D documentaries about travel, space and wildlife, lasting anywhere from 40 minutes to 1½ hours, as well as recently released blockbusters à la IMAX (DMR and digital titles cost £13.50/8.75). The drum-shaped building sits on 'springs' to reduce vibrations and traffic noise from the traffic circle and subways beneath it, and the exterior changes colour at night.

🛍 SHOPPING

If you like household and fashion design, head for Oxo Tower, home to two dozen small design studios with clothes, jewellery and quirky housewares. Gabriel's Wharf has some sweet boutiques, and inquisitive fashionistas might appreciate a quick scout in and around Bermondsey St.

KONDITOR & COOK
FOOD & DRINK

Map p436 (www.konditorandcook.com; 22 Cornwall Rd SE1; ⏰7.30am-6.30pm Mon-Fri, 8.30am-3pm Sat; ⊖Waterloo) This elegant cake shop and bakery produces wonderful cakes – lavender and orange, lemon and almond – massive raspberry meringues, cookies (including gingerbread men!) and loaves of warm bread with olives, nuts and spices. Six other K&C shops include a **Borough Market branch** (Map p436; Stoney St SE1; ⊖London Bridge).

BERMONDSEY MARKET
MARKET

Map p436 (Bermondsey Sq; ⏰5am-1pm Fri; ⊖Borough or Bermondsey) Reputedly it's legal to sell stolen goods here before dawn, but late risers will find this market altogether upright and sedate, with cutlery and other old-fashioned silverware, antique porcelain, paintings and some costume jewellery.

Kensington & Hyde Park

KNIGHTSBRIDGE | KENSINGTON | HYDE PARK | CHELSEA | BELGRAVIA | VICTORIA | PIMLICO

Neighbourhood Top Five

1 Culturally immersing yourself in the riveting **Victoria & Albert Museum** (p183) with its astonishing collection of decorative and design works.

2 Sizing yourself up next to the awesome diplodocus skeleton in the **Natural History Museum** (p187).

3 **Shopping** (p199) till dropping in Knightsbridge's big-name department stores or turning up surprises in the shops along the King's Road (p193).

4 Nurturing a wide-eyed fascination for the mysteries of the world and the cosmos in the **Science Museum** (p190).

5 **Dining** (p195) out at some of London's best-loved, most diverse and most mouth-watering restaurants.

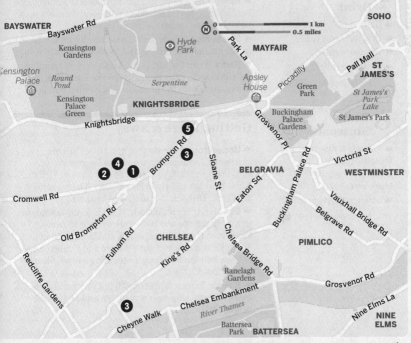

For more detail of this area, see Map p440 ➡

Lonely Planet's Top Tip

Catch the Queen's Life Guard (Household Cavalry) departing for Horse Guards Parade at 10.32am (9.32am on Sunday) from Hyde Park Barracks for the daily Changing of the Guard, performing a ritual that dates to 1660. They troop via Hyde Park Corner, Constitution Hill and the Mall.

✖ Best Places to Eat

➡ Zuma (p196)

➡ Gordon Ramsay (p197)

➡ Dinner by Heston Blumenthal (p196)

➡ Launceston Place (p195)

➡ Penny Black (p197)

For reviews, see p195 ➡

🍸 Best Places to Drink

➡ Galvin at Windows (p198)

➡ Drayton Arms (p198)

➡ Orangery (p196)

➡ 606 Club (p198)

For reviews, see p198 ➡

◉ Best Museums

➡ Victoria & Albert Museum (p183)

➡ Natural History Museum (p187)

➡ Science Museum (p190)

For reviews, see p190 ➡

Explore: Kensington & Hyde Park

With its triumvirate of top museums, South Kensington is compulsory sightseeing land and you'll need several days to do it all justice. Museums open at 10am, so a super-early start is unnecessary, but being there when the doors open provides useful elbow room. With its excellent range of hotels in every budget bracket, South Kensington is also a handy and good-looking part of town in which to hang your hat.

Shoppers will adore the King's Road, mixing with the well-heeled up to Knightsbridge and Harrods via Sloane St, but there are escapes from the crowds, such as the tranquil Chelsea Physic Garden.

Earmark a sight-packed day for a visit to Hyde Park and conjoined Kensington Gardens – crucial to see why Londoners love their parks. Begin by exploring the opulence of Apsley House before walking across the park, via the Serpentine, to the Albert Memorial, Royal Albert Hall and Kensington Palace.

Dining is an experience in itself: Kensington, Knightsbridge and Chelsea truly are your oyster, and offer an astonishing breadth and depth of choice, whether you're grazing, snacking or plain feasting.

Local Life

➡ **Hang-outs** Escape to a literary haven at John Sandoe Books (p199) or rub shoulders with local drinkers at the Drayton Arms (p198).

➡ **Museums** Late-night Fridays at the Victoria & Albert (p183) mean fewer crowds and locals can get a look-in.

➡ **Parks** When the sun is out, Londoners just want to get outdoors to expanses of green like Hyde Park (p192), where they lie on the grass reading chunky novels.

Getting There & Away

➡ **Underground** Kensington and Hyde Park are excellently connected to the rest of London via stations at South Kensington, Sloane Square, Victoria, Knightsbridge and Hyde Park Corner. The main lines are Circle, District, Piccadilly and Victoria.

➡ **Bus** Handy routes include 74 from South Kensington to Knightsbridge and Hyde Park Corner, 52 from Victoria to High St Kensington, and bus 360 from South Kensington to Sloane Square and Pimlico, and 11 from Fulham Broadway to the King's Road, Sloane Square and Victoria.

➡ **Bicycle** Barclays Cycle (p393) is a very handy scheme for pedal powering your way in, out and around the neighbourhood.

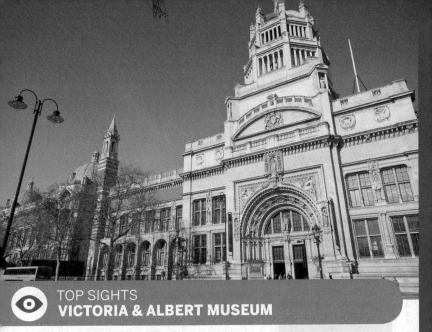

The Museum of Manufactures, as the V&A was known when it opened in 1852, specialises in decorative art and design, with some 4.5 million objects reaching back as far as 3000 years, from Britain and around the globe. It was part of Prince Albert's legacy to the nation in the aftermath of the successful Great Exhibition of 1851, and its original aims – which still hold today – were the 'improvement of public taste in design' and 'applications of fine art to objects of utility'. It's done a fine job so far.

Collection

Through 146 galleries, the museum houses the world's greatest collection of decorative arts, from ancient Chinese ceramics, to modernist architectural drawings, Korean bronze and Japanese swords, cartoons by Raphael, spellbinding Asian and Islamic art, gowns from the Elizabethan era, dresses straight from this year's Paris fashion shows, ancient jewellery, a Sony credit-card radio from 1985 – and much, much more.

Entrance

Entering under the stunning blue-and-yellow blown glass **chandelier** by Dale Chihuly, you can grab a museum map (free; £1 donation requested) at the information desk. (If the 'Grand Entrance' on Cromwell Rd is too busy, there's another around the corner on Exhibition Rd or you can enter from the tunnel in the basement, if arriving by tube).

DON'T MISS...

➡ Tipu's Tiger
➡ Jewellery Gallery
➡ Raphael Cartoons
➡ Ardabil Carpet
➡ Hereford Screen

PRACTICALITIES

➡ Map p440
➡ ☑7942 2000
➡ www.vam.ac.uk
➡ Cromwell Rd SW7
➡ admission free
➡ ⊘10am-5.45pm, to 10pm Fri
➡ ⊜South Kensington

V&A ARCHITECTURE

All the while look around you at the fabric of the Victoria & Albert Museum – tiled staircases and floors, painted, vaulted ceilings and astonishing murals – the museum is a work of art in itself.

When militant suffragettes threatened to damage exhibits at public museums in 1913, the V&A considered denying women entry to the museum, but instead opted for scrapping admission charges to the museum to boost visitor numbers and so help protect the V&A's collection.

V&A TOURS

Consider one of the free introductory guided tours, which last 45 minutes to an hour and leave the main reception area every hour from 10.30am to 3.30pm.

Level 1

Level 1 – street level – is mostly devoted to art and design from India, China, Japan, Korea and Southeast Asia, as well as European art. The museum has the best collection of Italian Renaissance sculpture outside Italy, as well as excellent French, German and Spanish pieces. One of the museum's highlights is the **Cast Courts** in room 46a, containing staggering plaster casts collected in the Victorian era, such as Michelangelo's David, acquired in 1858.

The awe-inspiring carved and painted wood **Tipu's Tiger** – a life-size (and mechanical) depiction of a European being savaged by a tiger – is in the South Asia Gallery (room 41). The **T.T. Tsui China collection** (rooms 44 and 47e) displays lovely pieces, including an art deco–style woman's jacket (1925–35) and exquisite Tang dynasty *sancai* porcelain. Within the subdued lighting of the **Japan Gallery** (room 45) stands a fearsome suit of armour in the Domaru style. More than 400 objects from the Islamic Middle East are within the **Islamic Middle East Gallery** (room 42), including ceramics, textiles, carpets, glass and woodwork from the 8th-century caliphate up to the years before WWI. The exhibition's highlight is the gorgeous mid-16th-century **Ardabil Carpet**, the world's oldest (and one of the largest) dated carpet, from Iran.

The highly celebrated **Raphael cartoons** belong in room 48a while the **photography collection** (room 38a) is one of the nation's best, with over 500,000 images collected since 1852.

Due to reopen in 2012, the **Fashion Room** (room 40) is among the most popular, with displays ranging from Elizabethan costumes to Vivienne Westwood gowns, dated 1980s Armani outfits and designs from contemporary catwalks.

For fresh air the landscaped **John Madejski Garden** is a lovely shaded inner courtyard where you can admire the museum's stunning red-brick architecture. Cross it to reach the original **Refreshment Rooms** (Morris, Gamble and Poynter Rooms), dating from the 1860s and redesigned by McInnes Usher McKnight Architects (MUMA), who also renovated the **Medieval and Renaissance galleries** (1350–1600) to the right of the Grand Entrance.

Level 2

The **British Galleries**, featuring every aspect of British design from 1500 to 1900, are divided between levels 2 (1500–1760) and 4 (1760–1900). They include **Henry VIII's writing box** (room 58e) and the so-called **Great Bed of Ware** (room 57) from the late 16th century, big enough to sleep five!

VICTORIA & ALBERT MUSEUM

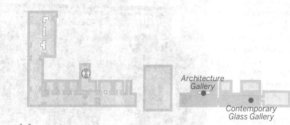

Architecture
Gallery

Contemporary
Glass Gallery

Level 4

British
Galleries

British
Galleries

British
Galleries
Great Bed
of Ware

**Henry VIII's
Writing Box**

Level 2

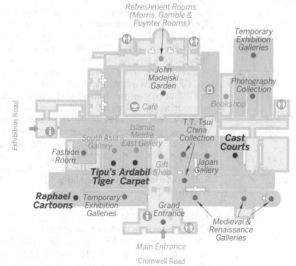

Refreshment Rooms
(Morris, Gamble &
Poynter Rooms)

Temporary
Exhibition
Galleries

John
Madejski
Garden

Photography
Collection

Café

Bookshop

T.T. Tsui
China
Collection

**Cast
Courts**

Exhibition Road

South Asia
Gallery

Islamic
Middle
East Gallery

Fashion
Room

**Tipu's
Tiger**

**Ardabil
Carpet**

Gift
Shop

Japan
Gallery

**Raphael
Cartoons**

Temporary
Exhibition
Galleries

Grand
Entrance

Medieval &
Renaissance
Galleries

Main Entrance

Cromwell Road

Level 1

TEMPORARY EXHIBITIONS & EVENTS

The V&A's temporary exhibitions are compelling, fun and bring lots of visitors (note that admission fees apply), so check the website to find out what's on. The V&A also has an excellent program of talks, workshops and events, plus one of the best museum shops around.

A Furniture Gallery will open in 2012.

OTHER LEVELS

Ceramics is on Level 6 and Europe and Medieval and Renaissance galleries (300–1500) are downstairs in Level 0.

Sculptures at the V&A Museum

Level 3

The **Jewellery Gallery** (rooms 91-93) in Materials and Techniques is outstanding, including pieces of exquisite intricacy, from early Egyptian, Greek and Roman jewellery to dazzling tiaras and contemporary designs. The upper level – accessed via the glass and perspex spiral staircase – glitters with jewel-encrusted swords, watches and gold boxes. **Sacred Silver and Stained Glass** (rooms 83-84) has a glittering collection of elaborate monstrances and other religious artefacts. The **Theatre and Performance Gallery** (rooms 103-106) displays a collection of marionettes, other theatrical pieces and Adam Ant's Prince Charming get-up. In rooms 70 to 73 you'll find part of the **Gilbert Collection** of gold, silver, mosaics and enamel miniatures, while the Gothic revival splendour of the **Hereford Screen,** weighing eight tonnes and designed by George Gilbert Scott, is also on this floor. The **20th Century Gallery** (rooms 74-76) embraces design classics from a Le Corbusier chaise longue to a Sony Walkman, Katherine Hamnett T-shirts and a Nike 'Air Max' shoe from 1992.

Level 4

The **Architecture Gallery** (rooms 127 to 128a) vividly describes architectural styles via models and videos, while the brightly illuminated **Contemporary Glass Gallery** (room 131) is quite spectacular. The British Galleries (1760–1900) continue on this floor.

TOP SIGHTS
NATURAL HISTORY MUSEUM

One of London's most-loved museums, this colossal landmark building is infused with the irrepressible Victorian spirit of collecting, cataloguing and interpreting the natural world. The main museum building, with its blue and sand-coloured brick and terracotta is as much a reason to visit as the world-famous collection within.

Your first impression is the dramatically over-arching **diplodocus skeleton** as you enter, which inspires children to yank their parents to the fantastic **dinosaur gallery**, with its impressive overhead walkway culminating in the museum's star attraction: the roaring animatronic T-rex.

The **Life galleries** are stuffed with fossils and glass cases of taxidermic birds. Ponder the enormity of the extinct giant ground sloth, visit the excellent **Creepy Crawlies** room, and admire the architecture.

The vast **Darwin Centre** focuses on taxonomy, showcases 28 million insects and six million plants in 'a giant cocoon'.

The **Earth galleries**, swap Victorian fustiness for sleek, modern design, the black walls of its **Earth Hall** lined with crystals, gems and precious rocks.

Ride out a tremor in the **Restless Surface gallery**, where the **mock-up of the Kobe earthquake**, a facsimile of a small Japanese grocery shop, shudders in replication of the 1995 earthquake where 6000 people perished.

Sensational Butterflies (adult/child/family £3.50/3.50/12; ☉10am-6pm mid Apr–mid Sep), a tunnel tent on the East Lawn, swarms with what must originally have been called 'flutter-bys'.

A slice of English countryside in SW7, the beautiful **Wildlife Garden** (☉ April to October) displays a range of British lowland habitats, even including a meadow with farm gates and a bee tree where a colony of honey bees fills the air.

DON'T MISS...

- ➡ Diplodocus skeleton
- ➡ Dinosaur Gallery
- ➡ Darwin Centre
- ➡ Earth Galleries
- ➡ Wildlife Garden

PRACTICALITIES

- ➡ Map p440
- ➡ ☎7942 5000; www.nhm.ac.uk; Cromwell Rd SW7
- ➡ admission free
- ➡ ☉10am-5.50pm
- ➡ 🛜
- ➡ ⊖South Kensington

Victoria & Albert Museum

The V&A boasts an unparalleled collection from the world's decorative arts. The museum setting is inspiring, as is the sheer diversity and rarity of its exhibits.

Ardabil Carpet

1 One of the world's most magnificent carpets, the Ardabil Carpet was completed in 1540, one of a pair commissioned by Shah Tahmaspthen, ruler of Iran. The carpet is most astonishing for the artistry of the detailing and the subtlety of design.

Hereford Screen

2 Designed by Sir George Gilbert Scott, this mighty choir screen is a labour of love, originally fashioned for Hereford Cathedral. An almighty conception of wood, iron, copper, brass and hardstone, there were few parts of the museum that could support its terrific mass.

Costumes & Clothing

3 The V&A displays an astonishing collection of historical costumes, from a 17th-century Belgian lace Christening forehead cloth to a gorgeous art deco era Chinese jacket to Adam Ant's outfits.

Henry VIII's Writing Box

4 This exquisitely ornate walnut and oak 16th-century writing box has been added to over the centuries but the original decorative motifs are superb, including Henry's coat of arms, flanked by Venus (holding Cupid) and Mars.

Tipu's Tiger

5 This disquieting 18th-century wood-and-metal mechanical automaton portrays a European being savaged by a tiger. When a handle is turned, an organ hidden within the feline mimics the cries of the dying man, whose arm also rises.

Clockwise from top left
1. Ardabil Carpet 2. Hereford Screen 3. Costumes worn by The Supremes 4. Henry VIII's writing box

⊙ SIGHTS

⊙ Knightsbridge, Kensington & Hyde Park

VICTORIA & ALBERT MUSEUM   MUSEUM
See p183.

NATURAL HISTORY MUSEUM   MUSEUM
See p187.

WELLINGTON ARCH   MONUMENT
Map p440 (⌖7930 2726; www.english-herit age.org.uk; Hyde Park Corner W1; adult/child £3.90/2.30, with Apsley House £7.90/4.70; ⊙10am-5pm Wed-Sun Apr-Oct, to 4pm Nov-Mar; ☎; ⊖Hyde Park Corner) This magnificent neo-classical 1826 arch, facing Apsley House in the green space strangled by the Hyde Park Corner roundabout, originally faced the Hyde Park Screen, but was shunted here in 1882 for road widening. The same year saw the removal of the disproportionately large equestrian statue of the duke crowning it, making way some years later for Europe's largest bronze sculpture: *Peace Descending on the Quadriga of War* (1912), three years in the casting.

Until the 1960s part of the monument served as a tiny police station (complete with pet moggy), but was restored and opened up to the public as a three-floor exhibition space, with exhibits on the **blue plaque scheme** of historical markers (on the 1st floor), the nearby Australian and New Zealand war memorials and triumphal arches around the world (3rd floor). The open-air balconies (accessible by lift) afford unforgettable views of Hyde Park, Buckingham Palace and the Houses of Parliament; the views get even better during the annual **Trooping the Colour** pageantry and the RAF fly-past.

FREE **SERPENTINE GALLERY**   GALLERY
Map p440 (⌖7402 6075; www.serpentinegallery. org; Kensington Gardens W2; ⊙10am-6pm; ☎; ⊖Knightsbridge) What resembles an unprepossessing 1930s tearoom in the midst of leafy Kensington Gardens is one of London's most important contemporary art galleries. Artists including Damien Hirst, Andreas Gursky, Louise Bourgeois, Gabriel

---

TOP SIGHTS
SCIENCE MUSEUM

With seven floors of interactive and educational exhibits, this spellbinding museum will mesmerise young and old.

The **Energy Hall**, on the ground floor, displays machines of the Industrial Revolution, including Stephenson's innovative rocket (1829). Nostalgic parents will delight in the **Apollo 10 command module** in the **Making the Modern World gallery**.

An intriguing detour on the 1st floor is **Listening Post**, a haunting immersion into the 'sound' and chatter of the internet interspersed with thoughtful silence.

The **History of Computing** on the 2nd floor displays some intriguing devices, from Charles Babbage's analytical engine to hulking valve-based computers.

The 3rd-floor **Flight Gallery** (free tours 1pm most days) is a favourite places for children, with its gliders, hot-air balloon and varied aircraft.

The hi-tech **Wellcome Wing** has an **IMAX Cinema** (£10) that shows the usual crop of travelogues, space adventures and dinosaur attacks in stunning 3-D.

If you've kids under the age of five, pop down to the basement and **The Garden**, where there's a fun-filled play zone, including a water-play area, besieged by tots in red waterproof smocks.

DON'T MISS...

➡ Apollo 10 command module

➡ Stephenson's Rocket

➡ Listening Post

➡ Charles Babbage's analytical engine

PRACTICALITIES

➡ Map p440

➡ ⌖0870 870 4868

➡ www.sciencemu seum.org.uk

➡ Exhibition Rd SW7

➡ admission free

➡ ⊙10am-6pm

➡ ☎

➡ ⊖South Kensington

TOP SIGHTS
APSLEY HOUSE

This stunning house, containing exhibits about the Duke of Wellington, was once the first building to appear when entering London from the west and was therefore known as 'No 1 London'. Still one of London's finest, Apsley House was designed by Robert Adam for Baron Apsley in the late 18th century, but later sold to the first Duke of Wellington, who lived here until he died in 1852.

In 1947 the house was given to the nation, which must have come as a surprise to the duke's descendants, who still live in a flat here; 10 of its rooms are open to the public. Wellington memorabilia, including his death mask, fills the basement gallery, while there's an astonishing collection of china and silver, including a stunning Egyptian service, a divorce present from Napoleon to Josephine (she declined it).

The stairwell is dominated by Antonio Canova's staggering 3.4m-high statue of a fig-leafed Napoleon with titanic shoulders, adjudged by the subject as 'too athletic'. The 1st-floor Wellington Gallery contains paintings by Velasquez, Rubens, Van Dyck, Brueghel and Murillo and Goya. Don't miss the elaborate Portuguese silver service, presented to Wellington in honour of his triumph over 'Le Petit Caporal'.

DON'T MISS...

➡ Egyptian service
➡ Canova's statue of Napoleon
➡ Wellington Gallery paintings

PRACTICALITIES

➡ Map p440
➡ www.english -heritage.org.uk
➡ 149 Piccadilly W1
➡ adult/child £6.30/3.80
➡ ⊙11am-5pm Wed- Sun Apr-Oct, to 4pm Nov-Mar
➡ ⊖Hyde Park Corner

Orozco, Tomoko Takahashi and Jeff Koons have all exhibited here.

Every year a leading architect (who has never built in the UK) is commissioned to build a new 'Summer Pavilion' nearby, open from May to October. Reading, talks and open-air cinema screenings take place here as well. A new 880-sq-metre exhibition space, the **Serpentine Sackler Gallery**, will open in 2012 in the Magazine, a former Palladian villa-style gunpowder depot on the far side of the Serpentine Bridge, built in 1805.

KENSINGTON GARDENS   PARK

Map p440 (☑7298 2000; www.royalparks.org.uk; ⊙6am-dusk; ⊖Queensway, High St Kensington or Lancaster Gate) Immediately west of Hyde Park and across the Serpentine lake, these gardens are technically part of Kensington Palace. If you have kids, the **Diana, Princess of Wales Memorial Playground**, in the northwest corner of the gardens, has some pretty ambitious attractions for children. Next to the playground is the delightful **Elfin Oak**, an ancient tree stump carved with elves, gnomes, witches and small animals.

George Frampton's celebrated **Peter Pan statue** is close to the lake. On the opposite side is a **statue of Edward Jenner**, who developed a vaccine for smallpox.

FREE ALBERT MEMORIAL   MONUMENT

Map p440 (☑7495 0916; 45min tours adult/ concession £6/5; ⊙tours 2pm & 3pm 1st Sun of the month Mar-Dec; ⊖Knightsbridge or Gloucester Rd) This splendid Victorian confection on the southern edge of Kensington Gardens, facing the Royal Albert Hall, is as ostentatious as the subject, Queen Victoria's German husband Albert (1819–61), was purportedly humble. Albert explicitly insisted he did not want a monument; ignoring the good prince's wishes, the Lord Mayor instructed George Gilbert Scott to build the 53m-high, gaudy Gothic memorial in 1872. The 4.25m-tall gilded statue of the prince, surrounded by 187 figures representing the continents (Asia, Europe, Africa and America), the arts, industry and science, was erected in 1876. An eye-opening blend of mosaic, gold leaf, marble and Victorian bombast, the renovated monument is topped with a crucifix. To step beyond the railings for a close-up of the 64m-long

TOP SIGHTS
HYDE PARK

London's largest royal park spreads itself over 142 hectares of neatly manicured gardens, wild expanses of overgrown grass and magnificent trees.

Henry VIII expropriated the park from the Church in 1536, after which it became a hunting ground for kings and aristocrats; later it became a popular venue for duels, executions and horse racing. It was the first royal park to open to the public in the early 17th century, the famous venue of the Great Exhibition in 1851, and during WWII it became an enormous potato bed.

West of the **Queen Elizabeth Gate** is the **Holocaust Memorial Garden**, a simple stone marker in a grove of trees. Hyde Park is separated from Kensington Gardens by the L-shaped **Serpentine**, a small lake that will host the Olympic triathlon and marathon swimming events in 2012. Rent a paddle boat from the **Serpentine boathouse** (☎7262 1330; adult/child per 30min £8/4, per 1hr £10/5). The **Serpentine solar shuttle boat** (adult/child £2.50/1.50) harnesses solar power to ferry you from the boathouse to the Princess Diana Memorial Fountain in Kensington Gardens.

Liberty Drives (☎07767 498096; free) also ferries visitors around the huge grounds in electric buggies.

DON'T MISS...

➡ Serpentine
➡ Serpentine solar shuttle boat

PRACTICALITIES

➡ Map p440
➡ ☎7298 2000
➡ www.royalparks.org.uk
➡ ⊙5.30am-midnight
➡ ⊖Hyde Park Corner, Marble Arch, Knightsbridge or Lancaster Gate

---

Frieze of Parnassus along the base, hop on one of the 45-minute tours.

ROYAL ALBERT HALL HISTORIC BUILDING
Map p440 (☎7589 3203, box office 0207 589 8212; www.royalalberthall.com; Kensington Gore SW7; ☎; ⊖South Kensington) This huge, domed, red-brick amphitheatre, adorned with a frieze of Minton tiles, is Britain's most famous concert venue (see p198) and home to the BBC's Promenade Concerts (the Proms) every summer. Built in 1871 the hall was never intended as a concert venue but as a 'Hall of Arts and Sciences', so it spent the first 133 years of its existence tormenting everyone with shocking acoustics. The huge mushroom-like acoustic reflectors first dangled from the ceiling in 1969 and a further massive refurbishment was completed in 2004. You can take a one-hour front-of-house **guided tour** (☎7959 0558; adult/concession £8.50/7.50; ⊙tours hourly 10.30am-4.30pm most days) of the hall from the box office at door 12. Ninety-minute **backstage tours** (☎0845 401 5045; adult £12) are also available, but are far less frequent (roughly one day a month; check website).

PRINCESS DIANA MEMORIAL FOUNTAIN MEMORIAL
Map p440 (Kensington Gardens W2; ⊖Knightsbridge) Opposite Kensington Gardens' Serpentine Gallery and across West Carriage Dr is this memorial fountain dedicated to the late Princess of Wales. Envisaged by the designer Kathryn Gustafson as a 'moat without a castle' and draped 'like a necklace' around the southwestern edge of Hyde Park near the Serpentine Bridge, the circular double stream is composed of 545 pieces of Cornish granite, its waters drawn from a chalk aquifer more than 100m below ground.

SPEAKERS' CORNER LANDMARK
Map p440 (⊖Marble Arch) The northeastern corner of Hyde Park is traditionally the spot for oratorical acrobatics and soapbox ranting. It's the only place in Britain where demonstrators can assemble without police permission, a concession granted in 1872 as a response to serious riots 17 years before when 150,000 people gathered to demonstrate against the Sunday Trading Bill before Parliament only to be unexpectedly ambushed by police concealed within Marble Arch. Speakers' Corner was

frequented by Karl Marx, Vladimir Lenin, George Orwell and William Morris. If you've got something to get off your chest, do so on Sunday, although you'll mainly have fringe dwellers, religious fanatics and hecklers for company.

MARBLE ARCH
MONUMENT

Map p440 (⊖Marble Arch) Lending its name to the surrounding area, this huge white arch was designed by John Nash in 1827. Facing Speakers' Corner, it was moved here from its original spot in front of Buckingham Palace in 1851, when adjudged too unimposing an entrance to the royal manor. If you're feeling anarchic, walk through the central portal, a privilege reserved by (un-enforced) law for the Royal Family and the ceremonial King's Troop Royal Horse Artillery. The arch contains three rooms (inaccessible to the public) and was used as a police hideout. A plaque on the traffic island at Marble Arch indicates the spot where the infamous **Tyburn Tree**, a three-legged gallows, once stood. An estimated 50,000 people were executed here between 1571 and 1783, many having been dragged from the Tower of London. During the 16th century many Catholics were executed for their faith and it later became a place of Catholic pilgrimage.

FREE TYBURN CONVENT
CONVENT

Map p440 (☎7723 7262; www.tyburnconvent. org.uk; 8 Hyde Park Pl W2; ◎6.30am-8.30pm, crypt tours 10.30am, 3.30pm & 5.30pm daily; ⊖Marble Arch) A convent was established here in 1903, close to the site of the Tyburn Tree gallows. The crypt contains the relics of 105 martyrs, along with paintings commemorating their lives and recording their deaths. A closed order of Benedictine sisters still forms a community here.

BROMPTON ORATORY
CHURCH

Map p440 (☎7808 0900; www.bromptonoratory. com; 215 Brompton Rd SW7; ◎7am-8pm; ⊖South Kensington) Also known as the London Oratory and the Oratory of St Philip Neri, this Roman Catholic church is second in size only to the incomplete Westminster Cathedral. Built in Italian baroque style in 1884, the impressive interior is swathed in marble and statuary; much of the decorative work predates the church and was imported from Italian churches. The incense-infused services are spellbinding, especially the Solemn Mass in Latin on Sundays (11am).

Intriguingly the church was employed by the KGB during the Cold War as a dead-letter box. If you want to get married here, apply six months in advance. There are five daily Masses on weekdays, four on Saturday and seven on Sunday between 7am and 8pm.

FREE MICHELIN HOUSE
HISTORIC BUILDING

Map p440 (81 Fulham Rd SW3; ⊖South Kensington) Even if dinner at the Bibendum (p196) restaurant isn't on your menu, pop into this breathtaking art nouveau building. Built for Michelin between 1905 and 1911 by François Espinasse, and completely restored in 1985, the building blurs the line between art nouveau and art deco. The iconic roly-poly Michelin Man (Bibendum) appears in the exquisite modern stained glass (the originals were removed at the outbreak of WWII and subsequently vanished), while the mesmerising lobby is decorated with tiles showing early-20th-century cars.

⊙ Chelsea & Belgravia

KING'S ROAD
STREET

Map p440 (⊖Sloane Sq or South Kensington) In the 17th century Charles II fashioned a love nest here for himself and his mistress Nell Gwyn, an orange seller turned actress at the Drury Lane Theatre. Heading back to Hampton Court Palace at eventide, Charles would employ a farmer's track that inevitably came to be known as the King's Road. The street was at the forefront of London fashion during the technicolour '60s and anarchic '70s, and continues to be trendy now, albeit in a more self-conscious way.

Near the Sloane Sq end, the **Saatchi Gallery** (☎7823 2363; www.saatchi-gallery.co.uk; Duke of York's HQ, King's Rd SW3 4SQ; admission free; ◎10am-6pm) offers 6500 sq metres of space for temporary exhibitions.

CHELSEA PHYSIC GARDEN
GARDEN

Map p440 (☎7352 5646; www.chelseaphysic garden.co.uk; 66 Royal Hospital Rd SW3; adult/child £8/5; ◎noon-5pm Tue-Fri (to 10pm Wed Jul & Aug), noon-6pm Sun Apr-Oct); ☎; ⊖Sloane Sq) This walled pocket of botanical enchantment was established by the Apothecaries' Society in 1676 for students working on medicinal plants and healing. One of Europe's oldest of its kind, the small

TOP SIGHTS
KENSINGTON PALACE

Built in 1605 the palace became the favourite royal residence under William and Mary of Orange in 1689, and remained so until George III became king and relocated to Buckingham Palace.

In the 17th and 18th centuries, Kensington Palace was variously renovated by Sir Christopher Wren and William Kent. At the time of writing the palace and its garden were undergoing costly restoration in preparation for a grand reopening in late March 2012. For most visitors the highlight is the **Royal Ceremonial Dress Collection**.

Most beautiful of all the quarters is the **Cupola Room**. The **Queen's Apartments** nearby are where Queen Mary entertained her visitors.

The **King's Gallery** displays some of the royal art collection, including the only known painting of a classical subject by Van Dyck.

The **King's Drawing Room** is dominated by a painting of **Cupid and Venus** by Giorgio Vasari (1511–74). There are lush views of the park and gardens from here.

The **Sunken Garden** near the palace is at its prettiest in summer; the nearby Orangery (p196) is a bright, rather formal place for tea. A new cafe will be added to the palace once renovations are complete in 2012.

DON'T MISS...

➡ Royal Ceremonial Dress Collection

➡ Cupola Room

➡ King's Gallery

➡ Queen's Apartments

PRACTICALITIES

➡ Map p440

➡ ☑0844 482 7777

➡ www.hrp.org.uk

➡ adult/child £12.50/6.25, park & gardens free

➡ ⊙10am-6pm Mar-Sep, to 5pm Oct-Feb

➡ ⊜Queensway, Notting Hill Gate or High St Kensington

grounds are a compendium of botany from carnivorous pitcher plants to rich yellow flag irises, a cork oak from Portugal, delightful ferns and a treasure trove of rare trees and shrubs. The fascinating pharmaceutical garden grows plants used in contemporary Western medicine; the world medicine garden has a selection of plants used by tribal peoples in Australia, China, India, New Zealand and North America; and there's a heady perfume and aromatherapy garden. Enter from Swan Walk. Free tours are held three times daily and a host of courses and lectures detail plant remedies.

FREE ROYAL HOSPITAL
CHELSEA   HISTORIC BUILDING
Map p440 (☑7881 5200; www.chelsea-pensioners.co.uk; Royal Hospital Rd SW3; ⊙10am-noon & 2-4pm, closed Sun Oct-Mar; ☎; ⊜Sloane Sq) Designed by Christopher Wren, this superb structure was built in 1692 to provide shelter for ex-servicemen. Since the reign of Charles II it has housed hundreds of war veterans, known as Chelsea Pensioners. They're fondly regarded as national treasures, and cut striking figures in the dark-blue greatcoats (in winter) or scarlet frock coats (in summer) that they wear on ceremonial occasions.

The museum contains a huge collection of war medals bequeathed by former residents and you'll get to peek at the hospital's Great Hall refectory, Octagon Porch, chapel and courtyards. Opening times of the grounds vary wildly through the year, but they are usually open from 10am to between 4.30pm and 8.30pm Monday to Saturday and from 2pm on Sunday.

CARLYLE'S HOUSE   HISTORIC BUILDING
Map p440 (☑7352 7087; www.nationaltrust.org.uk; 24 Cheyne Row SW3; adult/child £5.10/2.60; ⊙11am-5pm Wed-Sun Mar-Oct; ⊜Sloane Sq) From 1834 until his death in 1881, the eminent Victorian essayist and historian Thomas Carlyle dwelled in this three-storey terrace house, bought by his parents when surrounded by open fields in what was then a deeply unfashionable part of town. The lovely Queen Ann house – built in 1708 – is magnificently preserved as it looked in 1895, when it became London's first literary shrine. It's not big but has been left much as it was when Carlyle was living here and Chopin, Tennyson and Dickens came to call.

Carlyle unsuccessfully soundproofed his attic room from the hullabaloo of street criers, organ grinders and Italian ice-cream sellers and against this acoustic backdrop penned his famous history of the French Revolution. The first chapter was inadvertently tossed onto the fire by John Stuart Mill's maid; the stoic Carlyle took up his quill and wrote it again.

The family managed to get through 32 maids in as many years (one was an old soak who collapsed comatose in the hall, blocking the door, while another went into labour in the China room).

FREE NATIONAL ARMY MUSEUM MUSEUM

Map p440 (☑7881 2455, 7730 0717; www.nam. ac.uk; Royal Hospital Rd SW3; ☉10am-5.30pm; ☏; ☉Sloane Sq) This museum's four levels tell the history of the British army from the perspective of its servicemen and servicewomen. Standout pieces include the life and times of the 'Redcoat', the tactical battle at Waterloo between victor and vanquished and the skeleton of Napoleon's horse. In the Conflicts of Interest, 1969–Present section on level 4, hunt down the distinctly Darth Vaderish 'Fedayeen' helmet from 2003, worn by members of a paramilitary unit loyal to Saddam Hussein.

CHELSEA OLD CHURCH CHURCH

Map p440 (☑7795 1019; cnr Cheyne Walk & Old Church St SW3; ☉during church services & 2-4pm Tue, Wed & Thu, 1.30-5.30pm Sun; ☏; ☉Sloane Sq) This church stands behind a bronze monument to Thomas More (1477–1535). More's body is thought to be buried somewhere within the church; his head, having been hung out on London Bridge, is now at rest far away in St Dunstan's Church, Canterbury. Original features in the church include the Tudor More Chapel. At the western end of the south aisle don't miss the only chained books in a London church (chained, of course, to stop anyone making off with them).

☉ Victoria & Pimlico

WESTMINSTER CATHEDRAL CHURCH

Map p440 (☑7798 9055; www.westminsterca thedral.org.uk; Victoria St SW1; admission free, exhibition adult/concession £5/2.50, joint ticket with tower £8/4, tower £5/2.50; ☉cathedral 7am-7pm, tower 9.30am-12.30pm & 1-5pm daily Apr-

Nov, Thu-Sun Dec-Mar, exhibition 9.30am-5pm Mon-Fri, to 6pm Sat & Sun; ☏; ☉Victoria) With its distinctive candy-striped red-brick and white-stone tower features, John Francis Bentley's 19th-century cathedral, the mother church of Roman Catholicism in England and Wales, is a splendid example of neo-Byzantine architecture. Although construction started here in 1896 and worshippers began attending services seven years later, the church ran out of money and the gaunt interior remains largely unfinished.

The assumption of colour by the gloomy interior is a painfully slow process. The **Chapel of the Blessed Sacrament** and other parts of the interior are ablaze with Eastern Roman mosaics and ornamented with 100 types of marble; other areas are just bare brick. The work is also expensive, with £500,000 needed to decorate the exposed bricks of St George's Chapel alone.

The highly regarded stone bas-reliefs of the **Stations of the Cross** (1918) by Eric Gill and the marvellously sombre atmosphere make this a welcome haven from the traffic outside. The views from the 83m-tall **bell tower** – thankfully, accessible by lift – are impressive. Six Masses are said daily from Sunday to Friday and five on Saturday.

 EATING

Quality gravitates to where the money is, and you'll find some of London's finest establishments in the swanky hotels and ritzy mews of Chelsea, Belgravia and Knightsbridge. Chic and cosmopolitan South Kensington has always been reliable for pan-European options.

☒ Knightsbridge, Kensington & Hyde Park

LAUNCESTON PLACE MODERN EUROPEAN ££

Map p440 (☑7937 6912; www.launceston place-restaurant.co.uk; 1a Launceston Pl W8; 3-course lunch/Sun lunch/dinner £18/24/42; ☉closed lunch Mon; ☉Gloucester Rd or Kensington High St) This exceptionally handsome restaurant on a picture-postcard Kensington street of Edwardian houses is superchic. The food, prepared by chef Tristan Welch, a protégé of Marcus Wareing, tastes as divine as it looks. The adventurous (and flush) will go for the tasting menu (£52).

ZUMA
JAPANESE £££

Map p440 (☎7584 1010; www.zumarestaurant. com; 5 Raphael St SW7; mains £15-75; ⊖Knightsbridge) A modern-day take on the traditional Japanese *izakaya* ('a place to stay and drink sake'), where drinking and eating go together in relaxed unison, Zuma oozes style and sophistication. Traditional Japanese materials – wood and stone – combine with modern pronunciation for a highly contemporary feel. The private *kotatsu* room is the place for large dinner groups, or dine alongside the open-plan kitchen at the sushi counter. Ultimately it's the sushi, sashimi and robata dishes, all excellent and outstandingly presented, that steal the show. With more than 40 different types of sake at the bar, drinkers will find themselves in capable hands.

DINNER BY HESTON BLUMENTHAL
MODERN BRITISH £££

Map p440 (☎7201 3833; www.dinnerbyheston. com; Mandarin Oriental Hyde Park, 66 Knightsbridge SW1; set lunch £28, mains £32-72; ⊙lunch & dinner; ⊖Knightsbridge) The most eagerly awaited restaurant opening of recent years, sumptuously presented Dinner, on the ground floor of the Mandarin Oriental, is a gastronomic tour de force, taking diners on a tour of British culinary history (with inventive modern inflections). Dishes carry historical dates to provide context and a sense of tradition, while the restaurant interior is a design triumph, from the glass-walled kitchen and its overhead clock mechanism to the large windows onto the park. The broth of lamb (c 1730) is a lovingly prepared infusion of flavour, and the cod in cider (c 1940) is a joy, but unless you order the set lunch, your bill may quickly spiral out of control. Book ahead.

RACINE
FRENCH ££

Map p440 (www.racine-restaurant.com; 239 Brompton Rd SW3; mains £15.75-29.75, 2-/3-course set lunch £15.50/17.75; ⊖Knightsbridge or South Kensington) Regional French cooking is the vehicle at this good-looking brasserie. Expect the likes of *tête de veau* (the classic French veal dish; £17.75) and grilled rabbit with mustard (£16.75). Being French and very classic, dishes might feel heavy to some, but the sauces and the desserts are all spot on.

BIBENDUM
MODERN EUROPEAN £££

Map p440 (7589 1480; www.bibendum.co.uk; Michelin House, 81 Fulham Rd SW3; lunch £21-29.50, 2-/3-course set lunches £26.50/30; ⊙lunch & dinner; ⊖South Kensington) Named after the roly-poly Michelin man, Bibendum offers upstairs dining in a spacious environment illuminated by sunlight through magnificent stained-glass windows. The heritage-listed art nouveau Michelin House (p193) setting is unique, but the food is also very good. The Bibendum Oyster Bar on the ground floor offers a front-row seat from which to admire the building's lovely foyer while lapping up terrific native and rock oysters (per half-dozen £12).

MIN JIANG
CHINESE £££

Map p440 (www.minjiang.co.uk; 10th fl, Royal Garden Hotel, 2-24 Kensington High St W8; mains £10.50-48; ⊖Kensington High St) Min Jiang serves up seafood, excellent Peking duck (half/whole £27.50/53.50) – cooked in a wood-burning stove – and has sumptuously regal views over Kensington Palace and Gardens. The menu is diverse, with a sporadic accent on spice (the Min Jiang is a river in Sichuan), but vaults alarmingly across China from dim sum to stir-fried Mongolian-style ostrich.

KAZAN
TURKISH ££

Map p440 (www.kazan-restaurant.com; 93-94 Wilton Rd SW1; mains £11.95-15.95, set meals £25.95-39.95; ⊖Victoria) Excellent and enjoyable, Kazan gets repeated thumbs up for its set meze platters, shish kebabs and *karni-yarik* (lamb-stuffed aubergines). Flavours are rich and full, service attentive and the refreshingly unaffected setting allows you to focus on dining, with one eye on the evening belly dancers that occasionally swivel into view. Seafood and vegetarian options available.

TOM'S KITCHEN
MODERN EUROPEAN ££

Map p440 (www.tomskitchen.co.uk; 27 Cale St SW3; mains £13.90-30; ⊙8-11am & noon-3pm Mon-Fri, 10am-4pm Sat & Sun, plus 6-11pm daily; ⊖South Kensington) Celebrity chef Tom Aikens' restaurant serves excellent food (including award-winning breakfasts and pancakes).

ORANGERY
CAFE ££

Map p440 (www.hrp.org.uk; Kensington Palace, Kensington Gardens W8; mains £9.50-14; ⊙10am-6pm

Mar-Sep, to 5pm Oct-Feb; ⊜Queensway, Notting Hill Gate or High St Kensington) The Orangery, housed in an 18th-century conservatory on the grounds of Kensington Palace, is lovely for lunch, especially if the sun is beaming. The standout experience is tea, ranging in price from the Signature Orange Tea (£14.85 per person) to the indulgent heights of the Tregothnan English Tea (£33.75), a champagne-laced feast.

DAQUISE
POLISH £

Map p440 (20 Thurloe St SW7; mains £6.50-13.50, set lunch £9.50; ⊜South Kensington) This popular Polish cafe-cum-diner tempts with a good range of vodkas and reasonably priced dishes, including the oft-seen *bigos*, a 'hunter's stew' of cabbage and pork, and ravioli-like pierogi.

BYRON
BURGERS £

Map p440 (www.byronhamburgers.com; 300 King's Rd SW3; mains £6.50-8.75; ⊜Sloane Sq) Byron serves up only 'proper hamburgers' (or so says its sign). The Classic – 6oz of Aberdeen Angus beef – is chunky enough (and you shouldn't beef about the price), but you can double up for an extra £3.75.

✗ Chelsea & Belgravia

TOP CHOICE ⟩ GORDON RAMSAY
MODERN EUROPEAN £££

Map p440 (☎7352 4441; www.gordonramsay.com; 68 Royal Hospital Rd SW3; 3-course lunch/dinner £45/90; ☉lunch & dinner Mon-Fri; ⊜Sloane Sq) One of Britain's finest restaurants and London's longest-running with three Michelin stars, this is hallowed turf for those who worship at the altar of the stove. It's true that it's a treat right from the taster to the truffles, but you won't get much time to savour it all. Bookings are made in specific sittings and you dare not linger; book as late as you can to avoid that rushed feeling. The blowout tasting Menu Prestige (£120) is seven courses of absolute perfection.

PENNY BLACK
BRITISH ££

Map p440 (www.thepennyblack.com; 212 Fulham Rd SW10; mains £14-25; ☉noon-3pm & 6-11pm Tue-Sat, noon-10.30pm Sun; ⊜West Brompton or Gloucester Rd) Led by head chef Jan Chanter, this contemporary and stylish restaurant stimulates the senses with its combination of fresh, locally sourced ingredients, culinary excellence and highly appetising presentation. The beef Wellington, potato and fennel bake is a standout experience, but the desserts also demand attention. If you've kids in tow, the toad-in-the-hole obliges. Service is top of the range.

RASOI VINEET BHATIA
INDIAN £££

Map p440 (☎7225 1881; www.rasoi-uk.com; 10 Lincoln St SW3; 2-/3-/4-course lunch £21/27/32; ☉lunch Sun-Fri, dinner daily; ⊜Sloane Sq) When you eventually locate this gorgeous restaurant off the King's Road and ring the doorbell, it's like being invited round for dinner at someone's Chelsea residence with a handful of other guests. High on hospitality, seductively decorated and home to stunningly presented Indian cuisine (including a seven-course vegetarian gourmand menu for £79), this is truly what a fine dining experience should be. Book ahead.

✗ Victoria & Pimlico

ROUSSILLON
FRENCH £££

Map p440 (☎7730 5550; www.roussillon.co.uk; 16 St Barnabas St SW1; 3-course set lunch/dinner £35/55; ☉closed lunch Sat & all day Sun; ⊜Sloane Sq) On a quiet side street off Pimlico Rd, Michelin-starred Roussillon offers fine service, lovely muted decor and fresh English ingredients dexterously cooked *à la française*. There's no à la carte; choose from among four to six starters and main courses at lunch or dinner, or there's a more extravagant tasting menu (£48 to £58 at lunch, £75 at dinner) of eight courses. The Menu Légumes (£65) puts vegetarian cooking into the haute cuisine league.

HUNAN
CHINESE ££

Map p440 (☎7730 5712; 51 Pimlico Rd; lunch/dinner £28.80/41.80; ⊜Sloane Sq) In business since 1982 this understated Chinese restaurant imaginatively exercises a no-menu policy, so just present your preferences and let the *dachu* (chef) get cracking. If you need inspiration, however, staff assist with ideas, such as the appetising slow-cooked belly pork with Chinese spices and preserved vegetables. Named after a southwestern Chinese province celebrated for its piquant *xiangcai* cuisine (and birthplace of Chairman Mao), Hunan's dishes range across the chilli spectrum. Vegetarian tasting menu available.

🍷 DRINKING & NIGHTLIFE

GALVIN AT WINDOWS
COCKTAIL BAR

(www.galvinatwindows.com; London Hilton on Park Lane, 28th fl, 22 Park Lane W1; ☺10am-1am Mon-Wed, to 3am Thu-Sat, to 11pm Sun; ⊖Hyde Park Corner) This swish bar on the edge of Hyde Park opens onto stunning views, especially at dusk. Cocktail prices reach similar heights (£13.50 to £15.25) but the leather seats are comfortable and the marble bar is gorgeous.

DRAYTON ARMS
PUB

Map p440 (www.thedraytonarmssw5.co.uk; 153 Old Brompton Rd SW5; ☺noon-midnight Mon-Fri, 10am-midnight Sat & Sun; ⊖West Brompton or South Kensington, ☒430) This vast Victorian corner boozer is delightful inside and out, with some bijou art nouveau features (sinuous tendrils and curlicues above the windows and the doors), contemporary art on the walls and a fabulous coffered ceiling. The crowd is both hip and down-to-earth; great beer and wine selection.

NAG'S HEAD
PUB

Map p440 (53 Kinnerton St SW1; ⊖Hyde Park Corner) Located in a serene mews not far from bustling Knightsbridge, this gorgeously genteel early-19th-century drinking den has eccentric decor (think 19th-century cricket prints), traditional wood-panelled charm, a sunken bar and a no-mobile-phones rule. A dreamy delight, this one.

QUEEN'S ARMS
PUB

Map p440 (30 Queen's Gate Mews SW7; ⊖Gloucester Rd) The Queen's Arms wouldn't get much cover if situated elsewhere. But location, location, location, as they say: tucked down a quiet mews off Queen's Gate, this place wins bouquets from the many students living in the area as well as from concertgoers heading for the Royal Albert Hall (p198), around the corner. Add to that four hand pumps and a decent (mostly gastropub) menu.

⭐ ENTERTAINMENT

ROYAL ALBERT HALL
CONCERT VENUE

Map p440 (☎information 7589 3203, bookings 7589 8212; www.royalalberthall.com; Kensington Gore SW7; tickets £5-150, Proms tickets £5-75; ⊖South Kensington) This splendid Victorian concert hall hosts classical-music, rock and other performances, but is most famously the venue for the BBC-sponsored Proms. Booking is possible, but from mid-July to mid-September Proms punters also queue for £5 standing (or 'promenading') tickets that go on sale one hour before curtain-up. Otherwise the box office and prepaid ticket collection counter are both through door 12 (south side of the hall).

ROYAL COURT THEATRE
THEATRE

Map p440 (☎7565 5000; www.royalcourttheatre.com; Sloane Sq SW1; tickets free-£25; ⊖Sloane Sq) Equally renowned for staging innovative new plays and old classics, the Royal Court is among London's most progressive theatres and has continued to discover major writing talent across the UK under its inspirational artistic director, Dominic Cooke.

Tickets for concessions are £6 to £10, and £10 for everyone on Monday (four 10p standing tickets sold at the Jerwood Theatre Downstairs); tickets for under 26s are £8. Standby tickets are sold an hour before performances, but normally at full price.

CADOGAN HALL
CONCERT VENUE

Map p440 (☎7730 4500; www.cadoganhall.com; 5 Sloane Tce SW1; tickets £10-40; ⊖Sloane Sq) Home of the Royal Philharmonic Orchestra, Cadogan Hall is a major venue for classical music, opera and choral music, with occasional dance, rock and jazz.

CINÉ LUMIÈRE
CINEMA

Map p440 (☎7073 1350; www.institut-francais.org.uk; 17 Queensberry Pl SW7; ⊖South Kensington) Ciné Lumière is attached to South Kensington's French Institute, and its large art deco 300-seat *salle* (cinema) screens great international seasons (including the London Spanish Film Festival) and French and other foreign films subtitled in English.

606 CLUB
JAZZ

(☎7352 5953; www.606club.co.uk; 90 Lots Rd SW10; ☺7pm to late Mon-Thu & Sun, 8pm-late Fri & Sat, 12.30-4pm some Sundays; ⊖Fulham Broadway or Earl's Court) Named after its old address on Kings Road which cast a spell over jazz lovers London-wide back in the '80s, this fantastic, tucked-away basement jazz club and restaurant gives centre stage to contemporary British-based jazz musicians nightly. Hidden behind a nondescript brick wall, the club frequently opens until 2am, although at weekends you have to dine to gain admission (booking is advised). There is no entry charge, but a music fee (£10 during the week, £12 Friday and Saturday, £10 Sunday) will be added to your food/drink bill at the end of the evening.

SHOPPING

Frequented by models and celebrities and awash with new money (much from abroad), this well-heeled part of town is all about high fashion, glam shops, groomed shoppers and iconic top-end department stores. Even the charity shops along the chic King's Road resemble fashion boutiques.

HARRODS
TOP CHOICE   DEPARTMENT STORE

Map p440 (☑7730 1234; www.harrods.com; 87-135 Brompton Rd SW1; ☺10am-8pm Mon-Sat, 11.30am-6pm Sun; ⊖Knightsbridge) Both garish and stylish at the same time, perennially crowded Harrods is an obligatory stop for London's tourists, from the cash strapped to the big, big spenders. High on kitsch, the 'Egyptian Elevator' with its ex-owner Mohammed Al Fayed sphinxes, resembles something hauled in from an Indiana Jones epic, while the memorial fountain to Dodi and Di merely adds surrealism. Piped opera will be thrown at you as you recoil from the price tags: after an hour of browsing, you may just want to lie down on one of the doubles in the 2nd-floor bedroom department. But the stock is astonishing and you'll swoon over the spectacular food hall.

JOHN SANDOE BOOKS
TOP CHOICE   BOOKS

Map p440 (☑7589 9473; www.johnsandoe.com; 10 Blacklands Tce SW3; ☺9.30am-5.30pm Mon-Sat, to 7.30pm Wed, noon-6pm Sun; ⊖Sloane Sq) The perfect antidote to impersonal book superstores, this atmospheric little bookshop is a treasure trove of literary gems and hidden surprises. In business for decades, loyal customers swear by it and the knowledgeable booksellers spill forth with well-read pointers.

LIMELIGHT MOVIE ART   FILM POSTERS

Map p440 (☑7751 5584; www.limelightmovieart.com; 313 King's Rd SW3; ☺11.30am-6pm Mon-Sat; ⊖Sloane Sq or South Kensington) This fantastic shop is ideal for collectors of vintage film memorabilia, or merely nostalgic browsers. A framed *Dr Strangelove* (£850) would look good on anyone's wall, or there's 1979's *Alien* (£475), *Dr No* (£385, unframed) and many, many more.

CONRAN SHOP   DESIGN

Map p440 (☑7589 7401; Michelin House, 81 Fulham Rd SW3; ☺10am-6pm Mon, Tue & Fri, to 7pm Wed & Thu, to 6.30pm Sat, noon-6pm Sun; ⊖South Kensington) Located within iconic Michelin House, this splendid design shop constantly rewards visits with ideas, from chic canvases of literary first editions, quirky gifts for the kids, lovely deco-style furniture, trendy minimalist wristwatches and much more.

CHURCH'S   SHOES

Map p440 (☑7589 9136; www.church-footwear.com; 143 Brompton Rd SW3; ☺10.30am-6.30pm Mon-Sat, noon-6pm Sun; ⊖Knightsbridge) Everyone should possess something of quality that will never, ever let them down. It can take up to eight weeks to make a pair of Church's shoes, so they will cost an arm and, more appropriately, a leg, but they are lovingly produced in Northampton with such exquisite care and precision they can last decades.

RIPPON CHEESE STORES   FOOD

Map p440 (☑7931 0628; www.ripponcheese.com; 26 Upper Tachbrook St SW1; ☺8am-5.30pm Mon-Fri, 8.30am-5pm Sat; ⊖Victoria or Pimlico) A potently inviting aroma greets you as you approach this cheesemonger with its 500 varieties of English and European cheeses. The list is sensational, from Black Bomber to Idiazabal, Isle of Mull Truckle and way beyond, all ripened on site (you can taste before you buy).

HARVEY NICHOLS   DEPARTMENT STORE

Map p440 (☑7235 5000; www.harveynichols.com; 109-125 Knightsbridge SW1; ☺10am-8pm or 9pm Mon-Sat, 11.30am-6pm Sun; ⊖Knightsbridge) At London's temple of high fashion, you'll find Chloé and Balenciaga bags, the city's best denim range, a massive make-up hall with exclusive lines, great jewellery and the fantastic restaurant, Fifth Floor.

LULU GUINNESS

FASHION

Map p440 (☎7823 4828; www.luluguinness.com; 3 Ellis St SW1; ☺10am-6pm Mon-Fri, from 11am Sat; ⊖Sloane Sq) Quirky, whimsical and eye-catching British designs (the Japanese love them), from small evening bags resembling bright lips to fun umbrellas and cosmetic bags.

BUTLER & WILSON

ACCESSORIES

Map p440 (☎7352 3045; www.butlerandwilson. co.uk; 189 Fulham Rd; ☺10am-6pm Mon, Tue & Thu-Sat, 10am-7pm Wed, noon-6pm Sun; ⊖South Kensington) Bejewelled skulls, stunning bling bracelets and knockout necklaces; see p138.

Clerkenwell, Shoreditch & Spitalfields

CLERKENWELL | SHOREDITCH | HOXTON | SPITALFIELDS

Neighbourhood Top Five

❶ Wandering through wonderfully preserved Georgian **Spitalfields** (p208), before emerging onto exuberant and cacophonous Brick Lane to explore Banglatown and the hip bars, shops and cafes of the Old Truman Brewery.

❷ Squeezing into some skinny jeans and heading to **Shoreditch** (p211) for cocktails and carousing.

❸ Making the agonising choice between the exciting foodie options on **Exmouth Market** (p205).

❹ Stepping back through the living rooms of time at the **Geffrye Museum** (p204).

5. Market crawling on a sunny Sunday on **Brick Lane** and surrounds (p215).

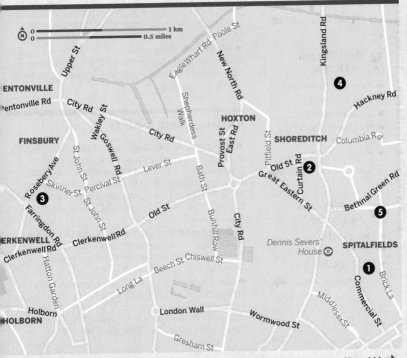

For more detail of this area, see Map p444 ➡

Lonely Planet's Top Tip

Fancy a late one? Clubs Aquarium and Fabric stay open until at least dawn. Brick Lane Beigel Bake will serve you munchies throughout the night, and for breakfast with a pint, the Fox & Anchor throws back its doors at 7am (Monday to Friday). Night buses run on all the major routes, and tubes from Old St, Farringdon and Liverpool St start running between 5am and 6am (7am to 7.30am Sunday).

Best Places to Eat

➡ Moro (p205)

➡ Leila's Shop (p207)

➡ St John (p205)

➡ Viet Grill (p209)

➡ Les Trois Garçons (p207)

For reviews, see p205 ➡

Best Places to Drink

➡ Jerusalem Tavern (p210)

➡ Book Club (p211)

➡ Golden Heart (p213)

➡ Worship St Whistling Shop (p212)

➡ Mason & Taylor (p211)

For reviews, see p210 ➡

Best Places to Dance

➡ Fabric (p210)

➡ Cargo (p211)

➡ XOYO (p212)

For reviews, see p210 ➡

Explore: Clerkenwell, Shoreditch & Spitalfields

These three redeveloped post-industrial areas northeast of the city contain a few key areas, sights and shops that you'll want to explore in the daytime, but none get too overrun so there's no compulsion to head out particularly early. Which isn't a bad thing, given this is a haven for night owls. All three neighbourhoods have a glut of excellent cafes, restaurants, bars and clubs catering to Londoners' desires at all hours. There are plenty of options sprinkled throughout Clerkenwell and Spitalfields, but Shoreditch remains the centre of the late-night activity. Sunday is a great day to join the crowds shrugging off their hangovers with a leisurely stroll through Spitalfields.

Local Life

➡ **The Pho Mile** Spend some time working out which is your favourite Vietnamese eatery on the Kingsland Rd (p209).

➡ **Nights Out with a Difference** Join the table footballers at Bar Kick (p211), learn to life draw at the Book Club (p211), or take in a moonlit flick on the roof of the Queen of Hoxton (p212).

➡ **Shopping Strip** Sashay down Redchurch St (p211), grab a coffee in Allpress Espresso (p208) and check out the designer shops for what the cool kids are wearing this season.

➡ **Big Brunch** There's nothing more restorative than a hearty breakfast and you're absolutely spoilt for choice here. Favourites include Leila's Shop (p207), Caravan (p205) and Luxe (p210).

Getting There & Away

➡ **Underground** Farringdon and Barbican are the stopping-off points for Clerkenwell, on the Circle, Hammersmith & City and Metropolitan lines. Old St is on the Bank branch of the Northern Line. Liverpool St, on the Central Line, gives you access to the City and the West End, as well as Bethnal Green and Stratford in the east.

➡ **Overground** Shoreditch High St and Hoxton are handy stops on the overground, running north to Dalston and Highbury & Islington, and south to Wapping.

➡ **Bus** Clerkenwell and Old St are connected with Oxford St by the 55 and with Waterloo by the 243. The 38 runs up Rosebery Ave, handy for Exmouth Market, on its way from Victoria to Islington. The 8 and 242 zip through the city and up Shoreditch High St.

👁 SIGHTS

👁 Clerkenwell

CHARTERHOUSE   HISTORIC BUILDING

Map p444 (www.thecharterhouse.org; Charterhouse Sq EC1; admission £10; ⊘guided tours 2.15pm Wed Apr-Aug; ⊜Barbican or Farringdon) You need to book six months in advance to see inside this former Carthusian monastery, where the centrepiece is a Tudor hall with a restored hammerbeam roof. Its incredibly popular two-hour guided tours begin at the 14th-century gatehouse on Charterhouse Square, before going through to the Preachers' Court, the Master's Court, the Great Hall and the Great Chamber, where Queen Elizabeth I stayed on numerous occasions.

The monastery was founded in 1371 by the Carthusians, the strictest of all Roman Catholic monastic orders, refraining from eating meat and taking vows of silence, broken only for three hours on Sunday. During the Reformation the monastery was oppressed, with at least three priors hanged at Tyburn (p193) and a dozen monks sent to Newgate, where they were chained upright and died of starvation. King Henry VIII confiscated the monastery in 1537, and it was purchased in 1611 by Thomas Sutton, known at the time as the 'richest commoner in England'. Sutton opened an almshouse for 'destitute gentlemen'; some three dozen pensioners (known as 'Brothers') live here today and lead the tours.

For tickets, you need to send a stamped, self-addressed envelope, a covering letter giving the dates of three Wednesdays between April and August when you would like to visit, and a cheque made payable to 'Charterhouse', to Tour Bookings, Charterhouse, Charterhouse Square, London EC1M 6AN. It's also possible to visit just the chapel during Open House Weekend.

FREE ST JOHN'S
GATE   MUSEUM/HISTORICAL BUILDING

Map p444 (⊜Farringdon) This surprisingly out-of-place medieval gate cutting across St John's Lane is no modern folly, but the real deal. During the 12th century, the crusading Knights of St John of Jerusalem (a religious and military order with a focus on providing care to the sick) established a priory on this site that originally covered around 4 hectares. The gate was built in 1504 as a grand entrance to the priory and although most of the buildings were destroyed when Henry VIII dissolved every monastery in the country between 1536 and 1540, the gate lived on. It had a varied afterlife, not least as a Latin-speaking coffee house run, without much success, by William Hogarth's father during Queen Anne's reign. Restored in the 19th century, it also housed the Old Jerusalem Tavern where writers and artists, including Charles Dickens, met. Inside is the small **Museum of the Order of St John** (www.museumstjohn. org.uk; St John's Lane EC1; ⊘10am-5pm Mon-Sat), which covers the history of the Order (including rare examples of the knights' armour), as well as the foundation of St John's Ambulance, set up in the 19th century to promote first aid and revive the Order's ethos of caring for the sick.

Across the road from the gate is the fine Norman crypt of the original **priory church** (free; ⊘10am-3pm Mon-Sat), which houses a sturdy alabaster effigy of a Castilian knight (1575) and a battered monument portraying the last prior, William Weston, as a skeleton in a shroud. There are also further displays on the history of the area and a lovely secluded garden.

Try to time your visit for one of the comprehensive **guided tours** (donation suggested; ⊘11am & 2.30pm Tue, Fri & Sat) of the gate and the restored church. You'll also be shown the sumptuous 1902 Chapter Hall and council chamber that are still used by the Order to this day.

BUNHILL FIELDS   CEMETERY

Map p444 (Bunhill Row EC1; ⊘7.30am-7pm Mon-Fri, 9.30am-7pm Sat & Sun Apr-Sep, closes 4pm Oct-Mar; ⊜Old St) This cemetery just outside the city walls has been a burial ground for over 1000 years (indeed 'Bunhill' supposedly comes from the rather macabre historical name for the area – 'Bone Hill'). It's probably the best-known 'dissenters' (ie non–Church of England) cemetery in the country. Here you can see the graves of such literary giants as Daniel Defoe, John Bunyan and William Blake. It's a lovely place for a stroll, and a rare green space in this built-up area. Across City Rd, to the east of the cemetery, is **Wesley's Chapel**, built in 1778. It was home and place of work and worship for John Wesley, the founder of Methodism.

⊙ Shoreditch & Hoxton

FREE **WHITE CUBE GALLERY** GALLERY

Map p444 (www.whitecube.com; 48 Hoxton Sq N1; ⊙10am-6pm Tue-Sat; ⊙Old St) Jay Jopling, dealer to the stars of the Brit Art firmament, made his reputation in the 1990s by exhibiting then-unknown artists such as Damien Hirst, Antony Gormley and Tracey Emin. This Hoxton Square cube is aptly named and, while the gallery is now part of Britain's 'new establishment', it's always worth a visit just to have a look at the latest shows. There's another White Cube (p104) in St James's.

⊙ Spitalfields

BRICK LANE STREET

Map p444 (⊙Shoreditch High St or Liverpool St) Full of noise, colour and life, Brick Lane is a vibrant mix of history and modernity, and a palimpsest of cultures. Today it is the centrepiece of a thriving Bengali community in an area nicknamed Banglatown. The southern part of the lane is one long procession of curry and balti houses intermingled with fabric shops and Indian supermarkets. Sadly the once-high standard of cooking in the curry houses is a distant memory, so you're probably better off trying subcontinental cuisine in Whitechapel (p224).

Just past Hanbury St is the converted **Old Truman Brewery**, a series of buildings on both sides of the lane that was once London's largest brewery. The Director's House on the left harks back to 1740, the old Vat House across the road with its hexagonal bell tower is early 19th century, and the Engineer's House next to it dates from 1830. The brewery stopped producing beer in 1989, and in the 1990s became home to a host of independent music businesses, small shops and hip clubs and bars. North of here Brick Lane is a very different place, stuffed with eclectic clothing stores, some of London's best bagel bakeries and plenty of cafes and bars.

BRICK LANE GREAT MOSQUE MOSQUE

Map p444 (Brick Lane Jamme Masjid; www.bricklanejammemasjid.co.uk; 59 Brick Lane E1; ⊙Shoreditch High St or Liverpool St) The best example of the changes in population that

TOP SIGHTS
GEFFRYE MUSEUM

This series of beautiful 18th-century ivy-clad almshouses, with an extensive and well-presented herb garden, was first opened as a museum in 1914, in a spot that was then in the centre of the furniture industry. The museum inside is devoted to domestic interiors, with each room of the main building furnished to show how the homes of the relatively affluent middle class would have looked from Elizabethan times right through to the end of the 19th century. A postmodernist extension completed in 1998 contains several 20th-century rooms (a flat from the 1930s, a room in the contemporary style of the 1950s and a 1990s converted warehouse complete with IKEA furniture) as well as a gallery for temporary exhibits, a shop and restaurant. The garden is also organised by era, mirroring the museum's exploration of domesticity through the centuries.

Be sure to time your visit in order to see the exquisite restoration of a historic **almshouse interior**. It's the absolute attention to detail that impresses, right down to the vintage newspaper left open on the breakfast table. The setting is so fragile, however, that **tours** (£2.50; ⊙hourly tours 11am-3pm 1st Sat, 1st & 3rd Wed, 2nd & 4th Thu) run only a few times a month.

DON'T MISS...

➜ Herb garden (Apr-Oct)

➜ Almshouse interior

PRACTICALITIES

➜ Map p444

➜ www.geffrye -museum.org.uk

➜ 136 Kingsland Rd E2

➜ admission free

➜ ⊙10am-5pm Tue-Sat, noon-5pm Sun

➜ ⊙Hoxton

this area has experienced over the past several centuries is this house of worship on Brick Lane. Built in 1743 as the New French Church for the Huguenots, it served as a Methodist chapel from 1819 until it was transformed into the Great Synagogue for Jewish refugees from Russia and central Europe in 1898. In 1976 it changed faiths yet again, becoming the Great Mosque.

CHRIST CHURCH SPITALFIELDS CHURCH

Map p444 (www.christchurchspitalfields.org; Commercial St E1; ⊙11am-4pm Tue, 1-4pm Sun; ⊖Shoreditch High St or Liverpool St) Diagonally opposite Spitalfields Market, on the corner of Commercial and Fournier Sts, is this restored church, where many of the area's weavers worshipped. The magnificent English baroque structure, with a tall spire sitting on a portico of four great Tuscan columns, was designed by Nicholas Hawksmoor and completed in 1729.

FREE 19 PRINCELET ST MUSEUM

Map p444 (www.19princeletstreet.org.uk; 19 Princelet St E1; ⊙limited; ⊖Shoreditch High St or Liverpool St) This unique Huguenot town house was built in 1719 and housed a prosperous family of weavers, before becoming home to waves of immigrants, including Polish, Irish and Jewish families, the last of which built a synagogue in the back garden in 1869. In keeping with the house's multicultural past, it's now home to a museum of immigration and diversity, with carefully considered exhibits aimed at both adults and children. Unfortunately the house is in urgent need of repair and, as such, opens only infrequently (usually no more than a dozen times a year). Check the website for dates.

EATING

As well as a wealth of fantastic cafes and restaurants, this area also hosts a number of food markets where you can grab a real variety of dishes and cuisines, from deliciously moist chocolate brownies to fiery Thai curries and overflowing burritos. Streets to check out include **Exmouth Market** (⊙noon-3pm Thu & Fri; ⊖Farringdon or Angel), **Whitecross St Market** (⊙11am-3pm Mon-Fri; ⊖Old St) and Brick Lane and the surrounding streets (see p215).

✗ Clerkenwell

MORO FUSION ££

Map p444 (☑7833 8336; www.moro.co.uk; 34-36 Exmouth Market EC1; mains £15.50-19.50; ☜; ⊖Farringdon or Angel) Still a frequent award winner 15 years after it launched, Moro serves Moorish cuisine, a fusion of Spanish, Portuguese and North African flavours. The restaurant is always full and buzzing, and the food is generally fabulous, with such dishes on its constantly evolving menu as wood-roasted chicken with chermoula, and charcoal-grilled lamb with garlic purée. Reservations are essential.

ST JOHN BRITISH ££

Map p444 (☑3301 8069; www.stjohnrestaurant.co.uk; 26 St John St EC1; mains £17-23.80; ⊙closed dinner Sun; ⊖Farringdon) This London classic is wonderfully simple – its light bar and cafe area giving way to a surprisingly small dining room where 'nose to tail eating' is served up courtesy of celebrity chef Fergus Henderson. This was one of the places that launched Londoners on the quest to rediscover their culinary past, and it's a place for anyone who wants an off-piste eating experience. Don't miss the signature roast bone-marrow salad with parsley and follow it with one of the tasty daily specials – middlewhite, chard and mustard, for example, or pigeon, peas and bacon. The traditional British puddings are similarly superb.

CARAVAN BRASSERIE ££

Map p444 (☑7833 8115; www.caravanonexmouth.co.uk; 11-13 Exmouth Market EC2; small plates £4.50-8, big plates £12.50-16; ⊙8am-10.30pm Mon-Fri, 10am-10.30pm Sat & Sun; ☜; ⊖Farringdon) Perfect for a sunny day when the sides of the restaurant are opened onto bustling Exmouth Market, this place is a relaxed affair, offering all-day dining and drinking. The menu offers a real variety of dishes to suit your appetite, combining global flavours and carefully sourced ingredients. The coffee, roasted in the basement, is fantastic.

MORITO TAPAS £

Map p444 (☑7278 7007; 32 Exmouth Market EC1; tapas £4-6; ☜; ⊖Farringdon or Angel) Little sister to the mighty Moro (p205), this is an authentic take on a Spanish tapas bar. Seats are at the bar, along the window, or

TOP SIGHTS
DENNIS SEVERS' HOUSE

This quirky hotchpotch of a cluttered house is named after the late American eccentric who restored and turned it into what he called a 'still-life drama'. Severs was an artist, and lived in the house (in a similar way to the original inhabitants) until his death in 1999. Visitors today find they have entered the home of a 'family' of Huguenot silk weavers, who were common to the Spitalfields area in the 18th century. However, while they see the fabulous restored Georgian interiors, with meals and drinks half-abandoned and rumpled sheets, and while they smell cooking and hear creaking floorboards, their 'hosts' always remain tantalisingly just out of reach. Each of the 10 rooms re-creates a specific time in the house's history from 1724 to 1914; and from the cellar to the bedrooms, the interiors demonstrate both the original function and design of the rooms, as well as the highs and lows of the area's history. It's a unique and intriguing proposition by day, but 'Silent Night' tours by candlelight every Monday evening (bookings essential) are even more memorable.

DON'T MISS...

➡ Silent Night tours
➡ House cat

PRACTICALITIES

➡ Map p444
➡ ☑7247 4013
➡ www.dennissevershouse.co.uk
➡ 18 Folgate St E1
➡ Sun/Mon/Mon evening £8/5/12
➡ ⏲noon-4pm Sun, noon-2pm Mon following 1st & 3rd Sun of the month, 6-9pm Mon
➡ ❸Liverpool St

on one of the small tables inside or out. It's relaxed, convivial and often completely crammed. Chefs furiously prepare grilled delights, as well as slower-cooked options and smaller bites. While the quality is top-notch, portions aren't generous, so you may want more than the recommended three per person. You can book at lunch but not in the evening.

LOOK MUM NO HANDS
CAFE £

Map p444 (www.lookmumnohands.com; 49 Old St EC1; dishes £4-8; ⏲7.30am-10pm Mon-Fri, 10am-10pm Sat & Sun; 🖐; ❸Old St) Cyclists and non-cyclists alike adore this cafe-bar-workshop, in a light, airy space looking out onto Old St. Excellent homemade pies and wholesome salads are accompanied by a small range of daily specials, cakes, pastries, sarnies and good coffee. There are also a few outdoor tables and they'll loan you a lock if you need to park your wheels.

MEDCALF
BRITISH ££

Map p444 (☑7833 3533; www.medcalfbar.co.uk; 40 Exmouth Market EC1; mains £12.50-16.50; ⏲closed dinner Sun; 🖐; ❸Farringdon or Angel) Medcalf is one of the best-value hang-outs in Exmouth Market. Housed in a beautifully converted butcher shop dating back to 1912, it serves up innovative and well-realised British fare, such as hand-picked Dorset crab and Welsh rarebit.

MODERN PANTRY
FUSION ££

Map p444 (☑7553 9210; www.themodernpantry.co.uk; 47-48 St John's Sq EC1; mains £15-20; ⏲8am-11pm Mon-Sat, 10am-10pm Sun; 🖐; ❸Farringdon) This three-floor Georgian town house in the heart of Clerkenwell has a cracking all-day menu, which gives almost as much pleasure to read as to eat from. Ingredients are combined sublimely into unusual dishes such as tamarind miso marinated onglet steak or panko and parmesan crusted veal escalope. The breakfasts are great, too, though sadly portions can be on the small side. Reservations recommended for the evenings.

BISTROT BRUNO LOUBET
MODERN FRENCH ££

Map p444 (☑7324 4455; www.bistrotbrunoloubet.com; The Zetter, 86-88 Clerkenwell Rd EC1; mains £16-21.50; ⏲from 7.30am; 🖐; ❸Farringdon) Overlooking St John's Square, this is an elegant hotel restaurant with much-lauded chef Bruno Loubet at the helm. High-quality ingredients are transformed into hearty dishes full of interesting and gutsy flavour combinations. As you'd expect, there's a well-chosen wine list and the service is impeccable.

COACH & HORSES GASTROPUB ££
Map p444 (www.thecoachandhorses.com; 26-28 Ray St EC1; mains £10.50-16.50; ⊘closed lunch Sat & dinner Sun; ☎; ⊖Farringdon) One of Clerkenwell's best gastropubs, sacrificing none of its old-world pub charm in attracting a well-heeled foodie crowd for its range of daily changing dishes.

ST ALI CAFE £
Map p444 (www.stali.co.uk; 27 Clerkenwell Rd EC1; mains £5.75-15; ⊘7am-6pm Mon-Fri, 10am-5pm Sat & Sun; ⊖Farringdon) This Australian cafe is something of a legend among Melbourne coffee aficionados and its first branch in the UK aims to bring a taste of the good stuff to Londoners. Baristas use beans roasted on site from an extensive menu, and the tempting food menu takes inspiration from all round the globe, with a focus on quality ingredients.

EAGLE GASTROPUB ££
Map p444 (☎7837 1353; 159 Farringdon Rd EC1; mains £9.50-18; ⊘closed dinner Sun; ⊖Farringdon) London's first gastropub may have seen its original owners move on, but it's still a great place for a bite to eat and a pint, especially at lunchtime, when it's relatively quiet. Watch the chefs work their magic right behind the bar, above which is chalked the menu.

CLARK'S BRITISH £
Map p444 (46 Exmouth Market EC1; mains £3.50-5.50; ⊘10.45am-4pm Mon-Sat; ⊖Farringdon or Angel) One of London's famous pie and mash shops. With old-school booths, benches and tiled walls, Clark's has been serving up this favourite East End staple since 1910.

✕ Shoreditch & Hoxton

LEILA'S SHOP CAFE £
TOP CHOICE
Map p444 (17 Calvert Ave E2; dishes £5-7; ⊘10am-6pm Wed-Sun; ⊖Shoreditch High St) Tucked away on up-and-coming Calvert Ave, Leila's Shop feels like a bohemian country kitchen. For breakfast, go for the eggs and ham, which come beautifully cooked in their own little frying pan. Sandwiches are freshly made with superior produce, and there's homemade lemonade and great coffee. Fresh flowers, large windows and outdoor seating complete the gorgeous little setup. At the shop next door you can pick up super-fresh and seasonal vegetables as well as hams, fruit, bread and cheese.

LES TROIS GARÇONS MODERN FRENCH £££
Map p444 (☎7613 1924; www.lestroisgarcons.com; 1 Club Row E1; 2/3 courses £39.50/45.50; ⊘closed dinner Sun; ⊖Shoreditch High St) The name may prepare you for the French menu, but nothing on Earth could prepare you for the camp decor inside this made-over Victorian pub. A virtual menagerie of stuffed or bronze animals fills every surface, while chandeliers dangle between a set of suspended handbags. The food is excellent, if a tad overpriced, and the small army of waiters unobtrusively delivers complimentary bread and tasty gifts from the kitchen. Weekday set menus (two/three courses £17.50/22) are good value.

PRINCESS OF SHOREDITCH GASTROPUB ££
Map p444 (☎7729 9270; www.theprincessof shoreditch.com; 76 Paul St EC2; mains £10-13; ☎; ⊖Old St) Handsome pub with a buzzy

CLERKENWELL, SHOREDITCH & SPITALFIELDS EATING

GEORGIAN SPITALFIELDS

Crowded around its eponymous market and the marvellous Hawksmoor Christ Church, Spitalfields is a layer cake of immigration from all over the world. Waves of French Huguenots, Jews, Irish and, more recently, Indian and Bangladeshi immigrants have made Spitalfields home, and it remains one of the capital's most multicultural areas. A walk down Brick Lane is the best way to get a sense of today's Bangladeshi community, but to get a taste of what Georgian Spitalfields was like, branch off to Princelet, Fournier, Elder and Wilkes Sts. Having fled persecution in France, the Huguenots set up shop here from the late 1600s, practising their trade of silk weaving. The attics of these grand town houses were once filled with clattering looms and the area became famous for the quality of its silk – even providing the material for Queen Victoria's coronation gown. To see inside one of these wonderful old buildings, visit Dennis Severs' House (p206), or, if it's open, 19 Princelet St (p205). Also make sure to check out the weavers' impressive place of worship, Christ Church Spitalfields (p205).

atmosphere, frequented by a mix of City suits and media types. Food is gastropub standard but very well done, with daily specials and polite service. There's a comprehensive wine list and a good ale selection. Head up the spiral staircase to the more refined (and slightly pricier) 1st-floor dining space (reservations advised).

ALBION
BRITISH £

Map p444 (www.albioncaff.co.uk; 2-4 Boundary St E2; mains £6-11; ⊙8am-11pm; 🖢; ⊜Shoreditch High St) Opened in 2008 Boundary (p333) marked Sir Terence Conran's re-entry to the capital's eating scene – with a combination of two eateries, a hotel and a fantastic rooftop terrace. Albion, the ground-floor 'caff' combines a bright and stylish canteen-style restaurant with a terrific deli. The menu features feel-good British food, cooked to perfection, with plenty of attention to detail, including accompanying English wines and beers, quirky crockery and some classic British desserts. Bread is baked on site and breakfasts are a little more adventurous than most, with kippers, kidneys and duck eggs on offer. The subterranean **Boundary** restaurant is the spot for a glamorous meal of French and British cooking, with a focus on seafood, cheese and charcuterie. And the rooftop terrace is an excellent choice for a sunset drink on a sunny evening.

EYRE BROTHERS
SPANISH-PORTUGUESE ££

Map p444 (📞7613 5346; www.eyrebrothers. co.uk; 70 Leonard St EC2; mains £16-21; ⊙closed lunch Sat & all day Sun; 🖢; ⊜Old St) The cuisine at this elegant Shoreditch restaurant is Iberian with a touch of African flair, courtesy of the eponymous brothers' upbringing in Mozambique, and it's every bit as exciting as it sounds. The rare acorn-fed Ibérico pork, in particular, is top-notch. It's all accompanied by an extensive list of Portuguese and Spanish wines.

FIFTEEN
ITALIAN ££

Map p444 (📞3375 1515; www.fifteen.net; 15 Westland PI N1; mains £10-21; 🖢; ⊜Old St) It would be easy to dismiss Jamie Oliver's nonprofit training restaurant as a gimmick, but on our latest visit the kitchen was in fine fettle. Here young chefs from disadvantaged backgrounds train with experienced professionals, creating an ambitious and interesting Italian menu. The ground-floor trattoria is a relaxed venue, while the underground dining room is more formal. Reservations are usually essential.

ALLPRESS ESPRESSO
CAFE

Map p444 (www.allpressespresso.com; 58 Redchurch St E2; dishes £4-6; ⊙9am-5pm Tue-Sun; ⊜Shoreditch High St) Neat-as-a-pin roastery and coffee shop, selling superior coffee, pastries and sandwiches.

✗ Spitalfields

ST JOHN BREAD & WINE
BRITISH ££

Map p444 (📞3301 8069; www.stjohnbreadand wine.com; 94-96 Commercial St E1; mains £14-19; ⊙9am-10.30pm Mon-Sat, to 9pm Sun; ⊜Liverpool St) Little sister to St John (p205), this place is cheaper and more relaxed but offers similar 'nose to tail' traditional fare (potted pork, venison and trotter pie, blood cake) in a simple, clean and bright space popular with

Spitalfields creative types. It also has an excellent selection of British cheeses and puddings.

POPPIES
FISH & CHIPS ££

Map p444 (www.poppiesfishandchips.co.uk; 6-8 Hanbury St E1; mains £9-13; ⏰11am-11pm; 📶; ⊜Shoreditch High St or Liverpool St) Glorious re-creation of a 1950s East End chippy, complete with waitresses in pinnies and hairnets, and retro memorabilia. As well as the usual fishy suspects, it also does jellied eels, homemade tartare sauce and mushy peas, and you can wash it all down with a glass of wine or beer. Also does a roaring takeaway trade.

HAWKSMOOR
STEAK £££

Map p444 (📞7247 7392; 157 Commercial St E1; mains £20-30; ⏰closed dinner Sun; 📶; ⊜Shoreditch High St or Liverpool St) You could easily miss discretely signed Hawksmoor, on an unlovely stretch of Commercial St, but carnivores will find this impressive steak restaurant worth seeking out. The dark wood, bare bricks and velvet curtains make for a handsome setting in which to gorge yourself on the best of British meat, cooked to perfection over charcoal. Make sure you try one of the equally impressive cocktails. The meaty brunch (11am to 4pm Saturday and Sunday) is a great weekend option.

NUDE ESPRESSO
CAFE £

Map p444 (www.nudeespresso.com; 26 Hanbury St E1; dishes £2.50-9; ⏰7.30am-5pm Mon-Fri, 10am-6pm Sat & Sun; ⊜Shoreditch High St or Liverpool St) A simply styled, well-run coffee shop serving excellent Australasian-influenced breakfasts and lunches that focus on seasonal and natural ingredients. It roasts and blends its own coffee just round the corner at its roastery, off Brick Lane.

ROSA'S
THAI £

Map p444 (www.rosaslondon.com; 12 Hanbury St E1; mains £7-12.50; ⊜Shoreditch High St or Liverpool St) Red-fronted Rosa's is a cosy Thai restaurant, over two floors, just off Commercial St, simply kitted out with low benches, banquettes and red stools. Go for its signature pumpkin curry, one of the super-fresh and zingy salads or delicious chargrills.

BRICK LANE BEIGEL BAKE
CAFE £

Map p444 (159 Brick Lane E2; filled bagels £1.50-3.50; ⏰24hr; ⊜Shoreditch High St or Liverpool St) You won't find fresher (or cheaper) bagels anywhere in London than at this bakery and delicatessen; just ask any taxi driver (it's their favourite nosherie). It's always busy: with market shoppers on Sunday and Shoreditch clubbers by night.

THE PHO MILE

Vietnamese refugees first started to arrive in the UK in 1975, after the Vietnam War, with communities setting up in Lewisham, Southwark and throughout the borough of Hackney. Some worked in the clothing industry, others in factories, but families also took over restaurants and started serving traditional Vietnamese cuisine to Londoners. The Kingsland Rd has become famous for its string of Vietnamese cafes and restaurants, many of which are BYO and serve authentic and great-value cuisine. Quality varies and most people tend to have a personal favourite. These are ours:

Viet Grill (Map p444; 📞7739 6686; www.vietnamesekitchen.co.uk; 58 Kingsland Rd E2; mains £6.50-10; ⊜Hoxton) One of the more upmarket options along the road, Viet Grill is a low-lit, modern restaurant over two floors with a buzzy atmosphere and colonial decor. On our last visit the mango and squid salad was particularly good, as were sake lamb skewers and the mighty feudal beef.

Sông Quê (Map p444; 📞7613 3222; www.songque.co.uk; 134 Kingsland Rd E2; mains £6.70-8.60; ⊜Hoxton) With the kind of demand for seats that most London restaurants can only dream of, this perennial favourite always has a line of people waiting for a table. Service is frenetic, but the food is great and good value.

Cây Tre (Map p444 (📞7729 8662; www.vietnamesekitchen.co.uk; 301 Old St EC1; mains £7-9; ⊜Old St) Sister to Viet Grill, Cây Tre serves up all the classics to a mix of Vietnamese diners and Hoxton scenesters in a simple but nicely decorated and tightly packed space. Across the road its cafe, **Kêu!** (332 Old St; baguettes £4.50; ⏰8am-8pm), offers up lip-smacking banh mi (baguettes) to eat in or takeaway, as well as soups, salads and specials.

LUXE
CAFE/BAR £

Map p444 (☎7101 1751; www.theluxe.co.uk; 109 Commercial St E1; mains £8-10; ☺8am-late; 🖱; ◉Liverpool St) With a terrace on the edge of Old Spitalfields Market, this is celebrity chef John Torode's newest London venture. Housed in the Old Flower Market building, there's a 1st-floor dining room (reservations advised) with a central kitchen and lovely corner booths, a more relaxed ground-floor cafe and bar, and a basement venue hosting live music and club nights. The cafe serves a good range of breakfasts, sandwiches and salads and it's a great choice for a weekend brunch.

🍷 DRINKING & ⚓ NIGHTLIFE

🍷 Clerkenwell

⎡TOP CHOICE⎦ JERUSALEM TAVERN
PUB

Map p444 (www.stpetersbrewery.co.uk; 55 Britton St EC1; ☺Mon-Fri; 🖱; ◉Farringdon) Starting life as one of the first London coffee houses (founded in 1703), with the 18th-century decor of occasional tile mosaics still visible, the JT is an absolute stunner, though sadly it's both massively popular and tiny, so come early to get a seat. There's good lunch food and, this being the only London outlet of St Peter's Brewery (based in North Suffolk), it has a brilliant range of drinks – organic bitters, cream stouts, wheat and fruit beers – many of which are dispensed in green apothecary-style bottles.

⎡TOP CHOICE⎦ FABRIC
CLUB

Map p444 (www.fabriclondon.com; 77a Charterhouse St EC1; ☺10pm-6am Fri, 11pm-8am Sat, 11pm-6am Sun; ◉Farringdon) This most impressive of superclubs is still the first stop on the London scene for many international clubbers, as the lengthy queues attest. A warren of three floors, three bars, many walkways and unisex toilets, room one also contains a kidney-shaking 'bodysonic' dance floor. The crowd is hip and well dressed without overkill, and the music – mainly electro, techno, house, drum and bass and dubstep – is as superb as you'd expect from London's top-rated club. Superstar DJs often sell out Friday night's FabricLive, when big names such as Goldie or DJ Hype take over. WetYourSelf!,

a hedonistic techno and house night, is a real Sunday night treat.

YE OLDE MITRE
PUB

Map p444 (1 Ely Ct EC1; ☺Mon-Fri; 🖱; ◉Chancery Lane or Farringdon) A delightfully cosy historic pub, tucked away in a backstreet off Hatton Garden (look for a Fullers sign above a low archway on the left), Ye Olde Mitre was built for the servants of Ely Palace. There's still a memento of Elizabeth I – the stump of a cherry tree around which she once danced. There's no music, so the rooms only echo to the sound of amiable chit-chat.

FILTHY MACNASTY'S
PUB

Map p444 (www.filthymacnastys.co.uk; 68 Amwell St EC1; 🖱; ◉Angel or Farringdon) The local of 'Amwell Village', tucked between Clerkenwell and Islington, is this stellar Irish music pub and whiskey bar that's every bit as cool as its name suggests. The two-room pub attracts an up-for-it young crowd that comes for live bands in the back room, the great whiskey list and the 'filthy food'.

FOX & ANCHOR
PUB

Map p444 (☎7250 1300; www.foxandanchor.com; 115 Charterhouse St EC1; ☺7am-11pm Mon-Fri, 8.30am-11pm Sat & Sun; 🖱; ◉Farringdon or Barbican) A revamped Victorian pub that has retained its three beautiful snugs at the back of the bar. Fully celebrating its proximity to Smithfield Market, food here is gloriously meaty and the pub opens at 7am during the week. Only the brave will opt for the All Day City Boy Breakfast – a veritable meat feast, washed down with a pint of stout (£16.95). It's also a good place to stay (p332).

THREE KINGS
PUB

Map p444 (7 Clerkenwell Close EC1; ☺closed Sat daytime & all day Sun; 🖱; ◉Farringdon) Down-to-earth and welcoming pub, attracting a friendly bunch of relaxed locals for its quirky decor, great music and good times.

VINOTECA
WINE BAR

Map p444 (www.vinoteca.co.uk; 7 St John St EC1; ☺closed Sun evening; 🖱; ◉Farringdon) Simple yet elegant oak decor, an astonishingly comprehensive wine list and amiable service make this a popular choice with suited City workers and local creatives. At the on-site shop you can also buy bottles of all of the wines available in the bar – and the Modern European food is very good too.

SHOREDITCH COOL

The Shoreditch phenomenon began in the late 1990s, when creative types chased out of the West End by prohibitive rents began buying warehouses in this then urban wasteland, abandoned after the collapse of the fabrics industry. Within a few years the area was seriously cool, boasting superslick bars, cutting-edge clubs, galleries and restaurants that catered to the new media-creative-freelance squad. Despite the general expectation that the Shoreditch scene would collapse under the weight of its own trucker hats, the regenerated area is flourishing more than ever, with new developments bringing life to some of London's poorest corners, spilling over into nearby Hackney and Bethnal Green. Once the site of one of London's most notorious slums (known as the Old Nichol), the area just to the east of Shoreditch High St, is currently enjoying most of the attention. Redchurch St is lined with a slew of new cafes and trendy shops, with Calvert Ave and Boundary St, just to the north, following suit.

PRUFROCK   CAFE **£**

Map p444 (www.prufrockcoffee.com; 23-25 Leather Lane EC1; ☺8am-6pm Mon-Fri, 10am-4pm Sat; ☎; ⊖Chancery Lane or Farringdon) Run by 2009's World Barista Champion Gwilym Davies, this large, serene space is a temple to coffee. Check out the line of equipment that looks like a lab and ask the helpful staff to advise on your choice of filter coffee, with a method chosen specifically to maximise the qualities of each different variety of bean.

🍸 Shoreditch & Hoxton

TOP CHOICE BOOK CLUB   BAR-CLUB

Map p444 (www.wearetbc.com; 100 Leonard St EC2; ☺8am-midnight Sun-Wed, to 2am Thu-Sat; ☎; ⊖Old St) This former Victorian warehouse has been transformed into an innovative temple to good times. Spacious and whitewashed with large windows upstairs and a basement bar below, it hosts a real variety of offbeat events, such as spoken word, dance lessons and life drawing, as well as a varied program of DJ nights (from punk, ska and '60s pop to electro, house and disco). Table tennis and pool add to the friendly, fun atmosphere. Breakfast is served from 8am, and food is available throughout the day and evening.

TOP CHOICE GEORGE & DRAGON   GAY

Map p444 (2-4 Hackney Rd E2; ⊖Shoreditch High St or Old St) Once a scuzzy local pub, the George was taken over and decorated with the owner's grandma's antiques (antlers, racoon tails, old clocks), cardboard cut-outs of Cher and fairy lights, turning this one-room pub into what has remained

the epicentre of the Hoxton scene for more than a decade. Some of the best DJ nights in London are on offer here, with cabaret performances taking place on window sills. It's total fun and mindless hedonism. Expect mustachioed media types and fashion-forward youths. Definitely not a place for a quiet pint, there's a great jukebox, and it tends to get packed out at the weekends.

MASON & TAYLOR   BAR

Map p444 (www.masonandtaylor.co.uk; 51-55 Bethnal Green Rd E1; ☎; ⊖Shoreditch High St) On a corner where Banglatown grinds up against Shoreditch, this designer beer bar offers an extraordinary range of cask and bottled beers. The selection is sourced from some interesting breweries, with welcome support for London's new breed of craft brewers, such as Kernel and Camden Town. A tasting 'flight' of three or six one-third pints allows you to sample a real variety. Staff are keen, knowledgeable and helpful, and there's tasty food on offer too.

BAR KICK   BAR

Map p444 (www.cafekick.co.uk; 127 Shoreditch High St E1; ☎; ⊖Old St or Shoreditch High St) A much larger sister venue to Clerkenwell's **Café Kick** (Map p444; 43 Exmouth Market EC1; ⊖Farringdon or Angel), this place has a slightly edgier Shoreditch vibe. This time, too, there was some floor space left over after four footy tables were installed, so there's room for leather sofas and simple tables and chairs.

CARGO   CLUB

Map p444 (www.cargo-london.com; 83 Rivington St EC2; ☺noon-1am Mon-Thu, noon-3am Fri, 6pm-3am Sat, noon-midnight Sun; ⊖Old St or Shoreditch High St) Cargo is one of London's

THE COCKTAIL HOUR

While mojitos and caipirinhas are these days two-a-penny in Shoreditch bars, there are some places that take their shaking far more seriously. Here is a list of our favourites. It's worth booking ahead at them all. Cocktails usually range from £7 to £10.

Worship St Whistling Shop (Map p444; ☑7247 0015; www.whistlingshop.com; 63 Worship St EC2; ☺noon-1am Mon-Thu, to 2am Fri & Sat; ☉Old St or Liverpool St) A 'Victorian' drinking den that takes cocktails to a molecular level, the Whistling Shop (as Victorians called a place selling illicit booze) serves expertly crafted and highly unusual concoctions using potions conjured up in its on-site lab. Try a Panacea, Black Cat Martini or the Bosom Caresser (made with formula milk). There's an incredible array of interesting spirits, as well as a Dram Shop for a private party, and an Experience Room for the really adventurous.

Happiness Forgets (Map p444; ☑7613 0325; www.happinessforgets.com; 8-9 Hoxton Sq N1; ☺5-11pm Mon-Sat; ☎; ☉Old St or Hoxton) The menu promises you mixed drinks and mischief at this low-lit, basement bar with good-value cocktails in a relaxed and intimate setting.

Nightjar (Map p444; ☑7253 4101; www.barnightjar.com; 129 City Rd EC1; ☺6pm-1.30am Tue & Wed, to 3.30am Thu-Sat; ☉Old St) Slick, wood-panelled speakeasy offering nightly live music. The well-executed cocktails are divided into four eras: before and during prohibition, postwar and Nightjar signatures.

Zetter Townhouse (Map p444; ☑7324 4545; www.thezettertownhouse.com; 49-50 St John's Sq EC1; ☺8am-1am; ☎; ☉Farringdon) Cocktail lounge of the Zetter Townhouse (p332), this ground-floor bar is quirkily decorated with plush armchairs, stuffed animal heads and a legion of lamps. The cocktail list takes its theme from the area's distilling history; recipes of yesteryear and homemade ingredients (such as nettle cordial) are used to create interesting and unusual tipples.

Callooh Callay (Map p444; ☑7739 4781; www.calloohcallaybar.com; 65 Rivington St EC2; ☺6pm-midnight Sun-Wed, to 1am Thu-Sat; ☉Old St) Given it's inspired by *Jabberwocky*, Lewis Carroll's nonsense poem, this bar's eccentric decor doesn't come as a surprise. Try the Ale of Two Cities, which comes in a half-pint beer mug.

Loungelover (Map p444; ☑7012 1234; www.lestroisgarcons.com; 1 Whitby St E1; ☺6pm-midnight Sun-Thu, to 1am Fri & Sat; ☎; ☉Liverpool St or Shoreditch High St) The drinks and the look are both faultless at this Shoreditch institution, where it's all about the superb cocktails and the junk-shop chic of the decor.

most eclectic clubs. Under its brick railway arches you'll find a dance-floor room, bar and outside terrace. The music policy is innovative and varied, with plenty of up-and-coming bands also on the menu. Food is available throughout the day.

PLASTIC PEOPLE
CLUB

Map p444 (www.plasticpeople.co.uk; 147-149 Curtain Rd EC2; ☉Old St) This is a tiny club with just a dance floor and bar and a booming sound system that experts say easily kicks the butts of bigger clubs. Head here on Fridays and Saturdays for nights that are often given over to one long DJ set by the likes of Kieran Hebden, Kode 9 or Mr Scruff, smashing out mainly house and electronica.

XOYO
CLUB

Map p444 (www.xoyo.co.uk; 32-37 Cowper St EC2; ☉Old St) Run by a group of music professionals, this lofty venue plays host to a finely chosen selection of gigs and club nights, as well as exhibiting art. The varied program – expect indie bands, hip hop, electro, dubstep and much in between – attracts a mix of clubbers from skinny-jeaned hipsters to more mature hedonists.

QUEEN OF HOXTON
BAR

Map p444 (www.thequeenofhoxton.co.uk; 1-5 Curtain Rd EC2; ☺to 2am Thu-Sat; ☎; ☉Liverpool St) Industrial-chic bar with a games room, basement and varied music nights, though the real drawcard is the vast rooftop bar, decked out with flowers, fairy lights and even a fish pond, with fantastic views across the city and a popular **outdoor film club** (www.rooftopfilmclub.com; ☺Jun-Sep).

DREAMBAGSJAGUARSHOES   DJ BAR

Map p444 (www.jaguarshoes.com; 32-36 Kingsland Rd E2; ☺noon-1am; ⊜Old St or Hoxton) The bar is named after the two shops whose two-floor space it now occupies, and this nonchalance is a typical example of the we-couldn't-care-less Shoreditch chic. The small interior is filled with sofas and formica-topped tables, and art exhibitions deck the walls. You can also order a pizza from the excellent Due Sardi, next door.

RED LION   PUB

Map p444 (www.redlionhoxtonst.com; 41 Hoxton St N1; ☺5-11pm Mon-Fri, noon-11pm Sat & Sun; ☎; ⊜Old St or Hoxton) This stalwart of the scene is run by the team behind both 333 and Mother Bar, and despite being spitting distance from Hoxton Square, it's well enough tucked away down a side street to avoid being overrun by the suburban crowd that now dominates the area at the weekends. Inside it's pure kitsch fun, with a well-balanced mix of down-to-earth and trendy folk. The top-floor roof terrace is a real draw.

CATCH   CLUB

Map p444 (www.thecatchbar.com; 22 Kingsland Rd E2; ☺6pm-midnight Mon-Wed, to 2am Thu-Sat, 7pm-1am Sun; ⊜Old St or Shoreditch High St) It doesn't look like much, but Catch is one of the best nights out in Shoreditch. Upstairs you'll hear anything from '90s to funk and hip hop, as well as a great selection of new and established bands. Downstairs you get a big house-party vibe with DJs who mix up pretty much anything from chart hits to electro and techno. Downstairs is free, it's open late and it's really fun.

HORSE & GROOM   PUB/CLUB

Map p444 (www.thehorseandgroom.net; 28 Curtain Rd EC2; ☺noon-midnight Mon-Wed, to 2am Thu & Sun; ⊜Liverpool St) A relaxed pub/club, in an underwhelming backstreet location, with two intimate spaces serving up hedonistic nights where you're most likely to hear disco, house, funk or soul.

333   CLUB

Map p444 (www.333mother.com; 333 Old St EC1; ⊜Old St) Hoxton's true old-timer, 333's stripped-down manner doesn't bow to Shoreditch's silly cool and just keeps going, despite not being what it once was in terms

of pulling power. The club still hosts great nights that are simultaneously scruffy and innovative, covering indie, electro, dubstep and hip hop. Upstairs the separate **Mother Bar** (☺8pm-3am) is a good, late-opening bar with a lounge, dance floor and fun, up-for-it crowd.

MACBETH   PUB

Map p444 (www.themacbethuk.co.uk; 70 Hoxton St N1; ☺11am-1am Mon-Thu, 5pm-2am Fri-Sun; ☎; ⊜Hoxton) This enormous old boozer on a still-to-be-yuppified street, just a short walk north of Hoxton Square, is an established stop on the ever-changing Hoxton scene. Run by musicians and providing a great platform for up-and-coming talent, as well as the occasional big name on its downstairs stage, Macbeth is an intimate venue, with a second bar upstairs and a large roof terrace as well.

OLD BLUE LAST   PUB

Map p444 (www.theoldbluelast.com; 38 Great Eastern St EC2; ☺to midnight Mon-Wed, to 12.30am Thu & Sun, to 1.30am Fri & Sat; ☎; ⊜Old St or Shoreditch High St) Frequently crammed with a hip teenage-and-up crowd of Hoxtonites, this beautiful old corner pub's trendy credentials are courtesy of *Vice* magazine, the bad-boy rag that owns the place. It hosts some of the best Shoreditch parties and has a rocking jukebox.

EAST VILLAGE   CLUB

Map p444 (www.eastvillageclub.co.uk; 89 Great Eastern St EC2; ⊜Old St) Basement club that sees house lovers flocking from all over London, especially for one-off nights featuring some of New York's finest. Other events range from disco to dancehall and dubstep to drum and bass.

AQUARIUM   CLUB

Map p444 (www.clubaquarium.co.uk; 256-264 Old St EC1; ⊜Old St) The real attraction at this big and brash club is the swimming pool and Jacuzzi (towels provided) and the often very-late opening hours (selected nights until 9am). DJs play mainly house and techno to a mainstream, dressed-up crowd. Trainers are not welcome here.

⛴ Spitalfields

GOLDEN HEART   PUB

Map p444 (110 Commercial St E1; ⊜Liverpool St) It's an unsurprisingly trendy Hoxton crowd that mixes in the surprisingly untrendy

MORE THAN A COFFEE

Local musician Chantal Hill lives in Hoxton, and still manages to regularly trip over new favourite hang-outs:

Chantal's Pick

I had assumed the **Bridge** (Map p444; 15 Kingsland Rd E2; ☺noon-1am Sun-Thu, to 2am Fri & Sat; ☏; ⊕Old St or Hoxton) was just another (albeit very elaborate) coffee shop until I actually went in and discovered the magical truth. It does sell coffee, along with a selection of snacks, but its main draw is the Aladdin's cave upstairs, a Rococo salon-cum-boudoir that looks like it has been decorated by the bastard love child of Louis XIV and your eccentric auntie with all the cats. The downstairs bar retains a distinctive Italian theme, with Joe di Maggio slugging it out on a loop above the door, and the most fantastic old-fashioned till you will probably ever see. It also sells beer, wine and spirits. A total find.

interior of this brilliant Spitalfields boozer. While it's famous as the watering hole for the cream of London's art crowd, our favourite part about any visit is a chat with Sandra, the landlady-celebrity who talks to all comers and ensures the bullshit never outstrips the fun.

TEN BELLS
PUB

Map p444 (www.tenbells.com; 84 Commercial St E1; ⊕Liverpool St) This landmark Victorian pub, with its large windows and beautiful tiles, is perfect for a pint after a wander round Spitalfields Market. It's famous for being one of Jack the Ripper's pick-up joints, although these days it attracts a rather more salubrious and trendy clientele.

93 FEET EAST
CLUB

Map p444 (www.93feeteast.co.uk; 150 Brick Lane E2; ☺5-11pm Mon-Thu, to 1am Fri & Sat, 3-10.30pm Sun; ⊕Liverpool St or Shoreditch High St) This great venue has a courtyard, three big rooms and an outdoor terrace that gets crowded on sunny afternoons, packed with a cool East London crowd.

VIBE BAR
DJ BAR

Map p444 (www.vibe-bar.co.uk; Old Truman Brewery, 91-95 Brick Lane E1; ☺until late Fri & Sat; ☏; ⊕Liverpool St or Shoreditch High St) Once the epicentre of the Hoxton scene, the Vibe is part bar, part club, part outdoor drinking arena complete with fast-food stalls. While its '90s time in the sun is long past, it's still popular and good fun outside in the summer. There are live acts most nights, and DJs at other times in the spacious interior.

 ENTERTAINMENT

SADLER'S WELLS
DANCE

Map p444 (☏0844 412 4300; www.sadlerswells.com; Rosebery Ave EC1; ⊕Angel) The theatre site dates from 1683 but was completely rebuilt in 1998; today it is the most eclectic and modern dance venue in town, with experimental dance shows of all genres and from all corners of the globe. The Lilian Baylis Studio stages smaller productions.

COMEDY CAFÉ
COMEDY

Map p444 (☏7739 5706; www.comedycafe.co.uk; 66-68 Rivington St EC2; ☺Tue-Sat; ⊕Old St or Shoreditch High St) A major venue, the Comedy Café is purpose built for, well, comedy, hosting some good comedians. It can be a little too try-hard and wacky, but it's worth seeing the Wednesday night try-out spots for some wincing entertainment.

 SHOPPING

This is a great area for discovering cool boutiques and market stalls for vintage clothes and up-and-coming designers. There are tonnes of shops off Brick Lane, especially in burgeoning Cheshire St, Hanbury St and the Old Truman Brewery on Dray Walk. Each December there's a major showcase of the latest products, clothes, jewellery and art at Shoreditch Town Hall; see www.eastlondondesignshow.co.uk. Clerkenwell is mostly known for its jewellery. For classic settings and unmounted stones, visit London's traditional jewellery and diamond trade area, **Hatton Garden** (Map p444; www.hatton-garden.net; ⊕Chancery Lane).

⬛ TOP CHOICE SPITALFIELDS MARKET
MARKET

Map p444 (www.oldspitalfieldsmarket.com; Commercial St, btwn Brushfield & Lamb Sts E1; ⏰10am-4pm Sun-Fri; ⬛Liverpool St) One of London's best markets, with traders hawking their wares here since the early 17th century. The covered market that you see today was built in the late 19th century, with the more modern development added in 2006. The market is open six days a week, with a particular focus on each day, but the best days to come are Thursdays (for antiques), Fridays (fashion) and Sundays, when the market is at its bustling best and filled with fashion, jewellery, food and music stalls.

ROUGH TRADE EAST
MUSIC

Map p444 (www.roughtrade.com; Dray Walk, Old Truman Brewery, 91 Brick Lane E1; ⏰8am-8pm Mon-Fri, 11am-7pm Sat & Sun; ⬛Liverpool St) This vast record store has an impressive selection of CDs and vinyl across all genres, as well as an interesting offering of books. There are stacks of knowledgeable recommendations and staff are happy to help. It also sells good coffee and stages live events.

TATTY DEVINE
JEWELLERY

Map p444 (www.tattydevine.com; 236 Brick Lane E2; ⏰11am-6pm Tue-Sun; ⬛Shoreditch High St) Harriet Vine and Rosie Wolfenden make hip and witty jewellery that's become the favourite of many young Londoners. Their original designs feature all manner of fauna-and-flora inspired necklaces, as well as creations sporting moustaches, dinosaurs and bunting. Perspex name necklaces (made to order; £27.50) are also a treat.

LABOUR & WAIT
HOMEWARES

Map p444 (www.labourandwait.co.uk; 85 Redchurch St E2; ⏰11am-6pm Tue-Sun; ⬛Liverpool St or Shoreditch High St) Dedicated to simple and functional, yet scrumptiously stylish, traditional British homewares, Labour & Wait specialises in items by independent manufacturers who make their products the old-fashioned way. There are school tumblers, enamel coffee pots, luxurious lambswool blankets, elegant ostrich-feather dusters and even kitchen sinks.

LADEN SHOWROOM
FASHION

Map p444 (www.laden.co.uk; 103 Brick Lane E1; ⬛Liverpool St or Shoreditch High St) The unofficial flagship for the latest Hoxton street wear, Laden was once 'London's best-kept secret', though a raft of celebrity endorsements have made the showroom's reputation soar and the large number of independent designers it stocks much in demand. A perfect one-stop shop for both womenswear and menswear.

ABSOLUTE VINTAGE
VINTAGE

Map p444 (www.absolutevintage.co.uk; 15 Hanbury St E1; ⏰11am-7pm; ⬛Liverpool St or Shoreditch High St) Check out the mammoth vintage shoe collection here – there are colours and sizes for all, with footwear ranging from designer vintage to something out of your grandma's storage. Clothes for men and women line the back of the shop.

MAGMA
BOOKS

Map p444 (www.magmabooks.com; 117-119 Clerkenwell Rd EC1; ⏰Mon-Sat; ⬛Farringdon) This much-loved shop sells books, magazines, T-shirts and almost anything on the design cutting edge. Great for present shopping.

CLERKENWELL, SHOREDITCH & SPITALFIELDS SHOPPING

SUPER MARKET SUNDAY

Head out east on a Sunday and it might feel that you can't move for markets. Starting at **Columbia Road Flower Market** (p231) and working your way south makes for a colourful and thrifty retail crawl. Spilling out into its surrounding streets, **Brick Lane Market** (Map p444; ⏰8am-3pm Sun; ⬛Shoreditch High St) takes over a vast area with household goods, bric-a-brac, secondhand clothes and cheap fashion. You can even stop off and play carrom. Just off Brick Lane, you'll find the **Backyard Market** (Map p444; www.backyardmarket.co.uk; ⏰11am-5pm Sat & Sun; ⬛Shoreditch High St), with stalls full of vintage clothes, ceramics and furniture. A little further south, on the other side of the lane, is the **Sunday UpMarket** (Map p444; www.sundayupmarket.co.uk; ⏰10am-5pm Sun), where young designers sell wonderful clothes, music and crafts, and the excellent food hall has worldwide grub, from Ethiopian vegie dishes to Japanese delicacies. If you've got the stamina, top it all off with a browse round Spitalfields.

ECONE
JEWELLERY

Map p444 (www.econe.co.uk; 41 Exmouth Market EC1; ⊘Mon-Sat; ⊖Farringdon or Angel) Husband-and-wife team Jos and Alison Skeates sell gorgeous contemporary collections by British and international jewellery designers on funky Exmouth Market.

START
FASHION

Map p444 (www.start-london.com; 42-44 Rivington St; ⊖Old St or Shoreditch High St) 'Where fashion meets rock n roll' is the appropriate tagline to this group of three boutiques brought to you by former Fall guitarist Brix Smith, a cult rocker who loves girly clothes. Designer labels such as Mulberry and Helmut Lang dominate, and Smith prides herself on her selection of flattering jeans, for which the store offers a fitting service. A similarly excellent store, **Start Menswear** (Map p444; 59 Rivington St), is over the road, and there's a third location, **Mr Start** (Map p444; 40 Rivington St), which is a men's tailoring shop.

PRESENT
FASHION

Map p444 (www.present-london.com; 140 Shoreditch High St E1; ⊖Old St or Shoreditch High St) Everything for the hip gentleman, including designer gear, shoes, books and bike accessories. You can also grab a great cup of coffee here.

NO-ONE
FASHION

Map p444 (www.no-one.co.uk; 1 Kingsland Rd E2; ⊖Old St or Shoreditch High St) This boutique, brought to you by the same people as hip nearby drinkery Dreambagsjaguarshoes (p213), can be found inside the Old Shoreditch station bar. It's all ultrahip, with fashion magazines, quirky accessories and shoes, and stocks Cheap Monday, House of Dagmar and new labels for women and men.

🖉 123 BETHNAL GREEN ROAD
FASHION

Map p444 (www.123bethnalgreenroad.co.uk; 123 Bethnal Green Rd E2; ⊘11.30am-7pm; ⊖Old St or Shoreditch High St) Housed in a grand, corner building that dates to the late 19th century, this three-floor store brings together designs by Dr Noki and the house collection 123, both of which comprise original and striking pieces using recycled materials. You'll find further rails on the ground floor along with homewares, and there's a cafe and bar in the basement.

LESLEY CRAZE GALLERY
JEWELLERY

Map p444 (www.lesleycrazegallery.co.uk; 33-35a Clerkenwell Green EC1; ⊘Tue-Sat; ⊖Farringdon) Considered one of Europe's leading centres for arty, contemporary jewellery, this gallery has exquisitely understated and sometimes pricey designs.

The East End & Docklands

WHITECHAPEL | BETHNAL GREEN | HACKNEY | MILE END | VICTORIA PARK | HACKNEY WICK | STRATFORD | WAPPING | LIMEHOUSE | DOCKLANDS

Neighbourhood Top Five

1 Taking in the landscaped majesty, incredible architecture and fauna-filled wetlands of East London's mighty **Olympic Park** (p222).

2 Stopping to smell the roses at London's most fragrant market, **Columbia Rd** (p231).

3 Investigating the fascinating history and contrasting landscapes of the **Docklands** (p223).

4 Imagining life as a 17th-century sailor on a swagger through **Wapping** (p223).

5 Heading to **Whitechapel** (p219) for a burst of multicultural London and authentic Bangladeshi cuisine.

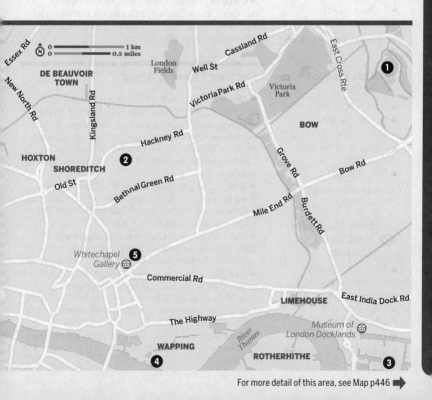

For more detail of this area, see Map p446 ➡

Lonely Planet's Top Tip

The most genial way to get around the East End is along the water. Cyclists and pedestrians can drop down to Regent's Canal at the bottom of Broadway Market and follow the waterway to Limehouse. Branching east of this at Victoria Park, the Hertford Union Canal will deliver you to Hackney Wick and the Olympic Park. From Limehouse Basin you can also pick up the Thames Path and follow it along the river to St Katharine Docks.

Best Places to Eat

➡ Wapping Food (p229)
➡ Formans (p228)
➡ Tayyabs (p224)
➡ E Pellici (p225)
➡ Gun (p229)

For reviews, see p224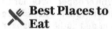

Best Places to Drink

➡ Dove Freehouse (p229)
➡ Grapes (p230)
➡ Carpenter's Arms (p230)
➡ Royal Inn on the Park (p230)
➡ Palm Tree (p230)

For reviews, see p229 ➡

Best Places for East End History

➡ Museum of London Docklands (p224)
➡ Sutton House (p220)
➡ Ragged School Museum (p221)
➡ House Mill (p221)

For reviews, see p219 ➡

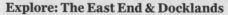

Explore: The East End & Docklands

A vast area, the East End and Docklands has a few standout sights but will really repay those happy to wander and soak up the unique character of each of its neighbourhoods. Handily, the recent opening of the overground lines has made East London much easier to traverse. The three main areas to head for are the all-new Olympic Park (and neighbouring Hackney) the Docklands (and adjoining waterside Limehouse and Wapping) and Whitechapel (from which Bethnal Green is just a short hop away). Each of these has a few don't-miss attractions but also plenty of places to linger over a coffee, lazy lunch or a few jars of ale.

Local Life

➡ **London Fields** On a sunny Saturday, East Enders of all ages grab some goodies from Broadway Market (p231) and head to London Fields (p220) for a picnic and a dip in the lido.

➡ **Whitechapel Gallery** With no permanent collection, there's always something new to check out here (p219), before heading to Tayyabs (p224) for the daily special.

➡ **Cabaret** From lip-synching trannies to trashy burlesque, Bistrotheque (p231) and the Bethnal Green Working Men's Club (p230) always provide a hugely fun reason to get your glad rags on.

Getting There & Away

➡ **Underground** Central Line runs from the West End and the City to Bethnal Green, Mile End and Stratford.

➡ **Overground** From Camden and Highbury, the overground affords a quick link to Hackney, Hackney Wick and Stratford. A separate branch connects Dalston and the southerly stops of Whitechapel and Wapping.

➡ **DLR** Starting at Tower Gateway or Bank, the DLR provides a scenic link to Limehouse and Docklands, as well as joining the dots with Stratford Domestic and International stations further north.

➡ **Bus** The 55 from Oxford St is a handy route to Hackney, as is the 38 from Victoria via Islington. The 277 runs from Hackney to the Docklands, via Victoria Park.

➡ **Rail** A quick ride to London Fields, Cambridge Heath or Stratford from Liverpool St. The high-speed link from St Pancras (to be known as the Javelin during the Olympics) whisks you to Stratford International in just seven minutes.

➡ **Boat** During the Games you can catch a barge from Limehouse to the Olympic Park.

SIGHTS

⊙ Whitechapel

WHITECHAPEL BELL FOUNDRY
HISTORIC BUILDING

Map p446 (www.whitechapelbellfoundry.co.uk; 32-34 Whitechapel Rd E1; tours per person £11; ⊙tours 10am & 1.30pm selected Wed & Sat, shop 9.30am-4.15pm Mon-Fri; ⊜Aldgate East or Whitechapel) The Whitechapel Bell Foundry has been standing on this site since 1738, although an earlier foundry nearby is known to have been in business in 1570. Both Big Ben (1858) and the Liberty Bell (1752) in Philadelphia were cast here, and the foundry also cast a new bell for New York City's Trinity Church, damaged in the terrorist attacks of 11 September 2001. The 1½-hour guided tours (maximum 25 people) are conducted on particular Saturdays and Wednesdays (check the website) but are often booked out a year in advance. During weekday trading hours you can view a few small but informative exhibits in the foyer and buy bell-related items from the shop.

WHITECHAPEL ROAD
STREET

Map p446 (⊜Whitechapel) The East End's main thoroughfare, Whitechapel Rd hums with a cacophony of Asian, African and Middle Eastern languages, its busy shops and market stalls selling everything from Indian snacks to Nigerian fabrics and Turkish jewellery, as the East End's multitudinous ethnic groupings rub up against each other more or less comfortably. It's a chaotic and poor place, but it's full of life. Within a few minutes' walk of Whitechapel tube station you'll find the large **East London Mosque** (www.eastlondonmosque.org.uk; 46-92 Whitechapel Rd E1), and, behind it, the **Great Synagogue** (41 Fieldgate St E1), built in 1899. Further down Fieldgate St, the enormous **Tower House** (81 Fieldgate St E1) was once a hostel and then a dosshouse but is now a redeveloped apartment block. Past residents include Joseph Stalin and authors Jack London and George Orwell. The latter describes it in detail in *Down and Out in Paris and London* (1933).

North along Whitechapel Rd itself sits the **Blind Beggar** (337 Whitechapel Rd E1), where the notorious gangster Ronnie Kray shot George Cornell dead in 1966, in a turf

THE EAST END & DOCKLANDS SIGHTS

⊙ TOP SIGHTS
WHITECHAPEL GALLERY

This ground-breaking gallery, which moved into its main art nouveau building in 1899, extended into the library next door in 2009, doubling its exhibition space to 10 galleries. Founded by the Victorian philanthropist Canon Samuel Barnett at the end of the 19th century to bring art to the people of East London, it has made its name by putting on exhibitions by both established and emerging artists, cartoonists and architects, including Jackson Pollock (his first UK show), Gary Hume, Robert Crumb, Mies van der Rohe and Picasso (whose *Guernica* was exhibited here in 1939). The gallery's ambitiously themed shows change every couple of months – check the program online – and there's also live music, poetry readings, talks and films till late on Thursday. Don't miss the phenomenal 'social sculptures' in various (and ephemeral) spaces throughout – there's even one on the roof of the building. Ask at the front desk about Janet Cardiff's *The Missing Voice (Case Study B)*, an audio walk that takes you into the surrounding streets – a surreal but exciting interaction of art and context (you need to leave a bank card as security). Other features are an excellent bookshop, the Whitechapel Gallery Dining Room (p225) and an uberdesigned cafe on the mezzanine level.

DON'T MISS...
➡ Social sculptures
➡ Bookshop
➡ A meal in the Dining Room

PRACTICALITIES
➡ Map p446
➡ www.whitechapelgallery.org
➡ 77-82 Whitechapel High St E1
➡ admission free
➡ ⊙11am-6pm Tue-Sun, to 9pm Thu
➡ ⊜Aldgate East

CABLE STREET

Cable St, just south of Commercial Rd, takes its name from the use of the length of the thoroughfare to twist hemp rope into ships' cables. Similarly named, but shorter and narrower, Twine Ct runs south from here. Cable St is most famous for the Battle of Cable St (1936), in which the British fascist Oswald Mosley led a bunch of his blackshirts into the area, supposedly as a celebration of the fourth anniversary of the British Union of Fascists. Although pockets of fascist supporters existed in the East End, the march was ferociously repelled by local people – thousands of Jews, communists, dockers, trade unionists and other East Enders turned out in solidarity against them. At No 236 you'll find St George's Town Hall building, its west wall sporting a large mural commemorating the riots. The church just behind this building is **St George-in-the-East** (www.stgite.org.uk; 16 Cannon St Rd E1), erected by Nicholas Hawksmoor in 1729 and badly damaged in the Blitz of WWII; all that now remains is a shell enclosing a smaller modern core.

war over control of the East End's organised crime. He was jailed for life and died in 1995. After the intersection with Cambridge Heath Rd, this traditionally poor area's history takes a more philanthropic turn, with a statue of **William Booth** (1829–1912), who established his Salvation Army Christian Mission here in 1865, and the **Trinity Green Almshouses**, poorhouses built for injured or retired sailors in 1695. The two rows of almshouses run at right angles away from the street, facing a village-type green and a chapel with a clock tower.

◉ Bethnal Green & Hackney

FREE V&A MUSEUM OF
CHILDHOOD   MUSEUM
Map p446 (www.vam.ac.uk/moc; cnr Cambridge Heath & Old Ford Rds E2; ☺10am-5.45pm; 🚇; ❸Bethnal Green) Housed in a renovated Victorian-era building moved from South Kensington in 1866, this branch of the Victoria & Albert Museum is aimed at both kids (with activity rooms and interactive exhibits, including a dressing-up box and sandpit) and nostalgic grown-ups who come to admire the antique toys. From teddies, doll's houses and dolls (one dating from 1300 BC) to Meccano, Lego and computer games, it's a wonderful toy-cupboard trip down memory lane. There's a good cafe on the ground floor too.

SUTTON HOUSE   HISTORIC BUILDING
Map p446 (www.nationaltrust.org.uk/sutton house; 2 & 4 Homerton High St E9; adult/child £3/1; ☺10am-5pm Thu & Fri, noon-5pm Sat & Sun, closed Jan; ❸Hackney Central, 🚌394)

Abandoned and taken over by squatters in the 1980s, what was originally known as Bryk Place when built in 1535 by a prominent courtier of Henry VIII, Sir Ralph Sadleir, could have been tragically lost to history, but it's since been put under the care of the National Trust and magnificently restored. The first historic room you enter, the Linenfold Parlour, is the highlight, where the Tudor oak panelling on the walls has been carved to resemble draped cloth. Other notable rooms include the panelled Great Chamber, the Victorian study, the Georgian parlour and the intriguing mock-up of a Tudor kitchen. There's a shop and pleasant cafe on site.

West of Sutton House, in the restored St John's Churchyard Gardens, is 13th-century **St Augustine's Tower** (www.hhbt.org.uk; Mare St E8), all that remains of a church that was demolished in 1798. On the last Sunday of the month (2.30pm to 4.30pm) you can climb the tower's 135 steps for fantastic views across Hackney (free).

LONDON FIELDS   PARK
Map p446 (www.hackney.gov.uk/cp-londonfields; 🚉London Fields, 🚌55 or 277) A strip of green amid a popular residential area of Hackney, London Fields was historically a place for the grazing of animals. A well-frequented public space at any time, it can be thronged with crowds on sunny weekend days as locals hang out after a meander up Broadway Market (see p231). Built in the 1930s, and abandoned by the '80s, **London Fields Lido** (www.hackney.gov.uk/c-london fields-lido; London Fields Westside E8; adult/child £4.10/2.45; ☺usually 6.30am-8pm) reopened to local delight in 2006. It gets packed with

swimmers and sunbathers during the summer months. The park also has two children's play areas and a decent pub.

⊙ Mile End & Victoria Park

VICTORIA PARK   PARK
Map p446 (www.towerhamlets.gov.uk; ⊙dawn-dusk; ⊜Mile End, ☐277 or 425) The 'Regent's Park of the East End', Victoria Park is an 86-hectare leafy expanse opened in 1845 – the first public park in the East End that came about after a local MP presented Queen Victoria with a petition of 30,000 signatures. In the early 20th century it was known as the Speaker's Corner of the East End, and during WWII the park was largely closed to the public and was used as an anti-aircraft shelling site as well as an internment camp for Italian and then German prisoners of war. At the time of writing, the park was undergoing a £12-million revamp, which will improve both the lakes, introduce a skate park and create a hub building housing a cafe, community room and park offices in the eastern section of the park.

FREE RAGGED SCHOOL MUSEUM   MUSEUM
Map p446 (www.raggedschoolmuseum.org.uk; 46-50 Copperfield Rd E3; ⊙10am-5pm Wed & Thu, 2-5pm 1st Sun of month; ⊜Mile End) Both adults and children are inevitably charmed by this combination of mock Victorian schoolroom – with hard wooden benches and desks, slates, chalk, inkwells and abacuses – recreated East End kitchen and social history museum below. 'Ragged' was a Victorian term used to refer to pupils' usually torn, dirty and dishevelled clothes, and the museum celebrates the legacy of Dr Thomas Barnardo, who founded this school for destitute East End children in the 1870s. The school closed in 1908 but you can experience what it would have been like on the first Sunday of the month, when a Victorian lesson in which 'pupils' (adults and children alike) are taught reading, writing and 'rithmetic by a strict school ma'am in full Victorian regalia called Miss Perkins. It takes place at 2.15pm and 3.30pm (suggested donation £2). There's also a tiny towpath cafe and shop where you can pick up your own slate and chalk. Friendly staff are on hand to pass on plenty of local information and background.

HOUSE MILL   HISTORIC BUILDING
Map p446 (www.housemill.org.uk; Three Mill Lane E3; adult/concession £3/1.50; ⊙11am-4pm Sun May-Oct, 1st Sun only Mar, Apr & Dec; ⊜Bromley-by-Bow) The House Mill (1776) operated as a sluice tidal mill, grinding grain for a nearby distillery until 1941, and is one of two remaining mills from a trio that once stood

---

A HERO RISES IN THE EAST

Daniel Mendoza (1764–1836), the father of 'scientific boxing' who billed himself as 'Mendoza the Jew', was the first bare-knuckle boxer to employ strategy and speed in the ring. Mendoza was born in Aldgate and left school at age 13, taking odd jobs as a porter, being taunted as an 'outsider' and getting into scrapes. He was eventually discovered by 'gentleman boxer' Richard Humphreys, 20 years his senior, who took him under his wing and started him training. Mendoza developed a style of fighting in direct opposition to the norm of the day, where two fighters would stand face to face and slug it out until one collapsed.

Mendoza began a highly successful career in the ring, but eventually fell out with his mentor. His most infamous fight came during a grudge match in 1788 with Humphreys. Just as Mendoza was about to administer the coup de grâce, Humphreys' second grabbed Mendoza's arm, a moment caught in a contemporary print called *Foul Play* on display in the National Portrait Gallery (p97). Mendoza went on to fight Humphreys fairly two more times, emerging the victor and moral superior.

Mendoza was the first sportsman in Britain to achieve cult status – a veritable David Beckham of 18th-century London. He made (and lost) a fortune, wrote his memoirs and a how-to book called *The Art of Boxing,* mixed with the high and mighty (including royalty) and sold branded trinkets and images of himself. Most importantly he advanced the cause of Jews in a country that had only allowed them back the century before. People learned for the first time that a Jew could and would fight back – and win.

COCKNEY RHYMING SLANG

Traditionally cockneys were people born within earshot of the Bow Bells – the church bells of St Mary-le-Bow (p152) on Cheapside. Since few people actually live in the City, this definition has broadened to take in those living further east. The term cockney is often used to describe anyone speaking what is also called estuarine English (in which 't' and 'h' are routinely dropped and glottal stops – what the two 't's sound like in 'bottle' – abound). In fact the true cockney language also uses something called rhyming slang, which may have developed among London's costermongers (street traders) as a code to avoid police attention. This code replaced common nouns and verbs with rhyming phrases. So 'going up the apples and pears' meant going up the stairs, the 'trouble and strife' was the wife, 'telling porky pies' was telling lies and 'would you Adam and Eve it?' was would you believe it? Over time the second of the two words tended to be dropped so the rhyme vanished. Few, if any, people still use pure cockney but a good many still understand it. You're more likely to come across it in residual phrases like 'use your loaf' ('loaf of bread' for head), 'ooh, me plates of meat' (feet) or 'e's me best china' ('china plate' for mate).

on this small island in the River Lea (the Clock Mill opposite has been converted into offices). Tours, which run according to demand and last about 45 minutes, take visitors to all four floors of the mill and offer a fascinating look at traditional East End industry. There's a small cafe and shop on site. To get to House Mill, exit the tube and head down the steps to the left. Continue into the underpass and at the top of the stairs turn right, down the hill. Take a right towards Tesco and right again into Three Mill Lane.

TOWER HAMLETS CEMETERY PARK
CEMETERY

Map p446 (www.towerhamletscemetery.org; Southern Grove E3; ☺8am-dusk; ☻Mile End or Bow Rd) Opened in 1841 this 13-hectare cemetery was the last of the 'Magnificent Seven', then-suburban cemeteries – including Highgate and Stoke Newington's Abney Park – created by an act of Parliament in response to London's rapid population growth and overcrowded burial grounds. Some 270,000 souls were laid to rest here until the cemetery was closed for burials in 1966 and turned into a park and local nature reserve in 2001. Today it is a quiet, restful site, its Victorian monuments slowly being consumed by vines. There are usually two-hour guided tours at 2pm on the third Sunday of the month.

MILE END PARK
PARK

Map p446 (www.towerhamlets.gov.uk; ☻Mile End) The 36-hectare Mile End Park is a long, narrow series of interconnected green spaces wedged between Burdett and Grove Rds and Regent's Canal. Landscaped to great effect during the millennium year, it incorporates a go-kart track, a children's centre, areas for public art, an ecology area, an indoor climbing wall and a sports stadium. The centrepiece, though, is architect Piers Gough's 'green bridge' linking the northern and southern sections of the park over busy Mile End Rd and planted with trees and shrubs.

⊙ Hackney Wick & Stratford

OLYMPIC PARK
PARK

Map p446 (www.london2012.com/olympic-park; ☻Stratford or Hackney Wick) From the mills of Cistercian monks in the 1st century, to the railway hub of the 1880s (from which goods from the Thames were transported all over Britain), the tidal Lower Lea Valley had long been the source of what Londoners required to fuel their industries. But until building work on the Olympic Park began in 2008, this vast area of East London had become derelict, polluted and largely ignored. Creating world-class sporting facilities for the 2012 Games was, of course, at the forefront of the development, but this was well balanced with the aim of regenerating this area for generations to come. More than 30 new bridges were built to criss-cross the Lea, its tributaries and the railway lines that divide up the parkland, and waterways in and around the park were upgraded, with waste cleared and contaminated soil cleaned on a massive scale.

The main focal point of the Queen Elizabeth Olympic Park, as it will be known from 2013, is the **Olympic Stadium**, with a Games capacity of 80,000, scaling back to approximately 60,000 seats post-Games. The striking **Aquatics Centre**, which will greet park visitors entering from Stratford, is the work of Clerkenwell-based architect Zaha Hadid and houses two 50m swimming pools and a diving pool. The equally impressive and award-winning **Velodrome** (aka the 'Pringle') has been praised for its aesthetic qualities, as well as its sustainable credentials and functional appeal. The 114m, spiralling red structure is Anish Kapoor's **ArcelorMittal Orbit**, or the 'Hubble Bubble Pipe', offering a vast panorama from its viewing platform.

The north of the park has been given over to wetlands, which provide a much wilder environment than the gardens and landscaping of the southern half of the park, which is home to the main venues. Set to open to the public in phases from 2013, the developments to transform the park into its promised legacy will take at least another 25 years to complete.

◉ Wapping & Limehouse

WAPPING
NEIGHBOURHOOD

Map p446 (◉Wapping) Once notorious for slave traders, drunk sailors and prostitutes, Wapping's towering warehouses, built at the beginning of the 19th century, still give an atmospheric picture of the area's previous existence. Although there's nothing to actually mark it, down on the riverside below Wapping New Stairs (near the marine police station) was **Execution Dock**, where convicted pirates were hanged and their bodies chained to a post at low tide, to be left until three tides had washed over their heads. Among the more famous people who died this way was Captain William Kidd, hanged here in 1701, and whose grisly tale you can read about in the nearby Captain Kidd pub (p231).

LIMEHOUSE
NEIGHBOURHOOD

Map p446 (DLR Limehouse or Westferry) There isn't much to Limehouse, although it became the centre of London's Chinese community – its first Chinatown – after some 300 sailors settled here in 1890. It gets a mention in Oscar Wilde's *The Picture of Dorian Gray* (1891), when the protagonist passes by this way in search of opium. The most notable attraction here is **St Anne's, Limehouse** (www.stanneslimehouse.org; cnr Commercial Rd & Three Colt St E1). This was Nicholas Hawksmoor's earliest church (1725) and still boasts the highest church clock in the city. In fact the 60m-high tower is still a 'Trinity House mark' for identifying shipping lanes on the Thames (thus it flies the Royal Navy's white ensign).

ST KATHARINE DOCKS
HARBOUR

Map p446 (www.skdocks.co.uk; ◉Tower Hill) The gateway to the warehouse district of Wapping, built in 1828 after 1250 'insanitary' houses were razed and 11,300 people made homeless, the dock's current incarnation – a marina for luxury yachts surrounded by cafes, restaurants and twee shops – dates from the 1980s. It's the perfect starting point for exploring Wapping and Limehouse.

◉ Docklands

ISLE OF DOGS
NEIGHBOURHOOD

Map p421 (DLR Westferry, West India Quay, Canary Wharf) Pundits can't really agree on whether this is really an island; strictly speaking it's a peninsula of land on the northern shore of the Thames, though without modern road and transport links it would *almost* be separated from the mainland at West India Docks. And etymologists are still out to lunch over the origin of the island's name. Some believe it's because the royal kennels were located here during the reign of Henry VIII. Others maintain it's a corruption of the Flemish word *dijk* (dyke), recalling the Flemish engineers who shored up the area's muddy banks.

THE EAST BY BARGE

A great way to see a different side of the East End is to climb aboard a barge and tour the canals and waterways. **Water Chariots** (www.waterchariots.co.uk; ⊙approx Apr–Oct) offer a program of pleasure cruises and, during the Olympic Games, a shuttle service for passengers travelling up the canal from Limehouse.

TOP SIGHTS
MUSEUM OF LONDON DOCKLANDS

Housed in a converted warehouse dating from 1802, this museum offers a comprehensive overview of the entire history of the Thames from the arrival of the Romans in AD 43. Well-organised with knowledgeable and helpful staff, it's at its best when dealing with specifics such as the docks during WWII, as well as their controversial transformation into the Docklands during the 1980s.

The tour begins on the 3rd floor (take the lift to the top) with the Roman settlement of Londinium and works its way downwards through the ages. Keep an eye out for the scale model of old London Bridge. Other highlights include Sailortown, a re-creation of the cobbled streets, bars and lodging houses of a mid-19th-century dockside community and nearby Chinatown, and more detailed galleries such as London, Sugar & Slavery, which examines the capital's role in the transatlantic slave trade.

There's lots for kids here, including the hands-on Mudlarks gallery, where children can explore the history of the Thames, tipping the clipper, trying on old-fashioned diving helmets and even constructing a simple model of Canary Wharf. The museum has special exhibitions every few months, for which there is usually a charge. There's also a great cafe on site.

DON'T MISS...

➡ Sailortown
➡ London, Sugar & Slavery
➡ Docklands at War
➡ New Port New City
➡ Scale model of London Bridge

PRACTICALITIES

➡ Map p421
➡ www.museumin docklands.org.uk
➡ No 1 Warehouse, West India Quay E14
➡ admission free
➡ ☺10am-6pm
➡ ◉Canary Wharf or DLR West India Quay

The centrepiece of the Isle of Dogs is Cesar Pelli's 244m-high **Canary Wharf Tower**, which was built in 1991. It's surrounded by more recent towers housing HSBC and Citigroup, and offices for Bank of America, Barclays, Morgan Stanley, Credit Suisse and more. Londoners are divided on their appreciation of this area, and although it is often thought of as soulless, there's certainly something impressive and noteworthy in the way that this 'isle' has been so radically developed.

FREE MUDCHUTE PARK & FARM FARM

Map p421 (www.mudchute.org; ☺farm 9am-5pm Tue-Sun; DLR Mudchute) Entering Mudchute Park from Eastferry Rd through the canopy of trees, you're greeted by a delightfully surprising sight of cows and sheep, roaming freely in this grassy 13 hectares of parkland. Looking back to the skyscrapers of Canary Wharf gives you a clear sense of the contrasts of this area of London. The lovely city farm has an array of animals, well kept, in spacious surrounds. Kids will love it, especially the llamas. There's also a neat cafe, serving excellent breakfasts and wholesome lunch options.

EATING

The East End's multiculturalism has ensured that its ethnic cuisine stretches far and wide, with some fantastic low-key eateries serving authentic and value-for-money fare. But the area's gentrification has introduced a slew of gastropubs and more upmarket eateries – the latest even earning a Michelin star. Trendy and excellent coffee shops have sprouted up all over the East End, but there are still plenty of places to get a decent fry and a cup of tea, or a traditional pie with mash and liquor. Places to head if you want to sniff out your own favourites include Columbia Rd, Broadway Market and the streets just to the north of Victoria Park (known to some as Hackney Village).

✗ Whitechapel

TOP CHOICE TAYYABS INDIAN, PAKISTANI £

Map p446 (☎7247 9543; www.tayyabs.co.uk 83-89 Fieldgate St E1; mains £6.50-10; ☺noon-midnight; ◉Whitechapel) This buzzing (OK crowded) Punjabi restaurant is in another league to its Brick Lane equivalents. Seek!

kebabs, masala fish and other starters served on sizzling hot plates are delicious, as are accompaniments such as dhal, naan and raita. Daily specials are also available. Tayyabs is hugely popular and queues often snake around the restaurant and out of the door.

CAFÉ-SPICE NAMASTÉ INDIAN ££

Map p446 (☎7488 9242; www.cafespice.co.uk; 16 Prescot St E1; mains £14-19, 2-course set lunch £15.95; ⊗closed lunch Sat & all day Sun; ⊖Tower Hill or DLR Tower Gateway) Chef Cyrus Todiwala has taken an old magistrates court just a 10-minute walk from Tower Hill and decorated it in carnival colours; the service and atmosphere are as bright as the walls. The Parsee and Goan menu is famous for its superlative *dhansaak* (lamb stew with rice and lentils; £14.95) but just as good are the tandoori dishes and the Goan king-prawn curry. Bonuses: it makes its own chutneys and there's a little garden behind the dining room open in the warmer months.

WHITECHAPEL GALLERY DINING ROOM MODERN EUROPEAN ££

Map p446 (☎7522 7896; www.whitechapelgallery.org; 77-82 Whitechapel High St E1; mains £12-15; ⊗lunch Tue-Sun, dinner Wed-Sat; ⊖Aldgate East) Housed in a small but perfectly formed dining room in the Passmore Edwards Library extension of the Whitechapel Gallery (p219), with high-profile chef Angela Hartnett acting as consultant. The menu offers small or large plates, to suit your appetite. Booking advised.

MIRCH MASALA INDIAN, PAKISTANI £

Map p446 (www.mirchmasalarestaurant.co.uk; 111-113 Commercial Rd E1; mains £4.50-11; ⊖Whitechapel) 'Chilli and Spice', part of a small chain based in the epicentre of London subcontinental food, Southall, is a less hectic alternative to Tayyabs and the food is almost up to the same level. Order the

prawn tikka (£9) as a 'warmer' followed by the *masala karella* (£5), a curry-like dish made from bitter gourd, and a *karahi* (stewed) meat dish.

KOLAPATA BANGLADESHI £

Map p446 (www.kolapata.co.uk; 222 Whitechapel Rd E1; mains £4.50-9.95; ⊖Whitechapel) This modest restaurant serves up excellent Bangladeshi cuisine. Try the *haleem* (lamb with lentils and spices) and the *sarisha elish* (fish cooked with mustard seed, onion and green chilli).

✖ Bethnal Green & Hackney

⬛TOP CHOICE E PELLICI CAFE £

Map p446 (332 Bethnal Green Rd E2; dishes £5-7.80; ⊗7am-4pm Mon-Sat; ⊖Bethnal Green, ☒8) There aren't many reasons to recommend a stroll down Bethnal Green Rd, but stepping into this diminutive, but larger-than-life, Anglo-Italian cafe is one of them. You're likely to be met by a warmer-than-average greeting as you squeeze onto a table among an amiable collection of East Enders. Opened in 1900 the wood-panelled caff is bedecked with museum-quality original fittings. Breakfasts are large and sustaining and the traditional English and Italian dishes are certain to satisfy the heartiest of appetites.

VIAJANTE FUSION £££

Map p446 (www.viajante.co.uk; Patriot Sq E2; tasting menu lunch £28-70, dinner £65-90; ⊗lunch Wed-Sun, 6-9.30pm Mon-Sun; ☏; ⊖Bethnal Green) Part of the Town Hall Hotel & Apartments (but with a completely separate entrance on Cambridge Heath Rd), this is an unexpected spot to find a Michelin-starred restaurant. The elegant dining room marries contemporary design with the original Edwardian features, and the very open

❶ LAZY MONDAYS

The East End is peppered with some fascinating and quirky sights, but unfortunately many of them have irregular opening hours, and a lot are closed on Mondays – as are a number of restaurants, cafes and some shops. Despite this there are plenty of parks, waterways and neighbourhoods perfect for exploring, and many a pub in which to rest your feet and grab a bite to eat. Two of the area's best sights, the Museum of Childhood (p220) and the Museum of London Docklands (p224), are luckily both open daily.

START **BETHNAL GREEN TUBE STATION**

END **OLYMPIC PARK**

DISTANCE **3 MILES**

DURATION **TWO HOURS**

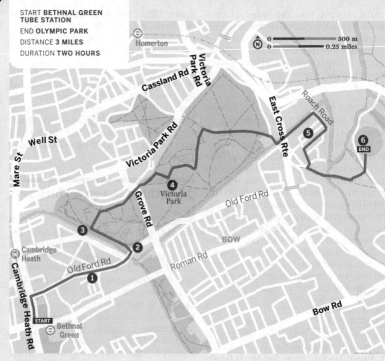

Neighbourhood Walk
East End Eras

This easy stroll offers an insightful view into the old and new of the East End. Exit the tube station towards the Museum of Childhood and head north. Take the first right and continue until you can take a right into Cyprus Pl. The surrounding area here was heavily bombed during WWII (due to its industry and proximity to the docks) and the tower blocks you can see if you raise your eyes skyward are a product of postwar redevelopment. But beautifully preserved **①** **Cyprus St** gives a taste of what Victorian Bethnal Green would have looked like. Continue left down Cyprus St and back onto Old Ford Rd.

Just over Regent's Canal lies **②** **Victoria Park**, built in the 1840s to improve the quality of life of East Enders. Take the path down to the road around the lake and head left to the **③** **Dogs of Alciabiades** howling on plinths, replicas of the originals that stood here from 1912. Turn right here and then again at the end of the road and continue to the grand Royal Inn on the

Park. Cross the road into the eastern section of the park and take a right towards the recently restored **④** **Burdett-Coutts Memorial** (1862), a gift of Angela Burdett-Coutts, once the richest woman in England and a prominent philanthropist.

From here, ramble on to the east lake and exit at the park's southeastern tip. Cross the road and pick up the canal path next to the Top O the Morning pub, crossing the canal at the first bridge you come to. Undergoing extensive redevelopment for the Olympic Games, **⑤** **Hackney Wick** is home to a warren of warehouses and a growing community of artists. Stop off at the Counter Cafe or Formans for views of the stadium, and check out their latest art exhibits. From here you're a mere shot-put from the **⑥** **Olympic Park**, heralding a whole new era for the East End.

kitchen (where food is 'assembled') offers only blind tasting menus. Chef Nuno Mendes' dishes are inventive, beautifully put together and a well-crafted and exciting fusion of flavours. Service is spot on. For a more relaxed (and cheaper) but similarly creative meal, try the **Corner Room** (mains £10-12), a great little dining room on the first floor of the hotel – it doesn't take reservations.

CLIMPSON & SONS
CAFE £

Map p446 (www.webcoffeeshop.co.uk; 67 Broadway Market E8; dishes £4-6.50; ⏰8am-5pm; ☒London Fields, ☐55 or 277) Small and simply decorated, this deservedly popular cafe is housed in what was once a butchers (and has retained the same name). Coffee is superb – it roasts its own just around the corner – and it also does a fine line in sandwiches, pastries and light meals, such as salads and couscous.

LAXEIRO
TAPAS ££

Map p446 (☎7729 1147; www.laxeiro.co.uk; 93 Columbia Rd E2; tapas £4.50-8.95, paella £21.50-24.50; ⏰lunch & dinner Tue-Sat, 9am-5pm Sun; ☒Hoxton) A homely yet stylish and buzzing restaurant with friendly staff providing great service. The menu offers up authentic and robust *raciones* – the barbecue lamb is a winner. The handful of more ambitious dishes includes paella to be shared. There are tables outside on the picturesque street in summer.

LITTLE GEORGIA
GEORGIAN £

Map p446 (87 Goldsmith's Row E2; dishes £4-8; ⏰closed dinner Mon; ☒Cambridge Heath, ☐55) A charming slice of the Caucasus in East London, this simple eatery on two floors is an excellent introduction to the cuisine of Georgia; try the mixed meze for two or four. The menu includes such classics as *nigziani* (red pepper or aubergine stuffed with walnuts, herbs and roast vegetables) and the staple *hachapuri* (cheese bread). The cafe is a good place for breakfast and has a delicious range of salads and sandwiches.

GREEN PAPAYA
VIETNAMESE £

Map p446 (191 Mare St E8; mains £6.50-8.50; ⏰dinner Tue-Sun; ☒London Fields, ☐55 or 277) This simple but friendly neighbourhood restaurant has been serving up high-quality Vietnamese food to Hackney diners

for years. The extensive menu is strong on vegetarian and seafood dishes.

F. COOKE
BRITISH £

Map p446 (9 Broadway Market; mains £3-4; ⏰10am-7pm; ☒Cambridge Heath, ☐55) If you want a glimpse of what eating out was like in Broadway Market before the street was gentrified, head to F. Cooke pie & mash shop. This family business has been going strong since 1900, and the shop has the original signage and tiles, along with plenty of family photographs around the walls and sawdust on the floor.

FRIZZANTE@CITY FARM
CAFE £

Map p446 (www.frizzanteltd.co.uk; Hackney City Farm, 1a Goldsmith's Row E2; dishes £4-9; ⏰10am-4.30pm Tue, Wed & Fri-Sun, 7-10pm Thu; ☎; ☒Cambridge Heath, ☐55) Award-winning restaurant serving excellent Italian food next door to one of London's half-dozen city farms, with a weekly agroturismo night offering special country dishes.

GALLERY CAFE
CAFE £

Map p446 (www.stmargaretshouse.org.uk; 21 Old Ford Rd E2; dishes £3.80-5.90; ⏰10am-6pm; ☎; ☒Bethnal Green) Tucked around the corner from the Museum of Childhood, the pretty Gallery Cafe is in the basement of a lovely Georgian building. It serves simple but delicious vegan and vegetarian fare to relaxed locals. There's a cute courtyard at the front for sunny days. Check the website for sporadic evening events such as jazz, world and acoustic music, and film nights.

Mile End & Victoria Park

FISH HOUSE
FISH & CHIPS £

Map p446 (www.fishouse.co.uk; 126-128 Lauriston Rd E9; mains £8.50-12.50; ⏰noon-10pm ☒Mile End, then ☐277) This combination seafood restaurant and chippy is just the sort of place you wish you had in your own neighbourhood. The freshest of fresh fish and crustaceans are dispensed from both a busy takeaway section (where a blackboard tells you from where your fish has come) and a cheerful sit-down restaurant. The lobster bisque and Colchester oysters are always good, while the generous fish pie bursting with goodies from the briny deep is exceptional.

DOCKLANDS DEVELOPMENT

You'd probably never guess it while gazing up at the ultramodern skyscrapers that dominate the Isle of Dogs and Canary Wharf, but from the 16th century until the mid-20th century this area was the centre of the world's greatest port, the hub of the British Empire and its enormous global trade. At the docks here, cargo from global trade was landed, bringing jobs to a tight-knit working-class community. Even up to the start of WWII this community still thrived, but that all changed when the docks were badly firebombed during the Blitz.

After the war the docks were in no condition to cope with the postwar technological and political changes as the British Empire evaporated. At the same time enormous new bulk carriers and container ships demanded deep-water ports and new loading and unloading techniques. From the mid-1960s, dock closures followed one another as fast as they had opened, and the number of dock workers dropped from as many as 50,000 in 1960 to about 3000 by 1980.

The financial metropolis that exists today was begun by the London Docklands Development Corporation (LDDC), a body established by the Thatcher government in the freewheeling 1980s to take pressure for office space off the City. This rather artificial community had a shaky start. The low-rise toytown buildings had trouble attracting tenants, the Docklands Light Railway – the main transport link – had teething troubles and the landmark Canary Wharf Tower itself had to be rescued from bankruptcy twice. Now, however, news media organisations and financial behemoths have moved in – with Citigroup and HSBC boasting their own buildings.

The Docklands today is a world of contrasts, futuristic but rich in history.

NAMÔ
VIETNAMESE £

Map p446 (☑8533 0639; www.namo.co.uk; 178 Victoria Park Rd E9; mains £8.50-9; ☻noon-10.30pm; ☻Mile End, then ☐277) This pretty place serves a carefully chosen selection of punchy Vietnamese dishes in a nicer-than-average setting. There's a lovely garden area with a retractable roof, great for English summers.

LOAFING
CAFE £

Map p446 (www.loafing.co.uk; 79 Lauriston Rd E9; dishes £4-5; ☻9am-6pm; ☻Mile End, then ☐277) Cute corner cafe with a glorious cake selection, lovingly displayed. Also offers sandwiches, pastries, Monmouth coffee and a great range of teas, served in mismatched fine bone china. The outdoor tables and huge windows make it perfect for people-watching and there's also a tiny garden to relax in out back.

PAVILION
CAFE £

Map p446 (www.the-pavilion-cafe.com; cnr Old Ford & Grove Rds E3; mains £4.50-8; ☻8.30am-5pm; ☻Mile End, then ☐277) Superb cafe overlooking an ornamental lake in Victoria Park, serving breakfasts and lunches made with locally sourced ingredients, and excellent coffee.

✖ Hackney Wick & Stratford

TOP CHOICE FORMANS
SEAFOOD ££

Map p446 (☑8525 2365; www.formans.co.uk; Stour Rd E3; mains £12-19.50; ☻dinner Thu & Fri, lunch & dinner Sat, noon-5pm Sun; ☎; ☻Hackney Wick) H Forman & Son have been curing fish here since 1905, and are notable for developing the much-celebrated London cure. Obliged to move to make way for the Olympic developments, they're now housed in appropriately salmon-pink premises that comprise their smokery, restaurant, bar and art gallery. The diminutive restaurant, with unrivalled views over the Olympic stadium, serves a fantastic variety of smoked salmon (the wild smoked salmon is exceptional), as well as an interesting range of dishes with ingredients sourced from within the British Isles. It also has a great selection of English wines and, unusually, spirits. Simpler sharing platters are available in the bar. Make sure to take a peek into the smokery next door and the art gallery upstairs.

COUNTER CAFE
CAFE £

Map p446 (www.thecountercafe.co.uk; 7 Roach Rd E3; dishes £4.50-8; ☻7.30am-5pm Mon-Fri, 9am-5pm Sat & Sun; ☎; ☻Hackney Wick) Housed within Stour Space (which hosts a variety of art exhibitions) and directly overlooking the Olympic stadium, this friendly local cafe serves up fantastic coffee and tasty breakfasts, sandwiches and pies. The mismatched, thrift-store furniture, painting-clad walls and relaxed atmosphere make this a firm favourite with the local artist community.

HACKNEY PEARL CAFE £
(www.thehackneypearl.com; 11 Prince Edward Rd E9; lunch dishes £5-7.50, dinner mains £10-13; ☺10am-11pm Tue-Sat, to 5pm Sun; ☎; ⊖Hackney Wick) In an unforgiving area, and on an equally unforgiving site, this cafe has created a cheerful and friendly atmosphere where you can enjoy tasty food and delicious coffee. With large windows, outdoor tables and de rigueur salvaged furniture, it's a relaxed place to have breakfast or lunch but is also open into the evening when there is a short but frequently changing menu that includes some good vegie options.

✗ Wapping & Limehouse

TOP CHOICE **WAPPING FOOD** MODERN EUROPEAN ££
Map p446 (☎7680 2080; www.thewapping project.com; The Wapping Project, Wapping Hydraulic Power Station, Wapping Wall E1; mains £14-21; ☎; ⊖Wapping) Stylish dining room set among the innards of a disused power station, creating a spectacular and unexpectedly romantic atmosphere. The high-quality, seasonal menu changes daily but might include guinea fowl wrapped in pancetta, or onglet with beetroot and horseradish. The owner is Australian, which accounts for the exclusively Australian wine list. The 'Project' (of which the restaurant is a part) also contains a regularly changing exhibition space (noon to 10pm Monday to Friday, 10am to 10pm Saturday), which is well worth popping into.

✗ Docklands

GUN GASTROPUB, PORTUGUESE £££
Map p421 (☎7515 5222; www.thegundocklands. com; 27 Coldharbour E14; mains £15-27; ☎; ⊖Canary Wharf) Set at the end of a pretty, cobbled street, this riverside pub has been seriously dolled up, but still manages to ooze history. Previously a local dockers pub, dating from the early 18th century, it

is claimed that Lord Nelson had secret assignations with Lady Emma Hamilton here (hence the naming of the toilets). Inside, the pub is mostly comprised of a dining area but there is a smaller room at the back as well as a terrace affording expansive views of the Thames. On a separate terrace, during summer months, the pub hosts the completely al fresco **A Grelha** (mains £15-28), grilling up dazzlingly fresh fish from Billingsgate Market, just a few streets away, as well as Portuguese classics such as *cataplana* and *estapada*. Call ahead if the weather's bad.

🍷 DRINKING & NIGHTLIFE

🍷 Whitechapel

RHYTHM FACTORY CLUB
Map p446 (www.rhythmfactory.co.uk; 16-18 Whitechapel Rd E1; ⊖Aldgate East) Perennially hip and popular, the Rhythm Factory is a club and venue hosting a variety of bands and DJs of all genres that keep the up-for-it crowd happy until late.

INDO PUB
Map p446 (133 Whitechapel Rd E1; ☺to 1am Sun-Thu, to 3am Fri & Sat; ☎; ⊖Whitechapel) Tiny, narrow pub bang opposite the East London Mosque, with battered old tables, pews and a couple of knackered Chesterfields under the only window. Friendly staff work the beautifully tat-cluttered bar, and serve decent pizzas (£5 to £7) to punters with the munchies. There's art for sale on the walls, DJs on weekend nights and interesting bands on an irregular schedule.

🍷 Bethnal Green & Hackney

DOVE FREEHOUSE PUB
Map p446 (www.belgianbars.com; 24-28 Broadway Market E8; ☎; ℝCambridge Heath, ☐55) This pub attracts at any time with its rambling series of rooms and wide range – 21 on draught – of Belgian Trappist, wheat and fruit-flavoured beers. Drinkers spill out onto the street in warmer weather, or hunker down in the low-lit back room with board games when it's chilly. Decent gastropub fare also on offer.

CARPENTER'S ARMS
PUB

Map p446 (www.carpentersarmsfreehouse.com; 73 Cheshire St E2; ⏰; ⊖Shoreditch High St, Ⓡ Bethnal Green) After a browse in the shops along Cheshire St, you'll probably end up outside this gorgeous corner pub. Once notorious – the pub was owned in the '60s by the Kray brothers, who gave it over to their mother – it has been well restored to a trendy, yet cosy and intimate pub combining traditional pub architecture with contemporary touches. A back room and small yard provide a little more space for the convivial drinkers. There's a great range of beers and lagers, as well as a menu offering quality drinking food.

BETHNAL GREEN WORKING MEN'S CLUB
CLUB

Map p446 (www.workersplaytime.net; 42-44 Pollard Row E2; ⏰8pm-2am, days vary; ⊖Bethnal Green) As it says on the tin, this is a true working men's club, which has opened its doors and let in all kinds of off-the-wall club nights, including trashy burlesque, vintage nights of all eras, beach parties and bake offs. Expect sticky carpets, a shimmery stage set and a space akin to a school-hall disco.

ROYAL OAK
PUB

Map p446 (www.royaloaklondon.com; 73 Columbia Rd E2; ⏰from 4pm Mon-Thu, from 12pm Fri-Sun; ⊖Hoxton) Lovely wood-panelled pub arranged around a handsome central bar with a good selection of bitter and a better-than-average wine list. There's also a little garden at the back and great food. It really gets into its stride on Sunday when London's famous flower market (p231) is just outside the door.

NELSONS HEAD
GAY

Map p446 (www.nelsonshead.com; 32 Horatio St E2; ⏰from 4pm Mon-Sat, 9am-11pm Sun; ⊖Hoxton) Small, down-to-earth locals' pub with quirky decor, a fun and friendly mixed clientele, and plenty of camp tunes.

JOINERS ARMS
GAY

Map p446 (www.joinershoreditch.com; 116-118 Hackney Rd E2; ⏰5pm-3am; ⊖Hoxton, Ⓡ55) Determinedly run-down and cheesy, the Joiners is Hoxton's only totally gay pub-club. It's a crowded, funky old boozer where hip gay boys hang out at the bar, dance and watch people play pool all night.

🍸 Mile End & Victoria Park

ROYAL INN ON THE PARK
PUB

Map p446 (111 Lauriston Rd E9; ⏰; ⊖Mile End, then Ⓡ277) On the northern border of Victoria Park, this excellent place, once a poster pub for Transport for London, has a half-dozen real ales and Czech lagers on tap, outside seating to the front and a recently made-over garden at the back. It's always lively and attracts a mixed boho/louche Hackney crowd.

PALM TREE
PUB

Map p446 (127 Grove Rd E3; ⏰to 2am Fri & Sat, to 1am Sun; ⊖Mile End, Ⓡ277) The Palm, the quintessential East End pub on the Regent's Canal, is loved by locals, students and trendies alike, with its comforting gold-flock wallpaper, photos of also-ran crooners and a handful of different guest ales every week. There's jazz on Friday and Saturday from around 9.30pm.

BRITANNIA
PUB

Map p446 (www.thebritanniapub.co.uk; 360 Victoria Park Rd E9; ⏰; ⊖Homerton, Ⓡ388) A large, rambling old pub, made-over in 2009, sporting a fabulous beer garden right on the park, with a barbecue running throughout the day on summer weekends. Also serves tasty gastropub dishes and a decent range of drinks.

🍸 Hackney Wick & Stratford

KING EDWARD VII
PUB

Off Map p446 (www.kingeddie.co.uk; 47 Broadway E15; ⊖Stratford) Built in the 19th century this lovely old boozer is a series of handsome rooms set around a central bar. The front bar and saloon are the most convivial, and there's a little leafy courtyard at the back. A decent selection of ales and wine, and some great pub grub, make this a real highlight of the area.

🍸 Wapping & Limehouse

GRAPES
PUB

Map p421 (www.grapeslondon.co.uk; 76 Narrow St E14; DLR Limehouse) One of Limehouse's renowned historic pubs – there's apparently been a drinking house here since 1583 – the Grapes is tiny, especially the riverside terrace, which can only really comfortably fit about a half-dozen close friends, but it's cosy inside and exudes plenty of old-world charm.

PROSPECT OF WHITBY PUB

Map p446 (57 Wapping Wall E1; ☎; ❷Wapping) Once known as the Devil's Tavern, the Whitby is said to date from 1520, making it the oldest riverside pub in London. It's firmly on the tourist trail now, but there's a smallish terrace to the front and the side overlooking the Thames, a decent restaurant upstairs and open fires in winter. Check out the wonderful pewter bar – Samuel Pepys once sidled up to it to sup.

CAPTAIN KIDD PUB

Map p446 (108 Wapping High St E1; ☎; ❷Wapping) With its large windows, fine beer garden and displays recalling the hanging nearby of the eponymous pirate in 1701, this is a favourite riverside pub in Wapping. Although cleverly done up, it actually only dates back to the 1980s.

WHITE SWAN GAY

Map p446 (www.bjswhiteswan.com; 556 Commercial Rd E14; DLR Limehouse) The White Swan is a fun East End kind of place, with a large dance floor as well as a more relaxed pub area. Its legendary amateur strip night takes place every Wednesday and there are also cabaret and karaoke nights. Club classics and cheesy pop predominate.

⭐ ENTERTAINMENT

WILTON'S THEATRE

Map p446 (☎7702 2789; www.wiltons.org.uk; 1 Graces Alley E1; ❷Tower Hill or DLR Tower Gateway) A gloriously atmospheric example of one of London's Victorian public-house music halls, Wilton's hosts a real variety of shows, from comedy and classical music to literary theatre and opera. You can also take a one-hour guided **tour** (£6; ⊘3pm & 6pm Mon) of the building to hear more about its fascinating history. The hall's **Mahogany Bar** (⊘5-11pm Mon-Fri) is a great way to get a taste of the place if you're not attending a performance.

BISTROTHEQUE BAR/CABARET BAR

Map p446 (☎8983 7900; www.bistrotheque.com; 23-27 Wadeston St E2; ❷Bethnal Green, ☐Cambridge Heath) This converted warehouse offers hilarious transvestite lip-synching in its ground-floor Cabaret Room and high-quality dining in its stylish whitewashed restaurant above. It's also worth coming just for the Napoleon bar, a moody, slightly decadent room with dark walls (the oak panels came from a stately home in Northumberland) and plush seating; the drinks are expertly mixed and the bar staff always friendly.

HACKNEY EMPIRE THEATRE

Map p446 (☎8985 2424; www.hackneyempire. co.uk; 291 Mare St E8; ☐Hackney Central, ☐38 or 277) The programming at this renovated Edwardian Music Hall (1901) is eclectic to say the least and certainly defines 'something for everyone' – from hard-edged political theatre to opera and comedy. The Empire is definitely one of the best places to catch a pantomime at Christmas.

🛍 SHOPPING

The boutiques and galleries lining Columbia Rd (which are usually open at the weekend only) and the shops along Broadway Market and Cheshire St are part of London's up-and-coming independent retail scenes. If you're after something a little more mainstream, Westfield Stratford City, currently Europe's largest urban shopping centre, can't fail to satisfy. There's also a shopping mall beneath the Canary Wharf skyscrapers, with similar shops, bars and restaurants.

COLUMBIA ROAD FLOWER MARKET MARKET

Map p446 (www.columbiaroad.info; ⊘8am-3pm Sun; ❷Hoxton) A real explosion of colour and life, this weekly market sells a beautiful array of flowers, pot plants, bulbs, seeds and everything you might need for the garden. A lot of fun, even if you don't buy anything, the market gets really packed so go as early as you can, or later on, when the vendors sell off the cut flowers cheaply. It stretches from Gossett St to the Royal Oak pub.

BROADWAY MARKET MARKET

Map p446 (www.broadwaymarket.co.uk; ⊘9am-5pm Sat; ☐London Fields, ☐55 or 277) There's been a market down this pretty street since the late 19th century, the focus of which has these days become artisan food, arty knick-knacks, books, records and vintage clothing.

JONES DAIRY   FOOD

Map p446 (www.jonesdairy.co.uk; 23 Ezra St E2; ⏺9am-1pm Fri-Sun; ⊖Hoxton) This wonderfully preserved shop, set on an atmospheric cobblestoned street, opened in 1902 and was once part of a chain of Welsh dairies across the capital. You can still choose from a quality selection of cheese, alongside bread, coffees, teas, jams and cakes. Perfect for stocking up on picnic food, there's also a cute little cafe round the back.

BEYOND RETRO   VINTAGE

Map p446 (www.beyondretro.com; 110-112 Cheshire St; ⊖Shoreditch High St, ⊠Bethnal Green) Huge selection of vintage clothes, including wigs, shoes, jackets and lin-gerie, expertly slung together in a lofty warehouse.

CARHARTT OUTLET STORE   FASHION

Map p446 (www.thecarharttstore.co.uk; 18 Ellingfort Rd E8; ⊖Hackney Central, ⊠London Fields) You'll find hoodies, sweats and jeans at this outlet of the street-wear label, as well as a small selection of similar brands. It's tucked away on a residential street, under the railway arches just north of London Fields station. Ring the bell to get in.

BURBERRY OUTLET SHOP   FASHION

Map p446 (29-31 Chatham Pl E9; ⊖Hackney Central, ⊠55) This outlet shop stocks seconds from the reborn-as-trendy Brit brand's current and last season's collections. Prices are around 30% lower than those on the high street. Service can be brusque.

Hampstead & North London

KING'S CROSS | EUSTON | REGENT'S PARK | CAMDEN | HAMPSTEAD | HIGHGATE | ISLINGTON | STOKE NEWINGTON | DALSTON

Neighbourhood Top Five

1 Walking in the gorgeous **Hampstead Heath** (p241); enjoying the sweeping views of London from Parliament Hill, getting your culture fix at the beautiful Kenwood House and slumping in a couch at the Garden Gate pub to recover.

2 Shopping at **Camden Market** (p240); having lunch at one of the food stalls and finishing your day with a leisurely stroll along Regent's Canal.

3 Discovering the treasures of the **British Library** (p235) and marvelling at the sheer amount of knowledge stored within its walls.

4 Enjoying a thought-provoking afternoon exploring the concepts of life, death and art at the **Wellcome Collection** (p238) and mulling it over a glass of wine at the wonderful Somers Town Coffee House (p248).

5 Going out in **Dalston** (p251) for superb kebabs and off-the-wall partying.

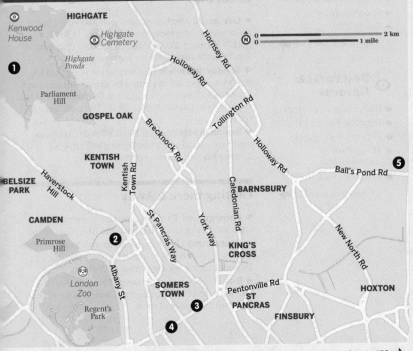

For more detail of this area, see Map p451, p448 and p452 ➡

Lonely Planet's Top Tip

North London is all about parks, so make sure you set aside a few hours during your stay to enjoy the greenery. Pack a picnic and do as Londoners do: head to the pub afterwards!

Best Places to Eat

➡ Ottolenghi (p245)
➡ Manna (p246)
➡ Mangal Ocakbasi (p247)
➡ Gaucho Grill (p244)
➡ Market (p243)

For reviews, see p243 ➡

Best Places to Drink

➡ Edinboro Castle (p248)
➡ Garden Gate (p249)
➡ Proud Camden (p248)
➡ Boogaloo (p249)
➡ Bull (p250)

For reviews, see p248 ➡

◉ Best Parks & Gardens

➡ Hampstead Heath (p241)
➡ Primrose Hill (p239)
➡ Regent's Park (p238)
➡ Abney Park Cemetery (p242)
➡ Alexandra Park (p244)

For reviews, see p238 ➡

Explore: Hampstead & North London

North London is a big place – you could spend a week here exploring its parks, checking the sights, lounging in gastropubs and sampling the nightlife. So if you're short on time, you'll have to pick and choose carefully.

Hampstead Heath and Camden Market should be top of your list; Camden is a major sight and its energy is intoxicating, while Hampstead Heath will offer you a glorious day out and an insight into how North Londoners spend their weekend. The Wellcome Collection and the British Library are also highly recommended and are easily accessible, thanks to their more central location.

Because this part of London is predominantly residential, it is at its busiest at the weekend. This means that most sights are relatively quiet during the week, with the exception of the Wellcome Collection and the British Library.

On the whole, North London is a wealthy area, full of 20- or 30-somethings (Camden, Islington, Dalston), young families (Hampstead, Highgate, Stoke Newington) and celebrities (Primrose Hill). The nightlife is excellent wherever you go, with edgy and offbeat bars in Dalston, excellent pubs in Hampstead or Islington and great live music in Camden.

Local Life

➡ **Live music** North London is well-known for being the home of indie rock. Music fans flock to Barfly (p252), Forum (p252) and the Bull & Gate (p252) to watch bands aiming for the big time.

➡ **Sunday pub lunch** This institution of English life has been embraced in earnest by gastropubs making a brisk trade. Favourites include the Garden Gate (p249), the Edinboro Castle (p248) and the Duke of Cambridge (p246).

➡ **Swimming** Hampstead Heath's Ponds (p254) are open year-round and a small group of hard-core aficionados swim every day, rain or shine.

Getting there & Away

➡ **Underground** The Northern Line has stops in Camden, Hampstead, Highgate and Islington (Angel).

➡ **Overground** The Overground crosses North London from east to west and is useful for areas such as Dalston that are not connected to the tube.

➡ **Bus** There is a good network of buses in North London connecting various neighbourhoods together, and with the centre of town.

BRITISH LIBRARY

In 1998 the British Library moved to its new premises between King's Cross and Euston stations. At a cost of £500 million, it was Britain's most expensive building, and not one that is universally loved; Colin St John Wilson's exterior of straight lines of red brick, which Prince Charles reckoned was akin to a 'secret-police building', is certainly not to all tastes. But even those who don't like the building from the outside will be won over by the spectacularly cool and spacious interior.

The British Library is the nation's principal copyright library: it stocks one copy of every British and Irish publication as well as historic manuscripts, books and maps from the British Museum (the Bodleian Library at Oxford University and the Cambridge University Library fulfil the same functions).

As well as hosting excellent permanent collections, the British Library runs regular temporary exhibitions of various authors, genres and themes (science fiction, the census etc), all connected to its records.

King's Library

At the centre of the building is the wonderful King's Library, the 65,000-volume collection of King George III, displayed in the eerily beautiful six-storey, 17m-high **glass-walled tower** at the centre of the building.

The collection is considered one of the most significant of The Enlightenment period, and it was bequeathed to the nation by George III's son, George IV, in 1823. It was decided that the volumes would be kept at the British Museum, in the specially-built King's Library Gallery. But after a bomb fell on the collection during WWII, it was moved to the Bodleian

DON'T MISS...

➡ King's Library
➡ Sir John Ritblat Gallery
➡ Philatelic Exhibition
➡ Guided tours

PRACTICALITIES

➡ Map p448
➡ www.bl.uk
➡ 96 Euston Rd NW1
➡ admission free
➡ ⊘9.30am-6pm Mon & Wed-Fri, to 8pm Tue, to 5pm Sat, 11am-5pm Sun
➡ ⊖King's Cross St Pancras

LIBRARY CAFES

All the catering at the British Library comes courtesy of the wonderful **Peyton & Byrne**, the progeny of Irish chef Oliver Peyton. There are three main outfits: the first floor **restaurant** (☉9.30am-5pm Mon-Fri, to 4pm Sat), with spectacular views of the King's Library Tower and treats such as made-to-order stir-fries; **Café** (☉daily) on the ground floor, which serves hot drinks, pastries and sandwiches; and the **Espresso Bar** (Euston Rd; ☉daily) which serves similar fare as Café as well as fresh *churros*.

What you can see of the British Library is basically the tip of the iceberg. Under your feet, on four basement levels run some 186 miles of shelving where the library keeps its records and treasures. The library currently contains 14 million books, 920,000 journal and newspaper titles, 58 million patents, and some 3 million sound recordings.

FREE WI-FI

The British Library has wi-fi throughout the building. You need to register to use it but it is free of charge.

Library in Oxford and only finally moved back to London in 1998 when the new British Library opened.

Sir John Ritblat Gallery: treasures of the British Library

For visitors, the highlight of a visit to the British Library is the Sir John Ritblat Gallery where the library keeps its most precious and high-profile documents. The collection spans almost three millennia of history and contains manuscripts, religious texts, maps, music scores, autographs, diaries and more.

Rare texts from all the main religions include the **Codex Sinaiticus**, the first complete text of the New Testament, written in Greek in the 4th century; a **Gutenberg Bible** (1455), the first Western book printed using movable type; and the stunningly illustrated **Jain sacred texts**.

There are also historical documents, including one of four remaining copies of **Magna Carta** (1215), the charter credited with setting out the basis of human rights in English law. Not so important but poignant is **Captain Scott's final diary** including an account of fellow explorer Lawrence Oates's death.

Literature is also well represented, with **Shakespeare's First Folio** (1623) and manuscripts by some of Britain's best-known authors (such as Lewis Carroll, Jane Austen, George Eliot and Thomas Hardy). Music fans will love the **Beatles' earliest handwritten lyrics** and original scores by Handel, Mozart amd Beethoven.

The Philatelic Exhibition

The Philatelic Exhibition, next to the Sir John Ritblat Gallery, is based on collections established in the 19th century and now consists of more than 80,000 items, including postage and revenue stamps and postal stationery from almost every country and from all periods.

Tours

There are **guided tours** (☎01937 546 546; adult/child £8/6.50; one hour) of the library's public areas at 3pm Monday, Wednesday and Friday and at 10.30am and 3pm Saturday, and another that includes a visit to one of the **reading rooms** at 11.30am and 3pm Sunday. The tours include fascinating background information on the building, its controversial design and the role the library plays in public life.

Further tours, including free tours of the reading rooms (☉11am Mon, Wed & Fri), and tours of the conservation studios, are also regularly available. Bookings are recommended for all tours.

 TOP SIGHTS **BRITISH LIBRARY**

Established in 1828, these zoological gardens are among the oldest in the world. This is where the word 'zoo' originated but the emphasis nowadays is firmly placed on conservation, education and breeding, with fewer species and more spacious conditions.

The newest development is **Penguin Beach**, a huge and beautifully landscaped enclosure featuring a pool with cool underwater viewing areas. The new facility is a key element to London Zoo's breeding program of Humboldt, macaroni, black-footed and rockhopper penguins.

Another highlight is **Gorilla Kingdom**, a project that involves a gorilla conservation program in Gabon and the Democratic Republic of Congo in central Africa. The zoo has four gorillas who live on their own island.

For a more inclusive experience, head to the lovely **Clore Rainforest Lookout and Nightzone**, a slice of the South American rainforest complete with marmosets, monkeys, fruitbats and other creatures wandering and flying freely among the visitors inside the humid, tropical-climate room. We loved the hot and humid **Butterfly Paradise** where myriads of butterflies and moths flutter from flower to flower.

There are feeding sessions or talks throughout the day, which are a great way to learn more about bird-eating spiders, cheeky squirrel monkeys or predatory birds.

There is also plenty to see indoors, with an **aquarium**, a **reptile house** and a building called Bugs full of creepy-crawlies.

The zoo is constantly redeveloping enclosures or building new ones. Its next big project is a tiger enclosure that will recreate the Sumatran jungle. Planned for Easter 2013, the new tiger enclosure will be five times as big as the current one.

DON'T MISS...

➡ Penguin Beach
➡ Gorilla Kingdom
➡ Butterfly Paradise
➡ Clore Rainforest

PRACTICALITIES

➡ Map p452
➡ www.zsl.org/london-zoo
➡ Outer Circle, Regent's Park NW1
➡ adult/child £19/15 plus optional £2 donation to protect endangered species
➡ ⊙10am-4pm Nov-Mar, to 5.30pm Apr-mid-Jul, Sep & Oct, to 6pm mid-Jul & Aug
➡ ⊖Regent's Park or Camden Town

◉ SIGHTS

North London is a collection of small neighbourhoods, ancient villages that were slowly drawn into London as the metropolis expanded. King's Cross has historically been a blight on the capital's landscape, but the opening of the beautiful St Pancras International train terminal and the urban renewal behind the station (the University of London will move there in 2014) is making this part of town more attractive. The rest of North London certainly doesn't suffer from an image problem: with wonderful parks, amazing views and some of the best pubs around, it's a great place for a more sedate day out.

◉ King's Cross & Euston

BRITISH LIBRARY CULTURAL BUILDING
See p235.

LONDON CANAL MUSEUM MUSEUM
Map p448 (www.canalmuseum.org.uk; 12-13 New Wharf Rd N1; adult/child £4/2; ☺10am-4.30pm Tue-Sun & bank holidays; ☻King's Cross St

Pancras) This quirky but fascinating museum is in an old ice warehouse (with a deep well where the frozen commodity was stored) dating from the 1860s. It traces the history of Regent's Canal, the ice business and the development of ice cream via models, photographs, exhibits and documentaries from the archives. (The ice trade was huge in late Victorian London, with 35,000 tonnes imported from Norway in 1899.)

You can access the wharf at the back of the museum where a number of narrow boats are moored. The exhibits in the stables upstairs are dedicated to the history of canal transport in Britain.

◉ Regent's Park

LONDON ZOO ZOO
See p237.

REGENT'S PARK PARK
Map p452 (www.royalparks.gov.uk; ☺5am-dusk; ☻Baker St or Regent's Park) The most elaborate and ordered of London's many parks, this one was created around 1820 by John Nash, who planned to use it as an estate to

---

◉ TOP SIGHTS
WELLCOME COLLECTION

The Wellcome Collection styles itself as a 'destination for the incurably curious', a pretty accurate tag for an institution that seeks to explore the links between medicine, science, life and art. It's a serious topic but the genius of the museum is that it presents it in an accessible way. The building is light and modern, with varied and interactive displays ranging from interviews with researchers, doctors and patients to art depicting medicine, models of human organs, etc.

The heart of the permanent collection is Sir Henry Wellcome's collection of objects from around the world. Wellcome (1853–1936), a pharmacist, entrepreneur and collector, was fascinated with medicine and amassed more than a million objects from different civilisations associated with life, birth, death and sickness.

The museum also runs outstanding temporary exhibitions on topics exploring the frontiers of modern medicine, its place in society and its history; highlights of the last few years include exhibitions on sleeping and dreaming, dirt, drugs (of the mind-altering kind), the heart, and a controversial series of beautiful black-and-white portraits of individuals before and after their death.

DON'T MISS...

➡ Temporary exhibitions

➡ Sir Henry Wellcome's collection

PRACTICALITIES

➡ Map p426

➡ www.wellcome collection.org

➡ 183 Euston Rd NW1

➡ admission free

➡ ☺10am-6pm Tue-Sat, to 10pm Thu, 11am-6pm Sun

➡ ☻Euston Sq or Euston

WALKING ALONG REGENT'S CANAL

The canals that were once a trade lifeline for the capital have now become a favourite escape for Londoners, providing a quiet walk away from traffic and crowds. For visitors, an added advantage of Regent's Canal towpath is that it provides an easy (and delightful) shortcut across North London.

You can, for instance, walk from Little Venice (p259) to Camden (p239) in less than an hour; on the way, you'll pass Regent's Park (p238), London Zoo (p237), Primrose Hill (p239), beautiful villas designed by architect John Nash as well as redevelopments of old industrial buildings into trendy blocks of flats. Allow 15 to 20 minutes between Camden and Regent's Park, and 25 to 30 minutes between Regent's Park and Little Venice. There are plenty of exits along the way and there are signposts all along.

If the canals have piqued your curiosity, make a beeline for the London Canal Museum in King's Cross (p238) to learn more about their fascinating history.

build palaces for the aristocracy. Although the plan never quite came off – like so many at the time – you can get some idea of what Nash might have achieved from the buildings along the Outer Circle, and in particular from the stuccoed Palladian mansions he built on Cumberland Tce.

Like many of the city's parks, this one was used as a royal hunting ground, and then as farmland, before becoming a place for fun and leisure during the 18th century. These days it's well organised but relaxed, lively but serene, and a local but cosmopolitan haven in the heart of the city. Among its many attractions are the London Zoo, Regent's Canal along its northern side, an ornamental lake, an open-air theatre in Queen Mary's Gardens where Shakespeare is performed during the summer months, ponds and colourful flowerbeds, rose gardens that look spectacular in June, and sports pitches where Londoners regularly meet to play football, rugby and volleyball.

On the western side of the park is the impressive **London Central Islamic Centre & Mosque** (www.iccuk.org; 146 Park Rd NW8; ⊖Marylebone), a huge white edifice with a glistening dome. Provided you take your shoes off and dress modestly you're welcome to go inside, although the interior is fairly stark.

LORD'S CRICKET GROUND   CRICKET GROUND
off Map p452 (www.lords.org; St John's Wood Rd NW8; tours adult/child £15/9; ⊗tours when no play 10am, noon & 2pm Apr-Sep; ⊖St John's Wood) The 'home of cricket' is a must for any devotee of this peculiarly English game: book early for the test matches here, but

it's also worth taking the absorbing and anecdotal 90-minute tour of the ground and facilities.

Tours take in the famous Long Room – where members watch the games surrounded by portraits of cricket's great and good – and a museum featuring evocative memorabilia that will appeal to fans old and new. The famous little urn containing the Ashes, the prize of the most fiercely contested competition in cricket, resides here when in English hands.

The ground itself is dominated by a striking media centre that looks like a clock radio, but you should also keep an eye out for the famous weathervane in the shape of Father Time and the remarkable tentlike modern Mound Stand. For the London Olympic Games in 2012, Lord's will change its vocation slightly to host the archery event.

◉ Camden

PRIMROSE HILL   NEIGHBOURHOOD
Map p452 Wedged between well-heeled Regent's Park and edgy Camden, the little neighbourhood of Primrose Hill is high on the wish list of most Londoners – but utterly unaffordable. With its independent boutiques (from interior design to bookshops, children's clothes to pet accessories, not a franchise in sight), lovely restaurants and good pubs, it has a rare village feel.

The proximity of the gorgeous, eponymous **park**, with fabulous views of London, is another draw. On summer weekends, it is absolutely packed with revellers enjoying a picnic with a view; but on weekdays, there's

TOP SIGHTS
CAMDEN MARKET

Although – or perhaps because – it stopped being cutting-edge several thousand cheap leather jackets ago, Camden market gets a whopping 10 million visitors each year and is one of London's most popular attractions.

What started out as a collection of attractive craft stalls by Camden Lock on the Regent's Canal now extends in various shape or form most of the way from Camden Town tube station to Chalk Farm tube station. There are four main market areas, **Buck Street Market**, **Lock Market**, **Canal Market** and **Stables Market**, although they seem to blend into one with the crowds snaking along and the 'normal' shops lining the streets. You'll find a bit of everything: clothes (of variable quality) in profusion, bags, jewellery, arts and crafts, candles, incense and a myriad of decorative titbits. For a more detailed breakdown of what you might find, see p253.

There are dozens of food stalls at the Lock Market and the Stables Market; virtually every type of cuisine is offered, from French to Argentinian, Japanese and Caribbean. Quality varies but is generally pretty good and affordable and you can eat on the big communal tables or by the canal.

DON'T MISS...

➡ Lock Market
➡ Stables Market
➡ Lunch at the food stalls

PRACTICALITIES

➡ Map p452
➡ Camden High St NW1
➡ ⊙10am-6pm
➡ ⊖Camden Town or Chalk Farm, 🚊Camden Rd

---

mostly dog walkers and nannies and it's a lovely place to enjoy a quiet stroll or an alfresco sandwich.

Famous residents include supermodels Kate Moss and Agyness Deyn, actors Jude Law, Helena Bonham-Carter, Sienna Miller and many more. Part of the fun is to come here and celebrity-spot.

⊙ Hampstead & Highgate

NO 2 WILLOW ROAD   HOUSE

Map p451 (2 Willow Rd NW3; adult/child £6/3; ⊙noon-5pm Wed-Sat Mar-Oct, guided tours 11am, noon, 1pm & 2pm; ⊖Hampstead or 🚊Hampstead Heath) Fans of modern architecture will want to swing past this property, the central house in a block of three, designed by the 'structural rationalist' Ernö Goldfinger in 1939 as his family home. Many people think it looks uncannily like the sort of mundane 1950s architecture you see everywhere. It may look similar now, but 2 Willow Rd was in fact a forerunner in this style.

The interior has cleverly designed storage space, amazing light (rooms that couldn't have a side window have a skylight) and collection of artworks by Henry Moore, Max Ernst and Bridget Riley. It's accessible to all, thanks to hugely knowledgeable staff. Entry is by guided tour only until 3pm, after which nonguided viewing is allowed.

FENTON HOUSE   HISTORIC BUILDING

Map p451 (Windmill Hill, Hampstead Grove NW3; adult/child £7/3; ⊙11am-5pm Wed-Sun Mar-Oct; ⊖Hampstead) One of the oldest houses in Hampstead, this late-17th-century merchant's residence has a charming walled garden with roses and an orchard, fine collections of porcelain and keyboard instruments – including a 1612 harpsichord played by Handel. The interior is very evocative thanks to original Georgian furniture and period art, such as 17th-century needlework pictures.

KEATS HOUSE   HISTORIC BUILDING

Map p451 (www.keatshouse.org.uk; Wentworth Pl, Keats Grove NW3; adult/child £5/free; ⊙1-5pm Tue-Sun May-Oct, Fri-Sun Nov-April; ⊖Hampstead or 🚊Hampstead Heath) Reopened mid-2009 following redevelopment, this elegant Regency house was home to the golden boy of the Romantic poets from 1818 to 1820. Never short of generous mates, Keats was persuaded to take refuge here by Charles Armitage Brown, and it was here that he met his fiancée Fanny Brawne, who was literally the girl next door.

Keats wrote his most celebrated poem, *Ode to a Nightingale*, while sitting under a plum tree in the garden, no longer there, in 1819. The house is sparsely furnished but does a good job of conveying what daily life would have been like in Keats' day.

FREE BURGH HOUSE   MUSEUM

Map p451 (www.burghhouse.org.uk; New End Sq NW3; ⊙noon-5pm Wed-Fri & Sun; ⊝Hampstead) If you happen to be in the neighbourhood, this late-17th-century Queen Anne mansion houses the Hampstead Museum of local history, a small art gallery and the delightful **Buttery Garden Café** (⊙11am-5.30pm Wed-Sat), where you can get a decent and reasonably priced lunch (sandwiches £5).

HIGHGATE WOOD   OUTDOORS

Map p451 (Archway Rd; ⊙7.30am-sunset; ⊝Highgate) With more than 28 hectares of ancient woodland, this park is a wonderful spot for a walk any time of the year. It's also teeming with life, and some 70 different bird species have been recorded here, along with five types of bat, 12 types of butterfly and 80 different kinds of spider. It also has a huge clearing in the centre for sports, a popular playground and nature trail for kids and a range of activities – from falconry to bat-watching – throughout the year.

⊙ Islington

ESTORICK COLLECTION OF MODERN ITALIAN ART   GALLERY

Map p448 (www.estorickcollection.com; 39a Canonbury Sq N1; adult/child £5/free; ⊙11am-6pm Wed-Sat, noon-5pm Sun; ⊝Highbury & Islington) The only museum in Britain devoted to Italian art, and one of the leading collections of futurist painting in the world, the Estorick Collection is housed in a listed Georgian building and stuffed with works by such greats as Giacomo Balla, Umberto Boccioni, Gino Severini and Ardengo Soffici.

The collection of paintings, drawings, etchings and sculpture, amassed by American writer and art dealer Eric Estorick and his wife Salome, also includes drawings and a painting by the even more famous

TOP SIGHTS
HAMPSTEAD HEATH

Sprawling Hampstead Heath, with its rolling woodlands and meadows, feels a million miles away – despite being approximately four – from the City of London. It covers 320 hectares, most of it woods, hills and meadows, and is home to about 180 bird species, 23 species of butterflies, grass snakes, bats and a rich array of flora. It's a wonderful place for a ramble, especially to the top of **Parliament Hill**, which offers expansive views across the city and is one of the most popular places in London to fly a kite. Alternatively head up the hill in North Wood or lose yourself in the West Heath.

If walking is too pedestrian for you, another major attraction is the **bathing ponds** (separate beautiful ones for men and women and a slightly less pleasant mixed pond – see p254).

Those of a more artistic bent should make a beeline for **Kenwood House** (p242) but stop to admire the **sculptures by Henry Moore and Barbara Hepworth** on the way.

Once you've had your fill of fresh air and/or culture, do as Londoners do and head to one of the wonderful nearby pubs (p249) for a restorative pint.

DON'T MISS...

➡ Views from Parliament Hill

➡ Strolling in the woodlands

➡ Swimming in the bathing ponds

➡ Kenwood House

➡ Henry Moore and Barbara Hepworth sculptures

PRACTICALITIES

➡ Map p451

➡ ⊝Hampstead, ⊠Gospel Oak or Hampstead Heath, ⊞214 or C2 to Parliament Hill Fields

TOP SIGHTS
KENWOOD HOUSE

This magnificent neoclassical mansion stands at the northern end of the heath in a glorious sweep of land-scaped gardens leading down to a picturesque lake, around which concerts take place during the summer months (see p251).

The house was remodelled by Robert Adam in the 18th century, and rescued from developers by Lord Iveagh Guinness, who donated it to the nation in 1927, including the wonderful collection of art it contains. The Iveagh Bequest, as it is known, contains paintings by such greats as Rembrandt (one of his many self-portraits), Constable, Turner, Hals, Vermeer and Van Dyck and is one of the finest small collections in Britain.

Robert Adam's Great Stairs and the library, one of 14 rooms open to the public, are especially fine. The Suffolk Collection occupies the 1st floor. It includes Jacobean portraits by William Larkin and royal Stuart portraits by Van Dyck and Lely. There are **guided tours** (adult/concession £2/1) of the house daily at 2.30pm.

Located in what was once the servants' wing of Kenwood House, the **Brew House Café** has delicious food, from light snacks to full meals (mains around £7.50), and plenty of room on the lovely garden terrace.

DON'T MISS...

➡ Self-Portrait by Rembrandt

➡ *Hampstead Heath* by Constable

➡ Kenwood House's summer concerts

➡ Strolling in the landscaped gardens

PRACTICALITIES

➡ Map p451

➡ Hampstead Lane NW3

➡ admission free

➡ ⊘11.30am-4pm

➡ ⊖Archway or Golders Green, then ⊒210

Amedeo Modigliani. Well-conceived special exhibitions have included many 20th century art movements and lesser-known artists from Italy and beyond. The museum also encompasses an extensive library, cafe and shop.

cruising ground and a hang-out for some of Hackney's least salubrious drug users, as a delightfully overgrown ruin. The derelict chapel at its centre could be right out of a horror film, and the atmosphere of the whole place is nothing short of magical.

⊙ Stoke Newington

ABNEY PARK CEMETERY   CEMETERY
(www.abney-park.org.uk; Stoke Newington Church St N16; ⊘8am-dusk; ⊒Stoke Newington, ⊒73, 106, 149, 243, 276, 476) Unfairly dubbed 'the poor man's Highgate' by some, this magical place was bought and developed by a private firm from 1840 to provide burial grounds for central London's overflow. It was a dissenters (ie non-Church of England) cemetery and many of the most influential Presbyterians, Quakers and Baptists are buried here, including the Salvation Army founder, William Booth, whose grand tombstone greets you as you enter from Church St.

Since the 1950s the cemetery has been left to fend for itself and, these days, is as much a bird and plant sanctuary, a gay

⊙ Dalston

EASTERN CURVE GARDENS   OUTDOORS
Map p448 (http://dalstongarden.site11.com; 13 Dalston Lane E8; ⊘11am-6pm; ⊒Dalston Junction or Dalston Kingsland) This lovely garden is typical of the kind of regeneration happening around Dalston: a project led by the community, for the community, and a roaring success. There are workshops and events almost every day, from gardening sessions to building a greenhouse or benches for the garden, to a pizza-making afternoon using the wood-fired oven.

The site used to be a derelict railway line and the garden has used the old sleepers to make a boardwalk and raised beds for the vegie patch. It's nice place to just sit down for a while or to meet friendly locals.

RIDLEY ROAD MARKET   MARKET

Map p448 (Ridley Rd E8; ⊗8.30am-6pm Mon-Sat; ⒭Dalston Kingsland or Dalston Junction) Massively enjoyed by the ethnically diverse community it serves, this market is best for its exotic fruit and vegetables, specialist cuts of meat and colourful fabrics. You'll also find the usual assortment of plastic tat, cheap clothing and mobile phone accessories.

EATING

North London is full of eating gems. From historic pubs to smart eateries catering for some of the capital's most sought-after residential neighbourhoods, this is not a place where you'll be left without options. While Islington is no longer London's foodie capital, it still has more than its fair share of excellent restaurants. Elsewhere you'll find a large choice running from Afghani and Greek to Russian and Turkish.

King's Cross & Euston

MESTIZO   MEXICAN ££

Map p452 (www.mestizomx.com; 103 Hampstead Rd NW1; mains £10-20; ⊗lunch & dinner; ⊖Warren St) If your idea of Mexican food is tacos and gluggy refried beans, think again. At this large and very attractive restaurant and tequila bar you'll find everything from *quesadillas* (cheese-filled pasties) to filled corn enchiladas. But go for the specials: *pozole* (a thick fresh corn soup with meat) and several different preparations of *mole* (chicken or pork cooked in a rich chocolate sauce).

RAVI SHANKAR   INDIAN £

Map p426 (133-135 Drummond St NW1; mains £6-10; ⊗lunch & dinner; ⊖Euston or Euston Sq) Another reliable *bhel poori* house (a vegetarian restaurant named after the dish of the same name containing puffed rice and a mix of vegetables) on Drummond St, this place with the memorable name is a good second choice if you can't get a table at Diwana (p246).

Camden

MARKET   MODERN BRITISH ££

Map p452 (www.marketrestaurant.co.uk; 43 Parkway NW1; mains £10-14; ⊗closed dinner Sun; ⊖Camden Town) This fabulous restaurant is an ode to great, simple British food with a a hint of European thrown in. The light and airy space with bare brick walls, steel tables and basic wooden chairs reflects this simplicity. The menu manages to make classic cookery memorable with delights such as roast poussin with baby spring vegetables, and whole plaice with caper butter and chips.

YORK & ALBANY   BRASSERIE ££

Map p452 (www.gordonramsay.com/yorkandalbany; 127-129 Parkway NW1; mains £13-19; ⊗breakfast, lunch & dinner;⊖Camden Town) This chic brasserie, part of chef Gordon Ramsay's culinary empire, serves classics with a Mediterranean twist such as roast leg of rabbit with potatoes and lemony anchovies, and confit lamb shoulder with soft polenta. The restaurant also does divine pizzas in its wood-fired oven. The food is pitch-perfect and the setting informal; you can eat at the bar, in the lounge or the more formal dining room.

BAR GANSA   SPANISH ££

Map p452 (⒥7267 8909; www.bargansa.co.uk; 2 Inverness St NW1; tapas £5; ⊗10am-12.30am Sun-Wed, to 1.30am Thu-Sat; ⊖Camden Town) Decked out in loud yellow and red, Bar Gansa is a focal point of the Camden scene and is howlingly popular. The menu is mostly tapas, which makes it very popular with small groups of friends. Bigger specialities include traditional favourites such as Paella Valenciana. There's live flamenco on Monday evening. It stays open late (12.30am or 1.30am) and so doubles up as a bar.

MANGO ROOM   CARIBBEAN ££

Map p452 (www.mangoroom.co.uk; 10-12 Kentish Town Rd NW1; mains £10-13; ⊗lunch & dinner; ⊖Camden Town) With delightful pastel decor and genteel service, Mango Room is a kind of decaf Caribbean experience,

COMBINED TICKET

Visitors interested in seeing both No 2 Willow Rd and Fenton House (highly recommended!) should get a combined ticket (£9) to save a few pounds. The two sights are only about 15 minutes' walk from each other across leafy Hampstead.

HAMPSTEAD & NORTH LONDON EATING

although there's no holding back with the food: grilled sea bass with coconut milk and sweet pepper sauce, salt fish with *ackee* (a yellow-skinned Jamaican fruit that has an uncanny resemblance to scrambled eggs), and curried goat with hot pepper and spices. The restaurant plays great ska music from the '50s and old reggae tunes.

MARINE ICES   ITALIAN £

Map p452 (www.marineices.co.uk; 8 Haverstock Hill NW3; mains £7-15; ⊙ lunch & dinner Tue-Sun; ⊖Chalk Farm) As its name suggests, this Chalk Farm institution started out as an ice-cream parlour (in fact, a Sicilian *gelateria*) but these days it does some savoury dishes as well, including pizzas and hearty pasta dishes. Be sure to try some of the excellent ice cream (Caribbean coconut and maple walnut come highly recommended); the parlour is particularly popular at weekends when a long line snakes down Haverstock Hill.

BELGO NOORD   BELGIAN ££

Map p452 (www.belgo-restaurants.co.uk; 72 Chalk Farm Rd NW1; mains £9-16; ⊙ noon-11pm; ⊖Chalk Farm) This branch of the Belgian restaurant chain does a mean *moules frites* (mussels and chips; £12), which you can wash down with one of the many Belgian beers on offer.

HACHÉ   BURGERS £

Map p452 (www.hacheburgers.com; 24 Inverness St NW1; mains £7-13; ⊙noon-10pm Sun-Wed, to 11pm Thu-Sat; ⊖Camden Town) A sister establishment to the Fulham branch (p304).

✖ Hampstead & Highgate

TOP CHOICE GAUCHO GRILL   STEAKHOUSE £££

Map p451 (✆7431 8222; www.gauchorestaurants. co.uk; 64 Heath St NW3; mains £15-52; ⊙noon-11pm Mon-Sat, from 10am Sun; ⊖Hampstead) Carnivores, rejoice: this is one of the finest places for steak in London. There are several branches of this Argentinian grill across the capital but this one has the advantage of being less busy than its counterparts, thanks to its residential setting. The Gaucho sampler (£89.95) is well worth sharing between three or four to taste the different cuts of meat (rump, sirloin, fillet and rib eye). We love the glitzy modern decor too, although the cowhide chairs are a little spiky!

WELLS TAVERN   GASTROPUB ££

Map p451 (✆7794 3785; www.thewellshampstead.co.uk; 30 Well Walk NW3; mains £10-16; ⊙lunch & dinner; ⊖Hampstead) This popular gastropub, with a surprisingly modern interior (given its traditional exterior), is a

---

WORTH A DETOUR

ALEXANDRA PARK & PALACE

Built in 1873 as North London's answer to Crystal Palace (p284), **Alexandra Palace** (www.alexandrapalace.com; Alexandra Palace Way N22; ⊠Alexandra Palace) suffered the ignoble fate of burning to the ground only 16 days after opening. Encouraged by attendance figures, investors decided to rebuild and it reopened just two years later. Although it boasted a theatre, museum, lecture hall, library and Great Hall with one of the world's largest organs, it was no match for Crystal Palace. Alexandra Palace housed German prisoners of war during WWI and in 1936 was the scene of the world's first TV transmission – a variety show called *Here's Looking at You*. The palace burned down again in 1980 but was rebuilt for the third time and opened in 1988.

Today 'Ally Pally' (as it is affectionately known) is a multipurpose conference and exhibition centre with additional facilities, including an indoor ice-skating rink, the panoramic Phoenix Bar & Beer Garden and funfairs in summer. It hosts occasional club nights and concerts too.

The park in which it stands sprawls over some 196 hectares consisting of public gardens, a nature conservation area, a deer park and various sporting facilities including a boating lake, pitch-and-putt golf course and skate park, making it a great place for a family outing. There is also a farmers market on Sundays.

Many locals come to enjoy the sweeping views of London. The fireworks held here on Bonfire Night (p29) are some of the most spectacular in town, lighting up the city skyline.

TOP SIGHTS
HIGHGATE CEMETERY

Most famous as the final resting place of Karl Marx, George Eliot (pseudonym of Mary Ann Evans) and other notable mortals, Highgate Cemetery is set in 20 wonderfully wild and atmospheric hectares, with dramatic and overdecorated Victorian family crypts. It is divided into two parts on either side of Swain's Lane. On the eastern side you can visit the **grave of Karl Marx**. The real draw however is the overgrown western section of this Victorian Valhalla. To visit it, you'll have to take a **tour** (☏8340 1834; adult/child £7/3; 1 hr; ☉1.45pm Mon-Fri, hourly from 11am to 3pm Sat & Sun Nov-Mar, to 4pm Apr-Oct). Note that children under eight are not allowed to join. It is a maze of winding paths leading to the **Circle of Lebanon**, rings of tombs flanking a circular path and topped with a majestic cedar of Lebanon tree. Guides will point out the various symbols and the eminent dead occupying the tombs.

Highgate remains a working cemetery – the most recent well-known addition was Russian dissident Alexander Litvinenko, who died under sinister circumstances in 2006, when the radioactive isotope Polonium 210 somehow made its into his tea in a Mayfair hotel.

DON'T MISS...

➡ Karl Max's grave
➡ Tour of the West Cemetery
➡ Circle of Lebanon

PRACTICALITIES

➡ Map p451
➡ ☏8340 1834
➡ www.highgate-cemetery.org
➡ Swain's Lane N6
➡ adult/child £3/free
➡ ☉10am-5pm Mon-Fri, 11am-5pm Sat & Sun Apr-Oct, closes 4pm daily Nov-Mar
➡ ⊖Highgate

HAMPSTEAD & NORTH LONDON EATING

real blessing in good-restaurant-deprived Hampstead. The menu is proper posh English pub grub – Cumberland sausages, mash and onion gravy, or just a full roast with all the trimmings. At the weekends you'll need to fight to get a table or, more wisely, book.

LA GAFFE
ITALIAN £

Map p451 (www.lagaffe.co.uk; 107-111 Heath St NW3; mains £7-15; ☉lunch Thu-Sun, dinner daily; ⊖Hampstead) This Hampstead landmark is a comfortable, family-run restaurant in an 18th-century cottage. Don't be put off by the faux Italian decor; the food is reliably good, particularly the fresh pasta dishes, and you can upgrade their size by adding £2 to the price. A three-course set lunch (£12.50) is available weekdays.

✖ Islington

TOP CHOICE OTTOLENGHI
ITALIAN ££

Map p448 (☏7288 1454; www.ottolenghi.co.uk; 287 Upper St N1; mains £7-12; ☉8am-11pm Mon-Sat, 9am-7pm Sun; ⊖Highbury & Islington or Angel) This is the pick of Upper Street's many eating options – a brilliantly bright, white space that's worth a trip merely to

see the eye-poppingly beautiful cakes in the deli. But get a table at this temple to good food and you'll really appreciate it. At lunch, you can choose from the deli counter, while in the evening there's à la carte dining, with fusion, meze-sized dishes to share. Weekend brunch is fabulous, though you'll usually have to wait for a table. Reservations are essential in the evenings.

GEORGIAN IBERIAN RESTAURANT
RUSSIAN ££

Map p448 (www.iberiarestaurant.co.uk; 294-296 Caledonian Rd; mains £8.50-16; ☉dinner Tue-Sun, lunch Sat & Sun; ⊖Caledonian Rd or Highbury & Islington) There isn't much going on in this part of town but this restaurant alone justifies the 10 minutes' walk from Islington. Georgian food is infused with flavours from neighbouring Russia (smoked ingredients, beans, walnuts, cabbage, dill) and the Middle East (mezes, flatbread and lots of spices). The food is divine and service is the friendliest you'll find in North London.

LE MERCURY
FRENCH £

Map p448 (www.lemercury.co.uk; 140a Upper St N1; mains £8; ☉lunch & dinner; ⊖Angel or Highbury & Islington) An excellent and wildly

NORTH LONDON'S BEST VEGETARIAN RESTAURANTS

Not a hint of rabbit food in sight – instead, creative, filling and absolutely delicious vegetarian cuisine to suit all tastes. Of the options listed, Addis is not – strictly speaking – vegetarian but Ethiopian cuisine has a rich vegetarian tradition, well represented in the restaurant's menu.

Manna (Map p452; ☑7722 8082; www.mannav.com; 4 Erskine Rd NW3; mains £11-14; ☺lunch Sat & Sun, dinner Tue-Sun; ⊜Chalk Farm) Tucked away on a side street in Primrose Hill, this little place does a brisk trade in inventive vegetarian cooking. The menu features such mouthwatering dishes as green korma, wild garlic and pea risotto cake and superb desserts. There are excellent vegan options too and everything comes beautifully presented, from fan-shaped salads to pyramidal mains. Reservations are usually essential.

Diwana Bhel Poori House (Map p426; www.diwanabhelpoori.co.uk; 121-123 Drummond St; mains £7-9; ☺noon-midnight; ⊜Euston or Euston Sq) Arguably one of the best Indian vegetarian restaurants in London, Diwana specialises in Bombay-style *bhel poori* (a sweet-and-sour, soft and crunchy 'party mix' snack) and dosas (filled pancakes made from rice flour). You can try thalis (a meal consisting of lots of small dishes, with a focus on vegetables), which offer a selection of tasty treats (£7 to £9) and the all-you-can-eat lunchtime buffet (£7) is legendary.

Woodlands (Map p451; www.woodlandsrestaurant.co.uk; 102 Heath St NW3; mains £7-19; ☺lunch Fri & Sat, dinner Mon-Sat; ⊜Hampstead) This South Indian vegetarian restaurant, whose rallying cry is 'Let Vegetation Feed the Nation', is determined to prove that South Indian vegetarian food can be as inventive as any meat-based cuisine and it does a pretty convincing job of it.

Rasa (www.rasarestaurants.com; 55 Stoke Newington Church St N16; mains £4-6; ☺lunch Sat & Sun, dinner daily; ℝStoke Newington, then 🚌73) Flagship restaurant of the Rasa chain, this South Indian vegetarian eatery is Stoke Newington's best known restaurant. Friendly service, a calm atmosphere, jovial prices and outstanding food from the Indian state of Kerala are its distinctive features. The multicourse Keralan Feast (£16) is for ravenous tummies only.

Addis (Map p448; www.addisrestaurant.co.uk; 40-42 Caledonian Rd N1; mains £8-11; ☺lunch & dinner; ⊜King's Cross St Pancras) Cheery Addis serves pungent Ethiopian dishes such as *ayeb be gomen* (cottage cheese mixed with spinach and spices) and *fuul musalah* (crushed fava beans topped with feta cheese, falafel and sautéed in ghee), which are eaten on a platter-sized piece of soft but slightly elastic *injera* bread. The restaurant is normally full of Ethiopian and Sudanese punters, which is always a good sign.

popular budget French eatery, Le Mercury seems to have a winning formula: romantic atmosphere with candlelit, small tables and plants everywhere combined with superb French food (try the roast duck breast with red wine jus) at unbeatable prices. Londoners have long known about this place, so reservations are advised.

🌱 DUKE OF CAMBRIDGE GASTROPUB ££

Map p448 (www.dukeorganic.co.uk; 30 St Peter's St N1; mains £13-19; ☺lunch & dinner; ⊜Angel) The UK's first certified organic pub is a great place to avoid the crowds, as it's tucked some way down a side street off the Essex Rd where casual passers-by rarely tread. There's a fantastic selection of beers and ales on tap, a great wine list and an interesting organic menu with a Mediterranean bent. You can eat in the pub proper for a relaxed meal, or enjoy more formal service in the restaurant at the back (reservations are a good idea in the evenings).

AFGHAN KITCHEN MIDDLE EASTERN £

Map p448 (35 Islington Green N1; mains £7; ☺lunch & dinner Tue-Sat; ⊜Angel) This minute two-floor eatery serves up some of Islington's best-value and most interesting cuisine. It features traditional Afghan dishes such as *qurma suhzi gosht* (lamb cooked with spinach) and *qurma e mahi* (fish stew) alongside a generous vegetarian selection, including *borani kado* (pumpkin with yoghurt) and *moong dall* (lentil dhal). In the evenings, there is freshly baked bread to go with the dishes instead of rice.

MASALA ZONE
INDIAN **££**

Map p448 (www.masalazone.com; 80 Upper St N1; mains £8-12; ⊙lunch & dinner; ⊜Angel) This spacious place with outside seating set back from Upper St is one of the best budget Indian options in London. Thoroughly modern in design, it serves up meals centred on its famous thalis, as well as tandoor and grilled dishes. There are now several other branches throughout the capital.

MORGAN M
FRENCH **£££**

Map p448 (☑7609 3560; www.morganm.com; 489 Liverpool Rd N1; set lunch/dinner £28/43; ⊙dinner Tue-Sat, lunch Wed-Fri & Sun; ⊜Highbury & Islington) This gourmet French restaurant in Highbury used to be an old pub. It has retained an old-school feel to it but the cuisine is resolutely modern and so very French. It's all about the set menus here, which run from a relatively restrained two courses at lunchtime to the full gastronomic blow out of the six-course tasting menu in the evening.

BREAKFAST CLUB
CAFE **£**

Map p448 (www.thebreakfastclubangel.com; 31 Camden Passage N1; dishes £3-9; ⊙8am-10pm Mon-Fri, 9.30am-10pm Sat & Sun; ⊜Angel) Despite the name, breakfast (£3 to £8.30) is not the only game here (although many people do come to nurse a hangover): it also does sandwiches, salads and decent pies, all dished out in an oasis of bright and quirky decor. Staff are all smiles and there's generally good, chilled-out music for relaxing.

RODIZIO RICO
BRAZILIAN **£££**

Map p448 (www.rodiziorico.com; 77-78 Upper St N1; per person £24; ⊙dinner Mon-Sun, lunch Sat & Sun; ⊜Angel) This all-you-can-eat Brazilian grill will be prized by carnivores with a huge appetite. Gourmets or vegetarians may not be so enthusiastic. Customers help themselves at the salad bar; skewered meat is then brought to the table by a constant stream of waiters. Everyone gets given a card, green on one side, red on the other. Green means 'keep bringing the meat', red means 'no thanks I'm about to burst'.

GALLIPOLI
MIDDLE EASTERN **££**

Map p448 (www.gallipolicafe.com; 102 Upper St N1; mains £10-15; ⊙lunch & dinner; ⊜Angel or Highbury & Islington) The draw here is decent Middle Eastern dishes at reasonable prices (there's a good selection of meze and a large range of kebabs). The drawback is the crowds (unbearable on a Friday and Saturday night, when birthday parties take over the place) and the very loud music.

✗ Stoke Newington

BLUE LEGUME
CAFE **£**

(101 Stoke Newington Church St N16; mains £5-12; ⊙9.30am-11pm Mon-Sat, to 6pm Sun; ⊠Stoke Newington, ⊒73) This lively Stokey mainstay has mosaic tables and rather hippie decor, with a bright conservatory at the back, and a scattering of tables outside on the street. The breakfasts are rightly popular – and there's a full Mediterranean menu ranging from lunches to a weekly paella night.

✗ Dalston

TOP CHOICE MANGAL OCAKBASI
TURKISH **£**

Map p448 (www.mangal1.com; 10 Arcola St E8; mains £5-12; ⊙noon-midnight; ⊠Dalston Kingsland) Mangal is the quintessential Turkish *ocakbasi* (open-hooded grill, the mother of all BBQs) restaurant: cramped and smoky and serving superb meze, grilled lamb chops, quail and a lip-smacking assortment of kebabs. There's no menu as such: you choose from the meat counter and then go and sit down. It's been here for almost 20 years and is always busy. Takeaway is also available if you can't get a table.

A LITTLE OF WHAT YOU FANCY
BRITISH **££**

Map p448 (www.alittleofwhatyoufancy.info; 464 Kingsland Rd E8; mains £9-18; ⊙9am-11pm Tue-Fri, 10am-midnight Sat, 12-6pm Sun, 7-11pm Mon; ⊠Dalston Junction or ⊒149) This twee little restaurant in Dalston is a breath of fresh air in an area better known for its kebabs than its cuisine. The decor is simple vintage and the food follows a similar philosophy of 'less is more' (actually the portions are on the 'more' side): risottos, soups, tarts, all simple but divine.

CAFÉ OTO
CAFE **£**

Map p448 (www.cafeoto.co.uk; 18-22 Ashwin St E8; mains £5-7; ⊙9.30am-5.30pm Mon-Fri, from 10.30am Sat & Sun; ⊠Dalston Junction or Dalston Kingsland, ⊒149, 38) This well-known music venue by night is a gorgeous cafe by day.

It's run by a Japanese–British couple so you'll find teriyaki wraps cohabiting with traditional soups and chunky bread on the menu. It's a similar story for drinks: sake and Japanese whisky feature as well as Kernel beers (a London-based microbrewery).

DRINKING & NIGHTLIFE

Camden Town is one of North London's favoured drinking areas, with more bars and pubs pumping music than you can manage to crawl between. The hills of Hampstead are a real treat for old-pub aficionados, while painfully hip Dalston is currently London's coolest place to drink.

King's Cross

SOMERS TOWN COFFEEHOUSE PUB

Map p448 (www.somerstowncoffeehouse.co.uk; 60 Chalton St NW1; King's Cross St Pancras) French bistro meets English pub is perhaps the best way to describe this gorgeous 'bistro pub'. As you would expect from such a mix, there is an equally good selection of beers and wines (all French, *bien sûr*). It's a beautiful building too, with a wood-panelled interior and terraces at the front and back.

CAMINO BAR

Map p448 (www.camino.uk.com; Regent Quarter, off Caledonian Rd N1; King's Cross St Pancras) This new venture in the Regent Quarter development is very popular with London's Spanish community and therefore feels quite authentic. Drinks too are representative of what you'd find in Spain: Cava, Estrella on tap, and a long, all-Spanish wine list. In summer, the courtyard is absolutely crammed. Sadly the food is nowhere near as good as the atmosphere.

BIG CHILL HOUSE DJ BAR

Map p448 (www.bigchill.net; 257-259 Pentonville Rd N1; until midnight Sun-Wed, until 1am Thu, until 3am Fri & Sat; King's Cross St Pancras) A three-floor space with a good selection of live music and DJs, and a great terrace for hanging out, this place is run by the same people behind the popular Big Chill festival and record label. The music choice is always

varied and international, the sound system is fantastic, plus entry is free most nights. Food is also served throughout the day. The kitchen also churns out good burgers.

EGG CLUB

Map p448 (www.egglondon.net; 5-13 Vale Royal N1; 10pm-7am Fri, 10pm-11am Sat & Sun; King's Cross St Pancras or Caledonian Rd) Egg has the most superb layout with three exposed concrete rooms (across three floors), a garden and two gorgeous tropical roof terraces (relieving the edgy, exiled smokers). It specialises in house, dance, techno and drum and bass. On Sunday morning, there's a breakfast after-party. At weekends, Egg runs a free shuttle every 30 minutes between 10pm and 2am from outside American Carwash on York Way.

RUBY LOUNGE DJ BAR

Map p448 (33 Caledonian Rd N1; to midnight Thu, to 2am Fri & Sat; King's Cross St Pancras) King's Cross is being gentrified slowly, so what was once an area frequented only by hardened clubbers, prostitutes and junkies is now turning into a three-Starbucks-per-square-metre neighbourhood. But the Ruby Lounge was around when the going was tough and is here to stay. It's a great place, with a fantastic boutique-design interior, excellent DJs and an up-for-it pre-clubbing crowd.

Camden

TOP CHOICE EDINBORO CASTLE PUB

Map p452 (www.edinborocastlepub.co.uk; 57 Mornington Tce NW1; Camden Town) A reliable Camden boozer, the large and relaxed Edinboro has a refined Primrose Hill atmosphere. It boasts a full menu, gorgeous furniture designed for slumping and a fine bar. Where the pub comes into its own however, is in its huge beer garden, complete with BBQ and table football and adorned with fairy lights for long summer evenings.

TOP CHOICE PROUD CAMDEN BAR

Map p452 (www.proudcamden.com; The Horse Hospital, Stables Market, Chalk Farm Rd NW1; to 1.30am Mon-Wed, to 2.30am Thu-Sat, to 12.30am Sun; Camden Town or Chalk Farm) Camden's former Horse Hospital, which looked after horses injured pulling barges on nearby Grand Union Canal, is now one of Camden's most brilliant bars. The stables have been converted into individual booths in which you can drink, play table football or pool or watch sports on the large screens. There are live bands and DJs in the large main room (see p251), and art exhibits adorn the walls. It's fantastic in summer, when the terrace is open.

LOCK TAVERN
PUB

Map p452 (www.lock-tavern.co.uk; 35 Chalk Farm Rd NW1; to 1am Fri & Sat; ⊖Chalk Farm or Camden Town) An institution in Camden, the black-clad Lock Tavern rocks for several reasons: it's cosy inside, has an ace roof terrace from where you can watch the market throngs, the food is good, the beer plentiful and it also has a roll-call of guest bands and DJs at the weekend to spice things up.

CROWN & GOOSE
PUB

Map p452 (www.crownandgoose.co.uk; 100 Arlington Rd NW1; ⊖to 2am Fri & Sat; ⊖Camden Town) One of our favourite London pubs, this square room has a central wooden bar surrounded by British-racing-green walls studded with gilt-framed mirrors and illuminated by big shuttered windows. More importantly, it combines a friendly, quietly cool crowd, easy conviviality, great food and a good range of inexpensive beers.

BAR VINYL
DJ BAR

Map p452 (www.barvinyl.com; 6 Inverness St NW1; ⊖to 1am Thu-Sat; ⊖Camden Town) Bar Vinyl is the epicentre for Camden's young and urban crowd, with cool kids behind the decks, a record shop downstairs and graffiti whirling along narrow walls. But it's superfriendly at the same time. Weekends are packed and buzzing, midweek nights are quieter, and the music is always good. There is happy hour every night of the week between 5pm and 9pm.

BLACK CAP
GAY

Map p452 (www.faucetinn.com/blackcap; 171 Camden High St NW1; ⊖noon-2am Mon-Thu, to 3am Fri & Sat, to 1am Sun; ⊖Camden Town) This friendly, sprawling place is Camden's premier gay venue, and attracts people from all over North London. There's a great outdoor terrace, the pleasantly pub-like upstairs Shufflewick bar and the downstairs club, where you'll find plenty of hilarious camp cabaret as well as decent dance music.

QUEEN'S
PUB

Map p452 (www.thequeensprimrosehill.co.uk; 49 Regent's Park Rd NW1; ⊖11am-11pm; ⊖Camden Town or Chalk Farm) Perhaps because this is Primrose Hill, the interior is more cafe than pub. Still, it's a good one, with a nice wine list, ales and lagers and, more importantly, plenty of people-watching to do with your pint; Jude Law and many of Primrose Hill's fashionistas come here for a tipple.

🍸 Hampstead & Highgate

BOOGALOO
TOP CHOICE
BAR

Map p451 (www.theboogaloo.org; 312 Archway Rd N6; ⊖to 1am Thu, to 2am Fri & Sat; ⊖Highgate) 'London's Number 1 Jukebox' is how Boogaloo flaunts itself and how it's been described in the local media: its celebrity-musician-fiddled-with jukebox playlists feature the favourite 10 songs of the likes of Nick Cave, Sinead O'Connor, Howie B and Bobbie Gillespie, to name but a few. There's plenty to boogie to, with live music on every night of the week. If you're into music in a big way, you won't regret the trek to come here.

GARDEN GATE
PUB

Map p451 (www.thegardengatehampstead.co.uk; 14 South End Rd NW3; ⊖noon-11pm; ⊟Hampstead Heath) At the bottom of the heath hides this gem of a pub, a 19th century cottage with a gorgeous beer garden. The interior is wonderfully cosy, with dark wood tables, upholstered turquoise chairs and an assortment of distressed sofas. It serves Pimms and lemonade in summer and mulled wine in winter, both ideal after a long walk on the heath. The pub also does excellent food.

SPANIARD'S INN
PUB

Map p451 (www.thespaniardshampstead.co.uk; Spaniards Rd NW3; ⊖11am-11pm; ⊖Hampstead then ⊟21) This marvellous tavern dates from 1585 and has more character than a West End musical. It was highwayman Dick Turpin's hang-out between robbing escapades, but it's also served as a watering hole for more savoury characters, such as Dickens, Shelley, Keats and Byron. There's a big, blissful garden, and although it's often full at the weekend, note that the food is overpriced and a little disappointing.

HOLLY BUSH PUB

Map p451 (22 Holly Mount NW3; ⏰11am-11pm; 🚇Hampstead) A beautiful pub that makes you envy the privileged residents of Hampstead, the Holly Bush has an antique Victorian interior, a secluded hilltop location, open fires in winter and a knack for making you stay longer than you had intended. Set above Heath St, it's reached via the Holly Bush Steps.

FLASK TAVERN PUB

Map p451 (77 Highgate West Hill N6; ⏰11am-11pm; 🚇Highgate) This weekend favourite is a brilliant place to end a walk in either Hampstead Heath or Highgate Wood. In the summer months it's all about its large courtyard where delicious burgers are served up along with pints. In the winter, huddle down in the cosy interior and enjoy its much-loved Sunday roast.

🍸 Islington

BULL PUB

Map p448 (www.thebullislington.co.uk; 100 Upper St N1; ⏰to midnight Wed & Thu, to 1am Fri & Sat; 🚇Angel or Highbury & Islington) One of Islington's liveliest pubs, the Bull serves 27 different kinds of draught lager, real ales, fruit beers, ciders and wheat beer, plus a large selection of bottled drinks and wine. The mezzanine is generally a little quieter than downstairs, although on weekend nights you'll generally struggle to find a seat.

CASTLE PUB

Map p448 (www.geronimo-inns.co.uk/thecastle; 54 Pentonville Rd N1; ⏰to midnight Fri & Sat; 🚇Angel) A gorgeous, boutique pub, all wooden floors, designer wallpaper, soft furnishings and bookshelves, with a winning formula of lovely decor, good gastropub food, a rotating selection of ales and lagers and to top it all off, a roof terrace.

PUBLIC HOUSE BAR

Map p448 (www.boutiquepubs.com; 54 Islington Park St N1; ⏰to midnight Sun-Thu, to 1am Fri & Sat; 🚇Highbury & Islington) This handsome bar adds a lovely splash of boudoir/burlesque to an area better known for its rowdy pubs than sophisticated drinking dens. Everything is obviously fabulous at Public House, from the carefully prepared cocktails (all seasonal) to the exquisite menu and long list of after-dinner drinks (brandies, whiskies, dessert wines).

BARRIO NORTH DJ BAR

Map p448 (www.barrionorth.com; 45 Essex Rd N1; ⏰to 2am Fri & Sat, closed Mon; 🚇Angel or Highbury & Islington) This cocktail/DJ bar is one of the most fun in Islington. The atmosphere, decor and music are a celebration of all things Latino with a hint of London and New York thrown in (if you can, grab a seat in the fairy-lit cut-out caravan). The cocktails are unrivalled with selections from South, Central and North America, the Caribbean and Europe. 'Amigo hour' is between 5pm and 8pm.

JUNCTION PUB

Map p448 (2a Corsica St N5; ⏰to 1am Fri & Sat; 🚇Highbury & Islington) This warehouse-sized venue isn't exactly full of character but it certainly is fun. It's a favourite of Arsenal fans and is therefore a brilliant place to watch football games, particularly those featuring Arsenal. It's obviously rammed on football nights but the atmosphere is amazing. There is plenty of seating and a beer garden, and the kitchen churns out good pizzas (two for one on Tuesdays).

GREEN GAY

Map p448 (www.thegreenislington.co.uk; 74 Upper St N1; ⏰to 2am Fri & Sat; 🚇Angel) The Green is a funky, friendly two-floor place where the young of N1 hang out, meet friends and warm up for a night out. It's happy hour until midnight on 'thirsty Thursdays'. There are regular DJ sets at weekends, when there's usually a cover charge after 11pm.

🍸 Stoke Newington

AULD SHILLELAGH PUB

(www.theauldshillelagh.com; 105 Stoke Newington Church St N16; 🚌73) The Auld Shillelagh is one of the best Irish pubs in London and full of old-style liver pounders. The staff are sharp, the Guinness is good, and the live entertainment is frequent and varied. There is also a beer garden where you can catch some rays.

FOX REFORMED BAR

(www.fox-reformed.co.uk; 176 Stoke Newington Church St N16; ⏰until midnight; 🚉Stoke Newington, 🚌73) Stoke Newington's firm favourite for more than two decades, the Fox has all the qualities of a good local: a friendly landlord, loyal regulars, good food, wine and beer, and a cosy back garden. The quiet atmosphere and chess and backgammon boards for entertainment on relaxing afternoons always bring new converts to its charms.

🍷 Dalston

TOP CHOICE PASSING CLOUDS CLUB

Map p448 (www.passingclouds.org; 1 Richmond Rd E8; ⊙10pm-4am Fri & Sat, hr vary Mon-Fri; ℞Dalston Junction or Dalston Kingsland, ⊠243, 76) One of those little flickers of nightlife brilliance, Passing Clouds throws legendary parties that go on until the early hours of the morning. The music is predominantly world oriented, with a lot of African influence and regular Afrobeat bands, and a reputed jam session on Sunday nights (from 9pm); the parties are a healthy mix of DJs and live music with a multicultural crowd that really makes you feel you're in London. The decor is makeshift bar, colourful lanterns and tropical titbits, and the atmosphere is just exhilarating.

BAR 23 BAR

Map p448 (23 Stoke Newington Rd N16; ⊙until 1am Sun-Thu, until 2am Fri & Sat; ℞Dalston Kingsland or Dalston Junction, ⊠76, 149) Film stars bedeck the walls of this, at first, unremarkable Turkish-run bar on Dalston's coolest stretch. But, come the evenings, the place is always full, DJs play and drinks are served up to the friendly crowd late into the evening.

DALSTON SUPERSTORE DJ BAR

Map p448 (117 Kingsland High St E8; ⊙to 2am; ℞Dalston Kingsland or Dalston Junction, ⊠76, 149) This two-level industrial space, with the feel of New York's meat-packing district, is open all day but really comes into its own after dark when there are club nights in the basement and DJs spinning upstairs.

JAZZ BAR DALSTON COCKTAIL BAR

Map p448 (4 Bradbury St N16; ⊙to 1am Mon-Thu, to 3am Fri & Sat, to midnight Sun; ℞Dalston Kingsland or Dalston Junction, ⊠76, 149) Jazz Bar is Dalston's most excellent and unexpected find, hidden just off the chaos of

Dalston Junction. Housed within glass walls, it's not really a jazz bar but a cocktail place where the neighbourhood's hip and friendly inhabitants congregate at the weekends to party on to hip-hop, R&B and reggae.

☆ ENTERTAINMENT

TOP CHOICE PROUD CAMDEN LIVE MUSIC

Map p452 (www.proudcamden.com; The Horse Hospital, Stables Market, Chalk Farm Rd NW1; ⊙ to 1.30am Mon-Thu, 2.30am Fri & Sat, and 12.30am Sun; ⊖Camden Town or Chalk Farm) It's very trendy indeed at Proud, with gorgeous Camdenites heading to the sunset-watching terrace for outdoor gigs in summer or indoor booths in winter. Proud is a great venue in North London that combines live music and exhibitions, and it's really best in summer, when the terrace is open. Also see p248.

TOP CHOICE KENWOOD HOUSE LIVE MUSIC

Map p451 (www.picnicconcerts.com; Hampstead Lane NW3; ⊖Archway or Golders Green, then ⊠210) Attending an outdoor concert in the grounds of Hampstead's Kenwood House has been a highlight of any good summer in London for years. These days the so-called Picnic Concerts sponsored by English Heritage focus as much on jazz (Ray Davies, Gypsy Kings, Jools Holland) and pop (Simply Red) as they do classical music and opera.

Concerts take place on Friday and Saturday evenings from late June to late August; bring your picnic and bubbles to make it a brilliant night. The last concert concludes with a massive fireworks display.

KOKO CONCERT VENUE

Map p452 (www.koko.uk.com; 1a Camden High St NW1; ⊙7-11pm Sun-Thu, to 4am Fri & Sat; ⊖Mornington Cres) Once the legendary Camden Palace, where Charlie Chaplin, the Goons, the Sex Pistols and Ryan Adams have all performed in the past, Koko is keeping its reputation as one of London's better gig venues – Madonna played a Confessions on a Dance Floor gig here in 2006 and Prince gave a surprise gig in 2007. The theatre has a dance floor and decadent balconies, and attracts an indie crowd with Club NME on

ROCK!

North London is the home of indie rock; many a famous band started playing in the area's grungy bars. Here's where to go for some of the best gigs in town. Doors generally open around 7.30pm but bands may not come on until 9pm, sometimes later. Closing time is normally around 2am, although this can vary depending on the event.

Barfly (Map p452; www.barflyclub.com; Monarch, 49 Chalk Farm Rd NW1; ⊖Chalk Farm or Camden Town) This typically grungy, indie-rock Camden venue is well known for hosting small-time artists looking for their big break. The focus is on rock from the US and UK, with alternative-music radio station Xfm hosting regular nights. The venue is small, so you'll feel like the band is just playing for you and your mates.

Electric Ballroom (Map p452; www.electricballroom.co.uk; 184 Camden High St NW1; ⊖Camden Town) One of Camden's historic venues, the Electric Ballroom has been entertaining North Londoners since 1938. Many great bands and musicians have played here, from Blur to Paul McCartney, The Clash and U2. There are club nights on Fridays (Sin City: metal music) and Saturdays (Shake: a crowd pleaser of dance anthems from the 70s, 80s and 90s).

Forum (Map p451; www.meanfiddler.com; 9-17 Highgate Rd NW5; ⊖Kentish Town) You can find your way to the Forum – once the famous Town & Country Club – by the ticket touts that line the way from Kentish Town tube. It's a really popular venue for seeing new big bands, and the medium-sized hall, with stalls and a mezzanine, is spacious enough and perfectly intimate.

Bull & Gate (Map p451; www.bullandgate.co.uk; 389 Kentish Town Rd NW5; ⊖Kentish Town) The best place to see unsigned but promising talent, the legendary Bull & Gate's old-school music venue still pulls in the punters eager to see guitar bands that might just turn out to be the next big thing.

Friday. There are live bands almost every night of the week.

CAFÉ OTO
LIVE MUSIC

Map p448 (www.cafeoto.co.uk; 18-22 Ashwin St E8; ☺8pm-1am; ®Dalston Junction or Dalston Kingsland, ☐149, 38) Café Oto is one of London's most idiosyncratic and interesting music venues. Set in a converted print warehouse and run by a Japanese–British couple, this place dedicates itself to promoting experimental and alternative international musicians. You'll find lots of Japanese stars of experimental, jazz and pop music, as well as legendary 1960s folk and rock stars.

ROUNDHOUSE
PERFORMING ARTS

Map p452 (www.roundhouse.org.uk; Chalk Farm Rd NW1; ⊖Chalk Farm) The Roundhouse was once home to 1960s avant-garde theatre, then a rock venue, then it fell into oblivion for a while before reopening a few years back. It holds great gigs and a smattering of brilliant performances, from circus to stand-up comedy, poetry slam and improvisation sessions. The round shape of the building is unique and generally well used in the staging.

RIO CINEMA
CINEMA

Map p448 (www.riocinema.org; 107 Kingsland High St E8; ®Dalston Kingsland) The Rio is Dalston's neighbourhood art-house, classic and new-release cinema, and *the* venue for offbeat festivals, such as the East End Film Festival in April and the Turkish Film Festival in December. It also holds regular Q&A sessions with film directors, such as the East End's very own Asif Kapadia who directed the acclaimed *Senna* documentary about Ayrton Senna in 2011.

EVERYMAN HAMPSTEAD
CINEMA

Map p451 (www.everymancinema.com; 5 Holly Bush Vale NW3; ⊖Hampstead) Ever dream of having your own private cinema? For the next best thing, go to the Everyman. The two auditoriums have comfy armchairs and sofas where you can sprawl out and watch a film with your cup of tea or glass of wine. The program has a wide range of films, from *Singing in the Rain* and opera on film to current blockbusters.

VORTEX JAZZ CLUB   JAZZ

Map p448 (www.vortexjazz.co.uk; 11 Gillet St N16; ⓇDalston Kingsland or Dalston Junction, ⓪73) The Vortex has a good program of musicians from the UK, US and Europe, and hosts jazz musicians, singers and songwriters. It's a small venue so make sure you book if there is an act you particularly fancy.

LOWDOWN AT THE ALBANY   COMEDY

Map p452 (www.lowdownatthealbany.com; 240 Great Portland St W1; ⊖Great Portland St or Regent's Park) This basement venue with just 100 seats hosts stand-up and sketch sets, Edinburgh previews and theatre. The pub above, The Albany, is excellent for a bite and a pint before the show. Check the website for the listings.

ARCOLA THEATRE   THEATRE

Map p448 (www.arcolatheatre.com; 27 Arcola St E8; ⓇDalston Kingsland or Dalston Junction, ⓪73) The Arcola's location in Dalston in the East End makes it a bit of a trek, but many still flock to this innovative theatre. The director, Mehmet Ergen has been staging adventurous and eclectic productions since founding the theatre in 2000.

The program focuses on cutting-edge, international productions (such as work by young Turkish, Swedish and Austrian playwrights) and a unique annual feature is **Grimeborn**, a music and opera festival in August/September, the antithesis of the world-famous annual Glyndebourne opera festival taking place around the same time.

UNION CHAPEL   PERFORMING ARTS

Map p448 (www.unionchapel.org.uk; Compton Tce N1; ⊖Highbury & Islington) One of London's most atmospheric and individual music venues, the Union Chapel is an old church that still holds services, and concerts – mainly acoustic – and a monthly comedy night. It was here that Björk performed one of her most memorable concerts to a candlelit audience in 1999.

HAMPSTEAD THEATRE   THEATRE

(www.hampsteadtheatre.com; Eton Ave NW3; ⊖Swiss Cottage) Not only is this Ewan McGregor's favourite London theatre, the Hampstead is famed for putting on new writing and taking on emerging directors. It staged Harold Pinter's new work way back in the 1960s, which shows it knows a good thing when it sees one. More recently, it staged Mike Leigh's revival of Ecstasy, which was so popular the play had to transfer to the West End.

JAZZ CAFÉ   LIVE MUSIC

Map p452 (www.jazzcafe.co.uk; 5 Parkway NW1; ⊖Camden Town) Though its name would have you think that jazz is this club's main staple, its real speciality is the crossover of jazz into the mainstream. It's a trendy industrial-style restaurant with jazz gigs around once a week, while the rest of the month is filled with Afro, funk, hip hop,

HAMPSTEAD & NORTH LONDON ENTERTAINMENT

WHICH CAMDEN MARKET?

Camden Market comprises four distinct market areas; they tend to sell similar kinds of things although each has its own specialities and quirks.

Stables Market (Map p452; Chalk Farm Rd NW1; ☉10am-6pm daily; ⊖Chalk Farm) Just beyond the railway arches, opposite Hartland Rd, the Stables is the best part of the market, with antiques, Asian artefacts, rugs and carpets, pine furniture and vintage clothing.

Lock Market (Map p452; www.camdenlockmarket.com; Camden Lock Pl NW1; ☉10am-6pm daily; ⊖Camden Town) Right next to the canal lock, with diverse food, ceramics, furniture, oriental rugs, musical instruments and designer clothes.

Canal Market (Map p452; cnr Chalk Farm Rd & Castlehaven Rd NW1; ☉10am-6pm Thu-Sun; ⊖Chalk Farm or Camden Town) Just over the canal bridge, Canal Market has bric-a-brac from around the world. This is the part of the market that burnt down in 2008; we love the scooter seats by the canal.

Buck Street Market (Map p452; cnr Camden High & Buck Sts NW1; ☉9am-5.30pm Thu-Sun; ⊖Camden Town) This covered market houses stalls for fashion, clothing, jewellery and tourist tat. It's the closest to the station but the least interesting.

CAMDEN PASSAGE

Not to be confused with Camden Market, Camden Passage is a series of four arcades selling antiques and curios, located in Islington, at the junction of Upper St and Essex Rd. There is an **antiques market** (Map p448; Camden Passage N1; ⏰7am-2pm Wed, 8am-4pm Sat; ⊖Angel) twice a week; stallholders know their stuff, so bargains are rare.

There are also plenty of vintage, boutique and antique shops along the passage and some great cafes.

R&B and soul styles with big-name acts and a faithful bohemian Camden crowd.

LONDON'S LITTLE OPERA HOUSE AT THE KING'S HEAD THEATRE
OPERA

Map p448 (www.kingsheadtheatre.com; 115 Upper St N1; ⊖Angel) This stalwart pub-theatre in the heart of the Islington party district has recently taken a musical turn with a new resident, OperaUpClose, which produces classical opera with new interpretations such as *La Bohème*, *The Barber of Seville* and *Così Fan Tutte*.

O2 ACADEMY ISLINGTON
CONCERT VENUE

Map p448 (www.o2academyislington.co.uk; N1 Centre, 16 Parkfield St N1; ⊖Angel) Many complain about Islington Academy's lack of atmosphere – it is, after all, set in a shopping centre – but all agree that the artist line-up is pretty top class: Franz Ferdinand, Kings of Leon and even Eminem have played here. The acoustics are excellent and the discerning crowd is serious about its music. The adjacent Academy 2 hosts up-and-coming groups and can be a great place to see new talent.

 SHOPPING

Shopping in Camden is more about cheap, disposable fashion and made-for-tourist trinkets at the huge market (p240), although you might occasionally be tempted to pop into one of the many clothes boutiques lining the high street.

GILL WING
GIFTS

Map p448 (www.gillwing.co.uk; 190 Upper St N1; ⊖Highbury & Islington) Gill Wing's three wonderfully individual boutiques are a must-see on this strip of Upper St – her shoe shop is much loved, the gift shop is full of amusing and garishly designed presents, but the real favourite is her stylish cook shop that has launched the dreams of many an aspirant Islington homemaker.

ANNIE'S VINTAGE COSTUMES & TEXTILES
VINTAGE

Map p448 (www.anniesvintageclothing.co.uk; 12 Camden Passage N1; ⊖Angel) One of London's most enchanting vintage shops, Annie's has costumes to make you look like Greta Garbo. Many a famous designer has come here for inspiration so you might also get to do some celebrity spotting.

PAST CARING
HOMEWARES

Map p448 (76 Essex Rd N1; ⏰noon-6pm Mon-Sat; ⊖Angel) Stuffed full of second-hand, retro bric-a-brac – from ashtrays and 1970s LPs to mannequins and loud china – this wonderful shop is like a snapshot from three or four decades ago.

HOUSMANS
BOOKS

Map p448 (www.housmans.com; 5 Caledonian Rd N1; ⊖King's Cross St Pancras) This long-standing, not-for-profit bookshop, where you'll find books that are unavailable on the shelves of the more mainstream stockists, is a good place to keep up to date with all sorts of progressive, political and social campaigns, and with your more radical reads. The forthcoming owner is a mine of local information.

 SPORTS & ACTIVITIES

TOP CHOICE **HAMPSTEAD HEATH PONDS**
SWIMMING

Map p451 (Hampstead Heath, Gordon House Rd NW5; adult/concession £2/1; ⧪Gospel Oak or Hampstead Heath, ⧉214, C2 or 24) Set in the midst of the gorgeous heath, the three ponds offer a slightly chilly dip surrounded by wild shrubbery; the men's pond is a bit of a gay cruising area (but it's also a fantastic, beautiful place for a swim), the secluded women's pond is less cruisy. The mixed pond can sometimes get rather crowded and isn't so scenically located.

The men's and ladies' ponds are open all year-round and are supervised by a lifeguard. Opening times vary with the seasons, from 7am or 8am in the morning until 3.30pm in the winter but until 8.30pm at the height of summer. The mixed pond is open to members only in winter. Despite what you might think from its murky appearance, the water is tested every day and meets stringent quality guidelines.

PARLIAMENT HILL LIDO
SWIMMING

Map p451 (Hampstead Heath, Gordon House Rd NW5; adult/concession £2/1; ⊘7am-noon Sep-Apr, to 8pm May-Aug; ℝGospel Oak, ⊒214 or C2) More conventional than the ponds, this classic lido on Hampstead Heath is a wonderful place to come for a bracing morning swim during the summer months. It attracts a friendly but dedicated bunch of locals and boasts a children's paddling pool and sunbathing area.

LORD'S CRICKET GROUND
CRICKET

off Map p452 (www.lords.org; St John's Wood Rd NW8; ⊖St John's Wood) A trip to Lord's, aka 'the home of cricket', is often as much a pilgrimage as anything else. As well as being home to Marylebone Cricket Club, the ground hosts test matches, one-day internationals and domestic finals. For more on Lord's see p239.

Notting Hill & West London

NOTTING HILL | WESTBOURNE GROVE | HIGH STREET KENSINGTON | EARL'S COURT | WEST BROMPTON | SHEPHERD'S BUSH | HAMMERSMITH | ST JOHN'S WOOD | MAIDA VALE | PADDINGTON | BAYSWATER

Neighbourhood Top Five

1 Spending a Saturday afternoon browsing the stalls of **Portobello Road Market** (p259) for beautiful vintage clothes, fabulous street food and perhaps even an antique bargain.

2 Relaxing with a drink by the Grand Union Canal at the **Waterway** (p263).

3 Taking a **boat trip** (p259) between Little Venice and Camden along Regent's Canal.

4 Blowing the budget with a night out at the sensational **Kensington Roof Gardens** (p263).

5 Cosying up on a leather sofa for two with a glass of wine and watching the latest hit movie at the **Electric Cinema** (p264), the UK's oldest picture house.

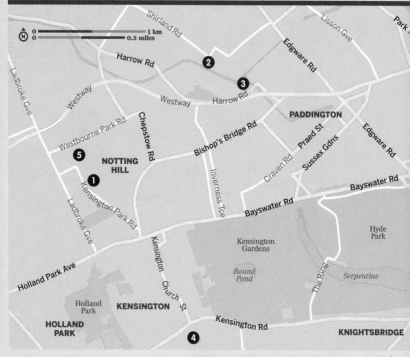

For more detail of this area, see Map p454 and p456

Explore West London

Most people come to West London for one of two reasons: to go to Portobello Road Market (definitely a highlight) or because they're sleeping in one of the many hotels dotting the area.

West London is not very dense in terms of sights, but if you can you should allow half a day for Portobello Road Market and another half day to walk along the Grand Union Canal towards Little Venice, maybe with a picnic on the way or a recuperative pint at one of the waterside pubs.

For those staying in the area, there are some excellent dining and entertainment options, which will save you from going into the West End (although you're definitely close enough to do so if you want). For eating, Notting Hill is where you'll find the greatest concentration of good addresses, but there are some real gems in Hammersmith, Shepherd's Bush and Earl's Court that are also worth a visit.

For nightlife, Notting Hill and Shepherd's Bush are the most vibrant, whilst Kensington is home to one of the capital's most stunning clubs. Other areas will be pretty quiet once the pubs have rung the bell at 11pm.

Local Life

➡ **Fruit and vegetable markets** Although also popular with tourists, many Notting Hill residents shop for their daily fruit and veg at Portobello Road Market (p259). Another good fruit and veg market is Shepherd's Bush Market (p266).

➡ **Waterside strolling** Little Venice (p259) is very popular at the weekend when families go for a walk along the canal's tow paths.

➡ **Affordable pampering** The Porchester Spa (p267) is run by Westminster Council and is cheaper than typical commercial spas. Local residents get additional discounts so it gets very busy in the evenings with the after-work crowd.

Getting There & Away

➡ **Underground** The Central Line, which crosses London from west to east, stops at Queensway (Bayswater), Notting Hill Gate and Shepherd's Bush. For Paddington, Westbourne Grove, and the western end of Shepherd's Bush, you'll have to rely on the painfully slow Hammersmith & City Line. Earl's Court and Hammersmith are on the speedy Piccadilly Line.

➡ **Barclays Bikes** Useful to get from one neighbourhood to another; there are docking stations across West London so you shouldn't have problems picking up and dropping off a bike.

Lonely Planet's Top Tip

To make the best of your time at Portobello Road Market, it's best to do a one-way circuit between Notting Hill Gate and Ladbroke Rd tube stations. The flow tends to go from Notting Hill to Ladbroke Grove, but either way works fine.

 Best Places to Eat

➡ Gate (p261)
➡ Tatra (p261)
➡ Taquería (p259)
➡ Tendido Cero (p261)

For reviews, see p259 ➡

Best Places to Drink

➡ Troubadour (p264)
➡ Windsor Castle (p264)
➡ Dove (p263)
➡ Waterway (p263)
➡ Beach Blanket Babylon (p263)

For reviews, see p263 ➡

Best Guided Tours

➡ BBC Television Centre (p258)
➡ Regent's Canal by boat (p259)
➡ Linley Sambourne House in period costume (p258)

For reviews, see p258 ➡

NOTTING HILL & WEST LONDON

⊙ SIGHTS

⊙ Notting Hill & Westbourne Grove

MUSEUM OF BRANDS, PACKAGING AND ADVERTISING
MUSEUM

Map p454 (www.museumofbrands.com; 2 Colville Mews, Lonsdale Rd W11; adult/child £6.50/2.25; ⊙10am-6pm Tue-Sat, 11am-5pm Sun; ⊖Notting Hill Gate) This unexpected find in the heart of Notting Hill is the brainchild of designer Robert Opie, who has been collecting advertising memorabilia since the age of 16. It's fairly low-tech, but very eye-catching, and visitors of every age will enjoy the hunt for familiar products. There are sponsored displays at the end of the gallery, with exhibits showing the evolution of packaging of certain well-known products such as Johnson's Baby Powder, Guinness, Kellogg's Cornflakes and Cadbury's chocolates.

⊙ High Street Kensington

LEIGHTON HOUSE
HOUSE

Map p456 (www.leightonhouse.co.uk; 12 Holland Park Rd W14; adult/child £5/3; ⊙10am-5.30pm Wed-Mon; ⊖High St Kensington) Sitting on a quiet street near Holland Park and designed in 1866 by George Aitchison, Leighton House was home to the eponymous Frederic, Lord Leighton (1830–96), a painter belonging to the Olympian movement. The ground floor is decorated in an Orientalist style, with the exquisite Arab Hall added in 1879 and densely covered with blue and green tiles from Rhodes, Cairo, Damascus, and Iznik in Turkey; a fountain trickles away in the centre. Even the wooden latticework of the windows and gallery was brought from Damascus. The house contains notable pre-Raphaelite paintings by Burne-Jones, Watts, Millais and Lord Leighton himself.

LINLEY SAMBOURNE HOUSE
HOUSE

Map p456 (www.rbkc.gov.uk/linleysambourne house; 18 Stafford Tce W8; adult/child £6/1; ⊙tours 11.15am & 2.15pm Wed, 11.15am, 1pm, 2.15pm, 3.30pm Sat & Sun mid-Sep–mid-Jun; ⊖High St Kensington) Tucked away behind Kensington High St, this was the home of *Punch* cartoonist and amateur photographer Linley Sambourne and his wife Marion from 1875 to 1914. It's one of those houses whose owners never redecorated or threw anything away. What you see is pretty much the typical home of a comfortable middle-class Victorian family, with dark wood, Turkish carpets and rich stained glass throughout.

You can visit some nine rooms, by 90-minute guided tour only. (On the weekend, the guide on all but the first tour is in period costume.)

⊙ Earl's Court & West Brompton

BROMPTON CEMETERY
CEMETERY

Map p456 (www.royalparks.gov.uk; Old Brompton Rd SW5; ⊙8am-dusk daily; ⊖West Brompton or Fulham Broadway) As London's vast population exploded in the 19th century, seven new cemeteries – the 'Magnificent Seven' – opened, among them Brompton Cemetery, a long expanse running between Fulham Rd and Old Brompton Rd. The chapel and colonnades at one end are modelled on St Peter's in Rome.

While the most famous resident is Emmeline Pankhurst, the pioneer of women's suffrage in Britain, the cemetery is most interesting as the inspiration for many of Beatrix Potter's characters. A local resident in her youth before she moved to the north, Potter seems to have taken many names from the deceased of Brompton Cemetery and immortalised them in her world-famous books. They include Mr Nutkin, Mr McGregor, Jeremiah Fisher, Tommy Brock – and even a Peter Rabbett.

BBC TELEVISION CENTRE

If you're interested in TV production, this is the perfect chance to visit the vast complex of **studios and offices** (off Map p456, www.bbc.co.uk/tours; Wood Lane W12; tours adult/child £9.95/7.75; ⊙tours Mon-Sat; ⊖White City) that bring the BBC's TV programs to the world. Visit is by two-hour guided tour only and bookings are essential (no children under nine).

You'll see the BBC News and Weather Centres as well as studios where shows are being made, dressing rooms and green rooms. Keep your eyes peeled all the while as you're very likely to spot a celebrity or familiar presenter wandering the corridors.

TOP SIGHTS
PORTOBELLO ROAD MARKET

Like Camden and Spitalfields, Portobello Road Market is an iconic London attraction with the usual mix of street food, fruit and veg, antiques, colourful fashion, and trinkets you'd never thought you'd need. Although the shops along Portobello Road open daily and the fruit and veg stalls (from Elgin Cres to Talbot Rd) only close on Sunday, the busiest day by far is Saturday, when antique dealers set up shop (from Chepstow Villas to Elgin Cres). This is also when the fashion market (beneath Westway from Portobello Road to Ladbroke Rd) is in full swing – although you can also browse for fashion on Friday and Sunday.

Among the vintage and 'first hand' fashion stalls of Westway, you'll also find accessories, shoes, jewellery and CDs. For something more upmarket, **Portobello Green Arcade** (281 Portobello Rd W10; ⊙daily) is home to some cutting-edge clothing and jewellery designers and is well worth a look.

If you continue on Portobello Road towards Golborne Rd (famous for its vintage furniture and clothes shops), you'll hit the 'new goods' section, with kitchenware, bric-a-brac and more fruit and veg stalls, as well as second-hand goods despite this being the 'new goods' market!

DON'T MISS...

➡ Fashion market
➡ Designers at Portobello Green Arcade
➡ Fruit and veg stalls
➡ Antiques market

PRACTICALITIES

➡ Map p454
➡ Portobello Rd W10
➡ ⊙8am-6pm Mon-Wed, 9am-1pm Thu, 7am-7pm Fri & Sat, 9am-4pm Sun
➡ ⊖Notting Hill Gate or Ladbroke Grove

NOTTING HILL & WEST LONDON EATING

Free tours lasting 90 minutes depart at 2pm Sunday from the South Lodge, near the Fulham Rd entrance.

⊙ St John's Wood & Maida Vale

LITTLE VENICE   CANAL
Map p454 It was poet Robert Browning who came up with this evocative phrase to describe the junction between Regent's Canal and the Grand Union Canal. No doubt he was inspired by the beautiful mansions, the tree-lined canals and the colourful narrow boats.

The canals go back to the early 19th century when the government was trying to develop new transport links across the country. Horse-drawn barges were ideal to carry coal and other bulk commodities such as grain or ice.

The barges are now long-gone and the horses have given way to pedestrians and cyclists along the tow paths, but Little Venice retains a certain bucolic charm. It is an important mooring point for narrow boats (many of them are permanent homes), which keeps the boating spirit alive.

LONDON WATERBUS COMPANY   CRUISE
Map p454 & p452 (www.londonwaterbus.co.uk; 2 Middle Yard, Camden Lock NW1; adult/child one-way £6.90/5.70, return £9.90/7.90; ⊙hourly 10am-5pm Apr-Sep; ⊖Warwick Ave or Camden Town) This enclosed barge runs 90-minute trips on Regent's Canal between Little Venice and Camden Lock, passing through Regent's Park and London Zoo. It's a very pleasant way to spend a couple of hours. Trips can be one-way or return. There are fewer departures outside of high season – check the website for schedules.

✕ EATING

✕ Notting Hill & Westbourne Grove

TAQUERÍA   MEXICAN **£**
Map p454 (www.taqueria.co.uk; 139-143 Westbourne Grove W11; tacos £5.50-7.50; ⊙closed Sun; ⊖Bayswater or Notting Hill Gate) You won't find fresher, limper (they're not supposed to be crispy!) tacos anywhere in London

NOTTING HILL CARNIVAL

Every year, for three days during the last weekend of August, Notting Hill echoes to the beats of calypso, ska, reggae and soca sounds of **Notting Hill Carnival** (www. nottinghill-carnival.co.uk). Launched in 1964 by the local Afro-Caribbean community keen to celebrate its culture and traditions, it has grown to become Europe's largest street festival (up to one million people) and a highlight of the annual calendar in London.

The carnival includes events highlighting the five main 'arts': the 'mas' (derived from masquerade), which is the main costume parade; pan (steel bands); calypso music; static sound systems (anything goes, from reggae to drum and bass); and the mobile sound systems. The 'mas' is generally held on the Monday and is the culmination of the carnival's celebrations. Processions finish around 9pm, although parties in bars, restaurants and seemingly every house in the neighbourhood go on late into the night.

Another undisputed highlight of the carnival is the food: there are dozens of Caribbean food stands and celebrity chefs such as Levi Roots often make an appearance.

because they're made on the premises. It's a small casual place with a great vibe; Taquería is also a committed environmental establishment. The eggs, chicken and pork are free-range, the meat is British, the fish MSC certified and the restaurant only uses organic milk and cream.

MARKET THAI   THAI £
Map p454 (1st fl, 240 Portobello Rd W11; mains £6.50-14; ⊜Ladbroke Grove) Drippy white candles, carved arches and wrought-iron chairs mark out the interior of this delightful restaurant. It occupies the 1st floor of the Market Bar, but is independent of it (and way classier). Hospitable staff and fresh delicately spiced Thai cuisine make this place a little money very well spent. Enter from Lancaster Rd.

ARANCINA   ITALIAN £
Map p454 (www.arancina.co.uk; 19 Pembridge Rd W11; dishes £2.70-5.20; ⊘7.30am-10pm; ⊜Notting Hill Gate) A fantastic place to indulge in Sicilian snacks, Arancina stops people dead in their tracks on the way to Portobello market thanks to the whiffs of freshly baked pizzas and the cut-out orange Fiat 500 in the window. Try the *arancini* (fried balls of rice with fillings; £2) and the creamy desserts known as *cannoli siciliano*.

ELECTRIC BRASSERIE   MODERN EUROPEAN ££
Map p454 (www.electricbrasserie.com; 191 Portobello Rd W11; mains £12.50-36; ⊜Ladbroke Grove or Notting Hill Gate) Whether it's for breakfast (£5 to £10) or brunch over the weekend, a hearty lunch or a full dinner, the Electric draws a trendy and wealthy Notting Hill

crowd with its Modern British/European cuisine. If you're feeling decadent, lobster and chips (£36) is the way forward.

MEDITERRANEO   ITALIAN ££
Map p454 (www.mediterraneo-restaurant.co.uk; 37 Kensington Park Rd W11; mains £13-22; ⊜Ladbroke Grove) For authentic Italian food, it hardly gets better than Mediterraneo: the pasta is home-made and there is plenty of veal on the menu (a meat that's almost unheard of in English cooking). The veal escalope in Marsala sauce is simply divine. Chefs use black and white truffles when in season.

E&O   ASIAN ££
Map p454 (www.rickerrestaurants.com; 14 Blenheim Cres W11; mains £9.50-28; ⊜Ladbroke Grove) This Notting Hill hot spot offers Asian fusion fare presented as artfully as an elaborate origami. The decor is equally attractive: black-and-white minimalist. You can do dim sum (£3.75 to £7.75) at the bar if no tables are available in the evening.

⬩DAYLESFORD   ORGANIC ££
Map p454 (www.daylesfordorganic.com; 208-212 Westbourne Grove W11; mains £10-15; ⊘8.30am-7pm Mon-Sat, 10am-4pm Sun; ⊜Westbourne Park) Daylesford is a farm in the Cotswolds that's been organic for nearly three decades. This Notting Hill outfit combines a shop selling products from the farm back in Gloucestershire and other organic suppliers, with a deli and restaurant. Both serve organic food exclusively, with

offerings such as beef burgers, soups and spring lamb with baby vegetables.

KENSINGTON PLACE MODERN EUROPEAN ££
Map p454 (www.kensingtonplace-restaurant. co.uk; 201-209 Kensington Church St W8; mains £13-22; ⊖Notting Hill Gate) The impressive glass frontage and design-driven interior look a little corporate to our taste, but the food certainly has soul. The emphasis is on seafood, with the adjoining fishmonger's providing the goods, although there are some very decent vegetarian and meat options, too.

GEALES FISH & CHIPS ££
Map p454 (www.geales.com; 2 Farmer St W8; set lunch Tue-Fri £11.95, mains £8-26.95; ⊙closed lunch Mon; ⊖Notting Hill Gate) Going since 1939, Geales has long enjoyed fame for its succulent fish. Service can be impatient, but the quiet location, tucked away off energetic Notting Hill Gate, is appetising. The fish in crispy batter remains the menu's main draw although the chips disappointingly cost extra (outside of the set lunch) on what should be a standard combination. There's outside seating.

COW GASTROPUB ££
Map p454 (www.thecowlondon.co.uk; 89 Westbourne Park Rd W2; mains £7.50-21; ⊖Westbourne Park or Royal Oak) Owned by Tom Conran, son of celebrated former restaurateur Sir Terence, this attractive boozer was one of London's original gastropubs. Name of the game both upstairs and downstairs at the main bar is seafood: Irish rock oysters, haddock fishcakes, and pasta with cuttlefish and samphire.

CHURRERÍA ESPAÑOLA CAFE £
Map p454 (177-179 Queensway W2; mains £5.95-8.95; ⊙8am-8pm Mon-Fri, from 9am Sat & Sun; ⊖Bayswater) This extremely popular cafe with open frontage serves a variety of cheap dishes, from English breakfasts to a range of Spanish tapas (£2.50 to £6.50).

✖ Earl's Court & West Brompton

TENDIDO CERO SPANISH ££
Map p456 (☑7370 3685; www.cambiodetercio. co.uk; 174 Old Brompton Rd SW5; tapas £3.75-20; ⊖Gloucester Rd) This stylish place (think clean lines in black and purple), limboed somewhere between South Kensington and Earl's Court, serves traditional tapas in just about the trendiest Spanish restaurant you've seen outside the Iberian Peninsula. It's popular and there are two sittings, so book ahead at all times.

MR WING CHINESE ££
Map p456 (www.mrwing.com; 242-244 Old Brompton Rd SW5; mains £12-35; ⊖Earl's Court or West Brompton) Mr Wing is a smart Chinese restaurant offering the full spectrum of Chinese cuisine, from dim sum to Cantonese hot plates and northern delights such as aromatic crispy duck. There is live jazz Thursday to Saturday nights.

✖ Shepherd's Bush & Hammersmith

GATE VEGETARIAN ££
Map p456 (☑8748 6932; www.thegate.tv; 51 Queen Caroline St W6; mains £10.50-13.50; ⊙lunch Mon-Fri, dinner Mon-Sat; ⊖Hammersmith) Widely considered the best vegetarian restaurant in town, this destination eatery has a poor location behind the Hammersmith Apollo and is surrounded by flyovers, but the inventive dishes (aubergine teriyaki, shitake wonton and pumpkin laksa, rocket cannelloni), friendly and welcoming staff, and the relaxed atmosphere make the trek here worthwhile. Bookings essential.

TATRA POLISH ££
Map p456 (www.tatrarestaurant.co.uk; 2 Goldhawk Rd W12; mains £8.90-15.50; ⊙ lunch Fri-Sun, dinner daily; ⊖Goldhawk Rd) Despite the surfeit of Poles in West London, upmarket Polish eateries remain as scarce as hens' teeth. Tatra is one major exception, with its designer-driven decor and ever-so-cool waiting staff. The menu offers all the usual favourites as well as less familiar treats, such as *kaszanka* (grilled black pudding with toast and apple) and a risotto of *kasza* (buckwheat groats) and wild mushrooms.

BLAH BLAH BLAH VEGETARIAN £
Map p456 (www.blahvegetarian.com; 78 Goldhawk Rd W12; mains £8.95-10.95; ⊙closed Sun; ⊖Goldhawk Rd) This vegetarian institution has been packing them in for years with imaginative, well-realised food and informal and very upbeat surrounds. Dishes feature vegetarian specialities from around the world (Caribbean curry,

NOTTING HILL CARNIVAL LIKE A LOCAL

Ancil Barclay is one of the directors of Notting Hill Carnival. He's worked on the carnival for 27 years. As a Trinidadian, he says that the carnival is simply part of his DNA.

Be an Actor, Not a Spectator
Few people realise that they don't just have to watch, they can actually take part in one of the floats. We sell **packages** (www.nottinghill-carnival.co.uk) where people get access to the float for two days, food and drink and even a costume (£100)! All they need is a good attitude and some comfortable shoes. We really want to encourage people from non-Caribbean backgrounds to take part.

Relaxed Carnival Experience
To make the best of the carnival, come early. Go to the Calypso tent, have some food, and come on children's day – Sunday, which is generally less busy.

Where to Go When it's Not Carnival
I love the atmosphere at the Thai restaurant **Garden & Grill** (Map p454; www.thairiver.co.uk/portobello.html; 235a Portobello Rd W11; mains £6-9; ⊖Notting Hill Gate or Ladbroke Grove). The balcony overlooks Portobello Rd and it's like a small carnival every day. The food is better at Market Thai (p260), however.

aubergine schnitzel, pasta etc). You can bring your own bottle (corkage £1.45 per person).

RIVER CAFÉ
ITALIAN £££
Map p456 (☑7386 4200; www.rivercafe.co.uk; Thames Wharf, Rainville Rd W6; mains £12-35; ⊗closed dinner Sun; ⊖Hammersmith) The Thames-side restaurant that spawned the world-famous eponymous cookery books offers simple, precise cooking that showcases seasonal ingredients sourced with fanatical expertise; the menus change daily. Booking is essential, as it's a favourite of the Fulham set.

ESARN KHEAW
THAI ££
Map p456 (www.esarnkheaw.com; 314 Uxbridge Rd W12; mains £6.95-16.50; ⊗lunch Mon-Fri, dinner daily; ⊖Shepherd's Bush) Welcoming you back into the 1970s is the very green interior of this superb restaurant serving food from the Esarn, the northeast of Thailand where people munch on chillies like chewing gum. The house-made Esarn Kheaw sausage and *som tom* (green papaya salad) are sublime.

PATIO
POLISH ££
Map p456 (www.patiolondon.com; 5 Goldhawk Rd W12; mains £8.50-14.90, set meal with glass of vodka £16.50; ⊗lunch Mon-Fri, dinner daily; ⊖Shepherd's Bush or Goldhawk Rd) This cosy restaurant is cluttered with curios and antiques and serves fairly authentic home-style Polish food. It is presided over by a kindly matriarch who knows and sees all.

✗ St John's Wood & Maida Vale

SUMMERHOUSE
MODERN EUROPEAN ££
Map p454 (☑7286 6752; www.frgroup.co.uk; Grand Union Canal, opposite 60 Blomfield Rd W9; mains £14-18.50; ⊗Apr-Oct; ⊖Warwick Ave) It would be unfair to say that the Summerhouse is all show and no substance, although it's true that this restaurant impresses more by its stunning, waterside alfresco setting than by its cuisine. If you do get a balmy summer evening, however, this is definitely the place to enjoy it, with a chilled glass of rosé on the side.

✗ Paddington & Bayswater

PEARL LIANG
CHINESE ££
Map p454 (www.pearlliang.co.uk; 8 Sheldon Sq W2; mains £7-28; ⊖Paddington) Touted by some as London's best Chinese restaurant, this stylish eatery, located in the new waterside development of Sheldon Sq, serves up Chinese with a modern slant. The dim sum (£2.50 to £3.50) is excellent, but the decor, with its water features, oversized abacus and dreadful waiting-room music, is a bit of a let-down.

COUSCOUS CAFÉ
MOROCCAN ££
Map p454 (7 Porchester Gardens W2; mains £9.95-15.95; ⊖Bayswater) This cosy and

vividly decorated basement place excels in Moroccan-style couscous and *tagines* (spicy stews cooked in an earthenware dish), *pastillas* (filled savoury pastries) and slightly exaggerated service. Try the mixed meze plate (small/large £6.95/11.95). Alcohol is served or you can BYO (no corkage fee).

DRINKING & NIGHTLIFE

Notting Hill & Westbourne Grove

EARL OF LONSDALE   PUB

Map p454 (277-281 Portobello Rd W11; ⊖Notting Hill Gate or Westbourne Park) Despite being in the middle of the Portobello Road Market, the Earl is peaceful during the day, with a mixture of old biddies and young hipsters inhabiting the reintroduced snugs. There are Samuel Smith's ales, and a fantastic backroom with sofas, banquettes and open fires, as well as a recently extended beer garden.

BEACH BLANKET BABYLON   BAR

Map p454 (www.beachblanket.co.uk; 45 Ledbury Rd W11; ⊖Notting Hill Gate) This truly fabulous bar, decorated in baroque and rococo styles, is the place to come for a decadent night out. It's a favourite of Princes William and Harry and the moneyed set of the royal boroughs so come with your wallet at the ready and your very best attire.

NOTTING HILL ARTS CLUB   CLUB

Map p454 (www.nottinghillartsclub.com; 21 Notting Hill Gate W11; ⊖Notting Hill Gate) London simply wouldn't be what it is without places like NHAC. Cultivating the underground music scene, this small basement club attracts a musically curious and experimental crowd. The famous monthly Thursday Yo-Yo night, where singer Lily Allen and producer Mark Ronson met, is one of the best nights for R&B, '80s boogies, hip hop, ragga and diverse live sets.

High Street Kensington

TOP CHOICE KENSINGTON ROOF GARDENS   CLUB

Map p456 (www.roofgardens.virgin.com; 99 Kensington High St W8; ⊖Kensington High St) High above Kensington High St, at the top of

---

WATERSIDE DRINKING

With canals and the Thames, West London boasts some atmospheric drinking options by the waterside.

Dove (Map p456; 19 Upper Mall W6; ⊖Hammersmith or Ravenscourt Park) A 17th-century coffee house– cum– pub, the Dove has many claims to fame, including that it was in the *Guinness Book of Records* in 1989 for having the smallest bar in England (though there are larger areas, including a terrace, lounge and conservatory). It was Graham Greene's local and Hemingway drank here, too; William Morris lived next door. There are good river views from the charming dark-wood interior, but if the sun is shining, fight for a place in the garden.

Waterway (Map p454; www.thewaterway.co.uk; 54 Formosa St W9; ⊙noon-1am; ⊖Warwick Ave) Don't come here for the selection of beer or ales or the overly expensive nosh; this place, hard by the Grand Union Canal in Little Venice, is all about location, and it's hard to imagine a better place to while away a weekend afternoon.

Old Ship (off Map p456; 25 Upper Mall W6; ⊖Hammersmith or Ravenscourt Park) This restful towpath pub is the prime stop-off for families and couples on their weekend walks by the Thames. It looks south across the lazy bend of the river to Putney, and it's popular during the rest of the week, especially on spring and summer days, thanks to its outdoor dining area, terrace and 1st-floor balcony.

Grand Union (Map p454; www.grandunionlondon.co.uk; 45 Woodfield Rd W9; ⊖Westbourne Park) With just the right mix of shiny gastropub, rough-and-ready local appeal and a splendid location on the Grand Union Canal with a waterside terrace, this pub is a fabulous place to enjoy a couple of pints on your way to or from Portobello Road Market.

an inconspicuous building, hides one of the most enchanting venues in London – a nightclub with 0.6 hectares of gardens. There are three different gardens: the stunningly beautiful Spanish gardens inspired by the Alhambra in Grenada; the Tudor gardens, all nooks and crannies, and fragrant flowers; and the Woodlands gardens, home to ancient trees and four resident flamingos.

The gardens are only open from May to September; they have their own bars and often host live bands. The indoor part is the club proper (open year-round) where commercial dance music keeps the crowd of young socialites boogying until the early hours.

All of this wow-factor comes at a premium: entry is £25, you must register on the guest list before going and the drinks are £10 a pop. Still, it's a once-in-a-lifetime place to experience. Entrance is on Derry St. Dress to impress.

WINDSOR CASTLE   PUB

Map p456 (www.thewindsorcastlekensington. co.uk; 114 Campden Hill Rd W8; ⊖Notting Hill Gate) A wonderful, relatively out-of-the-way tavern between Notting Hill and Kensington High St, this place has history, nooks and charm on tap. It's worth the search for its historic interior, roaring fire (in winter), delightful beer garden (in summer) and friendly regulars (most always).

CHURCHILL ARMS   PUB

Map p456 (119 Kensington Church St W8; ⊖Notting Hill Gate) You can't miss the Churchill Arms – with its cascade of geraniums and Union Jack flags swaying in the breeze, it's quite a sight on Kensington Church St! The pub is renowned for its Winston memorabilia and dozens of knick-knacks on the walls. It's a favourite of both locals and tourists. The attached conservatory has been serving excellent Thai food for two decades (mains £6-10).

🍸 Earl's Court & West Brompton

TOP CHOICE TROUBADOUR   BAR

Map p456 (www.troubadour.co.uk; 265 Old Brompton Rd SW5; ⊙9am-midnight; ⊖Earl's Court) Bob Dylan and John Lennon have performed here and this friendly cafe-bar remains a wonderfully relaxed boho hangout decades later. There's still live music (folk, blues) most nights and a large, pleasant garden open in summer. You'll be spoilt for choice with the wine list – Troubadour runs a wine club and has a wine shop next door.

ATLAS   PUB

Map p456 (www.theatlaspub.co.uk; 16 Seagrave Rd SW6; ⊖West Brompton) This cosy Victorian-era pub attracts a younger

---

INDIE CINEMAS

If you love cinema, you're in for a treat with West London's quirky picture houses. Q&A events with directors, sofas, alcoholic drinks allowed, and much more, this is how cinema should be. Tickets are slightly more expensive than in run-of-the-mill cinemas, but it's worth the expense.

Electric Cinema (Map p454; www.electriccinema.co.uk; 191 Portobello Rd W1; ⊖Ladbroke Grove or Notting Hill Gate) The Electric is the UK's oldest cinema, updated with luxurious leather armchairs, footstools, tables for food and drink in the auditorium, and the upmarket Electric Brasserie (p260) next door.

Gate Picturehouse (Map p454; www.picturehouses.co.uk; 87 Notting Hill Gate W1; ⊖Notting Hill Gate) The Gate's single screen has one of London's most charming art deco cinema interiors. Despite its retro-cutesy name, this cinema takes its programming seriously, with director Q&As and live opera screenings from the famous Glyndebourne Festival.

Coronet (Map p454; www.coronet.org; 103 Notting Hill Gate W8; ⊖Notting Hill Gate) A lovesick Hugh Grant munches popcorn here while watching Julia Roberts on the big screen in *Notting Hill*. The wonderful Edwardian interior, including a gorgeous balcony and even boxes, recalls the glory days of cinema, when filling a 400-seat house for every showing was easy.

local crowd with its real ales, excellent food, and a lovely side courtyard. The gastropub menu features essentially Mediterranean-inspired dishes (mains £8-15).

🍸 Shepherd's Bush & Hammersmith

GREEN ROOM   BAR
Map p456 (www.greenroom-london.co.uk; 45a Goldhawk Rd W12; ⏰5-11.30pm Mon-Fri, noon-11.30pm Sat & Sun; Ⓢ Goldhawk Rd or Shepherd's Bush) Originally a milk bottling factory, this large, warehouse-like venue offers a fresh take on nights out in Shepherd's Bush, with regular live music (ranging from jazz to DJ sets), six American pool tables and a kitchen churning out juicy burgers.

🍸 St John's Wood & Maida Vale

PRINCE ALFRED   PUB
Map p454 (5a Formosa St W9; Ⓢ Warwick Ave) Pubs don't really come much better than this charming place. Originally designed in Victorian times to separate the classes and sexes, the semicircular bar is divided into five gorgeous booths, each with its own waist-high door. The pub is always busy with adoring locals, many of whom make their way up to the stunning Formosa Dining Room.

WARRINGTON   PUB
Map p454 (93 Warrington Cres W9; Ⓢ Warwick Ave or Maida Vale) This former hotel and brothel is now an ornate, art nouveau pub with heaps of character. The huge saloon bar, dominated by a marble-topped hemispherical counter with a carved mahogany base and a huge stained-glass window by Tiffany, is a fabulous place to sample a range of four real ales. There's also outdoor seating.

⭐ ENTERTAINMENT

O2 SHEPHERD'S BUSH
EMPIRE   CONCERT VENUE
Map p456 (www.o2shepherdsbushempire.co.uk; Shepherd's Bush Green W12; Ⓢ Shepherd's Bush)

WESTFIELD SHOPPING CENTRE
This gigantic shopping mecca is London's first mall and the promoters spared no expense developing it. As well as the 300-odd shops that reside here (all franchises), **Westfield** (Map p456; http://uk.westfield.com/london; ⏰10am-9pm Mon-Wed, to 10pm Thu & Fri, 9am-9pm Sat, noon-6pm Sun) has a raft of eateries (again, chains only), bars, a cinema, and regular events, from fashion shows to book signings. It's big, brash and Londoners love it.

What distinguishes it perhaps from your average mall is The Village, an aisle of the building put aside for a coterie of designers and couture brands, from Louis Vuitton to Jimmy Choo, Prada and Tiffany & Co.

Top musicians (such as PJ Harvey or Antony and the Johnsons) perform in this midsized venue (capacity is 2000), and there's always something interesting going on. The downer is the fact that the floor doesn't slope, so if you're not so tall it can be impossible to see from up the back in the stalls – it's worth paying for the balcony.

BUSH THEATRE   THEATRE
Map p456 (www.bushtheatre.co.uk; 7 Uxbridge Rd W12; Ⓢ Shepherd's Bush) This West London theatre is renowned for encouraging new talent. Its success over the past three decades – it recently moved to larger premises to accommodate its prolific programming – is down to strong writing from the likes of Jonathan Harvey, Conor McPherson, Stephen Poliakoff and Mark Ravenhill.

OPERA HOLLAND PARK   OPERA
Map p456 (www.operahollandpark.com; Holland Park W8; Ⓢ High St Kensington) This is Ye Olde England, with picnics on the grass, opera on stage and frightfully posh surroundings. Sit under the 800-seat canopy, which is temporarily erected every summer for a nine-week season in the middle of Holland Park, and enjoy a mix of crowd pleasers and rare (even obscure) works.

NOTTING HILL & WEST LONDON ENTERTAINMENT

RIVERSIDE STUDIOS
PERFORMING ARTS

Map p456 (www.riversidestudios.co.uk; Crisp Rd W6; ⊖Hammersmith) Once a film and TV studio, where such classics as *Dr Who* and *Hancock's Half-Hour* were shot, the Riverside now hosts an eclectic mix of performing arts, from circus to theatre and comedy, and also doubles as an art-house cinema.

EARL'S COURT EXHIBITION CENTRE
SPECTATOR SPORT

Map p456 (www.eco.co.uk; Warwick Rd SW5; ⊖Earl's Court) This multipurpose venue hosts a range of events from sports fixtures to trade shows and concerts. In 2012, it will be the home of volleyball for the London Olympics.

 ## SHOPPING

BOOKS FOR COOKS
BOOKS

Map p454 (www.booksforcooks.com; 4 Blenheim Cres W11; ⊙10am-6pm Tue-Sat; ⊖Ladbroke Grove) All the recipe books from celeb and non-celeb chefs you can imagine are sold here – perfect for more adventurous cooks or for those looking for 'exotic' cookbooks. The cafe has a test kitchen where you can sample recipes at lunch and teatime.

RELLIK
VINTAGE

Map p454 (www.relliklondon.co.uk; 8 Golborne Rd W10; ⊖Westbourne Park) Incongruously located at the foot of one of London's most notorious tower blocks – the god-awful-yet-heritage-listed concrete Trellick Tower – Rellik is a fashionista favourite retro store. It stocks vintage numbers from the 1920s to the 1980s and, while you rummage among the frippery, it's not unusual to find an Yves

SHEPHERD'S BUSH MARKET
This fruit and veg **market** (Map p456; ⊙9.30am-5pm Mon-Wed, Fri & Sat, to 1pm Thu), stretches underneath the Hammersmith & City and Circle Lines between Goldhawk Rd and Shepherd's Bush tube stations. It's popular with local African and Afro-Caribbean communities and is therefore stockpiled with mangoes, passion fruit, okra, plantains, sweet potatoes and other exotic fare.

Saint-Laurent coat, a Chloe suit or an Ossie Clark dress. This is a real treasure trove for those in the know.

SPICE SHOP
FOOD

Map p454 (www.thespiceshop.co.uk; 1 Blenheim Cres W11; ⊖Ladbroke Grove) The smell coming from the Spice Shop says it all: from run-of-the-mill curry powder and herbs to much rarer spices and ready-made combinations (for fajitas, jerk seasoning, Cajun etc), this is a treasure trove of exotic flavours.

CERAMICA BLUE
HOMEWARES

Map p454 (www.ceramicablue.co.uk; 10 Blenheim Cres W11; ⊖Ladbroke Grove) A wonderful place for original and beautiful crockery, imported from more than a dozen countries. There are Japanese eggshell-glaze teacups, serving plates with tribal South African designs, gorgeous table cloths from Provence and much more.

RETRO WOMAN
VINTAGE

Map p454 (20 Pembridge Rd W11; ⊖Notting Hill Gate) More secondhand than vintage, but very popular, Retro Woman has racks upon racks of hand-me-down fashion, including a huge selection of shoes.

RETRO MAN
VINTAGE

Map p454 (34 Pembridge Rd W11; ⊖Notting Hill Gate) Part of the same outfit as Retro Woman, this caters to fashionable gents, with shirts, ties, trilby hats and trousers from way back.

ORSINI
VINTAGE

Map p456 (76 Earl's Court Rd W8; ⊖Earl's Court) One of the best vintage designer collections in town, Orsini is small, beautiful and friendly. It's a little out of the way, but worth the effort if you're looking for a gem. Alterations are available in-store.

AL SAQI
BOOKS

Map p454 (www.alsaqibookshop.com; 26 Westbourne Grove W2; ⊖Bayswater) Located in a beautiful building topped with a dozen busts, this shop specialises in books in English about the Arab world and Islam, including the full catalogue of books it publishes itself.

ROUGH TRADE
MUSIC

Map p454 (130 Talbot Rd W11; ⊖Ladbroke Grove) With its underground, alternative and vintage rarities, this home of the eponymous punk-music label remains a haven for vinyl junkies who get misty-eyed about the days before CDs (also on sale) and MP3 players.

SPORTS & ACTIVITIES

PORCHESTER SPA
SPA

Map p454 (Porchester Centre, Queensway W2; admission £24; ⊙10am-10pm; ⊖Bayswater or Royal Oak) Housed in a gorgeous, art deco building, the Porchester is unusual in the sense that it is a no-frills spa run by Westminster Council. It's used mostly by residents wanting to unwind and use the great facilities (a 30m swimming pool, a large Finnish-log sauna, two steam rooms, three Turkish hot rooms and a massive plunge pool). There are plenty of affordable treatments on offer including massages and male and female pampering/grooming sessions.

It's ladies only on Tuesdays, Thursdays and Fridays all day and between 10am and 4pm on Sundays; men only on Mondays, Wednesdays and Saturdays. Couples are welcome from 4pm to 10pm on Sundays.

K SPA
SPA

Map p456 (www.k-west.co.uk; Richmond Way W12; ⊖Shepherd's Bush) This is where to come for a pampering session, complete with candles and Zen music. The K Spa is an important part of the K West hotel (p335), and has a good range of facilities, including a hydro-therapy pool, eucalyptus steam room, sauna and even a snow room. The list of treatments available is an arm-long.

Greenwich & South London

GREENWICH | CHARLTON | WOOLWICH | LAMBETH | BRIXTON | BATTERSEA | WANDSWORTH | CLAPHAM | KENNINGTON | OVAL | STOCKWELL | DULWICH | FOREST HILL

Neighbourhood Top Five

1 Feasting on delicious views of London from beneath the statue of General Wolfe in **Greenwich Park** (p270), next to the **Royal Observatory** (p270).

2 Snacking and delving your way through the stalls and browse-worthy shops of **Greenwich Market** (p282).

3 Charting an eye-opening course through the oceanic exhibits of the standout **National Maritime Museum** (p273) at Greenwich.

4 Encountering the eclectic collection of the **Horniman Museum** (p279) before discovering what the glorious gardens have to offer.

5 Browsing, shopping, snacking and eating your way around fun and funky **Brixton Village** (p289).

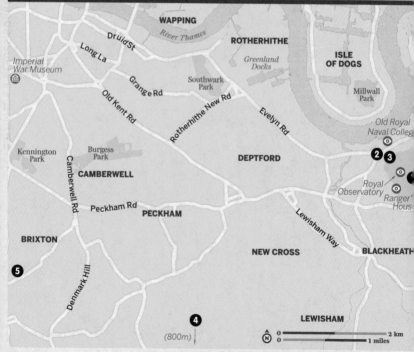

For more detail of this area, see Map p460, Map p462 and Map p463

Explore Greenwich & South London

The existential divide between north and south London remains as stark as the Watford Gap, but growing numbers of North Londoners have warmed to South London's more affordable property prices, leafy charms and relaxed tempo. Quaint Greenwich (*gren*-itch) is packed with grand architecture, while some gorgeous parks and standout museums bring growing fleets of visitors, including ticket-holders for South London venues of the 2012 Games. With the Royal Observatory and the fabulous National Maritime Museum, Greenwich should be one of the highlights of any visit to London; allow a day, particularly if you want to head down the river to the Thames Barrier, passing the stunning O2 along the way.

Find time for edgy and artistic Brixton and, of course, Clapham, with its upmarket restaurants and bars. Battersea is home to a magnificent and fun park while Lambeth boasts both the episcopal seat of the Church of England and one of London's finest museums. Dulwich and Forest Hill's excellent galleries and museums are ideally rounded off with a pint of beer in charming Dulwich Village, while Eltham chips in with an art deco palace alongside a Tudor one dating back to the 14th century.

Local Life

➡ **Hang-outs** Engagingly combining Victorian splendour with an Afro-Caribbean vibe, the Effra (p286) is a landmark Brixton local.

➡ **Live Music & Clubbing** Brixton clubs Plan B (p286) and Dogstar (p286) swarm with London clubbers.

➡ **Shopping** Funky and art-inclined Brixton Village (p289) has emerged as a vibrant and eclectic hub of local life. Retro clothing stores in Greenwich are cheaper than their West End equivalents.

Getting There & Away

➡ **Underground, DLR & Train** Most sights in Greenwich can be easily reached from the Cutty Sark DLR station; a quicker way from central London is via one of the mainline trains from Charing Cross or London Bridge to Greenwich railway station.

➡ **Walking** If coming from Docklands to Greenwich, consider walking under the river (p286).

➡ **Bus** From Greenwich, bus 177 or 180 is handy for the Thames Barrier. In Forest Hill, the P4 links the Horniman Museum and the Dulwich Picture Gallery.

➡ **Boat** Thames Clipper (p394) boats run to Greenwich and Woolwich Arsenal from London Eye Millennium Pier.

Lonely Planet Top Tip

Join the harvesters in October scouring Greenwich Park for its huge bounty of windfall edible chestnuts (it's legal to pick them up off the ground, but illegal to swat them from the trees). A fun way to reach Docklands from Greenwich is via the Foot Tunnel under the Thames (p286).

✖ Best Places to Eat

➡ Franco Manca (p283)
➡ Chez Bruce (p284)
➡ Honest Burgers (p283)
➡ Nevada Street Deli (p282)
➡ Old Brewery (p282)
➡ Trinity (p285)

For reviews, see p281 ➡

🍺 Best Places to Drink

➡ Greenwich Union (p285)
➡ Draft House (p287)
➡ Cutty Sark Tavern (p286)
➡ Effra (p286)
➡ Old Brewery (p282)

For reviews, see p285 ➡

◉ Best Guided Tours

➡ National Maritime Museum (p273)
➡ Ranger's House (Wernher Collection; p270)
➡ Imperial War Museum (p276)
➡ Horniman Museum (p279)
➡ Dulwich Picture Gallery (p281)
➡ Astronomy Centre at the Royal Observatory (p270)

For reviews, see p273 ➡

GREENWICH & SOUTH LONDON

ROYAL OBSERVATORY & GREENWICH PARK

One of London's most-visited attractions and part of the National Maritime Museum, the Royal Observatory is where the study of the sea and the stars converge within gorgeous Greenwich Park, London's oldest royal park. The Prime Meridian charts its line through the grounds of the observatory, chosen quite arbitrarily in 1884, cleaving the globe into the eastern and western hemispheres. The observatory sits on a hill within leafy and regal Greenwich Park, with its fabulous views, 73 hectares of trees and lush greenery.

Royal Observatory

Following an ambitious £15-million renovation, the excellent Royal Observatory is divided into two sections.

Flamsteed House & Meridian Courtyard

You now need to pay to access the sites of the northern portion, dedicated to horology. Charles II ordered construction of the Christopher Wren–designed **Flamsteed House** – the original observatory building – on the foundations of Greenwich Castle in 1675; it contains the magnificent Octagon Room, where timepieces are housed. Also within Flamsteed House are absorbing galleries dedicated to timekeeping and longitude.

Outside Flamsteed House, the globe is decisively sliced into east and west, where visitors can delightfully straddle both hemispheres in the **Meridian Courtyard**, with one foot either side of the meridian line. Every day at 1pm the red time-ball at the top of the Royal Observatory continues to drop as it has done since 1833.

Astronomy Centre & Peter Harrison Planetarium

The southern half contains the highly informative and free **Astronomy Centre**, where you can touch the oldest object you will ever encounter: part of the Gibeon meteorite, a mere 4.5 billion years old! Other engaging exhibits include an orrery (mechanical model of the solar system, minus Uranus and Neptune) from 1780, astronomical documentaries, a first edition of Newton's *Principia Mathematica* and the opportunity to view the Milky Way in multiple wavelengths. To take stargazing further, pick up a Skyhawk telescope from the shop.

Also here is the state-of-the-art **Peter Harrison Planetarium** (☑8312 8565; www.nmm.ac.uk/astronomy; adult/child £6.50/4.50; ☻hourly shows 12.45-3.45pm Mon-Fri, 11am-4.15pm Sat & Sun) – London's sole planetarium, with a digital laser projector that can cast entire heavens onto the inside of its roof.

Greenwich Park

Handsome venue of the 2012 Games equestrian events, this **park** (Map p463; ☑8858 2608; www.royal parks.gov.uk; ☻dawn-dusk, cars from 7am; ☒Greenwich or Maze Hill, DLR Cutty Sark) is one of London's loveliest expanses of green, with a rose garden, picturesque walks and astonishing views from the crown of the hill near the **statue of General Wolfe**, opposite the Royal Observatory. Covering a full 73 hectares, this is the oldest enclosed royal park and is partly the work of André Le Nôtre, the landscape architect who designed the palace gardens of Versailles for Louis XIV, the Sun King. The park is rich in historic sights, including a teahouse near the Royal Observatory, a cafe behind the National Maritime Museum, a deer park, tennis courts in the southwest and a boating lake at the Queen's House end. In October, look out for edible chestnuts on the ground (p269).

Ranger's House (Wernher Collection)

This elegant Georgian villa (Map p463; ☑8853 0035; www.english-heritage.org.uk; Greenwich Park, Chesterfield Walk SE10; adult/child £6.30/3.80; ☻tours 11.30am & 2.30pm Mon-Wed, 11am-5pm Sun early Apr-Sep), built in 1723, once housed the park's ranger and now contains a collection of 700 works of art (medieval and Renaissance paintings, porcelain, silverware, tapestries) amassed by Julius Wernher (1850–1912), a German-born railway engineer's son who struck it rich in the diamond fields of South Africa in the 19th century. The Spanish Renaissance **jewellery collection** is the best in Europe, and the **rose garden** fronting the house defies description.

PRIME TARGET

On 15 February 1894, the Royal Observatory was the unexpected target of an anarchist bomb plot. The bomber – a 26-year old French anarchist by the name of Martial Bourdin – managed to blow his left hand off in the bungled attack, and died from his wounds soon afterwards. The choice of the Royal Observatory as a target was never understood, but it was undamaged in the attack. The bombing later found literary recognition in Joseph Conrad's novel *The Secret Agent*.

The Greenwich Meridian was selected as the global Prime Meridian at the International Meridian Conference in Washington D.C. in 1884. Greenwich therefore became the world's common zero for longitude and standard for time calculations, replacing the multiple meridians that had previously existed. Greenwich was assisted in its bid by the earlier US adoption of Greenwich Mean Time for its own national time zones. Furthermore, the majority of world trade already used sea charts that identified Greenwich as the Prime Meridian.

GREENWICH & SOUTH LONDON ROYAL OBSERVATORY & GREENWICH PARK

TOP SIGHTS
OLD ROYAL NAVAL COLLEGE

When Christopher Wren was commissioned by William and Mary to construct a naval hospital here in 1692, he conceived it in two separate halves to protect the river views from the Queen's House, Inigo Jones' miniature masterpiece to the south. Built on the site of the Old Palace of Placentia, where Henry VIII was born in 1491, the hospital was initially intended for those wounded in the victory over the French at La Hogue. In 1869 the building was converted to a Naval College; today it is home to the University of Greenwich and Trinity College of Music, with two main rooms open to the public.

DON'T MISS...
➡ Painted Hall
➡ Nelson Room
➡ Chapel

PRACTICALITIES
➡ Map p463
➡ ☎8269 4747
➡ www.oldroyalnaval college.org
➡ King William Walk SE10
➡ admission free
➡ ⍰Greenwich or DLR Cutty Sark

Painted Hall

Designed as a dining hall for sailors, the **Painted Hall** (☺10am-5pm) in the King William Building is one of Europe's greatest banquet rooms, dressed in decorative 'allegorical Baroque' murals by artist James Thornhill, who also painted the cupola of St Paul's Cathedral. The magnificent ceiling mural above the Lower Hall is a feast, showing William and Mary enthroned amid symbols of the Virtues. Beneath William's feet grovels the defeated French king Louis XIV, furled flag in hand. Head up to the Upper Hall where, on the western wall, George I is depicted with his family. Children can embark on an animal trail to identify over 180 creatures in Thornhill's decorations.

Off the Upper Hall is the **Nelson Room**, originally designed by Nicholas Hawksmoor. In January 1806 the brandy-soaked (for embalming purposes, of course) body of the great naval hero lay in state here before his funeral at St Paul's. Today the room contains a plaster replica of the statue atop Nelson's column in Trafalgar Square, plus other memorabilia, including lots of hospital silver. Look to the courtyard through the window; the cobbles form an outline of the Union Flag (Union Jack).

A 90-minute **guided tour** (☎8269 4791; adult/child £5/free; ☺tours 11.30am & 2pm) from the Painted Hall will take you to places not normally open to the public: the Jacobean undercroft of the former Placentia palace and the 140-year-old Victorian Skittle Alley, featuring enormous hand-carved wooden bowling balls and pins.

Chapel

With its mix of ancient Greek and naval motifs, the beautiful **chapel** (☺10am-5pm Mon-Sat, 12.30-5pm Sun) in the Queen Mary Building is decorated in an elaborate rococo style with turquoise, gold and fawn to the fore. The eastern end of the chapel is dominated by a painting by the 18th-century American artist Benjamin West showing *The Preservation of St Paul after Shipwreck at Malta*. If possible come on the first Sunday of the month, when there's a free 50-minute **organ recital** at 3pm, or time your visit for sung Eucharist at 11am on Sunday.

Discover Greenwich

The new and mildly-diverting **Discover Greenwich** (The Pepys Bldg, King William Walk; ☺10am-5pm; admission free) exhibition delves into the history of Greenwich with models and hands-on exhibits, many aimed at children. The Greenwich Tourist Information Centre is also here. If you need a drink or a bite to eat, pop into the Old Brewery (p282) next door.

👁 SIGHTS

Greenwich

ROYAL OBSERVATORY
See p270.

GREENWICH PARK
See p271.

 FREE QUEEN'S HOUSE   HISTORIC BUILDING

Map p463 (☑8858 4422, recorded information 8312 6565; www.nmm.ac.uk/places/queens-house; Romney Rd SE10; ⏰10am-5pm; 🚇Greenwich or DLR Cutty Sark; 🚱) The first Palladian building by architect Inigo Jones after he returned from Italy, what was at first called the 'House of Delight' is indeed far more enticing than the art collection it contains, even though it includes some Turners, Holbeins, Hogarths and Gainsboroughs. The house was begun in 1616 for Anne of Denmark, wife of James I, but was not completed until 1638, when it became the home of Charles I and his queen, Henrietta Maria. The ceremonial **Great Hall** is the principal room – a gorgeous cube shape, with an elaborately tiled floor dating to 1637; the ceiling was originally decorated with nine paintings by Orazio Gentileshci. The beautiful helix-shaped **Tulip Staircase** (named for the flowers on the wrought-iron balustrade; sadly no photos allowed) leads to a gallery on level 2, hung with paintings and portraits with a sea or seafaring theme from the National Maritime Museum's fine art collection. Look out for the strikingly modernist *Sixty Degrees South* by Herbert Barnard John Everett.

CUTTY SARK   SHIP
Map p463 (☑8858 2698; www.cuttysark.org.uk; Cutty Sark Gardens SE10; 🚇Greenwich or DLR Cutty Sark) This Greenwich landmark, the last of the great clipper ships to sail between China and England in the 19th century, was due to reopen in spring 2012 after serious fire damage. Luckily half of the ship's furnishings and equipment, including the mast, had been removed for conservation at the time of the conflagration.

FAN MUSEUM   MUSEUM
Map p463 (☑8305 1441, 8858 7879; www.fan-museum.org; 12 Crooms Hill SE10; adult/child

---

👁 TOP SIGHTS
NATIONAL MARITIME MUSEUM

Narrating the long and eventful history of seafaring Britain, this museum is one of Greenwich's top attractions. Museum space increased with the Sammy Ofer Wing, which opened in late 2011.

The exhibits are arranged thematically and highlights include **Miss Britain III** (the first boat to top 100mph on open water) from 1933, the 19m-long **golden state barge** built in 1732 for Frederick, Prince of Wales, and the huge ship's propeller installed on level 1. The museum also owns the uniform coat that Britain's greatest seafaring hero, Horatio Nelson, was wearing when he was fatally shot (and the actual bullet), plus a replica of the lifeboat used by explorer Ernest Shackleton and some of his men after the *Endurance* sank on their epic mission in Antarctica. The restored stained glass from the **Baltic Exchange**, blown up by the IRA in 1992, is now a memorial to the victims of WWI.

The **Your Ocean** exhibit on level 1 examines the science, history, health and future of the sea. On level 2, kids will love firing a cannon in the All Hands exhibit or manoeuvring a tanker into port by using the Bridge Simulator. Tours depart from the ship's propeller at noon, 1pm and 3pm.

DON'T MISS...
➡ Frederick's golden state barge
➡ Nelson's uniform coat
➡ *Miss Britain III*
➡ Stained glass window from *Baltic Exchange*

PRACTICALITIES
➡ Map p463
➡ ☑8858 4422
➡ www.nmm.ac.uk
➡ Romney Rd SE10
➡ admission free
➡ ⏰10am-5pm
➡ 🚇Greenwich or DLR Cutty Sark

Parks & Gardens

Glance at a colour map of town and be struck by how much is olive green. London has some of the world's most superb urban parkland: most of it well-tended, accessible and a delight in any season.

Hyde Park

1 Perhaps London's most famous and easily-accessed expanse of urban greenery, Hyde Park is astonishing for the variety of its landscapes and trees. The Serpentine separates it from that other grand London park, Kensington Gardens.

Victoria Park

2 Named after its eponymous royal benefactor, Victoria Park is one of East London's most pleasant and popular parks and has recently had an expensive regeneration. In summer it becomes a venue for live music and festivals.

Kew Gardens

3 To fall for Kew Gardens, all you need is an eye for fine architecture, a fondness for exploration and a sense of natural curiosity and aesthetics. Children will adore the treetop walkway and winter iceskating.

Richmond Park

4 An epic expanse of greenery down southwest, royal Richmond Park is home to herds of deer, sublime views, a fantastic collection of trees, ponds, woodland and grass. Fling off the urban fumes and immerse yourself in its wild expanses.

Greenwich Park

5 Delightfully hilly, elegantly landscaped and bisected by the Meridian Line, Greenwich Park offers sweeping views from its highest point. London's oldest enclosed royal park, it is home to herds of

Clockwise from top left
1. Hyde Park (p192) 2. Victoria Park (p221) 3. Princess of Wales Conservatory, Kew Gardens (p296)
4. Richmond Park (p298)

TOP SIGHTS
IMPERIAL WAR MUSEUM

Fronted by a pair of intimidating 15in naval guns, this riveting museum is housed in what was once Bethlehem Royal Hospital, also known as Bedlam. Although the museum's focus is on military action involving British or Commonwealth troops during the 20th century, it rolls out the carpet to war in the wider sense. There's not just Lawrence of Arabia's 1000cc motorbike, but a **German V-2 rocket**, a Sherman tank and a lifelike replica of **Little Boy** (the atom bomb dropped on Hiroshima).

In the **Trench Experience** on the lower ground floor you walk through the grim reality of life on the Somme front line in WWI; the **Blitz Experience** has you cowering inside a mock bomb shelter during a WWII air raid before emerging through ravaged East End streets.

In **Secret War** on the first floor there's an intriguing rifle through the operations of the Secret Operations Executive (SOE), such as rubber soles resembling feet worn underneath boots to leave 'foot prints' on enemy beaches.

The two most harrowing sections are the extensive **Holocaust Exhibition** (not recommended for under 14s) on the third floor, and the stark **Crimes against Humanity** on the second floor.

DON'T MISS...
➡ Holocaust Exhibition
➡ Crimes against Humanity exhibition
➡ Blitz Experience
➡ German V-2
➡ Spitfire

PRACTICALITIES
➡ Map p462
➡ www.iwm.org.uk
➡ Lambeth Rd SE1
➡ admission free
➡ ⊙10am-6pm
➡ ⊖Lambeth North

£4/3; ⊙11am-5pm Tue-Sat, noon-5pm Sun; ⊞Greenwich or DLR Cutty Sark; ☎) The world's only museum entirely devoted to fans has a wonderful collection of ivory, tortoiseshell, peacock-feather and folded-fabric examples alongside kitsch battery-powered versions and huge ornamental Welsh fans. The temporary exhibits on the 1st floor are often choice; consult the website for details of fan-making classes. The setting, an 18th-century Georgian town house, also has a Japanese-style garden plus the **Orangery** (half-/full tea £5/6; ⊙3-5pm Tue & Sun), with lovely trompe l'œil murals and twice-weekly afternoon tea.

ST ALFEGE CHURCH
CHURCH
Map p463 (www.st-alfege.org; Church St SE10; admission free; ⊙10am-4pm Mon-Sat, 1-4pm Sun; ⊞Greenwich or DLR Cutty Sark) Designed by Nicholas Hawksmoor in 1714 to replace a 12th-century building, this glorious parish church features a restored mural by James Thornhill (whose work includes the Painted Hall at the Royal Naval College and St Paul's Cathedral), a largely wood-panelled interior and an intriguing 'Tallis' keyboard with middle keyboard octaves from the Tudor period.

O2
CONCERT VENUE
Map p421 (⊘8463 2000, bookings 0844 856 0202; www.theo2.co.uk; Millennium Way SE10; ⊖North Greenwich) The 380m-wide circular O2 cost £750 million to build and more than £5 million a year just to keep it erect. Once the definitive white elephant, it has hosted big acts like Madonna, Prince, Justin Timberlake and Barbara Streisand in its 23,000-seat **O2 Arena** and soul, pop and jazz bands in the 2350-seat **IndigO2**. Massive exhibitions (Tutankhamen and the Golden Age of the Pharaohs, The Human Body) and sporting events have made their temporary homes here, as well as a slew of bars, clubs and restaurants. During the Olympics, this venue will host the basketball and gymnastics events as the North Greenwich Arena.

BRITISH MUSIC EXPERIENCE
MUSEUM
(⊘0844 847 1761; www.britishmusicexperience.com; Millennium Way SE10; adult/child £15/12; ⊙11am-7.30pm; ⊖North Greenwich) This musical attraction in the O2 'bubble' traces the history of British popular music from 1945 to the present day. There's star-studded memorabilia: eye up Paul Weller's custom-made pop art Rickenbacker 330

guitar, David Bowie's Station to Station thin white duke togs and Duffy's Rockferry jacket. Film yourself playing guitar or pick up dance moves from a virtual instructor before standing next to holograms performing before a massive cheering (filmed) audience.

⊙ Charlton & Woolwich

FIREPOWER (ROYAL ARTILLERY MUSEUM) MUSEUM
(📞8855 7755; www.firepower.org.uk; Royal Arsenal, Woolwich SE18; adult/child £5.30/2.50; ⏰10.30am-5pm Wed-Sun; DLR Woolwich Arsenal, ⊖North Greenwich then 🚌161 or 472, DLR Cutty Sark then 🚌177 or 180) Loud and reeking of adrenaline – kids can't get enough of it – Firepower is an explosive display of the

evolution of artillery. The History Gallery traces artillery's development from catapults to nuclear warheads, while the multimedia, smoke-filled Field of Fire immerses you in the experience of artillery gunners from WWI to Bosnia in a 15-minute extravaganza. There's a Gunnery Hall packed with weapons and vehicles from the 20th century and the chance to take shots on a firing range, and take charge of a remote-control tank in the Camo Zone (£1.50 each, or £4.50 for four).

FREE GREENWICH HERITAGE CENTRE MUSEUM
(www.greenwichheritage.org; Royal Arsenal, Artillery Sq SE18; ⏰9am-5pm Tue-Sat; DLR Woolwich Arsenal, ⊖North Greenwich then 🚌161 or 472, DLR Cutty Sark then 🚌177 or 180) Next door to Firepower, this well-endowed centre

GREENWICH & SOUTH LONDON SIGHTS

WORTH A DETOUR

THAMES BARRIER

This sci-fi looking barrier is designed to protect London from flooding and, with rising sea levels and surge tides, vulnerable London is likely to become increasingly dependent on the barricade. Completed three decades ago, the barrier consists of 10 movable gates anchored to nine concrete piers, each as tall as a five-storey building. The silver roofs on the piers house the operating machinery that rotates the gates against excess water. Tested monthly, they make a glitteringly surreal sight, straddling the river in the lee of a giant warehouse.

London needs a flood barrier because water levels have been rising by as much as 60cm per century, while the river itself has been narrowing; furthermore, southeastern England is slowly tilting downwards at up to 2.1mm per year in a geological process known as 'isostatic rebound'. All of these factors combine to create major flood risks in London.

The Thames tide rises and falls quite harmlessly twice a day, and once a fortnight there's also a stronger 'spring' tide. The danger comes when the spring tide coincides with an unexpected surge, which pushes tons of extra water upriver. The barrier has been built to prevent that water pouring over the riverbanks and flooding nearby houses. Today environmentalists are already talking about a bigger, wider damming mechanism further towards the mouth of the river, before the current barrier comes to the expected end of its design life in 2030.

The barrier looks best when raised, and the only guaranteed time this happens is once a month, when the mechanisms are checked. For exact dates and times, contact the **Thames Barrier Information Centre** (📞8305 4188; 1 Unity Way SE18; adult/child £3.50/2; ⏰10.30am-5pm Apr-Sep, 11am-3.30pm Oct-Mar; ⊖North Greenwich, then 🚌472 or 161 or 🚇Charlton, then 🚌472).

If you're coming from central London, take a train to Charlton from Charing Cross or London Bridge. Then walk along Woolwich Rd to Eastmoor St, which leads northward to the centre. If you're coming from Greenwich, you can pick up bus 177 or 180 along Romney Rd and get off at the Thames Barrier stop (near Holborn College on Woolwich Rd). The closest tube station is North Greenwich, from where you can pick up bus 472 or 161. Boats also travel to and from the barrier, although they don't land here. For details see p395.

GREENWICH ARCHITECTURE

Greenwich is home to an extraordinary interrelated cluster of classical buildings. All the great architects of the Enlightenment made their mark here, largely due to royal patronage. In the early 17th century, Inigo Jones built one of England's first classical Renaissance homes, the Queen's House, which still stands today. Charles II was particularly fond of the area and had Sir Christopher Wren build both the Royal Observatory and part of the Royal Naval College, which John Vanbrugh then completed in the early 17th century.

examines the history of the Royal Arsenal and Woolwich Dockyards, with vivid eye-witness televised testimonials by former employees and local residents. Don't miss the stunning Millennium Embroideries, eight stitched panels from 1998 representing key periods in local history from the Celts and Romans to the late 20th century, at least one of which should be on display.

⊙ Lambeth

LAMBETH PALACE   HISTORICAL BUILDING

Map p462 (Palace Rd SE1; ⊖Lambeth North) This gorgeous red-brick Tudor gatehouse located beside the church of St Mary-at-Lambeth leads to Lambeth Palace, the London residence of the Archbishop of Canterbury. Although the palace is not usually open to the public, the gardens occasionally are; check with a tourist office for more details (see p402).

GARDEN MUSEUM   MUSEUM

Map p462 (☑7401 8865; www.gardenmuseum. org.uk; St Mary-at-Lambeth, Lambeth Palace Rd SE1; adult/concession £7/6; ☺10.30am-5pm Sun-Fri, 10.30am-4pm Sat; ⊖Lambeth North) Housed in the church of St Mary-at-Lambeth, this peaceful, green-fingered museum's trump card is its charming **knot garden**, a replica of a 17th-century formal garden, with topiary hedges clipped into an intricate, twirling design. Keen gardeners will enjoy the displays on the 17th-century Tradescant *père* and *fils* – a father-and-son team who were gardeners to Charles I and Charles II,

globetrotters and enthusiastic collectors of exotic plants (they introduced the pineapple to London). Captain William Bligh (of mutinous *Bounty* fame) is buried here (he lived and died nearby at 100 Lambeth Rd). The excellent **cafe** serves vegetarian food. Temporary exhibitions are also staged and tours are reserved for the last Tuesday of the month at 2pm.

FLORENCE NIGHTINGALE
MUSEUM   MUSEUM

Map p462 (☑7620 0374; www.florence-nightingale.co.uk; St Thomas's Hospital, 2 Lambeth Palace Rd SE1; adult/concession £5.80/4.80; ☺10am-5pm; ⊖Westminster or Waterloo; ☎) Attached to St Thomas's Hospital, this small, recently refurbished museum tells the story of feisty war heroine Florence Nightingale (1820–1910), who led a team of nurses to Turkey in 1854 during the Crimean War. There she worked to improve conditions for the soldiers before returning to London to set up a training school for nurses at St Thomas's in 1859. So popular did she become that baseball-card-style photos of the gentle 'Lady of the Lamp' were sold during her lifetime. There is no shortage of revisionist detractors who dismiss her as a 'canny administrator' and 'publicity hound'; Nightingale was, in fact, one of the world's first modern celebrities. But the fact remains she improved conditions for thousands of soldiers in the field and saved quite a few lives in the process. We can hardly think of a more glorious achievement. An audioguide is included in the admission price.

⊙ Battersea & Wandsworth

BATTERSEA PARK   PARK

Map p460 (www.batterseapark.org; ☺dawn-dusk; ☒Battersea Park) With its Henry Moore and Barbara Hepworth sculptures, these 50 hectares of gorgeous greenery stretch between Albert and Chelsea Bridges. The park's tranquil appearance belies a bloody past: it was the site of an assassination attempt on King Charles II in 1671 and of a duel in 1829 between the Duke of Wellington and an opponent who accused him of treason. The **Peace Pagoda**, erected in 1985 by a group of Japanese Buddhists to commemorate Hiroshima Day, displays the Buddha in the four stages of his life.

Refurbishment has seen the 19th-century landscaping reinstated and the grand riverside terraces spruced up. At the same time, the Festival of Britain pleasure gardens, including the spectacular Vista Fountains, have been restored. There are lakes, plenty of sporting facilities (including all-weather football pitches), an art space called the **Pump House Gallery** (Map p460; ☑8871 7572; www.wandsworth.gov.uk/gallery; Battersea Park SW11; admission free; ⊙11am-5pm Wed, Thu & Sun, 11am-4pm Fri & Sat) and a small **Children's Zoo** (Map p460; ☑7924 5826; www.batterseaparkzoo.co.uk; adult/child £7.95/6.50; ⊙10am-5.30pm Apr-Oct, to 4.30pm Nov-Mar). For funky horizontal biking around the grounds for kids and grown-ups, contact **London Recumbents** (☑7498 6543; per hr £7-15; ⊙Sat & Sun year round, daily in school holidays) in the northeast of the park.

BATTERSEA POWER STATION
HISTORIC BUILDING

Map p460 (www.batterseapowerstation.com; ☒Battersea Park) Its four smokestacks famously celebrated on Pink Floyd's *Animals* album cover, Battersea Power Station is one of south London's best known monuments. Built by Giles Gilbert Scott in 1933 with two chimneys (the other two were added in 1955), the power station was snuffed out in 1983 only to enter an existential limbo, slowly deteriorating as it passed from one optimistic developer to the next. The power station's future seems as uncertain as ever, with another 'master plan' in the pipeline.

WANDSWORTH COMMON
COMMON

(☒Wandsworth Common or Clapham Junction) Wilder and more overgrown than the nearby common in Clapham, Wandsworth Common is full of couples pushing prams on a sunny day. On the western side is a pleasant collection of streets known as the **toast rack**, because of their alignment. Baskerville, Dorlcote, Henderson, Nicosia, Patten and Routh Rds are lined with Georgian houses. There's a blue plaque at 3 Routh Rd, home to the former British prime minister David Lloyd George.

⊙ Clapham

CLAPHAM COMMON
COMMON

Map p460 (⊖Clapham Common) A magnificent expanse of green at the heart of the Clapham neighbourhood, huge Clapham Com-

TOP SIGHTS
HORNIMAN MUSEUM

Comprising the original collection of wealthy tea merchant Frederick John Horniman, this is a treasure-trove of discoveries, from a huge stuffed walrus to slowly undulating jellyfish, a fierce papier maché statue of Kali and a knock-out music exhibition.

On the ground and 1st floors is the **Natural History Gallery**, with animal skeletons and pickled specimens. When the magnificent 19th century **apostle clock** strikes 4pm, the apostles troop out past Jesus and only Judas turns away from him. Children adore the ground floor shop and the honey-bee hive in the **Nature Base**.

On the lower ground floor you'll find the **African Worlds Gallery**, and the **Music Gallery** displays instruments from 3500-year-old Egyptian clappers and early English keyboards, to Indonesian gamelan and Ghanaian drums, with touch screens so you can hear what they sound like and videos to see them being played in situ. The **aquarium** (adult/child £2/1) in the basement is small but state of the art. The cafe, with seating in the stunning conservatory, is a delight, as are the 6.5 hectares of magnificent hillside **gardens** (⊙7.30am-dusk Mon-Sat, from 8am Sun). Contact the museum for details of fun sleepovers at the Horniman.

DON'T MISS...
➡ Aquarium
➡ Music Gallery
➡ Gardens & Conservatory
➡ Apostle Clock
➡ Nature Base
➡ Shop

PRACTICALITIES
➡ ☑8699 1872
➡ www.horniman.ac.uk
➡ 100 London Rd SE23
➡ admission free
➡ ⊙10.30am-5.30pm
➡ ⊖Forest Hill

mon is a verdant venue for many outdoor summer events (see http://claphamhigh-street.co.uk) and sports. The main thoroughfare, Clapham High St, starts at the common's northeastern edge, lined with many of the bars, restaurants and shops that draw people to Clapham. It's much more pleasant to explore the more upmarket streets of **Clapham Old Town**, a short distance northwest of the tube station, and **Clapham Common North Side** at the common's northwesternmost edge.

Just west of the Pavement, the brick and stone **Holy Trinity Church** (1776) was home to the Clapham Sect, a group of wealthy evangelical Christians that included William Wilberforce, a leading antislavery campaigner, active between 1790 and 1830. The sect also campaigned against child labour and for prison reform.

⊙ Kennington, Oval & Stockwell

KENNINGTON PARK PARK

Map p462 (⊖Oval) This unprepossessing space of green has a great rabble-rousing tradition. Originally a common, where all were permitted entry, it served as a speakers' corner for South London. During the 18th century, Jacobite rebels trying to restore the Stuart monarchy were hanged, drawn and quartered here, and in the 18th and 19th centuries preachers used to deliver hellfire-and-brimstone speeches to large audiences; John Wesley, founder of Methodism and an antislavery advocate, is said to have attracted some 30,000 followers. After the great Chartist rally on 10 April 1848, where millions of working-class people turned out to demand the same voting rights as the middle classes, the Royal Family promptly fenced off the common as a park.

THE OVAL CRICKET GROUND

Map p462 (☑0871 246 1100; www.kiaoval.com; Surrey County Cricket Club SE11; international match £15-103, county £12-20; ⊙booking office 9.30am-12.30pm & 1.30-4pm Mon-Fri Apr-Sep; ⊖Oval) Home to the Surrey County Cricket Club, the Brit Oval is London's second cricketing venue after Lord's (p239). As well as Surrey matches, it also regularly hosts international test matches. The season runs from April to September.

⊙ TOP SIGHTS
ELTHAM PALACE

This art deco house was built between 1933 and 1937 by the textile merchant Stephen Courtauld (of Courtauld Institute fame) and his wife Virginia. From the impressive entrance hall with its dome and huge circular carpet with geometric shapes, to the black-marble dining room with silver-foil ceiling and burlwood-veneer fireplace, it appears the couple had taste as well as money. They also, rather fashionably for the times, had a pet lemur; the heated cage, complete with tropical murals and a bamboo ladder leading to the ground floor for the spoiled (and vicious) 'Mah-jongg' is also on view. Hour-long art deco **tours** (£12.30 incl admission; ⊙11.30am & 2pm) run periodically from April to October, but book well ahead.

A royal palace was built on this site in 1305 and was for a time the boyhood home of Henry VIII, before the Tudors decamped to Greenwich. Little of the palace remains, apart from the restored Great Medieval Hall. Its hammerbeam roof is generally rated the third best in the country, behind those at Westminster Hall (p90) and Hampton Court Palace (p293). The 8 hectares of gardens include a rockery and moat with working bridge.

DON'T MISS...

➡ Entrance Hall
➡ Dining Room

PRACTICALITIES

➡ www.english
-heritage.org.uk
➡ ⊙10am-5pm
Sun-Wed Apr-Oct,
11am-4pm Sun-Wed
Nov-late Dec, Feb
& Mar, closed late
Dec-Jan
➡ ⊠Eltham

◉ Brixton

BRIXTON NEIGHBOURHOOD

The years that most shaped contemporary Brixton were the post-WWII 'Windrush' years, when immigrants arrived from the West Indies. (*Windrush* was the name of one of the leading ships that brought these immigrants to the UK.) Economic decline and hostility between the police and particularly the black community led to riots in 1981, 1985 and 1995.

Although violence returned to Brixton during the London riots of August 2011, the mood today is upbeat. Soaring property prices have sent in house-hunters, and pockets of gentrification sit alongside the more run-down streets. Apart from some great restaurants and clubs, the big sights are the fantastic Brixton Village (p289) – a current south London culinary and shopping hotspot – and Brixton Market (p290).

◉ Dulwich & Forest Hill

DULWICH PICTURE GALLERY GALLERY

(☎8693 5254; www.dulwichpicturegallery.org.uk; Gallery Rd SE21; adult/child £5/free; ☺10am-5pm Tue-Fri, 11am-5pm Sat & Sun; ☒West Dulwich; ☻)
The UK's oldest public art gallery, the small Dulwich Picture Gallery was designed by the idiosyncratic architect Sir John Soane between 1811 and 1814 to house nearby Dulwich College's collection of paintings by Raphael, Rembrandt, Rubens, Reynolds, Gainsborough, Poussin, Lely, Van Dyck and others. Unusually, the collectors Noel Desenfans and painter Sir Peter Francis Bourgeois chose to have their mausoleums, lit by a moody *lumière mystérieuse* (mysterious light) created with tinted glass, placed among the pictures. In the Wolfson Room, seek out 'Bridge in an Italian Landscape' by Adam Pynacker, with its masterful use of light. Celebrating its bicentenary in 2011, the gallery's recent standout temporary exhibitions (additional £4 entry) have included the work of Norman Rockwell and Paul Nash. Free guided **tours** of the museum depart at 3pm on Saturday and Sunday. A cafe spills out onto the exquisite gardens to the rear, itself delightfully dotted with benches for sedentary enjoyment. Contact the gallery for details of art courses.

The museum is a 10-minute walk northwards along Gallery Rd, which starts

CHRIST'S CHAPEL

Part of the Edward Alleyn foundation and formerly the chapel of Alleyn's College of God's Gift, the gorgeous 17th century **Christ's Chapel** (☺1.30-3.30pm Tue) in the Dulwich Picture Gallery is permeated with the scent of seasoned wood. The wood-panelled chapel boasts an impressive copy of 'The Transfiguration' by Raphael. The chapel is only open on Tuesdays, for two hours in the afternoon.

almost opposite West Dulwich railway station. Bus P4 conveniently links the picture gallery with the Horniman Museum (p279).

DULWICH PARK PARK

(College Rd, SE21; ☺8am-dusk; ☒West Dulwich, North Dulwich) With its hectares of green space and much-loved bicycle hire putting fleets of novel, low-slung bikes under the feet of enthusiastic kids, Dulwich Park is one of London's most handsome and enjoyable parks. To find one of those nifty bikes everyone seems to be riding, head to **London Recumbents** (☎8299 6636; Ranger's Yard, Dulwich Park; per hr £7-15; ☺10am-dusk), near the Old College Gate in the west of the park, for your own set of head-turning wheels. The park playground is great for toddlers and sports enthusiasts. After exploring the park, exit onto College Rd by the Old College Gate in the west of the park for the Dulwich Picture Gallery and charming Dulwich Village.

✗ EATING

You may not be as spoiled for restaurant choice in South London as you are north of the Thames, but you can sit down to some supreme meals – Brixton has fantastic pizza, while you are simply guaranteed to run into a great meal in re-energised Brixton Village, busy attracting an almost ceaseless range of quality restaurants and cafes. Some of the restaurants in Battersea, Wandsworth and Clapham are simply destinations in their own right.

WORTH A DETOUR

DANSON HOUSE AND RED HOUSE

A couple of historic houses in Bexleyheath east of Eltham are well worth exploration. Highlights of **Danson House** (☎8303 6699; www.dansonhouse.org.uk; Danson Park, Bexleyheath DA6; adult/child/concession £6/free/5; ⊙11am-5pm Wed, Thu, Sun & bank holiday Mon late Mar-Oct, 11am-5pm Tue-Thu, Sun & bank holiday Mon Jun-Aug; Ⓡ Bexleyheath, then 20min walk southwest), a lovely Palladian villa dating to 1766, include the dining room's reliefs and frescoes celebrating love and romance; the library and music room, with its functioning organ; the dizzying spiral staircase; and the Victorian kitchens (open only occasionally). The English-style garden is a delight and you can hire boats on the large lake in Danson Park.

From the outside, **Red House** (☎8304 9878; www.nationaltrust.org.uk; 13 Red House Lane, Bexleyheath DA6; adult/child £7.20/3.60, gardens only adult/child 50p/free; ⊙11am-5pm Wed-Sun Mar-late Nov, 11am-5pm Fri-Sun late Nov- late-Dec; Ⓡ Bexleyheath, then 20min walk south), built by Victorian designer William Morris in 1859, conjures up a gingerbread house in stone. The nine rooms open to the public bear all the elements of the Arts and Crafts movement to which Morris adhered – a bit of Gothic art here, some religious symbolism there, an art nouveau–like sunburst over there. Furniture by Morris and the house's designer Philip Webb are in evidence, as are paintings and stained glass by Edward Burne-Jones. Entry prior to 1.30pm is by guided tour only, which must be pre-booked. The surrounding gardens were designed by Morris 'to clothe' the house. Don't miss the well with a conical roof inspired by the oast houses of nearby Kent.

✕ Greenwich

NEVADA STREET DELI — DELI £

Map p463 (www.nevadastreetdeli.co.uk; 8 Nevada St, SE10; ⊙9am-6pm; sandwiches £3.75-4; DLR Cutty Sark) There may be a sudden scramble for one of the few outside tables when the sun pops out, but this charming wedge-shaped space is a popular spot for sandwiches (especially bacon sandwiches), all-day breakfasts, mushrooms or gravadlax on toast, a plate of scrumptious handmade sausages in a wealth of varieties (smoked salmon, spinach and feta cheese) or merely a restorative cup of steaming coffee.

INSIDE — MODERN EUROPEAN ££

Map p463 (☎8265 5060; www.insiderestaurant.co.uk; 19 Greenwich South St SE10; mains £12.50-17.75, 2-/3-course set menu lunch £12.95/17.95, set menu early dinner £17.95/22.95; ⊙closed dinner Sun & all day Mon; DLR/Ⓡ Greenwich) With white walls, modern art and linen tablecloths, Inside is a relaxed kind of place and one of Greenwich's best restaurant offerings. The fine food hits the mark, ranging tastily and affordably from pumpkin and red lentil soup, to pan fried wild sea bass, and apple and rhubarb crumble.

GREENWICH MARKET — MARKET £

Map p463 (www.greenwichmarket.net; Greenwich Market, SE10; ⊙10am-5.30pm Wed, Sat & Sun; DLR Cutty Sark) Perfect for snacking your way through a world atlas of food while browsing the other market stalls, come here on Wednesdays, Saturdays and Sundays for delicious food-to go, from Spanish tapas to Thai curries, sushi, Polish doughnuts, French crêpes, Brazilian churros, smoked Louisiana sausages, chivitos and more; follow your nostrils and make your pick, and wash it all down with a glass of fresh farmhouse cider.

OLD BREWERY — MODERN BRITISH ££

Map p463 (☎3327 1280; Pepys Bldg, Old Royal Naval College, SE10; mains £11.50-26; ⊙cafe 10am-5pm Mon-Sun, restaurant 6-11pm Mon-Sat & 6-10.30pm Sun; DLR Cutty Sark) A working brewery with splendidly burnished 1000-litre copper vats at one end and a high ceiling lit with natural sunlight, the Old Brewery is perfectly located after staggering around Greenwich's top sights. Right next to the Discover Greenwich exhibition, it's a cafe by day, transforming into a restaurant in the evening, serving a choice selection of fine dishes carefully sourced from the best seasonal ingredients. The brickwork bar (p286) is an appetising prologue to dinner.

TAI WON MEIN   CHINESE £

Map p463 (39 Greenwich Church St, SE10; ⊙11.30am-11.30pm; mains from £4.95) The staff may be a bit jaded but this great snack spot – the Cantonese moniker just means 'Big Bowl of Noodles' – serves epic portions of carbohydrate-rich noodles to those overcoming Greenwich's titanic sights. Flavours are simple, but fresh, and the namesake *tai won mein* seafood noodles – with all manner of creatures from the deep hauled up to bob about in your broth – may have you applauding (but put your chopsticks down first).

SPREAD EAGLE   FRENCH ££

Map p463 (☑8853 2333; www.spreadeagle restaurant.co.uk; 1-2 Stockwell St SE10; set menu Sat & Sun 2-/3-course £12.95/15.95, lunch/early supper menu Mon-Fri 2-/3-course £16.50/19.50; DLR Cutty Sark) Smart, French-inspired restaurant opposite the Greenwich Theatre in what was once the terminus for the coach service to/from London.

✖ Brixton

TOP CHOICE FRANCO MANCA   ITALIAN £

Map p460 (☑7738 3021; www.francomanca. co.uk; 4 Market Row SW9; mains £4-6; ⊙noon-5pm Mon-Sat; ⊖Brixton) Voted as the best pizza in London by literally everybody, Franco Manca is worth coming specifically to Brixton for. Beat those queues by arriving early, avoiding lunch hours and Saturday, and delight in some fine, fine pizza. This place only uses its own sourdough (all made in the upstairs bakery with flour from a Neapolitan mill), fired up in a wood-burning 'tufae' brick oven. The choice of six excellent-value pizzas is all you need,

the source of every single delicious ingredient is accounted for – the vegetables are from a small London grocer, the organic olive oil brought from fincas in Spain and Sicily, the cheese is from Somerset, the tomatoes from Liguria in Italy and the meat from an independent London butcher. The beer and wine are organic (from Sussex and Piedmont, respectively) and the lemonade is homemade. Shame the opening times are so limiting. There's another branch in Chiswick (p304).

TOP CHOICE HONEST BURGERS   BURGERS £

Map p460 (www.honestburgers.co.uk; Unit 12, Brixton Village, Coldharbour Lane SW9; burgers from £6.50; ⊙noon-4pm Tue-Wed & Sun, noon-4pm & 6-10pm Thu-Sat; ⊖Brixton) This burger outfit has deftly hopped onto the enterprising Brixton Village bandwagon. Plaudits for their juicy and tender burgers and gloriously rosemary-seasoned triple-cooked chips have rained in from all corners and honest-to-God rightly so: they are well worth the wait for a table, which you could well have to do (it's titchy, seats around 30 and there are no bookings).

ROSIE'S DELI CAFÉ   CAFE £

Map p460 (www.rosiesdelicafe.com; 14e Market Row SW9; mains £4-6; ⊙9.30am-5.30pm Mon-Sat; ⊖Brixton) Park yourself on one of the mismatched wooden chairs at this much-loved Brixton cafe run by cook and author Rosie Lovell as it's a wholesome treat. She's certainly every bit as charming – and a real celebrity in Brixton Market and wider with her recipe book, *Spooning With Rosie* – and serves some fantastic cakes and biscuits. Quiches, wraps, ciabattas, sandwiches and steak and kidney pies also emerge from her kitchen.

CITY FARMS SOUTH

A couple of city farms (p33) – set up to introduce farmyard life to young urban tykes weaned on PlayStation – can be found south of the river. Full of farm animals, these farms are usually more popular with local people than with visitors, so they are a way of getting off the beaten track. Admission is always free (donations may be appreciated) and many have an education centre.

➡ **Surrey Docks Farm** (☑7231 1010; www.surreydocksfarm.org.uk; South Wharf, Rotherhithe St SE16; ⊙10am-5pm Tue-Sun; ⊖Rotherhithe) Working city farm on a 1 hectare site.

➡ **Vauxhall City Farm** (Map p462; ☑7582 4204; www.vauxhallcityfarm.org; 165 Tyers St SE11; ⊙10.30am-4pm Wed-Sun; ⊖Vauxhall) With more than 80 animals and riding opportunities.

WORTH A DETOUR

CRYSTAL PALACE PARK

Named after the prodigious glass and iron palace erected for the Great Exhibition in 1851 and moved here from Hyde Park in 1854, this huge **park** (⊖Crystal Palace, ⊠Crystal Palace) makes for intriguing exploration. Designed by Joseph Paxton, the palace burned down in 1936 with spectacular ferocity, the radiance of its conflagration visible across 10 counties. In just a few hours, the palace was reduced to a smoking ruin, its goldfish, which swam in the ornamental ponds 'missing – believed boiled', according to *The Times*. Winston Churchill, watching the destruction, lamented 'This is the end of an age'. Home of the first public flushing loos that cost 1p to use (possibly coining the British phrase 'to spend a penny'), nothing today remains of the Crystal Palace except the sublime Victorian terrace and its crumbling statues, including several weather-beaten sphinxes. Overlooked by the looming 219m-high transmitter tower, itself visible for miles around, the park is great for kids: hunt down the **stone dinosaurs** (carved by Benjamin Waterhouse Hawkins in 1854) in the southeast of the park, including the famously inaccurate Iguanodon; look out for the fun, restored but very low-standing **maze** (the original dated to 1870 and is London's largest maze); and in the west of the grounds, spend time moseying round the Victorian ruins of the terrace that supported the palace for over 80 years. Find out more about the palace at the **Crystal Palace Museum** (Anerley Hill; www.crystalpalacemuseum.org.uk; ⊙11am-4.30pm Sat & Sun; admission free) down Anerley Hill. To reach Crystal Palace from Rotherhithe, Forest Hill or Honor Oak Park, take an Overground train to Crystal Palace station.

FEDERATION COFFEE
CAFE **£**

Map p460 (Unit 46, Brixton Village SW9; ⊙8am-5pm Mon-Fri, 10am-5pm Sat, 9.30am-4pm Sun; ⊖Brixton) One of the fashionable new outlets in buzzing Brixton Village, funky Federation Coffee serves up cakes and a fantastic cup of coffee (with beans from micro-roastery Nude Espresso) in neat surroundings; it's an excellent spot to gauge the revitalized pulse of Brixton Village.

ASMARA
NORTH AFRICAN **£**

Map p460 (⊉7737 4144; 386 Coldharbour La SW9; mains £6.50-9, 6-/7-course set meals £27/28; ⊙5.30pm-late; ⊖Brixton) A rare Eritrean restaurant, unpretentious Asmara serves spicy chicken, lamb and beef stews and vegetable/vegan dishes that you scoop up with *injera,* the flat, slightly spongy sourdough bread that is a national dish. Staff add colour with traditional costumes, while the traditional *messob* meat dinner (£32 for two) with traditional coffee ceremony is pure enjoyment.

✕ Battersea & Wandsworth

TOP CHOICE CHEZ BRUCE
FRENCH **£££**

(⊉8672 0114; www.chezbruce.co.uk; 2 Bellevue Rd SW17; 3-4 course set menus £27.50-35; ⊠Wandsworth Common) Though Michelin -starred, Chez Bruce still insists on a winning quality local feel that accommodates all comers. The rustic facade, beside leafy Wandsworth Common, belies a crisp modern interior; the wine list is an all-star cast, the food sublime.

BUTCHER & GRILL
BRITISH **££**

Map p460 (www.thebutcherandgrill.com; 39-41 Parkgate Rd SW11; mains £6.50-48.50; ⊙closed dinner Sun; ⊖Sloane Sq, then ☐19 or 319; ⊛) This combi grill and butcher shop puts freshness to the fore and while not every carnivore wants to see their meat *au naturel* on entry, the quality of the ingredients, the wide choice of sauces and the views from the main dining room (all brickwork and exposed ducts) are more than compensation. Occasional live jazz and blues.

SANTA MARIA DEL SUR
ARGENTINE **££**

Map p460 (www.santamariadelsur.co.uk; 129 Queenstown Rd SW8; mains £10-23; ⊙lunch Sat & Sun, dinner daily; ⊠Queenstown Rd or Battersea Park, ☐77, 137 or 345) Catering to carnivores with grilled meats and sausages (and some token vegie dishes). Go for one of the *parrilladas* (mixed grill; £18 to £27.50 per person) to share.

✖ Clapham

TRINITY
TOP CHOICE
BRITISH **£££**

Map p460 (⌨7622 1199; www.trinityrestaurant.co.uk; 4 The Polygon, SW4; 3-course lunch menu £20, mains £17-45; ⊖Clapham Common) Named after the nearby church, Adam Byatt's good-looking Clapham Old Town restaurant is a light and delectable spot near the common. Service, attentive and unobtrusive, delivers a strong wine list and a mouth-watering menu displaying considerable culinary artistry; the Cornish plaice and mussels or the slow-cooked bavette are both delicious. A local classic, Trinity sees many returnees and also runs masterclasses in cookery. Reservations recommended.

MACARON BOULANGERIE & PATISSERIE
BAKERY **£**

Map p460 (22 The Pavement, SW4; ⊙7.30am-7pm Mon-Fri, 8am-7pm Sat, 9am-7pm Sun; ⊖Clapham Common) Among the spray of gift shops, cafes and delis along The Pavement, this gracious Parisian-style boulangerie welcomes with vast glass windows, an inviting sense of Gallic charm and a scattering of seats flung out front for delicious views of the common. The pastries, baguettes, croissants and ice creams are all tasty and tip-top fresh. Interlopers from other parts of town love it almost as much as locals.

✖ Kennington, Oval & Stockwell

LOBSTER POT
SEAFOOD **££**

Map p462 (www.lobsterpotrestaurant.co.uk; 3 Kennington Lane SE11; mains £16-23; ⊙closed Mon; ⊖Kennington or Elephant & Castle) This charming French-owned restaurant hidden in the wastelands south of Elephant & Castle reels in diners hook, line and sinker with finely prepared fish and seafood dishes *à la française* (think lashings of butter and garlic). An eight-course tasting menu with/without lobster is £50/45.

KENNINGTON TANDOORI
INDIAN **££**

Map p462 (www.kenningtontandoori.com; 313 Kennington Rd SE11; mains £7.95-13.95; ⊖Kennington) This local curry house is a favourite of MPs from across the river.

✖ Dulwich & Forest Hill

PIZZA EXPRESS
PIZZA **£**

(⌨8693 9333; 94 Dulwich Village, SE21; ⊙11.30am-11pm Sun-Thu, 11.30am-midnight Fri & Sat; mains £6.95-11.50; ⓘ) After feasting on art at the Dulwich Picture Gallery or cycling round Dulwich Park, this petite two-floor eatery is ideally located at the tranquil heart of Dulwich Village. Other local restaurants come and go or change hands but it may take some culinary imagination to unseat this perennially popular outpost of the chain. Kids are always more than welcome and service is always sprightly and efficient; reservations recommended.

☕ DRINKING & NIGHTLIFE

If you're looking for old-school pubs, this part of London can oblige – and will throw in some wonderful views to boot. We'd steer clear of the new bars in the area looking to accommodate recent arrivals – stick to traditional boozers and you can't go wrong. Of course there are always exceptions and we include at least one here.

☕ Greenwich

GREENWICH UNION
TOP CHOICE
PUB

Map p463 (www.greenwichunion.com; 56 Royal Hill SE10; DLR Cutty Sark) The award-winning Union plies six or seven local microbrewery beers, including raspberry and wheat varieties, and a strong list of ales, plus bottled international brews. It's a handsome place, with duffed up leather armchairs and a welcoming long, narrow aspect that leads to the conservatory and beer garden at the rear.

MUSIC FESTIVAL

The **Greenwich International Early Music Festival and Exhibition** (www.earlymusicfestival.com) – the world's largest celebration of early music – is held at the Old Royal Naval College in November.

CUTTY SARK TAVERN PUB

Map p463 (www.cuttysarktavern.co.uk; 4-6 Ballast Quay SE10; DLR Cutty Sark, 🚌177 or 180) Housed in a delightful bow-windowed, wood-beamed Georgian building directly on the Thames, the Cutty Sark is one of the few independent pubs left in Greenwich. Half a dozen cask-conditioned ales on tap line the bar, with an inviting riverside sitting-out area opposite. It's a 15-minute walk from the DLR station or hop on a bus along Trafalgar Rd and walk north.

TRAFALGAR TAVERN PUB

Map p463 (www.trafalgartavern.co.uk; 6 Park Row SE10; ⊙noon-11pm Mon-Thu, to midnight Fri & Sat, to 10.30pm Sun; DLR Cutty Sark) Lapped by the brown waters of the Thames, this cavernous pub with big windows looking onto the river is steeped in history. Dickens apparently knocked back a few here – and used it as the setting for the wedding breakfast scene in *Our Mutual Friend* – and prime ministers Gladstone and Disraeli used to dine on the pub's celebrated whitebait, when the start of the season was so keenly anticipated that Parliament would suspend sitting for a day. Try to make a beeline for a seat in the big bay window if you can.

OLD BREWERY BAR

Map p463 (Pepys Bldg, Old Royal Naval College, SE10; ⊙11am-11pm Mon-Sat, noon-10.30pm Sun; DLR Cutty Sark) Handily situated within the grounds of the old Royal Naval College, the brickwork bar at the Old Brewery is run by the Meantime Brewery, selling its own brew draught Imperial Pale Ale (brewed on site), along with a heady range of over 50 beers, from Belgian Trappist ales to fruity and flavoured brews, smoked beers and a wide-ranging menu of much more, with tables outside in the courtyard.

GREENWICH FOOT TUNNEL

Completed in 1902, the historic sub-river 370m-long foot tunnel (Map p463) running under the Thames from the Isle of Dogs is a fun way to travel. The lifts (under repair at the time of writing) down to the tunnel run between 7am and 7pm Monday to Saturday and 10am and 5.30pm on Sunday. Otherwise you're facing between 88 and 100 steps down and – shudder – up (open 24 hours).

MAYFLOWER PUB

(☎7237 4088; 117 Rotherhithe St SE16; ⊖Rotherhithe) Northwest of Deptford in Rotherhithe, this 15th-century pub, originally called the Shippe but rebuilt and renamed the Spread Eagle in the 18th century, is now named after the vessel that took the pilgrims to America in 1620; US visitors might want to make their own pilgrimage here. The ship set sail from Rotherhithe, and Captain Christopher Jones supposedly charted out its course here while supping schooners. There's seating on a small back terrace, from which you can view the Thames.

🍷 Brixton

Brixton remains one of the most vibrant and exciting places to go out drinking in South London.

EFFRA PUB

Map p460 (38A Kellet Rd SW2; ⊖Brixton) Behind the black, gold and cream exterior is a lovely old boozer that brings you closer to the heart of the Brixton Caribbean vibe than any other pub in the area, thanks to the spicy Jamaican menu, lively local regulars and live jazz in the evenings. A lovely garden with palm trees is out back, while the interior is all shabby and charming Victorian splendour.

DOGSTAR DJ BAR

Map p460 (☎7733 7515; www.antic-ltd.com/dogstar; 389 Coldharbour Lane SW9; ⊙4-11pm Tue, 4pm-2am Wed & Thu, 4pm-4am Fri, noon-4am Sat, noon-10.30pm Sun; ⊖Brixton) Downstairs, this long-running local institution has a cavernous DJ bar, mobbed by a young South London crowd. The main bar is as casual as you'd expect from a converted pub – comfortable sofas, big wooden tables – so dressing to kill is not obligatory. You'll have to push your way through the huge downstairs bar of this converted pub to get to the house-music club upstairs, but that's what all the Brixton clubbers do.

PLAN B CLUB

Map p460 (☎7737 7372; www.planb-london.com; 418 Brixton Rd, SW9; ⊖Brixton) Reverberating to its vast Funktion 1 sound system, this imaginative Brixton Rd club puts its small space on the Brixton nightlife map with a shaken up roll call of music line-ups for hip hop, dubstep, dancehall, r&b, house, old school, electro and more.

BABALOU BAR

Map p460 (www.babalou.net; St Matthew's Church, Brixton Hill SW2; ☺7pm-2am Wed & Thu, to 5am Fri & Sat; ⊝Brixton) The Bug Bar in the crypt of a Methodist church has turned into a bar-lounge-club called Babalou with fabulous cocktails and parties. The neogothic architecture stays but there are now North African touches and discreet little 'snugs' (OK, booths) in red velvet.

Battersea & Wandsworth

LOST SOCIETY BAR

Map p460 (www.lostsociety.co.uk; 697 Wandsworth Rd SW8; ☺5pm-midnight Mon-Wed, to 1am Thu & Sun, to 2am Fri & Sat; ⓡWandsworth Rd, Battersea Park or Queenstown Rd) A fantastic bar whose six rooms are dedicated to delightful decadence, it's all 1920s glamour and aristocratic glitz in Wandsworth these days. There's a garden at the back where many a summer drinking session goes on; DJs take over on weekends and create a good party atmosphere.

Clapham

With its restaurants, delis, middle class mums wheeling push prams and upmarket vibe, the long strip of Northcote Rd has some winning pubs and bars, or you can raise your glass in the genteel surrounds of Clapham Old Town on the far side of the common.

TOP **DRAFT HOUSE** PUB

(☎7924 1814; www.drafthouse.co.uk; 94 Northcote Rd, SW11; ☺noon-11pm Mon-Fri, 10am-11pm Sat, noon-10.30pm Sun; ⓡClapham Junction ⊝Clapham South; ⓦ) Its 18 ales, stouts and lagers on tap backed up by over 50 different bottled beers, Draft House, on the corner of Salcott Rd, is no slouch. A standout watering hole along urbane Northcote Rd, where middle-class cash and high expectations seamlessly dovetail, the seasonally-adjusted menu (served through the day) has also set local palates a quiver with excellent brunches and standout burgers (kids menu). The '60s and '70s retro posters suggest longevity of sorts, but it's abstract: this is a youngster (opened 2009) with a spring in its step. Outside seating.

PRINCE OF WALES PUB

Map p460 (38 Old Town SW4; ☺5-11pm Mon-Wed, 5pm-midnight Thu, 5pm-1am Fri, 1pm-1am Sat, 1-11pm Sun; ⊝Clapham Common) While some pubs that festoon their ceilings with bric-a-brac and hang London Underground station signs on the walls can be tiresome, the Prince of Wales remains a very pleasant Clapham hang-out, and its decor, unlike that of most pubs of the genre, is genuinely collected rather than supplied wholesale. Real ales appear regularly.

SO.UK BAR

Map p460 (www.soukclapham.co.uk; 165 Clapham High St SW4; ☺8pm-late Mon, 6pm-late Tue-Sun; ⊝Clapham Common) So.uk is a stylish, light and airy Moroccan-themed bar that serves unusual cocktails (Twisted Mojito, anyone?) and shooters. It's extremely popular, with house, soul, electro and funk in the air and the chance to spot a few well-known faces among the Clapham professionals on the pull.

TWO BREWERS GAY

Map p460 (www.the2brewers.com; 114 Clapham High St SW4; ☺noon-2am Sun-Thu, noon-4am Fri & Sat; ⊝Clapham Common or Clapham North) Clapham exudes an inner suburban feel, the High St in particular, but the longstanding Two Brewers endures as one of the best London gay bars outside the gay villages. Here there's a friendly, laid-back, local crowd who come for a quiet drink during the week and some madcap cabaret and dancing in the club at weekends.

Kennington, Oval & Stockwell

AREA GAY

Map p462 (www.areaclublondon.com; 67-68 Albert Embankment SE1; ☺10.30pm-6am Sat; ⊝Vauxhall) Home from home for circuit party boys but still very welcoming to all, Area describes itself as 'polysexual' and hosts some of the most inventive nights in town.

RVT GAY

Map p462 (☎7820 1222; www.rvt.org.uk; 372 Kennington Lane SE11; ☺7pm-midnight Mon, Wed & Thu, 6pm-midnight Tue, 9pm-2am Fri, 9pm-2am Sat, 2pm-midnight Sun; ⊝Vauxhall) Rough around the edges to say the least, the Royal Vauxhall Tavern is the perfect antidote to the gleaming new wave of gay venues now crowding

Vauxhall's gay village. Saturday's Duckie (www.duckie.co.uk), a wonderful indie performance night hosted by Amy Lamé, is rightly considered to be one of the best club nights in London. Also check out S.L.A.G.S. on Sundays, and keep an eye out on the website for other upcoming events – from cabaret nights to previews for the Edinburgh Fringe.

HOIST
GAY

Map p462 (☎7735 9972; www.thehoist.co.uk; Arches 47C, South Lambeth Rd SW8; ☺9pm-2am Wed, 8pm-midnight Thu, 10pm-3am Fri, 10pm-4am Sat, 10pm-2am Sun; ⊖Vauxhall) One of Europe's most famous fetish clubs, the Hoist is a one-stop shop for guys into leather and uniforms. The dress code is very strict – everyone has to wear boots, and rubber, leather or uniform. Check out the array of fetish nights on the website.

EAGLE
GAY

Map p462 (☎7793 0903; www.eaglelondon.com; 349 Kennington La SE11; ☺9pm-2am Mon-Thu, to 3am Fri & Sun, to 4am Sat; ⊖Vauxhall) This fantastic place is a haven of alternative queer goings-on in muscle-bound Vauxhall. Open nightly with a different feel throughout the week with Tonker every Friday, and Sunday night's legendary Horse Meat Disco.

🍷 Dulwich & Forest Hill

CROWN & GREYHOUND
PUB

(www.thecrownandgreyhound.co.uk; 73 Dulwich Village, SE21; ⊠North Dulwich, West Dulwich) With a resplendent position at the heart of leafy and dozy Dulwich Village, this imposing pub with a large garden is an excellent spot for a pint or a taste of its lovely Sunday roasts. In the old days this was in fact two pubs: The Crown for the upper classes and the Greyhound for the plebs; today all and sundry walk through the door for its cosy, warm ambience.

FIRE
CLUB

Map p462 (☎0790 503 5682; www.fireclub.co.uk; South Lambeth Rd SW8; ☺10pm-4am; ⊖Vauxhall) Sealing Vauxhall's reputation as the new gay nightlife centre of London, Fire is another expansive, smart space under the railway arches, hosting the centrepieces of the Vauxhall weekend: A:M on Friday, Later on Sunday afternoons, followed by the Sunday all-nighter, Orange.

☆ ENTERTAINMENT

Early September sees Greenwich play host to London's largest comedy festival, the Greenwich Comedy Festival (www.greenwichcomedyfestival.co.uk; p28) set in the grounds of the Old Royal Naval College.

TOP CHOICE BATTERSEA ARTS CENTRE
THEATRE

Map p460 (☎7223 2223; www.bac.org.uk; Lavender Hill SW11; ⊖Clapham Common, ⊠Clapham Junction, ☒77, 77A or 345) In the magnificent, mouldering old town hall, this is a friendly, homely, down-to-earth and old sofa-strewn community theatre where staff chat to you and actors mingle in the bar with the audience after the show. Playwrights see it as a valuable nurturer and crucible of new plays and talent. Artistic director David Jubb's famous 'Scratch' program is an excellent exercise in learning about the writing process: a developing play is shown to ever-increasing audiences until it's finished. Parents can take their kids (to five years old) to The Bee's Knees (☺10am-5pm Mon-Fri; free) cafe for toys, games, storytelling and music.

LABAN
DANCE

Map p463 (☎information 8691 8600, bookings 8469 9500; www.laban.org; Creekside SE8; admission £6-15; ⊠Deptford Bridge, DLR Greenwich) This is an independent dance training school, which also presents student performances, graduation shows and regu-

MINISTRY OF SOUND

Map p462 (☎7740 8600; www.ministryofsound.com; 103 Gaunt St SE1; admission £13-15; ☺10.30pm-6am Fri, midnight-9am Sat; ⊖Elephant & Castle) This legendary club-cum-enormous-global-brand (four bars, four dance floors) lost some 'edge' in the early noughties but, after pumping in top DJs, the Ministry has firmly rejoined the top club ranks. Fridays is the Gallery trance night, while Saturday sessions offers the crème de la crème of house, electro and techno DJs.

lar pieces by the resident troupe, Transitions Dance Company, as well as other assorted dance, music and physical performances. Its stunning £23 million home was designed by Herzog & de Meuron, designers of the Tate Modern (see p164).

UP THE CREEK COMEDY
Map p463 (☎8858 4581; www.up-the-creek.com; 302 Creek Rd SE10; admission £10-15; ☺Fri & Sat; ⓇGreenwich, DLR Cutty Sark) Bizarrely enough, the hecklers can be funnier than the acts at this great club. Up the Creek was established and is still living in the spirit of the legendary Malcolm Hardee. Hardee, who was the patron sinner of British comedy, famously stole Freddie Mercury's 40th birthday cake and donated it to his local old folks home. Mischief, rowdiness and excellent comedy are the norm with open mic nights on Thursdays (£4) and Sunday specials (www.sundayspecial.co.uk; £6).

RITZY PICTUREHOUSE CINEMA
Map p460 (☎0871 704 2065; www.picturehouses.co.uk; Brixton Oval, Coldharbour Lane SW2; ⊖Brixton) Still one of London's favourites, the Ritzy screens a good mix of mainstream and indie films. The Ritzy is an off–West End screen during the Times BFI London Film Festival, and alternative gigs are often held inside the large original auditorium. The ground floor cafe is frequently busy with a trendy crowd and there's a funky bar-cafe upstairs.

CLAPHAM PICTURE HOUSE CINEMA
Map p460 (☎0871 902 5727; www.picturehouses.co.uk; 76 Venn St, SW4; ⊖Clapham Common) This much-loved independent cinema stands out for its mix of art house cinema and mainstream movies, festival screenings and regular nods to kids. Even though the bar is excellent and a great place to hang out, you can take your wine glass into the screens with you.

O2 ACADEMY BRIXTON LIVE MUSIC
Map p460 (☎box office 0844 477 2000; www.o2academybrixton.co.uk; 211 Stockwell Rd SW9; ⊖Brixton) It's hard to have a bad night at the Brixton Academy, even if you leave with your soles sticky with beer, as this cavernous former art deco theatre (holding 5000) always thrums with bonhomie. There's a properly raked floor for good views, as well as plenty of bars. Massive acts show – including Madonna (once) and The Prodigy –

BRIXTON WINDMILL

Built for one John Ashby in 1816, Brixton Windmill (Blenheim Gardens SW2; ⊖Brixton) is the closest to central London still in existence. It was later powered by gas and milled as recently as 1934. It's been refitted with sails and machinery for a wind-driven mill and is not currently open to the public, but it can be admired from the outside.

---

but more likely artists are Band of Horses, Beady Eye or DJ Shadow.

O2 LIVE MUSIC
(☎0871 984 0002; www.theo2.co.uk; Peninsula Sq SE10; ⊖North Greenwich) One of the city's major concert venues, hosting all the biggies – the Rolling Stones, Britney Spears, Prince and many others inside the 20,000-capacity stadium. Ticket prices start at £25.

 SHOPPING

Greenwich is a paradise for lovers of retro clothes stores and secondhand bookshops; endlessly fascinating Greenwich Market (p282) rewards both casual and determined browsing. Brixton Market is a treasure trove for browsers and buyers and Brixton Village is a cheek-by-jowl array of shops, cafes and restaurants all stuffed together, selling allsorts from African fabrics to antique clothing, live crabs and conger eels. Northcote Rd in Wandsworth offers some quality food shopping.

[TOP CHOICE] BRIXTON VILLAGE INDOOR MARKET
Map p460 (☺10.30am-6pm Mon-Wed, to 10pm Thu-Sat, 10.30am-5pm Sun; ⊖Brixton) This revitalised market has enjoyed an eye-catching renaissance of late, prompted by an initiative to offer a period of free rent to outfits setting up in the dilapidated 1930s Granville Arcade. Restaurants and cafes have swarmed in, as well as a host of inventively inclined shops. Brick Box (☎7274 2211) is a community arts hub at the heart of the village that holds art events in the evenings. Shops worth popping into include Sweet Tooth (Unit 66), selling sweets from around the world, the Okido Doodle Shop (Unit 89)

ROYAL ARTILLERY BARRACKS

The Royal Artillery Barracks in Woolwich is the venue for the shooting events of the 2012 games.

and Leftovers (Unit 71), retailing antique French clothes. The Village is full of restaurants; dine at Honest Burgers (p283) or get caffeinated at Federation Coffee (p281).

TOP CHOICE VILLAGE BOOKS
BOOKS

(☑8693 2808; 1d Calton Avenue, Dulwich Village, SE21; ◷9am-5.30pm Mon-Sat, 11am-5pm Sun; ⓇNorth Dulwich) Very much the village bookshop that depends on the support of local and itinerant book-lovers, Village Books is so small you could swing the proverbial dead cat and dislodge books from all four walls. But tininess is this shop's forte, with a wealth of knowledge and experience from Hazel Broadfoot and other staff, who are never far away for literary queries, bookish pointers and excellent service. Stock is very strong, so you should find what you are looking for. There's also another branch in Wandsworth (☑8672 4413; 6 Bellevue Rd).

BRIXTON MARKET
MARKET

Map p460 (www.brixtonmarket.net; Reliance Arcade, Market Row, Electric Lane & Electric Ave SW9; ◷8am-6pm Mon-Sat, 8am-3pm Wed; ⊖Brixton) A heady, cosmopolitan blend of silks, wigs, knock-off fashion, Halal butchers and the occasional Christian preacher on Electric Ave. Tilapia fish, pig's trotters, yams, mangoes, okra, plantains and Jamaican *bullah* cakes (gingerbread) are just some of the exotic products on sale.

COMPENDIA
GIFTS, SOUVENIRS

Map p463 (☑8293 6616; www.compendia.co.uk; 10 Greenwich Market; ◷11am-5.30pm; DLR Cutty Sark) Compendia's owners are madly enthusiastic about games – board or any other kind – and they'll look for the rarest of things if you ask them to. The shop is excellent for gifts you can enjoy with your mates – backgammon, chess, Scrabble, solitaire and more fringe interests such as Mexican Train Domino, which claims to be the world's fastest game, Carrom (popular in South Asia) and Go. Look out for the Escher jigsaws and if you're Greenwich Parkbound, pick up a Frisbee, a kite, some juggling balls or even a diabolo.

EMPORIUM
FASHION

Map p463 (☑8305 1670; 330-332 Creek Rd SE10; ◷10.30am-6pm Wed-Sun; DLR Cutty Sark) Each piece is individual at this lovely vintage shop (unisex), where glass cabinets are crammed with costume jewellery, old perfume bottles and straw hats, while gorgeous jackets and blazers intermingle on the clothes racks.

ROULLIER WHITE
HOMEWARES, GIFTS

(☑8693 5150; www.roullierwhite.com; 125 Lordship Lane SE22; ◷10am-6pm Mon-Sat, 11am-5pm Sun; ⓇEast Dulwich) Back-to-basics shop with wooden floors and Victorian-style display cabinets flogging hard-to-find household products and gift items from often long-forgotten manufacturers (slippers, glassware, towelling, cleaning products). Worth the trip and you get the chance to see massively up-and-coming Lordship Lane.

BEEHIVE
VINTAGE

Map p463 (☑8858 1964; 320-322 Creek Rd, SE10; ◷10.30am-6pm Tue-Sun, 10.30am-6.30pm Sat & Sun; DLR Cutty Sark) Funky meeting ground of old vinyl (Bowie, Rolling Stones, vintage soul) and retro togs (frocks, blouses, leather jackets and overcoats).

JOY
CLOTHES, GIFTS

Map p460 (☑7787 9616; 432 Coldharbour Lane SW11; ◷10am-7.30pm Mon-Sat, 11am-7pm Sun; ⊖Brixton) This funky shop does a great line in retro floral frocks and blouses, hip T-shirts, polo shirts and an imaginative range of inventive gift ideas and quirky accessories.

🏃 SPORTS & ACTIVITIES

BROCKWELL PARK LIDO
SWIMMING

Map p460 (☑7274 3088; www.brockwell-lido.com; Dulwich Rd SE24; adult/child £3.10/5.20; ◷6.30am-7pm mid-Jun–Aug, weather dependent rest of year; ⊖Brixton, ⓇHerne Hill) A beautifully designed 1930s lido, Brockwell is one of London's best, drawing multitudes in summer months.

THE OVAL
CRICKET GROUND

Map p462 (☑0871 246 1100; www.kiaoval.com; Surrey County Cricket Club SE11; Kennington Oval SE11; ⊖Oval) County side Surrey plays at the Oval, known for its distinctive gasholders. For more on the Brit Oval, see p280.

Richmond, Kew & Hampton Court

RICHMOND | KEW | PUTNEY | BARNES | FULHAM | CHISWICK | TWICKENHAM | WIMBLEDON

Neighbourhood Top Five

1 Searching for ghosts and legends among the galleries and royal apartments of majestic **Hampton Court Palace** (p293), London's exquisitely wrought Tudor gem by the Thames.

2 Making it a day out among the green expanses, treetop walkways, tropical foliage and elegant architecture of **Kew Gardens** (p296).

3 Fleeing urban London to plunge into an exceptional range of bird and animal habitats at the outstanding **London Wetland Centre** (p301).

4 Sinking a pint of beer at the historic riverside **White Cross pub** (p305) while trying to avoid being cut off by the high tide.

5 Exploring London's wild side, roaming at will and hiking around immense **Wimbledon Common** (p302) or **Richmond Park** (p298).

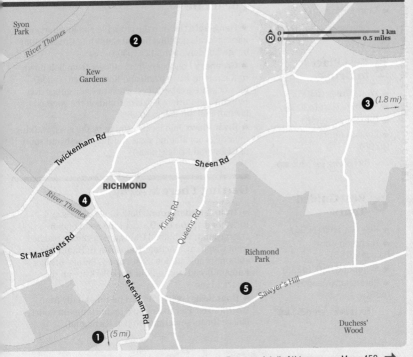

For more detail of this area, see Map p458 ➡

Lonely Planet's Top Tip

A manageable section of the fantastic Thames Path (p302) is the four miles between Putney Bridge and Barnes Footbridge. Taking around 90 minutes, most of the walk is very rural and at times you will only be accompanied by birdsong and the gentle swish of the river. From the footbridge, Chiswick train station is about 0.75 miles to the northwest. For more details, see the River Thames Alliance's **Visit Thames** (www.visit thames.co.uk) site.

✕ Best Places to Eat

➡ Al Boccon di'Vino (p302)

➡ Glasshouse (p303)

➡ Lots Road Pub & Dining Room (p304)

➡ Chez Lindsay (p303)

For reviews, see p302

⬤ Best Places to Drink

➡ White Cross (p305)

➡ Ye White Hart (p305)

➡ City Barge (p305)

➡ London Apprentice (p306)

For reviews, see p305 ➡

◉ Best Guided Tours

➡ Kew Gardens (p296)

➡ Hampton Court Palace (p293)

➡ Richmond Park (p298)

➡ Petersham Meadows (p300)

For reviews, see p298 ➡

Explore Richmond, Kew and Hampton Court

If anywhere in London could be described as a village, Richmond – with its delightful green, riverside vistas and white-painted two-storey cottages – is it. But the entire southwest from Putney to Twickenham is a revitalising and refreshing alternative to central London's urban and occasionally gridlocked density. Pastoral shades frequently pop into view and when the weather's fine, few London diversions can top time spent upriver by the Thames, whether exploring the major sights, walking along the riverbank or poking your head into a historic waterside pub. And if you really warm to the charms of London's green southwest, you'll find a few outstanding hotels to look after you.

You might not find yourself coming here to shop, but bring your wallet as there's no shortage of fine dining and you'll find pubs a plenty. But it's exploration that should top your agenda, whether it be getting lost in the maze at splendid Hampton Court Palace, finding endless botanic discoveries at Kew Gardens or walking the wilds of Richmond Park. Don't forget to pack your camera, friends back home may be amazed at how good-looking these parts of London are.

Local Life

➡ **Hang-outs** Get into the riverside pub lunch mood joining locals quaffing beer at the White Cross (p305) or the London Apprentice (p306).

➡ **Greenery** Londoners from all over town bolt down to Richmond Park (p298) and Kew Gardens (p296) for weekend great escapes; when the sun shines over Fulham and Putney, locals descend on the gorgeous lawn of Fulham Palace (p299).

➡ **River Views** Join locals jogging by the river, walking their dogs or catching some sunshine north and south of Richmond Bridge (p300).

Getting There & Away

➡ **Train & Underground** Both Kew Gardens and Richmond are on the District Line and London Overground; Richmond train station can be reached from Clapham Junction. Trains run to Hampton Court station from Waterloo. East Putney, Putney Bridge, Fulham Broadway and Chiswick Park are on the District Line.

➡ **Boat** Boats (p395) run several times daily from Westminster Pier to Kew and on to Hampton Court Palace (boats sometimes stop at Richmond).

 TOP SIGHTS
HAMPTON COURT PALACE

London's most spectacular Tudor palace, 16th-century Hampton Court Palace concocts an imposing sense of history, from the kitchens where you see food being prepared and the grand living quarters of Henry VIII to the spectacular gardens, complete with a 300-year-old maze. One of the best days out London has to offer, the palace should not be missed by anyone with any interest in British history, Tudor architecture or delicious landscaped gardens. Set aside plenty of time to do it justice (and if you arrive by boat from central London, half the day will have vanished already).

History of the Palace

Like so many royal residences, Hampton Court Palace was not built for the monarchy at all. In 1515 Cardinal Thomas Wolsey, Lord Chancellor of England, built himself a palace in keeping with his sense of self-importance. Unfortunately, even Wolsey couldn't persuade the pope to grant Henry VIII a divorce from Catherine of Aragon and relations between king and chancellor soured. With that in mind, you only need to glance at the palace to see why Wolsey felt obliged to present it to Henry, a monarch not too fond of anyone trying to outdo him. The hapless Wolsey was charged with high treason but died in 1530, before he could come to trial.

As soon as he had his royal hands upon the palace, Henry set to work expanding it, adding the Great Hall, the exquisite Chapel Royal and the sprawling kitchens. By 1540 it had become one of the grandest and most sophisticated

DON'T MISS...

→ Henry VIII's State Apartments
→ Great Hall
→ Chapel Royal
→ King's Apartments
→ Gardens & Maze
→ Haunted Gallery
→ Clock Court

PRACTICALITIES

→ off Map p291
→ 📞 0844 482 7777
→ www.hrp.org.uk/ HamptonCourtPalace
→ Hampton Court Rd, East Molesey KT8
→ all-inclusive ticket adult/child £15.95/8
→ ⏰ 10am-6pm late March-Oct, to 4.30pm Nov-late Mar
→ 🚉 Hampton Court

HAMPTON COURT PALACE BEER & JAZZ FESTIVAL

Real ale joins jazz at this entertaining jazz festival (www.hampton courtbeerandjazz.com), held at the palace in late August. The outdoor festival ranges through the octaves over roughly four days, taking whatever the London weather throws at it (so dress accordingly).

Out in London's southwestern outskirts, the wonderful Hampton Court Palace is pressed up against 445-hectare Bushy Park (www.royalparks.gov.uk), a semiwild expanse with herds of red and fallow deer.

HAUNTED HAMPTON COURT

With a history as old and as eventful as Hampton Court Palace, a paranormal dimension is surely par for the course. Arrested for adultery and detained in the palace in 1542, Henry's fifth wife, Catherine Howard, was dragged screaming down a gallery at the palace by her guards after an escape bid. Her ghost is said to do a repeat performance in the Haunted Gallery (she must be a tireless ghost as she also haunts the Tower of London).

palaces in Europe, but Henry only spent an average three weeks a year here. James I kept things ticking over at Hampton Court while Charles I put in a new tennis court and did some serious art-collecting, before finding himself a prisoner in the palace during the Civil War. After the war, puritanical Oliver Cromwell warmed to his own regal proclivities, spending weekends in the comfort of the former Queen's bedroom at the palace and flogging Charles I's art collection. In the late 17th century, William and Mary employed Sir Christopher Wren for extensions: the result is a beautiful blend of Tudor and 'restrained baroque' architecture.

Entering The Palace

Passing through the magnificent main gate (Trophy Gate) you arrive first in the **Base Court** and then the **Clock Court**, named after the 16th-century astronomical clock that still shows the sun revolving round the earth. The second court is your starting point; from here you can follow any or all of the six sets of rooms in the complex. Here behind the colonnade you'll also find the useful **Introductory Exhibition**, explaining what's where and how the compound functions.

Henry VIII's State Apartments

The stairs inside Anne Boleyn's Gateway lead up to Henry VIII's State Apartments, including the **Great Hall**, the largest single room in the palace, decorated with tapestries and what is considered the country's finest hammerbeam roof. The Horn Room, hung with impressive antlers, leads to the Great Watching Chamber where guards controlled access to the king.

Chapel Royal

Further along the corridor is the beautiful Chapel Royal, built in just nine months and still a place of worship after 450 years. The blue-and-gold vaulted ceiling was originally intended for Christ Church, Oxford, but was installed here instead; the 18th-century reredos was carved by Grinling Gibbons.

Tudor Kitchens

Also dating from Henry's day are the delightful Tudor kitchens, again accessible from Anne Boleyn's Gateway and once used to rustling up meals for a royal household of some 1200 people. The kitchens have been fitted out to resemble how they might have done in Tudor days and palace 'servants' turn the spits, stuff the peacocks and frost the marzipan with real gold leaf. Don't miss the Great Wine Cellar, which handled the 300 barrels each of ale and wine consumed here annually in the mid-16th century.

King's Apartments

West of the colonnade in the Clock Court is the entrance to the **Wolsey Rooms** and the **Young Henry VIII Exhibition**. East of the colonnade you'll find the stairs to the King's Apartments, completed by Wren for William III in 1702. A tour of the apartments takes you up the grand King's Staircase, painted by Antonio Verrio in about 1700 and flattering the king by comparing him to Alexander the Great. Highlights include the King's Presence Chamber, dominated by a throne backed with scarlet hangings. The King's Great Bedchamber, with a bed topped with ostrich plumes, and the King's Closet (where His Majesty's toilet has a velvet seat) should not be missed.

Queen's Apartments

William's wife, Mary II, had her own Queen's Apartments, accessible up the Queen's Staircase, decorated by William Kent. When Mary died in 1694, work on these was incomplete; they were finished during the reign of George II. The rooms are shown as they might have been when Queen Caroline used them for entertaining between 1716 and 1737. Compared with the King's Apartments, those for the queen seem austere, although the Queen's Audience Chamber has a throne as imposing as that of the king.

Georgian Rooms

Also worth seeing are the Georgian Rooms used by George II and Queen Caroline on the court's last visit to the palace in 1737. The first rooms were designed to accommodate George's second son, the Duke of Cumberland, whose bed is woefully tiny for its grand surroundings.

Other Palace Sights

In the **Cartoon Gallery**, the real Raphael Cartoons (now in the Victoria & Albert Museum, see p183) used to hang; nowadays it's just the late-17th-century copies.

Beyond the Cartoon Gallery are the **Queen's Private Apartments**: her drawing room and bedchamber, where she and the king would sleep if they wanted to be alone. Particularly interesting are the Queen's Bathroom, with its tub set on a floor cloth to soak up any spillage, and the Oratory, an attractive room with its exquisite 16th-century Persian carpet.

Garden & Maze

Beyond the palace are the stunning gardens. Look out for the **Real Tennis Court**, dating from the 1620s and designed for real tennis, a rather different version of the game from that played today. In the restored 24-hectare Riverside Gardens, you'll find the **Great Vine**. Planted in 1768, it's still producing just under 320kg of grapes per year. The **Lower Orangery** in the gardens houses Andrea Mantegna's nine *Triumphs of Caesar* paintings, bought by Charles I in 1629; the Banqueting House was designed for William III and painted by Antonio Verrio.

No-one should leave Hampton Court without losing themselves in the famous 800m-long **maze**, made of hornbeam and yew and planted in 1690. The average visitor takes 20 minutes to reach the centre. The maze is included in entry, although those not visiting the palace can enter for £3.85 (£2.75/11 for children/families). Last admission is 5.15pm in summer and 3.45pm in winter.

A whopping 24% of London is a green patchwork of domestic gardens, sprouting a staggering 2.5 million garden trees. Throw in London's parks, and this is one of the greenest cities on the planet. This 121-hectare gardens at Kew are the finest product of the British botanical imagination and really should not be missed, especially if you have kids. No worries if you don't know your golden slipper orchid from your fengoky or your quiver tree from your alang-alang, a visit to Kew is a journey of discovery for everyone.

Botanical Collection

As well as being a public garden, Kew is a pre-eminent research centre, maintaining its reputation as the most exhaustive botanical collection in the world.

Palm House

Assuming you come by tube and enter via Victoria Gate, you'll come almost immediately to a large pond overlooked by the enormous and iconic 700-glass-paned Palm House, a domed hothouse of metal and curved sheets of glass dating from 1848 and housing a splendid display of exotic tropical greenery; the aerial walkway offers a parrot's-eye view of the lush vegetation. Just northwest of the Palm House stand the tiny and irresistibly steamy **Waterlily House** (☺Mar-Dec), housing the gigantic *Victoria cruziana* waterlily.

DON'T MISS...

➜ Palm House
➜ Temperate House
➜ Rhizotron and Xstrata Treetop Walkway
➜ Princess of Wales Conservatory
➜ Pagoda

PRACTICALITIES

➜ Map p458
➜ www.kew.org
➜ adult/child £13.90/free
➜ ☺gardens 9.30am-6.30pm Mon-Fri, to 7.30pm Sat & Sun Apr-Aug, 9.30am-6pm Sep & Oct, 9.30am-4.15pm Nov-Feb, glasshouses 9.30am-5.30pm April-Oct, 9.30am-3.45pm Nov-Feb
➜ ⊖/⧉ Kew Gardens

Princess of Wales Conservatory

Further north, the stunning Princess of Wales Conservatory houses plants in 10 different climatic zones – everything from a desert to a mangrove swamp. Look out for stone plants, which resemble pebbles (to deter grazing animals), carnivorous plants, gigantic waterlilies, cacti and a collection of tropical orchids.

Temperate House

The beautiful Temperate House in the southeast of Kew Gardens (north of the pagoda) is the world's largest surviving Victorian glasshouse, an astonishing feat of architecture housing an equally sublime collection of plants. Nearby **Evolution House** traces plant evolution over 3500 million years.

Rhizotron and Xstrata Treetop Walkway

In the **Arboretum** – a short walk from Temperate House – this fascinating and much-enjoyed walkway takes you underground and then 18 metres up in the air into the tree canopy, for closer angles on tree anatomy.

Kew Palace

The smallest of the royal palaces, red-brick **Kew Palace** (adult/child £5.30/free; ☺10am-5.30pm late Mar-late Oct) in the northwest of the gardens is a former royal residence once known as Dutch House, and was built in 1631. It was the favourite home of George III and his family; his wife, Queen Charlotte, died here in 1818. Don't miss the Georgian rooms, restored to how they would have looked in 1804, and Princess Elizabeth's doll's house.

Other Highlights

Other highlights include the idyllic, thatched **Queen Charlotte's Cottage** (☺10am-4pm Sat & Sun Jul & Aug), which was popular with 'mad' George III and his wife. The **Marianne North Gallery** displays paintings on a botanical theme. Marianne North was one of those indomitable Victorian female travellers who roamed the continents from 1871 to 1885, painting plants and trees along the way. The results of her labour now cover the walls of this small purpose-built gallery. The **Orangery** near Kew Palace contains a restaurant, cafe and shop.

Getting Around

If you want a good overview of the gardens, jump aboard the **Kew Explorer** (adult/child £4/1), which allows you to hop on and off at stops along the way.

CHINESE PAGODA

Kew's celebrated 49.5m tall eight-sided Chinese Pagoda (1762), designed by William Chambers (who designed Somerset House), is one of the garden's architectural icons. It eluded a stick of Luftwaffe bombs during WWII that fell on Kew and was also secretly employed by the Ministry of Defence (MOD) to test bomb trajectories (which involved cutting holes in each floor!).

In 1985, a time-capsule containing an assortment of plant seeds was entombed within the foundations of the Princes of Wales Conservatory. It will not be dug up till 2085 and may provide a source of plant seeds that may then be extinct.

ROYAL BOTANIC GARDENS

The Royal Botanic Gardens at Kew is one of the most popular attractions in London. Spring may be the best time to visit, but any time of the year is fine at this truly delightful 120-hectare expanse of lawns, formal gardens and greenhouses. Grab a map from the ticket office.

RICHMOND, KEW & HAMPTON COURT KEW GARDENS

⊙ TOP SIGHTS
KEW GARDENS

⊙ SIGHTS

Richmond & Kew

RICHMOND PARK   PARK

Map p458 (www.royalparks.gov.uk; admission free; ⊙7am–dusk Mar-Sep, from 7.30am Oct-Feb; ⊖/ℝRichmond, then 🚌65 or 371) At 1012 hectares (the largest urban parkland in Europe), this park offers everything from formal gardens and ancient oaks to unsurpassed views of central London 12 miles away. It's easy to escape the several roads that slice up the rambling wilderness, making the park excellent for a quiet walk or a picnic with the kids, even in summer when Richmond's riverside can be heaving. Herds of more than 600 red and fallow deer basking under the trees are part of its magic, but they can be less than docile in rutting season (May to July) and when the does bear young (September and October). Birdwatchers will love the diverse habitats, from neat gardens to woodland and assorted ponds. Flower-lovers should visit **Isabella Plantation**, a stunning woodland garden created after WWII, in April and May when the rhododendrons and azaleas are in bloom.

Coming from Richmond, it's easiest to enter via Richmond Gate or from Petersham Rd. Take a map with you and wander the grounds.

Pembroke Lodge (www.pembroke-lodge. co.uk; ⊙9.30am-5.30pm summer, to just before dusk winter), the childhood home of Bertrand Russell, is now a cafe set in a beautiful 13-hectare garden and affording great views of the city from the back terrace.

The pastoral view from **Richmond Hill** has inspired painters and poets for centuries and still beguiles. It's the only view (which includes St Paul's Cathedral 10 miles away) in the country to be protected by an act of Parliament.

RICHMOND GREEN   PARK

Map p458 (⊖/ℝRichmond) A short walk west of the Quadrant, where you'll emerge from the tube, is Richmond Green with its mansions and delightful pubs. Cross the green diagonally for the attractive remains of **Richmond Palace**, just the main entrance and red-brick gatehouse, built in 1501. Henry VII's arms are visible above the main gate: he built the Tudor additions to the edifice, although the palace had been in use as a royal residence since 1125. Elizabeth I died here in 1603.

HAM HOUSE   HISTORIC BUILDING

(📞8940 1950; www.nationaltrust.org.uk; Ham St, Ham TW10; admission prices vary; ⊙house noon-4pm Mon-Thu, Sat & Sun late Mar-Oct, gardens 11am-4pm Jan–mid-Feb & Nov–mid-Dec, 11am-5pm mid-Feb–Oct; ⊖/ℝRichmond, then 🚌371; 🚲) Known as 'Hampton Court in miniature', Ham House was built in 1610 and became home to the first Earl of Dysart, unluckily employed as 'whipping boy' to Charles I. Inside it's furnished with grandeur; the Great Staircase is a magnificent example of Stuart woodworking. Look out for ceiling paintings by Antonio Verrio, who also worked at Hampton Court Palace, and for a miniature of Elizabeth I by Nicholas Hilliard. Other notable paintings are by Constable and Reynolds. The grounds of Ham House slope down to the Thames, but there are also pleasant 17th-century formal gardens. Just opposite the Thames and accessible by small ferry is Marble Hill Park and its splendid **mansion** (p301). House **tours** are run 11.30am to 3.30pm Monday to Thursday, Saturday and Sunday mid-February to March and from 11.30am to 3pm Monday, Tuesday, Saturday and Sunday in November. There is partial disabled access. Call for more information.

ST PETER'S CHURCH   CHURCH

Map p458 (Church Lane, Petersham TW10; admission free; ⊙3-5pm Sun; ⊖/ℝRichmond, then 🚌65) This Norman church has been a

---

ROYAL RICHMOND

Centuries of history, some stunning Georgian architecture and the graceful curve of the Thames has made this one of London's swankiest locales, home to ageing rock stars and city high-flyers alike.

Richmond was originally named Sheen, but Henry VII, having fallen in love with the place, renamed the village after his Yorkshire earldom. This started centuries of royal association with the area; the most famous local, Henry VIII, acquired nearby Hampton Court Palace (p293) from Cardinal Wolsey after the latter's fall from grace in 1529.

WORTH A DETOUR

SYON HOUSE

Just across the Thames from Kew Gardens, **Syon House** (www.syonpark.co.uk; Syon Park, Brentford TW7; adult/child £10/4, gardens only adult/child £5/2.50; ⊙11am-5pm Wed, Thu & Sun late Mar-Oct, gardens 10.30am-5pm daily mid-Mar-Oct, 10.30am-dusk Sat & Sun Nov–mid-Mar; ⊕/🚊Gunnersbury, then 🚌237 or 267) was once a medieval abbey named after Mt Zion. In 1542 Henry VIII dissolved the order of Bridgettine nuns who peacefully lived here and rebuilt it into a residence. (They say God had the last laugh in 1547 when Henry's coffin was brought to Syon en route to Windsor for burial and burst open during the night, leaving his body to be set upon by the estate's dogs.)

The house from where Lady Jane Grey ascended the throne for her nine-day reign in 1553 was remodelled in the neoclassical style by Robert Adam in the 18th century and has plenty of Adam furniture and oak panelling. The interior was designed on gender-specific lines, with pastel pinks and purples for the ladies' gallery, and mock Roman sculptures for the men's dining room. Guests at the house have included Thayandanegea (Joseph Brant), the great Mohawk chieftain, and Gunpowder Plot member Thomas Percy.

The estate's 16-hectare gardens, with a lake and the Great Conservatory (1820), were landscaped by Capability Brown. Syon Park is filled with attractions for children, including an adventure playground, aquatic park and trout fishery.

place of worship for 1300 years and parts of the present structure date from 1266. It's a fascinating place, not least for its curious Georgian box pews, which local landowners would rent, while the serving staff and labourers sat in the open seats in the south transept. Against the north wall of the chancel is the **Cole Monument**, depicting barrister George Cole, his wife and child, all reclining in Elizabethan dress – an unusual design for an English church. Of interest to Canadians, St Peter's is the burial place of Captain George Vancouver, who was laid to rest here in 1798; his simple tomb is on the southern wall of the cemetery.

⊙ Putney & Barnes

PUTNEY & BARNES   NEIGHBOURHOOD

Putney is best known as the starting point of the annual Oxford and Cambridge Boat Race (p27). Barnes is less well known and more 'villagey' in feel. The best way to approach Putney is to follow the signs from Putney Bridge tube station for the footbridge (which runs parallel to the rail track), admiring the gorgeous riverside houses, with their gardens fronting the Thames, and thereby avoiding the tatty High St until the last minute.

⊙ Fulham

FREE FULHAM PALACE   HISTORIC BUILDING

(📞7736 8140; www.fulhampalace.org; Bishop's Ave SW6; ⊙palace & museum 1-4pm Sat-Wed, gardens dawn-dusk daily; ⊕Putney Bridge; 🛜) Summer home of the bishops of London from 704 to 1975, Fulham Palace is an appealing blend of architectural styles set in beautiful gardens and, until 1924, when filled with rubble, enclosed by the longest moat in England (a 70m section is currently being restored). The oldest surviving part of the palace is the little red-brick Tudor gateway, but the main building you see today is from the mid-17th century, remodelled in the 19th century.

The lovely courtyard draws watercolourists on sunny days and the lovely **cafe** (⊙10am-4pm Mon-Fri, 9am-5pm Sat & Sun) in the drawing room at the rear, looking out onto the gorgeous lawn, is a superlative spot for some carrot cake and a coffee. There's also a pretty **walled garden** (undergoing restoration) and, detached from the main house, a Tudor Revival **chapel** designed by Butterfield in 1866.

You can learn about the history of the palace and its inhabitants in the museum. Guided **tours** (📞7610 7164; tickets £5; ⊙tours 2pm 2nd & 4th Sun, 3rd Tue of month), usually take in the Great Hall, the Victorian chapel, Bishop Sherlock's Room and the museum and last about 1¼ hours. There are also garden walks (£5) and evening walks (£10, booking essential) for a nightfall perspective.

The surrounding land, once totalling almost 15 hectares but now reduced to just over five, forms Bishop's Park, and consists of a shady promenade along the river, a bowling green, tennis courts, a rose garden, a cafe and even a paddling pond with fountain. Hiking around the long moat of the palace makes for an excellent walk, while summer sees a popular art fair and music festivals at the palace.

Located by the Thames a short walk northwest of Putney Bridge, the palace can be easily reached from Putney Bridge underground station.

⊙ Chiswick

CHISWICK HOUSE
HISTORIC BUILDING

(www.chgt.org.uk; Chiswick Park, Burlington Lane W4; adult/child/£5.50/3.30, gardens free; ⏰house 10am-5pm Sun-Wed Apr-Oct, gardens 7am-dusk daily; ⛎Chiswick or ⊜Turnham Green; 🚇P) This stunner of a neo-Palladian pavilion with an octagonal dome and colonnaded portico is a delight. The confection was designed by the third Earl of Burlington (1694–1753) fired up with passion for all things Roman after his grand tour of Italy.

Inside, some of the rooms are almost overpoweringly grand. The coffered dome of the main salon has been left ungilded and the walls are decorated with eight enormous paintings. With its stunningly painted ceiling (by William Kent), the Blue Velvet Room also has a portrait of architect Inigo Jones, much admired by Lord Burlington, over one of the doors. Look out for carvings of the pagan vegetative deity, the Green Man, in the marble fireplaces of the Green Velvet Room.

Lord Burlington also planned the house's original gardens, now Chiswick Park, surrounding the house, but they have been much altered since his time. The recently restored gardens are lovely and children will love them – look out for the stone sphinxes near the Cedar of Lebanon trees (another sphinx made of lead can be found in the Lower Tribuna) and the restored Cascade waterfall is bubbling again after being out of action for years. Chiswick House also has an excellent cafe.

The house is about a mile southwest of the Turnham Green tube station and 750m northeast of Chiswick train station.

FREE HOGARTH'S HOUSE
HISTORIC BUILDING

(🚇8994 6757; www.hounslow.info/arts/hogarthshouse; Hogarth Lane W4; ⏰1-5pm Tue-Fri, 1-6pm Sat & Sun Apr-Oct, 1-4pm Tue-Fri, 1-5pm Sat & Sun Nov, Dec, Feb & Mar; ⊜Turnham Green; P) Home between 1749 and 1764 to artist and social commentator William Hogarth, this house displays his caricatures and engravings, with such works as the haunting *Gin Lane*, *Marriage-à-la-mode* and a copy of *A Rake's Progress*. Here you'll also find the private engravings *Before* and *After* (1730), commissioned by the Duke of Montagu and bearing Aristotle's aphorism *Omne Animal Post Coitum Triste* (Every creature is sad after intercourse). Although the house and grounds are attractive, Hogarth's House has been closed for several years for refurbishment (an unfortunate fire during the current restoration delayed reopening); it was due to reopen in November 2011.

THAMES AT RICHMOND

The stretch of the river from Twickenham Bridge to Petersham and Ham is one of the prettiest in London. The action is mostly around five-span **Richmond Bridge**, built in 1777 and London's oldest surviving crossing, only widened for traffic in 1937. Just before it, along one of the loveliest stretches of the Thames, is tiny Corporation Island, colonised by flocks of feral parakeets. The lovely walk to Petersham can be crowded in nice weather; best to cut across **Petersham Meadows** – where cows still graze – and continue to Richmond Park for peace and quiet. There are several companies near Richmond Bridge, including **Richmond Boat Hire** (🚇8948 8270), that offer skiff hire (adult/child £5/2.50 per hour, £15/7.50 per day). Alternatively, walk north from Twickenham Bridge, alongside the Old Deer Park, past the two obelisks and climb onto **Richmond Lock** and footbridge, dating from 1894.

TOP SIGHTS
LONDON WETLAND CENTRE

One of Europe's largest inland wetland projects, with a terrific range of animal habitats, this highly rewarding 42-hectare centre run by the Wildfowl & Wetlands Trust (WWT) was successfully transformed from four Victorian reservoirs and attracts some 180 species of bird, as well as 300 types of moth and butterfly.

From the visitor centre and glassed-in observatory overlooking the ponds, meandering paths and boardwalks lead visitors around the grounds, taking in the habitats of its many residents, including ducks, swans, geese, sand martins, and coots and the rarer bitterns, herons and kingfishers. There's even a large colony of parakeets, which may or may not be the descendants of caged pets. Don't miss the **Peacock Tower**, a three-storey hide on the main lake's eastern edge. Though there are half-a-dozen hides sprinkled elsewhere around the reserve, the tower is the mecca for more serious birders. The wetland is also well-populated with different species of bats that feed on the abundant moths, but also look out for frogs, toads and grass snakes. Free daily **tours**, which are led by enthusiastic staff members depart at 11am and 2pm daily. Children's activities take place at weekends and during the school holidays.

DON'T MISS...
➡ Peacock Tower
➡ Daily Tours

PRACTICALITIES
➡ www.wwt.org.uk
➡ 9.30am-6pm Mar-Oct, 9.30am-5pm Nov-Feb, to 8pm Thu Jun-late Sep
➡ Hammersmith then 283 (Duck Bus), 33, 72 or 209, or Barnes

FULLER'S GRIFFIN BREWERY BREWERY
(8996 2063; www.fullers.co.uk; Chiswick Lane South W4; adult/concession incl tasting) £10/8; tours hourly 11am-3pm Mon-Fri; Turnham Green or Chiswick) If you're a total beer fiend, hop (excuse the pun) on a tour to see it being brewed up and join in a good-old tasting session (over-18s only). Fuller's is now the last working brewery in London; you can only visit on the two-hour guided tour (minimum four people), which must be booked in advance by phone.

Twickenham

MARBLE HILL HOUSE HISTORIC BUILDING
(8892 5115; www.english-heritage.org.uk; Richmond Rd TW1; adult/child £5.30/3.20; Sat tours 10.30am & noon Sat, 10.30am, 12pm, 2.15pm & 3.30pm Sun Apr-Oct; St Margaret's or Richmond, Richmond) An 18th-century Palladian gem, this majestic love nest was originally built for George II's mistress Henrietta Howard and later occupied by Mrs Fitzherbert, the secret wife of George IV. The splendid Georgian interior contains some magnificent touches, including the hand-painted Chinese wallpaper in the dining parlour and some gorgeous furniture. The poet Alexander Pope had a hand in designing the park, which stretches leisurely down to the Thames.

To get there from St Margaret's station, turn right along St Margaret's Rd. Then take the right fork along Crown Rd and turn left along Richmond Rd. Turn right along Beaufort Rd and walk across Marble Hill Park to the house. It is also easily accessible by pedestrian ferry from Ham House (p298). It's a 25-minute walk from Richmond station.

There is partial disabled access. Call for more information.

FREE ORLEANS HOUSE GALLERY GALLERY, HISTORIC BUILDING
(www.richmond.gov.uk/orleans_house_gallery; Riverside, Twickenham TW1; 1-5.30pm Tue-Sat, 2-5.30pm Sun Apr-Sep & 1-4.30pm Tue-Sat, 2-4.30pm Sun Oct-Mar; /Richmond then 33, 490, H22, R68, R70 or 290, Twickenham or St Margarets) With its temporary art exhibitions decorating the former stables buildings, this attractive historic house a short distance west of Marble Hill House by the river originally dates to the early 18th century, with the Octagon Room an

THAMES PATH

The Thames Path National Trail is a long-distance walk stretching from the river's source at Thames Head, near Kemble in the Cotswolds, to the Thames Barrier (p277), a distance of some 184 miles. It's truly magnificent, particularly in its upper reaches, but tackling the entire course is for the truly ambitious. The rest of us walk sections of it, such as the 16-mile chunk from Battersea to the barrier, which takes about 6½ hours. See p295 for details on the short riverside walk from Putney to Barnes.

eight-sided baroque highlight. For coffee and snacks, a **cafe** (◷10.30am-5pm Wed-Sun) is on the grounds.

◉ Wimbledon

WIMBLEDON COMMON   COMMON
(www.wpcc.org.uk; ◉/⒭Wimbledon, then ▭93) Running on into Putney Heath, Wimbledon Common covers a staggering 460 hectares of southwest London. An astonishing expanse of open, wild and wooded space for walking, nature trailing and picnicking – the best mode of exploration – the common has its own **Wimbledon Windmill** (www.wimbledonwindmill.org.uk; Windmill Rd SW19; adult/child £2/1; ◷2-5pm Sat, 11am-5pm Sun late Mar-Oct; ◉Wimbledon; Ⓟ), a fine smock mill (ie octagonal-shaped with sloping weatherboarded sides) dating from 1817, which now contains a museum with working models on the history of windmills and milling. It was during a stay in the mill in 1908 that Robert Baden-Powell was inspired to write parts of his *Scouting for Boys*. The adjacent **Windmill Tearooms** (◷9am-5.30pm Mon-Fri, 9am-6pm Sat, 9am-6.30pm Sun) can supply tea, caffeine and sustenance.

On the southern side of the common, the misnamed **Caesar's Camp** is what's left of a roughly circular earthen fort built in the 5th century BC.

WIMBLEDON LAWN TENNIS MUSEUM   MUSEUM
(▱8946 6131; www.wimbledon.org; Gate 3, Church Rd SW19; adult/child £11/7, museum & tour £20/12.50/17; ◷10am-5pm; ◉/⒭Wimbledon, then ▭93) Of specialist interest to tennis players, dwelling as it does on the minutiae and ephemera of the sport's history, traced back here to the critical invention of the lawnmower in 1830 and the India-rubber ball in the 1850s. It's a state-of-the-art presentation, with plenty of video clips to let fans of the game relive their favourite moments. Note that the museum is only open to ticket holders during the championships; it houses a tearoom and a shop selling all kinds of tennis memorabilia.

BUDDHAPADIPA TEMPLE   TEMPLE
(▱8946 1357; www.buddhapadipa.org; 14 Calonne Rd SW19; admission free; ◷temple 9am-6pm Sat & Sun; grounds 9am-5pm daily; ◉Wimbledon, then ▭93) A surprising sight in a residential neighbourhood half a mile from Wimbledon Village, this is as authentic a Thai Theravada Buddhist temple as ever graced this side of Bangkok. The Buddhapadipa Temple was built by an association of young Buddhists in Britain and opened in 1982. The *wat* (temple) boasts a *bot* (consecrated chapel) decorated with traditional scenes by two leading Thai artists. Remember to take your shoes off before entering. The temple holds regular meditation classes and retreats (see the website).

To reach the temple, take the tube or train to Wimbledon and then bus 93 up to Wimbledon Parkside. Calonne Rd leads off it on the right.

✖ EATING

✖ Richmond

TOP
CHOICE **AL BOCCON DI'VINO**   ITALIAN £££
Map p458 (▱8940 9060; http://nonsolovinoltd.co.uk; 14 Red Lion St, TW9; mains £40; ◷lunch & dinner Thu-Sun, dinner Tue-Wed; ◉/⒭Richmond) This stellar Venetian restaurant is generally stuffed with Richmond locals, coveting some of the very finest Italian food in London. Rather audaciously perhaps, there's neither menu nor wine list, but this just adds to the adventurousness of the occasion, as overseen by owner Riccardo. You may get pasta fresca ripiena or agnello al forno, it all depends on the availability of the freshest ingredients. You are however guaranteed a remarkable feast of fine

flavour so book well ahead, especially for weekends.

CHEZ LINDSAY
FRENCH ££

Map p458 (☎8948 7473; www.chezlindsay.co.uk; 11 Hill Rise TW10; mains £10-20.50, 2-/3-course set lunches £9.75/11.75;☻/ⓇRichmond) A tasty slice of Brittany at the bottom of Richmond Hill, Chez Lindsay's simply furnished dining room wins fans with its wholesome Breton cuisine, comfortable ambience and river views. Great for seafood, house specialities also include adorable galettes (buckwheat pancakes) with countless tasty fillings, washed down with a variety of hearty (and very dry) Breton ciders.

PETERSHAM NURSERIES CAFÉ
MODERN EUROPEAN £££

Map p458 (☎8605 3627; www.petershamnurseries.com; Church Lane, off Petersham Rd TW10; mains £18-29, 2-/3-course menu Wed-Fri £23/28; ☻lunch Tue-Sun; ☻/ⓇRichmond, then 🚌65 or 371) In a greenhouse at the back of the gorgeously situated Petersham Nurseries is this award-winning cafe straight out of the pages of *The Secret Garden*. Well-heeled locals tuck into confidently executed food that often began life in the nursery gardens – organic vegetable dishes, such as artichokes braised with preserved lemon sage and black olives, feature alongside seasonal plates of, say, roasted quail with walnut sauce or white polenta with squid and sherry butter. Booking in advance is essential. There's also a **teahouse** (☻10am-4.30pm Tue-Sat, from 11am Sun) for sandwiches, tea and cakes.

Because of local residents and council concerns about traffic increasing with the cafe's popularity, patrons are asked to walk here via the picturesque river towpath, or use public transport.

DON FERNANDO'S
SPANISH £

Map p458 (www.donfernando.co.uk; 27f The Quadrant TW9; mains £9-17; ☻from noon; ☻/ⓇRichmond; 🖉) The Izquierdo family has been serving superb cuisine from their native Andalucía for over two decades. There's cheerful service, a tip-top list of tapas (£3.95 to £7.95), Spanish beers, wines, cava and culinary specialities, and vegetarians are very well-provided for.

✖ Kew

GLASSHOUSE
MODERN EUROPEAN ££

(☎8940 6777; www.glasshouserestaurant.co.uk; 14 Station Pde TW9; 3-course lunch £26-32.50, 3-course dinner £39.50; ☻/ⓇKew Gardens; 🖈) Round off a day at Kew Gardens at this superb restaurant. The glass-fronted exterior reveals a delicately lit, low-key interior, where the focus remains on the divinely cooked food. Diners revel in a menu from chef Daniel Mertl that combines English mainstays with modern European innovation. With a great weekend kid's lunch menu, the Glasshouse is sister restaurant to Chez Bruce (p284) in Wandsworth.

NEWENS MAIDS OF HONOUR
CAFE £

(www.theoriginalmaidsofhonour.co.uk; 288 Kew Rd W9; set tea £6.95; ☻9am-6pm Mon-Fri, 8.30am-6pm Sat & Sun; ☻/ⓇKew Gardens) The name of this quirky Kew tearoom (bombed during the Blitz) a short distance from the main entrance to Kew Gardens comes from its famed dessert (£3), supposedly created by Anne Boleyn, Henry VIII's ill-fated second wife. Made of puff pastry, lemon, almonds and curd cheese, anyone visiting should try it at least once.

WIMBLEDON TICKETS

For a few weeks each June and July, the sporting world's attention is fixed on the quiet southern suburb of Wimbledon, as it has been since 1877. Unsurprisingly, **Wimbledon** (www.wimbledon.com) will be the venue of the tennis events of the 2012 Games.

Most show-court tickets for the Wimbledon Championships are allocated through public ballot, applications for which usually begin in early August of the preceding year and close at the end of December. Entry into the ballot does not mean entrants will get a ticket. A quantity of show court, outer court, ground tickets and late entry tickets are also available if you queue on the day of play, but if you want a show-court ticket it is recommended you camp the night before in the queue. See www.wimbledon.com/championships/tickets for details.

✘ Putney & Barnes

ENOTECA TURI   ITALIAN ££
(www.enotecaturi.com; 28 Putney High St SW15; mains £9.50-22.50, 2-course set lunches/dinners £16.50/26.50; ⊘closed Sun; ⊜Putney Bridge, ⓡPutney) The atmosphere at this stylish place is serene, the service charming. Enoteca Turi devotes equal attention to the grape as to the food, which means that each dish, be it a shellfish *tagliolini* or saddle of new season lamb, comes recommended with a particular glass of wine (or you can pick from the enormous wine list if you have ideas of your own).

MA GOA   INDIAN ££
(www.ma-goa.com; 242-244 Upper Richmond Rd SW15; mains £8.75-15.50, 2-course set meal £10 daily; ⊘lunch Tue-Fri, dinner Mon-Sun; ⊜Putney Bridge, ⓡPutney; ⊘) With almost two decades satisfying Putney punters, the speciality here is the subtle cuisine of Portugal's former colony on India's west coast. Winning dishes include the lovely *chini raan achari* (pot roasted lamb shank with spice) and, among the seafood options, *Ma's fish caldin* (swordfish with coconut, mustard & fenugreek sauce). Vegetable dishes available.

CHOSAN   JAPANESE ££
(292 Upper Richmond Rd SW15; mains £4-17; ⊘closed Mon; ⊜Putney Bridge, ⓡPutney) This understated traditional little Japanese restaurant turns out excellent sushi and sashimi, as well as tempura and *kushiage* (deep-fried meat or vegetable skewers) which you can pair nicely with a glass of *junmai daiginjo* (a kind of highly refined 'pure rice' sake).

✘ Fulham

LOTS ROAD PUB & DINING ROOM   GASTROPUB ££
(www.lotsroadpub.com; 114 Lots Rd SW10; mains £10.50-17, 2-course set meal £10 Sun pm & Mon; ⊘11am-11pm Mon-Sat, 12.30-10.30pm Sun; ⊜Fulham Broadway) Even this charmingly tucked-away gastropub's affectation of listing prices in hundreds of pence is forgiven as light floods through the windows into the high-ceilinged, wood-lined curved dining area and onto the black-and-chrome bar, where choice wines are sold by the glass. Service is tip-top and the regularly changing menu

may read as standard fare – beef, salmon, lamb – but it's all delicious; don't miss the sticky toffee pudding; Sunday roasts are deservedly popular, as are the cheap Sunday evening and Monday set meals for a tenner. The 606 Club round the corner provides jazz.

HACHÉ   BURGERS ££
Map p440 (www.hacheburgers.com; 329-331 Fulham Rd SW10; mains £6.95-12.95; ⊘noon-10.30pm Mon-Wed, to 11pm Thu, to 11.15pm Fri & Sat, to 10pm Sun; ⊜Sloane Sq, then ⊞19 or 319) This consistently popular Fulham burger joint cooks Scotch beefsteak burgers just the way they should be, from steak au naturel to filling steak le grand: fresh, plump, cooked as you want and oozing flavour.

BLUE ELEPHANT   THAI ££
(www.blueelephant.com; 3-6 Fulham Broadway SW6; mains £15-22, Sunday brunch £30; ⊘lunch & dinner; ⊜Fulham Broadway) The surroundings, attentive staff and most importantly, the superb food of this Fulham institution, with branches around the globe, make this a memorable Thai dining choice. The atmosphere hovers on the cusp of kitsch; the dazzlingly bling Blue Bar giving it the final shove.

✘ Chiswick

FRANCO MANCA   PIZZA £
(⊘8747 4822; www.francomanca.co.uk; 144 Chiswick High Rd W4; ⊘noon-11pm; pizzas £4.50-6.95; ⊜Turnham Green) Sister establishment to the outstanding (but undersized) Brixton pizzeria (p283), Franco Manca has brought its deliciously aromatic thin crust, sourdough pizzas (and culinary pizzazz) to Chiswick, with longer hours and more space. The superb flavour and value remain a highly satisfying constant, making this an excellent choice when at the mercy of the munchies.

BOLLO   GASTROPUB
(www.thebollohouse.co.uk; 13-15 Bollo Lane W4; ⊘from noon; ⊜Chiswick Park) On the Chiswick/Acton fringes, this backstreet gastropub has been a huge success, run by local restaurateurs who redeveloped it from a simple local, offering a great seasonal menu and an open fire in winter. It's best at weekends when liveliest, catering to a well-heeled, older crowd looking for a pub and dining room rolled into one.

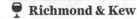 DRINKING & NIGHTLIFE

Richmond & Kew

WHITE CROSS
PUB

Map p458 (Water Lane TW9; Richmond) The riverside location, good food and fine ales make this bay-windowed pub on the site of a former monastery a winner. There are entrances for low and high tides, but when the river is at its highest, Cholmondeley Walk running along the Thames floods and the pub is out of bounds to those not willing to wade (very occasionally boats have to pick up stranded boozers). A chalkboard outside lists high tide times and depths. Quirky detail: there's a minute working fireplace *under* the window on your right as you enter.

CRICKETERS
PUB

Map p458 (8940 4372; The Green TW9; from noon; /Richmond) Delightfully facing Richmond Green from its southern side (where its very own team bats and bowls) and where you can decamp in warm weather with your pint, the Cricketers is a friendly and comfortable, themed (guess what) pub with a decent selection of ales, pub grub and a mixed clientele.

Putney & Barnes

YE WHITE HART
PUB

(The Terrace SW13; to midnight Fri & Sat; Barnes Bridge) This riverside Young's pub in Barnes was formerly a Masonic lodge; it's huge, traditional and welcoming downstairs, but the temptation in warmer months is to head to the balcony upstairs for choice Thames views and river breezes or plonk yourself down at one of the riverside tables. When Boat Race day arrives, the pub is deluged by beer-toting spectators angling for the best views.

JOLLY GARDENERS
PUB

(61-63 Lacy Rd SW15; Putney Bridge or Putney) With a terrific bamboo-shielded terrace fronting a quiet road, the JG has been lovingly and eclectically kitted out; you'd never guess that Victorian oak cabinets went quite so well with art deco lamps. The pub plays host to amiable 30-somethings

and boasts excellent wine and food menus, including full-on Sunday roasts.

COAT & BADGE
PUB

(www.geronimo-inns.co.uk; 8 Lacy Rd SW15; to midnight Fri & Sat; Putney Bridge or Putney) The Coat & Badge has gone for a tried and tested lounge-room approach (worn sofas, arm chairs, bare wood tables, secondhand books on shelves, standard lamps, stained glass, sports telly), all of which fashions a tempting comfort. There's a short but excellent menu, a marvellous front garden and live music every other Thursday evening.

SHIP
PUB

(8870 9667; www.theship.co.uk; 41 Jew's Row SW18; Wandsworth Town) Though the Ship is right by the Thames, the views aren't really spectacular along this stretch of the river – unless you're partial to retail parks and workaday bridges (which the owners freely admit). But all's otherwise shipshape: the outside area is large, the real ale goes down well, the barbecues in fine weather are a real treat and the conservatory bar is fun in any weather.

Fulham

FULHAM MITRE
PUB

(www.fulhammitre.com; 81 Dawes Rd SW6; Fulham Broadway) A beautiful, light-filled and airy pub with a large semicircular bar and walled courtyard at the back, the award-winning Mitre gets very crowded in the evenings and at the weekends, especially at lunchtime.

WHITE HORSE
PUB

(1-3 Parson's Green SW6; 9.30am-11.30pm Mon-Wed & Sun, to midnight Thu-Sat; Parsons Green;) Directly on Parsons Green, the White Horse is an inviting pub with a diverse clientele. Come here for good hearty fare, barbecues during summer, the warm and friendly atmosphere and – most important – the extensive range of beers (draught ales, Belgian Trappist beers). There's pleasant outside seating at the front.

Chiswick

CITY BARGE
PUB

(27 Strand on the Green W4; Gunnersbury) The Barge, perched dramatically close to – but

not on – the Thames, has existed as a pub since the Middle Ages (1484, to be exact), although the Luftwaffe gave it an unexpected facelift. Once known as the Navigators Arms, it is split into two bars (go for the old downstairs one) and there is a small waterside terrace. Little known fact: a scene from the Beatles' film *Help!* was shot here.

🍷 Twickenham

LONDON APPRENTICE
PUB

(www.thelondonapprentice.co.uk; 62 Church St TW7; 🚉Isleworth) This riverside pub (apparently unconnected with the Cornish village of the same name) has a history harking back to Tudor days, although the building is 18th century. Henry VIII is said to have dallied with wife-to-be No 5, Catherine Howard, at the tavern's older incarnation; other regulars included smugglers and highwaymen.

BARMY ARMS
PUB

(The Embankment TW1; 🚉Twickenham) This popular Twickenham pub gets packed to capacity on international match days; it claims to welcome *all* rugby fans. It's just by Eel Pie Island, a once-funky hippy hang-out that still attracts the alternative crowd, despite its heyday having long passed. It also has decent pub food and a charming beer garden to recommend it.

WHITE SWAN
PUB

(www.whiteswantwickenham.com; Riverside TW1; 🚉Twickenham) This traditional pub in Twickenham overlooks a quiet stretch of the Thames from what must be one of the most English-looking streets in London. It boasts a fantastic riverside location, a great selection of beer and a loyal crowd of locals. Even if you are not in Twickenham, the White Swan is worth a detour.

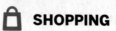

SHOPPING

📝 MORTIMER & BENNETT
FOOD

(📞8995 4145; www.mortimerandbennett.co.uk; 33 Turnham Green Tce W4; ⏰8.30am-6pm Mon-Fri, 8.30am-5.30pm Sat; 🚉Turnham Green) Tantalising range of speciality produce from across the world: St Felicien cheese from Lyon, Bonnat chocolates from Voiron, foie gras, avocado oil and lots more.

📝 CHISWICK FARMERS & FINE FOODS MARKET
MARKET

(Masonian Bowls Hall, Duke's Meadow W4; ⏰10am-2pm Sun; 🚉Turnham Green) Great Sunday farmers market with a large range of organic produce.

NORTH END ROAD MARKET
MARKET

(⏰9am-5pm Mon-Sat; 🚉Fulham Broadway or West Brompton) Great for fresh fruit and veg, cheap clothing and household goods.

🏃 SPORTS & ACTIVITIES

TWICKENHAM RUGBY STADIUM
STADIUM

(📞8892 2000; www.rfu.com; Rugby Rd, Twickenham TW1; 🚉Hounslow East, then 🚌281, 🚉Twickenham) The home of English rugby union. There is a **museum** here that showcases old matches in the video theatre and has a collection of 10,000 items of rugby memorabilia. You can go on a guided tour of the stadium and museum (adult/child/family £14/8/40) at 10.30am, noon, 1.30pm and 3pm Tuesday to Saturday and at 1pm and 3pm on Sunday. There are no tours on match days and the museum is closed on Mondays.

N

100km
60mi

50km
30mi

Oxford

Windsor & Eton

LONDON ★

Bath

Brighton

English Channel (La Manche)

Day Trips from London

Oxford p308

The world's oldest university town, Oxford's allure does not rest solely with its prestigious colleges, but with its delightful architecture and world-class museums too.

Brighton p312

With its heady mix of seediness and sophistication, Brighton is London's favourite seaside resort – and one with a trump card in the form of a mock-Mogul summer palace.

Windsor & Eton p315

An affluent town dominated by that nerve centre of British royalty, Windsor Castle, Windsor is a pleasant place to wander. Just minutes away is more laid-back Eton.

Bath p317

A cultural trendsetter and fashionable haunt for three centuries, Bath has so many architectural gems that the entire city has been named a World Heritage Site.

Oxford

Explore

The Victorian poet Matthew Arnold called Oxford 'that sweet city with her dreaming spires'. These days the spires coexist with a flourishing commercial city that has some typical urban social problems. But for visitors, the superb architecture and the unique atmosphere of the more than three dozen colleges – synonymous with academic excellence – and their courtyards and gardens remain major attractions.

The town dates back to the early 12th century (having developed from an earlier Saxon village) and has been responsible for educating some 26 British prime ministers, including Margaret Thatcher, Tony Blair and the current PM, David Cameron.

The Best...

➡ **Sight** Pitt Rivers Museum (p309)

➡ **Place to Eat** Jericho Tavern (p309)

➡ **Place to Drink** Turf Tavern (p309)

Top Tip

The only way to see the inside of what is the very symbol of Oxford – Radcliffe Camera – is to join an extended tour (£13) of the Bodleian Library departing at 9.30am on Wednesday, at 10am on Saturday and at 11.15am and 1.15pm on Sunday.

Getting There & Away

Bus Oxford Tube (☎772250; www.oxfordtube.com) and Oxford Espress (☎785400; www.oxfordbus.co.uk) buses depart every 10 to 30 minutes round the clock from London's Victoria coach station (return from £16) and can be boarded at various other points in London too, including Marble Arch, Notting Hill Gate and Shepherd's Bush. Journey time is an hour and 40 minutes.

Train There are two trains (☎0845 748 4950; www.nationalrail.co.uk) per hour from London's Paddington station (return from £16, one hour).

Need to Know

➡ **Area code** ☎01865

➡ **Location** 59 miles northwest of London

➡ **Tourist office** (☎252200; www.visitoxfordandoxfordshire.com; 15-16 Broad St; ⊗9.30am-5pm Mon-Sat, 10am-4pm Sun)

◉ SIGHTS

CHRIST CHURCH COLLEGE   COLLEGE

(www.chch.ox.ac.uk; St Aldate's; adult/child £7.50/6; ⊗9am-5.30pm Mon-Sat, 2-5.30pm Sun) Founded in 1525 and now massively popular with Harry Potter fans, having appeared in several of the films, Christ Church is the largest and grandest of all the 38 colleges. The main entrance is below **Tom Tower** (1681), designed by Christopher Wren and containing a 7-tonne bell called Great Tom. Visitors enter farther down St Aldate's via the wrought-iron gates of the War Memorial Gardens and Broad Walk. The college chapel is **Christ Church Cathedral**, the smallest in the country.

OTHER COLLEGES   COLLEGE

If time and opening hours permit (check www.ox.ac.uk/colleges for details), consider visiting any of the following important colleges: **Magdalen College** (www.magd.ox.ac.uk; High St; adult/child £4.50/3.50), pronounced *maud-lin*, with huge grounds bordering the River Cherwell; **Merton College** (www.merton.ox.ac.uk; Merton St; adult/child £2/free), with a 14th-century library where JRR Tolkien wrote much of the *Lord of the Rings;* **Trinity College** (www.trinity.ox.ac.uk; Broad St; adult/child £2/1), with an exquisitely carved chapel; and **Balliol College** (www.balliol.ox.ac.uk; Broad St; adult/child £2/1), founded in 1263 and thought to be the oldest college in Oxford.

BODLEIAN LIBRARY   LIBRARY

(www.bodleian.ox.ac.uk/bodley; Catte St; half-hour/one-hour tour £4.50/6.50; ⊗9am-5pm Mon-Fri, 9am-4.30pm Sat, 11am-5pm Sun) The early 17th-century Bodleian Library is one of the oldest public libraries in the world and one of just three copyright libraries in England. It is connected by tunnel with the Palladian-style **Radcliffe Camera** (1749), which functions as a reading room for the Bodleian and supports Britain's third-largest dome.

CAMBRIDGE: CLASSIC UNIVERSITY TOWN

If you liked Oxford, you'll love Cambridge. Awash in exquisite architecture, steeped in history and tradition and renowned for its quirky rituals, Cambridge is the quintessential English university town and has produced more Nobel prize winners than any other educational institution in the world. Must-see sites include 16th-century **King's College Chapel** (www.kings.cam.ac.uk), one of the most sublime buildings in Europe, and **Trinity College** (www.trin.cam.ac.uk), the largest and wealthiest of Cambridge's 31 colleges established by Henry VIII in 1546. But don't miss the rich **Fitzwilliam Museum** (www.fitzmuseum.cam.ac.uk), one of the first art museums in the UK, and a spot of punting (see p316), which is even more of a tradition than at Oxford. Some 60 miles north of London, Cambridge is accessible by bus from London's Victoria coach station (return from £18, two hours, every 10 mins) and by train from both Liverpool St station (return from £15) and King's Cross station (return from £21). The journey by rail takes between 45 minutes and 1¼ hours.

FREE ASHMOLEAN MUSEUM — MUSEUM

(www.ashmolean.org; Beaumont St; ⊙10am-6pm Tue-Sun) Britain's oldest public museum (1683) is now among its finest after a massive £60 million redevelopment. It contains everything from Egyptian artefacts and Chinese art to European and British paintings by the likes of Rembrandt, Michelangelo, Turner and Picasso. There's a wonderful rooftop terrace restaurant with stunning views of the city.

FREE OTHER MUSEUMS — MUSEUM

Oxford has some other excellent museums, including two housed in the same Victorian neogothic building on Parks Rd: the **Oxford University Museum of Natural History** (www.oum.ox.ac.uk; ⊙10am-5pm), famed for its dinosaur and dodo skeletons, and the incomparable **Pitt Rivers Museum** (www.prm.ox.ac.uk; ⊙12-4.30pm Mon, 1-4.30pm Tue-Sun), an Aladdin's cave of explorers' booty spread over three floors and crammed with such things as blowpipes, magic charms, voodoo dolls and shrunken heads from the Caribbean, Africa and the Pacific.

✖ EATING & DRINKING

QUOD — INTERNATIONAL ££

(☎202505; www.quod.co.uk; 92-94 High St; mains £12-16; ⊙7am-11pm Mon-Sat, 7am-10.30pm Sun) Perennially popular for its smart surroundings and buzzy atmosphere (not to mention its fine grills, fish dishes and pasta), this is the place Oxford students drag the rich relatives to when they're in town. Try its

afternoon tea (£6.95 to £20.95) from 3pm to 5.30pm.

JERICHO TAVERN — MODERN BRITISH ££

(☎311775; www.thejerichooxford.co.uk; 56 Walton St; mains £8-12) Chilled out, with big leather sofas, a large beer garden and a live-music venue upstairs (supposedly Radiohead played their first gig here), this old coaching inn just outside the city gates in the trendy Jericho district has added gastropub to its CV and it's a winner.

EDAMAME — JAPANESE £

(www.edamame.co.uk; 15 Holywell St; mains £6-9; ⊙lunch Wed-Sun, dinner Thu-Sat) It may not be the place for a leisurely dinner thanks to its cramped quarters, but the queue out the door speaks volumes for the quality of the food at this Japanese joint. The sushi (Thursday night only; £2.50 to £8) is divine. Last orders at 8.30pm.

JERICHO CAFÉ — MEDITERRANEAN ££

(www.thejerichocafe.co.uk; 112 Walton St; mains £8-12; ⊙8am-9.30pm Mon-Sat, 8am-8pm Sun) This relaxed cafe serves wholesome lunch and dinner specials, including everything from fish pie to falafel and meze. There are plenty of generous salads and lots of options for vegetarians too.

TURF TAVERN — PUB

(www.theturftavern.co.uk; 4 Bath Pl) Hidden away down a narrow alleyway off Holywell St, this tiny medieval pub is one of the town's best-loved and bills itself as 'an education in intoxication'. Home to real ales and student antics, it's always packed and is one of the few pubs in Oxford with plenty of outdoor seating.

Oxford

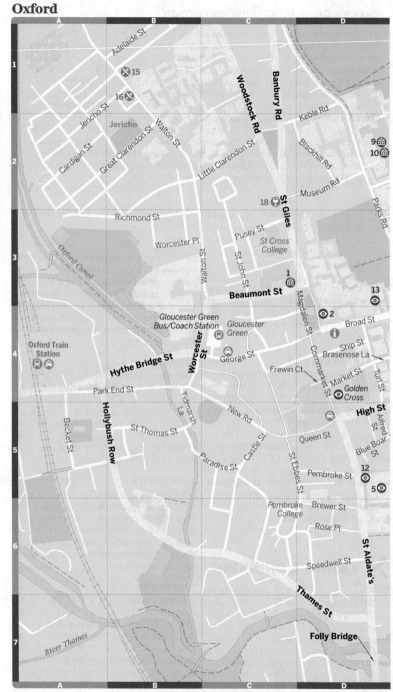

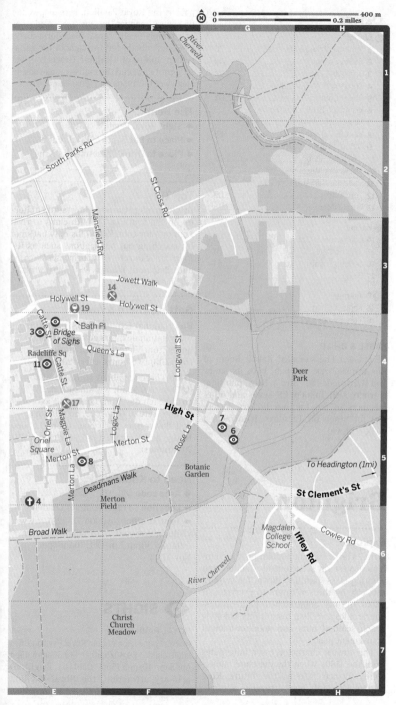

Oxford

EAGLE & CHILD PUB

(49 St Giles) The so-called Rabbit Room of this atmospheric old pub, with its snugs and Ganymede-like 'Bird & Baby' pub sign, is where JRR Tolkien, CS Lewis and other members of the Inklings literary society met for lunch on Tuesdays. It attracts a mellow crowd.

Brighton

••

Explore

With its large student population, the country's biggest gay scene outside London, and working-class families down for a jolly, this city by the sea caters to everyone. It offers in one outstretched hand atmospheric cafes, excellent restaurants, old-style beach seafood huts and good-for-a-laugh amusement pier

The town's character essentially dates from the 1780s when the dissolute, music-loving Prince Regent (the future King George IV) built his outrageous summer palace, the Royal Pavilion, here as a venue for lavish parties by the sea. And that charmingly seedy 'great-place-for-a-dirty-weekend' vibe lasted throughout the gang-ridden 1930s of Graham Greene's novel *Brighton Rock* and the mods-versus-rockers rivalry of the 1950s and '60s.

••

The Best...

➡ **Sight** Royal Pavilion (p312)
➡ **Place to Eat** Sam's of Brighton (p313)
➡ **Place to Drink** Basketmakers Arms (p315)

••

Top Tip

Brighton offers the best entertainment line-up on the south coast, with clubs to rival London's for cool. Keep tabs on what's hot by searching out publications such as the *Brighton Source* (www.brightonsource.co.uk) and *Brighton What's On* (http://whatson.brighton.co.uk).

••

Getting There & Away

Bus National Express (☑0871 781 8181; www.nationalexpress.com) runs hourly buses from Victoria coach station (return from £13, two hours, every 20 mins).

Train There are about 40 fast trains (☑0845 748 4950; www.nationalrail.co.uk) each day from London's Victoria station (return from £23, 50 minutes), and slower ones from Blackfriars, London Bridge and King's Cross (return from £10, 70 minutes).

••

Need to Know

➡ **Area code** ☑01273
➡ **Location** 53 miles south of London
➡ **Tourist office** (☑0906 711 2255; www.visitbrighton.com; 4-5 Pavilion Buildings; ☺9am-5.30pm Apr-Oct, 10am-5pm Nov-Mar)

◉ SIGHTS

ROYAL PAVILION PALACE

(www.royalpavilion.org.uk; Royal Pavilion Gdns; adult/child £9.80/5.60; ☺9.30am-5.45pm Apr-Sep, 10am-5.15pm Oct-Mar) Brighton's primary attraction, the Royal Pavilion, is an extraordinary folly – Indian palace on the outside and over-the-top chinoiserie within. The first pavilion, built in 1787, was a classical villa. It wasn't until the early 19th century, when things Asian were all the rage, that the current confection began to take shape under the direction of John Nash, architect of Regent's Park and its surrounding crescents. The entire over-the-top edifice, which Queen Victoria sold to the town in 1850 (apparently she found Brighton 'far too crowded'), is not to be missed. Of the dozen or so rooms, described in a concise, self-paced audioguide tour, have an especially good look on the ground floor at the **Long Gallery,** with its metal bamboo staircases; the **Banqueting Room** (especially the domed and painted ceiling and the rococo furnishings); the superb **Great Kitchen**; and the restored **Music Room**, with its nine lotus-shaped chandeliers and Chinese murals in vermilion and gold. Not to be missed on the 1st floor are the **South Galleries** and **Queen Victoria's Apartments** (including her water closet). Also keep an eye out for Rex Whistler's humorous painting *HRH The Prince Regent Awakening the Spirit of Brighton* (1944) in which the overweight (and all-but-naked) prince is rousing a nubile 'Brighton' with a lascivious look in his eye. It's just before the entrance to the tearoom.

BRIGHTON PIER   AMUSEMENT PARK
(www.brightonpier.co.uk; Madeira Dr) This grand old centenarian dating back to 1899 is the place to experience the tackier side of Brighton. There are plenty of stomach-churning fairground rides and dingy amusement arcades to keep you amused, and candy floss and Brighton rock (a type of hard candy) to chomp on while you're doing so.

BRIGHTON SEA LIFE CENTRE   AQUARIUM
(www.visitsealife.com/Brighton; Marine Pde; adult/child £16.20/11.40; ⊙10am-6pm Apr-Sep, 10am-5pm Oct-Mar) Just opposite the start of Brighton Pier is the world's oldest operating aquarium, with some 150 rays, octopuses, seahorses, turtles and other sea creatures in almost five dozen tanks and pools, as well as a glass-bottom boat walk-though tunnel.

FREE **BRIGHTON MUSEUM & ART GALLERY**   MUSEUM, GALLERY
(www.brighton-hove-museums.org.uk; Royal Pavilion Gdns; ⊙10am-5pm Tue-Sun) Of the 18 exhibition rooms here our favourites are

World Art, which effectively displays the spoils and souvenirs brought home by 19th-century colonialists; the excellent Brighton History Centre, with its 'naughty-but-nice' displays; and the Ancient Egypt collection. Other galleries display local pottery, fashion and costumes and fine art from the 15th to 20th centuries.

✕ EATING & DRINKING

SAM'S OF BRIGHTON   MODERN BRITISH **££**
(☑676222; www.samsofbrighton.co.uk; 1 Paston Pl; mains £11-18, 2-/3-course set lunch £10/14) Not exactly in the thick of things, this family-owned restaurant (those are pictures of the kids on the wall) in easternmost Kemp Town is well worth the journey for its innovative takes on dishes like roast breast of guinea fowl and braised Southdowns lamb. Brunch is served from 10am at the weekend.

TERRE À TERRE   VEGETARIAN **££**
(☑729051; www.terreaterre.co.uk; 71 East St; mains £14; ⊙noon-10.30pm Tue-Fri, noon-11pm Sat, noon-10pm Sun) A gourmet vegetarian restaurant is not an oxymoron; we enjoyed some of the most inventive meatless dishes we've ever had at this very popular and stylish eatery. The organic wine selection is a plus as are the coveted tables outside in warmer weather.

RIDDLE & FINNS   SEAFOOD **££**
(www.riddleandfinns.co.uk; 11 Meeting House Lane; mains £12-19; ⊙noon-10pm Sun-Thu, noon-11pm Fri & Sat) We're told that Gordon Ramsay called the fare served in this elegant champagne and oyster bar hidden in The Lanes 'seafood as it should be'. We don't care about that, but we'll come back for our favourite bivalves (from £12 a half-dozen), bubbly and candlelight by night. Weekday set lunch is a snip at £12.95. No bookings.

DUE SOUTH   INTERNATIONAL **£££**
(☑821218; www.duesouth.co.uk; 139 Kings Rd Arches; mains £17-28) Sheltered under a cavernous Victorian arch directly on the seafront, with a curved front window and small screened terrace on the promenade, this refined yet relaxed restaurant specialises in dishes cooked with wild, organic

Brighton

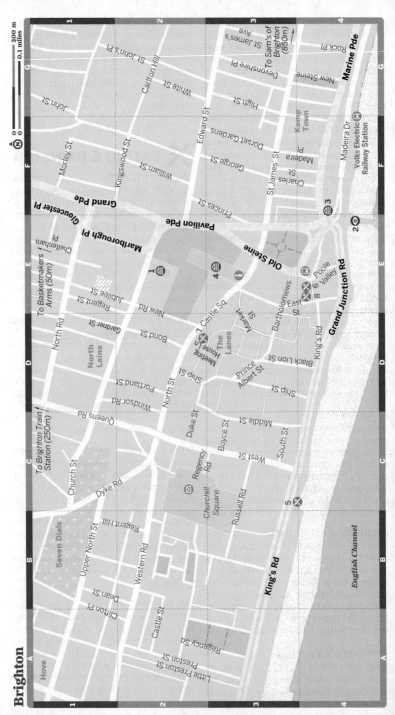

Hove

Seven Dials

To Brighton Train / Station (250m)

To Basketmakers Arms (50m)

North Laine

The Lanes

Kemp Town

Old Steine

English Channel

King's Rd

Grand Junction Rd

Marine Pde

To Sam's of Brighton (850m)

Volks Electric Railway Station

0   200 m
0   0.1 miles

Brighton

and free-range local produce, with an emphasis on fish.

MOCK TURTLE   CAFE £
(4 Pool Valley; mains £4-7; ◎9am-6pm Mon-Sat) Our favourite place in central Brighton for all-day breakfast (£6.95), a sandwich, a bowl of soup (from £3.50) or a cream tea (£5.65) is this almost-over-the-top tearoom done up in shades of blue and crammed with old furniture and mismatched crockery. Utterly charming.

BASKETMAKERS ARMS   PUB
(www.thebasketmakersarms.co.uk; 39 Cheltenham Pl) Probably the best traditional pub in Brighton, Basketmakers is in the North Laine district, southeast of the train station, and has eight ales on tap. Food (fish of the day, Mexican chilli) is way above average and served daily from noon to 8.30pm (7pm on Saturday, 6pm on Sunday).

Windsor & Eton

Explore

With its romantic architecture and superb state rooms, Windsor Castle is one of Britain's premier tourist attractions and, since it is so close to central London and easily accessible by rail and road, it crawls with tourists in all seasons. If possible, avoid visiting at weekends and during the peak months of July and August when the queues to get into Liz's humble abode are at their longest.

If you can't avoid these periods and need a respite from the crowds, cross the pedestrian Windsor Bridge over the Thames and head for Eton. By comparison it's far quieter. And while it, too, is a one-trick pony in the form of the world's most prestigious boys' school, its pedestrianised centre is lined with antique shops and art galleries rather than chain restaurants and high street brand shops.

The Best...

➡ **Sight** Windsor Castle (p316)
➡ **Place to Eat** Gilbey's (p317)
➡ **Place to Drink** Two Brewers (p317)

Top Tip

A must for any visitor is the **changing of the guard** (◎11am Mon-Sat Apr-Jul, alternate days Aug-Mar), a fabulous spectacle of pomp and ceremony that draws large crowds to the castle gates. You'll get a better view if you stay to the right of the crowd, and if you're just interested in watching the marching bands, find a spot along High or Sheet Sts; the guards leave from Victoria Barracks on the latter at 10.45am and return an hour later.

Getting There & Away

Bus Green Line buses (☑0844 801 7261; www.greenline.co.uk) Nos 701 and 702 link Victoria coach station with Windsor (return from £10, 1¼ hours) at least hourly every day.

Train Trains (☑0845 748 4950; www.nationalrail.co.uk) from Waterloo station go to Windsor Riverside station every 30 minutes, or hourly on Sunday (return from £10, 50 minutes). Trains from Paddington go via Slough to Eton and Windsor Central station (return from £9, 45 minutes).

Need to Know

➡ **Area code** ☑01753
➡ **Location** 25 miles west of London
➡ **Tourist office** (☑743900; www.windsor.gov.uk; Old Booking Hall, Windsor Royal Station, Thames St; ◎9.30am-5.30pm Mon-Sat, 10am-4pm Sun May-Aug, 10am-5pm Mon-Sat, 10am-4pm Sun Sep-Apr)

IN FOR A PUNT

Punting is the pastime of choice on the River Cherwell in Oxford and along the Backs in Cambridge. It looks fairly straightforward, but we've landed in the drink enough times to assure you that it ain't. Still, that shouldn't deter anyone who isn't afraid of getting a bit wet.

The secret to propelling the flat-bottomed boats is to push gently on the pole to get the punt moving and then to use the pole as a rudder to keep on course.

Punts are available daily from 9.30am to dusk, March to October. If you'd like to give it a go in Oxford, head for **Magdalen Bridge Boathouse** (www.oxfordpunting. co.uk; Magdalen Bridge; punting max 5 people per hr £16-20, chauffeured boat max 4 people per 30 min £23) just below the northeast end of Magdalen Bridge. In Cambridge, where punt hire costs £14 to £18 per hour and a 45-minute chauffeured trip is £15, two recommended firms are **Granta Punt Hire Company** (www.puntingincambridge. com; Newnham Rd) and **Scudamore's** (www.scudamores.com; Granta Pl & Mill La).

⊙ SIGHTS

WINDSOR CASTLE   CASTLE
(www.royalcollection.org.uk; adult/child £16.50/9.90, when State Apartments closed £9/6; ⊙9.45am-5.15pm Mar-Oct, 9.45am-4.15pm Nov-Feb) British monarchs have inhabited Windsor Castle for more than 900 years, and it is well known to be the Queen's favourite residence and the place she calls home after returning from her work 'week' (now just Tuesday to Thursday) at the 'office' (Buckingham Palace). A disastrous fire in 1992 nearly wiped out this incredible piece of English cultural heritage, luckily damage, though severe, was limited and a £37 million restoration, completed in 1997, has returned the state apartments to their former glory.

Starting out as a wooden castle erected around 1080 by William the Conqueror, and rebuilt in stone in 1170, this is one of the world's greatest surviving medieval castles, and its longevity and easy accessibility from London guarantee its popularity.

The castle area, covering more than five hectares, is divided into three wards. In the Upper Ward, the **State Apartments**, which are closed to the public at certain times (check the website), reverberate with history. The self-paced audioguide tour starts with the impossibly opulent **Grand Staircase** and weapons-filled **Grand Vestibule** and leads into the **Waterloo Chamber**, created to commemorate the Battle of Waterloo and filled with portraits of the great and the good by Sir Thomas Lawrence (1769–1830).

From here you move to the **King's Rooms** and **Queen's Rooms**. These are lessons in how the other half lives, with opulent furniture, tapestries and paintings by Canaletto, Dürer, Gainsborough, Van Dyck, Hogarth, Holbein, Rembrandt and Rubens. Next is the extraordinary **St George's Hall**, the structure most affected by the 1992 fire but now brought back to life, including its signature hammerbeam roof. This is where state banquets take place. The tour ends in the **Garter Throne Room**.

Outside on the North Terrace you can't help noticing the queues that form for the impossibly intricate **Queen Mary's Doll's House**, the work of architect Sir Edwin Lutyens. Built in 1923 on a 1:12 scale, it took 1500 craftsmen three years to finish and it's complete in every detail, right down to electric lights that work and flushing toilets.

Moving westward through the Middle Ward and past the distinctive **Round Tower**, rebuilt in stone from the original Norman keep in 1180, you enter the Lower Ward. Here one of Britain's finest examples of early English architecture, **St George's Chapel** (begun by Edward IV in 1475, but not completed until 1528) has a superb nave done in Perpendicular Gothic style, with gorgeous fan vaulting. The chapel contains **royal tombs** of 10 monarchs including Edward IV, Henry VIII, Charles I and George VI and the late Queen Mother.

South of the castle is beautiful **Windsor Great Park** (⊙8am-dusk) covering an area of some 10,500 hectares. The **Long Walk** is a 3-mile jaunt along a tree-lined path from King George IV Gate to the Copper Horse statue (of George III) on Snow Hill, the park's highest point.

ETON COLLEGE
COLLEGE

(www.etoncollege.com; Baldwins Shore; adult/child £6.50/5.50; ⊘guided tours 2pm & 3.15pm daily school holidays, Wed, Fri, Sat & Sun term time) Over the River Thames is arguably the world's most famous public (ie private) school, one that has educated 19 prime ministers and a host of explorers, authors and economists. Several buildings, including the **Lower School**, date from the founding in 1440.

 EATING & DRINKING

GILBEY'S
MODERN BRITISH £££

(☑854921; www.gilbeygroup.com; 82-83 High St, Eton; mains £16-24; 2-/3-course lunch £18.50/24; ⊘lunch & dinner Mon-Fri, afternoon tea Sat & Sun) This little restaurant just beyond the bridge in Eton is one of the area's finest. Terracotta tiling and a sunny courtyard garden lend a Continental cafe air, but the understated decor and menu are indisputably British. Excellent wine list.

TOWER
BRASSERIE ££

(☑848547; High St; mains £10.50-14.50; ⊘7am-11pm Mon-Fri, from 8am Sat & Sun) Giant windows with priceless views over Windsor Castle are the immediate allure at this eatery in the Harte and Garter Hotel. The menu is brasserie style with a choice of classic British dishes – grills, fish, steaks – simply and perfectly done.

DRURY HOUSE
BRITISH ££

(☑863734; www.druryhouse.co.uk; 4 Church St; mains £7.95-12.95; ⊘9.30am-5.30pm) What purports to be the oldest restaurant in Windsor (1645) enjoys pride of place on a delightful cobbled street some 50m from the castle. Food is simple but filling (puddings, pies, stews); come for the fabulous wood-panelled dining rooms over three floors. There's outside seating on the footpath in summer.

CROOKED HOUSE OF WINDSOR
TEAROOM £

(www.crooked-house.com; 51 High St; afternoon teas from £8.50; ⊘9.30am-6pm daily Apr-Oct, 11am-5pm Mon-Fri Nov-Mar) This is Windsor's most traditional (and central) tearoom, complete with sloping floors, wooden beams and royal cream teas.

TWO BREWERS
PUB

(www.twobrewerswindsor.co.uk; 34 Park St) This 17th-century inn perched on the edge of Windsor Great Park and the Long Walk is close to the castle's tradesmen's entrance and supposedly frequented by staff from the castle. It's a quaint and cosy place, with dim lighting, obituaries to castle footmen and royal photographs with irreverent captions on the wall. Great pub grub too.

Bath

Explore

This delightful city of honey-coloured stone has always been renowned for its architecture, especially its fine Georgian terraces. Nowadays, though, it is celebrated in equal measure for its association with the novelist Jane Austen – not so much for her actual works but for the films based on them. Sometimes it seems the crowds just can't get enough.

The Romans established the town of Aquae Sulis in AD 44 and built an extensive baths complex and a temple to the goddess Sulis Minerva. Throughout the Middle Ages, Bath was an ecclesiastical centre and a wool-trading town, but it was not until the early 18th century that Bath and its spas became the centre of fashionable society. Certain districts in Bath still vie with some in London as the nation's top 'des res' (desirable residences).

The Best...

➡ **Sight** Roman Baths (p319)
➡ **Place to Eat** Circus (p320)
➡ **Place to Drink** Star Inn (p321)

Top Tip

The Roman Baths have been off-limits to bathers since 1976 for health reasons. But should you want to take the plunge in Bath's thermal waters there is finally a way: **Thermae Bath Spa** (☑0844 888 0844; www.thermaebathspa.com; New Royal Bath, Bath St; New Royal Bath spa session per 2hr/4hr £25/35; ⊘9am-10pm, last entry 7.30pm), an

Bath

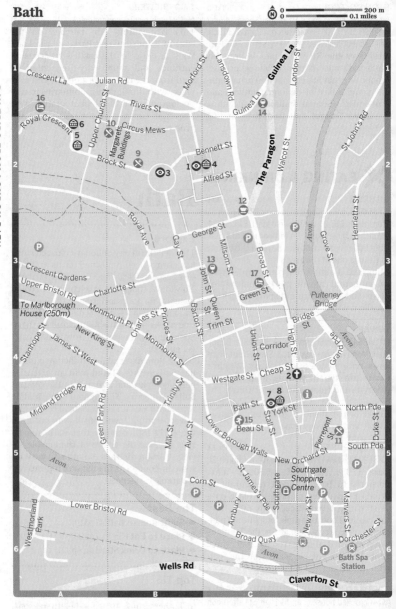

ultramodern shell of stone and glass sitting comfortably beside a Georgian spa building, that has steam rooms, waterfall showers and a choice of bathing venues, including an open-air rooftop pool with jaw-dropping views of Bath.

Getting There & Away

Bus National Express (☏0871 781 8181; www.nationalexpress.com) links London's Victoria coach station (one-way from £20, 3½ hours) with Bath up to 10 times a day.

Bath

Train There are direct trains (☏0845 748 4950; www.nationalrail.co.uk) from London Paddington and Waterloo stations (return from £34, 1½ hours) at least hourly.

Need to Know
➡ **Area code** ☏01225
➡ **Location** 115 miles west of London
➡ **Tourist office** (☏0906-711 2000; www.visitbath.co.uk; Abbey Churchyard; ⊙9.30am-6pm Mon-Sat & 10am-4pm Sun Jun-Sep, 9.30am-5pm Mon-Sat & 10am-4pm Sun Oct-May)

⊙ SIGHTS

ROMAN BATHS   MUSEUM
(www.romanbaths.co.uk; Abbey Churchyard; adult/child £12/7.80; ⊙9am-10pm Jul & Aug, 9am-6pm Mar, Jun, Sep & Oct, 9.30am-5.30pm Jan, Feb, Nov & Dec) Ever since the Romans arrived in Bath, life has revolved around the three natural springs that bubble up near Bath Abbey. The 2000-year-old baths now form one of the best-preserved ancient Roman spas in the world. The heart of the complex is the **Great Bath**; head down to water level and along the raised walkway to see the Roman paving. Other highlights are the vast **Temple of Sulis Minerva** with its gilded bronze head of the goddess and the 12th-century **King's Bath**, built around the original sacred spring, from which 1.5 million litres of hot water still pour into the pool every day.

Above the temple is the 18th-century **Pump Room** (Stall St), now a cafe-restaurant where you can take a drinking cure (50p) from 9.30am to 4.30pm daily. The water is hot and smelly but said to cure anything and everything.

ROYAL CRESCENT &
CIRCUS   HISTORIC BUILDING
The crowning glory of this city of architectural gems is the **Royal Crescent**, a semicircular terrace of majestic houses overlooking the green sweep of Royal Victoria Park. Designed by John Wood the Younger and completed in 1774, the houses would have originally been rented for the season by wealthy socialites. For a glimpse into the splendour of Georgian life, head for **No 1 Royal Crescent** (www.bath-preservation-trust.org.uk; adult/child £6.50/2.50; ⊙10.30am-5pm Tue-Sun late Feb-Oct, 10.30am-4pm mid-Nov–mid-Dec), which has been fully restored using only 18th-century materials. Some 200m east along Brock St is the **Circus**, a ring of 33 symmetrical houses divided into three terraces. Famous residents have included Thomas Gainsborough, Clive of India, David Livingstone and US actor Nicholas Cage.

BATH ABBEY   CHURCH
(www.bathabbey.org; requested donation £2.50; ⊙9am-6pm Mon-Sat Apr-Oct, 9am-4.30pm Nov-Mar, 1-2.30pm & 4.30-5.30pm Sun year-round) King Edgar was crowned in a church in Abbey Courtyard in 973 but the present Bath Abbey was built between 1499 and 1616, making it the last great medieval church erected in England. The nave's wonderful fan vaulting was added in the 19th century. Outside, the most striking feature is the west facade, where angels climb up and down stone ladders, commemorating a dream of the founder, Bishop Oliver King (note the crown and olive tree symbols).

SLEEPING IN BATH

You can reach Bath in just 1½ hours from London, but you might decide to spend the night. The tourist office (☎0844 847 5256; www.visitbath.co.uk) has a free accommodation-booking service.

➡ **Royal Crescent Hotel** (☎823333; www.royalcrescent.co.uk; 16 Royal Cres; d/ste £199/£700; P❄@☎) This exquisite hotel counts 45 guestrooms dripping in Georgian luxury, common rooms with ceilings that look like the inside of a Wedgwood bowl and the most desirable address in town. The private spa in a converted coach house and the spacious gardens to the rear are a positive delight.

➡ **Marlborough House** (☎318175; www.marlborough-house.net; 1 Marlborough Lane; s £75-110, d £85-135, tr £95-145; P☎) Our favourite B&B in Bath has six tastefully themed rooms and a welcoming host, Peter, who is a font of information. The Victorian (No 2) and Georgian (No 3) rooms have four-post beds and there's an extra bath on the 1st floor.

➡ **St Christopher Bath** (☎481444; www.st-christophers.co.uk/bath-hostels; 6 Green St; dm £16-19, d £55; @☎) A branch of a chain of successful UK-based hostels with the signature Belushi's pub on the ground floor, St Christopher Bath has a half-dozen dormitory rooms with six to 12 beds, a twin and two doubles (one with bath). The views from the chill-out room at the top are priceless.

ASSEMBLY ROOMS   HISTORIC BUILDING

(www.nationaltrust.org.uk/main/w-bathassemblyrooms; 19 Bennett St; adult/child £2/free; ◷10.30am-6pm Mar-Oct, 10.30am-5pm Nov-Feb) Opened in 1771, the glorious Assembly Rooms were where fashionable Bath socialites once gathered to waltz, play cards and listen to the latest chamber music. Highlights include the card room, tearoom and the truly splendid ballroom, all of which are lit by their original 18th-century chandeliers. If you really want to see what Jane Austen and her contemporaries wore, go downstairs to the **Fashion Museum** (www.fashionmuseum.co.uk; adult/child £7.25/5.25; ◷10.30am-5pm Mar-Oct, 10.30am-4pm Nov-Feb), which displays costumes worn from the 17th century onward, including some alarmingly oversized crinolines.

✗ EATING & DRINKING

CIRCUS   MODERN BRITISH ££

(☎466020; www.thecircuscafeandrestaurant.co.uk; 34 Brock St; mains lunch £5.50-10, dinner £11-14; ◷10am-midnight Mon-Sat) This appropriately named restaurant on the western edge of the Circus is our favourite place in Bath. The food, prepared by chef/owner Alison Golden, is excellent and beautifully presented, the welcome is warm, and you can choose to eat on the ground floor over-looking a small courtyard or in the intimate cellar dining room.

YAK YETI YAK   NEPALESE £

(☎442299; www.yakyetiyak.co.uk; 12 Pierrepont St; mains £7.50-9, 3-course lunch £10.50) You'd look for a month of Sundays for a Nepalese restaurant in London, but here's one serving excellent food in a colourful basement eatery just up from the train station. Try the pork dumplings with hemp-seed chutney, any of the cumin-heavy lamb dishes, and the *musurko dal* made with red lentils.

SALAMANDER   BRITISH ££

(☎428889; www.bathales.com/pubs/salamander.html; 3 John St; mains £9-13; ◷lunch daily, dinner to 9pm Mon-Thu, to 9.30pm Fri & Sat) Owned by the city's bespoke brewery, Bath Ales, the Sally's ground-floor bar is the place to sample amber-coloured Gem and Golden Hare and the stronger (5.2%) and darker Rare Hare. The supper room upstairs has moved on from 'steak and chops' to some far more adventurous dishes made with locally sourced meat and produce.

LIME LOUNGE   BRITISH ££

(☎421251; www.limeloungebath.co.uk; 11 Margarets Buildings; mains lunch £7-10, dinner £11-14.50; ◷8am-midnight Mon-Sat, 10am-10pm Sun) Though it's open later and longer than most, the greener-than-green Lime

Lounge works best as an upbeat place for lunch while exploring the Royal Crescent to the west and the Circus to the east. Oak-smoked kippers with poached egg, cheddar and bacon tartlets, lime-dusted chips... The food is truly divine.

JIKA JIKA
CAFE

(www.jikajika.co.uk; 4a Princes Buildings, George St; ☺8am-6.30pm Mon-Thu, 8am-7pm Fri, 8.30am-7pm Sat, 9am-5.30pm Sun) This shrine to the coffee bean is a must if you can't live without your latte. Beans are sourced from various rare estates and roasted by hand, ensuring that the espressos here are among the best outside London.

STAR INN
PUB

(www.star-inn-bath.co.uk; 23 The Vineyards, off the Paragon) Not many pubs can boast they serve 'ales from the vineyards' or retain their original 19th-century bar fittings. It's the brewery tap for Bath-based Abbey Ales; some ales are served straight from the barrel into traditional jugs, and you can ask for a pinch of snuff in the 'smaller bar'.

Sleeping

Finding the right accommodation is integral to your London experience, and there's no shortage of choice. But just because London is a city that never sleeps doesn't mean it doesn't go to bed: rooms in popular hotels often need to be booked well in advance. There are some fantastic hotels about, whatever the price tag, but plan ahead.

Hotels

London has some stunning hotels and many are experiences in their own right. The lead up to 2012 has seen some big-profile openings, while others remain under development. Standards across the top end and much of the boutique bracket are high, but so are prices. A host of more budget boutique hotels has explored a profitable niche, while a rung or two down in overall quality and charm, midrange chain hotels generally offer good locations and dependable comfort. Demand can often outstrip supply – especially at the bottom end of the market – so book ahead, particularly during holiday periods and in summer.

B&Bs

Bed and breakfasts dwell a tier below hotels, but often have boutique-style charm, are housed in lovely old buildings and offer a personal level of service. B&B clusters can be found in South Kensington, Victoria and Bloomsbury.

Hostels

After B&Bs the cheapest forms of accommodation are hostels, both the official Youth Hostel Association (YHA) ones and the (usually) hipper, more party-orientated independent ones. Hostels vary in quality so select carefully; most offer twins as well as dorms.

Rates & Booking

Deluxe hotel rooms will cost from around £350 per double but there's good variety at the top end, so you should find a room from about £180 offering superior comfort without the prestige. Some boutique hotels also occupy this bracket. There's a noticeable dip in quality below £180 for a double, but we have listed the best in this range. Under £100 and you're at the more serviceable, budget end of the market. Look out, though, for weekend deals that can put a better class of hotel within reach. Rates often slide in winter. Book through the hotels' websites for the best online deals or promotional rates. Unless otherwise indicated, accommodation prices quoted in this book include breakfast. International Youth Hostel Federation (IYHF) members net discounts on YHA accommodation. Be aware that room prices will skyrocket to unspecified heights during the 2012 Olympic Games.

Apartments

If you're in London for a week or more, a short-term or serviced apartment such as 196 Bishopsgate (p329) or Number 5 Maddox Street (p325) may make sense; rates at the bottom end are comparable to a B&B.

Websites

Lonely Planet (www.hotels.lonelyplanet.com) Bookings.

YHA central reservations system (✆0800 019 1700; www.yha.org.uk) Hostel room bookings.

Visit London (www.visitlondon.com) London tourist organisation's website, special deals and list of gay-friendly accommodation.

LondonTown (✆7437 4370; www.londontown.com)

Lonely Planet's Top Choices

York & Albany (p333) North London Georgian elegance meets luxurious comfort.

Haymarket (p325) Stunning composition, magnificent pool and central location.

Hoxton Hotel (p332) Excellent value, cool location, nifty looks.

Clink78 (p334) Heritage hostel and former magistrates court.

Best by Budget

£
Clink261 (p334)
Church Street Hotel (p337)
YHA Earl's Court (p335)

££
Dean Street Townhouse (p325)
Rough Luxe (p334)
Kennington B&B (p338)

£££
No 10 Manchester Street (p325)
One Aldwych (p325)
Rookery (p332)

Best Romantic Hotels

Portobello Hotel (p334)
Ritz (p327)
Gore (p330)
Twenty Nevern Square (p336)

Best for Families/Kids

Arran House Hotel (p326)
Brown's (p326)
Ridgemount Hotel (p328)

Best Boutique Hotels

Dean Street Townhouse (p325)
Rough Luxe (p334)
Zetter Hotel & Townhouse (p332)
Church Street Hotel (p337)

Best B&Bs

B+B Belgravia (p329)
Aster House (p330)
Number 16 St Alfege's (p338)
Kennington B&B (p338)

Best for Contemporary Cool

W (p326)
Hempel (p335)
Soho Hotel (p326)
K West (p335)

Best for Heritage

Claridge's (p326)
Ritz (p327)
Waldorf Hilton (p327)
St Pancras Renaissance Hotel (p334)

Best for Views

W (p326)
One Aldwych (p325)
The Bingham (p339)

Best for Swimming Pools

Shoreditch Rooms (p333)
Waldorf Hilton (p327)

Best for Hotel Restaurants

Claridge's (p326)
Dean Street Townhouse (p325)
W (p326) and Spice Market (p120)

NEED TO KNOW

Price Ranges
In our listings we've used the following codes to represent the price of an en suite double room in high season:

➡ £   under £80
➡ ££   £80-180
➡ £££   over £180

Reservations
Book rooms as far in advance as possible, especially for weekends and peak periods.
➡ **British Hotel Reservation Centre** (☎7592 3055; www.bhrconline.com; booking fee £5) has desks at airports and major train stations.
➡ **Visit London** (☎0870 156 6366; www.visitlondon.com) offers a free booking service with a wide range of accommodation options and has special deals.

Tax
Value-Added Tax (VAT, now a staggering 20%) is added to hotel rooms. Some hotels include this in their advertised rates, some don't. Prices in this chapter include VAT.

Checking In & Out
Check in is usually 2pm, though most places will let you check in earlier, or at least leave your luggage. Check out is usually between 10am and noon.

Breakfast
Breakfast may be included in the room rate. Sometimes this is a continental breakfast; full English breakfast could cost extra.

SLEEPING

Where to Stay

Neighbourhood	For	Against
The West End	Close to main sights; ubercentral; great transport links; wide accommodation range in all budgets; great restaurants	Busy, tourist areas; expensive
The City	St Paul's and Tower of London; good transport links; handy central location; quality hotels; some cheaper weekend rates	Very quiet at weekends; a business district so prices high during week
The South Bank	Near Tate Modern, London Eye and Southbank Centre; cheaper than West End; excellent pubs and views	Many chain hotels; choice and transport limited
Kensington & Hyde Park	Excellent for South Kensington museums and shopping; great accommodation range; stylish area; good transport	Quite expensive; drinking and nightlife options limited
Clerkenwell, Shoreditch & Spitalfields	Trendy area with great bars and nightlife; excellent for boutique hotels	Few top sights; transport options limited
The East End & Docklands	Well positioned for Olympic Park; markets, multicultural feel; great restaurants and traditional pubs	Rather limited sleeping options; some areas less safe at night
Hampstead & North London	Leafy feel; vibrant and energetic nightlife; pockets of village charm; excellent boutique hotels and hostels; great gastropubs; quiet during week	Non-central and away from main sights
Notting Hill & West London	Cool cachet; great shopping, markets and pubs; fab boutique hotels; good transport	Pricey; light on sights
Greenwich & South London	Ace boutique options; leafy escapes; near top Greenwich sights	Sights spread out beyond Greenwich; transport limited
Richmond, Kew & Hampton Court	Smart riverside hotels; semi-rural pockets; close to Kew Gardens, Hampton Court Palace and Richmond; quiet; fantastic riverside pubs	Sights spread out; long way from central London

🛏 The West End

TOP CHOICE HAYMARKET
BOUTIQUE HOTEL £££

Map p422 (📞7470 4000; www.haymarkethotel. com; 1 Suffolk Pl SW1; r £260-340, ste from £410; ⊖Piccadilly Circus; ✳🐕🛜📶) The progeny of hoteliers and designers Tim and Kit Kemp, the Haymarket is opulently beautiful, with hand-painted Gournay wallpaper, signature fuchsia and green designs in the room, a sensational 18m pool with mood lighting, an exquisite library lounge with honesty bar, and original artwork throughout. Wi-fi is £20 a day.

TOP CHOICE HAZLITT'S
HISTORIC HOTEL £££

Map p422 (📞7434 1771; www.hazlittshotel.com; 6 Frith St W1; s £185, d £230-360, ste £550-850; ⊖Tottenham Court Rd; ✳📶) Built in 1718 and comprising three original Georgian houses, this is the one-time home of essayist William Hazlitt (1778–1830). Bedrooms have been furnished with original antiques from the Georgian era and boast a wealth of seductive details, including panelled walls, mahogany four-poster beds, Victorian claw-foot tubs and sumptuous fabrics, as well as creature comforts such as complimentary wi-fi, iPod docking stations and flat-screen TVs.

TOP CHOICE DEAN STREET TOWNHOUSE
BOUTIQUE HOTEL £££

Map p422 (📞7434 1775; www.deanstreettown house.com; 69-71 Dean St W1; r £160-310; ⊖Tottenham Court Rd; ✳📶) This little gem at the heart of Soho has a wonderful boudoir atmosphere with its Georgian furniture, retro black-and-white tiled bathroom floors, beautiful lighting and girly touches (Cowshed bathroom products, hairdryer *and* straighteners in every room!). 'Medium' and 'bigger' rooms have king-sized beds and antique-style bathtubs.

NO 10 MANCHESTER STREET
BOUTIQUE HOTEL £££

Map p428 (📞7317 5900; www.tenmanchester streethotel.com; 10 Manchester St W1; d £225; ✳📶; ⊖Baker St) In a wonderful Edwardian town house, No 10 Manchester epitomises the definition of boutique hotel: print wallpaper, designer beiges and browns, splashes of colour, high-tech must haves (iPods, free wi-fi, DVD player – DVD collection in reception – Nespresso machines etc) and impeccable service. No 10 Manchester also prides itself on its humidor and outdoor heated lounge, where you can try one of the 60 different kinds of cigars and cigarillos.

FIELDING HOTEL
BOUTIQUE HOTEL ££

Map p432 (📞7836 8305; www.the-fielding-hotel.co.uk; 4 Broad Ct, Bow St WC2; s/d from £90/140; ✳📶; ⊖Covent Garden) Located in a pedestrianised court in the heart of Covent Garden, this pretty, 24-room hotel has been refurbished to a very high standard: the bathrooms have lovely walk-in showers, the rooms are beautifully done up, have free wi-fi and are fully air-conditioned. The hotel doesn't provide breakfast but considering the location, you'll be spoilt for your choice of cafe.

ONE ALDWYCH
LUXURY HOTEL £££

Map p432 (📞7300 1000; www.onealdwych. co.uk; 1 Aldwych WC2; d £275-370, ste from £585; ✳🐕🛜; ⊖Covent Garden or Charing Cross or Temple) Housed in what were once art nouveau newspaper offices (1907), One Aldwych is an upbeat hotel with 105 rooms and modern art everywhere. The spacious and stylish rooms are replete with raw silk curtains, natural tones, daily fresh flowers and huge bathtubs. The circular suites have fabulous views of The Strand and Waterloo Bridge. Unusually for a luxury hotel, wi-fi is complimentary. All rooms are fitted with British as well as American sockets.

NUMBER 5 MADDOX STREET
APARTMENT £££

Map p422 (📞7647 0200; www.5maddoxstreet. com; 5 Maddox St W1; ste £270-650; ✳📶; ⊖Oxford Circus) Right off Regent St, this luxury establishment, with 12 suites/apartments, will make you feel like you're living the high life in your own London pad. On show are Eastern themes, along with all the facilities the contemporary traveller could require (iPod docking stations, wi-fi etc). Every apartment has a fully equipped kitchen, and some even get their own little balcony or patio. There is no lift. Wi-fi is £15/50 per day/week.

YHA OXFORD ST
HOSTEL £

Map p422 (📞0845 371 9133; www.yha.org. uk; 3rd fl, 14 Noel St W1; dm £16-28, d £51-74; @📶; ⊖Oxford Circus or Tottenham Court Rd) The most central of London's seven YHA hostels is also one of its most attractive, thanks to a great refurbishment in 2011. It is also one of the most intimate, with only 93 beds and excellent shared facilities: we love the fuchsia kitchen and the bright, funky lounge. Dormitories are three and four beds and there are private doubles and twins. The shop sells coffee and beer, and internet costs £1 per 20 minutes on the fab new computers, or £5/9 per day/week for wi-fi.

ARRAN HOUSE HOTEL   HOTEL ££

Map p426 (☑7636 2186; www.arranhotel-london.com; 77-79 Gower St WC1; dm £30-35, s/d £80/120, with shared bathroom £70/97; @☎; ⊖Goodge St) This welcoming place in Bloomsbury provides excellent value for the location. The 28 rooms range from basic dormitory-style accommodation to bright, well-furnished doubles with bathrooms. There is a cosy lounge at the front of the house, with big leather sofas, piles of magazines and two guest computers. And last but not least, Arran House has two gorgeous gardens at the back, perfect for a few drinks or a quiet read. Guests can use the kitchen and dining room at their leisure and there are laundry facilities. Wi-fi is free.

COVENT GARDEN HOTEL   BOUTIQUE HOTEL £££

Map p432 (☑7806 1000; www.coventgardenhotel.co.uk; 10 Monmouth St WC2; r £250-355, ste from £400; ✷☎; ⊖Covent Garden or Tottenham Court Rd) This 58-room boutique hotel housed in an old French hospital uses antiques (don't miss the beautiful marquetry desk in the drawing room), gorgeous, bright fabrics and quirky bric-a-brac to stake out its individuality. There's an excellent bar-restaurant called Brasserie Max just off the lobby, and two stunning guest lounges on the 1st floor that come into their own in the winter. Wi-fi is £20 a day.

W   LUXURY HOTEL £££

Map p422 (☑7758 1000; www.whotels.com; 10 Wardour St W1; r from £329; ✷☎; ⊖Leicester Sq) Everything, it seems, has been designed for fun at the W: from the disco-ball adorned reception to the curved walls and furniture, the cartoon cushions and the room entrances via the bathroom (yes). The retro decor, with padded walls and red and gold themes, is slightly reminiscent of an Austin Powers film, but the W is definitely more sophisticated than that. Being right at the heart of the West End, room prices increase as you go up the building.

ACADEMY   BOUTIQUE HOTEL £££

Map p426 (☑7631 4115; www.theetoncollection.com; 21 Gower St WC1; d from £180; ✷☎; ⊖Goodge St) This beautiful, terribly English 49-room hotel is set across five Georgian town houses. The lovely rooms are kitted out with fluffy feather duvets, elegant furnishings and the latest in creature comforts (iPod docking stations in every room, flat-screen TVs and free wi-fi). There's a conservatory overlooking a leafy back garden with a fish pond, and a cosy breakfast room but no lift.

SOHO HOTEL   BOUTIQUE HOTEL £££

Map p422 (☑7559 3000; www.sohohotel.com; 4 Richmond Mews W1; r/ste from £295/415; ✷☎; ⊖Tottenham Court Rd) One of London's hippest hotels, the Soho is in a converted car park just off Dean St. All the hallmarks of the eclectically chic Tim and Kit Kemp have been writ large over 91 individually designed rooms; the colours lean towards the raspberries and puces, and there's original artwork throughout the hotel, including a stunning black-cat Botero sculpture at the entrance. Wi-fi is £20.

BROWN'S   HISTORIC HOTEL £££

Map p422 (☑7493 6020; www.brownshotel.com; 30 Albemarle St W1; r/ste from £485/915; ✷☎; ⊖Green Park) A stunner of a five-star number, this 117-room hotel was created in 1837 from 11 houses joined together. Each room has been individually decorated by designer Olga Polizzi and many feature antiques and original artworks. The rest of the hotel is similarly attractive: the traditional English Tea Room has retained wonderful Edwardian oak panelling and working fireplaces; the Donovan Bar features original prints by Terence Donovan and a stunning stained-glass window above the bar; while the restaurant, Hix at the Albermarle (by celebrity chef Mark Hix), is decorated with original art by Tracy Emin, Rankin and other illustrious contemporary names.

CLARIDGE'S   LUXURY HOTEL £££

Map p428 (☑7629 8860; www.claridges.co.uk; 55 Brook St W1; r/ste from £299/555; ✷@☎; ⊖Bond St) Claridge's, with 203 rooms, is one of the greatest of London's five-star hotels. Well known for its sumptuous art deco features (including 1930s vintage furniture that once graced the staterooms of the decommissioned SS *Normandie*), it recently added a more modern touch with a series of rooms and suites designed by fashion designer Diane von Furstenberg. Better known for her wrap dresses, this was her first interior-design project but it was a resounding success, with bold, colourful fabrics and elegant, classic furniture designs.

CHARLOTTE STREET HOTEL
BOUTIQUE HOTEL £££

Map p426 (☑7806 2000; www.charlottestreet hotel.com; 15-17 Charlotte St W1; r/ste from £240/410; ✳@🕏; ⊖Tottenham Court Rd) This wonderful 52-room hotel, where Laura Ashley goes postmodern and comes up smelling of roses, is a favourite of visiting media types. The Drawing Room, with its working fireplace and oversized sofas, is a delightful place to wind down. The Charlotte also has its own private cinema and has films every Sunday night (£35 for a three-course meal and film). Wi-fi is £20 a day.

RITZ
LUXURY HOTEL £££

Map p430 (☑7493 8181; www.theritzlondon.com; 150 Piccadilly W1; r/ste from £305/585; ✳🕏; ⊖Green Park) What can you say about a hotel that has lent its name to the English lexicon? Arguably London's most celebrated hotel, this 136-room caravanserai has a spectacular position overlooking Green Park and is supposedly the Royal Family's home away from home. All rooms have period interiors and antique furniture. The Long Gallery and Palm Court restaurant, done in Louis XVI themes, have a strict formal-dress code (shirt and tie).

CUMBERLAND HOTEL
HOTEL £££

Map p428 (☑0871 376 9014; www.thecumber land.co.uk; Great Cumberland Pl W1; s £169, d from £179; ✳🕏; ⊖Marble Arch) You'll be forgiven for thinking you've accidentally stumbled into a contemporary art gallery in the hangar-sized lobby with larger-than-life sculptures and backlit floor. This, however, is London's third largest hotel, with more than 1000 guest rooms. Many have views of nearby Hyde Park and all have cheerful, modern decor. It's worth paying the extra £40 for an executive room, which comes with free wi-fi, free pay TV, bathrobes, accessories and access to the executive lounge.

GENERATOR
HOSTEL £

Map p426 (☑7388 7655; www.generatorhostels. com; Compton Pl, opp 37 Tavistock Pl WC1; dm/ s/d/tr from £15/20/40/60; @🕏; ⊖Russell Sq)

With its industrial decor, blue neon lights and throbbing techno, the huge Generator (more than 800 beds) is one of the grooviest budget places in central London. The bar, complete with pool tables, stays open until 2am and there are frequent themed parties. Dorm rooms have between four and 16 beds. There is no kitchen but breakfast is provided and the large canteen serves bargain dinners from £4.50.

JESMOND HOTEL
B&B ££

Map p426 (☑7636 3199; www.jesmondhotel.org. uk; 63 Gower St WC1; s/d/tr £60/100/130, s/d with shared bathroom £50/80/105; @🕏; ⊖Goodge St) We've received more than a few letters from readers singing the praises of this family-run B&B in Bloomsbury. The 16 guest rooms – a dozen with bathroom – are basic but clean and cheerful, and it has a small, pretty garden. There's laundry service and internet's free, but wi-fi is a £10 flat rate.

HARLINGFORD HOTEL
HOTEL ££

Map p426 (☑7387 1551; www.harlingfordhotel. com; 61-63 Cartwright Gardens WC1; s/d £96/115; 🕏; ⊖Russell Sq) With its 'H' logo proudly sewn on your bedroom cushion, and a modern interior with lots of lavender and mauve, and green-tiled bathrooms, this stylish Georgian hotel with 43 rooms is arguably the best on a street where competition is fierce. Service is a little lacklustre but the price is unbeatable. The hotel has no lift and lots of stairs!

WALDORF HILTON
HISTORIC HOTEL £££

Map p432 (☑7836 2400; www.hilton.co.uk/ waldorf; Aldwych WC2; r from £350; ✳🕏🏊; ⊖Temple, Covent Garden or Charing Cross) The glorious Edwardian splendour of this renovated old pile still lives on in the heritage-listed Palm Court. The rooms feature some very contemporary designs but the hotel is working hard to make the best of its heritage and anecdote-filled history, with afternoon teas, historic tours, a pianist in the reception area, and a Louis XVI–style restaurant.

CHESTERFIELD
BOUTIQUE HOTEL £££

Map p428 (☑7491 2622; www.redcarnation hotels.com; 35 Charles St W1; s/d/ste from £275/375/585; ✳🕏; ⊖Green Park) Just a block west of Berkeley Sq, the 110-room Chesterfield comprises five floors of refinement and lustre hidden behind a fairly plain Georgian facade. It has ceilings with mouldings, marble floors, upholstered walls and period-style furnishings, as you'd expect from one of the grande dames of London digs.

HOTEL LA PLACE
HOTEL ££

Map p428 (☎7486 2323; www.hotellaplace.com; 11 Nottingham Pl W1; s/d from £99/145; ✳@☎; ⊖Baker St) The 18 rooms here are very much in the traditional mode, but impeccably cared for, and some have updated bathrooms. All double rooms have king-size beds with orthopaedic mattresses, and the friendly family management has installed a 24-hour wine bar downstairs, an ice machine on the 1st floor and a little computer room.

MORGAN HOTEL
HOTEL ££

Map p426 (☎7636 3735; www.morganhotel.co.uk; 24 Bloomsbury St WC1; s/d/ste/tr from £100/125/150/170; ✳@☎; ⊖Tottenham Court Rd) In a row of 18th-century Georgian houses alongside the British Museum, the family-owned Morgan has distinguished itself by its friendliness, great service (free wi-fi, free computer downstairs, breakfast fit for a king) and good value. The decor in the rooms is somewhat dated, but impeccably clean. The larger suites (no air-con) are well worth the extra money.

VICARAGE HOTEL
HOTEL ££

Map p456 (☎7229 4030; www.londonvicaragehotel.com; 10 Vicarage Gate W8; s/d/tr/q £102/130/170/185, with shared bathroom £60/102/130/140; @☎; ⊖High St Kensington or Notting Hill Gate) Gilt mirrors, sconces, chandeliers and striped red-and-gold wallpaper – this former Victorian home almost on Palace Gardens Tce (where the phenomenal cherry trees in spring have to be seen to be believed) is fantastically located. The 17 rooms are less lavish, but atmospherically old-world-English and slightly larger than usual. The 3rd- and 4th-floor rooms have shared bathrooms.

YHA HOLLAND HOUSE
HOSTEL £

Map p456 (☎7937 0748; www.yha.org.uk; Holland Walk W8; dm £23.65; @; ⊖High St Kensington) Built into the Jacobean wing of Holland House (1607) in the middle of Holland Park, this hostel has 201 beds in large rooms with between six and 20 beds. It's all about location here, as it's always busy and rather institutional. There's a cafe and kitchen.

AROSFA
HOTEL ££

Map p426 (☎7636 2115; www.arosfalondon.com; 83 Gower St WC1; s/d from £69/90; ⊖Euston Sq or Goodge St) The new owners have really spanked up old Arosfa, decking out the lounge with Philippe Starck furniture, blow-ups of the Manhattan skyline on the wall and a generally modern look. The rooms are less lavish, however, with cabinlike bathrooms in many of them. Some have been refurbished but they remain, on the whole, very small. It's good value, in any case.

RIDGEMOUNT HOTEL
HOTEL £

Map p426 (☎7636 1141; www.ridgemounthotel.co.uk; 65-67 Gower St WC1; s/d £60/86, with shared bathroom £48/66; @☎; ⊖Goodge St) This old-fashioned hotel offers its guests a warmth and consideration that you don't come across very often in the city these days. About half of its 30 utilitarian rooms have bathrooms; there are a number of triples and quadruples that will be useful for groups of friends and families. It also has a laundry service and complimentary wi-fi.

GRANGE BLOOMS HOTEL
HOTEL £££

Map p426 (☎7323 1717; www.grangehotels.com; 7 Montague St WC1; r from £225; ✳☎; ⊖Tottenham Court Rd or Russell Sq) This elegant 18th-century town house has the feel of a country home, which belies its position in the heart of London (in what used to be the grounds of the British Museum). The decor is all carpets and print fabrics and there's a delightful terrace garden at the back where breakfast can be served on sunny days. Wi-fi is £10 per day.

SEVEN DIALS HOTEL
HOTEL ££

Map p432 (☎7240 0823; www.sevendialshotellondon.com; 7 Monmouth St WC2; s/d £95/105; ☎; ⊖Covent Garden or Tottenham Court Rd) The Seven Dials is a clean and comfortable budget/midrange option in a very central location. Half of the 18 rooms face onto charming Monmouth St; the ones at the back don't get much of a view but are quieter. Wi-fi works up to the 1st floor.

🛏 The City

THREADNEEDLES
BOUTIQUE HOTEL £££

Map p438 (☎7657 8080; www.theetoncollection.com; 5 Threadneedle St EC2; r/ste from £390/606, weekend rate r/ste from £222/390, breakfast £15; ❄ 🛜; ⊖Bank) You have to know this place is here. It's wonderfully anonymous, though once through the doorway the grand circular lobby, which is furnished in a vaguely art deco style and covered with a hand-painted glass dome, comes into view. The 69 rooms are very pleasantly kitted out, all with high ceilings and dark, sleek furnishings.

ANDAZ LIVERPOOL STREET HOTEL £££
Map p438 (📞7961 1234; www.andaz.com; 40 Liverpool St EC2; r/ste from £234/396, breakfast £20; ❄ 🛜; ⊖Liverpool St) A Hyatt-branded property, this is the London flagship for its youth-oriented Andaz chain. There's no reception, just black-clad staff who check you in on mini laptops. Rooms are cool and spacious, with free nonalcoholic drinks and local calls. On top of this there are five restaurants and a subterranean Masonic temple discovered during the hotel's refit in the '90s. This is a solid choice, well located and a good compromise between business and boutique, with rates dropping over the weekend.

196 BISHOPSGATE APARTMENT £££
Map p438 (📞7621 8788; www.196bishopsgate. com; studio £232-245, 1-bed apt £276-288, cheaper after 6 nights; ❄ 🛜; ⊖Liverpool St) These 47 luxury serviced apartments are well equipped and in a very handy location opposite Liverpool St station. Two-bed and executive studios (with balcony) are also available. Apartments here are a good option for a longer stay.

YHA LONDON ST PAUL'S HOSTEL £
Map p438 (📞0845 371 9012; www.yha.org.uk; 36 Carter Lane EC4; dm £20-25, d £50; 🛜; ⊖St Paul's) This 208-bed hostel, housed in a heritage-listed building with a gorgeous facade, stands in the very shadow of St Paul's Cathedral and opposite the Tate Modern. Dorms have between three and 11 beds, and twins and doubles are available. There's a licensed cafeteria but no kitchen, plus a lot of stairs and no lift. It's also good for families and there's a seven-night maximum stay.

🛏 The South Bank

BERMONDSEY SQUARE HOTEL BOUTIQUE HOTEL ££
Map p436 (📞7378 2450; www.bermondsey squarehotel.co.uk; Bermondsey Sq, Tower Bridge Rd SE1; r £120-250, ste £300-500; ❄ @ 🛜; ⊖Lon-

don Bridge) Just the ticket for Bermondsey is this hip, purpose-built, 80-room boutique hotel. Lobby photos of Brigitte Bardot and a young Anthony Hopkins set the '60s mood. The smallish but stylish standard rooms are fine but the best are the far-pricier suites at the top, named after iconic '60s songs. Match your mood with a colour from delicious Lucy (black, with terrace and fun outside hot tub), Ruby (red, of course), Jude (pink), Lily (white) and Eleanor (yellow and orange, with Jacuzzi). Below, London's most famous flea market takes place on Fridays.

ST CHRISTOPHER'S VILLAGE HOSTEL £
Map p436 (📞7407 1856; www.st-christophers. co.uk; 161-163 Borough High St SE1; dm £15-30, d & tw £40-55; @ 🛜; ⊖Borough or London Bridge) This 185-bed place is the flagship of a hostel chain with basic, but cheap and clean accommodation. There's a roof garden with bar, barbecue and excellent views of the Thames, as well as a cinema (with high-profile comedy events) and Belushi's bar below for serious partying to 2am weekdays and 4am at the weekend. Dorms have four to 14 beds. Its two nearby branches (same contact details) are **St Christopher's Inn** (Map p436; 121 Borough High St SE1), with 50 beds, another pub and a small veranda; and the **Oasis** (Map p436; 59-61 Borough High St SE1), with 40 beds, a laundry, cafe and women-only dormitory.

MAD HATTER HOTEL ££
Map p436 (📞7401 9222; www.madhatterhotel. com; 3-7 Stamford St SE1; r £145-180, breakfast £8-13, weekend rate incl breakfast £130; ❄ @ 🛜; ⊖Southwark) Its 30 rooms across three floors are quite generic, but the solid Mad Hatter is well located and slightly more homely than most chain hotels (it's part of the Fuller's brewery group) thanks to its traditionally styled reception area and attached pub of the same name (open round the clock for guests).

🛏 Kensington & Hyde Park

🔝 B+B BELGRAVIA B&B ££
Map p440 (📞7259 8570; www.bb-belgra via.com; 64-66 Ebury St SW1; s/d/tw/tr/q £99/135/145/165/175; @ 🛜; ⊖Victoria) This spiffing six-floor Georgian B&B, remodelled with contemporary flair, boasts crisp common areas and a chic lounge echoing the black-and-white tiled floor. The 17 rooms

STUDENT DIGS

During university holidays (generally mid-March to late April, late June to September and mid-December to mid-January), student dorms and halls of residence are open to paying visitors. Choices include **LSE Vacations** (☎7955 7575; www.lsevacations. co.uk; s/tw/tr from £27/44/69), whose eight halls include the 800-bed **Bankside House** (Map p436; ☎7107 5750; 24 Sumner St SE1; ⊖Southwark); the 281-bed **Butler's Wharf Residence** (Map p436; ☎7107 5798; 11 Gainsford St SE1; ⊖Tower Hill or London Bridge); and **High Holborn Residence** (Map p432; ☎7107 5737; 178 High Holborn WC1; ⊖Holborn).

King's College Conference & Vacation Bureau (☎7248 1700; www.kcl.ac.uk/ kcvb; s £44, tw £65) handles the **Great Dover St Apartments** (Map p436; ☎7407 0068; 165 Great Dover St SE1; ⊖Borough) and the **Stamford St Apartments** (Map p436; ☎7633 2182; 127 Stamford St SE1; ⊖Waterloo).

Another option worth trying is **International Students House** (p334).

(some with shower, others with bath) aren't enormous but there's a further batch of studio rooms with compact kitchens at No 82 Ebury St (studio £99 to £145, apartment £270). A pleasant courtyard garden is out back and guests get to use hotel bicycles for free. No lift.

ASTER HOUSE　　　　　B&B £££
Map p440 (☎7581 5888; www.asterhouse.com; 3 Sumner Pl SW7; s £120, d & tw £180-250, ste £250; ❄@; ⊖South Kensington) This award-winning Singaporean-run property is truly excellent. From the lovely house and quintessential English aura, the welcoming staff, the comfortable rooms with quality furnishings and sparkling bathrooms to the delightful plant-filled Orangerie and Jemima the duck in the charming garden, it's all delightful. Furthermore, prices are reasonable and guests can borrow mobile phones.

NUMBER SIXTEEN　　　BOUTIQUE HOTEL £££
Map p440 (☎7589 5232; www.numbersixteen hotel.co.uk; 16 Sumner Pl SW7; s £120, d £165-270, breakfast £16-17.50; ❄@⊙; ⊖South Kensington) With cool grey muted colours, tasteful clarity and choice art throughout, Number Sixteen is four properties in one and a stunning (and rather labyrinthine) place to stay, with 42 individually designed rooms, a cosy drawing room and a fully stocked library. And wait till you see the idyllic, long back garden set around a fish pond with a few cosy snugs, or have breakfast in the conservatory.

HALKIN　　　　　　　HOTEL £££
Map p440 (☎7333 1000; www.halkin.como.bz; Halkin St SW1; r/ste from £450/650, breakfast £29; ❄@⊙; ⊖Hyde Park Corner) With very muted Asian influences and an excellent Thai restaurant (Nahm), the chichi Halkin is for business travellers of a minimalist bent. Bedroom doors are hidden within curved wooden hallways, and the 41 swish rooms are filled with natural light, cream walls, burlwood panelling and large all-marble bathrooms. The staff, wearing Armani-designed uniforms, are all obliging. There's no rear garden, though guests can use the key for nearby Belgrave Square.

BLAKES　　　　　　　HOTEL £££
Map p440 (☎7370 6701; www.blakeshotels.com; 33 Roland Gardens SW7; s £195, d £295-395, ste from £695, breakfast £12.50-19.50; Ⓟ❄@⊙; ⊖Gloucester Rd) For classic style one of your first choices in London should be black-painted Blakes: five Victorian houses cobbled into one hotel and incomparably designed by Anouska Hempel of the Hempel Hotel (p335). Each of its 48 guest rooms is elegantly decked out with a distinctive style: expect four-poster beds (with and without canopies), rich fabrics and antiques set on bleached hardwood floors.

GORE　　　　　　　　HOTEL £££
Map p440 (☎7584 6601; www.gorehotel.com; 190 Queen's Gate SW7; s £140-180, d £180-280, ste from £440, breakfast £12.95-16.95; ❄@⊙; ⊖Gloucester Rd or High St Kensington) Charismatically kooky, this splendid 50-room hotel is a veritable palace of polished mahogany, oriental carpets, antique-style bathrooms, potted aspidistras and portraits and prints (some 4500, in fact) covering every square centimetre of wall space. The attached **Bistrot One Ninety Queen's**

Gate (2-/3-course lunch £21.50/23.50) is a fine place for brunch or a pre- or post-concert drink for the nearby Royal Albert Hall.

LUNA SIMONE HOTEL　　　HOTEL ££
Map p440 (☑7834 5897; www.lunasimonehotel. com; 47-49 Belgrave Rd SW1; s £70-80, d £95-120, tr £130-150, q £150-170; @; ⊖Victoria or Pimlico) This central and welcoming 35-room hotel is a popular choice among the hotels along Belgrave Rd. Compact rooms come with clean showers, double-glazed windows and innocuous blonde-wood furniture. Luggage storage is free; no lift. English breakfast included.

KNIGHTSBRIDGE HOTEL　　　HOTEL £££
Map p440 (☑7584 6300; www.knightsbridge hotel.com; 10 Beaufort Gardens SW3; s £180-205, d & tw £230-320, ste £375-645, breakfast £18-19; P✳@☎; ⊖Knightsbridge) The lovely six-floor, 44-room Knightsbridge occupies a 200-year-old house just around the corner from Harrods (p199) on a particularly quiet, no-through-traffic, tree-lined street. Each room is different, with elegant and beautiful interiors done in a sumptuous, subtle and modern English style. Some of the singles, although beautifully furnished, are very small for the price. Check out is 11am (Sundays noon).

LANESBOROUGH　　　HOTEL £££
Map p440 (☑7259 5599; www.lanesborough. com; Hyde Park Corner SW1; s £395-455, d £525-615, ste from £745-14,000; ✳@☎; ⊖Hyde Park Corner) Where visiting divas doze and foreign royalty hang their crowns, this former hospital's (St George's) lavishly appointed guest rooms exude a regal opulence. All guests receive personal butlers, and staff are impeccably dressed in bowler hats and morning suits. The recently opened Lanesborough Suite ranges across an epic 380 sq metres, with four bedrooms, five and a half bathrooms, a kitchen, two living rooms, a dining room and a price tag of £14,000 per night.

SAN DOMENICO HOUSE　　　HOTEL £££
Map p440 (☑7581 5757; www.sandomenico house.com; 29-31 Draycott Pl SW3; s £210, d £235-255, ste £295-360; ✳☎; ⊖Sloane Sq) With 15 lovely rooms and some very imposing furniture, this elegant and boutique Italian-owned hotel has kept the feel of a family house. Each room is individual in colour and style, from the well-dressed doubles

to the grand split-level four-poster rooms. Ornate and splendid, with service that's top drawer. Three rooms have a balcony.

WINDERMERE HOTEL　　　HOTEL ££
Map p440 (☑7834 5163; www.windermere-hotel. co.uk; 142-144 Warwick Way SW1; s £125, d £145-185, tw £155-185, 3-bed f £195-215; @☎; ⊖Victoria) The attractive, award-winning and recently refurbished and expanded Windermere has 19 small but bright and individually designed rooms in a sparkling-white mid-Victorian town house (now with lift). A reliable and reasonably priced restaurant is downstairs.

CADOGAN HOTEL　　　HOTEL £££
Map p440 (☑7235 7141; www.cadogan.com; 75 Sloane St SW1; r £185-325, ste £395-850, breakfast £22-28; ✳@☎; ⊖Sloane Sq) This 64-room hotel is a wonderful hybrid, with two lower floors that are contemporary in style and the recently refurbished top two floors a wonderful vestige from Edwardian times, filled with polished oak panels, wing chairs, rich heavy fabrics and a refined drawing room for afternoon tea. Not surprisingly the most indulgent (and coveted) rooms are No 118, where Oscar Wilde was arrested for 'indecent acts' in 1895, and the Lillie Langtry room (No 109) – all rose wallpaper, feather boas and pink lace – where the actress (and mistress to Edward VII) once laid her head.

MEININGER　　　HOSTEL £
Map p440 (☑7590 6910; www.meininger-hostels. com; 65-67 Queen's Gate SW7; dm £15-27, s/tw/tr from £75/70/96; ✳@☎; ⊖Gloucester Rd or South Kensington) Opposite the Natural History Museum, this German-run 'city hostel and hotel' has 48 clean rooms, most of which are dorms with between four and 12 beds. The 11 private rooms all have bathrooms and a good-size working area. The service is efficient and correct, there's good security and a bar in-house plus a great roof terrace hosting barbecues in warm weather.

ASTOR HYDE PARK　　　HOSTEL £
Map p440 (☑7581 0103; 191 Queen's Gate SW7; dm/tw £22/28 Sun-Thu, dm/tw £35/40 Fri-Sat; @; ⊖Gloucester Rd or High St Kensington) With its wood-panelled walls, bay windows with leaded lights, 19th-century vibe and posh address just over from the Royal Albert Hall, this hostel has 150 beds in rooms

over five floors (no lift), including dorms with three to 12 beds, and a good kitchen complete with incongruous pool tables. Its sister property, the **Astor Kensington** (Map p440; ☎7373 5138; 138 Cromwell Rd SW7; dm £13-20, d £60-70; ☻Gloucester Rd), 1km or so to the southwest, is every bit as nice but in a modern, upbeat sort of way, and is closer to the action and a tube stop. It's got 121 beds (dorm rooms in bright primary colours have four to 10 beds), a huge and bright modern kitchen and (joy of joys) a lift.

ASTOR VICTORIA   HOSTEL £

Map p440 (☎7834 3077; 71 Belgrave Rd SW1; dm £18-20, d £45-90; ☻Pimlico) Mother ship of the Astor group of five hostels, this sedate place has 180 beds, including four- and eight-bed dorms and a handful of twins and doubles with shared shower and toilet. The hostel is helpfully staffed by travellers in between trips who are loaded with useful information.

🛏 Clerkenwell, Shoreditch & Spitalfields

TOP CHOICE ROOKERY   BOUTIQUE HOTEL £££

Map p444 (☎7336 0931; www.rookeryhotel.com; 12 Peter's Lane, Cowcross St EC1; s £222, d £276-300, ste £420-612, breakfast £11.95; ❄🛜; ☻Farringdon) This absolute charmer is a warren of 33 rooms that has been built within a row of 18th-century Georgian houses and fitted out with antique furniture (including a museum-piece collection of Victorian baths, showers and toilets), original wood panelling, statues in the bathrooms and artworks selected personally by the owner. There's a small courtyard garden and a wonderfully private and whimsical feel to the whole place.

ZETTER HOTEL & TOWNHOUSE   BOUTIQUE HOTEL £££

Map p444 (☎7324 4444; www.thezetter.com; 86-88 Clerkenwell Rd EC1; r £222-294, studio £294-438, breakfast £13.50-17.50; ❄🛜; ☻Farringdon) The Zetter comprises two quite different properties, both exemplary in their execution. The original Zetter is a temple of cool with an overlay of kitsch on Clerkenwell's titular street. Built using sustainable materials on the site of a derelict office, its 59 rooms are small but perfectly formed, with Penguin Classics on the bookshelves and

hi-tech flat screens and air-conditioning (using water from the hotel's very own bore hole). The rooftop studios are the real treat though, with terraces commanding superb views across the city. Top-quality fare is available in the ground-floor restaurant (p206).

The **Zetter Townhouse** (49-50 St John's Sq; r £222-294, ste £438-480), on a pretty square behind the Zetter, has just 13 rooms in a characterful Georgian pile, each uniquely decorated in period style but with witty touches such as headboards made from reclaimed fairground carousels. Further treats include the Roberts radios, beautiful roll-top baths and the hand-painted lifts. The fantastic hotel bar (p212) is a destination in itself.

TOP CHOICE HOXTON HOTEL   BOUTIQUE HOTEL ££

Map p444 (☎7550 1000; www.hoxtonhotels.com; 81 Great Eastern St EC2; r inc breakfast £1-199; ❄🛜; ☻Old St) This is hands down the best hotel deal in London. In the heart of Shoreditch, this sleek 208-room hotel aims to make its money by being full each night. You get an hour of free phone calls, free computer terminal access in the lobby, free printing and breakfast from Prêt à Manger. Rooms are small but stylish, with flat-screen TV, desk and fridge with complimentary bottled water and milk. Best of all is the price – while you have to be very lucky to get one of the £1 rooms (which sell out in minutes every three months), depending on the date you can find a room for £49 to £69 – still excellent deals for this level of comfort.

13 PRINCELET ST   APARTMENT £££

Map p444 (☎01628 825925; www.landmarktrust.org.uk; 13 Princelet St E1; r around £300; ☻Liverpool St) Built in 1719 this fantastic old town house was lovingly restored in 1987 before being bequeathed to the Landmark Trust, offering a rare opportunity to stay in a period property in this area. It's beautifully decorated, with tiled fireplaces and three large bedrooms (two twins, one double) set over four sloping floors. There's also a patio garden and fully equipped kitchen. Prices vary depending on dates and there's a minimum stay of three nights.

FOX & ANCHOR   BOUTIQUE HOTEL £££

Map p444 (☎0121 616 3614; www.foxandanchor.com; 115 Charterhouse St EC1; r £222-246, ste £324, weekend rate r £138-162, ste £234; ❄🛜; ☻Farringdon or Barbican) Characterful option in a handy location above a glorious pub (p210), this place offers just six small but sumptuous rooms, each individually decorated and with all mod cons.

SHOREDITCH ROOMS
BOUTIQUE HOTEL **£££**

Map p444 (2 7739 5040; www.shoreditchrooms. com; Shoreditch House, Ebor St E2; r around £225, breakfast £10; ❄ ❐ ☎; ⊖ Shoreditch High St) Part of private members' club Shoreditch House, but with rooms available to all, they're quite upfront here about the size of the rooms, categorising them tiny, small and small plus. While obviously not spacious, each room is freshly decorated in a beachhouse style, with light wood panelling and sparkly white linen. Small plus rooms have a balcony. Areas available to guests include the gorgeous rooftop pool, secret garden and lazy lawn. Prices vary considerably depending on the date and can go as low as £85 on selected nights.

BOUNDARY
BOUTIQUE HOTEL **£££**

Map p444 (2 7729 1051; www.theboundary.co.uk; 2-4 Boundary St E2; d £252-294, ste £450-570; ❄ ☎; ⊖ Shoreditch High St) Terence Conran's impressive design hotel in a converted factory towers over the shops on achingly hip Redchurch St. Each room or suite takes its theme from a particular designer or design style, such as Eames, Bauhaus or Scandinavian. Mod cons are as flash as you'd expect. Rates are reduced for all rooms on Sunday nights.

MALMAISON
HOTEL **£££**

Map p444 (2 7012 3716; www.malmaison-london. com; 18-21 Charterhouse Sq EC1; r £294-318, breakfast £15.50-18.50; ❄ ☎; ⊖ Farringdon) Facing a picture-postcard leafy square in Clerkenwell, this conservatively chic 97-room hotel feels more like a dangerously expensive cocktail bar when you enter its lobby. Public areas are moodily low-lit, with the exception of the luminous subterranean restaurant. Rooms are simple and elegant. Prices vary considerably and can be much cheaper at the weekends.

🛏 The East End & Docklands

TOP CHOICE **40 WINKS**
GUESTHOUSE **££**

Map p446 (2 7790 0259; www.40winks.org; 109 Mile End Rd E1; s/d £95/140; ☎; ⊖ Stepney Green) Short on space but not on style, this two-

room boutique guesthouse in less-than-desirable Stepney Green oozes charm. It is housed in an early 18th-century town house owned by a successful designer and has been used as a location for a number of fashion shoots. The rooms (the single is quite compact) are uniquely decorated with an expert's eye that has preserved the history of the building and married it with exquisite modern touches and a great sense of fun. Book early.

TOWN HALL HOTEL & APARTMENTS
LUXURY HOTEL, APARTMENT **£££**

Map p446 (2 7871 0460; www.townhallhotel.com; Patriot Square E2; d £348-384, apt £402-546, breakfast £15; ❄ ❐ ☎; ⊖ Bethnal Green) Set in an erstwhile Edwardian town hall (1910), updated with art deco features in the 1930s, it was the council's headquarters until 1965. The design aesthetic of the hotel combines these eras beautifully, with the addition of cutting-edge contemporary art by London-based artists. The marble lobby and central staircase are an impressive welcome and a world away from the scruffy neighbourhood outside. No rooms are the same, and in each you'll find quirks from the original structure, along with carefully designed contemporary features throughout. Apartments are extremely well equipped.

OLD SHIP
HOTEL **££**

Map p446 (2 8986 1641; www.urbaninns.co.uk; 2 Sylvester Path E8; s/d from £79.95/99.95; ☎; ᴙ Hackney Central, ☐ 38 or 55) This bright, 10-room place has surprisingly cheerful rooms and public areas, and represents good value for money, putting you close to the action of lively Broadway Market and surrounds. The pub of the same name below serves, among other things, excellent British 'tapas' and pies.

🛏 Hampstead & North London

TOP CHOICE **YORK & ALBANY**
BOUTIQUE HOTEL **£££**

Map p452 (www.gordonramsay.com/yorkandalbany; 127-129 Parkway NW1; r from £186; ❄ ☎; ⊖ Camden Town) Luxurious yet cosy, the York & Albany oozes Georgian charm: there are feature fireplaces in many of the rooms, antique furniture, beautiful floor-to-ceiling windows and lush bathrooms (with underfloor heating, ideal on cold winter days). All rooms have flat-screen TV, DVD player (and DVDs at reception) and free wi-fi. The hotel is right by Regent's Park, and just five minutes' walk from happening Camden.

TOP CHOICE CLINK78
HOSTEL £

Map p448 (℡7183 9400; www.clinkhostels.com; 78 King's Cross Rd WC1; dm £17-27, d £75; @⊛⊙; ⊖King's Cross St Pancras) This fantastic 500-bed hostel is housed in a 19th-century magistrates courthouse where Dickens once worked as a scribe and members of the Clash made an appearance in 1978. Some parts of it, including seven tiny cells converted to bedrooms and a pair of wood-panelled court rooms used as a TV lounge and an internet room, are heritage-listed. Rooms feature pod beds (including storage space) in colour-coded dormitories (four to 16 beds – there is a female aisle). Ther's a top kitchen with a huge dining area and a busy bar in the basement.

CLINK261
HOSTEL £

Map p448 (℡7833 9400; www.clinkhostels.com; 261-265 Gray's Inn Rd WC1; dm £18-22, d with shared bathroom £55; @⊛; ⊖King's Cross St Pancras) Clink261 underwent a thorough refurbishment in 2010, and the hostel is now top-notch, with bright, funky dorms, bunk beds fitted with a privacy panel and individual lockers for valuables, a brilliant self-catering kitchen that looks straight out of a design magazine, and a fab TV lounge and computer room. The bathroom refurbishment was planned for 2012.

ROUGH LUXE
BOUTIQUE HOTEL £££

Map p448 (℡7837 5338; www.roughluxe.co.uk; 1 Birkenhead St WC1; r from £200, with shared bathroom £177; ⊛; ⊖King's Cross St Pancras) Half rough, half luxury is the strapline of this unique hotel, and the interior is true to its words: scrapes of old newspaper adorn the walls along with original works of arts; the finest linen graces your bed but the vintage 1970s TV doesn't work; and salvaged furniture from the old Savoy in Paris mixes with divine bathroom fittings. The service is entirely luxe, however, from the little patio at the back and the shared glass of wine with the owners to the organic breakfast on the communal table.

ST PANCRAS RENAISSANCE HOTEL
LUXURY HOTEL £££

Map p448 (℡7841 3540; www.stpancrasrenaissance.co.uk; Euston Rd NW1; r from £228; ❄⊛⊠; ⊖King's Cross St Pancras) It took the best part of a decade and £150 million to revive the former Midland Grand into the St Pancras Renaissance but, boy, was it worth it. The Gothic, red-brick building was always stunning from the outside but the interior has now been returned to its former glory, with the grand staircase's ornate walls and gold-leaf ceilings, glazed-roof lobby, wood-panelled bar and Victorian-tiled pool. Disappointingly, only 38 of the 245 rooms are in the original building at the front; the rest are in an extension at the back and rather bland.

HAMPSTEAD GUESTHOUSE
GUESTHOUSE ££

Map p451 (℡7435 8679; www.hampsteadguesthouse.com; 2 Kemplay Rd NW3; s/d £75/95, with shared bathroom £65/80, studio apt s/d/tr/f £100/125/145/175, breakfast £7; ⊖Hampstead) This lovely nine-room guesthouse with a quirky character, rustic decor, a mountain of bric-a-brac, comfy beds and a delightful back garden makes for a great place to stay. There's also a studio apartment that can accommodate up to five people and the hosts are very welcoming.

INTERNATIONAL STUDENTS HOUSE
HOSTEL £

Map p452 (℡7631 8300; www.ish.org.uk; 1 Park Cres W1; per person s/d £44/34, with shared facilities dm/s/d/tr £19/39/31/27; @⊛; ⊖Great Portland St) The building may not be all that fancy and the rooms fairly standard but the facilities are great (quality, subsidised on-site restaurant and a bar that serves student-priced drinks), the staff are really friendly, the location (across the road from Regent's Park) is wonderful and there are people from every corner of the globe staying here. Oh, and did we mention the price?

YHA ST PANCRAS INTERNATIONAL
HOSTEL £

Map p448 (℡0845 371 9344; www.yha.org.uk; 79-81 Euston Rd NW1; dm from £29.65, d & tw £74; @⊛; ⊖King's Cross St Pancras) This 185-bed hostel has modern, clean dorms sleeping four to six (nearly all with private facilities) and some private rooms. There's a good bar and cafe, although there are no self-catering facilities.

🛏 Notting Hill & West London

PORTOBELLO HOTEL
BOUTIQUE HOTEL £££

Map p454 (℡7727 2777; www.portobello-hotel.co.uk; 22 Stanley Gardens W11; s/d/feature rooms from £174/234/288; ❄ @ 🛜; ⊖Notting Hill Gate) This beautifully appointed 21-room property is in a great location and has been a firm favourite with rock and rollers and movie stars down the years. Rooms and furnishings are done up in a stylish colonial decor and have an exclusive feel to them. Spectacular features include free-standing baths, a round bed and a four-poster bed so high you need stairs to access it. Rooms at the back have views of the neighbouring properties' beautiful gardens.

HEMPEL
BOUTIQUE HOTEL **£££**

Map p454 (☑7298 9000; www.the-hempel. co.uk; 31-35 Craven Hill Gardens W2; d/ste from £190/250; ❄ 🛜; ⊖Lancaster Gate or Queensway) This stunner of a boutique hotel – designer Anouska Hempel's minimalist symphony in white and natural tones – is effortlessly beautiful. The 50 rooms, suites and apartments are all unique (the Lioness Den even contains a bed within a cage suspended over a living area!) and the Japanese-style garden opposite is a restful oasis (it's where the wedding scene from *Notting Hill* was filmed).

COLONNADE
HOTEL **££**

Map p454 (☑7286 1052; www.theetoncollection. com; 2 Warrington Cres W9; s/d from £144/168; ❄ @ 🛜; ⊖Warwick Ave) A charmer in lovely Little Venice, the Colonnade is the handsome Victorian structure where Sigmund Freud sheltered after he fled Vienna in June 1938. Apart from the three rooms in the basement, the 43 guest rooms are light, spacious and decorated in classic, antique decor.

YHA EARL'S COURT
HOSTEL **£**

Map p456 (☑7373 7083; www.yha.org.uk; 38 Bolton Gardens SW5; dm from £19.65, tw/d from £48.50/50.50; @ 🛜; ⊖Earl's Court) On a quiet, leafy street in Earl's Court, the YHA is a cheerful place. Most accommodation (186 beds) is in clean, airy dormitories of between four and 10 bunk beds. Staff are friendly and there's a good-sized kitchen, two lounges, a bright and modern cafe, and a courtyard garden at the back. The hotel was in the midst of refurbishments in 2011 and planned to have brand new lounges and kitchen by 2012.

BASE2STAY
HOTEL **££**

Map p456 (☑7244 2255; www.base2stay.com; 25 Courtfield Gardens SW5; s/d & tw from £95/113; ❄ 🛜; ⊖Earl's Court or Gloucester Rd) base2stay has endeavoured to filter out all the 'unnecessary' extras most hotels offer and concentrate on the 'important' things like good wi-fi, music systems, kitchenettes and discounts at local restaurants. The result is a pared-down but extremely comfortable 67-room hotel. The hotel is committed to being as sustainable as possible (recycling, energy-saving light bulbs, water savings, fair-trade tea and coffee etc) and encourages guests to embrace the same principles. The hotel also has an electric car for hire (£30 for the weekend).

K WEST
HOTEL **££**

Map p456 (☑8008 6600; www.k-west.co.uk; Richmond Way W14; s/d/ste from £149/159/290; ❄ @ 🛜; ⊖Shepherd's Bush) This very stylish 220-room place, hard by Shepherd's Bush Green, combines dark wood, suede, stainless steel and sand-blasted glass, and somehow it all works. Many people come here to take advantage of the exquisite K Spa (see p267). Upper-range rooms have creature comforts such as Sony PlayStations, Nespresso machines and state-of-the-art iPod-compatible sound systems. The library with its complimentary (and huge) Mac computers is a treat.

ROCKWELL
BOUTIQUE HOTEL **££**

Map p456 (☑7244 2000; www.therockwell. com; 181-183 Cromwell Rd SW5; s/d/ste from £120/160/180; ❄ 🛜; ⊖Earl's Court) A very friendly establishment in Earl's Court, the 40-room Rockwell is a 'budget boutique' hotel par excellence. The decor puts a contemporary spin on English traditional (we love the 'jungle' wallpaper in the dining room!) and the three rooms (LG1, 2 and 3) giving on to the garden are particularly fine. Rooms on Cromwell Rd are triple-glazed to ensure a good night's sleep.

HOTEL INDIGO
BOUTIQUE HOTEL **££**

Map p454 (☑7706 4444; www.hipaddington. com; 16 London St W2; r from £152; ❄ 🛜; ⊖Paddington) This 64-room gem, part of the boutique division of the huge US Inter-Continental group of hotels, is a fabulous option in Paddington. The decoration takes its inspiration from the 13th-century Fibonacci sequence of numbers (ie pi) that apparently produces shapes in nature. Each of the four floors has its own colour scheme in the rooms. The bathrooms are stunning too, with great colour schemes and fabulous fittings.

VANCOUVER STUDIOS — HOTEL ££

Map p454 (☏7243 1270; www.vancouverstudios.co.uk; 30 Prince's Sq W2; s/d/tr studio £92/135/175, 3-bedroom apt £350; @☎; ☻Bayswater) Everyone will feel at home in this lovely terrace of 45 stylish and very affordable studios. Rooms all contain kitchenettes but otherwise differ wildly – ranging from a tiny but well-equipped single to a generously sized family room with balcony, and embracing all styles of decoration from faux-mink throws to Japanese. There's even a walled garden with small fountain. There are DVD players in each studio and DVDs for rent (£1).

PAVILION HOTEL — HOTEL ££

Map p454 (☏7262 0905; www.pavilionhoteluk.com; 34-36 Sussex Gardens W2; s £60-85, d/tr £100/120; ☻Paddington; ☎) The quirky Pavilion boasts 30 individually themed rooms: Honky Tonky Afro has a 1970s theme, Casablanca a Moorish one and Goldfinger a James Bond theme, while Enter the Dragon conjures up Shanghai nights and Indian Summer is a tribute to Bollywood. They're meant to reflect the hotel's slogan – 'Fashion, Glam & Rock 'n' Roll' – and are both good fun and good value.

NEW LINDEN HOTEL — BOUTIQUE HOTEL ££

Map p454 (☏7221 4321; 58-60 Leinster Sq W2; s/d from £95/119; ☎; ☻Notting Hill Gate) Light, airy and beautifully designed, the New Linden is a very classy option located between Westbourne Grove and Notting Hill. Some of the rooms are on the small side due to the Georgian buildings' quirky layout, but they feel cosy rather than cramped. Staff are charming too.

TWENTY NEVERN SQUARE — BOUTIQUE HOTEL ££

Map p456 (☏7565 9555; www.20nevernsquare.com; 20 Nevern Sq SW5; s/d from £79/89; ☎; ☻Earl's Court) One of London's cheaper boutique hotels, this place, overlooking a lovely square, is done up in colonial style, with imposing carved-wood beds (some of them four-poster), venetian blinds and heavy fabrics. There is a gorgeous conservatory where breakfast is served, and a tiny patio. Wi-fi is complimentary.

PARKWOOD HOTEL — HOTEL ££

Map p454 (☏7402 2241; www.parkwoodhotel.com; 4 Stanhope Pl W2; s/d/tr/f £79/97/115/130, with shared bathroom s/d/tr £59/79/95; ☎; ☻Marble Arch) You certainly get value for money at this small hotel. The rooms are rather simple but pretty spacious on the whole. The bathrooms are basic but the whole place is run with pride and the staff are very friendly. You're a hop and a skip from Oxford St and Hyde Park, and wi-fi is free.

RUSHMORE — HOTEL ££

Map p456 (☏7370 3839; www.rushmore-hotel.co.uk; 11 Trebovir Rd SW5; s/d £69/89; ☎; ☻Earl's Court) The soft pastel colours, draped fabrics and simple-yet-elegant designs of this modest hotel create a welcoming and charming atmosphere. All 22 guest rooms, which have renovated bathrooms, are of a decent size and are impeccably clean. Four rooms on the 1st floor have balconies: Nos 11 and 12 face the street and Nos 14 and 15, the courtyard.

MAYFLOWER — BOUTIQUE HOTEL ££

Map p456 (☏7370 0991; www.mayflowerhotel.co.uk; 26-28 Trebovir Rd SW5; s/d from £89/110; ☎; ☻Earl's Court) A sister hotel of Twenty Nevern Square, a block up the road, the 47-room Mayflower has chosen an updated colonial style, with wooden carvings from India, ceiling fans and black-tiled bathrooms. Rooms, particularly the bathrooms, are on the small side. The deluxe doubles all have private balconies. There is a small garden at the back.

ELYSEE HOTEL — HOTEL ££

Map p454 (☏7402 7633; www.hotelelysee.co.uk; 25 Craven Tce W2; s/d/tr from £69/99/144; ✳@☎; ☻Lancaster Gate) This hotel on a quiet street on the north side of Kensington Gardens, just 100m from Hyde Park, offers excellent value for its location and class (three stars). A new lift offers a less stressful access to the 55 guest rooms, and the flower-bedecked front facade is welcoming. The rooms are pretty standard.

GATE HOTEL — B&B ££

Map p454 (☏7221 0707; www.gatehotel.co.uk; 6 Portobello Rd W11; s/d from £60/85; ☎; ☻Notting Hill Gate) The half-dozen guest rooms in this old town house with classic frilly English decor and flowery facade all have private facilities. You're as close as you're going to get to the buying and selling of Portobello Road. It's worth noting that breakfast is continental only and served in the rooms since there is no dining room.

GARDEN COURT HOTEL
HOTEL **££**

Map p454 (☎7229 2553; www.gardencourtho
tel.co.uk; 30-31 Kensington Gardens Sq W2; s/d/
tr/f £76/125/150/175, s/d with shared bathroom
£50/79; @☎; ⊝Bayswater) Run by the same
family since 1954, the spotless Garden
Court is a reliable choice in its price range.
The decor is simple, with decorative wallpaper and basic furniture, and a great bonus
for guests is access to both the hotel garden
and the leafy square across the street. Wi-fi
is £5 per stay.

STYLOTEL
HOTEL **£**

Map p454 (☎7723 1026; www.stylotel.com;
160-162 Sussex Gardens W2; s/d/tr/q
£60/85/105/120, studio/1-bedroom ste £142/
185; ✻@☎; ⊝Paddington) The branding of
Stylotel is rather pretentious ('Not just a
hotel, a machine for living in') but the industrial design – scored aluminium treads,
opaque green glass, lots of stainless steel –
of this 47-room hotel is clean, contemporary
and refreshing at these prices. The eight
suites around the corner on London St are
a big plus for longer stays and families.

PORTOBELLO GOLD
GUESTHOUSE **££**

Map p454 (☎7460 4910; www.portobellogold.
com; 95-97 Portobello Rd W11; r/apt from £75/135;
☎; ⊝Notting Hill Gate) This friendly guesthouse above a pleasant restaurant and pub
has seven rooms of varying sizes and quality of furnishings. There are several small
doubles (with minuscule shower room). The
so-called Honeymoon Suite has antique
furnishings, a four-poster bed and open-
hearth fireplace. The Roof Terrace studio
has a microwave and fridge and exclusive
access to the roof.

W14
HOSTEL **£**

Map p456 (☎7602 6600; www.thew14hotel.co.uk;
16-22 Gunterstone Rd W14; dm £26.50-34.50,
with shared bathroom £21-27, d £105, with shared
bathroom £58-65; @☎; ⊝Barons Court or West
Kensington) Squeaky-clean and on a quiet
residential street west of Earl's Court (so
a bit in the middle of nowhere but close to
the tube), this 163-bed place has a contemporary, upbeat feel, with a great bar and a
fabulous back garden. Accommodation is in
dorms with between three and eight bunk
beds, and there is private accommodation
in four double rooms with bathroom, all
of which give on to a patio overlooking the
garden.

BARMY BADGER BACKPACKERS
HOSTEL **£**

Map p456 (☎7370 5213; www.barmybadger.com;
17 Longridge Rd SW5; dm £20-22, d & tw £50; ☎;
⊝Earl's Court) Smack bang in the middle of a
residential area, this Victorian town house
turned backpackers haven is smaller than
many other hostels in town, giving it a
homely feel. The lounge is definitely in need
of a little TLC but there is a lovely back garden, a great communal kitchen and friendly
owners. The weekly rates (from £110 in a
six-bed dorm) are a bargain. Wi-fi is just £2
per week.

OXFORD HOTEL
HOTEL **£**

Map p454 (☎7402 6860; www.oxfordhotel
london.co.uk; 13-14 Craven Tce W2; s/d/tr/q
£65/78/98/120; ⊝Lancaster Gate) For a humble establishment the 21-room Oxford sure
tries hard with its sunny yellow walls and
blue-checked bedspreads, although the
swirly carpets in the breakfast room and
the dodgy stairs are a reminder of how
tired things can get here. Reception is always welcoming.

ST CHRISTOPHER'S
SHEPHERD'S BUSH
HOSTEL **£**

Map p456 (☎8600 7500; www.st-christophers.
co.uk; 13-15 Shepherd's Bush Green; dm £19-21;
⊝Shepherd's Bush) St Christopher's Shepherd's Bush is slap bang on the massive
Shepherd's Bush roundabout. It's noisy
and not exactly scenic but you're right by
the tube station, the hostel has a very lively
pub and the staff are friendly. The accommodation is rather cramped, but there are
nifty lockable drawers under the beds and
the special offers mean you can find beds at
just over £10 per night.

🛏 Greenwich & South London

TOP CHOICE CHURCH STREET HOTEL
BOUTIQUE HOTEL **££**

(☎7703 5984; www.churchstreethotel.com; 29-33
Camberwell Church St SE5; s £70-90, d £90-170,
tw/f £90/190; P✻☎; ⓇDenmark Hill) One
of London's most individual boutique hotels, this vibrant establishment is a much
needed shot of tequila into the often sober
hotel landscape of southeast London. Brimful of colour, vibrant details and Mexicana,
the lovely tiled bathrooms will perk up anyone's day and so will the rooms. If you're

FEW FRILLS CHAINS

London has several discount hotel chains that offer clean and modern – if somewhat institutional – accommodation for reasonable rates.

➡ **Express by Holiday Inn** (☎0800 434 040; www.hiexpress.co.uk; weekday/weekend d £115/70) The most upmarket of the chains listed here, and notable for its clever locations.

➡ **Premier Inn** (☎0870 242 8000; www.premierinn.com; r £110) London's original cheap chain; in large numbers.

➡ **Travelodge** (☎0871 984 8484; www.travelodge.co.uk; r £75-105) Pleasant rooms, few public facilities.

➡ **Days Hotel** (☎0800 028 0400; www.daysinn.co.uk; r £69-125) Just three branches in central London.

➡ **easyHotel** (www.easyhotel.com; r £25-60) Functional, with orange plastic-moulded rooms, some without windows; five branches in town.

looking for somewhere to hang your sombrero, you couldn't do better and with prices generously kicking off at £70 for a single with shared bathroom (brekkie included), give yourself another reason to tuck into some *jamón iberico* at the hotel's terrific Angels & Gypsies restaurant.

PARK PLAZA WESTMINSTER BRIDGE
HOTEL £££

Map p462 (☎0844 415 6780; 200 Westminster Bridge Rd, London SE1; d £238; ✴🛜🏊) This snazzy new hotel has given things a shake up around Waterloo. Rooms are contemporary, stylish and very comfortable but the cheapest merely face unspectacularly into the atrium; otherwise upgrade to the best studio and penthouse rooms, which reward you with views of the Thames, Westminster Bridge, Big Ben and the London Eye. Service is hit and miss, but there's no doubt the location is phenomenal for sightseeing, while a snappy freshness runs throughout, including the snazzy Primo bar, a chilled-out area of leather furniture and geometric neatness.

KENNINGTON B&B
B&B ££

Map p462 (☎7735 7669; www.kenningtonbandb.com; 103 Kennington Park Rd SE11; d £120-150; 🛜; ⊝Kennington) With gorgeous bed linen, well-preserved Georgian features and just a small number of bedrooms, this lovely B&B in an 18th-century house is very tasteful in almost every regard, from the shining, tiled shower rooms and Georgian shutters to the fireplaces and cast-iron radiators. Free telephone calls to landlines abroad.

NUMBER 16 ST ALFEGE'S
B&B £

Map p463 (☎8853 4337; www.st-alfeges.co.uk; 16 St Alfege's Passage SE10; r from £75; ☐Greenwich, DLR Cutty Sark) One-time sweet shop and highly coveted Greenwich address since appearing on Channel 5's *Hotel Inspector*, this gay-owned B&B has two well-appointed doubles and a single, individually decorated in shades of blue, green or yellow and all with bathroom. The owners do their best to make everyone, gay or straight, feel at home, with chats and cups of tea in the charming basement kitchen. Turn the corner into Roan St to find the main door.

CAPTAIN BLIGH GUESTHOUSE
APARTMENT ££

Map p462 (100 Lambeth Rd SE1; www.captainblighhouse.co.uk; s £63-75, d £85-90; ⊝Lambeth North) With a minimum-stay policy of four nights and very helpful but nonintrusive owners, this late-18th-century property and former home of Bligh is excellently located for the Imperial War Museum. Pros: rooms are very shipshape and quiet; everything is well-maintained with elbow grease; and rooms have a kitchen. Cons: no credit cards; one night's nonrefundable deposit required; and you'll need to book well ahead. No lift. Look for the bright blue door.

YHA LONDON THAMESIDE
HOSTEL £

Map p463 (☎7232 2114; www.yha.org.uk; 20 Salter Rd SE16; dm £16-27, tw £39-67; @🛜; ⊝Canada Water or Rotherhithe) Facilities at this large flagship YHA hostel are very good, but the location is rather remote. There's a bar, a restaurant, kitchen facilities and a laundry. Dorm rooms have from four to 10 beds; the 20 twins have bathrooms.

ST CHRISTOPHER'S INN
GREENWICH
HOSTEL £

Map p463 (☏8858 3591; www.st-christophers.co.uk; 189 Greenwich High Rd SE10; dm £10-25, tw £40-55; ⊖/ℝGreenwich) The Greenwich branch of this successful chain of hostels has 55 beds and is quieter than some of its more centrally located sister properties (though it stands cheek by jowl to Greenwich train station). Dorms have six to eight beds, there's just two twin rooms (bunks) and there's a pub on site.

NEW CROSS INN
HOSTEL £

Off Map p463 (☏8691 7222; www.newcrossinn.co.uk; 323a New Cross Rd SE14; dm £12-15, tw £25; ℝ/⊖New Cross Gate or New Cross) This 75-bed hostel in far-flung New Cross, southwest of Greenwich, has basic rooms with basin and fridge, two kitchens, and a pub attached. Reachable by train from London Bridge station in about six minutes, or on the overground line. Dorms have four to eight beds and there are a few twins; all rooms are £3 pricier at weekends.

🛏 Richmond

TOP
CHOICE THE BINGHAM
BOUTIQUE HOTEL £££

Map p458 (☏8940 0902; www.thebingham.co.uk; 63 Petersham Rd TW10; s £170, d £190-285; P⚒🛜; ⊖Richmond, ℝRichmond then bus 65) Just upriver from Richmond Bridge, this lovely riverside Georgian town house is an enticing boutique escape from central London, with 15 very stylish and well-presented, art deco inspired rooms. Each room takes its name from a poem (the house holds a literary history). Riverside rooms are naturally pricier, but worth it, as roadside rooms – although deliciously devised and double-glazed – look out over busy Petersham Rd. Further treasures are the Michelin-starred restaurant and the lounge bar where some irresistible cocktail mixing takes place.

PETERSHAM
HOTEL £££

Map p458 (☏8940 0061; www.petershamhotel.co.uk; Nightingale Lane TW10; s £135-175, d £185-250, ste £320, weekend rate s £95-135, d £165; P🛜; ⊖Richmond, ℝRichmond then bus 65) Neatly perched on the slope down Richmond Hill leading across Petersham Meadows towards the Thames, the impressive Petersham offers stunning, Arcadian views at every turn. And its restaurant, with its large windows gazing down to the river, has some choice panoramas. The 60 rooms are classically styled but those with good river views are dearer.

Top: Natural History Museum (p187)
Bottom: Millennium Bridge (p170), a collaboration between Foster and partners, Sir Anthony Caro and Arup

DAVID TOMLINSON / LONELY PLANET IMAGES ©

Understand London

London Today

Since scooping its bid to host the 2012 Olympic Games, London has attracted a staggering amount of attention and scrutiny from talking heads, the media and the chattering classes. The city has been appraised, reappraised, examined and re-examined against a raft of expectations that would capsize a lesser city, especially one in the grip of recession. Yet London has reaffirmed itself as a capital of transformative ideas, cultural dynamism and staying power.

Best on Film

Withnail & I (1986) Cult black comedy about two unemployed actors in 1969 Camden.
Love Actually (2003) Saccharine romantic comedy with great shots of town.
An American Werewolf in London (1981) Classic offbeat horror comedy.
Notting Hill (1999) Soppy romcom with Hugh Grant and Julia Roberts in an atypically all-white Notting Hill.
Sliding Doors (1998) Gwyneth Paltrow stars in classic 'What if?' alternate-history drama.

Best in Print

London Fields (Martin Amis; 1989) Gripping, dark postmodern study of London lowlife.
Journal of the Plague Year (Daniel Defoe; 1722) Defoe's classic reconstruction of the Great Plague of 1665.
London: The Biography (Peter Ackroyd; 2001) Marvellously researched and well-written brick of a book.
Oliver Twist (Charles Dickens; 1837) Unforgettable characters and a vivid portrayal of Victorian London seen through the eyes of a hapless orphan.
Brick Lane (Monica Ali; 2003) A tale of an arranged marriage in London's Bangladeshi community.

The Olympic Games Effect

The recession may have double-dipped its way across the cityscape, leaving stalled projects and the occasionally immobile crane in its wake, but the Olympic project has proceeded to plan, reshaping parts of the East End of London, expanding the city's transport network, rejuvenating squares and parks and adding a bit of fizz to even the most remote of urban backwaters. A concurrent, unplanned economy has coalesced around the big occasion, unleashing new hotels, restaurants, bars and vast fleets of public bicycles onto the roads of a city preparing to entertain the world, when it comes to town.

Olympic Games work projects are notorious poisoned chalices, but London put its money on the massive regeneration of a derelict, polluted and neglected part of town, forging an emphasis on sustainability, the creation of wildlife and wetland habitats and affordable housing. To be renamed the Queen Elizabeth Olympic Park in 2013, the Olympic Park (p222) is designed to grow and flourish as soon as the last athlete takes his or her bow in 2012. It's an ambitious and bold long-term vision that will take decades to fully mature.

Economic Blues

The West's most crippling recession since the Great one of the 1930s has naturally promoted caution over risk-taking, but optimists say London may still emerge more even-keeled in the process. The UK is on the economic ropes but London is seemingly driven by its own reserves of economic vitality, given an extra shot of adrenaline by the approaching 2012 Games.

The property market – badly buffeted by the economic cyclone – has proved more resilient in London than many other parts of the UK. Parts of London seem to write their own economic laws, with property prices in many boroughs rising or staying level as the rest of

Great Britain sags. But with dark clouds over the European and US economies, the economic barometer remains set to overcast (with the possibility of a perfect storm).

Multiculturalism

Since the terrorist bombings by Muslim extremists on the London Transport network in 2005, multiculturalism became one of the fiercest debates in England's political history. A consensus emerged that aspects of multicultural integration have been politically mismanaged. Some say it all comes down to how Londoners, and British people, see themselves and their place in the world. Others lay the blame at the door of UK foreign policy. Others insist immigrants need to somehow conform to a national credo. Many Londoners are calling for greater efforts to promote integration of ethnic communities into British culture, but the subject remains a political minefield.

Political Change

The UK political landscape endured great upheaval in the 2010 general election as the Labour Party – in power since 1997 – was finally unseated by public discontent over the economy, foreign policy and a seeming absence of dynamic leadership. The resulting hung parliament saw the Conservative Party and Liberal Democrats forced into the same bed and the task of forging the first coalition cabinet since WWII, with David Cameron as prime minister. Rarely has a UK government taken charge in more economically blighted circumstances. With an economy essentially crippled by debt and overspend, a new Age of Austerity and unpopular public service cutbacks dawned, with rounds of belt-tightening gripping London and the UK. Some pundits linked the London riots of 2011 with the cutbacks and economic hardship, others blamed the erosion of social and personal responsibility in modern Britain.

Moving Forwards

An intelligent and nifty redesign of London's transport options is either on the drawing board or already on the streets. The Barclay's Cycle Hire Scheme (p393) has transformed the way a large number of people – including visitors – get about town. The East London Overground line has been extended and a cable car is planned to drape itself across the Thames between Greenwich and the Royal Docks. Crossrail will bring high-frequency underground trains linking east and west London along two brand new lines costing £15.9 billion, due to commence service in 2018. The old Routemaster buses have largely vanished – axed to great dismay in 2005 – but are due to reappear by 2012 in modernised, more environmentally-friendly form, replacing the much-mocked 'bendy buses'.

LONDON TODAY

if London were 100 people

60 would be white British
12 would be South Asian
11 would be white non-British
11 would be Africa or Afro-Caribbean
6 would be Other

belief systems
(% of population)

58 Christian

4 Hindu

26 Other

2 Jewish

8 Muslim

1 Buddhists

population per sq km

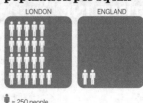

LONDON   ENGLAND

= 250 people

History

London's history is a long and turbulent narrative spanning two millennia that saw long-established settlements and villages gradually coalesce to form the immense city around the Roman core that still marks the city's heart today. Once indulging itself as capital of the world's largest empire, London has endured a dramatic voyage through conflict, apocalyptic plague, cataclysmic fires and bombardment with the world's first ever space rockets (the V-2).

LONDINIUM

The Romans are the real fathers of London, despite there being a settlement of some form or another along the Thames for several thousand years before their arrival. Amazingly, the Roman wall built around the settlement of Londinium still more or less demarcates the City of London from neighbouring London boroughs today.

The Romans first visited in the 1st century BC, traded with the Celts and had a browse around. In AD 43 they returned with an army led by Emperor Claudius and decided to stay, establishing the port of Londinium. They built a wooden bridge across the Thames (near the site of today's London Bridge), using the settlement as a base from which to capture other tribal centres, which at the time provided much bigger prizes. The bridge became the focal point for a network of roads fanning out around the region, and for a few years the settlement prospered from trade.

This growth was nipped in the bud around AD 60 when an army led by Boudicca, queen of the Celtic Iceni tribe based in East Anglia, exacted violent retribution on the Romans, who had attacked her kingdom, seized her land and raped her daughters. The Iceni overran Camulodunum (Colchester) – which had become capital of Roman Britannia – and then turned on Londinium, massacring its inhabitants and razing the settlement. Boudicca, however, was eventually defeated (and according to legend is buried under platform 10 of King's Cross station) and the Romans rebuilt Londinium around Cornhill.

A century later the Romans built the defensive wall around the city, fragments of which survive. The original gates – Aldgate, Ludgate, Newgate

TIMELINE	AD 43	47–50	c120–125
	The Romans invade Britain, led by Emperor Claudius himself. Before this the Britons paid tribute to Rome following an early incursion here by Julius Caesar in 55 and 54 BC.	The defensive fort at Londinium is built. The name Londinium is probably pre-Celtic and there is no evidence as to what it means, although 'settlement on the wide river' is one suggestion.	A vast fire, known as the 'Hadrianic Fire' (named after Emperor Hadrian) sweeps through Londinium, devastating the settlement.

and Bishopsgate – are remembered as place names in contemporary London. Excavations in the City suggest that Londinium, a centre for business and trade although not a fully fledged *colonia* (settlement), was an imposing metropolis whose massive buildings included a basilica, an amphitheatre, a forum and the governor's palace.

By the middle of the 3rd century AD, Londinium was home to some 30,000 people of various ethnic groups, with temples dedicated to a large variety of cults. When Emperor Constantine converted to Christianity in 312, the Middle Eastern religion became the official faith of the entire empire, although the remains of the Temple of Mithras survive in the city, a testament to London's pagan past.

Overstretched and worn down by ever-increasing barbarian invasions, the Roman Empire fell into decline, as did Londinium. When the embattled Emperor Honorius withdrew the last soldiers in 410, the remaining Romans scarpered and the settlement was reduced to a sparsely populated backwater.

LUNDENWIC

What happened to Londonium after the Roman withdrawal is still the subject of much historical debate. While the Dark Ages have become considerably better illuminated in the past two decades with archaeological finds and improved technology, there remain several key unknowns, including whether or not the Roman walled city was ever entirely abandoned. Most historians now think that some form of Romano-British continuity survived even as Saxon settlers, Germanic tribes that colonised the southeast of England from the 5th century onwards, established themselves in the wake of the Roman abandonment.

Lundenwic (or London marketplace) was established due west of Londinium (around present-day Aldwych and Charing Cross) as a Saxon trade settlement and by the early 7th century the Saxons were converted from paganism to Christianity after Rome sent Augustine to convert the British. Rome designated Lundenwic as a diocese and the first St Paul's Cathedral was established at the top of Ludgate Hill.

The settlement became the victim of its own success when it attracted the Vikings of Denmark, who raided the city in 842 and burned it to the ground 10 years later. Under the leadership of King Alfred the Great of Wessex, the Saxon population fought back, drove the Danes out in 886 and re-established what soon became Lundunburg as the major centre of trade.

Saxon London grew into a prosperous and well-organised town divided into 20 wards, each with its own alderman, and resident colonies

Historical Reads

London: The Biography (Peter Ackroyd)

London at War (Philip Ziegler)

London in the Twentieth Century (Jerry White)

The Newgate Calender (Clive Emsley)

Restoration London, Elizabethan London and Dr Johnson's London (Liza Picard)

122	190–225	410	c600
Emperor Hadrian pays a visit to Londinium and many impressive municipal buildings are constructed. Roman London reaches its peak, with temples, bathhouses, a fortress and a port.	London Wall is constructed around Londinium to defend it from outsiders, who had breached Hadrian's Wall. The wall encloses an area of just 132 hectares and is 5m high.	The Emperor Honorius decrees that the colony of Britannia should take care of its own defences, thus effectively ending the Roman presence in Londinium.	The Saxon trade settlement of Lundenwic – literally 'London trading town' – has formed to the west of the Roman site of Londinium.

BRIDGES

of German merchants and French vintners. But the Danes wouldn't let it lie, and Viking raids finally broke the weakening Saxon leadership, which was forced to accept the Danish leader Canute as king of England in 1016.

With the death of Canute's son Harthacanute in 1042, the throne passed to the Saxon Edward the Confessor, who went on to found an abbey and palace at Westminster on what was then an island at the mouth of the River Tyburn (which now flows underground). When Edward moved his court to Westminster, he established divisions that would – geographically, at least – dominate the future of London. The port became the trading and mercantile centre (the area now known as the City), while Westminster became the seat of politics and administration.

THE NORMANS

The most famous date in English history, 1066 marks the real birth of England as a unified nation state. After the death of Edward the Confessor in 1066, a dispute over who would take the English throne spelled disaster for the Saxon kings. Harold Godwinson, the Earl of Wessex, was anointed successor by Edward on his deathbed, but this enraged William, the Duke of Normandy, who believed Edward had promised him the throne. William mounted a massive invasion of England from France and on 14 October defeated Harold at the Battle of Hastings, before marching on London to claim his prize. William the Conqueror was crowned king of England in Westminster Abbey on 25 December 1066, ensuring the Norman conquest was complete. He subsequently found himself in control of what was by then the richest and largest city in the kingdom.

William distrusted 'the fierce populace' of London and built several strongholds, including the White Tower, the core of the Tower of London. Cleverly, he kept the prosperous merchants on side by confirming the city's independence in exchange for taxes. Sometime following the Norman conquest, London became the principal town of England, overtaking Winchester, the ancient capital of Wessex.

MEDIEVAL LONDON

Successive medieval kings were happy to let the City of London keep its independence as long as its merchants continued to finance their wars and building projects. When Richard I (known as 'the Lionheart') needed funds for his crusade to the Holy Land, he recognised the City as a

Work on the first stone London Bridge was completed in 1209 after the earlier Norman wooden bridge was destroyed twice, once by a storm in 1091 and again by fire in 1136.

604	852	886	1016
The first Christian cathedral dedicated to St Paul is built (on the site of the current cathedral); fashioned from wood, it burns down in 675 and is later rebuilt.	Vikings settle in London, having attacked the city a decade previously. This is a period of great struggle between Wessex and Denmark for control of the Thames.	King Alfred the Great, first king of England, reclaims London for the Saxons and founds a new settlement within the walls of the old Roman town.	The Danes return to London and Canute is crowned king of England. Most famous in English folklore for failing to command the waves, Canute ushered in two decades of peace.

self-governing commune, and the appreciative merchants duly coughed up. The City's first mayor, Henry Fitz Aylwin, was elected sometime around 1190. A city built on money and commerce, London would always guard its independence fiercely, as Richard's successor, King John, learned the hard way. In 1215 John was forced to cede to the powerful barons, and to curb his excessive demands for pay-offs from the City. Among those pressing him to seal the landmark Magna Carta of 1215 (which effectively diluted royal power) was the by then powerful mayor of the City of London. Amazingly, two copies of this document can be seen in the British Library.

Trade and commerce boomed, and the noblemen, barons and bishops built lavish houses for themselves along the prime real estate of The Strand, which connected the City with the Palace of Westminster, the new seat of royal power. The first stone London Bridge was built in 1176, although it was frequently too crowded to cross, and most people traversed the river with waterboatmen (who plied their trade until the 18th century). Their touting shouts of 'Oars? Oars?' are said to have confused many a country visitor tempted by more carnal services.

Fire was a constant hazard in the cramped and narrow houses and lanes of 14th-century London, but disease caused by unsanitary living conditions and impure drinking water from the Thames was the greatest threat to the burgeoning city. In 1348 rats on ships from Europe brought the Black Death, a bubonic plague that wiped out almost two-thirds of the population of 100,000 over the following decades.

With their numbers subsequently down, there was growing unrest among labourers, for whom violence became a way of life, and rioting was commonplace. In 1381, miscalculating – or just disregarding – the mood of the nation, Richard II tried to impose a poll tax on everyone in the realm. Tens of thousands of peasants, led by the soldier Wat Tyler and the priest Jack Straw, marched in protest on London. The Archbishop of Canterbury was dragged from the Tower and beheaded, several ministers were murdered and many buildings were razed before the Peasants' Revolt ran its course. Tyler died at the end of the mayor's blade, while Straw and the other ringleaders were executed at Smithfield. However, there was no more mention of a poll tax (until Margaret Thatcher, not heeding the lessons of history, tried to introduce one in the 1980s).

London gained wealth and stature under the Houses of Lancaster and York in the 15th century, also the era of the charitable mayor Dick Whittington, immortalised for many children in the fairy tale of his rise to power from poverty. William Caxton set up the first printing press at Westminster in 1476.

The stench on the streets of medieval London would have been unbearable, an overpowering and grotesque blend of urine, excrement, rotting meat, muck, offal, blood and the hideous aromas that emanated from the tanneries.

1065

Westminster Abbey is first consecrated, even though the building is not completed for a further 25 years.

1066

After his great victory over King Harold at the Battle of Hastings, William, Duke of Normandy, aka William the Conqueror, is crowned in Westminster Abbey.

DOUG MCKINLAY / LONELY PLANET IMAGES ©

Westminster Abbey (p80)

BEGGING

The century's greatest episode of political intrigue occurred in 1483. The 12-year-old Edward V, of the House of York, reigned for only two months before vanishing with his younger brother into the Tower of London, never to be seen again. Whether or not their uncle, Richard III – who became the next king – murdered the boys has been the subject of much conjecture over the centuries. (In 1674 workers found a chest containing the skeletons of two children near the White Tower, which were assumed to be the princes' remains and were reburied in Innocents' Corner in Westminster Abbey.) Richard III didn't have long to enjoy the hot seat: he was killed in 1485 at the Battle of Bosworth Field by Henry Tudor, first monarch of the eponymous dynasty.

TUDOR LONDON

London became one of the largest and most important cities in Europe during the Tudor reign, which coincided with the discovery of the Americas and thriving world trade.

Henry's son and successor, Henry VIII, was the most ostentatious of the clan, instructing new palaces to be built at Whitehall and St James's, and bullying his lord chancellor, Cardinal Thomas Wolsey, into gifting him Hampton Court.

His most significant contribution, however, was the split with the Catholic Church in 1534 after the Pope refused to annul his marriage to the non-heir-producing Catherine of Aragon. Thumbing his nose at Rome, he made himself the supreme head of the Church of England and married Anne Boleyn, the second of his six wives. He 'dissolved' London's monasteries and seized the church's vast wealth and property. The face of the medieval city was transformed: much of the land requisitioned for hunting later became Hyde, Regent's and Richmond Parks, while many of the religious houses disappeared, leaving only their names in particular areas, such as Whitefriars and Blackfriars (after the colour of the monks' habits).

Despite his penchant for settling differences with the axe (two of his six wives and Wolsey's replacement as lord chancellor, Thomas More, were beheaded) and his persecution of both Catholics and fellow Protestants who didn't toe the line, Henry VIII remained a popular monarch until his death in 1547. The reign of Mary I, his daughter by Catherine of Aragon, saw a brief return to Catholicism, during which the queen sanctioned the burning to death of hundreds of Protestants at Smithfield and earned herself the nickname 'Bloody Mary'. By the time Elizabeth I, Henry VIII's daughter by Anne Boleyn, took the

Begging was treated very harshly in 16th century London. Henry VIII instructed that able-bodied beggars and vagabonds be whipped, beaten or even imprisoned, but such policies failed to stem the tide of vagrants.

1091	1097	1176	1189
The Great London Tornado sweeps through town, destroying much of the original church of St Mary-le-Bow and sweeping away the wooden London Bridge and countless houses.	William Rufus commences the construction of Westminster Hall; the hall, possibly the largest in Europe at the time, is completed two years later.	The first stone London Bridge is built, although it was frequently too crowded to cross, and most people traversed the river with waterboatmen.	The coronation of Richard I sees a pogrom against Jewish people in which Jews of both sexes and all ages are killed in London.

throne, Catholicism was a waning force, and hundreds of people who dared to suggest otherwise were carted off to the gallows at Tyburn.

ELIZABETHAN LONDON

The 45-year reign (1558–1603) of Elizabeth I is still looked upon as one of the most extraordinary periods in English history, and it was just as significant for London. During these four decades English literature reached new and still unbeaten heights, and religious tolerance gradually became accepted doctrine, although Catholics and some Protestants still faced persecution. England became a naval superpower, having defeated the Spanish Armada in 1588, and the City established itself as the premier world trade market with the opening of the Royal Exchange in 1566.

London was blooming economically and physically; in the second half of the 16th century the population doubled to 200,000. The first recorded map of London was published in 1558, and John Stow produced *A Survey of London,* the first history of the city, in 1598.

This was also the golden era of English drama, and the works of William Shakespeare, Christopher Marlowe and Ben Jonson packed new playhouses, such as the Rose (built in 1587) and the Globe (1599). Both were built in Southwark, a notoriously 'naughty' place at the time, teeming with brothels and bawdy taverns. Most importantly, they were outside the jurisdiction of the City, which frowned upon and even banned theatre as a waste of time.

When Elizabeth died without an heir in 1603, she was succeeded by her second cousin, who was crowned James I. Although the son of Catholic Mary, Queen of Scots, James was slow to improve conditions for England's Catholics and drew their wrath. He narrowly escaped death when Guy Fawkes' plot to blow up the Houses of Parliament on 5 November 1605 was uncovered. The discovery of the audacious plan is commemorated on this date each year with bonfires, fireworks and the burning of Guy Fawkes effigies throughout England.

Sanitation in London could have taken an evolutionary leap forwards in 1596 when Sir John Harrington invented a flushing loo with a cistern, but the novel concept failed to find a market.

THE ENGLISH CIVIL WARS

When James I's son, Charles I, came to the throne in 1625, his intransigent personality and total belief in the 'divine right of kings' set the monarchy on a collision course with an increasingly confident parliament at Westminster and a City of London tiring of extortionate taxes. The crunch came when Charles tried to arrest five antagonistic

FIRST TOILET

1215	1241	1340	1348
King John signs the Magna Carta (literally 'the Great Charter'), an agreement with England's barons forming the basis of constitutional law in England.	Cock Lane in Smithfields effectively becomes London's first red light district.	The population of London reaches between 50,000 and 80,000, similar to other large cities in Europe at the same time.	Rats on ships from Europe brought the Black Death, a bubonic plague that wiped out almost two-thirds of the 100,000 residents over the following decades.

members of parliament, who fled to the City, and in 1642 the country slid into civil war.

The Puritans (extremist Protestants) and the City's expanding merchant class threw their support behind General Oliver Cromwell, leader of the Parliamentarians (the Roundheads), who battled against the Royalist troops (the Cavaliers). London was firmly with the Roundheads, and Charles I was defeated in 1646, although a Second Civil War (1648–49) and a Third Civil War (1649–51) continued to wreak havoc on what had been a stable and prosperous nation.

Charles I was beheaded for treason outside Banqueting House in Whitehall on 30 January 1649, famously wearing two shirts on the cold morning of his execution so as not to shiver and appear cowardly. Cromwell ruled the country as a republic for the next 11 years, during which time Charles I's son, Charles II, continued fighting for the restoration of the monarchy. During the Commonwealth of England, as the English republic was known, Cromwell banned theatre, dancing, Christmas and just about anything remotely fun.

For a real-time experience of Samuel Pepys diary entries, click on The Diary of Samuel Pepys (www.pepysdiary.com), where a new entry written by the diarist is published daily.

THE RESTORATION: PLAGUE & FIRE

After Cromwell's death, parliament decided that the royals weren't so bad after all and restored the exiled Charles II in 1660. Death was deemed too good for Cromwell, whose exhumed body was hung, drawn and quartered at Tyburn. His rotting head was displayed on a spike at Westminster Hall for two decades.

Despite the immense wealth that London experienced during the reign of the Tudors, the capital remained a crowded and filthy place where most of the population lived in poverty. A lack of basic sanitation (urine and faeces were routinely poured into the streets from the slop bucket), dirty water and overcrowding all contributed to recurrent outbreaks of deadly illnesses and fevers. The city had suffered from outbreaks of bubonic plague since the 14th century, but all previous incidences were dwarfed by the Great Plague of 1665.

As the plague spread, the panicked population retreated behind closed doors, only venturing out for supplies and to dispose of their dead. Previously crowded streets were deserted, the churches and markets were closed, and an eerie silence descended on London. To make matters worse, the mayor believed that dogs and cats were the spreaders of the plague and ordered them all killed, thus in one stroke ridding the disease-carrying rats of their natural predators. By the time the winter cold arrested the epidemic, 100,000 people had perished, their

1558	1569	1599	1605
The first detailed map of London is commissioned by a group of German merchants. In the same year the Elizabethan age begins when Queen Elizabeth I takes the throne.	In order to raise money, Elizabeth I holds the world's first national lottery, with a top prize of $5000. Tickets cost 10 shillings and the draw took place next to old St Paul's Cathedral.	The Globe Theatre opens in Southwark alongside other London stages. Most of Shakespeare's plays written after 1599 are staged here, including *Macbeth*, *King Lear* and *Hamlet*.	A Catholic plot to blow up James I by hiding gunpowder under the House of Commons is foiled. Guy Fawkes, one of the plotters, is executed in 1606.

corpses collected and thrown into vast 'plague pits', many of which stand empty of buildings to this day.

The plague finally began to wane in late 1665, leaving the city's population devastated and superstitious that the deaths had been a punishment from God for London's moral squalor. Just as Londoners breathed a sigh of relief, another disaster struck. The city had for centuries been prone to fire, as nearly all buildings were constructed from wood, but the mother of all blazes broke out on 2 September 1666 in a bakery in Pudding Lane in the City.

It didn't seem like much to begin with – the mayor himself dismissed it as 'something a woman might pisse out' before going back to bed – but the unusual September heat combined with rising winds created a tinderbox effect, and the fire raged out of control for days, reducing some 80% of London to carbon. Only eight people died (officially at least), but most of London's medieval, Tudor and Jacobean architecture was destroyed. The fire was finally stopped at Fetter Lane, on the very edge of London, by blowing up all the buildings in the inferno's path. It is hard to overstate the scale of the destruction – 89 churches and more than 13,000 houses were razed, leaving tens of thousands of people homeless. Many Londoners left for the countryside, or sought their fortunes in the New World.

HISTORY WREN'S LONDON

Hidden London (www.hidden london.com) explores and exposes London's 'minor districts and localities' to the light of day, seasoned with some fascinating historical nuggets and details.

WREN'S LONDON

One positive outcome of the inferno was that it created a blank canvas upon which master architect Christopher Wren could build his magnificent churches. Wren's plan for rebuilding the entire city was unfortunately deemed too expensive, and the familiar pattern of streets that had grown up over the centuries since the time of the Romans quickly reappeared (by law, brick and stone designs replaced the old timber-framed, overhanging Tudor houses, to avoid a repeat of 1666; many roads were widened for the same reason). At this time, Charles II moved to St James's Palace, and the surrounding area was taken over by the gentry, who built the grand squares and town houses of modern-day Mayfair and St James's in order to be close to the court.

By way of memorialising the blaze – and symbolising the restoration and resurgence of the subsequent years – the Monument, designed by Wren, was erected in 1677 near the site of the fire's outbreak. At the time it was by far the highest structure in the city, visible from everywhere in the capital.

In 1685 some 1500 Huguenot refugees arrived in London, fleeing persecution in Catholic France. Many of them turned their hands to

1661	1665	1666
Oliver Cromwell's body is dug up from Westminster Abbey and treated to a posthumous execution. Cromwell's head is then stuck on a spike and displayed above Westminster Hall.	The Great Plague ravages London, wiping out a fifth of the population. While less dire than the 14th-century Black Death, it is remembered as one of Europe's last outbreaks.	The Great Fire of London burns for five days, destroying the city Shakespeare had known and loved and changing London forever, leaving four-fifths of the metropolis in smoking ruins.

The Great Fire of London

LEBRECHT/ALAMY©

ST PAUL'S CATHEDRAL

the manufacture of luxury goods such as silks and silverware in and around Spitalfields and Clerkenwell, which were already populated with Irish, Jewish and Italian immigrants and artisans. London was fast becoming one of the world's most cosmopolitan places.

The Glorious (ie bloodless) Revolution in 1688 brought the Dutch king William of Orange to the English throne. He relocated from Whitehall Palace to a new palace in Kensington Gardens, and the surrounding area smartened itself up accordingly. In order to raise finances for his war with France – and as a result of the City's transformation into a centre of finance rather than manufacturing – William III established the Bank of England in 1694.

London's growth continued unabated, and by 1700 it was Europe's largest city, with 600,000 people. The influx of foreign workers brought expansion to the east and south, while those who could afford it headed to the more salubrious environs of the north and west. London remains today, more or less, divided along these lines.

The crowning glory of the 'Great Rebuilding', Wren's St Paul's Cathedral, was completed in 1710 – one of the largest cathedrals in Europe, it remains one of the city's most prominent and visible landmarks.

For superb city views from London's most iconic piece of ecclesiastical architecture, climb the 528 stairs into the dome of Sir Christopher Wren's *magnum opus*: the newly restored, three century-old St Paul's Cathedral.

GEORGIAN LONDON

When Queen Anne died without an heir in 1714, the search began for a Protestant relative (the 1701 Act of Settlement forbade Roman Catholics to occupy the throne). Eventually George of Hanover, the great-grandson of James I, arrived from Germany and was crowned king of England, though he never learned to speak English. Meanwhile, the increasingly literate population got their first newspapers, which began to cluster around Fleet St.

Robert Walpole's Whig Party controlled parliament during much of George I's reign, and Walpole effectively became Britain's first prime minister. He was presented with 10 Downing St, which has been the official residence of nearly every prime minister since.

London grew at a phenomenal pace during this time, and measures were taken to make the city more accessible. When Westminster Bridge opened in 1750 it was only the second spanning of the Thames after London Bridge, first built by the Romans. The old crossing itself was cleared of many of its buildings, and the Roman wall surrounding the City torn down.

Georgian London saw a great creative surge in music, art and architecture. Court composer George Frederick Handel wrote *Water Music* (1717) and *Messiah* (1741) while living here, and in 1755 Dr Johnson pro-

1702	1707	1711	1759
The *Daily Courant*, London's first daily newspaper, is published in Fleet Street, consisting of a single page of news.	The first ever sitting of the Parliament of the Kingdom of Great Britain occurs in London as the 1707 Acts of Union brings England and Scotland together under one parliament.	Sir Christopher Wren's St Paul's Cathedral is officially completed, 35 years after old St Paul's Cathedral is entirely gutted in the Great Fire.	The British Museum opens to the public for the first time, housed in Montagu House in Bloomsbury and levying no admission fee to all 'studious and curious persons'.

duced the first English dictionary. William Hogarth, Thomas Gainsborough and Joshua Reynolds produced some of their finest engravings and paintings, and many of London's most elegant buildings, streets and squares were erected or laid out by the likes of John Soane and the incomparable John Nash (see p363).

All the while, though, London was becoming ever more segregated and lawless. George II himself was relieved of 'purse, watch and buckles' during a stroll through Kensington Gardens. This was Hogarth's London, in which the wealthy built fine mansions in attractive squares and gathered in fashionable new coffee houses while the poor huddled together in appalling slums and drowned their sorrows with cheap gin. To curb rising crime, two magistrates established the 'Bow Street Runners' in 1749, a voluntary group – effectively a forerunner to the Metropolitan Police Force (set up in 1829) – that challenged the official marshals (thief-takers), who were suspected (often correctly) of colluding with the criminals themselves.

In 1780 parliament proposed to lift the law preventing Catholics from buying or inheriting property. One MP, Lord George Gordon, led a 'No Popery' demonstration that turned into the Gordon Riots. A mob of 30,000 went on a rampage, attacking Irish labourers, and burning prisons, 'Papishe dens' (chapels) and several law courts. At least 300 people died during the riots, including some who drank themselves to death after breaking into a Holborn distillery, and the army managed to restore order only after five days of rioting.

As the 18th century drew to a close, London's population had mushroomed to almost a million.

For trivia, little-known facts and endless specialist information on the history of the East End and its personalities, click on East London History (www.eastlondonhistory.com).

VICTORIAN LONDON

While the growth and achievements of the previous century were impressive, they paled in comparison with the Victorian era, which began when the 19-year-old Victoria was crowned in 1838. During the Industrial Revolution, when small 'cottage' industries were suddenly overtaken by the advance of the great factories, spurring the creation of the first industrialised society on earth, London became the nerve centre of the largest and richest empire the world has ever known, one that covered a quarter of the earth's surface area and ruled more than 500 million people.

New docks in East London were built to facilitate the booming trade with the colonies, and railways began to fan out from the capital. The world's first underground railway opened between Paddington and Farringdon Rd in 1863 and was such a success that other lines quickly

1812	1814	1829	1838
Charles Dickens, Victorian England's greatest novelist, is born. Many of the author's novels paint London in all its Victorian squalor.	The Great Beer Flood of London saw a flash-flood of almost 1.5 million litres of beer causing death and destruction in the streets around a brewery in St Giles when vats ruptured.	London's first regular bus service – the 'omnibus' – commences, running from Paddington to Bank. Fares cost one shilling.	The coronation of Queen Victoria at Westminster Abbey ushers in a new era for London. The British capital becomes the economic and political centre of the world.

followed. Many of London's most famous buildings and landmarks were built at this time: the Clock Tower (popularly known as 'Big Ben', 1859), Royal Albert Hall (1871) and the magnificent Tower Bridge (1894).

The city, however, heaved under the burden of its vast size, and in 1858 London was in the grip of the 'Great Stink', when the population explosion so overtook the city's sanitation facilities that raw sewage seeped in through the floorboards of wealthy merchants' houses. Leading engineer Joseph Bazalgette tackled the problem by creating an underground network of sewers in the late 1850s, which was copied around the world. London had truly become the first modern metropolis.

Though the Victorian age is chiefly seen as one of great imperial power founded on industry, trade and commerce, intellectual achievement in the arts and sciences was enormous. The greatest chronicler of the times was Charles Dickens, whose *Oliver Twist* (1837) and other works explored the themes of poverty, hopelessness and squalor among the working classes. In 1859 Charles Darwin published the immensely controversial *On the Origin of Species* here, in which he outlined his epoch-making theory of evolution.

This was also the era of some of Britain's most capable and progressive prime ministers, most notably William Gladstone (four terms between 1868 and 1894) and Benjamin Disraeli (who served in 1868 and again from 1874 to 1880).

Waves of immigrants, from Chinese to Eastern Europeans, arrived in London during the 19th century, when the population exploded from one million to six million people. This breakneck expansion was not beneficial to all – inner-city slums housed the poor in atrocious conditions of disease and overcrowding, while the affluent expanded out to leafy suburbs, where new and comfortable housing was built. The inner suburbs of London are still predominantly made up of Victorian terraced housing.

Queen Victoria lived to celebrate her Diamond Jubilee in 1897, but died four years later aged 81 and was laid to rest in Windsor. Her reign is seen as the climax of Britain's world supremacy, when London was the de facto capital of the world.

FROM EMPIRE TO WORLD WAR

Victoria's self-indulgent son Edward, the Prince of Wales, was already 60 by the time he was crowned Edward VII in 1901. London's belle époque was marked with the introduction of the first motorised buses, which replaced the horse-drawn versions that had plodded their trade

You may worry about today's vehicle emissions, but at the end of the 19th century, 1000 tonnes of horse dung would fall on the streets of London daily. In 1894 *The Times* estimated that the streets of London would be 9ft deep in horse manure within 50 years.

1843	1878	1884	1893
Connecting Rotherhithe and Wapping, the Thames Tunnel opens; it is the first tunnel to be constructed under a navigable river.	London's first electric lights are installed in Billingsgate Fish Market, using Jablochkoff Candles; Holborn Viaduct and Victoria Embankment are also illuminated at the same time.	Greenwich Mean Time is established, making Greenwich Observatory the centre of world time, against which all clocks around the globe are set.	The Shaftesbury Memorial Fountain, topped with a statue of Eros (more accurately Anteros), the world's first ever public aluminium statue, is unveiled in Piccadilly Circus.

since 1829, and a touch of glamour came in the form of luxury hotels, such as the Ritz in 1906, and department stores, such as Selfridges in 1909. The Olympics were held at White City Stadium in 1908 – a rather different spectacle to those planned for just over a century later. The stadium was demolished in 1985 to make way for a new British Broadcasting Corporation (BBC) building.

What became known as the Great War (WWI) broke out in August 1914, and the first German bombs fell from zeppelins near the Guildhall a year later, killing 39 people. Planes were soon dropping bombs on the capital, killing in all some 650 Londoners (half the national total of civilian casualties).

While the young, moneyed set kicked up their heels after the relative hardships of the war, the 'roaring '20s' brought only more hardship for most Londoners, with an economic slump increasing the cost of living.

The population continued to rise, reaching nearly 7.5 million in 1921. The London County Council (LCC) busied itself clearing slums and building new housing estates, while the suburbs encroached ever deeper into the countryside.

Unemployment rose steadily as the world descended into recession. In May 1926 a wage dispute in the coal industry escalated into a nine-day general strike, in which so many workers downed tools that London virtually ground to a halt. The army was called in to maintain order and to keep the city functioning, but the stage was set for more than half a century of industrial strife.

Despite the economic woes, the era brought a wealth of intellectual success. The 1920s were the heyday of the Bloomsbury Group, which counted writer Virginia Woolf and economist John Maynard Keynes in its ranks. The spotlight shifted westwards to Fitzrovia in the following decade, when George Orwell and Dylan Thomas clinked glasses with contemporaries at the Fitzroy Tavern on Charlotte St.

Cinema, TV and radio arrived. The BBC aired its first radio broadcast from the roof of Marconi House on The Strand in 1922, and the first TV program from Alexandra Palace 14 years later.

The Royal Family took a knock when Edward VIII abdicated in 1936 to marry a woman who was not only twice divorced but, heaven save us, an American. The same year Oswald Mosley attempted to lead the British Union of Fascists on an anti-Jewish march through the East End but was repelled by a mob of around half a million at the famous Battle of Cable St.

GAMES TRIFECTA

In 2012, London will be the first city in the world to host the Olympic Games for the third time.

1901	1908	1928	1936
Queen Victoria dies after reigning more than 63 years – the longest reign (so far) in British history. As Victoria was averse to black funerals, London is festooned in purple and white.	London hosts its first Olympic Games, in the now demolished White City Stadium. A total of 22 teams take part and the entire budget is £15,000.	Parts of central London are deluged as the River Thames floods, killing 14 people and inundating streets and properties.	George VI becomes king following the abdication of his brother, Edward VIII, who gave up his throne for Wallis Simpson, an American divorcée unacceptable to the British establishment.

WWII & THE BLITZ

Prime Minister Neville Chamberlain's policy of appeasing Adolf Hitler during the 1930s eventually proved misguided as the Führer's lust for expansion appeared insatiable. When Germany invaded Poland on 1 September 1939, Britain declared war, having signed a mutual assistance pact with the Poles a few days beforehand. WWII (1939–45), Europe's darkest hour, had begun.

The Underground was turned into a giant bomb shelter

The first year of the war was one of anxious waiting for London; although more than 600,000 women and children had been evacuated to the countryside, no bombs fell to disturb the blackout. On 7 September 1940 this 'phoney war' came to a swift and brutal end when the German Air Force, the Luftwaffe, dropped hundreds of bombs on the East End, killing 430 people.

The Blitz (from the German '*blitzkrieg*' or 'lightning war') lasted for 57 nights, and then continued intermittently until May 1941. The Underground was turned into a giant bomb shelter, although one bomb rolled down the escalator at Bank station and exploded on the platform, killing more than 100 people. Londoners responded with legendary resilience and stoicism. The Royal Family – still immensely popular and enormously respected – were also to play their role, refusing to leave London during the bombing. Begged to allow her children to leave the capital, Queen Elizabeth (the present monarch's late mother) apparently replied, 'the children could not possibly go without me, I wouldn't leave without the King, and the King won't leave'. The king's younger brother, the Duke of Kent, was killed in active service in 1942, while Buckingham Palace took a direct hit during a bombing raid, famously prompting the Queen to announce that 'now we can look the East End in the face'. Winston Churchill, prime minister from 1940, orchestrated much of the nation's war strategy from the Cabinet War Rooms deep below Whitehall, and it was from here that he made his stirring wartime speeches.

London's spirit was tested again in January 1944, when Germany launched pilotless V-1 bombers (known as doodlebugs) over the city. By the time Nazi Germany capitulated in May 1945, up to a third of the East End and the City had been flattened, 32,000 Londoners had been killed and a further 50,000 had been seriously wounded. The scale of the destruction can only really be felt by taking a walk around the City – where postwar buildings (many of them monstrous) have been erected: this is most probably where German bombs hit.

1940–41

London is devastated by the Blitz, although miraculously St Paul's Cathedral and the Tower of London escape the bombing unscathed.

1944

The Blackout is downgraded to a Dim-out over London in autumn. Big Ben is again illuminated in Apr of the following year, along with full street lighting

SCIENCE & SOCIETY PICTURE LIBRARY/GETTY ©

St Paul's Cathedral (c 1943; p147)

POSTWAR LONDON

Once the celebrations of Victory in Europe (VE) day had died down, the nation began to confront the war's appalling toll. The years of austerity had begun, with the rationing of essential items and the building of high-rise residences on bomb sites in Pimlico and the East End to solve the chronic housing problem. Hosting the 1948 Olympics and the Festival of Britain in 1951, however, boosted London's morale.

The gloom returned, quite literally, on 6 December 1952 in the form of the Great Smog. A lethal blend of fog, smoke and pollution descended, and some 4000 people died of smog-related illnesses. This prompted the 1956 Clean Air Act, which introduced zones to central London where only smokeless fuels could be burned.

Rationing of most goods ended in 1953, the year the current queen, Elizabeth II, was crowned following the death of her much-loved father King George VI the year before.

Immigrants from around the world – particularly the former British colonies – flocked to postwar London, where a dwindling population had led to labour shortages, and the city's character changed forever. However, as the Notting Hill race riots of 1958 attest, despite being officially encouraged to come, new immigrants weren't always welcomed on the streets.

Some economic prosperity returned in the late 1950s, and Prime Minister Harold Macmillan told Britons they'd 'never had it so good'. London became the place to be during the 1960s, when the bottled-up creative energy of the postwar era was spectacularly uncorked. London found itself the epicentre of cool in fashion and music: the streets were awash with colour and vitality, the iconic Mini (1959) became a British icon and the Jaguar E-type (1961) was launched to adoring crowds. In the early 1960s, Mods danced to Motown, Jamaican Ska and R&B, turning their well-dressed backs on rock 'n roll and embracing new immigrant sounds.

Social norms underwent a revolution: the introduction of the contraceptive pill, the legalisation of homosexuality, and the popularisation of drugs such as marijuana and LSD through the hippy movement created an unprecedentedly permissive and liberal climate. Popular music in mid-to-late 1960s London became increasingly alloyed with drug use, political activism and a counter-cultural mindset. The Beatles recording at Abbey Rd and the Rolling Stones performing free in front of half a million people in Hyde Park were seminal moments. Carnaby St was the most fashionable place on earth, and pop-culture figures from Twiggy and David Bailey to Marianne Faithfull and Christine Keeler became the icons of the new era.

The night of 29th December 1940 has been called the 'Second Great Fire of London', when German bombers dropped over 100,000 bombs on London in a few hours, starting 1500 fires raging across the City – which became a furnace – and up to Islington. St Paul's escaped largely due to the bravery of firefighters.

1951	1952	1953	1956
The Festival of Britain is opened by King George VI; the festival celebrates the centenary of the Great Exhibition and aims to lift the national mood after the destruction of WWII.	London is brought to a virtual standstill for four days in December by a thick pea-souper smog that smothers and chokes the city.	Queen Elizabeth II's coronation is held at Westminster Abbey, the first major live event to be broadcast around the world on TV, for which many English families bought their first televisions.	Red Routemaster double-decker buses make their first appearance in London and instantly become an iconic symbol of the city.

THE WORLD IN ONE CITY

London is historically made up of immigrants. Whether Roman, Viking, Anglo-Saxon, Norman, Huguenot, Irish or Jamaican, the city has always assimilated large numbers of ethnically diverse people. Africans are well documented to have served in the Roman army, but they first came to England in significant numbers as slaves in Elizabethan times. The first truly large influx of foreigners was in the late 17th century, when Huguenots, French Protestant refugees fleeing religious persecution at home, settled in Spitalfields and Soho. Jews have arrived over the past four centuries; their traditional areas have been the East End (particularly Spitalfields and Stamford Hill) and northwest London. WWII brought Poles, Ukrainians and other Eastern Europeans to London, and today the Poles are a long-established community in Hammersmith and Shepherd's Bush. The single biggest wave of immigration came in the 1950s, when, facing a labour shortage, the government allowed anyone born in a UK colony to have British citizenship. This brought a huge black population from the Caribbean and a large Asian diaspora from India, Bangladesh and Pakistan. The black population settled in West London and South London, while Asians were concentrated in the East End.

PUNK LONDON

The party didn't last long, however, and London returned to the doldrums in the harsh economic climate of the 1970s, a decade disfigured by unemployment and Irish Republican Army (IRA) bombs. Post-1960s music became more formulaic as glam rock ruled, despite the blossoming of London legends Mark Bolan and David Bowie. Economic stagnation, cynicism and the superficial limits of disco and glam rock however spawned a novel London aesthetic: punk.

Despite the sexual liberation of the swinging '60s, London had remained a relatively conservative place, and the generation that had witnessed flower power as kids recognised their own need for action. Largely white, energetic, abrasive and fast, punk transformed popular music and fashion at one stroke as teenagers traded in denim bell bottoms for black drainpipes. The late 1970s were exhilarating times for London youth as punk opened the door for new wave, a punchy mod revival and the indulgent new romantics.

While the music and fashion scene was popping, torpor had set into Britain's body politic. Seen as weak and in thrall to the all-powerful trade unions, the brief and unremarkable Labour premiership of James Callaghan (1976–79) was marked by crippling strikes in the late 1970s, most significantly the 'Winter of Discontent' in 1978–79.

1959

The Notting Hill Carnival is started by Claudia Jones to promote good race relations following the riots of 1958 when white and African Caribbean communities clashed.

Notting Hill Carnival (p260)

1966

England beats Germany to win the World Cup at Wembley – possibly the greatest day in the history of British sport and one seared into the consciousness of every schoolboy.

1979

Margaret Thatcher is elected prime minister. Her policies will transform Britain beyond recognition – part vital modernisation, part radical right-wing social policy.

THE THATCHER & MAJOR YEARS

Recovery began – at least for the business community – under the iron fist of Margaret Thatcher, the leader of the Conservative Party, who was elected Britain's first female prime minister in 1979. In power for the whole of the 1980s and embarking on an unprecedented program of privatisation, Margaret Thatcher – aka the 'Iron Lady' – is easily the most significant of Britain's post-war leaders. While her critics decry her approach to social justice and the large gulf that developed between the haves and have nots during her time in power, her defenders point to the massive modernisation of Britain's lumbering trade-union-dominated infrastructure under her leadership and the vast wealth creation her policies generated.

The Greater London Council (GLC), under the leadership of 'Red' Ken Livingstone, proved to be a thorn in Thatcher's side. Thatcher responded in 1986 by abolishing the GLC, leaving London as the only European capital without a unified local government, a bizarre situation that would continue for 14 years until Ken Livingstone re-emerged as a thorn in Tony Blair's side in 2000.

While poorer Londoners suffered under Thatcher's significant trimming back of the welfare state, things had rarely looked better for the wealthy and London underwent explosive economic growth. New property developers proved to be only marginally more discriminating than the Luftwaffe, though some outstanding modern structures, including the Lloyd's of London building went up.

Like previous booms, the one of the late 1980s proved unsustainable. As unemployment started to rise and people found themselves living in houses worth much less than they had paid for them, Thatcher introduced a flat-rate poll tax. Protests around the country culminated in a 1990 march on Trafalgar Square that ended in a fully fledged riot. Thatcher's subsequent forced resignation brought to an end a divisive era in modern British history, and her successor, the former Chancellor of the Exchequer, John Major, employed a far more collective form of government.

In 1992, to the amazement of most Londoners, the Conservatives were elected for a fourth successive term in government, without the inspiring leadership of Thatcher. The economy went into a tailspin shortly after, the IRA detonated two huge bombs, one in the City in 1992 and another in the Docklands four years later and by 1995 the writing was on the wall for the Conservatives, as the Labour Party, apparently unelectable for a decade, came back with a new face.

For a fascinatingly informative blog reviewing the social, musical and popular cultural history of London, take a look at Another Nickel in the Machine (www.nickelinthemachine.com): it covers everything from vintage Bowie to suffragettes.

1981	1984	1987	1990
Brixton sees the worst race riots in London's history. Lord Scarman, delivering his report on the events, puts the blame squarely on 'racial disadvantage that is a fact of British life'.	The Thames Barrier, designed to protect London from flooding as a consequence of high tides and storm surges, is officially opened by the Queen.	A fire, probably started by a dropped match, at King's Cross underground station causes the death of 31 people.	Britain erupts in civil unrest, culminating in the poll tax riots in Trafalgar Square. Thatcher's deeply unpopular poll tax is ultimately her undoing and she is forced to resign in November.

MILLENNIUM DOME

BLAIR'S BRITAIN

Invigorated by its sheer desperation to return to power, the Labour Party elected the thoroughly telegenic Tony Blair to lead it, who reinvented the brand as New Labour, finally leading to a landslide win in the May 1997 general election. The Conservatives were atomised, and the Blair era had begun.

Most importantly for London, Labour recognised the legitimate demand the City had for local government, and created the London Assembly and the post of mayor. Former leader of the GLC Ken Livingstone stood as an independent candidate and stormed the contest. For London, this meant big change. Livingstone introduced a successful congestion charge and sought to bring London's backward public transport network into the 21st century.

London's resurgence as a great world city seemed to be going from strength to strength, culminating in the International Olympic Committee selection of London to host the 2012 games. London's buoyant mood was however shattered the very next morning when terrorists detonated a series of bombs on the city's public transport network, killing 52 innocent people. Triumph turned to terror, followed quickly by anger and then defiance. Just two weeks later the attempted detonation of several more home-made bombs on London's public transport system sent the city into a state of severe unease, which culminated in the tragic and shocking shooting by the Metropolitan Police of an innocent Brazilian electrician Jean Charles de Menezes, mistaken for Hussain Osman, one of the failed bombers from the previous day. Summer 2005 definitely marked London's lowest ebb for some time.

Championed by Tony Blair as a 'triumph of confidence over cynicism, boldness over blandness, excellence over mediocrity', the Millennium Dome on the Greenwich Peninsula failed to match the hype when it opened in 2000. Designed by Richard Rogers and sometimes mockingly referred to as the Millennium Tent, the dome eventually triumphed when rebranded as the O2 in 2007.

THE ERA OF BORIS

Ken Livingstone's campaign to get a third term as London mayor in 2008 was fatally undermined when the Conservative Party fielded maverick MP and popular TV personality Boris Johnson as its candidate. Even more of a populist than Livingstone, Eton-educated Johnson, portrayed by the media as a gaffe-prone toff, actually proved to be a deft political operator and shocked everyone by sailing past Livingstone to become the first Conservative mayor of London.

With his wild mop of blond hair, shapeless suits and in-your-face eagerness, Johnson cuts an almost eccentric and oddball appearance, a persona Londoners warmed to. The disastrous scenarios hand-wringing left-wing Londoners predicted never quite materialised. He disagreed with Livingstone on many things, but Johnson actually continued to support several of his predecessor's policies, including the congestion

1997	2000	2003	2005
Labour sweeps to victory after almost two decades of Tory power. Tony Blair's radical relaunch of the once left-wing Labour Party as centrist 'New Labour' gives him a majority of 179.	Ken Livingstone is elected mayor of London as an independent, despite the government's attempts to shoehorn its own man into the job.	London's congestion charge is introduced by Livingstone, creating an outcry that soon disappears as traffic in London's streets begins to flow smoothly again.	A day after London is awarded the 2012 Olympics, 52 people are killed by Muslim extremist suicide bombers attacking the London transport network on 7 July.

charge and the expansion of bicycle lanes. A keen cyclist, Boris's name is forever associated with the Barclay's Cycle Hire Scheme (p393), although Livingstone proposed it first. Johnson pledged to replace Livingstone's unloved 'bendy buses' with remodelled Routemasters and the new mayor also oversaw the banning of alcohol consumption on London Transport.

Johnson's first mayoral term coincided with London's transformation for the 2012 Olympic Games, as neglected areas of this recession-hit city were showered with investment and a vast building program in East London took shape (p342). The era also saw a transferral of government power from the lacklustre Labour Party under Gordon Brown's leadership to a Conservative–Liberal Democrat coalition government with fellow Etonian David Cameron as prime minister. But with so much to play for in the next mayoral election, it's likely that Ken vs Boris, round two, in 2012 will be even more of a spectacle.

2008	2009	2010	2011
Boris Johnson, a Conservative MP and journalist famed for his gaffes and rather eccentric appearance, beats Ken Livingstone to become London's new mayor.	Construction starts on The Shard at London Bridge; when completed in 2012, the dramatic skyscraper will be the tallest building in the European Union.	Labour is defeated in the 2010 general elections which result in a hung parliament and a Conservative-Liberal Democrat coalition government with David Cameron as prime minister.	A peaceful demonstration in Tottenham on 6 August turns into a riot and episodes of mass looting which then spreads to numerous London boroughs and towns across the UK.

Architecture

Unlike other world-class cities, London was never methodically planned, despite being largely burned to the ground in 1666. The city has instead developed in an organic (read: haphazard) fashion, so although you will lose track of the historical narrative, London is sprinkled with architectural refrains from every period of its long history. This is a city for explorers: keep your eyes peeled and you'll spot part of a Roman wall enclosed in the lobby of a postmodern building near St Paul's, say, or a galleried coaching inn dating from the Restoration tucked away in a courtyard off a high street in Borough.

LAYING THE FOUNDATIONS

Celebrating buildings with a range of events, walks, talks, tours and debates, the London Festival of Architecture has been held every two years since kicking off in 2004 and will be staged from 23 June to 8 July 2012. A description of the 2010 festival can be read online at www.lfa2010.org.

London's architectural roots lie within the walled Roman settlement of Londinium, established in AD 43 on the northern banks of the River Thames, roughly on the site of today's City. Few Roman traces survive outside museums, though you can see the relocated Temple of Mithras, built in AD 240, at the eastern end of Queen Victoria St in the City. Stretches of the Roman wall (Map p438) remain as foundations to a medieval wall outside Tower Hill tube station and in a few sections below Bastion highwalk, next to the Museum of London.

The Saxons, who moved into the area after the decline of the Roman Empire, found Londinium too small and built their communities further up the Thames. Excavations carried out by archaeologists from the Museum of London during renovations at the Royal Opera House in the late 1990s uncovered extensive traces of the Saxon settlement of Lundenwic, including some wattle-and-daub housing. But the best place to see in situ what the Saxons left behind is the church of All Hallows-by-the-Tower, northwest of the Tower of London, which boasts an important archway, the walls of a 7th-century Saxon church and a Roman pavement.

With the arrival of William the Conqueror in 1066, the country received its first example of Norman architecture with the White Tower, the sturdy keep at the heart of the Tower of London. The church of St Bartholomew-the-Great at Smithfield also has Norman arches and columns marching down its nave. The west door and elaborately moulded porch at the Temple Church in Inner Temple are other outstanding details of Norman architecture.

MEDIEVAL LONDON

Enlarged and refurbished between the 12th and 14th centuries, Westminster Abbey is a splendid reminder of the craftsmanship of master masons in the Middle Ages. Perhaps the finest surviving medieval church in the city is the 13th-century church of St Ethelburga-the-Virgin near Liverpool St station, heavily restored after Irish Republican Army (IRA) bombings in 1993. The 15th-century Church of St Olave (Map p438), northwest of Tower Hill, is one of the City's few remaining Gothic parish churches, while the crypt at the largely restored Church of St Ethelreda, north of Holborn Circus, dates from about 1250. Southwark Cathedral includes some 12th- and 13th-century remnants.

Secular medieval buildings are even scarcer, although the ragstone Jewel Tower (Map p430), opposite the Houses of Parliament, dates from 1365, and most of the Tower of London goes back to the Middle Ages. Staple Inn (Map p438) in Holborn dates from 1378, but the half-timbered shopfront facade (1589) is mostly Elizabethan, heavily restored in the mid-20th century. Part of the 12th century great hall of Winchester Palace, including the Rose Window, survives in Clink St on the South Bank.

A TRINITY OF ARCHITECTS

The finest London architect of the first half of the 17th century was Inigo Jones (1573–1652), who spent a year and a half in Italy and became a convert to Palladian Renaissance architecture. His *chefs-d'œuvre* include Banqueting House (1622) in Whitehall and Queen's House (1635) in Greenwich. Often overlooked is the much plainer church of St Paul's (Map p432) in Covent Garden, which Jones designed in the 1630s and described as 'the handsomest barn in England'.

The greatest architect ever to leave his mark on London was Sir Christopher Wren (1632–1723), responsible not just for his masterpiece and monument St Paul's Cathedral (1710) but also for many of central London's finest churches. He oversaw the building of dozens of them, many replacing medieval churches lost in the Great Fire, as well as the Royal Hospital Chelsea (1692) and the Old Royal Naval College, begun in 1694 at Greenwich. His neoclassical buildings and churches are taller, lighter and generally more graceful than their medieval predecessors.

Nicholas Hawksmoor (1661–1736) was a pupil of Wren, and worked with him on several churches before going on to design his own masterpieces. The restored Christ Church (1729) in Spitalfields and the 1731 St George's Bloomsbury (Map p426), as well as St Anne's, Limehouse (1725) and St George-in-the-East (1726) at Wapping, are among his finest works, which are usually defined as English baroque.

GEORGIAN MANNERS

The Georgian period saw the return of classicism (or neo-Palladianism). Among the greatest exponents of this revived style was Robert Adam (1728–92), much of whose work was demolished by the Victorians, but an excellent example that managed to survive is Kenwood House (1773) on Hampstead Heath.

Adam's fame has been eclipsed by that of John Nash (1752–1835), whose contribution to London's architecture compares to that of Wren. Nash was responsible for the layout of Regent's Park and its surrounding elegant crescents. To give London a 'spine', he created Regent Street as a straight north–south axis from St James's Park in the south to the new Regent's Park in the north. This grand scheme also involved the formation of Trafalgar Square, and the development of the Mall and the western end of The Strand.

The lovely row of houses at 52–55 Newington Green (N16) are London's oldest surviving brick terraced houses. Predating the Great Fire of London, they were built in 1658.

ARCHITECTURE A TRINITY OF ARCHITECTS

OPEN SESAME

If you want to stick your nose inside buildings you wouldn't normally be able to see, September is the time to visit London. One weekend that month (usually the third), the charity **Open House London** (☑3006 7008; www.londonopenhouse.org) arranges for owners of more than 700 private buildings to throw open their front doors and let in the public free of charge. Major buildings, some of them included in this section (eg, 30 St Mary Axe, City Hall, Lloyd's of London, Royal Courts of Justice), have also participated as well as the BT Tower (p102). The full program becomes available in August. An architectural London Night Hike winds its way through London during the same period and three-hour, architect-led tours are held on Saturdays year-round.

Nash's contemporary, John Soane (1753–1837), was the architect of the Bank of England (Map p438), completed in 1833 (though much of his work was lost during the bank's rebuilding by Herbert Baker, 1925–39), as well as the Dulwich Picture Gallery (1814). Robert Smirke (1780–1867) designed the British Museum in 1823, one of the finest expressions anywhere of the Greek Revivalist style.

A 'GOTHICK' RETHINK

In the 19th century a reaction emerged in the form of the highly decorative neo-Gothic style, also known as Victorian High Gothic or 'Gothick'. Champions were George Gilbert Scott (1811–78), Alfred Waterhouse (1830–1905), Augustus Pugin (1812–52) and Charles Barry (1795–1860). Scott was responsible for the elaborate Albert Memorial (1872) in Kensington Gardens and the 1874 St Pancras Chambers (Map p448). Waterhouse designed the flamboyant Natural History Museum (1880), while Pugin and Barry worked together from 1840 on the Houses of Parliament after the Palace of Westminster burned down in 1834. The last great neo-Gothic public building to go up in London was the Royal Courts of Justice (1882), designed by George Edmund Street.

The emphasis on the artisanship and materials necessary to create these elaborate neo-Gothic buildings led to the so-called Arts and Crafts movement – 'British art nouveau', for lack of a better term – of which William Morris (1834–96) was the leading exponent. Morris' work can be enjoyed in the Green Dining Room of the Victoria & Albert Museum. The 1902 Euston Fire Station (Map p448), opposite St Pancras New Church, is a wonderful example of Arts and Crafts architecture.

London's smallest house – 3ft wide at its narrowest point – is 10 Hyde Park Pl, now part of Tyburn Convent (8 Hyde Park Pl, W2). Despite being such a small target, it was damaged by a German bomb during WWII.

FLIRTING WITH MODERNISM

Few notable public buildings emerged from the first 15 years of the 20th century, apart from Admiralty Arch (1910) in the Edwardian baroque style of Aston Webb (1849–1930), who also designed the 1911 Queen Victoria Memorial (Map p430), opposite Buckingham Palace, and worked on the front facade of the palace itself. County Hall, designed by Ralph Knott in 1909, was not completed until 1922. More modern imagination is evident in commercial design, for example the superb art-nouveau design of Michelin House on Fulham Rd, dating from 1911.

In the period between the two world wars, English architecture was barely more creative, though Edwin Lutyens (1869–1944), whose work is sometimes classified as British art deco, designed the Cenotaph (1920) in Whitehall as well as the impressive 1927 Britannic House (Map p444), now Triton Court, in Moorgate. Designed by US architect Harvey Wiley Corbett (1873–1954), Bush House (Map p432) – current home of the BBC World Service – at the southern end of Kingsway, was built between 1923 and 1935. The delicious curves of the Daily Express Building (120 Fleet St; Ellis & Clarke with Sir Owen Williams) are a splendid example of art deco grace. Designed by HS Goodhart-Rendel in 1928, iconic St Olaf House (Map p436), an office block fronting the Thames, is an art-deco classic; Eltham Palace is another lovely art-deco treasure.

Russian architect Berthold Lubetkin (1901–90) is perhaps best remembered for his Penguin Pool at the London Zoo, with its concrete spiral ramp. Built in 1934, it is considered to be London's earliest modernist structure.

PANCAKE / ALAMY©

30 St Mary Axe (the Gherkin; p151), designed by Foster and Partners

POSTWAR RECONSTRUCTION

Hitler's bombs during WWII wrought the worst destruction on London since the Great Fire and the immediate postwar problem was a chronic housing shortage. Low-cost developments and ugly high-rise housing were thrown up on bomb sites and many of these blocks still scar the London horizon today.

The Royal Festival Hall, designed by Robert Matthew (1906–75) and J Leslie Martin (1908–99) for the 1951 Festival of Britain and overhauled more than half a century later, attracted as many accolades as brickbats when it opened as London's first major public building in the modernist style. However, hardly anyone seems to have a good word to say about Denys Lasdun's (1914–2001) brutalist National Theatre, begun in 1966 and finished a decade later.

The 1960s saw the ascendancy of the workaday glass-and-concrete high-rises exemplified by the mostly unloved 1967 Centre Point (Map p422) by Richard Seifert (1910–2001). But one person's muck is another's jewel; the once-vilified modernist tower has been listed by English Heritage, meaning that it represents a particular style, is of great value to the patrimony and largely cannot be altered outside (and in some cases inside as well). The 1964 BT Tower (p102), formerly known as the Post Office Tower and designed by Eric Bedford (1909–2001), has also received Heritage-listed status.

The 1970s saw very little building in London apart from roads, and the recession of the late 1980s and early 1990s brought much development and speculation to a standstill. Helping to polarise traditionalists and modernists still further was Prince Charles, who described a proposed extension to the National Gallery as being like 'a monstrous carbuncle on the face of an elegant and much loved friend'. For these and other reasons, the London skyline had little to compare with that of New York or Hong Kong.

The famous art-nouveau stained glass of the Michelin Building was removed for storage at the start of WWII, but subsequently vanished. The current stained glass are reproductions, based on photographs. The hunt for the original stained glass continues (www.michelinon line.co.uk/cen tenary/amnesty .htm).

RAZORS AND MUTANT TROMBONES

The *Evening Standard* newspaper makes a sport of nicknaming new towers – whether built or planned – and Londoners accept them with alacrity. Here are some of the popular ones inspired, of course, by the building's proposed or actual outline:

Hubble-Bubble Tower 'Twisted spaghetti', 'Meccano on crack' and 'supersized mutant trombone' are some of the other verdicts on the proposed 115m-tall tangle-of-metal ArcelorMittal Orbit (a public work of art, rather than a building) under construction at Olympic Park.

Cheese Grater (Map p438; Leadenhall Bldg; 122 Leadenhall St EC3) Piling work finally commenced in 2011 for this recession-delayed 48-storey, 224m-tall tower in the form of a stepped wedge to face architect Richard Rogers' other icon, the Lloyd's of London building.

Flatiron (South Molton St W1) The West End's answer to Manhattan's iconic eponymous building (1902) – though only six storeys high – is planned along Oxford St.

Gherkin (30 St Mary Axe; p151) The bullet-shaped tower that seems to pop up at every turn has also been known as the Swiss Re Tower (after its first major tenants), Cockfosters (after its architect, Norman Foster), the exotic pickle etc.

Helter Skelter (Map p438; Bishopsgate Tower; 22-24 Bishopsgate EC2) At 288m and 63 storeys, this fabulously twisting tower (Kohn Pedersen Fox Associates) is also called the Pinnacle. It is due for completion in 2013, when it will be the City's tallest building.

Shard (Map p436; London Bridge Tower; 32 London Bridge St SE) This needle-like, 310m-tall tower (by Renzo Piano) is one mother of a splinter you wouldn't want to tussle with. The EU's tallest building when complete, it should be finished in 2012.

Walkie Talkie (Map p438; 20 Fenchurch St EC3) This 36-storey, 160m-tall tower, expected in 2012, bulges in and bulges out, vaguely resembling an old-fashioned walkie talkie.

Razor (8 Walworth Rd, Southwark SE1) One of our favourite towers in South London is this 43-storey, turbine-topped tower (officially the Strata building) rising over Elephant & Castle, resembling an electric razor and completed in 2010.

POSTMODERNISM LANDS

London's contemporary architecture was born in the City and the re vitalised Docklands in the mid-1980s. The former's centrepiece was the 1986 Lloyd's of London (Map p438), Sir Richard Rogers' 'inside-out' masterpiece of ducts, pipes, glass and stainless steel. Taking pride of place in the Docklands was Cesar Pelli's 244m-high 1 Canada Square (1991), commonly known as Canary Wharf and easily visible from central London.

With a youthful New Labour in power at the end of the 1990s, Britain's economy on the up and the new millennium looming, attention turned to public buildings, including several landmarks that would define London in the early 21st century.

From the disued Bankside Power Station (Sir Giles Gilbert Scott, 1947–1963), the Tate Modern (Herzog & de Meuron, 1999) was refashioned as an art gallery that scooped international architecture's most prestigious prize, the Pritzker. The stunning Millennium Bridge (Sir Norman Foster and Antony Caro, 2000), the first new bridge to cross the Thames in central London since Tower Bridge in 1894, is much loved and much used. Even the once-maligned Millennium Dome (Sir Richard Rogers), the class dunce of 2000, won a new lease of life as the 02 concert and sports hall.

The graceful British Library (Colin St John Wilson, 1998), with its warm red-brick exterior, Asian-like touches and its wonderfully bright interior, met a very hostile reception. It has now become a popular and much loved London landmark.

TODAY & TOMORROW

More recent structures such as the 2002 glass 'egg' of City Hall (Map p436) and the ever-popular, ever-present 2003 30 St Mary Axe (Map p438) – or 'the Gherkin' – gave the city the confidence to continue planning more heady buildings.

Topped out in 2010, the 230m-tall Heron Tower in the City is London's third tallest building, even though some critics find it uninspiring. Home of the *Guardian* newspaper, Kings Place (90 York Way, London N1), a music and arts venue and office development in the King's Cross area, is a further recent architectural addition to London's burgeoning cultural firmament. With its 133m-high arch and 1km stadium circumference, redesigned Wembley Stadium (designed by Lord Foster) has re-emerged as a dramatic sporting icon.

The recession has, however, undermined what was the most ambitious building program in London since WWII. Even buildings so iconic as to already have nicknames (see boxed text, p366) have been cancelled, delayed or shrunk considerably in size.

Unstoppable, though, is London's biggest urban development project, the 200-hectare Olympic Park (Map p446) in the Lea River Valley near Stratford, where most of the events of the 2012 Summer Olympiad will take place. Front and centre will be Zaha Hadid's stunning Aquatics Centre, a breathtaking structure suitably inspired by the fluid geometry of water.

The spotlight may be over East London, but parts of South London are undergoing energetic and perhaps even visionary urban renewal. A vastly expensive commercial, business and transport regeneration scheme, the London Bridge Quarter (www.londonbridgequarter.com) in Borough consists of the Shard, a brand new piazza, The Place – the so-called Baby Shard (a misnomer) – and the transformation of London Bridge Station as the focal point of access. Although still a glass-clad concrete stub at the time of writing, the spike-like Shard will poke dramatically into Borough skies from 2012, its sharp form visible from across London. When finally unveiled, the Shard will house a five-star hotel, restaurants and London's highest public viewing gallery. The new Tate Modern Project extension will add a dramatically modern and inspirational add-on to the southern facet of the Tate Modern when it opens in 2016.

Other innovative designs include top-heavy Palestra House, at 197 Blackfriars Rd, and Bankside 123, which includes the Blue Fin Building (Building 1), with its vertical aluminium fins, and London's tallest residential building, the distinctive Strata building (see boxed text, p366), with built-in wind turbines. Projects awaiting starter's orders include Beetham Tower (1 Blackfriars), a visually unusual concept that has been stymied by the tentative financial climate and triple-dip recession fears.

For a look at what architectural exhibitions, events or talks are happening in London, access the handy London Architecture Diary (www .londonarchitec turediary.com).

Literary London

Over six centuries, London has been endlessly captured in prose; a history of London writing has become a history of the city itself. The capital has been the inspiration for the masterful imaginations of Shakespeare, Defoe, Dickens, Thackeray, Wells, Orwell, Conrad, Eliot, Greene and Woolf, to name but a few. Ever changing, yet somehow eerily consistent, London has left its mark on some of the most influential writing in the English language.

OLD LITERARY LONDON

Top Literary Sites
....
Shakespeare's Globe
....
Dickens House Museum
....
Keats House
....
Carlyle's House
....
Sherlock Holmes Museum

It's hard to reconcile the bawdy portrayal of London in Geoffrey Chaucer's *Canterbury Tales* with Charles Dickens' bleak hellhole in *Oliver Twist,* let alone Daniel Defoe's plague-ravaged metropolis in *Journal of the Plague Year* with Zadie Smith's multiethnic romp in *White Teeth.* London's ever-changing zeitgeist and state of mind has been conjured up by literary thought since quill first met parchment.

Chaucerian London

The first literary reference to London appears in Chaucer's *Canterbury Tales,* written between 1387 and 1400, where the pilgrims of the tale gather for their trip to Canterbury at the Tabard Inn in Southwark. Sadly, the inn burned down in 1676; a blue plaque marks the site of the building today.

Shakespearian London

William Shakespeare spent most of his life as an actor and playwright in London around the turn of the 17th century, when book publishing was beginning. He trod the boards of several Southwark theatres and wrote his greatest tragedies, among them *Hamlet, Othello, Macbeth* and *King Lear,* for the original Globe theatre on the South Bank. Although London was his home for most of his life, Shakespeare was an ardent fantasist and set nearly all his plays in foreign or make-believe lands. Even his English historical plays are hardly ever set in the capital; only *Henry IV: Part II* includes a London setting – a tavern called the Boar's Head in Eastcheap.

18th-Century London

Daniel Defoe was perhaps the first true London writer, both living in and writing about the city during the early 18th century. He is most famous for *Robinson Crusoe* (1720) and *Moll Flanders* (1722), which he wrote while living in Church St in Stoke Newington. Defoe's *Journal of the Plague Year* is his most absorbing account of London life, documenting the horrors of the Great Plague in London during the summer and autumn of 1665, when the author was a child.

Dickensian & 19th-Century London

Two early 19th-century poets drew inspiration from London. John Keats wrote *Ode to a Nightingale* while living near Hampstead Heath in 1819 and *Ode on a Grecian Urn* after inspecting the Portland Vase in the British Museum. William Wordsworth visited in 1802, discovering inspiration for the poem *On Westminster Bridge.*

Charles Dickens (1812–70) was the definitive London author. When his father and family were imprisoned for not paying their debts, the 12-year-old Charles was forced to fend for himself on the streets. His family was released three months later, but that grim period was seared into the boy's memory and provided a font of experiences on which to draw. His novels most closely associated with London are *Oliver Twist,* with its gang of thieves led by Fagin in Clerkenwell, and *Little Dorrit,* whose heroine was born in the Marshalsea (the same Southwark prison where his family was interned). *Our Mutual Friend* is a scathing criticism of modern values, both monetary and social, and a spirited attack on the corruption, complacency and superficiality of 'respectable' London.

Sir Arthur Conan Doyle (1858–1930) portrayed a very different London, his pipe-smoking, cocaine-snorting sleuth, Sherlock Holmes, coming to exemplify a cool and unflappable Englishness. Letters to the mythical hero still arrive at 221b Baker St, where there's a museum to everyone's favourite Victorian detective.

London at the end of the 19th century appears in many books. HG Wells' *The War of the Worlds* captures the sense and mood of the times. W Somerset Maugham's first novel, *Liza of Lambeth,* was based on his experiences as an intern in the slums of South London, while *Of Human Bondage,* so English, provides a portrait of late-Victorian London.

20TH-CENTURY WRITING

American Writers & London

Of Americans who wrote about London at the turn of the century, Henry James, who settled and died here, stands supreme with *Daisy Miller* and *The Europeans. The People of the Abyss,* by American socialist writer Jack London, is a sensitive portrait of poverty and despair in the East End. And we couldn't forget Mark Twain's *The Innocents Abroad,* in which the inimitable humorist skewers both the Old and New Worlds. St Louis–born TS Eliot settled in London in 1915, where he published his poem 'The Love Song of J Alfred Prufrock' almost immediately and moved on to his groundbreaking epic *The Waste Land,* where London is portrayed as an 'unreal city'.

The Primrose Hill address 23 Fitzroy Rd NW1 is a double literary landmark: Irish poet and playwright WB Yeats lived here and tragic US poet Sylvia Plath died here.

LITERARY READINGS, TALKS & EVENTS

A host of literary events are regularly held across London, ranging from book and poetry readings to talks, open-mic performances, writing workshops and other occasions celebrating the written word.

To catch established and budding authors, attend the monthly **Book Slam** (www. bookslam.com) held at **Tabernacle** (☏7221 9700; 34-35 Powis Sq W11; admission £8-10; ☺6pm last Thu of the month), and hosted by founder-author Patrick Neate. Guests have included Nick Hornby, Hari Kunzru and Mil Millington, and the event features readings, slam poetry, live music and DJs.

Covent Garden's **Poetry Café** (Map p432; ☏7420 9880; www.poetrysociety.org.uk; 22 Betterton St WC2; ⊖Covent Garden) is a favourite for lovers of verse, with almost daily readings and performances by established poets, open-mic evenings and writing workshops.

The **Institute of Contemporary Arts** (ICA; ☏information 7930 6393, bookings 7930 3647; www.ica.org.uk; Nash House, the Mall SW1; ⊖Charing Cross or Piccadilly Circus) has excellent talks every month, with well-known writers from all spectrums, from the hip to the seriously academic.

Bookshops, particularly **Waterstone's** (p137) and **Foyle's** (p137), often stage readings. Some major authors also now appear at the **Southbank Centre** (p170). Many are organised on an ad-hoc basis, so keep an eye on the listings in *Time Out* or any of the weekend newspaper supplements, including the *Guardian Guide* distributed with Saturday's edition.

Held in the first two weeks of July, the **London Literary Festival** (www.londonlitfest. com) at the Southbank Centre holds talks and events featuring writers and the literati.

Council plaque marking TS Eliot's former residence

Interwar Developments

Between world wars, PG Wodehouse (1881–1975), the most quintessentially British writer of the early 20th century, depicted London high life with his hilarious lampooning of the English upper classes in the Jeeves stories. Quentin Crisp, the self-proclaimed 'stately homo of England', provided the flipside, recounting in his ribald and witty memoir *The Naked Civil Servant* what it was like to be openly gay in the sexually repressed London of the 1920s. George Orwell's experience of living as a beggar in London's East End coloured his book *Down and Out in Paris and London* (1933), while the sternly modernist Senate House on Malet St, Bloomsbury, was the inspiration for the Ministry of Truth in his classic dystopian 1949 novel *Nineteen Eighty-Four*.

Literary Pubs

Newman Arms
(West End)

George Inn
(South Bank)

Museum Tavern
(West End)

Coach and Horses
(West End)

French House
(West End)

Dove (Notting Hill
& West London)

The Modern Age

The End of the Affair, Graham Greene's novel chronicling a passionate and doomed romance, takes place in and around Clapham Common just after WWII, while *The Heat of the Day* is Elizabeth Bowen's sensitive, if melodramatic, account of living through the Blitz.

Colin MacInnes described the bohemian, multicultural world of 1950s Notting Hill in *City of Spades* and *Absolute Beginners,* while Doris Lessing captured the political mood of 1960s London in *The Four-Gated City,* the last of her five-book *Children of Violence* series. She also provided some of the funniest and most vicious portrayals of 1990s London in *London Observed*. Nick Hornby found himself the voice of a generation, nostalgic about his days as a young football fan in *Fever Pitch* and obsessive about vinyl in *High Fidelity*.

Before it became fashionable, Hanif Kureishi explored London from the perspective of ethnic minorities, specifically young Pakistanis, in his best-known novels *The Black Album* and *The Buddha of Suburbia*. He also wrote the screenplay for the groundbreaking film *My Beautiful Laundrette*. Author and playwright Caryl Phillips won plaudits for his description of the Caribbean immigrant's experience in *The Final Passage*, while Timothy Mo's *Sour Sweet* is a poignant and funny account of a Chinese family in the 1960s trying to adjust to English life.

The late 1970s and 1980s were a great time for British literature, bringing a dazzling new generation of writers to the fore. Martin Amis *(Money, London Fields)*, Julian Barnes *(Metroland, Talking it Over)*, Ian McEwan *(Atonement, Enduring Love)*, Salman Rushdie *(Midnight's Children, The Satanic Verses)*, AS Byatt *(Possession, Angels & Insects)*, Alan Hollinghurst *(The Swimming Pool Library, The Line of Beauty)* and Hanif Kureishi all need little introduction to keen readers.

Millenium London

Helen Fielding's *Bridget Jones's Diary* founded the 'chick lit' genre, one that transcended the travails of a young single Londoner to become a worldwide phenomenon. Will Self – enfant terrible and incisive social commentator – has long been the toast of London. His *Grey Area* is a superb collection of short stories focusing on skewed and surreal aspects of the city, while *The Book of Dave* is his hilarious, surreal story of a bitter, present-day London cabbie burying a book of his observations, which are later discovered and regarded as scripture by the people on the island of Ham (future Britain is an archipelago due to rising sea levels).

Peter Ackroyd is regarded as the quintessential London author and names the city as the love of his life. *London: The Biography* is his inexhaustible paean to the capital, while his most recent book, *The Clerkenwell Tales,* brings to life the 14th-century London of Chaucer. *Thames: Sacred River* is Ackroyd's fine monument to the muck, magic and mystery of the river through history.

Finally, Iain Sinclair is the bard of Hackney, who, like Ackroyd, has spent his life obsessed with and fascinated by the capital. His acclaimed and ambitious *London Orbital,* a journey on foot around the M25, London's mammoth motorway bypass, is required London reading, while his latest work, *Hackney, That Rose-Red Empire,* is an exploration of London's most notorious borough, one that underwent enormous changes in the approach to 2012.

CURRENT SCENE

Home to most of the UK's major publishers and its best bookshops, London remains a vibrant place for writers and readers alike. But the frustrating predominance of several powerful corporations within publishing can occasionally limit pioneering writing. The desperation with which agents and publishers seek 'the next big thing' is a sign of the times. Spending large fees on a few gambles makes it harder for other writers with less marketable qualities to get into print.

This state of affairs has, however, stimulated an exciting literary fringe, which, although tiny, is very active and passionate about good writing. London still has many small presses where quality and innovation are prized over public relations skills, and events kick off in bookshops and in the back rooms of pubs throughout the week.

Back in the mainstream, the big guns of the 1980s, such as Martin Amis, Ian McEwan, Salman Rushdie and Julian Barnes, are still going strong, although new voices have broken through in the last decade – indeed, there have been some outstanding new London writers in recent years, from Monica Ali, who brought the East End to life in *Brick Lane,* to Jake Arnott's intelligent Soho-based gangster yarn *The Long Firm* and Gautam Malkani's much-hyped *Londonstani.*

Browse any London bookshop and you should find a London Writing section, where you will find many of these titles.

US poet and playwright TS Eliot is commemorated with a blue plaque at the Faber & Faber offices at 24 Russell Square, just east of London's School of Oriental and African Studies in Bloomsbury.

Built in 1567, the Old Curiosity Shop (13-14 Portsmouth Street, WC2), made famous by Charles Dickens' eponymous book, can still be seen today (although some say the name was added after publication).

Theatre & Dance

London has more theatrical history than almost anywhere else in the world, and it's still being made nightly on the stages of the West End, the South Bank and the vast London fringe. No visit to the city is complete without taking in a show, and a mere evening walk through 'theatreland' in the West End is an electrifying experience as thousands of people make their way to one of London's many playhouses. And if dance also tops your list, there are numerous London venues where you can applaud classical and contemporary repertoires.

THEATRE

Dramatic History

Elizabethan Period

Very little is known about London theatre before the Elizabethan period, when a series of 'playhouses', including the Globe, were built on the south bank of the Thames and in Shoreditch. Although the playwrights of the time – Shakespeare, Christopher Marlowe *(Doctor Faustus, Edward II)* and Shakespeare's great rival, Ben Jonson *(Volpone, The Alchemist)* – are now considered timeless geniuses, theatre then was more about raucous popular entertainment, where the crowd drank and heckled the actors. The Puritans responded by shutting the playhouses down after the Civil War in 1642.

Restoration

Three years after the return of the monarchy in 1660, the first famous Drury Lane theatre was built and the period of 'restoration theatre' began, under the patronage of the rakish Charles II. Borrowing influences from Italian and French theatre, Restoration theatre incorporated drama, including John Dryden's *All For Love* (1677), and comedy. The first female actors appeared (in Elizabethan times men played female roles), and Charles II is recorded as having had an affair with at least one, Nell Gwyn.

Victorian Period

Despite the success of John Gay's *The Beggar's Opera,* (1728), Oliver Goldsmith's 1773 farce *She Stoops to Conquer* and Richard Sheridan's *The Rivals* and *The School for Scandal* (also in the 1770s) at Drury Lane, popular music halls replaced serious theatre during the Victorian era. Light comic operetta, as defined by Gilbert and Sullivan *(HMS Pinafore, The Pirates of Penzance, The Mikado)*, was all the rage. A sea change only arose with the emergence at the end of the 19th century of such compelling playwrights as Oscar Wilde *(An Ideal Husband, The Importance of Being Earnest)* and George Bernard Shaw *(Pygmalion)*.

The 20th Century

Comic wits, including Noel Coward *(Private Lives, Brief Encounter)*, and earnest dramatists, such as Terence Ratigan *(The Winslow Boy, The Browning Version)* and JB Priestley *(An Inspector Calls)*, followed. However, it wasn't until the 1950s and 1960s that English drama yet again experienced such a fertile period as the Elizabethan era.

Perfectly encapsulating the social upheaval of the period, John Osborne's *Look Back in Anger* at the Royal Court theatre in 1956 heralded a rash of new writing, including Harold Pinter's *The Homecoming*, Joe Orton's *Loot*, Tom Stoppard's *Rosencrantz and Guildenstern are Dead* and

Alan Ayckbourn's *How the Other Half Loves*. During the same period many of today's leading theatre companies were formed, including the National Theatre.

Somewhat eclipsed by the National Theatre, today's Royal Court Theatre retains a fine tradition of new writing. In the past decade it has nurtured such talented playwrights as Jez Butterworth *(Mojo, The Night Heron)*, Ayub Khan-Din *(East is East)*, Conor McPherson *(The Weir, Shining City)* and Joe Penhall *(Dumb Show)*.

Current Scene

London remains a thrilling place for theatre-lovers. Nowhere else, with the possible exception of New York, offers such a diversity of high-quality drama, first-rate musical theatre and such a sizzling fringe. Whether it's Hollywood A-listers gracing tiny stages and earning Equity minimum for their efforts, or lavish West End musicals, London remains an undisputed theatrical world leader and innovator.

West End

In recent years the mainstream West End has re-established its credentials, with extraordinary hits, while the smarter end of the fringe continues to shine with risky, controversial and newsworthy productions. The hottest tickets are still for the National Theatre, which has gone from strength to strength under Nicholas Hytner, with productions enjoying both huge box-office success and critical acclaim.

Off West End

Other innovative venues are off–West End theatres such as the Arcola, the Almeida, the Royal Court Theatre, the Soho Theatre and the Donmar Warehouse. Big names can often be seen treading these hallowed boards – think Jude Law playing Hamlet at the Donmar, Ethan Hawke playing Treplev in Tom Stoppard's translation of Chekhov's *The Seagull* at the Old Vic, or Dame Judi Dench in Mishima's *Madame de Sade* at the Wyndham's Theatre.

There's something for all dramatic tastes in London's Theatreland, from contemporary political satire to creative reworking of old classics and all shades in between. Recent productions that have won critical acclaim include the National Theatre's fine revival of *After the Dance*, by Terence Rattigan, the triumphant musical *Passion* (Stephen Sondheim) at the Donmar Warehouse, Mikhail Bulgakov's *The White Guard* at the Lyttelton and *The Railway Children* (staged at Waterloo Station). *Into the Woods* (Stephen Sondheim) at Regent's Park Open Air Theatre was also much praised, as was Shakespeare's *Henry IV* at the Globe and Kevin Spacey's powerful performance in the title role of *Richard III* at the Old Vic (where he is artistic director).

If innovation and change are too much for you, drop by St Martin's Theatre where the same production of *The Mousetrap* has been running since 1952!

Shakespearean Offerings

Shakespeare's legacy is generously honoured on the city's stages, most notably by the Royal Shakespeare Company (RSC) and at the Globe Theatre. The RSC stages one or two of the bard's plays in London annually, although it currently has no London home (its productions are based in Stratford-upon-Avon and usually transfer to the capital later on in the run), while the open-air Shakespeare's Globe on the South Bank attempts to re-create the Elizabethan theatre experience. Artistic director Dominic Dromgoole, having taken over the reins at the start of 2006, has ensured that Shakespeare's plays remain at the core of the theatre's program, but at the same time has produced a wider range of European and British classics, as well as new material.

For full theatre listings by area, see the Entertainment section of each neighbourhood chapter, and for ticketing information and other details see p61.

Consult London's weekly 'what's on' bible, *Time Out*, for current theatrical offerings.

DANCE

Contemporary, classical or crossover – London will have the right dance moves for you. As one of the world's great dance capitals, London's artistic habitat has long created and attracted talented choreographers with both the inspiration and aspiration to fashion innovative dance.

London's most celebrated choreographer is award-winning Matthew Bourne *(Swan Lake, Play Without Words, Edward Scissorhands, Dorian Gray, Oliver!, Cinderella)*, who has been repeatedly showered with praise for his reworking of classics. Other leading London-based talents who have helped take London's dance message to the wider world include Rafael Bonachela, who scripted Kylie Minogue's Showgirl tour, and Wayne McGregor, who worked as movement director on *Harry Potter and the Goblet of Fire*.

However, Bonachela and McGregor are not alone in the vanguard. The Place (p131) in Euston was the original birthplace of modern British dance, and the training school Laban (p288) has emerged with strong cutting-edge performances. Meanwhile, the revamped Sadler's Wells (p214) – the birthplace of English classical ballet in the 19th century – continues to stage an exciting program of various styles featuring dance performances choreographed by Carlos Acosta, Twyla Tharp and Alvin Ailey and international troupes such as the Dance Theatre of Harlem.

Covent Garden's redeveloped Royal Opera House (p130) is the stunning home of London's leading classical-dance troupe, the world-famous Royal Ballet. The company largely sticks to the traditional, but more contemporary influences occasionally seep into productions. Back-to-back anniversaries have meant retrospectives devoted to choreographers George Balanchine and Frederick Ashton, as well as to dancers Sergei Diaghilev and Dame Ninette de Valois (the latter was the ballet's founder). All the same, the Royal Ballet has also made itself more accessible by dropping some ticket prices to £10 (as at the National Theatre).

Running for six weeks from early October, Dance Umbrella (www.danceumbrella.co.uk) is one of the world's leading dance festivals of its kind.

For more cutting-edge work, the innovative **Rambert Dance Company** (☎ 8630 0640; www.rambert.org.uk) is the UK's foremost contemporary dance troupe. It is possibly the most creative force in UK dance and although currently based in Chiswick, Rambert will move to purpose-built premises in Doon St (behind the National Theatre) in the far more creative milieu of the South Bank in 2013, making its dance concepts that much more accessible.

One of the world's best companies, the **English National Ballet** (www.ballet.org.uk), is a touring ballet company. You may be fortunate enough to catch it at one of its various venues in London – principally at the London Coliseum.

Another important venue for experimental dance is the Barbican (p160); for the latest of what's on, check www.londondance.com.

Art & Fashion

London today is the art capital of Europe, with a vibrant gallery scene and some of the world's leading modern-art collections. Many of the world's greatest artists have spent time in London, including Monet and Van Gogh. Although Britain's artists have historically been eclipsed by their European confreres, some distinctly innovative artists have emerged from London, a city also considered to be a major citadel of contemporary fashion.

ART

Holbein to Turner

It wasn't until the rule of the Tudors that art began to take off in London. The German Hans Holbein the Younger (1497–1543) was court painter to Henry VIII, and one of his finest works, *The Ambassadors* (1533), hangs in the National Gallery. A batch of great portrait artists worked at court during the 17th century, the best being Anthony Van Dyck (1599–1641), who painted *Charles I on Horseback* (1638), now in the National Gallery. Charles I was a keen collector and it was during his reign that the Raphael Cartoons, now in the Victoria & Albert Museum, came to London.

Local artists began to emerge in the 18th century, including landscapist Thomas Gainsborough (1727–88), William Hogarth (1697–1764), and poet, engraver and watercolourist William Blake (1757–1827). A superior visual artist to Blake, John Constable (1776–1837) studied the clouds and skies above Hampstead Heath, sketching hundreds of scenes that he'd later match with subjects in his landscapes.

JMW Turner (1775–1851), equally at home with oils and watercolours, represented the pinnacle of 19th-century British art. Through innovative use of colour and gradations of light he created a new atmosphere that seemed to capture the wonder, sublimity and terror of nature. His later works, including *Snow Storm – Steam-boat off a Harbour's Mouth* (1842), *Peace – Burial at Sea* (1842) and *Rain, Steam and Speed – The Great Western Railway* (1844), now in the Tate Britain and the National Gallery, were increasingly abstract, and although widely vilified at the time, later inspired the impressionist works of Claude Monet.

Since 1999, the Fourth Plinth Project in Trafalgar Square has offered a platform for novel, and frequently controversial, works by contemporary artists.

The Pre-Raphaelites to Hockney

The brief but splendid flowering of the Pre-Raphaelite Brotherhood (1848–54) took its inspiration from the Romantic poets, abandoning the pastel-coloured rusticity of the day in favour of big, bright and intense depictions of medieval legends and female beauty. The movement's main proponents were William Holman Hunt, John Everett Millais and Dante Gabriel Rossetti; artists Edward Burne-Jones and Ford Madox Brown were also strongly associated with the movement.

In the early 20th century, cubism and futurism helped generate the short-lived Vorticists, a modernist group of London artists and poets that was centred on the dapper Wyndham Lewis (1882–1957) and sought to capture dynamism in artistic form.

Sculptors Henry Moore and Barbara Hepworth both typified the modernist movement in British sculpture, but by the post-WWII years, art had transformed yet again. In 1945, the tortured, Irish-born painter Francis Bacon (1909–92) caused a stir when he exhibited his *Three Studies for Figures at the Base of a Crucifixion* – now on display at the Tate Britain – and afterwards continued to spook the art world with his repulsive yet mesmerising visions.

Australian art critic Robert Hughes has eulogised Bacon's contemporary, Lucian Freud (1922–2011), as 'the greatest living realist painter'. Freud's early work was often surrealist, but from the 1950s the bohemian Freud exclusively focused on pale, muted portraits – often nudes, and frequently of friends and family (although he has also painted the Queen).

Popular art classes are held at the Dulwich Picture Gallery and other museums and galleries around London.

London in the swinging 1960s was perfectly encapsulated by pop art, its vocabulary best articulated by the brilliant David Hockney (b 1937). Hockney gained a reputation as one of the leading pop artists through his early use of magazine-style images (although he rejected the label), but after a move to California, his work became increasingly naturalistic. Two of his most famous works, *Mr and Mrs Clark and Percy* (1971) and *A Bigger Splash* (1974), are displayed at the Tate Britain.

Gilbert & George were quintessential English conceptual artists of the 1960s. The Spitalfields odd couple are still at the heart of the British art world, having now become a part of the establishment themselves by representing Britain at the 2005 Venice Biennale, and holding a very successful retrospective at the Tate Modern in 2007.

Brit Art

Despite its incredibly rich collections, Britain had never led, dominated or even really participated in a particular artistic epoch or style. That all changed in the twilight of the 20th century, when 1990s London became the beating heart of the art world.

Brit Art sprang from a show called *Freeze*, which was staged in a Docklands warehouse in 1988, organised by artist and showman Damien Hirst and largely featuring his fellow graduates from Goldsmiths' College. Influenced by pop culture and punk, this loose movement was soon catapulted to notoriety by the advertising guru Charles Saatchi, who came to dominate the scene and bought an extraordinary number of works.

London's Greatest Artworks

Sunflowers by Vincent Van Gogh (National Gallery)

Fighting Temeraire by JMW Turner (National Gallery)

Whaam! By Roy Lichtenstein (Tate Modern)

Ophelia by Sir John Everett Millais (Tate Britain)

Three Studies for Figures at the Base of a Crucifixion by Sir Francis Bacon (Tate Britain)

Brit Art was brash, decadent, ironic, easy to grasp and eminently marketable. Hirst chipped in with a cow sliced into sections and preserved in formaldehyde; flies buzzed around another cow's head and were zapped in his early work *A Thousand Years*. Chris Ofili provoked with *The Holy Virgin Mary,* a painting of the black Madonna made partly with elephant poo; brothers Jake and Dinos Chapman produced mannequins of children with genitalia on their heads; and Marcus Harvey created a portrait of notorious child-killer Myra Hindley, made entirely with children's hand-prints, whose value skyrocketed when it was repeatedly vandalised with ink and eggs by the general public.

The areas of Shoreditch, Hoxton and Whitechapel – where many artists lived, worked and hung out – became the epicentre of the movement, and a rash of galleries moved in. Among these was White Cube, owned by one of the most important patrons of early Brit Art, Jay Jopling.

For the 10 years or so that it rode a wave of publicity, the defining characteristics of Brit Art were notoriety and shock value. Damien Hirst and Tracey Emin inevitably became celebrities.

One critic argued the hugely hyped movement as the product of a 'cultural vacuum' and became like *The Emperor's New Clothes*, with people afraid to criticise the works for fear they'd look stupid.

Beyond Brit Art

On the fringes of Brit Art, a lot of less stellar but equally inspiring artists exploring other directions. A highlight was Richard Wilson's iconic installation *20:50* (1987) – now a permanent installation at the Saatchi Gallery – a room filled waist-high with recycled oil, where you walk in and feel as if you've just been shot out into space. In his most famous work, *24 Hour Psycho* (1993), Scottish video artist Douglas Gordon slowed Alfred Hitchcock's masterpiece down so much it was stripped of its narrative and viewed more like a moving sculpture. Gary Hume first came to prominence with his *Doors* series which are full-size paintings of hospital doors, powerful allegorical descriptions of despair – or just perfect reproductions of doors.

The biggest date on the art calendar is the controversial Turner Prize at the Tate Britain. Any British artist under the age of 50 is eligible to enter, although there is a strong preference for conceptual art – a sound installation from Susan Philipsz won in 2010, attracting considerable cynicism from the general public – rather than painting.

FASHION

The British fashion industry has always been about younger, directional and more left-field designs. London fashion focuses on streetwear and the wow factor, with a few old reliables keeping the frame in place and mingling with hot new designers, who are often unpolished through in-experience, but bursting with talent and creativity. As a result, London is definitely exciting in a global sense and nobody with an interest in street fashion will be disappointed.

London weathered a tough few years that saw its status as an international fashion centre drop, but the city has returned to the heart of the fashion universe, boasting a bright new firmament of young stars.

London's Who's Who

With his witty designs and eclectic references, St Martin's graduate Giles Deacon took London by storm with his own label, Giles. Other Brit stars making a buzz are Henry Holland, Jonathan Saunders, Christopher Kane and Greek-Austrian import Marios Schwab. Nu-rave darling Gareth Pugh is also someone to look out for, another St Martin's alumnus who took the underground club fashions of Shoreditch and transposed them for the shop floor.

The popular Palace Art Fair (www.palaceartfair.co.uk), held in stunning surroundings at Fulham Palace in October every year, showcases over 100 contemporary artists working across a variety of media.

LONDON ARTISTS TODAY

London continues to generate talent across a range of artistic media, keeping critics on their toes. These are some of the biggest-name artists working in contemporary London:

Banksy The anonymous street artist whose work is a worldwide phenomenon.

Antony Gormley This sculptor is best known for the 22m-high *Angel of the North*, beside the A1 trunk road near Gateshead in northern England.

Anish Kapoor An Indian sculptor working in London since the 1970s, whose fantastic installations and sculpture are extremely popular with Londoners and who is well represented in the Tate Modern.

Marc Quinn A London artist whose work includes *Self*, a sculpture of his head made from the artist's own frozen blood, which Quinn recasts every five years. *Self* can be seen – in all its refrigerated glory – at the National Portrait Gallery.

Chantal Joffe This London-based artist is wellknown for her naive, expressionist portraits of women and children.

FASHIONPIX / ALAMY©

London Fashion Week

London Fashion Abroad

The influence of London's designers continues to spread well beyond the capital. The 'British Fashion Pack' still work at, or run, many of the major Continental fashion houses such as Chanel, Givenchy and Chloé. Meanwhile, regardless of whether they send models down the local catwalks, fashion houses such as Alexander McQueen retain design studios in London, and erstwhile defectors to foreign catwalks, such as Luella Bartley and Matthew Williamson, have returned to London to show their collections.

Fame & Celebrity

With its eccentricity when compared to the classic feel of the major Parisian and Milanese houses or the cool street-cred of New York designers, the London fashion spirit was best exemplified by Isabella Blow, the legendary stylist who discovered Alexander McQueen, Stella Tennant and Sophie Dahl (among many others) during her career at *Vogue* and *Tatler*. Blow sadly committed suicide in 2007 and her tragic loss was deeply felt in the fashion industry of the city she worked in. A further shock for the industry was the tragic suicide of Alexander McQueen in 2010 at the age of 40, just nine days after the death of his mother.

The fashion world thrives on notoriety and John Galliano's much-publicised arrest in 2011 for an anti-Semitic diatribe against a couple in a Paris cafe was a nadir for Dior's chief designer. Dior consequently dropped the South London fashion guru. But despite being buffeted by recent tragic losses and scandal, London retains all the innovative ingredients for exhilarating developments in fashion, today and tomorrow.

The high point on the London fashion calendar is London Fashion Week (www. londonfashion week.co.uk), held twice a year, in February and September. The main venue is Somerset House.

The Music Scene

Drawing upon a deep and often gritty reservoir of talent, London's modern music scene is one of the city's greatest sources of artistic power and a magnet for bands and hopefuls from all musical hemispheres. Periodically a worldleader in musical fashion and innovative soundscapes, London blends its homegrown talent with a continuous influx of styles and cultures, keeping currents flowing and inspiration percolating upwards.

THE SWINGING '60S

London's prolific output began with the Kinks and their North London songwriter Ray Davies, whose lyrics read like a guide to the city. 'You Really Got Me', 'All Day and All of the Night' and 'Dedicated Follower of Fashion' brilliantly capture the anti-establishment mood of the '60s, while 'Waterloo Sunset' is the ultimate feel-good London song.

Another London band, the Rolling Stones, first stepped up to a paying audience at the old Bull & Bush in Richmond in 1963. An R&B band with frequent trajectories into American blues and rock and roll, the Stones quickly set up as a more rough-edged counterpoint to the cleaner boy-next-door image of The Beatles (famously from Liverpool but recorded most of their best-known songs in London).

Struggling to be heard above the din was inspirational mod band the Small Faces, formed in 1965. The Who, from West London, innovated by smashing guitars on stage ('instrument destruction'), propelling TVs from hotel windows and driving cars into swimming pools. Jimi Hendrix came to London and took guitar playing to unseen heights before tragically dying in a flat in the Samarkand Hotel in West London in 1970. In some ways, the swinging '60s ended in July 1969 when the Stones famously staged their free concert in Hyde Park in front of over 250,000 liberated fans.

THE '70S

A local band called Tyrannosaurus Rex had enjoyed moderate success throughout the '60s. In 1970 they changed their name to T. Rex, frontman Marc Bolan donned a bit of glitter and the world's first 'glam' band had arrived. Glam encouraged the youth of uptight Britain to come out of the closet and be whatever they wanted to be. Baritone-voiced Brixton boy David Jones (aka David Bowie) then altered the rock landscape with his astonishing *The Rise and Fall of Ziggy Stardust and the Spiders from Mars* in 1972, one of decade's

LONDON IN MUSIC THROUGH THE YEARS

1967
Waterloo Sunset (The Kinks) Unimpeachable classic from the '60s.

1978
(I Don't Want to Go to) Chelsea (Elvis Costello) Punchy Costello classic from the early years.

1978
Hong Kong Garden (Siouxsie and the Banshees) Stirring goth-punk ode to a Chinese takeaway in Chislehurst High St.

1978
Baker Street (Gerry Rafferty) With an iconic and roof-raising saxophone riff.

1978
Down in the Tube Station at Midnight (The Jam) Possibly The Jam's best-known song.

1979
London Calling (The Clash) Raw and potent punk anthem.

1984
West End Girls (Pet Shop Boys) Smooth and glossy first chart success from the British pop duo.

1989
Twenty-four Minutes from Tulse Hill (Carter the Unstoppable Sex Machine) SW2 finds fame in this throbbing indie track.

seminal albums. Genre-spanning Roxy Music, blending art rock and synth pop, generated a more sophisticated glam sound.

Back at the rock face, a little band called Led Zeppelin (formed in 1968) was busy cultivating the roots of heavy metal. Seventeen-year-old Farok Bulsara changed his name to Freddie Mercury and led Queen to become one of the greatest rock-and-roll stars of all time. British-American band Fleetwood Mac left blues for pop rock and stormed the charts in the US as well as in Britain; their landmark *Rumours* became the fifth-highest-selling album in history.

Overpriced, oversexed and way overdone, '80s London was a roll-call of hair-gelled pop

Punk's unexpected arrival kicked in the complacent mid-'70s commercial edifice of disco, rock and glam. Few saw it coming but none missed its appearance. The Sex Pistols were the most notorious of a wave of bands that began pogoing around London in 1976.

Fellow Londoners The Clash harnessed the raw anger of the time into a collar-grabbing brand of political protest that would see them outlast their peers, treading the fine line between angry punks and great songwriters. The disillusioned generation finally had a plan and a leader in frontman Joe Strummer; *London Calling* is a spirited call to arms.

Punk cleared the air and into the oxygen-rich atmosphere swarmed a gaggle of late '70s acts. London band The Damned sought out an innovative niche as Goth punk pioneers. The Jam deftly vaulted the abyss between punk and mod revivalism (lead singer and 'Modfather' Paul Weller followed up with a hugely successful solo career after middle-of-the road sophisti-pop hits with The Style Council) and Madness put the nutty sound on the London map. New Wave and the New Romantics quickly shimmied into the fast-changing music scene... And before London knew it, the '80s had arrived.

THE '80S

Guitars disappeared, swiftly replaced by keyboard synthesisers and drum machines. Fashion and image became indivisible from music. Thin ties, winklepickers, velcro-lace white sneakers, spandex, densely-pleated trousers and make-up dazzled at every turn. Big hair was big. Overpriced, oversexed and way overdone, '80s London was a roll-call of hair-gelled pop: Spandau Ballet, Culture Club, Bananarama, Wham! and Howard Jones. Wham!'s Georgios Panayiotou changed his name to George Michael and gained massive success as a solo artist.

Depeche Mode broke new ground in dark neo-synth pop, while northern-lads-turned-Londoners the Pet Shop Boys found success and an impressive longevity, Neneh Cherry started rapping and southeast London samplers Colourbox strongly hinted at things to come.

While the late '80s brought blond boy band Bros and the anodyne starlets and one-hit wonders of the Hit Factory: Stock Aitken Waterman, relief had already been assured from up north with the arrival of The Smiths and their alternative rock innovations. In the closing years of the decade, the Stone Roses and the Happy Mondays devised a new sound that had grown out of the recent acid-house raves. Dance exploded in 1988's summer of love, with dilated pupils and a stage set for rave anthems such as the KLF's mighty 'What Time is Love?' A generation was gripped by dance music and a new lexicon ruled: techno, electronica, hip hop, garage, house and trance.

BRITPOP

The early 1990s saw the explosion of yet another scene: Britpop, a genre broadly defined as back to (Beatles) basics. A high-profile battle between two of the biggest bands, Blur from London and Oasis from Manchester, drew a line in the musical sand.

Also weighing in for the London side were the brilliant and erratic Suede and Elastica (fronted by the punky, poppy Justine Frischmann), not to mention Sheffield defectors to the capital, Pulp (with their irrepressible lead man, Jarvis Cocker). Skirting around the edges, doing their own thing, were Radiohead (from Oxford, close enough to London).

As the Britpop bands and fans became more sophisticated, the genre expired around 1997 as the zeitgeist disappeared and the Britpop musical muse called it a day. But as Britpop ebbed away, other currents were flowing into town and electronica found an anthem-packed sound with London band Faithless stylishly seeing out the millennium.

THE NOUGHTIES

London band Coldplay – melodic rockers led by the falsetto front man Chris Martin – first made a big splash in the UK at the dawn of the new century, before finding international fame. After four best-selling albums, their position as one of London's leading rock bands appears unshakeable.

But other musical styles were cooking. London's Asian community made a big splash in the early 21st century, with Talvin Singh and Nitin Sawhney fusing dance with traditional Indian music to stunning effect, and Asian Dub Foundation brought their unique brand of jungle techno and political comment to an ever-widening audience.

Pete Doherty and Carl Barât single-handedly renewed interest in guitar music despite its post-Britpop malaise. Doherty's band, The Libertines created a huge splash with their 2002 debut single 'What a Waster', and their first album went platinum. Kicked out, Doherty went on to form Babyshambles.

Fronted by eponymous Alison, Goldfrapp brought a seductive and sensual electronica to the fore (*Black Cherry, Supernature*) before abruptly departing in a mystical pastoral-folk direction on the band's much-applauded *Seventh Tree* (2008). The band then backpedaled with 2010's *Head First* as Goldfrapp rediscovered 1980's synthpop.

Other London noughties talents include art rockers Bloc Party, Anglo-Swedish group Razorlight, the ever-rotating line-up of the Sugababes and quirky West London singer-songwriter Lily Allen and extraordinary but ultimately troubled (passing away in July 2011, aged just 27) Southgate chanteuse Amy Winehouse.

LONDON IN MUSIC THROUGH THE YEARS

1993
Buddha of Suburbia (David Bowie; 1993) One of the Thin White Duke's most sublime songs.

2004
Hype Talk (Dizzee Rascal; 2004) Voluble track from the Bow rapper.

2004
Round Here (George Michael; 2004) Moving song drawing on the singer's recollections of his first day at school.

2006
LDN (Lily Allen; 2006) Catchy ska-beat hit from the London popster.

2007
Hometown Glory (Adele; 2007) Exquisite celebration of West Norwood from the Tottenham-born songstress.

2007
London Town (Kano; 2007) London rapper on his hometown.

2008
Warwick Avenue (Duffy; 2008) The beautiful voice of this Welsh starlet puts Warwick Avenue tube station on the musical map.

A MUSICAL JOURNEY THROUGH LONDON

➡ **Zebra crossing on Abbey Road, St John's Wood** – the Beatles' most famous album cover

➡ **Heddon Street, Soho** – where the cover for *Ziggy Stardust* was photographed

➡ **23 Brook Street, Mayfair** – former home to composers Handel and Hendrix

➡ **St Martin's College, Mayfair** – first Sex Pistols gig

➡ **Tree on Queen's Ride, Barnes** – where Marc Bolan died as a passenger in a Mini in 1977

➡ **3 Savile Row, Mayfair** – site of the last Beatles performance on the roof of the Apple building in 1969

London Music Today

The London scene has fought its way back from being an overhyped late-'90s destination for those seeking cool by association and is again one of the major creative musical hubs on earth.

With her 2nd album released, Tottenham-born soulstress-songwriter Adele has won not just the nation's hearts but spent 10 weeks at No 1 in the US album charts with *21* (2011), the first time since *Faith* (1987) from fellow Londoner George Michael.

Grime – and its successor genre, dubstep (two real indigenous London musical forms born in the East End out of a fusion of hip-hop and Asian influences) – are at the cutting edge of London music. Dizzee Rascal, Lady Sovereign, Lethal Bizzle, Roll Deep, GoldieLocks and Kano are perhaps the best-known singers and groups working in the genre.

Pigeonhole-defying James Blake won critical acclaim for his eponymous and soulful first album, along with songstress Jessie J for her 2011 pop debut *Who You Are*. Popular London folk rock ensemble Mumford & Sons have also assailed the American charts, and Londoner Tinie Tempah is the first British rapper to make it big in the US. London indie-punk newcomers The Vaccines arrived in 2011 with their *What Did You Expect from the Vaccines?* while London indie-rock-pop band The Noisettes have recently found more mainstream fame despite having been around since the mid-1990s.

La Roux, Florence and the Machine, Little Boots, Hot Chip, MIA and the Klaxons, and Anna Calvi all back up London's claim to be a world centre for musical innovation.

For a list of venues, see p61.

Film & Media

The UK punches well above its weight for its presence on the international film scene, but London is far from the glittering hub of the film industry that it might be, despite notable celluloid triumphs. Nonetheless, London forms the backdrop to a riveting spectrum of films while the city's media sphere is a vibrant and influential force.

LONDON & FILM

The Local Cinematic Industry

Londoners are proud of their hometown, but few see London at the forefront of the film industry. British films can be hit and miss; there are commercial triumphs, for sure, including recent Oscar-winners *The King's Speech* and *The Queen,* and further back the '90s older monster hits such as *Four Weddings and a Funeral* and *Shakespeare in Love,* but a frustrating inconsistency persists (despite the disproportionate influence of Brits in Hollywood).

Film fans nostalgically dwell on the golden – but honestly rather brief – era of Ealing comedies, when the London-based Ealing Studios turned out a steady stream of hits. Between 1947 and 1955, after which the studios were sold to the BBC, it produced enduring classics such as *Passport to Pimlico, Kind Hearts and Coronets, Whisky Galore, The Man in the White Suit, The Lavender Hill Mob* and *The Ladykillers.* This was also the time of legendary film-makers Michael Powell and Emeric Pressburger, the men behind *The Life and Death of Colonel Blimp* and *The Red Shoes.*

Today the industry seems stuck in a groove of romantic comedies *(Love Actually),* costume dramas and dire gangster pics. Producers, directors and actors complain about a lack of adventurousness in those holding the purse strings, while film investors claim there are not enough scripts worth backing.

A system of public funding through the UK Film Council exists alongside private investment, and although in 2002 it only accounted for a minority of the £570 million spent on film in the UK, some critics object to the scheme. The *Evening Standard's* late, lamented former film critic Alexander Walker was one of those who suggested that it led to poor projects being made, simply because the money was there.

> Get the low-down on British films, as well as films made in London and the UK, at the London Film Museum (www.londonfilmmuseum.com).

BEST CINEMATIC FESTIVALS

A host of London festivals celebrating cinema and ranging across the film spectrum entertains film enthusiasts from the popcorn crowd to arthouse buffs.

London Film Festival (www.bfi.org.uk/lff) held in October is the highlight of London's many festivals celebrating cinema.

Raindance Festival (www.raindance.co.uk) is Europe's leading independent film-making festival. It's a terrific celebration of independent, non-mainstream cinema from across the globe, screening just before the London Film Festival.

Portobello Film Festival (www.portobellofilmfestival.com) in September features largely independent works by London film-makers and international directors. It is free to attend.

London Lesbian & Gay Film Festival (www.bfi.org.uk/llgff) is one of the best of its kind with hundreds of independent films from around the world shown over a fun, party-intensive fortnight at BFI Southbank.

OUTDOOR CINEMA

Meanwhile, well-known British actors such as Ewan McGregor, Ian McKellen, Ralph Fiennes, Jude Law, Liam Neeson, Hugh Laurie, Kristin Scott Thomas, Keira Knightley, Orlando Bloom and Emily Watson spend time working abroad, as do many British directors, such as Tony Scott (*Crimson Tide, True Romance*), Ridley Scott (*Blade Runner, Alien, Thelma & Louise, Black Hawk Down*), Michael Winterbottom (*The Claim, The Killer Inside Me*) and Sam Mendes (*American Beauty, Revolutionary Road*).

London on the Screen

London remains one of the most popular places to make films in the world. Newfound converts have included that most die-hard of New Yorkers, Woody Allen, who made *Match Point, Scoop* and *Cassandra's Dream* in the capital in recent years before moving on to Barcelona.

The city's blend of historic and modern architecture works to its advantage. Ang Lee's *Sense and Sensibility* retreated to historic Greenwich for its wonderful parkland and neoclassical architecture. Merchant Ivory's costume drama *Howard's End* and the biopic *Chaplin* feature the neo-Gothic St Pancras Chambers, while David Lynch's *The Elephant Man* took advantage of the moody atmosphere around the then-undeveloped Shad Thames (the site of today's Butler's Wharf). *Withnail & I* (1987) remains a quintessential classic of offbeat British comedy, partly set in Camden.

London also serves as an effective backdrop to the horror genre and dystopian cinema. Danny Boyle's shocking *28 Days Later* (2002) haunted viewers with images of an entirely deserted central London in its opening sequences, scenes rekindled in the gore-splattered sequel *28 Weeks Later* (2006). Much of Stanley Kubrick's controversial and bleak *A Clockwork Orange* (1971) was filmed in London, while Alfonso Cuarón's *Children of Men* (2006) forged a menacing and desperate vision of a London to come.

Other parts of town to look out for include the eponymous West London neighbourhood in *Notting Hill* (1999) and the Dickensian backstreets of Borough that feature in such polar opposites as chick-flick *Bridget Jones's Diary* and Guy Ritchie's gangster-romp *Lock, Stock and Two Smoking Barrels,* while Smithfield is given a certain bleak glamour in *Closer*.

For an overview of cinemas in London see the Entertainment chapter (p61), and check the Entertainment sections within each neighbourhood chapter for local cinema details.

Outdoor cinema is rolled out in London in the warmer months at Somerset House Summer Screen (www.somersethouse.org.uk/film; tickets £14.50), where films can be enjoyed in a sublime setting.

TELEVISION

Most countries would give their eye teeth to have TV this good, from the extraordinary films of the BBC natural history unit to the cutting-edge comedy and drama across the channels.

When it comes to televisual output, London plays with a stronger hand than it does in film: a huge amount of global TV content originates in Britain, from the *Teletubbies* to *Planet Earth* and *Who Wants to be a Millionaire*. There are five free-to-air national TV stations: BBC1, BBC2, ITV1, Channel 4 and Five.

First airing on BBC1 in 2007 and currently in its 4th series, award-winning *Outnumbered*, a charmingly comic portrayal of life in a South London middle-class family, is much-loved for its its uncontrived yet painfully amusing insights into parenthood.

RADIO

BBC London (94.9 FM) is largely a talk station with great sports coverage, broadcasting across the capital. BBC Radio 4 (93.5 FM) is an excellent spoken word station with first-rate news coverage. If you're stuck in the traffic, tune into Capital FM (95.8 FM), the most popular pop station in the city and the commercial equivalent of the BBC's national Radio 1 (98.8 FM). For indie music, there's Xfm (104.9 FM), for dance tune into Kiss (100 FM) and for soul, there's Choice FM (96.9 FM). Classical listeners can turn to Classic FM (100.9 FM).

MEDIA

Newspapers & Magazines

National newspapers in England and London are almost always financially independent of any political party, although their political leanings are quite clear. There are two broad categories of newspapers, most commonly distinguished as broadsheets (or 'qualities') and tabloids (the distinction is more about content than physical size).

Daily Papers

The main London newspaper is the centre-right *Evening Standard,* a free tabloid published between Monday and Friday and handed out around mainline train stations, tube stations, retailers and stands. *Metro* (published Monday to Friday) is another skimpy morning paper designed to be read in 20 minutes, littering tube stations and seats, giving you an extra excuse to ignore your fellow passengers.

Broadsheet readers are extremely loyal to their paper and rarely switch from one to another. Liberal and middle-class, the *Guardian* has excellent reporting, an award-winning website and a progressive agenda. A handy small-format entertainment supplement, the *Guide,* comes with Saturday's paper. Dubbed the 'Torygraph', the right-wing *Daily Telegraph* is the unofficial Conservative party paper, and fogeyish perhaps, but with first-rate foreign news coverage. The *Times* is a stalwart of the British press and part of the Murdoch stable; a decent read with a wide range of articles and strong foreign reporting. Not aligned with any political party, the *Independent* is a left-leaning serious-minded tabloid with a focus on lead stories that other papers ignore. The *Financial Times* is a heavyweight business paper with a fantastic travel section in its weekend edition.

For sex and scandal over your bacon and eggs, turn to the *Mirror,* a working class and Old Labour paper; the *Sun,* the UK's bestseller, a gossip-hungry Tory-leaning tabloid legendary for its sassy headlines; or the lowbrow *Daily Star.* Other tabloid reads include the midlevel *Daily Express* and the centre-right *Daily Mail.*

Sunday Papers

Most dailies have Sunday stablemates, and (predictably) the tabloids have bumper editions of trashy gossip, star-struck adulation, fashion extras and mean-spirited diatribes. The *Observer,* established in 1791, is the oldest Sunday paper and sister of the *Guardian.* The *Sunday Telegraph* is as serious and politically blue as its weekly sister paper, while the *Sunday Times* is brimful of fashion and scandal.

Observer Sunday-only paper similar in tone and style to the *Guardian,* which owns it, with a great Sunday arts supplement (the *Review*).
Sunday Telegraph As serious and politically blue as its weekly sister.
Sunday Times Full of fashion and scandal. Probably destroys at least one rainforest per issue, but most of it can be arguably tossed in the recycling bin upon purchase.

New Media Websites

Londonist (www.londonist.com) London-centric blog.

Urban 75 (www.urban75.com) Outstanding and original.

Indymedia (www.uk.indymedia.org) Global network of alternative news.

Magazines

An astonishing range of magazines is published and consumed in London, from celebrity gossip to ideological heavyweights.

Political magazines are particularly strong. The satirical *Private Eye* has no political bias and lampoons everyone equally, although anyone in a position of power is preferred. The excellent weekly *Economist* cannot be surpassed for international political and business analysis. Claiming to be Britain's oldest running magazine, the right-wing weekly *Spectator* is worshipped by Tory voters, but its witty articles are often loved by left-wingers too. The *New Statesman* is a stalwart left-wing intellectual news magazine.

Time Out is the listings guide par excellence and great for taking the city's pulse, with strong arts coverage, while the *Big Issue,* sold on the streets by the homeless, is not just an honourable project but a damned fine read.

London loves celebrities with *Heat, Closer* and *OK!* the most popular purveyors of the genre. US import *Glamour* is the queen of the women's glossies; *Marie Claire, Elle* and *Vogue* are regarded as the thinking woman's glossies. The smarter men's magazines include *GQ* and *Esquire*, while less edifying reads are the so-called 'lads' mags': *FHM, Loaded, Maxim* and *Nuts*. A slew of style magazines are published here, including *i-D,* an ubercool London fashion and music gospel and *Dazed & Confused*.

Survival Guide

Transport

GETTING TO LONDON

Most passengers arrive in London by air. The city has five airports: Heathrow, which is the largest, to the west; Gatwick to the south; Stansted to the northeast; Luton to the northwest; and London City in the Docklands.

Most trans-Atlantic flights land at Heathrow (average flight time from the east coast is about seven to eight hours, 10 to 11 hours from the west coast; slightly more on the way back).

Visitors from Europe are more likely to arrive in Gatwick, Stansted or Luton (the latter two are used exclusively by low-cost airlines such as easyJet and Ryanair). Most flights to continental Europe last two to three hours.

An increasingly popular form of transport is the Eurostar between London and Paris or Brussels (Channel Tunnel train). The journey lasts 2¼ hours to Paris and less than two hours to Brussels, and takes visitors directly to/from the centre of each city.

Check any of the websites below for good deals on airline tickets:

www.cheapflights.co.uk

www.ebookers.com

www.expedia.com

www.lastminute.com

www.opodo.co.uk

www.skyscanner.net

Or try the following for rail bookings:

www.eurostar.com

www.raileurope.co.uk

Flights, tours and rail tickets can be booked online at lonely planet.com/bookings.

Air

Heathrow Airport

Some 15 miles west of central London, **Heathrow** (LHR; www.heathrowairport.com) is the world's busiest international airport and now has five terminals (although Terminal 2 is closed for refurbishment until 2014).

Each terminal has currency-exchange facilities, information counters and accommodation desks.

Left-luggage Facilities in each terminal. The charge per item is £5 for up to four hours, £8.50 for 24 hours (or part thereof), up to a maximum of 90 days.

Hotels There are three international hotels that can be reached on foot from the terminals, and another 20 or so nearby. The **Hotel Hoppa bus** (adult/child £4/free; every 15 to 30 minutes; from 4.30am to midnight) links nearby hotels with the airport's terminals.

GETTING TO/FROM HEATHROW AIRPORT

Train Underground (www. tfl.gov.uk) Three Piccadilly line stations serve the airport: one for Terminals 1, 2 and 3, another for Terminal 4, and a third for Terminal 5. The Underground, commonly referred to as 'the tube' (one way £5, from central London one hour, every three to nine minutes) is the cheapest way of getting to Heathrow. It runs from just after 5/5.45am from/to the airport (5.50/7am Sunday) to 11.45pm/12.30am (11.30pm Sunday in both directions). Buy tickets from the station.

Heathrow Express (www. heathrowexpress.com) This ultramodern train (one way/ return £16.50/32, 15 minutes, every 15 minutes) whisks passengers from Heathrow Central station (serving Terminals 1, 2 and 3) and Terminal 5 to Paddington. Terminal 4 passengers should take the free shuttle train available to Heathrow Central and board the Heathrow Express there. Trains run approximately from just after 5am in both directions between 11.45pm (from Paddington) and just after midnight (from the airport).

Heathrow Connect (www. heathrowconnect.com) Travelling between Heathrow and Paddington station, this modern passenger train service (one way £8.50, 25 minutes, every 30 minutes) makes five stops en route at places like Southall and Ealing Broadway. The first trains leave Heathrow at about 5.20am (6am Sunday) and the last service is around midnight. From Paddington, services leave between approximately 4.30am (6am Sunday) and 11pm.

Taxi Black cab A metered black cab trip to/from central London will cost between £45 and £65 (£55 from Oxford St) and takes 45 minutes to an hour, depending on your departure point.

Bus National Express (www.nationalexpress.com) Coaches (one way/return from £5/9, tickets valid three months, 45 minutes to 90 minutes, every 30 minutes to one hour) link the Heathrow Central Bus Station with **Victoria coach station** (164 Buckingham Palace Rd SW1; ⊖Victoria) about 45 times per day. The first bus leaves the Heathrow Central Bus station (at Terminals 1, 2 and 3) at 5.25am, with the last departure at 9.40pm. The first bus leaves Victoria at 7.15am, the last at 11.30pm.

At night the N9 bus (£1.30, 1¼ hr, every 20 minutes) connects Heathrow with central London.

Gatwick Airport

Located some 30 miles south of central London, **Gatwick** (LGW; www.gatwick airport.com) is smaller than Heathrow. The North and South Terminals are linked by a 24-hour shuttle train, with the journey time about three minutes. There are left-luggage facilities in both terminals. The charge is £8 per item for 24 hours (or part thereof), up to a maximum of 90 days' storage.

GETTING TO/FROM GATWICK AIRPORT

Train (www.nationalrail. co.uk) There are regular train services to/from London Bridge (30 minutes, every 15

to 30 minutes), King's Cross (45 minutes, every 15 to 30 minutes) and London Victoria (30 minutes, every 10 to 15 minutes). Fares vary depending on the time of travel and the train company, but allow £7 to £10 for a single.

Gatwick Express (www. gatwickexpress.com) This dedicated train service (one way/return £17.90/30.80, 30 minutes, every 15 minutes) links the station near the South Terminal with Victoria station in central London. From the airport, there are services between 4.30am and 1.35am. From Victoria, they leave between 3.30am and 12.30am.

Bus National Express (www.nationalexpress.com) Coaches (one way/return £7.50/15, tickets valid three months, 65 minutes to 90 minutes) run from Gatwick to Victoria coach station about 18 times per day. Services leave the airport at least once an hour between 6am and 9.45pm and operate hourly on the hour from Victoria between 7am and 7pm, with fewer services until 11.30pm.

easyBus (www.easybus. co.uk) This budget outfit runs 19-seater minibuses (one way £10, from £2 online, 70 minutes, every 20 minutes) from Earl's Court/West Brompton to Gatwick from 3am to 11.30pm daily. Departures from Gatwick are between 4.30am and 1am. Tickets can be purchased from the driver and there are ticket outlets at the airport in both the North and South Terminals.

Taxi A metered trip to/from central London costs about £90 and takes just over an hour.

Stansted Airport

Stansted (STN; www.stan stedairport.com) is 35 miles northeast of central London, heading towards Cambridge.

GETTING TO/FROM STANSTED AIRPORT

Train Stansted Express (www.standstedexpress.com) This rail service (one way/ return £21/29.70, 45 minutes, every 15 to 30 minutes) links the airport and Liverpool St station. From the airport the first train leaves at 5.30am, the last just before midnight. Trains depart Liverpool St station from 4.10am to just before 11.30pm; from Stansted, trains run between 5.30am and 12.30am.

Bus National Express (www.nationalexpress.com) Coaches run around the clock, offering some 120 services per day. The A6 runs to Victoria coach station (one way/ return £10.50/17.50, 85 to 110 minutes, every 10 to 20 minutes) via North London. The A9 runs to Stratford (£8.50/15, 45 minutes to one hour, every 30 minutes), from where you can catch a Jubilee line tube (20 minutes) into central London.

easyBus (www.easybus. co.uk) Minibuses (one way £10, from £2 online, 75 minutes, every 20 to 30 minutes) from Baker St to Stansted run 24 hours a day.

Terravision (www.terravi sion.eu) Coaches (one way/ return £9/14) link Stansted to both Liverpool St rail station (bus A51; 55 minutes) and Victoria coach station (bus A50; 75 minutes) every 20 to 40 minutes between 6am and 1am.

Taxi A metered trip to/from central London costs around £90.

Luton Airport

A smallish airport 32 miles northwest of London, **Luton** (LTN; www.london-luton.co.uk) caters for cheap charter flights and discount airlines.

CLIMATE CHANGE & TRAVEL

Every form of transport that relies on carbon-based fuel generates CO_2, the main cause of human-induced climate change. Modern travel is dependent on aeroplanes, which might use less fuel per kilometre per person than most cars but travel much greater distances. The altitude at which aircraft emit gases (including CO_2) and particles also contributes to their climate change impact. Many websites offer 'carbon calculators' that allow people to estimate the carbon emissions generated by their journey and, for those who wish to do so, to offset the impact of the greenhouse gases emitted with contributions to portfolios of climate-friendly initiatives throughout the world. Lonely Planet offsets the carbon footprint of all staff and author travel.

GETTING TO/FROM LUTON AIRPORT

Train (www.nationalrail.co.uk) Services (off-peak one way/return £12.50/21.50, 30 to 40 minutes, every six to 15 minutes, from 7am to 10pm) run from London Bridge and King's Cross St Pancras stations to Luton Airport Parkway station, from where an airport shuttle bus will take you to the airport in eight minutes.

Bus easyBus (www.easybus.co.uk) Minibuses (one way £10, from £2 online, 80 minutes, every 30 minutes) from Victoria coach station to Luton via Marble Arch, Baker St and Finchley Rd tube stations every half-hour round the clock, with the same frequencies coming from the airport.

Green Line bus 757 (www.greenline.co.uk) Buses to Luton (one way/return £16/22, tickets valid three months, 60 to 90 minutes) run from Buckingham Palace Rd just south of Victoria station, leaving approximately every half-hour round the clock.

Taxi A metered trip to/from central London costs about £90.

London City Airport

Its proximity to central London, which is just six miles to its west, as well as to the commercial district of the Docklands, means **London City Airport** (LCY; www.londoncityairport.com) is predominantly a gateway airport for business travellers, although it does also serve holidaymakers with its two dozen continental European and seven national destinations.

GETTING TO/FROM LONDON CITY AIRPORT

Train Docklands Light Railway (DLR; www.tfl.gov.uk/dlr) Stops at the London City Airport station (one way £4, with an Oyster card £2.20 to £2.70). The journey to Bank takes just over 20 minutes, and trains go every eight to 15 minutes from 5.30am to 12.30am Monday to Saturday, and 7am to 11.30pm Sunday.

Taxi A metered trip to or from the City/Oxford St/Earl's Court costs about £25/30/40.

Rail

Main national rail routes are served by InterCity trains, which are neither cheap nor particularly punctual. Check **National Rail Enquiries** (www.nationalrail.co.uk) for timetables and fares.

Eurostar (www.eurostar.com) The high-speed passenger rail service links St Pancras International station with Gare du Nord in Paris (or Bruxelles Midi in Brussels), with up to two-dozen daily departures. Fares vary enormously, from £69 for the cheapest return to more than £300 for a fully flexible return at busy periods. There are services to Avignon in the south of France (seven hours) in summer and to the French Alps in winter (eight to 10 hours).

Eurotunnel (www.eurotunnel.com) Transports motor vehicles and bicycles between Folkestone in England and Coquelles (near Calais) in France. Services run up to every 15 minutes during the day (but hourly 1am to 6am). Booking online is cheapest, where day-overnight return fares start at £44 and two- to five-day excursion fares from £84. All prices include a car and passengers.

Bus

Eurolines (www.eurolines.com; 52 Grosvenor Gardens SW1) Has National Express–operated buses to continental Europe leaving from **Victoria coach station** (Map p440; 164 Buckingham Palace Rd SW1; ⊖Victoria).

National Express (www.nationalexpress.com) The main coach operator, with comfortable and reliable services.

Megabus (www.megabus.com) Operates a no-frills airline style of seat pricing, where some tickets go for as little as £1.

Green Line (www.greenline.co.uk) Another national coach operator on main UK routes.

GETTING AROUND LONDON

Public transport in London is excellent, if pricey. It is managed by **Transport for London** (www.tfl.gov. uk), which has an excellent, multilingual website with live updates on traffic, a journey planner, maps and detailed information on every mode of transport in the capital.

The cheapest way to travel is with an Oyster card, a smart card. Paper tickets still exist and although day travel cards cost the same on paper as on Oyster, paper singles or returns are substantially more expensive than with Oyster.

The tube, DLR and Overground network are ideal for zooming across different parts of the city; buses and the new Barclays bikes are great for shorter journeys.

Left-luggage facilities **Excess Baggage** (☎0800 783 1085; www.left-baggage. co.uk) are available at London's main train stations: St Pancras, Paddington, Euston, Victoria, Waterloo, King's Cross, Liverpool St and Charing Cross. The service costs £8.50 per bag for the first 24 hours and £5 for each additional day.

Underground, DLR & Overground

Despite the never-ending upgrades and weekend closures, the London Underground ('the tube'; 11 colour-coded lines), Docklands Light Railway (DLR; a driverless train operating in the eastern part of the city) and Overground network (mostly outside of Zone 1) are overall the quickest and easiest way of getting around the city, if not the cheapest.

The first trains operate from around 5.30am Monday to Saturday and 7am Sunday. The last trains leave around 12.30am Monday to Saturday and 11.30pm Sunday.

There are regular line closures at weekends when upgrade work is carried out; schedules, maps and alternative route suggestions are posted in every station and staff are at hand to help redirect you.

Some stations, most famously Leicester Square and Covent Garden, are much closer in real life than they appear on the map.

Fares

➡ London is divided into nine concentric fare zones.

➡ It will always be cheaper to travel with an Oyster card than a paper ticket.

➡ Children under the age of 10 travel free.

➡ If you're in London for a longer period and plan to travel every day, consider a weekly or monthly travel card.

➡ If you're caught without a valid ticket, you're liable for an on-the-spot fine of £50. If paid within 21 days, the fine is reduced to £25.

Bus

London's iconic double-decker Routemaster was phased out in 2005 except for two 'heritage routes' (9 and 15). But today's modern double-deckers offer just as good a view of the city as the old ones. Just beware that the going can be slow, thanks to traffic jams and dozens of commuters getting on and off at every stop.

There are excellent 'bus spider maps' at every bus stop detailing every route and destination available from that particular area (generally a few bus stops within two to three minutes' walk, shown on a local map).

Bus services normally operate from 5am to 11.30pm.

Night bus

➡ More than 50 night bus routes (prefixed with the letter 'N') run from midnight to 4.30am.

➡ There are also another 60 bus routes operating 24 hours; the frequency decreases between 11pm and 5am.

➡ Oxford Circus, Tottenham Court Rd and Trafalgar Square

OYSTER CARD

The Oyster card is a smart card on which you can store credit towards so-called 'prepay' fares, as well as Travelcards. Oyster cards are valid across the entire public transport network in London. All you need to do when entering a station is touch your card on a reader (which has a yellow circle with the image of an Oyster card on them) and then touch again on your way out. The system will then deduct the appropriate amount of credit from your card, as necessary. For bus journeys, you only need to touch once upon boarding.

The benefit lies in the fact that fares for Oyster-users are lower than standard ones. If you are making many journeys during the day, you will never pay more than the appropriate Travelcard (peak or off peak) once the daily 'price cap' has been reached.

Oyster cards can be bought (£5 refundable deposit) and topped up at any Underground station, travel info centre or shop displaying the Oyster logo.

Simply return your Oyster card at a ticket booth to get your deposit back, as well as any remaining credit.

TRAVEL FARES

ZONE	NON-OYSTER SINGLE	OYSTER PEAK SINGLE	OYSTER OFF-PEAK SINGLE	PEAK CAP (OYSTER DAY TRAVEL CARD)	OFF-PEAK CAP (OYSTER DAY TRAVEL CARD)
Zone 1 only	£4	£1.90	£1.90	£8	£6.60
Zone 1&2	£4	£2.50	£1.90	£8	£6.60
Zone 1-3	£4	£2.90	£2.50	£10	£7.30
Zone 1-4	£5	£3.40	£2.50	£10	£7.30
Zone 1-5	£5	£4.10	£2.70	£15	£8
Zone 1-6	£5	£4.50	£2.70	£15	£8
Children 11-15	£2	£0.70	£0.65	£4	£1.30

are the main hubs for night routes.

➡ Night buses can be infrequent and stop only on request, so remember to ring for your stop.

Fares

➡ Oyster cards are valid on all bus services, including night buses, and are cheaper than cash fares. Bus journeys cost a flat fare (non-Oyster/Oyster £2.20/1.30) regardless of how far you go.

➡ At bus stops with a yellow background, if you don't have an Oyster card, you must buy your ticket before boarding the bus at the stop's ticket machine (you will need the exact amount in coins).

➡ Children under 11 travel free; those aged 11 to 18 years do as well but require an Oyster photocard.

➡ If you only travel by bus, the daily cap is £4.

Bicycle

Thousands of Londoners cycle to work every day, and it is generally a good way to get around the city, although traffic can be intimidating for less confident riders. The city has tried hard to improve the cycling infrastructure however, and it is gradually getting better. Recent highlights include the opening of new 'cycle superhighways'

for commuters in 2010 and 2011, and the launch of the Barclays Cycle Hire scheme (p393) in 2010. The latter is particularly useful for visitors.

Transport for London (www.tfl.gov.uk) publishes free London cycle guides, which are in effect 14 maps of London cycle routes. You can order them via the website or by ringing ☑7222 1234.

Hire

London Bicycle Tour Company (Map p436; ☑7928 6838; www.londonbicycle.com; 1a Gabriel's Wharf, 56 Upper Ground SE1; ⊖Waterloo or Blackfriars) Rentals cost £3.50 per hour or £20 for the first day, £10 for days two and three, £5 for days four and five, £50 for the first week and £15 for subsequent weeks. It also offers daily bike tours of central London for £19.95 (East London and Royal London tours also available weekends). Routes are on its website. You will need to provide credit card details as a deposit and must show ID.

On Your Bike (Map p436; ☑7378 6669; www.onyourbike.com; 52-54 Tooley St SE1; ⊖London Bridge) Rentals cost £18 for the first day, £10 for subsequent days, £45 per week. Prices include hire of a helmet and lock. A deposit of

£150 (via credit card) is necessary and you will be required to show ID.

Bicycles on Public Transport

Bicycles can be taken only on the Circle, District, Hammersmith & City and Metropolitan tube lines, though not during peak times (7.30am to 9.30am and 4pm to 7pm Monday to Friday). Folding bikes can be taken on any line at any time, however. Bicycles can also travel on the Overground but not on the DLR.

Restrictions on taking a bike on suburban and main-line trains vary from company to company but many now have carriages with very generous handicapped sections that cyclists can take advantage of when not in use. For details call ☑0845 748 4950.

Pedicabs

You'll find three-wheeled cycle rickshaws, seating two or three passengers, have been a regular, if much-cursed, part of the Soho scene in the past 10 years. They're less a mode of transport than a gimmick for tourists and the occasional drunk on a Saturday night. Expect to pay about £5 for a trip across Soho. For more information visit www.londonpedicabs.com.

Taxi

Black Cabs

The London **black cab** (www.londonblackcabs. co.uk) is as much a feature of the cityscape as the red double-decker bus. Licensed black-cab drivers have 'The Knowledge', acquired after rigorous training and a series of exams. They are supposed to know every central London street and the 100 most visited spots of the moment, including sights, clubs and restaurants.

➡ Cabs are available for hire when the yellow sign above the windscreen is lit; just stick your arm out to signal one.

➡ Fares are metered, with the flag-fall charge of £2.20 (covering the first 336m during a weekday), rising by increments of 20p for each subsequent 168m.

➡ Fares are more expensive in the evenings and overnight.

➡ You can tip taxi drivers up to 10% but few Londoners do, simply rounding up to the nearest pound.

➡ To order a cab by phone, try **Computer Cabs** (☎cash 7908 0207, credit card 7432 1432; www.comcablondon. com); it charges a £2 booking fee.

➡ **Zingo Taxi** (☎0870 070 0700; http://pda.london-taxi. co.uk) uses GPS to connect your mobile phone to that of the nearest free black-cab driver. This service costs £2; you will also be charged what it cost the cab to reach you (maximum £3.80).

Minicabs

Minicabs, which are licensed, are (usually) cheaper freelance competitors of black cabs.

➡ Minicabs cannot legally be hailed on the street; they must be hired by phone or directly from one of the minicab offices (every high street has at least one and most clubs work with a minicab firm to send revellers home safely).

➡ Don't accept unsolicited offers from individuals claiming to be minicab drivers – they could be anyone.

➡ Minicabs don't have meters; there's usually a fare set by the dispatcher – ask before setting off.

BARCLAYS CYCLE HIRE SCHEME

Following the success of cycling hire schemes in Paris and other European cities, London got in on the act in 2010, and unveiled its very own **Barclays bikes**. Also nicknamed 'Boris bikes' after the mayor, Boris Johnson, who launched the initiative, the bikes have proved as popular with Londoners as with visitors.

The idea is simple: pick up a bike from one of the 400 docking stations dotted around the capital. Cycle. Drop it off at another docking station.

The access fee costs £1 for 24 hours, £5 for a week. All you need is a credit or debit card.

Hire rates:

Up to 30min	free
Up to 1hr	£1
Up to 2hrs	£4
Up to 3hrs	£15
Up to 24hrs (maximum)	£50

You can take as many bikes as you like during your access period (24 hours or one week), leaving five minutes between each trip.

The pricing structure is designed to encourage short journeys rather than longer rentals. You'll also find that although easy to ride, the bikes only have three gears and are quite heavy. You must be 18 to buy access and at least 14 to ride a bike.

Hiring a Bike

➡ Insert your debit or credit card in the docking station to pay your access fee (only once for the access period).

➡ Request a cycle release code slip at the docking station (every time you want to take a bike during your access period).

➡ Enter the release code at your chosen bike dock; wait for the green light to release the bike.

➡ Ride!

➡ Return the bike at any free dock; wait for the green light to make sure the bike is locked.

If the docking station is full, consult the terminal to find available docking points nearby. iPhone users may also want to download the free cyclehire app, which locates nearby docking stations and shows you how full they are.

For more information, check www.tfl.gov.uk.

→ Ask a local or your hotel to recommend a reputable mini-cab company in the neighbourhood or phone a large 24-hour operator such as **Addison Lee** (0844 800 6677; www.addisonlee.com).

→ Women travelling alone at night can choose **Lady Mini Cabs** (7272 3300; www.ladyminicabs.co.uk), which has women drivers.

Boat

There are a number of companies operating along the Thames. Only the **Thames Clippers** (www.thamesclippers.com) really offers commuter services, however. It's fast, pleasant and you're always guaranteed a seat and a view.

Boats run from 6am to just after 10pm (later when there is an event at the O2), every 20 to 30 minutes. The route goes from London Eye Millennium Pier to Woolwich Arsenal Piers, serving London Eye, Tate Modern, Shakespeare's Globe, Borough Market, Tower Bridge, Canary Wharf, Greenwich and the O2.

Fares cost £3.50 to £5.50 for adults, £1.70 to £2.80 for children; pay-as-you-go Oyster card holders get a 10% discount, while travelcard holders (paper ticket or on an Oyster card) get a third off.

For sightseeing tours, see p395.

Car & Motorcycle

As a visitor, it's unlikely you'll need to drive in London. Mayors Ken Livingstone (2000–08) and Boris Johnson (elected in 2008 and in office until 2012) have done everything in their power to encourage Londoners to get out of their car and into public transport (or on their bikes!) and the same disincentives should keep you

firmly off the road: extortionate parking charges, congestion charge, traffic jams, high price of petrol, fiendishly efficient traffic wardens and wheel clampers etc.

If you get a parking ticket or your car gets clamped, call the number on the ticket. If the car has been removed, ring the free 24-hour service called **TRACE** (Tow-Away Removal & Clamping Enquiries; 0845 206 8602) to find out where your car has been taken to. It will cost you at least £200 to get your vehicle back on the road.

Driving

ROAD RULES

→ Get a copy of *Highway Code*, available at Automobile Association (AA) and Royal Automobile Club (RAC) outlets, as well as some bookshops and tourist offices.

→ A foreign driving licence is valid in Britain for up to 12 months from the time of your last entry into the country.

→ If you bring a car from Europe, make sure you're adequately insured.

→ All drivers and passengers must wear seatbelts, and motorcyclists must wear a helmet.

CONGESTION CHARGE
London was the world's first major city to introduce a congestion charge to reduce the flow of traffic into its centre. For full details log on to www.tfl.gov.uk/roadusers/congestioncharging.

→ The congestion charge zone encompasses Euston Rd, Pentonville Rd, Tower Bridge, Elephant & Castle, Vauxhall Bridge Rd, Marylebone Rd and Park Lane.

→ As you enter the zone, you will see a large letter 'C' in a red circle.

→ If you enter the zone between 7am and 6pm Monday to Friday (excluding public holidays), you

must pay the £10 charge (payable in advance or on the day) or £12 on the first charging day after travel to avoid receiving a fine (£120 or £60 if paid within two weeks).

→ You can pay online, at newsagents, petrol stations or any shop displaying the 'C' sign, by telephone on 0845 900 1234 and even by text message/SMS once you've registered online.

Hire

There is no shortage of car rental agencies in London. Book in advance for the best fares, especially at weekends. The following agencies have several branches across the capital:

Avis (www.avis.com)
easyCar (www.easycar.com)
Hertz (www.hertz.com)

A godsend for those who need a car for just a couple of hours or half a day is the self-service pay-as-you-go scheme, **Streetcar** (0845 644 8475; www.streetcar.co.uk). After registering and paying the £59.50 annual membership, you locate the closest available Streetcar vehicle to where you are staying, unlock the car with your membership card, release the key with a PIN and drive on. Prices start at £5.25/52.50 per hour/day. You get 20 miles of free petrol per day for bookings of less than 72 hours, and about 500 miles per week for longer bookings.

Tram

South London has a small network called **London Tramlink** (www.tfl.gov.uk). There are three routes running along 28km of track, including Wimbledon to Elmers End via Croydon; Croydon to Beckenham; and Croydon to New Addington. Single tickets cost £2.20 (£1.30 with an Oyster card).

TOURS

From traditional to wacky, there is a huge range of tours on offer to see the sights of London. The bus and cab tours, although not particularly cool, are good for those who are short on time.

Air

Adventure Balloons
(☎01252-844222; www.adventureballoons.co.uk; Winchfield Park, London Rd, Hartley Wintney, Hampshire) Weather permitting, there are weekday morning London flights (£185 per person) shortly after dawn from late April to mid-August. The flight lasts one hour, but allow four to six hours, including take-off, landing and recovery.

Cabair Helicopters
(☎8953 4411; www.cabairhelicopters.com; Elstree Aerodrome, Borehamwood, Hertfordshire) Thirty-minute flights over London twice a month on Saturday or Sunday for £150. Call for schedule details.

Boat

Travel-card holders get one-third off all boating fares listed here, except RIB. Boat services cruise along the Thames in central London but also go as far as the Thames Barrier and Hampton Court. You can also explore London's lesser known canals.

Circular Cruise
(☎7936 2033; www.crownriver.com; adult/child/family £11/5.50/33; ☺11am-6.30pm late May-early Sep, to 5pm early Apr-late May & early Sep-Oct, to 3pm Nov-early Apr) Vessels travel east from Westminster Pier to St Katharine's Pier near the Tower of London and back, calling at Embankment, Festival, Bankside and London Bridge Piers. You can use the boat as a hop-on/hop-off service to visit sights on the way. Tours depart half-hourly late May to early September and less frequently the rest of the year.

RIB London Voyages
(☎7928 8933; www.londonribvoyages.com; Boarding Gate 1, London Eye, Waterloo Millennium Pier, Westminster Bridge Rd SE1; adult/child £32.50/19.50; ☺hourly 9am-4pm) Feel like James Bond on this high-speed inflatable boat that flies down the Thames at 30 to 35 knots. RIB also does a Captain Kidd–themed trip between the London Eye and Canary Wharf at the same price.

Thames River Services
(☎7930 4097; www.westminsterpier.co.uk; Westminster Pier, Victoria Embankment SW1; adult/child one way £8.40/4.20, return £11/5.50, family £28; ☺tours every 30min 10am-4pm or 5pm Apr-Oct) These cruise boats leave Westminster Pier for Greenwich, stopping at the Tower of London. Every second service continues on from Greenwich to the Thames Barrier (one way adult/child £10.40/5.20, return £12.80/6.40, hourly 11.30am to 3.30pm) but does not land there, passing the O2 along the way. From Westminster it's a two-hour round trip to Greenwich, three hours to the Thames Barrier; from Greenwich the round trip to the barrier takes one hour. From November to March there's a reduced service from Westminster to Greenwich, with eight daily departures between 10.40am and 3.20pm.

Thames River Boats
(☎7930 2062; www.wpsa.co.uk; Westminster Pier, Victoria Embankment SW1; Kew adult/child/family one way £12/6/30, return £18/9/35, Hampton Court one way £15/7.50/37.50, return £22.50/11.25/56.25; ☺10.30am, 11.30am, noon & 2pm Apr-Oct) These boats go upriver from Westminster Pier to the Royal Botanic Gardens at Kew (1½ hours) and on to Hampton Court Palace (another 1½ hours, noon boat only). It's possible to get off the boats at Richmond but it depends on the tides; check before you sail.

Bus

The following companies offer commentary and the chance to get off at each sight and rejoin the tour on a later bus. Tickets are valid for 24 hours.

Big Bus Tours
(www.bigbustours.com; adult/child £27/12; ☺every 15min 8.30am-6pm) Informative commentaries in eight languages. The ticket includes a free river cruise with City Cruise and four thematic walking tours (Royal London, Harry Potter film locations, the Beatles, and the Ghosts by Gaslight).

Original Tour
(www.theoriginaltour.com; adult/child/family £26/13/91; ☺every 20min 8.30am-5.30pm)

Specialist

Black Taxi Tours of London
(☎7935 9363; www.blacktaxitours.co.uk; 2hr for up to 5 passengers day/night £115/125; ☺8am-midnight) Hire your own black cab with a trained tour guide at the wheel (although you are likely to hear equally amusing tales from any other cabbie in the city).

London Duck Tours
(☎7928 3132; www.londonducktours.co.uk; adult/child/family from £21/14/62; ⊜Waterloo) Amphibious craft based on D-Day landing vehicles depart from behind the London Eye and cruise the streets of central London before making a dramatic descent into the

Thames at Vauxhall. Tours last 80 minutes.

Open City (☎7383 2131; www.open-city.org.uk; prices vary; ⊙10am Sat) This architectural charity organises architectural tours to one of four different areas (Square Mile, South London, the West End or Docklands) weekly. The tours (2½ to three hours) include lively, well-informed commentary.

Walking

Association of Professional Tourist Guides

(APTG; ☎7611 2545; www.touristguides.org.uk; half/full day £127/200) Hire a prestigious Blue Badge Guide, know-it-all guides who have studied for two years and passed written exams to do their job.

London Walks (☎7624 3978; www.walks.com; adult/child £8/free) A huge array of walks, including Jack the Rip-

per tours at 7.30pm daily and 3pm Saturday, Beatles tours at 11.20am Tuesday and Saturday and a Sherlock Holmes tour at 2pm Friday.

London Mystery Walks

(☎0795 738 8280; www.tourguides.org.uk; adult/child/family £10/9/25; ⊖Aldgate) Tour Jack the Ripper's old haunts at 7pm on Monday, Wednesday and Friday. You must book in advance.

Directory
A–Z

Business Hours

The following table summarises standard opening hours. Reviews in this book won't list opening hours unless they significantly differ from these.

Information	9am-5pm Mon-Fri
Sights	10am-6pm
Banks	9am-5pm Mon-Fri
Shops	9am-7pm Mon-Sat, 11am-5pm Sun
Restaurants	noon-2.30pm & 6-11pm
Pubs & bars	11am-11pm

Children

London offers a wealth of sights and museums that appeal to children. It's a city with many green spaces, which often include safe areas for children to play, and swings and slides. See p30.

There is nearly always a special child's entry rate to paying attractions, although ages of eligibility may vary. Children also travel more cheaply on public transport.

The only places where children may not be accepted are pubs; gastropubs generally welcome kids but not city-centre pubs.

Babysitting

All the top-range hotels offer in-house babysitting services. Prices vary enormously, so enquire with your concierge. The following recommendations are also good:

Sitters (☎0800 389 0038; www.sitters.co.uk) A quarterly registration fee costs £13.85 and prices vary between £5.95 (weekdays) and £6.95 per hour (Saturdays), with an additional £4 booking charge per session.

Childcare (www.childcare. co.uk) This is an online forum designed to match parents with childcare providers. Registration is free.

Courses

British Council (Map p432; ☎7389 4385; www.britishcoun cil.org; 10 Spring Gardens SW1; ⊖Charing Cross) Publishes a free list of accredited colleges teaching English whose facilities and teaching reach the required standards. It can also advise foreign students on educational opportunities in the UK.

Floodlight (www.floodlight. co.uk) Lists courses from needle-work to Nietzsche, photography and politics.

Hotcourses (www.hotcourses. com) Another good miscellaneous course listing.

Careers Advice (☎0800 100 900; www.careersadvice.direct. gov.uk) Advises on vocational courses.

Customs Regulations

The UK distinguishes goods bought duty-free outside the EU and those bought in another EU country where taxes and duties have already been paid.

If you exceed your duty-free allowance, you will have to pay taxes. For European goods, there is officially no limit to how much you can bring but customs use certain guidelines (boxed text, p399) to distinguish between personal and commercial use.

Discount Cards

Possibly of most interest to visitors who want to take in

PRACTICALITIES

➜ **Weights & Measures** The UK uses a confusing mix of metric and imperial systems.

➜ **Smoking** Forbidden in all enclosed public places in England. Most pubs have a smoking area outside.

lots of sights is the **London Pass** (www.londonpass.com). Passes start at £15.83 per day (for six days), although they can be altered to include use of the Underground and buses. The pass offers free entry and queue-jumping to all major attractions; check the website for details.

Electricity

240V/50HZ

Embassies

Australia (☏7379 4334; www.uk.embassy.gov.au; Australia House, The Strand WC2; ⊖Holborn or Temple)

Canada (☏7258 6600; www.canada.org.uk; 1 Grosvenor Sq, W1; ⊖Bond St)

France Consulate (☏7073 1200; www.ambafrance-uk.org; 21 Cromwell Rd SW7; ⊖South Kensington)

Germany (☏7824 1300; www.london.diplo.de; 23 Belgrave Sq SW1; ⊖Hyde Park Corner)

Ireland (☏7235 2171; www.embassyofireland.co.uk; 17 Grosvenor Pl SW1; ⊖Hyde Park Corner)

Netherlands (☏7590 3200; www.netherlands-embassy.org. uk; 38 Hyde Park Gate SW7; ⊖Gloucester Rd)

New Zealand (☏7930 8422; www.nzembassy.com; New Zealand House, 80 Haymarket SW1; ⊖Piccadilly Circus)

South Africa (☏7451 7299; www.southafricahouseuk.com; South Africa House, Trafalgar Sq WC2; ⊖Charing Cross)

Spain (☏7589 8989; www.conspalon.org; 20 Draycott Pl SW3; ⊖Sloane Sq)

USA (☏7499 9000; www.usembassy.org.uk; 24 Grosvenor Sq W1; ⊖Bond St)

Emergency

Dial ☏999 to call the police, fire brigade or ambulance in an emergency.

Holidays

Public Holidays

Most attractions and businesses close for a couple of days over Christmas. Places that normally shut on Sunday will probably close on bank holiday Mondays.

New Year's Day 1 January

Good Friday Late March/April

Easter Monday Late March/April

May Day Holiday First Monday in May

Spring Bank Holiday Last Monday in May

Summer Bank Holiday Last Monday in August

Christmas Day 25 December

Boxing Day 26 December

School Holidays

These change from year to year and often from school to school. As a general rule, however, they are as follows:

Spring half term One week in mid-February

Easter holidays One week either side of Easter Sunday

Summer half term One week during end of May/early June

Summer holiday Late July to early September

Autumn half term Last week of October

Christmas holidays Roughly 20 December to 6 January

Internet Access

➡ The vast majority of hotels in London now provide wi-fi, although many, particularly top-end places, charge for the service.

➡ A number of hotels, hostels especially, also provide computer terminals for guests who may not be travelling with a laptop.

➡ A huge number of cafes now offer free wi-fi to customers, including chains such as Starbucks, Pret a Manger, McDonalds and Le Pain Quotidien.

➡ The City of London is one big wi-fi zone (see www.thecloud.net); it's free for iPhone users but not for other devices.

➡ Islington's Upper St is a 'technology mile' of free wi-fi access.

➡ Most major train stations and airport terminals also have wi-fi access, but it can be quite pricey.

Legal Matters

Should you face any legal difficulties while in London, visit any one of the **Citizens Advice Bureaux** (www.citizensadvice.org.uk).

Driving Offences

The laws against drink-driving are very strict and are treated seriously. Currently the limit is 80mg of alcohol in 100mL of blood. The safest approach is not to drink anything at all if you're planning to drive.

Drugs

Illegal drugs of every type are widely available in London, especially in clubs. Nonetheless, all the usual drug warnings apply. Cannabis was downgraded to a Class C drug in 2004 but reclassified as a Class B drug in 2009 following new studies that prompted a government rethink. If you're caught with pot today, you're likely to be arrested. Possession of harder drugs, including heroin and cocaine, is always treated seriously. Searches on entering clubs are common.

Fines

In general you rarely have to cough up on the spot for an offence. The exceptions are trains, the tube and buses, where people who can't produce a valid ticket for the journey when asked to by an inspector can be fined there and then. No excuses are accepted, though if you can't pay, you'll be able to register your details (if you have ID with you) and be sent a fine in the post.

Maps

The *London A-Z* series produces a range of excellent maps and hand-held street atlases. Online, www.street map.co.uk and Google Maps are also very comprehensive.

Medical Services

➡ EU nationals can obtain free emergency treatment on presentation of a **European Health Insurance Card** (www.ehic.org.uk).

➡ Reciprocal arrangements with the UK allow Australian residents, New Zealand nationals, and residents and nationals of several other countries to receive free emergency medical treatment and subsidised dental care through the **Na-**

IMPORT RESTRICTIONS

ITEM	DUTY-FREE	TAX & DUTY PAID
Tobacco	200 cigarettes or 100 cigarillos or 50 cigars or 250g tobacco	3200 cigarettes, 200 cigars, 400 cigarillos, 3kg tobacco
Spirits & liqueurs	1L spirit or 2L of fortified wine	10L spirit, 20L fortified wine
Beer & wine	16L beer, 4L still wine	110L beer, 90L still wine
Other goods	Up to a value of £390	n/a

tional Health Service (NHS; ☎0845 4647; www.nhsdirect. nhs.uk). They can use hospital emergency departments, GPs and dentists (check the Yellow Pages).

➡ Visitors staying 12 months or longer, with the proper documentation, will receive care under the NHS by registering with a specific practice near their residence.

➡ Travel insurance is advisable for non-EU residents as it offers greater flexibility over where and how you're treated and covers expenses for an ambulance and repatriation that won't be picked up by the NHS.

Dental Services

➡ For emergency dental care, call into **University College Hospital** (☎3456 7890; 253 Euston Rd NW1; ⊖Euston Sq).

➡ Note that many travel insurance schemes do not cover emergency dental care.

Hospitals

The following hospitals have 24-hour accident and emergency departments. However, in an emergency just call ☎999 and an ambulance will normally be dispatched from the hospital nearest to you.

Charing Cross Hospital (☎3311 1234; Fulham Palace Rd W6; ⊖Hammersmith)

Chelsea & Westminster Hospital (☎8746 8000; 369 Fulham Rd SW10; ⊖South Kensington, then ⛟14 or 414)

Guy's Hospital (☎7188 7188; Great Maze Pond SE1; ⊖London Bridge)

Homerton Hospital (☎8510 5555; Homerton Row E9; ⊕Homerton)

Royal Free Hospital (☎7794 0500; Pond St NW3; ⊖Belsize Park)

Royal London Hospital (☎7377 7000; Whitechapel Rd E1; ⊖Whitechapel)

University College Hospital (☎3456 7890; 253 Euston Rd NW1; ⊖Euston Sq)

Pharmacies

The main pharmacy chains in the UK are Boots, Superdrug and Lloyd's Pharmacy. The first two can be found on virtually every high street.

The **Boots** on Piccadilly Circus (44-46 Regent St; ⊙9am-8pm Mon-Sat, noon-6pm Sun; ⊖Piccadilly Circus) is a one of the biggest and most centrally located.

Money

➡ Despite being a member of the EU, the UK has not signed up to the euro and has retained the pound sterling (£) as its unit of currency.

➡ One pound sterling is made up of 100 pence (called 'pee', colloquially).

➡ Notes come in denominations of £5, £10, £20 and £50, while coins are 1p, 2p, 5p, 10p, 20p, 50p, £1 and £2.

➡ Unless otherwise noted, all prices in this book are in pounds sterling.

ATMs

ATMs are everywhere and will generally accept Visa, MasterCard, Cirrus or Maestro cards, as well as more obscure ones. There is nearly always a transaction surcharge for cash withdrawals with foreign cards. There are nonbank-run ATMs that charge £1.50 to £2 per transaction. These are normally found inside shops and are particularly expensive for foreign bank card holders. The ATM does warn you before you take money out that it'll charge you so you don't get any surprises on your bank statement.

Also, always beware of suspicious-looking devices attached to ATMs. Many London ATMs have now been made tamperproof, but certain fraudsters' devices are capable of sucking your card into the machine, allowing the fraudsters to release it when you have given up and left.

Changing Money

➡ The best place to change money is in any local post office branch, where no commission is charged.

➡ You can also change money in most high-street banks and some travel-agent chains, as well as at the numerous bureaux de change throughout the city.

➡ Compare rates and watch for the commission that is not always mentioned. The trick is to ask how many pounds you'll receive in total before committing – you'll lose nothing by shopping around.

Credit & Debit Cards

Londoners live off their debit cards, which can be used to get 'cash back' from supermarkets. Visitors should know that:

➡ Credit and debit cards are accepted almost universally in London, from restaurants and bars to shops and even some taxis.

➡ American Express and Diner's Club are less widely used than Visa and MasterCard.

Post

The **Royal Mail** (www.royal mail.co.uk) is generally very reliable.

Postcodes

The unusual London postcode system dates back to WWI. The whole city is divided up into districts denoted by a letter (or letters) and a number. For example, W1, the Mayfair and Soho postcode, stands for 'West London, district 1'. EC1, on the other hand, stands for 'East Central London, district 1'. The number a district is assigned has nothing to do with its geographic location, but rather its alphabetical listing in that area. For example, in north London N1 and N16 are right next to each other. While in West London W2 is very central, W3 is further out.

Relocating

The following are great for job and/or flat hunting:

Loot (www.loot.com) As well as the website, the paper comes out three times a week.

Gumtree (www.gumtree. com) Flats, secondhand furniture, jobs, the works.

SpareRoom (www.spare room.co.uk) Ideal for flat-sharing.
Check the weekly freebies *TNT Magazine, Southern* *Cross* or *SA Times*, with Australasian and South African news and sports results. They are also useful for their entertainment listings, travel sections and classified ads for jobs, cheap tickets, shipping services and accommodation, and can be found outside most tube stations.

Expat communities have traditionally favoured certain areas of London; here's a rough guide to find kindred spirits.

Aussie, US & Kiwi	West London (Earl's Court, Acton, Shepherd's Bush, Fulham)
Carribean	Brixton, Dalton
Cypriot & Turkish	Dalston, Stoke Newington, Green Lane
French	South Kensington
Middle Eastern	Edgware Rd
Portuguese	Stockwell
South African	Putney
Spanish	Notting Hill
Polish	Balham, Hammersmith

Safe Travel

London's a fairly safe city, considering its size, so exercising common sense should keep you safe.

If you're getting a cab after a night's clubbing, make sure you go for a black cab or a licensed minicab firm. Many of the touts operating outside clubs and bars are unlicensed and can therefore be unsafe. The areas where you should avoid wandering alone at night are King's Cross, Dalston and Peckham, though sticking to the main roads offers a certain degree of safety.

Pickpocketing does happen in London, so keep an eye on your handbag, especially in bars and nightclubs, and in crowded areas such as the Underground.

POSTAL RATES

POSTCARD & LETTERS	PRICE	DELIVERY
Domestic 1st class	46p	Next working day
Domestic 2nd class	36p	3 working days
Europe	68p	3-5 working days
North America, Asia, Oceania	£1.10	5 working days

Taxes & Refunds

Value-added tax (VAT) is a 20% sales tax levied on most goods and services except food, books and children's clothing. Restaurants must, by law, include VAT in their menu prices, although VAT is not always included in hotel room prices so always ask when booking to avoid surprises at bill time.

It's sometimes possible for visitors to claim a refund of VAT paid on goods. You're eligible if you have spent fewer than 365 days out of the two years prior to making the purchase living in the UK, and if you're leaving the EU within three months of making the purchase.

Not all shops participate in the VAT refund scheme, called the Retail Export Scheme or Tax-Free Shopping, and different shops will have different minimum purchase conditions (normally around £75 in any one shop). On request, participating shops will give you a special form (VAT 407). This must be presented with the goods and receipts to customs when you depart the country (VAT-free goods can't be posted or shipped home). After customs has certified the form, it should be returned to the shop for a refund (minus an administration or handling fee), which takes about eight to 10 weeks to come through.

Telephone

British Telecom's famous red phone boxes survive in conservation areas only (notably Westminster).

Some BT phones still accept coins, but most take phonecards (available from retailers, including most post offices and some newsagents) or credit cards.

Useful phone numbers (charged calls):

Directory enquiries, international (☑118 661, 118 505)

Directory enquiries, local & national (☑118 118, 118 500)

Operator, international (☑155)

Operator, local & national (☑100)

Reverse charge/collect calls (☑155)

Phone codes worth knowing:

International dialling code (☑00)

Local call rate applies (☑08457)

National call rate applies (☑0870, 0871)

Premium rate applies (☑09) From 60p per minute.

Toll-free (☑0800)

Calling London

➜ London's area code is ☑020, followed by an eight-digit number beginning with ☑7 (central London), ☑8 (Greater London) and ☑3 (non-geographic).

➜ You only need to dial the ☑020 when you are calling London from elsewhere in the UK or if you're calling from a mobile.

➜ To call London from abroad, dial your country's international access code, then ☑44 (the UK's country code), then ☑20 (dropping the initial ☑0), followed by the eight-digit phone number.

International Calls & Rates

➜ International direct dialling (IDD) calls to almost anywhere can be made from nearly all public telephones. Direct dialling is cheaper than making a reverse-charge (collect) call through the international operator (☑155).

➜ Many private firms offer cheaper international calls than BT. In such shops you phone from a metered booth and then pay the bill. Some cybercafes and internet shops also offer cheap rates for international calls.

➜ International calling cards with a PIN (usually denominated £5, £10 or £20), which you can use from any phone by dialling a special access number, are usually the cheapest way to call abroad. These cards are available at most corner shops.

➜ Note that the use of Skype can be restricted in hostels and internet cafes because of noise and/or band-width issues.

Local & National Call Rates

➜ Local calls are charged by time alone; regional and national calls are charged by both time and distance.

➜ Daytime rates apply from 6am to 6pm Monday to Friday.

➜ The cheap rate applies from 6pm to 6am Monday to Friday; weekend rates apply from 6pm Friday to 6am Monday.

Mobile Phones

➡ The UK uses the GSM 900 network, which covers Europe, Australia and New Zealand, but is not compatible with the North American GSM 1900 or Japanese mobile technology.

➡ If you have a GSM phone, check with your service provider about using it in the UK and enquire about roaming charges.

➡ It's usually better to buy a local SIM card from any mobile-phone shop, though in order to do that you must ensure your handset is unlocked before you leave home.

Time

Wherever you are in the world, the time on your watch is measured in relation to the time at Greenwich in London – Greenwich Mean Time (GMT). British Summer Time, the UK's form of daylight-saving time, muddies the water so that even London is ahead of GMT from late March to late October.

Paris	GMT +1
New York	GMT -5
San Francisco	GMT -8
Sydney	GMT +10

Tipping

➡ Many restaurants now add a 'discretionary' service charge to your bill. It's legal for them to do so but this should be clearly advertised.

➡ In places that don't, you are expected to leave a 10% to 15% tip unless the service was unsatisfactory.

➡ You never tip to have your pint pulled in a pub.

➡ Some guides and/or drivers on Thames boat trips will solicit you for their commentary. Whether you pay is up to you.

➡ You can tip taxi drivers up to 10% but most people round up to the nearest pound.

Toilets

It's an offence to urinate in the streets. Train stations, bus terminals and attractions generally have good facilities, providing also for people with disabilities and those with young children. You'll also find public toilets across the city, some operated by local councils, others automated and self-cleaning. Some charge 20p.

Tourist Information

Britain Visitor Centre (off Map p422; www.visitbritain.com; 1 Regent St SW1; ⏱9.30am-6pm Mon, 9am-6pm Tue-Fri, 9am-4pm Sat, 10am-4pm Sun & bank holidays Sep-May, to 5pm Sat Jun-Sep; 🚇Piccadilly Circus) London's main tourist office has comprehensive information, in eight languages, on London and the whole of the UK. It can arrange accommodation, tours, and train, air and car travel. It also has a theatre ticket agency, a bureau de change, international telephones and an internet cafe (£1 per 20 minutes).

Visit London (☎0870 156 6366; www.visitlondon.com) Can fill you in on everything from tourist attractions and events (such as the Changing of the Guard) to river trips and tours, accommodation, eating, theatre, shopping, children's London, and gay and lesbian venues.

Heathrow Airport (Terminal 1, 2 & 3 Underground station; ⏱7.15am-9pm)

King's Cross St Pancras station (Map p448; ⏱7.15am-9.15pm Mon-Sat, 8.15am-8.15pm Sun)

Liverpool Street station (Map p438; ⏱7.15am-9.15pm Mon-Sat, 8.15am-8.15pm Sun)

Victoria train station (Map p430; ⏱7.15am-9.15pm Mon-Sat, 8.15am-8.15pm Sun) Local tourist offices:

City Information Centre (Map p438; www.visitthecity.co.uk; St Paul's Churchyard EC4; ⏱9.30am-5.30pm Mon-Sat, 10am-4pm Sun; 🚇St Paul's) Opposite St Paul's Cathedral.

Greenwich Tourist Office (Map p463; www.greenwich.gov.uk; Pepys House, 2 Cutty Sark Gardens SE10; ⏱10am-5pm; DLR Cutty Sark)

Travellers With Disabilities

For disabled travellers London is an odd mix of user-friendliness and downright disinterest. New hotels and modern tourist attractions are legally required to be accessible to people in wheelchairs, but many historic buildings, B&Bs, guesthouses are in older buildings, which are hard (if not impossible) to adapt.

Transport is equally hit and miss, but slowly improving:

➡ Only 62 of London's tube stations have step-free access; the rest have escalators or stairs.

➡ The DLR is entirely accessible for wheelchair users.

➡ All buses are low-floor vehicles: they are lowered to street level when the bus stops; wheelchair users travel free.

➡ Guide dogs are universally welcome in public transport, hotels, restaurants, attractions etc.

➡ Transport for London publishes the *Getting Around London* guide, which contains the latest information on accessibility for passengers with disabilities. Download it from www.tfl.gov.uk.

The following organisations can provide helpful information ahead of travel:

Royal Association for Disability & Rehabilitation (Radar; ☎7250 3222; www.radar.org.uk; Unit 12, City Forum, 250 City Rd EC1) This is an umbrella organisation for voluntary groups for people with disabilities. Many disabled-user toilets across London can be opened only with a special key, which can be obtained from tourist offices or for £3.50 (plus a brief statement of your disability) via the Radar website.

Royal National Institute for the Blind (☎7388 1266; www.rnib.org.uk; 105 Judd St WC1) This is the best point of initial contact for sight-impaired visitors to London. It can also be contacted via its confidential **helpline** (☎0303 123 9999; ◷8.45am-5.30pm Mon-Fri).

Royal National Institute for Deaf People (☎freephone 0808 808 0123, textphone 0808 808 9000; www.rnid.org.uk; 19-23 Featherstone St EC1) This is the main organisation working with deaf and hard of hearing people in the UK. Many ticket offices and banks are fitted with hearing loops to help the hearing-impaired; look for the ear symbol.

Visas

Immigration to the UK is becoming tougher, particularly for those seeking to work or study. The following table indicates who will need a visa for what, but make sure you check www.ukvisas.gov.uk or with your local British embassy for the most up-to-date information.

Visa Extensions

Tourist visas can only be extended in clear emergencies (eg an accident, death of a relative). Otherwise you'll have to leave the UK (perhaps going to Ireland or France) and apply for a fresh one. To extend (or attempt to extend) your stay in the UK, ring the **Visa & Passport Information Line** (☎0870 606 7766; Home Office's Immigration & Nationality Directorate, Lunar House, 40 Wellesley Rd, Croydon CR9 2BY; ◷8am-4pm Mon-Fri; ᵣEast Croydon) before your current visa expires. The process takes a few days in France and Ireland, longer in the UK.

Women Travellers

In general, London is a fairly laid-back place, and you're unlikely to have too many problems provided you take the usual city precautions. Don't get into an Underground carriage with no one else in it or with just one or two men. And if you feel unsafe, you should hang the expense and take a taxi. Archway-based **Lady Mini Cabs** (☎7272 3300) has women drivers.

Apart from the occasional wolf whistle and unwelcome body contact on the tube, women will find male Londoners reasonably enlightened. Going into pubs alone may not always be a comfortable experience, though it's in no way out of the ordinary.

Marie Stopes International (☎0845 300 8090; www.mariestopes.org.uk; 108 Whitfield St W1; ◷8.30am-5pm Mon, Wed & Fri, 9.30am-6pm Tue & Thu, 9am-4pm Sat; ⊖Warren St) provides contraception, sexual health checks and abortions.

Work

Looking For Work

Whether skilled or unskilled, you're likely to find work in London. Traditionally, unskilled visitors have worked in pubs, restaurants, admin or as nannies. A minimum wage (£5.93 per hour, £4.92 for those aged 18 to 21) exists, but if you're working illegally, no one's obliged to pay you that.

➡ The free *TNT Magazine* (www.tntmagazine.com) is a good starting point for jobs and agencies aimed at travellers.

➡ Other good resources for job listings include www.loot.co.uk and www.gumtree.com/london.

➡ For au pair and nanny work, try the quaintly titled the *Lady* (www.lady.co.uk).

➡ Registering with temporary agencies such as Reed, Office Angels or Kelly Services is a good idea if you're looking for short-term contracts.

VISA REQUIREMENTS

COUNTRY	TOURISM	WORK	STUDY
European Economic Area (except Romania & Bulgaria)	X	X	X
Australia, Canada, New Zealand, South Africa, USA	X (up to 6 months)	√	√
Other nationalities	√	√	√

BUSKING IT

If you play a musical instrument or have other artistic talents, busking could make you some pocket money. However, to perform in Underground stations, you have to go through a rigorous process taking several months. After signing up at www.tfl.gov.uk, you will have to go through an audition and get police security clearance (£10) before being granted a licence to perform and then getting yourself on a rota of marked pitches.

Buskers also need to have a permit to work at top tourist attractions and popular areas such as Covent Garden and Leicester Square. Contact the local borough council for details.

➡ Teachers should contact the individual London borough councils, which have separate education departments, although some schools recruit directly.

➡ Trained nurses or midwives have to apply to the **UK Nursing & Midwifery Council** (☑7333 9333; www.nmc-uk.org).

➡ Government-operated **Jobcentres**, which are scattered throughout London, are listed under 'Employment Services' in the phone directory.

➡ Newspapers also have job listings, notably on their website.

Tax

➡ Income tax and National Insurance are automatically deducted from your pay packets.

➡ Deductions will be calculated on the assumption that you're working for the entire financial year (which runs from 6 April to 5 April). If you don't work as long as that, you may be eligible for a refund. Visit the website of the **HM Revenue & Customs** (www.hmrc.gov.uk) to locate your nearest tax office.

Work Permits

➡ EU and Swiss nationals don't need a work permit to work in London but everyone else does.

➡ If you're a citizen of Australia, Canada, Japan, New Zealand or Monaco, aged between 18 and 31, you can apply to take part in the Youth Mobility Scheme, which allows you to live and work in the UK for up to 24 months. You will need to have £1600 of available maintenance funds when you apply. Check the UK Border Agency's website (www.ukba.homeoffice.gov.uk) for more information.

➡ If you're a Commonwealth citizen and have a grandparent born in the UK (or a grandparent born before 31 March 1922 in what is now the Republic of Ireland), you may be eligible to live and work in the UK for up to five years. You must apply for 'entry clearance' before coming to the UK.

➡ The Blue Card Internship Programme of the **British Universities North America Club** (Bunac; ☑203 264 0901; www.bunac.org; PO Box 430, Southbury CT 06488, USA) Blue Card Internship Programme offers US students (or students of any nationality studying in the US) who are at least 18 years old, studying full time or a recent graduate, the chance to get a six-month internship in the UK for US$750. Eligible candidates must find their internship before applying to Bunac for support.

➡ Most other travellers wishing to work and not fitting into any of the aforementioned categories will need a work permit (awarded through a point-based system to favour skilled workers) and to be sponsored by a British company. See www.ukba.homeoffice.gov.uk for more details.

➡ If you have any queries once you're in the UK, contact the Home Office's **UK Border Agency** (☑0870 606 7766).

Behind the Scenes

SEND US YOUR FEEDBACK

We love to hear from travellers – your comments keep us on our toes and help make our books better. Our well-travelled team reads every word on what you loved or loathed about this book. Although we cannot reply individually to postal submissions, we always guarantee that your feedback goes straight to the appropriate authors, in time for the next edition. Each person who sends us information is thanked in the next edition – and the most useful submissions are rewarded with a free book.

Visit **lonelyplanet.com/contact** to submit your updates and suggestions or to ask for help. Our award-winning website also features inspirational travel stories, news and discussions.

Note: We may edit, reproduce and incorporate your comments in Lonely Planet products such as guidebooks, websites and digital products, so let us know if you don't want your comments reproduced or your name acknowledged. For a copy of our privacy policy visit lonelyplanet.com/privacy.

OUR READERS

Many thanks to the travellers who used the last edition and wrote to us with helpful hints, useful advice and interesting anecdotes:

David, Maja, Badong Abesamis, Jeanne Aguilera, Dana Beyer, Heather Brandon, Phelan Chatterjee, William Cookson, Sarah-Jayne Dominic, Katherine Green, Joe Macdonagh, Ngaire Moore, Denise Pulis, Sebastien Simard, Olivia Thomas, Christopher Webb.

AUTHOR THANKS

Damian Harper

I would like to thank Daisy Harper, Rob Howell, Kevin Fallows, Kerry Brown, Bill Moran, my co-authors plus Jo Cooke and all the staff at Lonely Planet. I would also like to proffer a warm handshake and thumbs-up to the engaging people of London (on both sides of the river). Thanks, of course, to Timothy and Emma.

Steve Fallon

Several of my fellow Blue Badge (then) trainee guides made helpful suggestions for this chapter, especially Claudia Crovace and Myra Morgan. Many thanks to co-authors Damian Harper and Emilie Filou for their help, especially on the technical side. As always, I'd like to state my admiration, gratitude and great love for my partner and, for this edition, travelling buddy, Michael Rothschild.

Emilie Filou

My thanks go to the many friends who came along for the ride, chipped in with recommendations and made research so much fun: Catherine, Chris, Karine, Nikki, Sid, Thibault and Van. Thanks also to fellow journalist Stephen Unwin for his insight on gay London, and Ancil Barclay of Notting Hill Carnival for his top carnival tips. And finally, thanks to chief critic and husband extraordinaire, Adolfo, for his patience and company.

Vesna Maric

I would like to thank Jo Cooke for giving me the opportunity to work on this guide, and to Damian Harper for being kind and helpful at all times. This is for Frida.

Sally Schafer

Thanks to Imogen and Jo for letting me out the door, to Ed for his silvery words, Chantal (and her mum) for extensive knowledge and appreciation of the finer things in life, Ian for his late-night reviews of the facilities, Mum and Dad for their wine and mushroom expertise, Clare and Eric for the tour, Freya for the walk, and to James, and especially Kate, for still being my anchor after all these years.

ACKNOWLEDGMENTS

Cover photograph: St Paul's Cathedral and Millenium Bridge over the River Thames/ Alan Copson.

The Millennium Bridge is a collaboration between Foster and partners, Sir Anthony Caro and Arup.

Artwork, 'Guns' by Andy Warhol, as seen in photograph of Tate Modern museum, page 9, © The Andy Warhol Foundation for the Visual Arts, Inc/ARS. Licensed by Viscopy, 2011.

Illustrations p166-7, p144-5 by Javier Zarracina.

Many of the images in this guide are available for licensing from Lonely Planet Images: www.lonelyplanetimages.com.

THIS BOOK

This 8th edition of London was researched and written by Damian Harper, Emilie Filou, Sally Schafer, Steve Fallon and Vesna Maric. The 7th and 6th editions were written by Tom Masters, Steve Fallon and Vesna Maric. Sarah Johnstone and Tom Masters wrote the 5th edition. Martin Hughes, Sarah Johnstone and Tom Masters wrote the 4th edition. Steve Fallon wrote the 2nd and 3rd edition. Pat Yale wrote the 1st edition.

This guidebook was commissioned in Lonely Planet's London office, and produced by the following:

Commissioning Editor Joanna Cooke

Coordinating Editor Karyn Noble

Coordinating Cartographer Jolyon Philcox

Coordinating Layout Designer Kerrianne Southway

Managing Editors Kirsten Rawlings, Tasmin Waby McNaughtan

Managing Cartographer Amanda Sierp

Managing Layout Designer Chris Girdler

Assisting Editors Andrew Bain, Kate Daly, Cathryn Game, Carly Hall, Jocelyn Harewood, Lauren Hunt,

Martine Power, Saralinda Turner, Kate Whitfield

Assisting Cartographers Ildiko Bogdanovits, Csanad Csutoros, Katalin Dadi-Racz, Joelene Kowalkski, Peter Shields

Cover Research Naomi Parker

Internal Image Research Sabrina Dalbesio

Illustrator Javier Zarracina

Thanks to Janine Eberle, Ryan Evans, Liz Heynes, Briohny Hooper, Gabrielle Innes, Laura Jane, David Kemp, Anna Metcalfe, Trent Paton, Piers Pickard, Lachlan Ross, Michael Ruff, Dianne Schallmeiner, Julie Sheridan, Laura Stansfeld, John Taufa, Gerard Walker, Jeanette Wall, Clifton Wilkinson

See also separate subindexes for:

🍴 **EATING P412**

🍷 **DRINKING & NIGHTLIFE P413**

☆ **ENTERTAINMENT P414**

🔒 **SHOPPING P415**

🏃 **SPORTS & ACTIVITIES P416**

🛏 **SLEEPING P416**

Index

Sights p000
Map Pages **p000**

London Maps

Map Legend

Sights
- 🏖 Beach
- 🔱 Buddhist
- 🏰 Castle
- ✝ Christian
- 🕉 Hindu
- ☪ Islamic
- ✡ Jewish
- ❶ Monument
- 🏛 Museum/Gallery
- ⚭ Ruin
- 🍷 Winery/Vineyard
- 🐨 Zoo
- ◉ Other Sight

Eating
- 🍴 Eating

Drinking & Nightlife
- ☕ Drinking & Nightlife
- ☕ Cafe

Entertainment
- ✪ Entertainment

Shopping
- 🛍 Shopping

Sleeping
- 🛏 Sleeping
- ⛺ Camping

Sports & Activities
- 🤿 Diving/Snorkelling
- 🚣 Canoeing/Kayaking
- ⛷ Skiing
- 🏄 Surfing
- 🏊 Swimming/Pool
- 🚶 Walking
- 🏄 Windsurfing
- 🤸 Other Sports & Activities

Information
- ✉ Post Office
- ❶ Tourist Information

Transport
- ✈ Airport
- ⊗ Border Crossing
- 🚌 Bus
- 🚡 Cable Car/ Funicular
- 🚴 Cycling
- ⛴ Ferry
- Ⓜ Metro
- 🚝 Monorail
- Ⓟ Parking
- Ⓢ S-Bahn
- 🚕 Taxi
- 🚆 Train/Railway
- 🚊 Tram
- Ⓣ Tube Station
- Ⓤ U-Bahn
- • Other Transport

Routes
- Tollway
- Freeway
- Primary
- Secondary
- Tertiary
- Lane
- Unsealed Road
- Plaza/Mall
- Steps
-)=(Tunnel
- Pedestrian Overpass
- Walking Tour
- Walking Tour Detour
- Path

Boundaries
- International
- State/Province
- Disputed
- Regional/Suburb
- Marine Park
- Cliff
- Wall

Geographic
- 🏠 Hut/Shelter
- 🗼 Lighthouse
- 👁 Lookout
- ▲ Mountain/Volcano
- 🌴 Oasis
- ❶ Park
-)(Pass
- 🏕 Picnic Area
- 🌊 Waterfall

Hydrography
- River/Creek
- Intermittent River
- Swamp/Mangrove
- Reef
- Canal
- Water
- Dry/Salt/ Intermittent Lake
- Glacier

Areas
- Beach/Desert
- Cemetery (Christian)
- Cemetery (Other)
- Park/Forest
- Sportsground
- Sight (Building)
- Top Sight (Building)

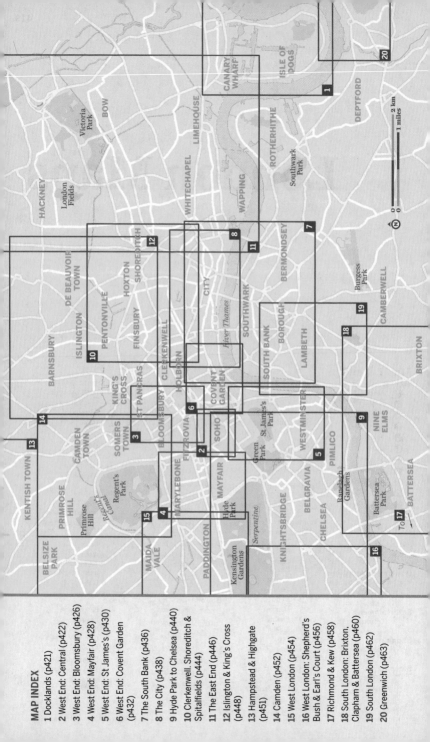

MAP INDEX

DOCKLANDS

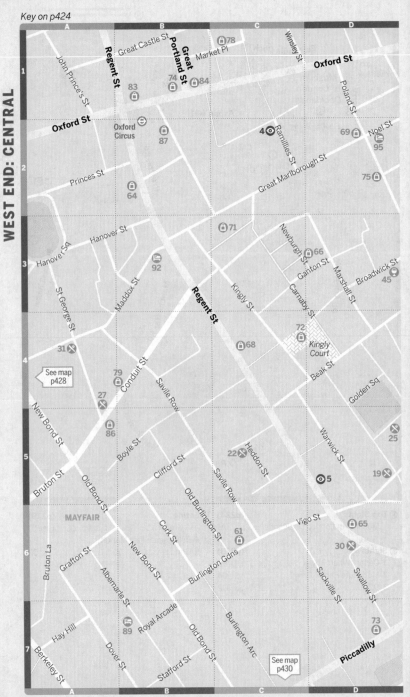

WEST END: CENTRAL

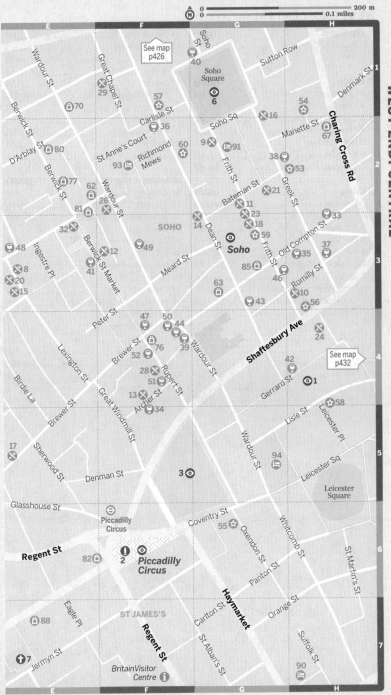

WEST END: CENTRAL *Map on p422*

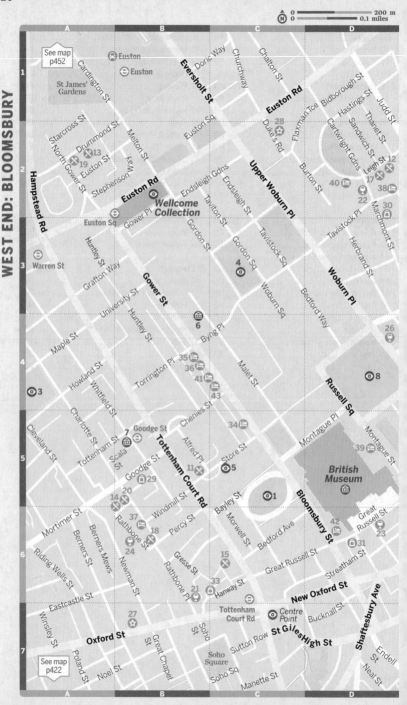

WEST END: BLOOMSBURY

Map labels
Argyle St
Tonbridge St
Cromer St
Harrison St
Hunter St
Handel St
Brunswick Sq
St George's Gardens
St Pancras Coram's Fields
Bernard St
Grenville St
Russell Sq
Guildford St
Queen Sq
Southampton Row
Bedford Pl
Bloomsbury Square
Bury Pl
Bloomsbury Way
New Oxford St
Museum St
High Holborn
Stukely St
Macklin St
Drury La
Betterton St

To Bea's of Bloomsbury (400m)

See map p432

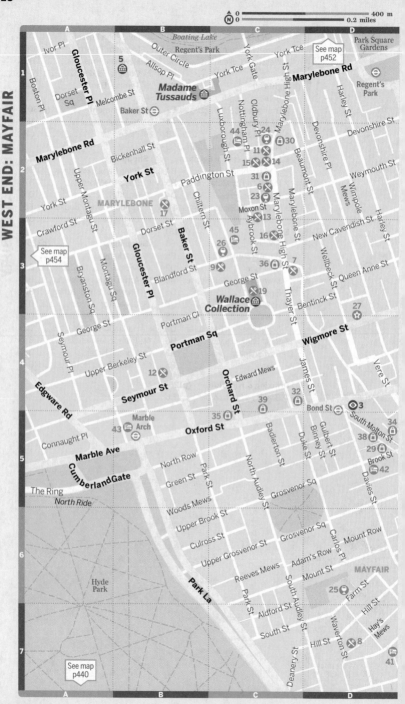

See map
p422

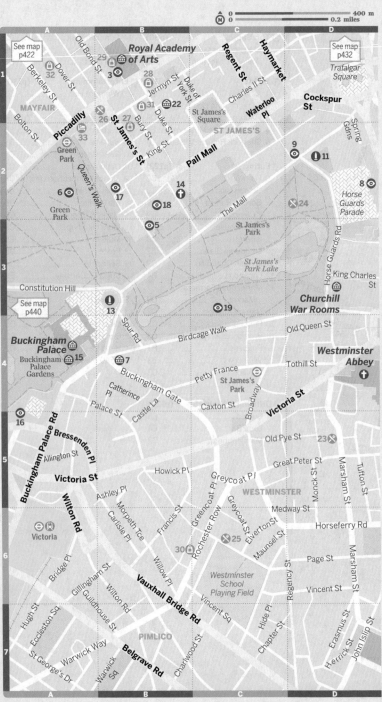

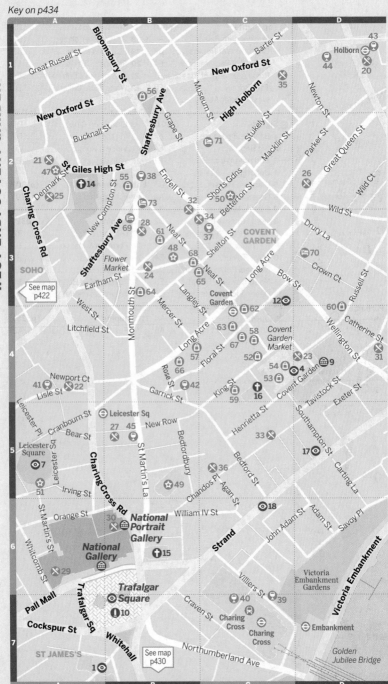

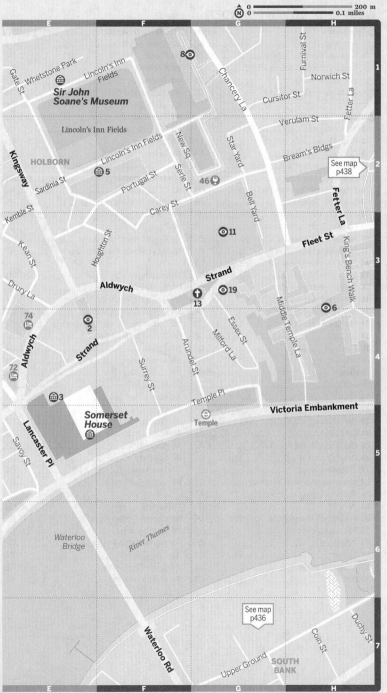

WEST END: COVENT GARDEN *Map on p432*

THE SOUTH BANK *Map on p436*

Key on p435

THE SOUTH BANK

A   B   C   D

High Holborn

Holborn

Kingsway

HOLBORN

Lincoln's
Inn Fields

Chancery La

New Fetter La

Farringdon St

Newgate St

St Paul's

1

Fleet St

COVENT
GARDEN

Aldwych

City
Thameslink

Queen Victoria St

Blackfriars

White Lion Hill

2

Strand

Temple

Victoria Embankment

River Thames

Blackfriars
Bridge

Millennium
Bridge

13

**Shakespeare's
Globe**

Waterloo
Bridge

30

1

47

**Tate
Modern**

3

See map
p430

Hungerford
Bridge

53

45

41 43

48

46

**Southbank
Centre**

34

Upper Ground

Stamford St

Blackfriars Rd

59

Park St

54

Southwark St

57

Great Suffolk St

Southwark St

Waterloo
Millennium
Pier

20

40

65

36

Hatfields St

Roupell St

Southwark

Union St

4

15

**London
Eye**

12   62

11   4

17

York Rd

51

London Visitor
Centre

Cornwall Rd

Waterloo
East

49

22

The Cut

33

Southwark

Belvedere Rd

Waterloo

44

Blackfriars Rd

26

BOROUGH

Webber St

5

Westminster
Bridge

39

Bayliss Rd

Waterloo Rd

29

Southwark Bridge Rd

Westminster Bridge Rd

Lambeth North

Borough Rd

Lambeth Palace Rd

Carlisle La

Hercules Rd

Archbishop's
Park

Lambeth Rd

St George's Rd

London Rd

Newington Causeway

6

Elephant
& Castle

Lambeth
Bridge

LAMBETH

Kennington Rd

Brook Dr

Oswin St

Newington Butts

Newport St

See map
p462

Newington Butts

Hampton St

7

A   B   C   D

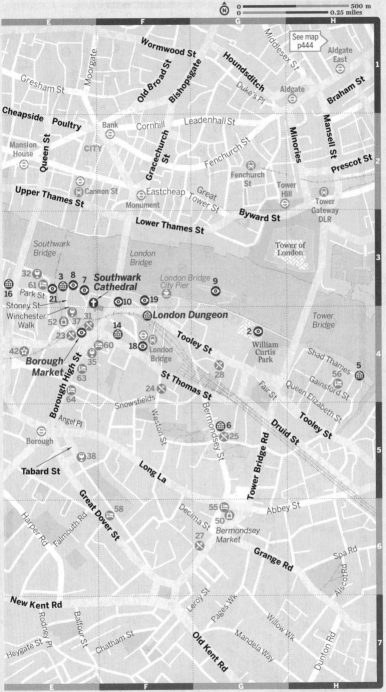

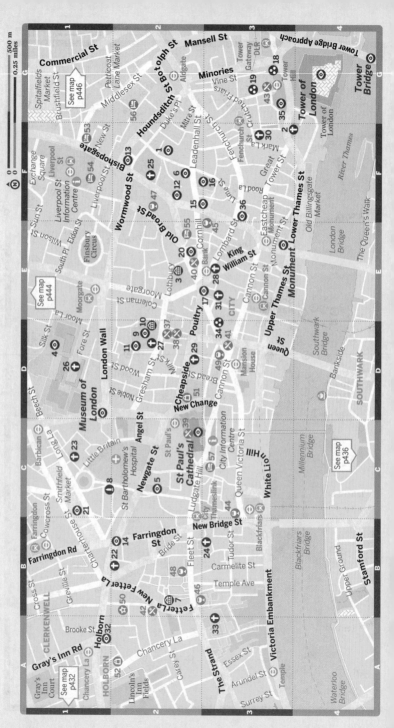

See map p446

See map p444

See map p432

See map p436

N

0   500 m
0   0.25 miles

Commercial St

Spitalfields
Market

Brushfield St

Petticoat
Lane Market

Middlesex St

Mansell St

Minories

Tower
Gateway
DLR

Tower
Hill

Tower Bridge Approach

**Tower
Bridge**

Bishopsgate

Houndsditch

Bishopsgate

Duke's Pl

Mitre St

Vine St

Crutched Friars

**Tower of
London**

Tower of
London

River Thames

Wormwood St

Old Broad St

Leadenhall St

Lime St

Fenchurch St

Mark La

Great Tower St

Eastcheap

Monument

Lower Thames St

Old Billingsgate
Market

London
Bridge

The Queen's Walk

Exchange
Square

Liverpool St

Liverpool St
Information
Centre

Sun St

Wilson St

Eldon St

South Pl

Finsbury
Circus

Moorgate

Moor La

Silk St

Fore St

London Wall

**Museum of
London**

Beech St

Barbican

Long La

Smithfield
Market

St Bartholomew's
Hospital

Little Britain

Newgate St

Angel St

**St Paul's
Cathedral**

Cheapside

New Change

Cornhill

Lothbury

Coleman St

Bank

**King
William St**

Lombard St

Cannon St

CITY

Cannon St

Upper Thames St

Queen
St

Southwark
Bridge

SOUTHWARK

Bankside

Millennium
Bridge

Poultry

Mansion
House

Bread St

White Lion Hill

City Information
Centre

Queen Victoria St

St Paul's

Ludgate Hill

City
Thameslink

New Bridge St

Fleet St

Bride La

Fleet La

New Fetter La

**Farringdon
St**

Farringdon

Cowcross St

Farringdon Rd

Cross St

Greville St

Charterhouse St

CLERKENWELL

Brooke St

Holborn

Gray's Inn Rd

Gray's
Inn Court

Chancery La

HOLBORN

Lincoln's
Inn Fields

Carey St

Essex St

The Strand

Arundel St

Surrey St

Victoria Embankment

Temple Ave

Carmelite St

Tudor St

Temple

Blackfriars
Bridge

Blackfriars

Upper Ground

Stamford St

Waterloo
Bridge

Chancery La

THE CITY

Key on p442

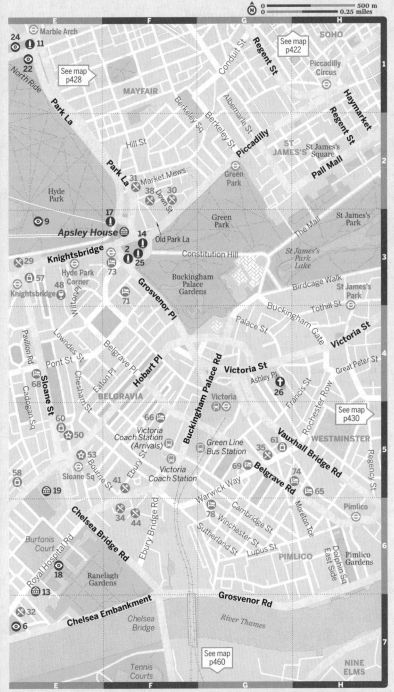

See map p422

See map p428

Marble Arch

24
11
22

MAYFAIR

Park La

North Ride

Conduit St

Regent St

SOHO

Piccadilly Circus

Haymarket

Regent St

Hill St

Berkeley Sq

Berkeley St

Albemarle St

Piccadilly

ST JAMES'S

St James's Square

Pall Mall

Park La

31
Market Mews
38
30
Down St

Green Park

Hyde Park

9

Apsley House

17

14
Old Park La

2
25

29

Knightsbridge

57

48

Knightsbridge

73

71

Grosvenor Pl

Hyde Park Corner

Green Park

Constitution Hill

Buckingham Palace Gardens

St James's Park

The Mall

St James's Park Lake

St James's Park

Birdcage Walk

Buckingham Gate

Palace St

Tothill St

Victoria St

Palace St

68

Sloane St

Cadogan Sq

Pavilion Rd

Pont St

Lowndes St

Chesham St

Belgrave Pl

Eaton Pl

Hobart Pl

BELGRAVIA

Buckingham Palace Rd

Victoria St

Ashley Pl

26

Francis St

Rochester Row

Great Peter St

See map p430

WESTMINSTER

Regency St

60

50

53

Sloane Sq

Bourne St

58

19

41

66

Victoria Coach Station (Arrivals)

Ebury St

Victoria Coach Station

Victoria

Green Line Bus Station

69

Belgrave Rd

35
61

Vauxhall Bridge Rd

74

65

Pimlico

Moreton Terr

34
44

Warwick Way

78

Cambridge St

Winchester St

Sutherland St

Lupus St

PIMLICO

Dolphin Sq East Side

Pimlico Gardens

Chelsea Bridge Rd

Ebury Bridge Rd

Burton's Court

Royal Hospital Rd

18

Ranelagh Gardens

13

32

6

Chelsea Embankment

Chelsea Bridge

Grosvenor Rd

River Thames

See map p460

Tennis Courts

NINE ELMS

0   500 m
0   0.25 miles

N

HYDE PARK TO CHELSEA *Map on p440*

CLERKENWELL, SHOREDITCH & SPITALFIELDS *Map on p444*

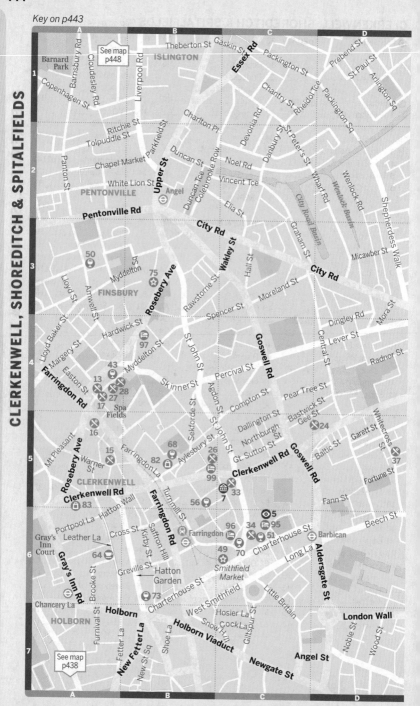

CLERKENWELL, SHOREDITCH & SPITALFIELDS

Barnard Park

Copenhagen St

Barnsbury Rd

Cloudesley Rd

See map p448

Liverpool Rd

Theberton St

Gaskin St

Essex Rd

Packington St

Prebend St

St Paul St

Arlington Sq

ISLINGTON

Chantry St

Rheidol Tce

Packington Sq

Charlton Pl

Devonia Rd

St Peter's St

Danbury St

Wharf Rd

Wenlock Rd

Shepherdess Walk

Ritchie St

Tolpuddle St

Panton St

Chapel Market

Parkfield St

Duncan St

Noel Rd

Duncan Tce

Colebrooke Row

Vincent Tce

City Road Basin

Wenlock Basin

White Lion St

Upper St

Angel

Ella St

PENTONVILLE

Pentonville Rd

City Rd

Wakley St

Graham St

City Rd

Micawber Walk

50

Myddelton Sq

75

Roseberry Ave

Rawstorne St

Hall St

Moreland St

Mora St

FINSBURY

Lloyd St

Amwell St

Spencer St

Dingley Rd

Lever St

Central St

Radnor St

Lloyd Baker St

Hardwick St

97

Myddelton St

St John St

Percival St

Goswell Rd

Margery St

Easton St

43

13

28

Skinner St

Compton St

Pear Tree St

Bastwick St

Gee St

24

Farringdon Rd

27

17

Sekforde St

Agdon St

St John St

Dallington St

Northburgh St

Gt. Sutton St

Whitecross St

Garett St

16

Spa Fields

68

Aylesbury St

26

Clerkenwell Rd

Goswell Rd

Baltic St

Fortune St

37

15

Warner St

Farringdon La

82

99

Clerkenwell Rd

Mt Pleasant

Roseberry Ave

CLERKENWELL

7

33

Fann St

Beech St

Clerkenwell Rd

83

Tunmill St

56

5

Gray's Inn Court

Portpool La

Hatton Wall

Cross St

Farringdon Rd

Kirby St

Saffron Hill

Farringdon

96

34

95

Charterhouse St

51

Barbican

Aldersgate St

Leather La

64

Hatton Garden

49

70

Long La

Gray's Inn Rd

Brooke St

Greville St

Smithfield Market

Little Britain

Chancery La

Charterhouse St

73

West Smithfield

London Wall

HOLBORN

Holborn

Hosier La

Cock La

Giltspur St

Snow Hill

Noble St

Wood St

See map p438

Fetter La

New Fetter La

New St Sq

Shoe La

Holborn Viaduct

Newgate St

Angel St

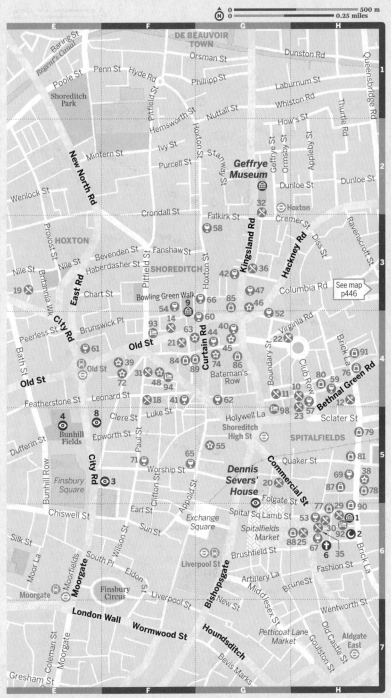

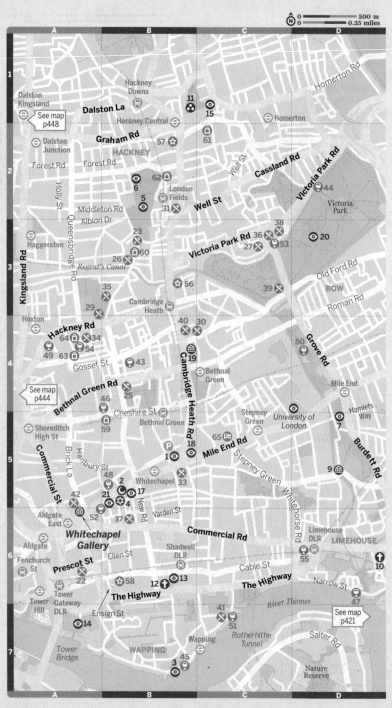

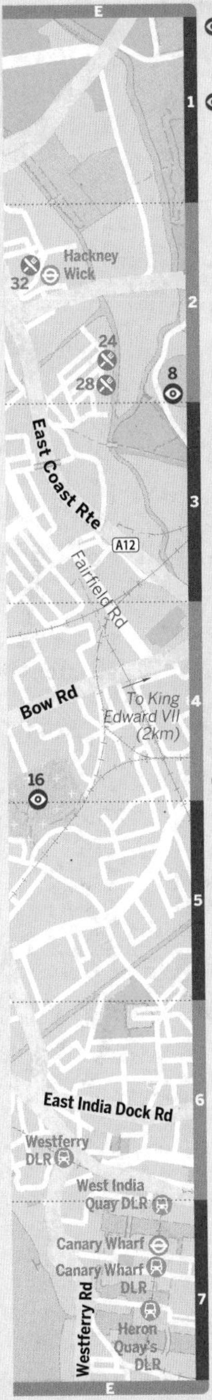

E
1
2
3
4
5
6
7
Hackney Wick
32
24
28
8
East Coast Rte
A12
Fairfield Rd
Bow Rd
To King Edward VII (2km)
16
East India Dock Rd
Westferry DLR
West India Quay DLR
Canary Wharf
Canary Wharf DLR
Westferry Rd
Heron Quays DLR
E

Top Sights (p219)
Whitechapel Gallery A6

Sights (p219)
1 Blind Beggar B5
2 East London Mosque B5
3 Execution Dock.................... B7
4 Great Synagogue................. B5
5 London Fields B2
6 London Fields Lido B2
7 Mile End Park....................... D5
8 Olympic Park E2
9 Ragged School Museum..... D5
10 St Anne's, Limehouse D6
11 St Augustine's Tower........... B1
12 St George-in-the-East......... B6
13 St George's Town Hall Building B6
14 St Katharine Docks A7
15 Sutton House........................C1
16 Tower Hamlets Cemetery Park E4
17 Tower House........................ B5
18 Trinity Green Almshouses .. B5
19 V&A Museum of Childhood........................... B4
20 Victoria Park D3
21 Whitechapel Bell Foundry... B5
William Booth Statue . (see 18)

Eating (p224)
22 Café Spice Namasté............ A6
23 Climpson & Sons B3
Corner Room ....(see 40)
24 Counter Cafe.........................E2
25 E Pellici B4
26 F. Cooke B3
27 Fish House C3
28 Formans...............................E2
29 Frizzante@City Farm A3
30 Gallery Cafe......................... C4
31 Green Papaya B2
32 Hackney Pearl.......................E2
33 Kolapata B5
34 Laxeiro.................................. A4
35 Little Georgia B3
36 Loafing.................................. C3
37 Mirch Masala........................ B6
38 Namô C3
39 Pavilion C3
Tayyabs ....(see 17)
40 Viajante B4
41 Wapping Food...................... C7
42 Whitechapel Gallery Dining Room A5

Drinking & Nightlife (p229)
43 Bethnal Green Working Men's Club B4
44 Britannia............................... D2
45 Captain Kidd B7
46 Carpenter's Arms B4
Dove Freehouse..........(see 60)
47 Grapes D6
48 Indo....................................... B5
49 Joiners Arms......................... A4
Nelsons Head.............(see 64)
50 Palm Tree D4
51 Prospect of Whitby.............. C7
52 Rhythm Factory.................... A6
53 Royal Inn on the Park C3
54 Royal Oak A4
55 White Swan D6

Entertainment (p231)
56 Bistrotheque......................... B3
57 Hackney Empire B2
58 Wilton's................................. B6

Shopping (p231)
59 Beyond Retro........................ B5
60 Broadway Market B3
61 Burberry Outlet Shop.......... C2
62 Carhartt Outlet Store B2
63 Columbia Road Flower Market A4
64 Jones Dairy A4

Sleeping (p333)
65 40 Winks C5
Old Ship ....(see 57)
Town Hall Hotel & Apartments..............(see 40)

ISLINGTON & KING'S CROSS

See map p452

See map p444

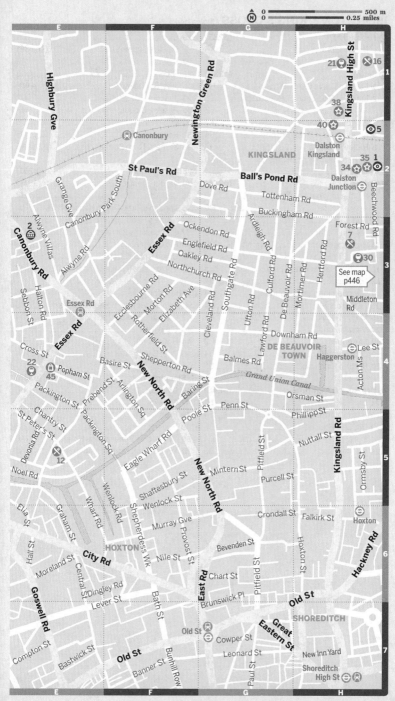

ISLINGTON & KING'S CROSS *Map on p448*

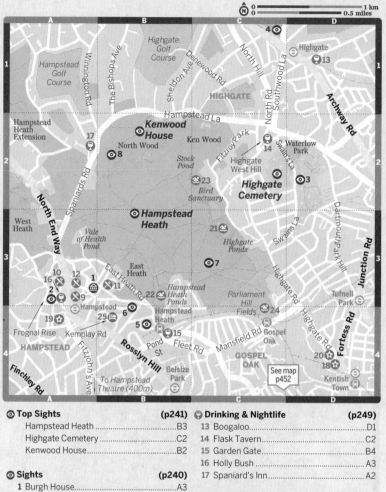

◎ Top Sights	(p241)
Hampstead Heath	B3
Highgate Cemetery	C2
Kenwood House	B2

◎ Sights	(p240)
1 Burgh House	A3
2 Fenton House	A3
3 Highgate Cemetery Entrances	D2
4 Highgate Wood	C1
5 Keats House	B4
6 No 2 Willow Road	B4
7 Parliament Hill	C3
8 Sculptures by Henry Moore & Barbara Hepworth	B2

⊗ Eating	(p244)
9 Gaucho Grill	A3
10 La Gaffe	A3
11 Wells Tavern	B3
12 Woodlands	A3

◎ Drinking & Nightlife	(p249)
13 Boogaloo	D1
14 Flask Tavern	C2
15 Garden Gate	B4
16 Holly Bush	A3
17 Spaniard's Inn	A2

★ Entertainment	(p251)
18 Bull & Gate	D4
19 Everyman Hampstead	A4
20 Forum	D4

◆ Sports & Activities	(p254)
21 Hampstead Heath Men's Pond	C3
22 Hampstead Heath Mixed Pond	B3
23 Hampstead Heath Women's Pond	C2
24 Parliament Hill Lido	C4

⊟ Sleeping	(p334)
25 Hampstead Guesthouse	B4

CAMDEN

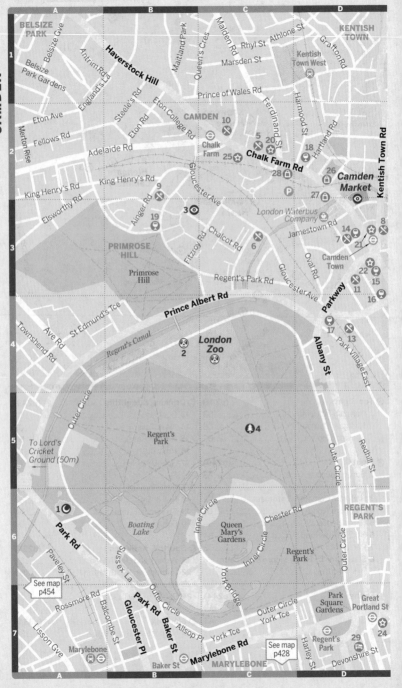

0 — 500 m
0 — 0.25 miles

See map p448

◉ **Top Sights** **(p237)**
Camden Market.....................................D3
London Zoo..C4

◉ **Sights** **(p238)**
1 London Central Islamic Centre &
Mosque..A6
2 London Zoo (Entrance).....................B4
3 Primrose Hill.....................................B3
4 Regent's Park....................................C5

✖ **Eating** **(p243)**
Bar Gansa..(see 14)
5 Belgo Noord.......................................C2
6 Engineer...C3
7 Haché..D3
8 Mango Room......................................D3
9 Manna...B2
10 Marine Ices..C2
11 Market...D3
12 Mestizo...E6
13 York & Albany.....................................D4

🍷 **Drinking & Nightlife** **(p248)**
14 Bar Vinyl..D3
15 Black Cap..D3
16 Crown & Goose..................................D4
17 Edinboro Castle..................................D4
18 Lock Tavern.......................................D2
Proud Camden...............................(see 28)
19 Queen's...B3

🎭 **Entertainment** **(p251)**
20 Barfly..C2
21 Electric Ballroom...............................D3
22 Jazz Café..D3
23 Koko..E4
24 Lowdown at the Albany......................D7
25 Roundhouse.......................................C2

🛍 **Shopping** **(p254)**
Buck Street Market.........................(see 21)
26 Canal Market......................................D2
27 Lock Market.......................................D2
28 Stables Market...................................C2

🛏 **Sleeping** **(p333)**
29 International Student House...............D7
York & Albany.................................(see 13)

WEST LONDON

WEST LONGON

WEST LONDON

Hyde Park

Buck Hill Walk

The Long Water

Lancaster Walk

Kensington Gardens

The Broad Walk

Bayswater Rd

Queensway

Pembridge Rd

Notting Hill Gate

Kensington Church St

Holland Park Ave

Ladbroke Rd

Ladbroke Sq Gdns

Lansdowne Rd

Clarendon Rd

Portland Rd

◎ **Top Sights** (p259)
Portobello Road Market.....................B4

◎ **Sights** (p258)
1 Little Venice.....................E2
2 London Waterbus Company.....................E2
3 Museum of Brands, Packaging and Advertising.....................B4

✕ **Eating** (p259)
4 Arancina.....................C5
5 Churreria Española.....................D3
6 Couscous Café.....................D4
7 Cow.....................C3
8 Daylesford.....................B4
9 E&O.....................A4
Electric Brasserie.....................(see 26)
10 Garden & Grill.....................A3

11 Geales.....................C5
12 Kensington Place.....................C5
13 Market Thai.....................A3
14 Mediterraneo.....................A4
15 Pearl Liang.....................E3
16 Summerhouse.....................D2
17 Taqueria.....................C4

🍸 **Drinking & Nightlife** (p263)
18 Beach Blanket Babylon.....................B4
19 Earl of Lonsdale.....................C5
20 Grand Union.....................B2
21 Notting Hill Arts Club.....................C5
22 Prince Alfred.....................D1
23 Warrington.....................B4
24 Waterway.....................D2

✦ **Entertainment** (p264)
25 Coronet.....................C5
26 Electric Cinema.....................B4
27 Gate Picturehouse.....................C5

🛍 **Shopping** (p266)
28 Al Saqi.....................D3
Books for Cooks.....................(see 29)
29 Ceramica Blue.....................A3
30 Portobello Green Arcade.....................A3
31 Rellik.....................A2
Retro Man.....................(see 32)
32 Retro Woman.....................C5
33 Rough Trade.....................B3
34 Spice Shop.....................B4

✦ **Sports & Activities** (p267)
35 Porchester Spa.....................D3

🛏 **Sleeping** (p334)
36 Colonnade.....................D2
37 easyHotel Paddington.....................F3
38 Elysee Hotel.....................E4
39 Garden Court Hotel.....................C4
40 Gate Hotel.....................B5
41 Hempel.....................E4
42 Hotel Indigo.....................F4
43 New Linden Hotel.....................C4
44 Oxford Hotel London.....................E4
45 Parkwood Hotel.....................G4
46 Pavilion Hotel.....................F3
47 Portobello Gold.....................B4
48 Portobello Hotel.....................B4
49 Stylotel.....................F3
50 Stylotel Suites.....................F4
51 Vancouver Studios.....................C4

WEST LONDON: SHEPHERD'S BUSH & EARL'S COURT

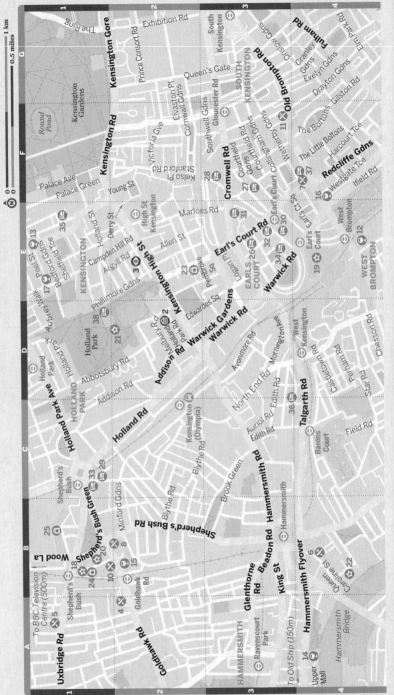

WEST LONDON: SHEPHERD'S BUSH & EARL'S COURT

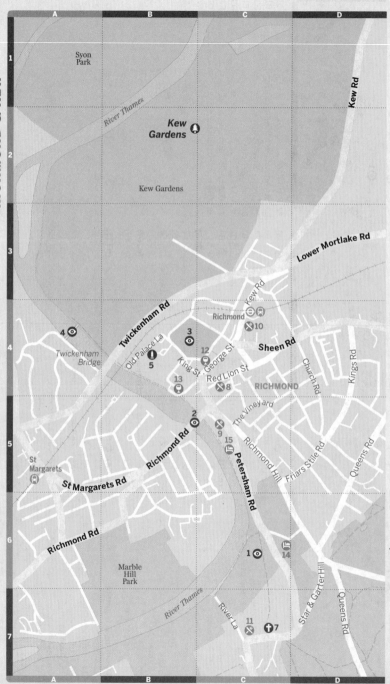

Syon Park

River Thames

Kew Gardens

Kew Gardens

Kew Rd

Lower Mortlake Rd

Twickenham Rd

Richmond

10

Kew Rd

Sheen Rd

4

Twickenham Bridge

Old Palace La

3

5

12

King St

George St

Red Lion St

RICHMOND

Church Rd

Kings Rd

13

8

The Vineyard

2

9

15

Richmond Rd

Richmond Hill

Friars Stile Rd

Queens Rd

St Margarets

St Margarets Rd

Petersham Rd

Richmond Rd

Marble Hill Park

1

14

River Thames

River La

11

7

Star & Garter Hill

Queens Rd

N 0 ____ 500 m
0 ____ 0.25 miles

Kew
Gardens

Mortlake Rd

Sandycombe Rd

Fulham
Cemetery

Lower Richmond Rd

Clifford Ave

Manor Rd

North
Sheen

Sheen Rd

Richmond &
East Sheen
Cemetery

Richmond Park

6 ◎

Sawyer's Hill

SOUTH LONDON: BRIXTON, CLAPHAM & BATTERSEA

See map p462

See map p440

1 km
0.5 miles

CHELSEA

Kennington Open Space

Kennington Park

Camberwell New Rd

Clayton St

The Oval

Oval

Vassall Rd

Caldwell St

Mostyn Gardens

Mostyn Rd

Cowley Rd

Brixton Rd

Overton Rd

Max Roach Park

Wiltshire Rd

Gresham Rd

Clayton Rd

Clapham Rd

Hillyard St

Groveway

Lorn Rd

Stockwell Park Rd

Sidney Rd

Robsart Rd

Rumsey Rd

BRIXTON

17

18

Claylands Rd

Fentiman Rd

Dorset Rd

Stockwell

Landsdowne Way

Binfield Rd

Studley Rd

Stockwell Rd

Dalyell Rd

Hargwyne St

Hubert Gve

Edithna St

Landor Rd

Puiross Rd

Vauxhall

Parry St

Vauxhall Park

Miles St

Wyvil Rd

South Lambeth Rd

Guildford Rd

Hartington Rd

Lingham St

Jeffreys Rd

Clapham Rd

Clapham High St

Clapham North

River Thames

Nine Elms La

Wandsworth Rd

NINE ELMS

Priory Gve

Larkhall Park

Larkhall La

Union Rd

Albion Ave

Edgeley Rd

Voltaire Rd

Grosvenor Rd

Cringle St

Battersea Park Rd

Thessaly Rd

Deeley Rd

Stewarts Rd

Queenstown Rd

Killyon Rd

Wandsworth Rd

Clapham Manor St

2

Heathbrook Park

Silverthorne Rd

Robertson St

Turret Gve

Orlando Rd

16

19

Queenstown Rd

Chelsea Bridge

Chelsea Embankment

Chelsea Physic Garden

Ranelagh Gardens

Battersea Park

Tennis Courts

Carriage Dr East

Carriage Dr North

Duck Pond

Ladies Pond

Boating Lake

7

1

3

6

The Parade

Albert Bridge

Albert Bridge Rd

Rosenau Rd

Elcho St

Battersea Bridge Rd

Queenstown Rd

St Phillip St

Stanley Gve

BATTERSEA

Warriner Gardens

Prince of Wales Dr

Carriage Dr South

Carriage Dr West

Battersea Park Rd

Battersea Park Rd

Battersea Park Rd

Everleigh Rd

Ashbury Rd

Elsley Rd

Lavender Hill

Latchmore Rd

22

Battersea Bridge Rd

Falcon Rd

9

SOUTH LONDON: BRIXTON, CLAPHAM & BATTERSEA

SOUTH LONDON

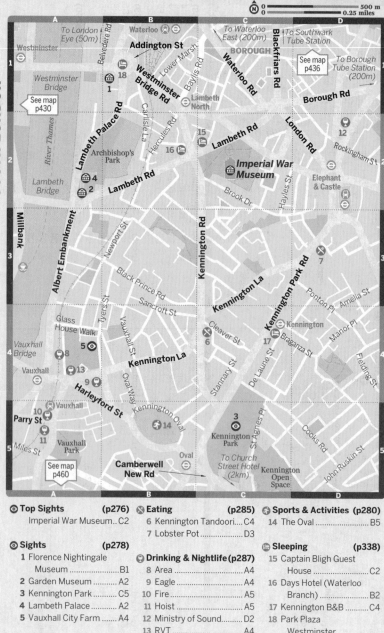

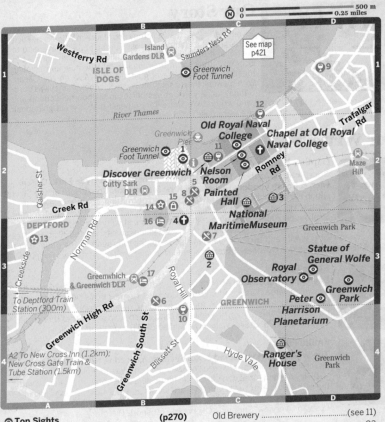

Our Story

A beat-up old car, a few dollars in the pocket and a sense of adventure. In 1972 that's all Tony and Maureen Wheeler needed for the trip of a lifetime – across Europe and Asia overland to Australia. It took several months, and at the end – broke but inspired – they sat at their kitchen table writing and stapling together their first travel guide, *Across Asia on the Cheap*. Within a week they'd sold 1500 copies. Lonely Planet was born.

Today, Lonely Planet has offices in Melbourne, London and Oakland, with more than 600 staff and writers. We share Tony's belief that 'a great guidebook should do three things: inform, educate and amuse'.

Our Writers

Damian Harper

Coordinating Author, The South Bank; Kensington & Hyde Park; Greenwich & South London; Richmond, Kew & Hampton Court Born off the Strand within earshot of Bow Bells (favourable wind permitting), Damian grew up in Notting Hill way before it was discovered by Hollywood. A Wykehamist, former Shakespeare and Company bookseller and linguist with two degrees, Damian has been authoring guidebooks for Lonely Planet since the late 1990s. He lives in South London with his wife and two kids. Damian also wrote the Plan section, the Understand section, Museums & Galleries Overview, Entertainment Overview, Sports & Activities Overview.

Steve Fallon

Day Trips from London After more than a decade of living in the centre of the known universe (East London) Steve Cockney-rhymes in his sleep, eats jellied eel for brekkie, drinks lager by the bucketful and dances round the occasional handbag. For this edition he went bush and is happy to report that there is life beyond the M25. Steve is a newly qualified Blue Badge London guide.

Emilie Filou

The West End, Hampstead & North London, Notting Hill & West London Emilie was born in Paris, where she lived until she was 18. Following her three-year degree and three gap years, she found herself in London, fell in love with the place and never really left. She now works as a journalist, specialising in Africa. Emilie also wrote Eating Overview, Drinking & Nightlife Overview, Gay & Lesbian Overview, Shopping Overview, Transport, Directory.

Read more about Emilie at:
lonelyplanet.com/members/emiliefilou

Sally Schafer

The City, Clerkenwell, Shoreditch & Spitalfields, East End & Docklands Having lived in east London for over 10 years, in the shadow of the emerging Olympic Park for four, and worked in Clerkenwell and Old St for the last six, Sally had a whale of a time re-exploring her own backyard. She usually goes by the title of Associate Publisher in Lonely Planet's London office but has also written about London, Spain and Portugal on previous office flits.

Contributing Writer

Vesna Maric wrote the With Kids chapter and has lived in London for 15 years. She has been delighted to discover an entirely new side of the city since having her daughter Frida, a year and a half ago. She looks forward to showing her the city's wonderful array of offerings in the years to come.

Published by Lonely Planet Publications Pty Ltd
ABN 36 005 607 983
8th edition – Feb 2012
ISBN 978 1 74179 898 2
© Lonely Planet 2012   Photographs © as indicated 2012
10 9 8 7 6 5 4 3 2
Printed in China